Human Relations

CONCEPTS AND CASES IN

CONCRETE SOCIAL SCIENCE

 CONCEPTS

Hugh Cabot ▪ *Joseph A. Kahl*

IN ASSOCIATION WITH Joseph C. Bailey, Robert F. Bales, Wallace B. Donham, Frances Mulhearn Fuller, George C. Homans, Ralph M. Hower, Florence Rockwood Kluckhohn, George F. F. Lombard, William G. Perry, Jr., Fritz J. Roethlisberger, Harriet O. Ronken, Jerome F. Scott, Philip E. Slater, Charles P. Whitlock

Harvard University Press
Cambridge, Massachusetts
1953

CORRECTION

The diagram at the bottom of page 133 should be arranged as follows:

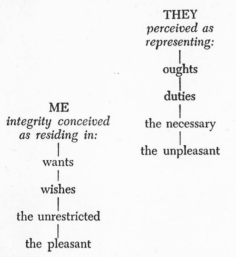

THEY
*perceived as
representing:*

|

oughts

|

duties

|

the necessary

|

the unpleasant

ME
*integrity conceived
as residing in:*

|

wants

|

wishes

|

the unrestricted

|

the pleasant

**To
N. H. C.
and
S. K.**

445937

Preface

Our present undergraduate course at Harvard College, Social Sciences 112 — Human Relations, is the outgrowth of three years of experimental teaching by the case method begun at the college in 1945. The course is a way of teaching selected concepts from the social sciences that apply to face-to-face human interaction, together with skills in the application of these concepts to concrete situations. During the two decades preceding the start of our course in the college, the utility of case teaching had been demonstrated at Harvard's Graduate School of Business Administration under the leadership of Professor Wallace B. Donham, then Dean. His leadership, together with the inspiration of the late Professor Elton B. Mayo in the specific area of human relations, provided impetus for the inclusion of this type of study in the newly developing undergraduate program in General Education in Harvard College. The philosophic ideas which underlay these early years can be found in Donham's *Education for Responsible Living* (Harvard University Press, 1944) and in the Harvard Committee report, *General Education in a Free Society* (Harvard University Press, 1945).

For the early thinking in the development of the course, we are particularly indebted to Professor Donham, to Fritz J. Roethlisberger, and to George F. F. Lombard, who compiled the first *Reading Notes* distributed to students. We are perhaps equally indebted to the early teaching staffs, which, in addition, included Joseph C. Bailey, Frances Mulhearn Fuller, Ralph M. Hower, Harriet O. Ronken, and Jerome F. Scott, and to the visiting Fellows from the University of Kansas, Colgate University, and Ohio University.

For their thoughtful reading of our manuscript during its many revisions and for their invaluable suggestions both in ideas and expression, we are deeply grateful to our current teaching colleagues, Frances Mulhearn Fuller, George C. Homans, William G. Perry, Jr., Philip E. Slater, and Charles P. Whitlock. They have met with us repeatedly in our endeavor to clarify and to communicate our ideas effectively and have given endlessly of their time.

For their understanding and encouragement, we are sincerely indebted to Florence R. Kluckhohn and Robert F. Bales of Harvard University, and David Riesman of the University of Chicago. Dr. Kluckhohn has read much of the manuscript and has graciously rewritten to fit our particular needs her two papers which appear herein. Dr. Bales, in addition to his interest in the manuscript, has studied groups of students drawn from our classes in connection with his general research on social interaction in small discussion groups. It appears from his findings that many of our students are able to use theoretical ideas communicated by case discussion in their interaction with each other. He has also helped us to develop operational ways of defining classroom interactions which previously we had observed and felt to be important but could not adequately describe. In this way our "clinical intuition," that useful but risky tool of those who like to work with people, has been sharpened. Dr. Riesman's sensitive appraisal of our manuscript through its various stages of development has helped us immeasurably in bringing it to its present form.

These brief acknowledgments will, we hope, make it evident that many minds have been productively associated in the development of this book and the teaching methods on which it is based. Our colleagues together with hundreds of our students have provided the proving ground for the communicability of the concepts presented here and their applicability to specific situations. We have profited so greatly during the past seven years from the accumulated experience of our many colleagues and students that it is difficult to express adequately our obligations to them. Where we have disagreed with them, our own skills and knowledge have been increased; where we have agreed with them, our work has been enriched.

The cases in Volume II are the result of research by many people. We are indebted both to our professional colleagues and to the graduate and undergraduate students who have been willing to record carefully a bit of their experience so that others might share it. Because of the necessity of keeping the cases anonymous, many of the contributors to them cannot be mentioned by name. We can, however, express our obligations for case material to John B. Fox, Frances Mulhearn Fuller, George F. F. Lombard, Fritz J. Roethlisberger, Harriet O. Ronken, and Philip E. Slater, all of Harvard University; to Carroll D. Clark, Edwin O. Stene, Robert K. Ready, and Gerald Raines, of the University of Kansas; to Jerome F. Scott, of the British Institute of Management, London, England; to William F. Whyte, of Cornell University; and to H. L. Creek, of Purdue University.

We wish to thank Mr. William Steig and *Nation's Business* for graciously allowing us to use the illustrations Mr. Steig originally prepared for John Kord Lagemann's article about our course, "Why Do People Act Like That?" in the May 1951 issue of that magazine. We think Mr. Steig has, with his usual high skill, captured in graphic form fundamental aspects of human relations.

We have been fortunate in the expert editorial assistance of Patricia E. Hungerford, recently of our staff, and of Elizabeth Treeman of the Harvard University Press. Our thanks also go to our secretarial assistants, particularly Margery L. Johnson, who have worked with such diligence on this manuscript.

We are grateful to the following individuals, publishers, and periodicals for permission to use copyrighted material. They have been unfailingly coöperative, and without their help this book in its present form would not have been possible. Unless otherwise indicated, the material is copyrighted in the name of the publisher listed. Our additional obligations to the copyright holders of the case material are expressed at the beginning of each case.

American Sociological Review, New York, for Talcott Parsons, "Age and Sex in the Social Structure of the United States," October 1942; and for excerpts from James C. Worthy, "Organizational Structure and Employee Moral," April 1950.

Appleton-Century-Crofts, Inc., New York, for excerpts from Ralph Linton, *The Study of Man,* copyright, 1936; and Appleton-Century-Crofts, Inc., and Routledge and Kegan Paul Ltd., London, for excerpts from Ralph Linton, *The Cultural Background of Personality,* copyright, 1945.

Chester I. Barnard, editor, for Lawrence J. Henderson's unpublished "Procedures in a Science."

Natalie Harris Cabot, for her translation of excerpts from Emile Durkheim, *Le Suicide,* translation copyright, 1948, by the President and Fellows of Harvard College.

Joyce Cary and Curtis Brown, Ltd., New York, for Mr. Cary's story, "A Special

Occasion," first printed in *Harper's Magazine*, September 1951, copyright, 1951, by Harper and Brothers.

University of Chicago Press, Chicago, for Charles H. Cooley, "The Roots of Social Knowledge," *American Journal of Sociology*, July 1926; for excerpts from Edward Sapir, "Culture, Genuine and Spurious," *American Journal of Sociology*, January 1924; and for excerpts from Hugh Cabot and Joseph A. Kahl, "Teaching Human Relations," *Journal of General Education*, July 1951.

Columbia University Press (King's Crown Press), New York, for excerpts from Morris Opler's contribution to *Science for Democracy*, edited by Jerome Nathanson, copyright, 1946.

The Delphian Society, Chicago, for Florence R. Kluckhohn, "The American Family" and "America's Women," from *Psychological Patterns*, edited by O. H. Mowrer, copyright, 1952.

Harcourt, Brace and Company, Inc., New York, and George Allen and Unwin Ltd., London, for excerpts from S. I. Hayakawa, *Language in Thought and Action*, copyright, 1949; Harcourt, Brace and Company, Inc., and Routledge and Kegan Paul Ltd., London, for excerpts from George C. Homans, *The Human Group*, copyright, 1950; and Harcourt, Brace and Company, Inc., Martin Secker and Warburg, London, and Lewis Mumford, for Mr. Mumford's article, "The Fallacy of Systems," first printed in the *Saturday Review of Literature*, October 1, 1949, and later incorporated in his book, *The Conduct of Life*, copyright, 1951, by Lewis Mumford.

Harper and Brothers, New York, for excerpts from Lowell J. Carr, *Situational Analysis*, copyright, 1948; for Mary Parker Follett, "The Psychology of Control," chapter 9 of *Dynamic Administration, The Collected Papers of Mary Parker Follett*, edited by Henry C. Metcalf and L. Urwick, copyright, 1942; and for excerpts from Arnold M. Rose, *The Negro in America*, copyright, 1948.

Harper's Magazine, New York, for excerpts from Elton Mayo, "Civilization — The Perilous Adventure," October 1924.

Harvard University, Graduate School of Business Administration, Division of Research, for excerpts from Elton Mayo, *The Human Problems of an Industrial Civilization*, second edition, copyright, 1946, by the President and Fellows of Harvard College; first published by the Macmillan Company, 1933.

Harvard University Press, for excerpts from Chester I. Barnard, *The Functions of the Executive*, copyright, 1938, by the President and Fellows of Harvard College; for excerpts from Abbott Lawrence Lowell, *Conflicts of Principle*, copyright, 1932, by the President and Fellows of Harvard College; for excerpts from Elton Mayo, *Some Notes on the Psychology of Pierre Janet*, copyright, 1948, by the President and Fellows of Harvard College, and for the Appendix to that book, "Frightened People," originally published in the Harvard Medical Alumni Association *Bulletin*, January 1939; and for excerpts from William G. Perry, Jr., "Conflicts in the Learning Process: The Student's Response to Teaching," chapter 2 of *A Handbook for College Teachers*, edited by Bernice B. Cronkhite, copyright, 1950, by the President and Fellows of Harvard College.

Henry Holt and Company, Inc., New York, and Pearn, Pollinger and Higham Ltd., London, for excerpts from L. L. Whyte, *The Next Development in Man*, copyright, 1950, by the New American Library.

Hermitage House, Inc., New York, for excerpts from Patrick Mullahy, *Oedipus: Myth and Complex*, copyright, 1948; and Hermitage House, Inc., and Margaret Mead, for Ruth Benedict, "Continuities and Discontinuities in Cultural Conditioning," from *A Study of Interpersonal Relations*, edited by Patrick Mullahy, copyright, 1949, by Hermitage Press, Inc., first printed in *Psychiatry*, May 1938.

Houghton Mifflin Company, Boston, and Carl R. Rogers, for excerpts from Dr. Rogers' book, *Counseling and Psychotherapy*, copyright, 1942, by Carl R. Rogers.

Alfred A. Knopf, Inc., New York, for excerpts from Volume I of William I.

Thomas and Florian Znaniecki, *The Polish Peasant in Europe and America*, 2 vols., copyright, 1927; first published in five volumes by Richard Badger, Boston, 1918.

Little, Brown and Company, Boston, for excerpts from Jacques Barzun, *The Teacher in America*, copyright, 1945, by Little, Brown and Company — Atlantic Monthly Press.

George F. F. Lombard, for material from *Notes on the Reading Assignments for Social Sciences 12a and 12b*, copyright, 1946, by the President and Fellows of Harvard College; and for "The Veteran Himself," from *Rehabilitation: The Man and the Job*, Report of the Subcommittee on Rehabilitation of the Committee on Work in Industry, National Research Council publication no. 121, printed by the Lord Baltimore Press, 1945, no copyright claimed.

The Macmillan Company, New York, for excerpts from Hadley Cantril, *The "Why" of Man's Experience*, copyright, 1950.

McGraw-Hill Book Company, Inc., New York, for excerpts from Benjamin M. Selekman, *Labor Relations and Human Relations*, copyright, 1947.

National Conference of Social Work, Columbus, Ohio, for Florence R. Kluckhohn, "Dominant and Variant Cultural Value Orientations," an address to the 78th Annual Meeting of the National Conference of Social Work, published in *The Social Welfare Forum, 1951*, copyright, 1951.

W. W. Norton and Company, Inc., New York, for excerpts from Walter B. Cannon, *The Wisdom of the Body*, copyright, 1939, by Walter B. Cannon; and for excerpts from Karen Horney, *Our Inner Conflicts*, copyright, 1945.

The Psychoanalytic Quarterly, New York, for excerpts from Milton H. Erickson, "Experimental Demonstrations of the Psychopathology of Everyday Life," July 1939.

The Reader's Digest, Pleasantville, New York, and James Finan, for Mr. Finan's article, "Inside the Prison — A New Spark of Hope for Remaking Men," *Reader's Digest*, May 1950.

Rinehart and Company, Inc., New York, and Routledge and Kegan Paul Ltd., London, for excerpts from Erich Fromm, *Escape from Freedom*, copyright, 1941, published in England as *Fear of Freedom*.

Carl R. Rogers, for "A Counseling Viewpoint for the USO Worker," published as a pamphlet by the Program Services Division, United Service Division, United States Organizations, Inc., ca. 1943, no copyright claimed.

Routledge and Kegan Paul Ltd., London, for excerpts from Jean Piaget, *Language and Thought of the Child*, copyright, 1926; *Judgment and Reasoning in the Child*, copyright, 1928; *Moral Judgment of the Child*, copyright, 1932; published in the United States by Harcourt, Brace and Company, Inc.; reprint edition of *Moral Judgment of the Child* issued by The Free Press, Glencoe, Illinois, 1948.

Society for Applied Anthropology, New York, for excerpts from Sidney Garfield and William F. Whyte, "The Collective Bargaining Process: A Human Relations Analysis," *Human Organization*, Summer 1950.

Yale University Press, New Haven, and Oxford University Press, London, for excerpts from James B. Conant, *Science and Common Sense*, copyright, 1951; Yale University Press, for excerpts from W. Lloyd Warner and Paul S. Lunt, *"The Social Life of a Modern Community*, copyright, 1941.

Since the selections in this book have been reprinted from many different sources, no attempt has been made to standardize spelling, annotation, or style. Obvious typographical errors and a few other irregularities have been corrected.

Cambridge, Massachusetts   HUGH CABOT
October 1952   JOSEPH A. KAHL

Contents

CONTENTS

Integrated Readings

These articles and books form an integral part of the discussion in each chapter; the shorter items, marked with an asterisk, are reprinted herein.

I. THE CLINICAL APPROACH

* Abbott Lawrence Lowell, *Conflicts of Principle,* selections
* Lawrence J. Henderson, "Procedure in a Science"
* Mary Parker Follett, "The Psychology of Control"

II. DIFFICULTIES IN CLINICAL OBSERVATION

Earl C. Kelley, *Education for What Is Real,* selections
S. I. Hayakawa, *Language in Thought and Action,* selections
* Charles H. Cooley, "The Roots of Social Knowledge"

III. CULTURAL VALUES AND SOCIAL ROLES

* Emile Durkheim, "Anomie"
* Florence R. Kluckhohn, "Dominant and Variant Cultural Value Orientations"
* Ralph Linton, "Status and Role"
W. Lloyd Warner and Paul S. Lunt, *The Social Life of a Modern Community,* selections
* Ruth Benedict, "Continuities and Discontinuities in Cultural Conditioning"
* Talcott Parsons, "Age and Sex in the Social Structure of the United States"
Ruth Benedict, *Patterns of Culture,* selections

IV. THE RESPONSIBILITY OF DECISION

Erich Fromm, *Escape from Freedom,* selections
* William G. Perry, Jr., "The Student's Response to Teaching"

V. OUR DEVELOPING SOCIAL INTERACTIONS

* Jean Piaget, "The Rules of the Game"

VI. THOUGHT PROCESSES

* Elton Mayo, "Notes on Consciousness and Attention"
* Lewis Mumford, "The Fallacy of Systems"
Sigmund Freud, *A General Introduction to Psychoanalysis,* selections

VII. THE INDIVIDUAL'S RESPONSE TO STRESS

* George F. F. Lombard, "The Veteran Himself"
* Elton Mayo, "Frightened People"

Cases in Volume II

Introduction

Active attack on the environment is the most prominent fact in [man's] existence . . . The explanation of
this active attack . . . is a three-fold urge: (i) to live,
(ii) to live well, (iii) to live better. In fact the art of life
is *first* to be alive, *secondly* to be alive in a satisfactory
way, and *thirdly* to acquire an increase in satisfaction.

—Alfred North Whitehead
in *The Function of Reason*

MANY NOTIONS about social science, both our own and those of others, have
been gathered together in these pages. Many other notions, perhaps
equally important, have been intentionally omitted. "Human Relations," which
is often used to refer to various areas of social science, is here defined and
limited to a consideration of the face-to-face interactions which occur between
individual men and women in their immediate social environment.

We have selected certain concepts from the broad field of social science
which many people on the basis of their daily experience find understandable
and useful. Instead of dealing with a group of concepts from a single social
science discipline, such as sociology or psychology, we are presenting here
certain interrelated concepts from several of these disciplines. No tightly reasoned system of social theory is put forward, but rather a series of ideas found
to be fruitful in developing within the individual an increased comprehension
of the social situations in which he interacts. Many of these ideas may appear
to be obvious — and this seems to us desirable. A greater understanding of the
implications of the obvious is of prime importance in the area of human relations. Such learning can come from the knowledge gained in ordinary social
life — and insofar as we all live and observe we are all social scientists — combined with more formal, articulate, and communicable ideas from an ever-
growing theoretical tradition. As social life becomes more complex, the need
grows for theoretical comprehension and practical skill in human interaction.

It is perhaps axiomatic that as living organisms become more effective in
dealing with their environment, they also become increasingly complex. Simple
cellular entities move with their environment and wait for food and nourish-
ment; multicellular organisms are able to seek sustenance and, finally, even to
make material modification of their environment. They not only live, but they
can live well and may aspire to live better. This generalization seems to be as
valid of social organizations as of physical organisms. Small, isolated groups

of men drift with the seasons and depend largely upon chance to bring food within their grasp. An increased control of the environment — with a greater permanence of location, increased specialization of labor, improved technology — awaits the larger and less isolated groups. Greater interdependence between men, with an increase in the complexity of organization, seems to be inherent in the process of transition from living to living well. And the aspiration to live better seems to have resulted in still greater complexity. In the current social organizations of man, this complexity is now enormous.

Organizational complexity is a relative matter; a development that may under certain circumstances be too complex for the environment to sustain or for the minds of the men involved to grasp, may under other circumstances become stable and comprehensible. A complexity of forces with survival value becomes an organism *or* an organization when the interactions between its elements mutually improve their lot. These interactions are never wholly effective or ineffective, good or bad; rather, their net result is a practical working arrangement between the elements which permits each of them to obtain some mutual benefits not otherwise available. In the physiological realm such a working arrangement has satisfied the demands of the individual cells in relation to their environment so fully that life in many forms has maintained itself from a distant past almost without change. In the social world also comparative stability has been attained — the ant society operates in its environment apparently as effectively today as it did thousands of years ago. Although such environmental responses are highly complex, a useful dynamic equilibrium has been attained and survival value developed.

Human society is still developing increasingly complex organizations. It is still attempting to live better within the physical environment, and there can be no question that social organization has produced great successes to this end over a long period of years. Man has steadily extended the amount of work he can do in his limited lifetime by combining his energies with others through organization. Thereby the technical skills and practical energies of an increasing number of trained specialists have been productively interlocked. This meshing of knowledge would be impossible without a scientific method common to all the specialists. It accurately relates them to the physical environment they deal with and, because of conventional ways of communicating, to each other. Such a scientific method, vital in maintaining technical complexity, has been patently successful in solving many of the problems of the physical, inorganic environment. Similarly, in the organic environment, *except for some interactions with other humans*, this same method is solving many problems in medicine, biochemistry, and the related sciences. It is widely believed, and may be accepted as an asymptotic approach to truth, that with adequate time and money most such problems can be solved.

However, in that part of our environment dealing with many of our interactions with each other, the developing organizational complexity may have exceeded our ability to understand it. We do not have in most of our activities so methodical a basis for interaction as exists among natural scientists in their technical work. Indeed, they find it difficult to apply their usual scientific methods to an understanding of their own interactions with each other. The phenomena of natural and social sciences seem to have important differences. Perhaps it is particularly true of social sciences that the phenomena are more frequently a system of forces whose responsive interactions are difficult to classify into limited causal relationships. The distinctions may become more clear if we consider some of the problems of man in relation to his world.

Successful methods have been developed for studying many effects of outside forces on the human body — both such inorganic forces as cold and such organic forces as disease. It could be observed that these forces affect the human body in limited ways; and, as these forces were isolated, increasingly better methods could be developed for understanding them and modifying their effect. The internal bodily response to such forces is much less clearly understood. And, further, there seem to be some responses, in which the body is reacting as a whole to the total environment around it, that are hardly understood at all. These may be systemic internal responses to a large number of forces in the total external system that are not susceptible to isolation by any current scientific method. For example, psychic disturbances, rheumatoid arthritis, even the growth of cancer cells may be such systemic responses.

The limits of tolerance of the elements in the body's system to cold are definite and observable; but the limits of tolerance to internal forces are not so clear. Cancer cells may start on their deviant path in response to some obscure but limited set of forces from the outside world; if so, the scientific methods now developed will probably isolate these forces. On the other hand, the growth of cancer cells may result from a systemic modification of the body in response to practically unlimited combinations of external forces difficult to isolate. Or they may grow only in response to an internal modification of the body's system itself. The internal forces which hold the system together may at times get out of balance from a multiple of internal causes, with the result that certain elements of the system demand for themselves a greater modification of response on the part of the other cells than is possible for them. Thus, the cancer cells might only be cells that, because of changes in the internal system, no longer respond within the limits that can be tolerated by the other, noncancerous cells.

Such changes in the internal forces are the most difficult factors to observe about many systems, and they may be the critical factors in the operation of social systems. New elements are always being added to a social system which modify the balance of the internal forces that hold that system in operation. This increasing complexity demands some modification of responses by all the elements within the system. This modification, to be effective, must result in a new working arrangement in which the responses of *all* elements to each other are within expected and manageable proportions. Thus in a social system of men the understanding of their responses in face-to-face interactions is of importance. Threats to social systems as great as those of cancer cells to the body systems have occurred in history and have created similar destruction. Societies have died and disappeared.

However, human beings may be able to exert a unique control over the social system of which they are a part. They may be able, consciously or unconsciously, to restrain disruptive internal forces at their inception and keep them within manageable limits. By developing ethical standards based upon consistent behavior in response to the accumulated experience of countless generations, they may be able to maintain a social equilibrium without detailed understanding of the nature or operation of these mores. But — and this is a task of human relations — in addition, men and women in a society can learn to understand and to control some of the consequences of their behavior as it develops in relation to others.

The observation of social phenomena on which to base a methodical understanding has certain inherent difficulties not present in the observation of the natural sciences. First, the concrete phenomena of natural science remain comparatively stable over a long period of time. The movements of heavenly bodies, for example, although perhaps not unchanged, have modified so little that we today can feel we are observing the same phenomena studied by Copernicus and Galileo. We have developed good techniques and equipment for observing these particular phenomena and accumulating more and more carefully refined observations about them over a long period of years. Secondly, in the natural sciences, we as observers are not closely involved with a large part of the phenomena we are observing. We can, therefore, be trained to develop and make use of an "objectivity" about the data in a sense that makes possible identical observations by men of very different social training. A Chinese, a Frenchman, a Christian, or a Jew can all be trained to observe the sun within the framework of a limited methodology and to communicate their findings to each other in definite terms — in an international theoretical language.

In observing social phenomena, however, both aspects are different. The facts under observation may change materially from lifetime to lifetime in little-understood ways, and the "subjectivity" of observations becomes a nagging problem. It is impossible to view again the particular concrete data on which men with social skills throughout the ages based their hypotheses. Although we are still observing *men* in their interactions with others and use very similar words to describe our observations, it is difficult to believe that the phenomena have not changed materially with the years. The natural phenomena which Copernicus and Galileo viewed remain essentially unchanged; the men on whose interactions Heraclitus and Plato and Bacon based their social conceptualizations have long since died, and it seems likely that their counterparts have been greatly modified by a changing society. Such modifications certainly have not been so great that they invalidate all past social observations, yet it is patently impossible to observe the same concrete phenomena and determine the modifications of hypothesis necessary. This difficulty in reëxamining in detail identical concrete social phenomena over long periods has necessarily limited the number of minds that can appraise particular data and has led to generalizations on a very high level of abstraction. Such generalizations as "Love of one's fellow men is the strongest force for good in the world" or "The strongest motivation in man is fear of his fellow men" have the ring of truth. Yet the limits of their applicability are not inherent in their statement, and it is difficult to use them methodically in understanding the social phenomena we are observing. They leave out by their very nature differences of detail that may have made of them useful generalities about particular situations in the past.

Furthermore, the success which has been obtained in the natural sciences, where the factors observed are in a certain sense "outside ourselves," has led to many attempts at "objectivity" in the same sense in viewing social data. The difficulties of this attempt have become increasingly evident, and a suspicion seems to be growing that such "objectivity" is not only impossible but even undesirable. Our view of ourselves and of our interactions with others is materially different from our view of other types of phenomena. We are inevitably *part* of any social situation which we are observing, and, no matter how we minimize this part, we do change the situation by our presence. This change is in the forces internal to the system we are observing and is much more complex and more difficult to analyze than our effect upon other data. Yet our intimate connection with the many elements of the data may make more of them available to us for consideration and give us our best opportunity to understand them.

The fact that we interact with the social phenomena we are observing need not deter us from the attempt to understand the effects of that interaction. Many men, at some level of their being, have understood these effects and have behaved in response to them — although seldom have they been able to communicate their understanding clearly. They have observed their social world, have gathered useful generalities which have permitted them to relate themselves well to it, and have continued to interact skillfully with others over long periods of time. They have lived in many different ways all described as "successful" and have been greatly admired. As viewed by others, these men have not only lived and lived well but seem to have also lived better. Such men in their own lives have maintained no great objectivity in their observations of others. Rather, they have lived active lives, they have welcomed social intercourse, and their understanding has been expressed in the skills of their interactions. Such men are of utmost value to social organization. Often, those immediately around them learn many of their skills in the way that children learn from parents. However, this communication of skills is uncertain; much of the understanding of such wise practitioners perishes with them. It remains unformulated and unarticulated. Neither leader nor disciple is able to select the more from the less significant knowledge.

This very selection, however, is the necessary foundation of widespread communication of skills. In the field of human relations, the selection of fruitful hypotheses which lead to greater understanding has been slowly growing. Although the relevance to social behavior of many of these theories, such as those included in this book, has been established, the logical relation of one to the other is by no means so clearly evident.

At the present stage of social science, knowledge that can be used does not seem to develop merely from a logical exposition of ideas. Since in social science we always interact with social phenomena, notions are only fully understood as they lead to greater skills of interaction — to greater interpersonal competence. Just as we must learn the concepts of natural science in order to deal with the external world around us, so our learning of the concepts of social science has as its purpose more effective understanding of the human world within which we interact. Each student of human relations in this way becomes a judge of the validity of any given notion. Unless its presentation fits closely with other notions which he has already gathered from his own experience and helps him interact more effectively, he will tend to view it as "possibly sound but too theoretical" and to give it no further consideration. In human relations, more than in other areas of social science, every adult from eighteen to eighty has in fact vast amounts of personally tested knowledge and rightly feels that he is able to weigh against it all new notions presented to him.

The observation and communication of the material of human relations have, therefore, special problems. To those of the perishability of particular social phenomena and the impossibility of being wholly "objective" about them must be added the problems involved in the vast and frequently over-simplified knowledge with which we all start this specialized study. Most of us, if we were undertaking to study physics or astronomy or physiology, would expect to work in some organized way with a specialist in the field. We might read reports of his work, listen to him lecture, or watch him in the laboratory. We would expect him to point out to us, in one way or another, the premises on which his hypotheses rest, to weigh for us the relative importance of the various concepts based on these premises, to lead us clearly and carefully through a logical presentation to well-founded conclusions and finally, per-haps, to some understanding of basic problems that still remain unsolved. With this behind us we would feel that we had a sound foundation on which to form some opinions of our own about this field.

In human relations, however, and to some extent in all social science, much of the data considered by the specialist is already well known to us; we have considered more or less consciously many basic premises, developed concepts, weighed their relative importance, and discarded those that seem least useful to us. We have then on the basis of such considerations built the growing edifice of our own lives. The hypotheses of the specialist, dealing with much the same data and drawing more detailed and perhaps radically different con-clusions from our own, do in fact present us with a backhanded criticism of our own knowledge and skills. We may be trying to lead the best life we know how to live, possibly based on learning from many people we hold dear. Then this "specialist," knowing nothing at all about us, tries to tell us that we should be behaving in other and "better" ways.

A proper spirit of humility regarding the notions of human relations is, therefore, much more difficult to achieve than in other fields of study. Here, we must not only attempt to *evaluate* data in ways that the specialists have found to be productive but we must also try to *reëvaluate* very similar data that we have found for ourselves to be fundamentally important in our own lives.

On the basis of some such general considerations as have been presented in this introduction, we, the authors and our associates, have been working with groups of undergraduate and graduate students in the study of human rela-tions. Slowly, from our work, ways of observation and communication have evolved that seem to lead to an increased operational understanding on the part of both students and teachers.

Some years ago, we all took as our starting point the observation that case discussion produced learning in this area. As a result, we gathered together hundreds of cases to present as factually as possible concrete social phenomena. In working with this material, we discovered that there are certain character-istics which make a case "good" from our point of view. A case must be *real* in the sense that the reported interactions between the people in it have actu-ally occurred. The description of it should be brief but detailed, presenting verbatim conversations and sufficient background material to establish the so-cial context within which the interactions took place. Names and places should be disguised to prevent embarrassment to original participants, but always in a way that does not modify substantially the original situation. Value judgments — whether any particular social situation is good or bad — should be scrupulously kept at a minimum. No analysis should be included to indicate why things happened as they did, unless such an analysis is made by some character in the case whose relation to the social situation is evident. Nor should a case be written to illustrate any particular theory, but, by presenting the complexity of the original situation, exemplify, like life itself, many theories.

In addition to these criteria, a good case from our viewpoint must also be one which consistently produces good group discussion. Many cases that some of us felt were highly significant were quickly discarded after subjection to this test. Others that we considered only mildly interesting have become favorite cases after discussion; groups of people have been able to find in them many things of interest that we did not even suspect.

We have included in the second volume of this book thirty-three cases which fill these requirements. Each of them represents a report of an actual social interaction, and each has produced active discussion in groups of twenty to fifty people. Most of them have been discussed by dozens of such groups. These cases have been selected primarily to be of interest to men and women between the ages of eighteen and twenty-five, although many older groups have found them equally interesting. They represent a wide variety of social situations — from family, friendship, and social groups to administrative, business, and community activities. They consist largely of situations either close to the actual experience of many people or close to situations in which many people expect to become involved. Some of the cases are more interesting to men than to women and of some the obverse is true, but both men and women become interested in the discussion as they become aware of the mutuality of the problems involved.

Given this first point of interest, the cases then permit a more careful consideration of "what is going on here." These situations, with some of the complexity of all life situations, contain many elements which mutually affect each other in varying ways. Many readers have found techniques for understanding at least their own reactions to such brute facts. As the reader also learns to ask himself why the people in the cases are behaving as they do — be it like or unlike the way he himself would behave — further interest in the cases develops. If he can ask himself what reasonable inferences about the behavior in the case can be drawn from the material presented — inferences that are consistent with the material and not denied by any part of it — further understanding develops. With such an enlarged understanding, a wider view of the courses of action available to the people in the cases can be considered.

It may be evident that such an approach to the understanding of case material is a response to some of the problems already stated about the consideration of all social phenomena. The cases represent "permanent social data" which are readily available and to which ideas can be referred again and again as they develop. The social phenomena were selected as pertinent within careful limits, and interpretations are subject to denial or abandonment if they are not supported by the "facts" of the situation as reported.

These cases are "clinical" observations about social situations and bear some relation to similar observations in medicine which make possible the handling of malfunctions of the body. Such medical observations have not as yet led to any general theory which encompasses all the behavior of the body. They have led, however, to extensive skill and to detailed understanding of many medical problems. Similar objectives have been achieved in the social area through a consideration of case material.

Our experience has indicated that there is a substantial body of social theory in the area of human relations, imprecise as it is, that can be communicated productively. This group of concepts does seem to assist many individuals in reëvaluating and modifying their own ideas so that they become more useful to them. These men and women are then in a better position to develop, as their experience grows, new and more adequate social concepts.

We do not find that even these theories can be presented dogmatically or at all times wholly logically. It does not seem possible to express them so that they are equally evident to all readers. If, however, the concepts presented in Volume I are used together with such case material as we have presented in Volume II, then the theoretical concepts often spotlight observations that could not otherwise be made; they permit observations to be related together in ways wholly new to the reader. The theories and the cases are more useful in relation to each other than either would be alone.

This book is written in a manner that permits the reader to evaluate for himself the relevance of theoretical hypotheses to the accumulation of social knowledge he has previously acquired. This body of theoretical material is all interlocking — each theory tends to support and clarify others. Yet the *relative* importance of each individual notion can be weighed by the reader out of his own experience without serious damage to the material as a whole.

Our first two chapters deal with a detailed consideration of the clinical approach to social data which we have introduced here. The next five chapters discuss concepts which may be useful to the individual in understanding and observing his own motivations and their effect on his interactions with those immediately around him. The eighth chapter makes a transition from the individual to the group. These eight chapters are also pointed toward answering, in respect to case material, the basic question, "What is going on here?" The remaining five chapters undertake to consider more fully concepts about groups and their effects on the individuals within them. These latter chapters are also oriented more than are the earlier chapters toward the question, "What shall I do?" This order of presentation need not be followed rigidly. We have indicated frequently the relationship of one set of material to another, and some freedom can be felt to consider "interesting" ideas thoroughly and others more casually.

The order of presentation itself rests on assumptions which our own experience indicates to be important. We assume that an improvement in an individual's ability to observe social phenomena is necessary and desirable; that it can be accomplished if the issue is approached directly; that in turn this improved ability permits an increase in the choices of action possible; and that all this leads to more effective interactions between individuals. These assumptions are clearly not equally applicable to all individuals. In fact, there is considerable evidence to support an exactly opposite approach, and several of our chapters present ideas about ways in which such resistance to concepts develops. However, our experience indicates that resistance can be overcome and that our assumptions have important validity for a large proportion of the men and women with whom we have dealt.

We have used the words of other authors whenever possible in the first volume. We have quoted from them extensively; we have reprinted articles and even parts of books where such abstraction did not seem to violate the authors' material; we have referred the reader to substantial parts of other books when a more complete presentation of a related group of ideas by others seems desirable. We have used our own words only where it seemed others had not adequately formulated some concept of human relations that we felt to be useful, where we wished to indicate a point of view helpful to the consideration of case material, or where we considered that the interrelatedness of the concepts should be emphasized. We ask our reader not to consider these references to other books as simply "outside reading." These books do not just expand notions included here, but rather present ideas which we have not summarized but which we use somewhere in our discussion. These works are as much and as important a part of our book as if they had been reprinted within it. Strictly "outside reading" to assist in a more thorough understanding of some of the ideas presented will be found in the "Additional Readings" listed at the end of each chapter.

The cases in Volume II have been numbered to assist in reference to them, and their order is related in a very general way to the order of the readings. Since the cases contain much of the complexity of life situations and can, as we have already noted, be considered in relation to a large number of concepts, they might be arranged in many other ways. Their particular order here is one which we have recently used and which seems to have raised questions in a way that has led to productive discussion. We shall certainly modify this order in our own use whenever we feel that a particular group at a particular time might learn from the discussion of a particular case. In general, the early cases are less complex than the later ones. The early ones also seem more useful in improving observation about social situations than in deciding appropriate action. The later cases raise action questions more clearly.

We have found the first four cases a useful introduction for individual or group consideration and have used them in this order for several years. The first three cases present "problems" of widespread interest but do not indicate any clear path to equally wide agreement for the "solution" of the problems. They thus put before the reader some need for a further understanding of the complexity of social phenomena. The fourth case raises specific problems but indicates that some sort of solution satisfactory to the people in the case was reached. This absence of "unsolved problems" seems to heighten the impact of the other questions that can be raised about case material, such as the nature of the relationships among the different people in the case, the ways in which these relationships have been developed in the past, and their effect on the present situation. Basic questions of this sort are continually raised in the discussion of later cases, but we have developed no more than a general case order that has seemed useful.

Any reader who has followed our discussion thus far must realize that to us clinical observation forms a foundation for our entire work. The case material of Volume II presents social experiences that the reader and the authors may have in common, and reference to it at times will produce a clarification of ideas. The cases in some such order as presented were in the authors' minds as the chapters were written. Ideally, then, it would be useful if the reader began with the first case in Volume II and read two or three cases before he turned to Volume I. Further, if he interspersed two or three cases between each chapter, useful questions might arise that would make the chapters more meaningful. Such a mixture of the facts of concrete social phenomena with the abstractions of social concepts makes a reëvaluation of the reader's own ideas more productive for him.

We realize that, if the reader is to understand this material well, we have not suggested a simple program. We know that we are asking much more work of him than he is ordinarily willing to give to many books and more than he may be willing to give to this one. In extenuation we can only say that this approach does use the reader's own accumulated experience effectively and has intrigued people into investing the necessary amount of time for its comprehension.

We have indicated our opinion that, at the present stage of knowledge in social science, communication of the ideas of human relations in any form is difficult and that many of these difficulties lie in the reëvaluation of one's own concepts which must often precede understanding. This book both in its content and its method of presentation attempts to assist the process of reëvaluation. But such reëvaluation of one's own concepts is difficult to accomplish *alone*. People often feel they must defend their current evaluations with all the strength at their command. Further assistance in the process of reëvaluation can be developed through the discussion of case data in groups. Such discussions can point out an often present oversimplicity of numerous sensible but divergent notions about the same material, and the comparative stability of the case material can give many points of reference to help in the resolution of conflicting views.

Case discussions in groups differ materially from ordinary social conversation. This introduction is not the place to consider these differences in detail, but one important difference is worth consideration. In case discussions the interest is focused on the task of determining what is going on *here in this particular case*. In social conversations — serious or casual — such a task is seldom present, and the interaction usually enables the individual to relate himself to those around him in some meaningful way.

In social discussions without this task it does not matter that the data are present only in the mind of one of the participants and that he can modify the observations subtly to fit the trends of the discussion. It also does not matter that many social conversations proceed from the particular to the general in ways that would prevent either understanding or agreement if considered carefully. Important interactions certainly take place where neither agreement nor understanding is necessary. An eminent professional man recently argued socially in our presence that *all* sunglasses were bad for the eyes. His arguments were presented seriously and were twofold. First, he asserted that the eyes were built to accommodate adequately to variations in the intensity of light — an argument which is clearly not true without limit and does not express the limits of its validity. Secondly, he bolstered his argument by reference to authority and stated that his doctor, in fact, *all good* doctors, agreed that this was so — a claim which was for practical purposes empirically unassailable. In this social conversation such an argument could only be attacked by a statement of a contrary opinion — "I don't believe it" — with the consequent risk of unreconcilable disagreement. No such attack was made, and his relations with the group may even have been improved by his discussion. But the problem was not adequately analyzed.

Social conversations tend to repeat and defend the existing evaluations of the community, tend to force reëvaluations in this direction. The general task of understanding social data is not the prime objective of social discussion, although much of our prior learning about social data has taken place through it. Such conversation tends to be a solidarity-producing and tension-relieving process — a way of saying, "We are all more or less alike."

The task of determining "what is going on here" is, of course, often present in lectures on social phenomena as well as in discussions of it. The lecturer's method of communicating this task requires the presentation in a clear and logical manner of evaluations about the material that seem to him important in relation to the group before him. But the acknowledged existence of other evaluations *in the listener* about what may appear to be identical social phenomena makes communication of more careful formulations difficult. If this problem is as important as it seems to us at the present stage of knowledge in social science, then the answer to it cannot lie only in an improvement in the skills of the lecturer. Some important blocks to thorough communication can only be removed by the experience of the listener.

The lecturer tries to lead the ideas of his listeners down the paths that seem important to him by his skills of presentation to a particular audience, by the ways he arranges his ideas and feelings to follow one another. For general reasons which have been indicated earlier in this introduction, this method is quite effective for many subjects and in many situations. But it is not the only way in which the ideas of a group can be led. Interaction in discussion also accomplishes such leadership. Ideas can be modified, limited, or expanded, by the way in which one responds in discussion to the ideas of others. Discussions are, of course, never precise and the paths frequently wander, but the ideas of others may at times be directed even more effectively toward a desired goal. In general social interactions, such leadership of ideas is often used skillfully.

In case discussion, the task of understanding specific material is as present as it is in any lecture. Since this understanding must be related both to the ideas of the specialist and his listener, communication can be paced more carefully. Discussion permits a teacher to do what all teachers want but seldom have the opportunity to do: it allows him to be patient in his teaching and to find out what must be said again in other ways and in different contexts so as to increase the listeners' understanding. As the teacher learns to accept fully the fact that, because he has once stated something clearly, it does not follow that any of his listeners have necessarily comprehended it, he will then be able to listen more carefully. Productive disagreements can take place and clarifications of ideas can occur. In case discussions, arguments, although they frequently arise, can be resolved by direct reference to the case data. Either the points in question represent facts of the data, or fair inferences to be drawn from the data not denied by such facts or other equally good inferences, or they are possibly true but outside the data of the case and must be considered as undemonstrated.

Perhaps more important is the observation that ideas developed from a discussion of case data do carry conviction for a group. When, during a discussion, notions develop that are contrary to the prior beliefs of many of the group and that are unassailable by the data, modification in those beliefs appears. When a member of the group finds that some of his pet notions have become irrelevant to the discussion, he often starts to reconsider their value to him. A vivid example occurred in one of our groups a few years ago. A man had been disagreeing logically and forcefully with many of the ideas presented by other members of the group for about fifteen meetings. Finally, in the middle of one meeting, he interrupted the discussion of another member with: "Go on with what you're saying. It's interesting. If people really behave the way they seem to in these cases, I've got to change my whole idea about the world." He then became comparatively quiet for several discussion meetings and finally developed into one of the most useful members of the group.

Group discussion of case material in the way we are suggesting contains many anxiety-producing elements, both for the "specialist" and for the rest of the group, that do not develop for various reasons in either the lecture or the ordinary social discussion. In the organized teaching of social science the teacher is likely to be a man who has spent years in learning an academic discipline; he has found answers to many intellectual problems that have seemed important to him by turning to that discipline. He may well feel that he knows, or should know, the answers to the problems raised in the discussion and that he must spell them out for his students as quickly and precisely as possible. Yet the considerations we have been discussing here suggest that at least in the teaching of human relations the time when the teacher is ready to talk is not necessarily the time when the student is most likely to listen productively.

The students in the group also have new and difficult problems placed before them. Although the struggles in working through these problems seem to be a necessary part of the process of learning material which requires a reëvaluation of acceptable ideas, nevertheless such activity is anxiety-producing. Each member of the group must *first* sort out for himself the complexity of particular case material, much of which is close to his own experience. He must *secondly*, if he is to feel he is making sense in the discussion, develop some viewpoint about the material consistent with his own experience and with the general ideas presented in the prior discussions. He must *thirdly* determine some way of expressing these ideas to the particular group of which he is a part. All these activities are difficult and produce their own kind of anxiety which must be handled.

Individuals develop many ways of protecting themselves against the consequences of these anxieties, which may become productive or destructive forces. The most effective discussions seem to originate from an atmosphere, nurtured by both the teacher and the students, which steadily encourages sufficient conflict to challenge oversimplified thinking about specific material but also rewards the patient search for more adequate thinking. The active reëvaluation distinguishes this process of learning from both the ordinary social conversations and lectures.

The organized teaching of human relations by case discussion up to the present time has developed teachers who use techniques suited to themselves but which differ widely in detail. We are not yet able to understand sufficiently the group processes involved to state clearly the "best" way to lead discussion. All of the techniques appear to us effective when they are characterized, first, by a feeling of the necessity of taking into patient consideration the thoughts of the particular group about the brute facts of a particular situation, and secondly, by a realization that the anxiety-producing elements of this process cannot be ignored.

In our own experience one of the most serious obstacles to the development of an effective working arrangement within a discussion group which includes an instructor is the indiscriminate use by the instructor of the authority of his position. We are trying to create a situation where ideas pertinent to a course in human relations will develop and be rewarded at those times they appear important to the student. Yet many students have spent years learning to please or displease the teacher. They may even have internalized this learning to a point where they can see value only in a statement by them that produces either approval or disapproval from the teacher. They may have no clear standard in intellectual work other than the word of constituted authority. The teacher is thus encouraged to take a position of evaluating the discussion which he may rightly feel the group is demanding and would accept. But if he takes such a position he also takes with it the responsibility for future clarification of all ideas, which leads more to the development of his own thinking than to that of the students.

We have therefore in the early stages of the development of an effective working arrangement within a group limited our authoritative statements to those about the structure of the course rather than to its content. We tell the students that we require a particular case, which must have been read before class, to be discussed today. As discussion gets away from the case, we may bring the students back to the case; as it becomes evident that certain students have read the case only superficially, we ask embarrassing questions which suggest that a more thorough reading would be desirable. We ask the students to take the initiative about when they shall talk. We state that we want everyone to feel free to talk but that we will not call on anyone who does not want to talk. We set the limits within which the discussion takes place but are interested in *any* discussion that takes place within those limits.

Often, in the early weeks, the students, in trying to be "right," use all their skills to maneuver us into taking a stand. They want to know the best way to go about tackling a new case; they want an explicit statement of the difference between a case discussion and a book discussion; they occasionally burst out in angry phrases that this is all nonsense, that, in so far as each man is entitled to his own opinion, obviously they as a group are not going to reach any positive decisions or learn anything new.

Soon, however, the students become convinced that we mean what we have been saying and doing; that we are interested in *their* thoughts about *this* material; that we will help the discussion move forward along the lines of their interests whenever we can. They learn that we are not going to force our ideas on them. We can and will clarify statements advanced in a blurred fashion, perhaps sharpening the point made, to allow the student to develop his thinking or to be more adequately challenged by another student. We will make explicit unstated premises behind different statements. We will relate statements to others made earlier and thus encourage interactions within the group. We will point out contradictions. We will help the students understand the importance to the discussion of their own and other students' feelings as well as their ideas. We will help them express, if they wish, feelings that are painful or embarrassing. Thus by our actions we slowly help the students learn that the instructor's role is to help keep the discussion of this particular case moving clearly and productively for the whole group, rather than to indicate, either by positive statements of our own or by the leading questions we ask, just what we consider the "proper solution" of the case to be.

In this development of class initiative, there are many considerations that the instructor must keep in mind. In the early stages of his relationship with this group, the individual differences within the group are most important. The class is characterized, of course, by the students who are the most vocal. Intellectual skills and an ability to verbalize easily do not necessarily go together. A class may be led at the beginning by bright or dull students, and each must be handled carefully with respect to himself, to the group, and to the development of the subject matter. The bright student must be helped to make his points clear to the group. The dull student must not be discouraged, for he often has some point that can be most useful to the discussion.

One year the first student who spoke for an instructor on the opening day of case discussion talked steadily, scarcely stopping for breath until he had outlined the case brilliantly. The instructor felt that he could not have done a better job himself. From the point of view of a clear exposition of the case, nothing more remained to be done. From the point of view of teaching human relations, little had been accomplished. The instructor remarked only: "That is very interesting. Have we any other thoughts?" And the class, having at that time listened only casually to the first student, discussed the case actively for nearly two one-hour sessions before many of the points originally raised were generally understood. The first student also learned that the group in the classroom, as well as the individual brilliance of a single performer, has something to do with the situation. He started to observe the thoughts of others, and this stood him in good stead when cases outside his experience were under consideration.

As the group grows in creative independence and as the instructor develops his relationship with the group, the students begin to indicate important holes in their experience, gaps where the greater knowledge of the instructor can be helpful. At times the students show clearly that they need clarification, expansion, or perhaps "pulling together" of the thoughts they have been discussing in recent sessions. On these occasions the instructor can and must formulate the needed conceptualizations by short lectures. Even then care must be taken to present these theories as being potentially useful in the discussion of the case material rather than as dogmatically true.

We use the material in the chapters of this first volume to present the theoretical ideas we wish our students to consider. We lay aside one or two days every two or three weeks during an academic year for the specific discussion of the conceptualizations put forward in a particular chapter. During the interim, while we are discussing specific case material, we make clear our interest in any conceptual material from the reading that they are able to bring into the discussion. In our periodic reading discussions, while still directing our attention to the students' understanding, we are more free to explain briefly our opinion about the ideas that we feel a particular author had in mind. Still, we do assume that students can read for themselves if the material is significant to them, and we do not lecture on any of these reading assignments.

If these volumes are to be used in academic teaching in this general way, they include enough work for a full academic year. As we suggested for the general reader, we would expect any instructor who wished to use *Human Relations* in his own course to differ with some of our decisions regarding emphasis on particular ideas. He may well want to include more reading and spend more time on certain ideas than we do, and he may wish to omit other ideas altogether. He may wish to present the ideas in an order very different from the one we use. He may be more interested in the second half of Volume I than the first, or he may want to select certain chapters out of the entire volume. Such changes in use seem to us entirely appropriate, and we have tried to present this material so that individual instructors — and the general reader — can make any such choices as his own interests dictate. Anyone who reads these volumes carefully from cover to cover will in any event make similar choices by integrating certain parts of them into his thinking and entirely forgetting other parts. Any assistance in this selection process that would be clearly useful for a particular group would, of course, be very valuable. Although many references are made from one part of these books to another, the chapters and the cases are so written that they are to a considerable extent complete in themselves, and such modifications can be readily made.

Our entire approach to the task of communicating our ideas in human relations must indicate the value we place on interactions with others about the material. We feel that any further determination of the relative importance of the concepts we have presented can only be made through such interactions. The path we have taken may at times seem tortuous, but it has led us more surely to the objective we have in mind than other apparently more direct routes. We are sure that still more effective paths can be developed as the processes involved in this particular type of learning are more fully understood. We hope that many people familiar with this material will try various ways of using it and will let us know their results.

Human Relations

CONCEPTS IN CONCRETE

SOCIAL SCIENCE

CHAPTER I

The Clinical Approach

WE PUT a great deal of intellectual effort into the search for proper guides for action in everyday situations. We select from our past experiences certain generalizations that seem useful and retain them as signposts to direct our steps. These experiences are not only those in which we ourselves have been directly engaged but also those in which we have participated "secondhand" through the behavior, conversation, or writings of others. From these experiences we often form in our minds a body of "principles" which permits us to say, when faced with a specific situation, "It's against my principles," or "It's the principle of the thing." Many of these principles, however, seem to be both good in themselves and opposed to each other. Lowell, in the reading listed below, considers the nature of such conflicts. How do we know *when* and to *what degree* a principle is to be applied to the situation at hand? Read

ABBOTT LAWRENCE LOWELL, *Conflicts of Principle*, selections below.

Lowell, following Aristotle, describes the mean between two apparently equally good principles as the way to resolve conflict between them. But he adds:

> As a general maxim in life this is excellent, but imperfect because it does not determine where the mean actually lies . . .
> In fact the true mean may vary with the conditions in which men are placed, and the conditions change with the passing years . . . The object of these pages is, therefore, as a footnote to Aristotle, to point out by recent examples in various fields how the mean has changed, and how mankind is seeking for it amid the contrary principles between which it lies.[1]

Lowell's concept of "finding the proper limits between conjugate principles" is useful in trying to apply generalizations to particular cases. But the simplicity of his presentation is misleading. His illustrations are so clear that they make it seem obvious that principles can be carried only so far. It is very difficult, however, to observe any case with sufficient clarity so that the mean point for the application of conjugate principles becomes apparent. As Lowell points out, this mean is always changing from situation to situation. The development of skills in social observation is necessary in order to be able to determine the utility of any generalization in a specific situation. And in dealing with the world around us, we are always dealing with specific situations, never general ones. If we can observe a situation fully and understand its nature clearly, we will be able to act more effectively in it.

---

[1] Abbott Lawrence Lowell, *Conflicts of Principle* (Cambridge: Harvard University Press, 1932), pp. 6–7; see selections below.

Observing a constantly changing situation requires a different method from that usually used in the laboratory. There, techniques and instruments can be developed to isolate certain factors for careful analysis while all "other things" are held or assumed constant. Galileo, for example, conducted experiments in his laboratory which permitted him to observe similarities from which he formulated his laws of motion. In these experiments he studied the motion of cylinders rolling down inclined surfaces. In doing this he decided that it was helpful for his purpose to ignore the effects of friction. Now anyone knows that in a practical situation to ignore friction is folly. Yet Galileo could not have formulated the laws of motion without doing so.

In social observation this technique is seldom effective; we are usually dealing with many variables that are constantly interacting, not only with each other, but also with the observer: these variables are mutually dependent. Even a slight change of one factor, therefore, affects all other factors, and they in turn react on the original one. Thus there is rarely a simple cause followed by a simple effect, though it sometimes looks as if this had taken place. If we are to understand clearly what is happening, then we must study the nature of the interdependence of the variables and their relation to the whole. The method of studying social phenomena "as a whole" is often called clinical. The techniques of the clinic are as useful as those of the laboratory. When we are acting in life situations, we are never in a position to ignore completely one variable while we are observing the actions of the other variables. Whether we are in medicine, business, government, education, or family life, we are in situations where clinical rather than laboratory observations are important, and we must at all times be alert to the relevance of *all* the factors present.

Laboratory experimentation and observation is not more or less scientific than clinical observation. It is merely a different technique developed for different purposes. According to James B. Conant,

> Science is an interconnected series of concepts and conceptual schemes that have developed as a result of experimentation and observation and are fruitful of further experimentation and observations. In this definition the emphasis is on the word "fruitful." Science is a speculative enterprise. The validity of a new idea and the significance of a new experimental finding are to be measured by the consequences — consequences in terms of other ideas and other experiments. Thus conceived, science is not a quest for certainty; it is rather a quest which is successful only to the degree that it is continuous.[2]

Both laboratory and clinical observations seek to develop ideas that are useful in certain ways and within certain limits. The concepts of science and the ethical principles or maxims that have been developed by "common sense" observations over a long period of time have much in common — both are theoretical considerations about the world, and both are useful within the limits of their applicability. Often, however, they deal with only a limited area of the total situation with which we are concerned and consequently, although sound "in principle," fail in application.

The social scientist who reports the following example observes that the disregard of certain factors that were present in the situation but not present in the superintendent's view of the situation led to the failure of an entire project.

---

[2] *Science and Common Sense* (New Haven: Yale University Press, 1951), pp. 25–26.

I propose to present, from my own experience, a few of the reactions and obstacles which a social scientist meets when he attempts to apply his techniques and
his point of view to the problems of contemporary America.

During the last eleven years or so, my time has been divided rather equally
between teaching social science, principally anthropology and sociology, in colleges and universities and applying what I know of these subjects as an employee
in various government agencies. During the practical phase of these endeavors, I
have been an Anthropologist in the office of Indian Affairs, a Collaborator in the
Soil Conservation Service of the United States Department of Agriculture, a member of the Advisory Council in Human Relations to the United States Forest Service, a Community Analyst in the War Relocation Authority, and a Social Science
Analyst in the Office of War Information. During this period I have seen some of
the pioneer efforts to tap the resources of social science in government and public
affairs unfold, and I have personally felt many of the satisfactions and perplexities
which this development has brought. If these associations have done nothing more
for me, they have supplied me with a rich store of anecdotes and incidents. The
episodes which I shall describe, however, are chosen, not for their entertainment
value, but because each represents a type response and points to particular challenges which the social scientist faces in attempting to apply the lessons of his
field to matters of policy.

My thoughts go back almost ten years to a day when I was directed to make
a socio-economic study of conditions on a certain western Indian Reservation. I
was told in advance that the economic condition of the Indians seemed to be improving steadily but that drunkenness, assaults, and even homicides had also risen
in strange parallel. My findings, which were incorporated into a report, were briefly
these:

A superintendent who had long had a romantic desire to raise great herds of
cattle on western lands was administering the reservation. When he arrived he
found the tribal herd in poor condition and the Indians, whose traditions inclined
them toward a hunting rather than a pastoral outlook, largely indifferent to this
possible source of revenue. The superintendent sought to remedy matters in the
shortest possible time. He purchased good bulls, he halted over-grazing in certain
areas, he had the salt distributed more wisely, he had the fences repaired and kept
in repair, he saw that a more thorough job was done at branding and round-up
times. The tribal herd increased, the animals were heavier in average and brought
more per pound.

But this superintendent made little effort to enlist the help of the people in his
program. He was disgusted with their initial lack of interest and suspicious of their
abilities. On the whole, he ignored them and tended to hire experienced white men
from the surrounding country. Actually, he utilized Indian labor only twice a year
when a very large number of hands was needed for short periods. He managed
the industry as though it were his own private enterprise and as though efficiency
of operation were the only important concern.

In respect to the division of the earnings, however, this man was scrupulously
honest, and the per capita payments to the Indians rose as the stock improved. But
the reservation was isolated, and the Indians had little outside source of employment. To provide more income for them without finding an outlet for their energies was no great kindness, for the enforced idleness which prevailed simply led to
increased gambling, drunkenness, and disorder. The superintendent was puzzled
but not too greatly distressed by the social disorganization which existed. His reports were triumphant recitals of the progress of the tribal herd and the improvement of the grazing lands. In his state of single-mindedness he allowed the little
arable land (these Indians had some background in small-scale farming) which

the tribe possessed to go under water when a dam was built nearby. Thus, one of the few remaining channels of self-help and self-support was closed to these people.

In my report, I gave the superintendent full credit for his zeal, his excellent intentions, and his honesty. But I suggested that the people should have been more fully drawn into the conduct of their own affairs, even at the risk of temporary inefficiency, and that an educational program should have been initiated to foster an interest in conservation and a spirit of independence. But nothing praise-worthy which I had to say could mollify the superintendent. According to his view-point, he was a man unfairly attacked and betrayed from within his own organization. He argued that every figure, every sale, every common sense test showed him to be a successful administrator.

During this period of clash of ideas while policy was being formulated, I found many supporters of my view. But it was interesting to see that there were outspoken champions of the superintendent's position, too, persons who felt that because he had succeeded in one important phase of reservation life, the economic, he should not be too closely examined concerning other, less satisfactory, developments.[3]

The superintendent based his action on a very common starting point: the values from his past experience which were most important to him. He "knew" that the economic aspects of a situation were "always" the most vital, and he was therefore unable to recognize that they were not so in this instance. He failed completely to take into account the social organization — the way of life — of the Indians, which the experience of the anthropologist led him to emphasize. Data in this situation that seemed relevant to the superintendent did not seem equally relevant to the anthropologist — nor to the Indians for whom the project was designed. A clinical perspective that would look at situations as wholes was necessary.

L. J. Henderson, in the reading below, discusses some techniques for clinical observation. He undertakes to define a systematic way of thinking about the unique aspects of a particular situation. Many important scientific discoveries have originated from the careful study of one small or even "unimportant" fact. The traditional story of Newton's derivation of the law of gravity is one example; so too is the study that a shipboard operator made of a slight irregularity in the reception of some radio signals which led to the development of radar. Such men were skilled observers, and in order for them to recognize such significant data they needed, according to Henderson, "(1) an intimate, habitual, intuitive familiarity with things, (2) a systematic knowledge of things, and (3) an effective way of thinking about things." Read

LAWRENCE J. HENDERSON, "Procedure in a Science," below.

The intimate familiarity comes from personal experience with the data under consideration; the systematic knowledge is built up by patiently relating parts of the data to other parts in an orderly fashion; the effective way of thinking comes through the use of a "conceptual scheme" that supplies a framework for our specific observations. All three are necessary for good clinical observation. Without the first, we spin empty theories, "logically sound" but unconnected with reality. Without the second, our knowledge is piecemeal, chaotic, unorganized. Without the third, we have no frame of reference which tells us what is relevant to our problem — we don't know what to look for.

---

[3] From Morris Opler's contribution to *Science for Democracy*, ed. Jerome Nathanson (New York: King's Crown Press, 1946), pp. 118–120.

Henderson's lecture raises the question of the way to move from the particular to the general and back again. The former is often called "concrete," the latter "abstract." An abstraction is a selection of part of a real situation for attention; it purposely neglects other parts in order to focus on the aspect of especial interest. Only by so abstracting can we compare different situations; we have to ignore the ways they are different in order to describe the way they are similar. A specialist concerned with developing systematic knowledge in the purposely limited field of his discipline is primarily concerned with the similarities within his data.

Through the use of a conceptual scheme, Henderson's "effective way of thinking about things," we order the knowledge we have of concrete phenomena into systematic sets of abstractions. This allows us to meet new situations by comparing them with old ones with which we are already familiar. In dealing with human situations, however, we ignore the differences of the particular situation at our peril, since it is through these differences that we apply our systematic knowledge. It is only wide experience with concrete facts, Henderson's "intimate, habitual, intuitive familiarity with things," that will permit us to distinguish *significant* differences, such as those that led to the discovery of radar, from merely minor modifications of the similarities. Only an operator intimately familiar with the irregularities found in "normal" radio reception could detect a different kind of irregularity — a unique variation from the normal that necessitated a new explanation. Observation of this sort, however, is only the first step. Uniqueness must be related to some generalization if it is to be significant; in fact, something is unique only as we contrast it to the usual. Much experimental work must be undertaken before conceptualization adequate to explain a unique variation can be developed. Thus both clinical observation and experimental research are often necessary if the similarities and the differences of a particular situation are to be understood in relation to other situations.

The clinical approach to social situations is thus concerned with the consideration of all pertinent factors and the conceptualizations that make evident why these factors are deemed pertinent. This approach recognizes that in such observation we are always dealing with a concrete situation where the relations of individual factors to each other are as significant as the factors themselves.

Mary Parker Follett points out that while we used to describe people by naming a number of characteristics, such as selfishness, kindness, aggressiveness, and so forth, now we realize that it is the way these characteristics are related that makes a man's personality. She says that, although it is now common to insist that the total situation is important and that all factors must be included, actually the nature of the totality is the prime consideration. When we add or subtract a factor from a situation, we do not have that situation plus or minus that factor, because all the other factors will be changed. It is ineffective to attempt to characterize a concrete situation by any single aspect of it, be it usual or unique. She suggests that we view human situations not as psychological *or* ethical *or* economic, but as situations with psychological, ethical, economic, *and* many other aspects. Read

MARY PARKER FOLLETT, "The Psychology of Control," below.

The problems of the application of conjugate principles that Lowell considers may lie in their very simplicity. Such generalizations often clearly express important factors that are present in many situations, but omit from consideration other factors and their interactions that are critically important in the particular situation at hand. Follett goes on to discuss at a clinical level the effect that such conclusions have on the way in which we deal with the world around us. She touches upon many matters that we will consider in more detail in later chapters.

ADDITIONAL READINGS

Bernard, Claude, *An Introduction to the Study of Experimental Medicine* (New York: Henry Schuman, 1927).
This book is a classic description of the interplay between general theory and the careful observation of minute facts. Bernard's examples are from biology.

Cannon, Walter B., *The Way of an Investigator* (New York: W. W. Norton, 1945).
Chapter V, "The Role of Hunches," and Chapter VI, "Gains from Serendipity," show how a trained investigator focuses all of his experience on a particular situation in order to discover new factors in it that had previously gone unnoticed.

Homans, George C., *The Human Group* (New York: Harcourt, Brace, 1950).
In the first chapter, Professor Homans discusses the usefulness of conceptual schemes, and he also examines the distinction between clinical and laboratory (or "analytical") methods.

Johnson, Wendell, *People in Quandaries* (New York: Harper, 1946).
In Chapters II and III, Johnson discusses some of the difficulties engendered by our "scientific culture" and the conflicts it sometimes raises with our "traditional institutions, beliefs, and habits." He suggests that we consider science as a method by which we can learn to ask effective questions of our experience.

Conflicts of Principle*

BY ABBOTT LAWRENCE LOWELL

INTRODUCTION

What appears as a universal principle is in fact often true only within the limits of the conditions in which it is properly applied, and becomes partially true, or altogether inapplicable, under new and unfamiliar circumstances. Yet we find a difficulty in emancipating ourselves from a conviction of its absoluteness and tend to rely upon it as an infallible guide where it is so no longer.

Many years ago a student from one of the Southern states in the course of conversation assumed that the practice of

not eating at the same table with a negro — regarded as a principle inviolable in his home — should be followed everywhere. I suggested that while the system of caste in India, involving the rejection of food touched by anyone of an inferior caste, or casteless, might have a sound basis there in preserving the integrity of the more cultivated strains, yet for a Brahman to insist upon it in a hotel in Paris was carrying it out of the range of rational application into a region where the cause for it did not exist; and in the same way, for a Southerner to refuse to

* Selections from Abbott Lawrence Lowell, *Conflicts of Principle* (Cambridge: Harvard University Press, 1932), pp. 3–20, 28–36, 39–45, 94–105, 123–132, 145–151, 153–155.

dine at a Parisian table with Alexandre Dumas would be making a principle, justified, if at all, only by local conditions, into a universal dogma, to be followed where those conditions are absent and contrary principles rightly prevail. He said that he had never thought of the matter in that way.

One of the basic political assumptions of Americans is the right of all people to govern themselves, and hence to be independent of external control; resulting, as a friend of mine remarked, in sympathy with revolution in every country but their own. Now it is noteworthy that of the two greatest heroes in American history the popular reputation of Washington rests less on his great work as our first President than on the successful conduct of a struggle for independence, while Lincoln's rests on his success in suppressing one. Although pursuing diametrically opposite principles, both are adjudged right by posterity, even in the main by the descendants of the defeated side. Later events have caused the Civil War to be regarded as waged on the issue of slavery; but at the outset Lincoln asserted that it was fought, not to abolish slavery, but to maintain the Union — that is to resist the claim of the Southern states to independence. Such a claim, or right, has its limits, and to state the matter from the cold standpoint of political philosophy, the National Government believed that in this case the claim was not within the limits where the principle properly applied.

Considerations like these induce one to reflect upon the limited nature of principles commonly accepted as universal; upon the conflicts that arise when two inconsistent principles of that kind come into collision; and how far such conflicts may be avoided by recognizing that there are limits, with a debatable region in which neither can be rigorously applied.

GENERAL PRINCIPLE

After a wise caution that ethics is not an exact science, Aristotle stated his familiar principle that good in the moral world is destroyed by both defect and excess, and preserved by the mean between the two; and hence virtue is a middle state between two vices, one of which by defect falls short of, and the other exceeds, what is right. Recognizing that general statements are apt to be vague, he gives illustrations from a series of particular virtues, with the corresponding vices which carry to an extreme the contrasted qualities of which virtue is the mean. As a general maxim in life this is excellent, but imperfect because it does not determine where the mean actually lies; and in fact Aristotle says that the practical application of the principle is difficult, just as it is not in every man's power to find the centre of a circle. He indicates that much must depend upon the time, the case, the persons, the motive and the manner.

In fact the true mean may vary with the conditions in which men are placed, and the conditions change with the passing years, more rapidly now with man's growing control over the forces of nature than in the days of the Greeks. Mankind, being far from perfect, often advances by over-accentuation of one principle at a time, like a sailing vessel which can not head up in the eye of the wind, but first on one tack and then on the other is making to windward on both. An important maxim is not to hold too long on the same tack. The object of these pages is, therefore, as a footnote to Aristotle, to point out by recent examples in various fields how the mean has changed, and how mankind is seeking for it amid the contrary principles between which it lies.

Aristotle's own practice of virtue might not be quite suitable to the present day. He lived in an age when slavery was deemed both right and necessary. Physical power was derived mainly from the muscles of men or animals, and in an ancient industrial civilization laboring men were largely a source of brute force, a condition wholly changed by our mastery of the forces of nature, and by our mechanical devices for using them. The worker is more and more engaged in directing power, less and less in supplying it from his own body, a progress that has wrought a change in the whole position of the toilers. In this way steam and machinery made large scale industry possible without slavery. The pyramids of Egypt could be built only by masses of forced laborers, in a condition of virtual slavery, raising blocks of stone by their own strength; but now we construct enormous buildings where the lifting is done by the mechanical application of natural forces. This is only one example of a change in conditions that affect human relations and conduct. We should not condemn Greek slavery without a very intimate knowledge of the state of affairs at that time; but we can certainly say that what may have been right then would be clearly wrong now, and that while Aristotle's principle is in the abstract correct, its application has changed in many ways since his day.

The proper mean between opposite qualities not only varies at different periods, but is not always the same at one period. Take for example boldness and prudence. What would be rash under some conditions would be excessive caution in others. In an emergency risks must be taken that would be unpardonable if ample time were given for deliberation. The man in a position of responsibility who must act immediately with a partial knowledge of the facts is unable, like the historian, to judge the wisdom of an act after much study at his leisure. Many men who are wise when they have time for consideration cannot act suddenly in an emergency, and to some extent the reverse is also true.

Conditions may change gradually with the progress of time, or they may change rapidly with sudden events. An illustration of the latter is the attitude of Lee and Grant when the retreat of the Confederate Army had been cut off to the west of Appomattox. On the morning of that day General Alexander, the chief of the artillery, found General Lee before the camp fire, told him that the line of retreat was severed, and suggested that if an order were given to disband and reassemble in the mountains of North Carolina many of the men could escape

capture, reach there and keep up a guerrilla warfare for a long time. Lee admitted this was true, but said the cause for which they had fought was lost, that they must remember they were a Christian people and strive to restore a civilized state of peace. He added that he was about to meet General Grant and surrender the army. When they met Grant wrote into the terms of capitulation that the men should keep their horses, saying they would need them for the spring plowing. The day before Lee would have put in his last man had there been a prospect of success, and Grant would have seized all the horses of Lee's army if he could; but on that morning both realized that the war was over, and that the conditions and duties of peace are quite different from those of war. Everyone sees this after a time, but these men saw it as soon as the retreat of the Army of Northern Virginia was blocked.

Almost all our knowledge is relative, and while true in the conditions with which we are familiar is not necessarily true under others. Someone will object to this statement, arguing that two and two make four universally. But do they? If two transverse beams each capable of supporting two tons are welded together horizontally they will support four tons, if vertically they will support eight tons, because the power of beams is equal to the breadth multiplied by the square of the depth. The laws of physics are not simply arithmetical. In short the rules of addition are true only for things to which they are applicable. Without attempting to assert that there are no propositions of absolutely universal application, it is enough for our purpose to say that many are commonly stated as universal when in fact they are not. This is particularly true of rules of conduct. Often two inconsistent principles are declared by their advocates to be universal, although this certainly cannot be true of both; and in reality is true of neither. An illustration may be found in the comparison of Washington and Lincoln in the Introduction. Washington was right in conducting a revolution on the principle stated in the Declaration of Independence — generally believed by Americans to be of universal application — that all peoples are entitled to govern themselves and hence to separate from a power whose rule they dislike. Lincoln was right in the principle that a nation is entitled to maintain its integrity by resisting and suppressing a revolt. These principles are contradictory; both are true under the appropriate conditions, and neither is of universal application. They are what may be termed conjugate principles, and it is with such that we are here mainly concerned.

A pair of principles may be termed conjugate when they are mutually contradictory or inconsistent and yet each is partially, or under some conditions, true . . . Now it may well happen, and often does, that under some conditions one of the pair is for practical purposes applicable to the fullest extent, so that it may be regarded, and acted upon, as wholly true, while under very different circumstances this may not be the case. It may even happen that at another time the opposite principle is in the same position; or this may be true of both at one time in different places because of dissimilar conditions. For our discussion it is not necessary to assert that contrasts actually occur to this extent. It is enough if such conditions are so nearly reached that serious people may reasonably believe, and do believe, that one of a pair of conjugate principles is for practical purposes to be accepted as an axiom, a universal maxim of conduct, while other people, equally sincere, have the same conviction for the opposite principle. This is not uncommon, and when the two groups are confronted on questions requiring action controversies between good men arise.

We are concerned here with differences of opinion between good men. We are not considering selfish interests, the quarrels that arise over who shall enjoy the fruits of the earth, which nation shall exploit backward regions, or what industries shall be favored by a tariff. Of course selfish motives are always mixed with moral ones, but they do not as such concern us here. We are dealing with contests of principles earnestly held to be right. Nor are we touching those controversies that spring from differences of opinion about facts. That is quite another subject, although elements of this kind are almost always injected into the argument about a principle; and rightly so because they affect the question whether the conditions are such as to justify its application. We are dealing not with concrete cases, where facts are in dispute, but with abstract propositions and a theory of their appropriate limitation.

In any controversy about a principle it is a dictate of good sense to hear the other side, and yet this is an insufficient, and may be a fallacious, attitude, for it tends to assume that the principle discussed is either right or wrong, when in fact it is neither and both. Such a discussion often resembles that of the two knights who fought over the color of the shield, each being perfectly correct about what he had seen, but wrong in supposing the shield to be uniform. So each controversialist assumes the principle he advocates to be absolute and universal, when in fact it has limits. Each starts from conditions, real or believed, where his principle is true, or nearly enough so for practical purposes, and extends it beyond those limits to conditions in which its application is at least doubtful, if not clearly wrong; and there meets another coming from a situation where a contrary principle is equally true. It is in the debatable area between conjugate principles that many controversies arise, and the true problem in such a case is not to argue their inherent truth, but to discover their appropriate limits. In an orderly society the limits are fixed by law, often after a struggle between the advocates of divergent views. In international relations they are too frequently settled by a resort to war.

The extent to which we are constantly engaged in seeking and finding the limits of conjugate principles is largely concealed by the habit of giving different names to acts that fall on the two sides of the line we have drawn. "Thou shalt not kill" is too universal a statement to be literally applied, for everyone agrees that a man may kill a bandit or burglar if it is the only way to save his family from being slain. So we call killing that is not justified murder. It is on the wrong side of the limit, the jury being asked to decide, under instructions from the judge, whether the homicide was murder or not; and people who do not think a putting to death justified beg the question of whether or not it is beyond the limit by calling it a murder. The same is true of fraud, a word used to denote taking advantage of another beyond a limit imposed by law or conscience. Now, as we shall see later, the limits of these terms and the acts to which they are applied change with the progress of civilization. Homicide that would have been excusable in one age becomes murder in another, as for example killing in a duel; and deception tolerated at one time is fraud in a more scrupulous age.

Not only in obvious cases do the limits between conjugate principles vary from one period to another, but the same is generally true of almost all such limits. Mankind, as we have already remarked, is like a sailing vessel which can not point in the eye of the wind, but beats to windward on both tacks. A principle, with an institution that embodies it, is peculiarly needed at one time. It is therefore acclaimed as the panacea for all ills, the instrument for making a better world; it does its work, achieves the objects for which it is adopted, and is then discarded for something inconsistent with it that supplies a new want. Thus the need of orderly life on a national scale gave rise at the close of the Middle Ages to monarchy of a powerful type, and to the principle of the divine right of kings. The result in France was a more autocratic monarch than in England, partly because more arbitrary power was needed to bring the great feudatories into subjection. But the process was of the same nature over almost all Latin Christendom. Monarchy did its work, created modern states, brought civic order within them, and then gave way in form or substance to new aspirations which expressed themselves through popular government. This change has been sometimes gradual, sometimes abrupt and sometimes alternating. What further needs will arise, what form of government people will use as their instrument, we do not know. Utopia has not yet been reached; criticisms of the results attained by democracy have long been rife, not least among its most ardent advocates. It does not appear to produce leaders who can maintain continuously a commanding position, or stable majorities supporting a consistent policy. Such imperfections may be ephemeral, or they may be persistent, the precursors of a further and unknown evolution. Writing of democracy Edmond Scherer remarked, "C'est une étape dans cette marche fatale vers un but inconnu, et ne mérite dès lors ni les éloges qu'elle évoque ni les craintes qu'elle inspire."

As in the case of the rise of centralized monarchy in Europe, it often happens that in seeking the limit between conjugate principles men go too far in one direction and then in the other, and thus oscillate until a limit stable under existing conditions is reached. The ardent advocates of a change believe that it will go still farther their way, when in fact a retrocession may be in store toward a more appropriate limit, often on a higher plane. Extremists striving for an object which they believe to be absolutely right, when in fact it is partly right and partly wrong, are in error and may do more harm than good. If what they see were all, if the conditions were as they conceive them to be, they would be right. If not, they are in the position of the knight seeing one side of the shield and eager to fight about its color; or in that of people coming blindly from a condition where their principles are for practical purposes right to one where they are partially, if not wholly, inapplicable. One of the great difficulties in life is to know the eddy from the stream. Moreover the stream itself does not run straight. The man of his age thinks he is the man of the future; but he is not, for the future will be no more like the present than the present is like the past. If the present should create an enduring future the world would become stagnant. All we can do is to find the limits of principles correct for the conditions we see, and can foresee, trusting that posterity will not be less wise than ourselves.

One of the great difficulties in finding the proper limits between conjugate principles comes from the well-nigh universal tendency to associate in one complex system ideas that have only an historical or accidental connection, and to strive to apply them as a unit when in fact the limits of their application are not the same. Hence men are guided by one part of the complex in fields where another part does not apply, and thus wrongly object to innovations in the latter because they think it involves the former which may still be quite right. Such a confusion and error occurs in all forms of private and public thought and conduct; but it is most strikingly illustrated in religion where dogma is systematic and sensitiveness acute. Every religion strives for a complete philosophy and therefore incorporates into its system what is believed to be known of the physical world, in short the science of its day. But as knowledge grows the scientific ideas that religion has embodied in its theology become outgrown, and yet are so encased therein that the new theories are deemed subversive of the system, heretical, damnable. Yet it may be science, not religion, that has changed. Such was the attitude of the Church in condemning Galileo for advocating the heliocentric theory, although there was nothing in it inconsistent with the teaching of Christ, or with the essential principles of the Christian religion. Protestants did the same thing fifty years ago when the pulpits rang with refutations of Darwin's Origin of Species, whereof we have now a belated echo in parts of this country. The tendency works also conversely. The man who disbelieves in a part of a system of doctrine, or of an institution, is apt to extend his objections to other parts where they do not apply, and oppose the system or institution as a whole.

A great part of the art of life and of civilization lies in ascertaining the true limits of conjugate principles. That many contests, sometimes disastrous and often avoidable, flow from a failure to find those limits will appear [later] . . . One thing we should bear constantly in mind: Aristotle advocated the mean, not because it was worldly wise, but because it was the path of virtue; and we should seek the limit between conflicting principles to find, not what is expedient, but what is right.

PERSONAL LIBERTY AND UNIFORMITY

[Personal liberty and compulsory uniformity are conjugate principles of widespread interest.] During the Middle Ages, and still more after the great schism of the Reformation, the general welfare was supposed to require uniformity in religious belief and observance, and there is much to be said in favor of that point of view. A common basis for conduct, a common spiritual conviction, adds to the active momentum of a people and makes for the maintenance of civic order in a rough age. On the other hand the persecution of heretics, the crushing of dissent by punishment, causes intense suffering, and, stifling independent thought, brings intellectual stagnation. After an experience of centuries with attempts to enforce uniformity the modern world has come to the opinion that the general welfare is better promoted by liberty in religious ideas and practices. But this is true only so far as the doctrines do not involve grossly immoral conduct. A sect that openly preached arson, murder or suicide as a duty would probably be suppressed by force everywhere, and the plea of conscientious religious faith would not be accepted as a defence. This is a case where well-nigh universal opinion has changed in regard to the line to be drawn between the principles of uniformity and of personal liberty. Nor is the change due wholly or mainly to a decay in the strength of religious faith, although that has no doubt been an element in the process; for the objection to compulsory conformity is strong among people with deep religious fervor, as well as with the skeptic in such matters. The men of all churches who persecuted dissenters were perfectly sincere in their belief in the righteousness of their actions, but their ideas have been altered, first by the concept of toleration, and then by that of personal liberty in religion. This has now become almost as axiomatic as uniformity was formerly.

Not altogether, or everywhere. In some states in this country the Fundamentalists have sought to enact, and occasionally with success, a prohibition of teaching evolution, not only in public, but also in privately supported, institutions. This is a reversion to the earlier attitude in religious matters. More striking still is the condition in Russia, where the ideas of Europe have penetrated comparatively recently as an exotic, and have never kept pace with the march of Western thought. There the Soviet government is striving to produce a religious or philosophical uniformity by suppressing the old national orthodox Russian Church of the Tzardom, and inculcating the doctrines of the Bolshevist régime. No doubt the object is political rather than religious, but so it has usually been to some extent in such persecutions. The Soviet policy is a reversion to the ideas of Rousseau, who in his *Contrat Social* argued that there ought to be a state religion including among other tenets the sacredness of the social compact, — in other words his basic philosophic principle of the state. This religion, he said, everyone must accept on pain of banishment; and if any person, after having declared his belief in it, should behave as if he did not believe in it, he ought to be punished with death because he has lied before the law.

So much for liberty on the most important of human conceptions. Similar conjugate principles may be observed in other questions on which people differ. In all the more advanced nations there is at the present day no inquest by the public authorities into the personal opinions of the private citizen; that is, he is free to hold any views he pleases so long as he does not express them in a way deemed subversive of good morals or the safety of the community. But where the limit lies to the expression deemed subversive varies with different conditions, with the form the expression takes, and

the excitability of the public or its rulers. Naturally in war, especially a modern war, where the issues involved are momentous, where universal effort is strained to a common end, and where passions run high, tolerance of dissent is less than in peaceful times when decision can await discussion. Therefore the limit to the expression of opinion tends to be less liberal than in peace. But even after the war is over the state of nervous tension it has caused may not be at once allayed, as happened in this country, where it lasted two or three years, although largely transferred to a panic about red agitation.

Liberty of speech and of the press almost everyone agrees must have a limit somewhere. No one, not a fanatic, would maintain that murder of magistrates on one side, or of agitators on the other, may be advocated by speech or press with impunity; nor conversely would anyone in a free country suggest that all criticism of the government should be prohibited. But between these two extremes opinions of every kind are held, some people inclining toward a wider, others to a more restricted, application of the laws of libel and of the principle of free utterance. Aristotle's caution is here wise, to lean away from the side on which we have the most tendency to go wrong; and, as we are all prone to be irritated by opinions hostile to our personal convictions, it is well, in case of doubt about the limit, to err on the side of liberty. Differences of opinion even on fundamental matters are precious, and are of grave import in preventing the habits and state of mind generated under excitement from becoming permanent. Again it is a question of seeking the limit between conjugate principles, neither of which is absolute.

How about uniformity and liberty in conduct — the principle of discipline, obedience and concerted action in a common cause on one side; and, on the other, of personal conscience and judgment? In extreme cases there is no doubt. Everyone will agree that a man ought not to do an immoral or dishonorable act because his superior orders it. Everyone will also agree that a military officer is not justified in refusing to obey orders because his opinion of wise strategy differs from that of the commander-in-chief. But in both civil and military life there are limits to each of these principles, and a debatable region where doubtful cases arise. When the Titanic was ripped open by ice the California was not far off and could probably have saved all on board before the ship sank. The officer on the bridge received the SOS signal, and rapped on the door of the captain, who failed to heed. Ought the officer to have assumed command and gone to the rescue, disobeying or superseding the captain? When, in 1893, during a manoeuvre in the Mediterranean which was almost certain to have that result, the Camperdown rammed and sank the Victoria with a large loss of life, the court martial expressed a regret that her commander had not, before obeying the order, signalled the flagship his doubt about it, although it was perfectly clear, and in fact intentional.[1] In war the principle of obedience to commands extends farther than in peace; yet even here there are limits. It is related that on the second day at Gettysburg two adjoining regiments had orders to charge under conditions that meant destruction, and where no good object could be served. One of the colonels, saying, "It is murder, but it is the order," sprang over the entrenchment and led his men forward. The other, convinced there was a grave misapprehension, did not charge. Which was right? Such examples could be cited without end. One of the great arts of administration in every career is knowing how far — consonant with the general plan — to entrust discretion to subordinates, and this in effect is perceiving the limits between these conjugate principles.

That the limit between uniformity and personal liberty varies with the conditions is evident. Like that of obedience to orders, it is not the same in peace and war. Compulsion of individuals, restraints in their conduct, regulation of their movements and even of their food, may be perfectly proper in war, though to people accustomed to liberty intolerable in peace. Moreover the limit may depend upon the magnitude of the effort the nation has to make in a war. In England the Defence of the Realm Act, commonly known as DORA, was cheerfully accepted in the World War, but would no doubt have been regarded as tyranny in the Boer War; and the same is true in the United States of the conditions in the World War and the Spanish War. All sensible people would agree to this in the abstract, but diverse opinions always arise in regard to the limits in concrete cases.

Our country is struggling at this moment with the problem of the prohibition of liquor. Although obscured by other issues, at its base lies essentially that of finding the appropriate limit between compulsory uniformity and personal liberty. No one who reflects seriously believes that restraint of personal conduct in such matters is in all cases wrong; for there is no resistance to laws preventing the sale of drugs made from opium. Few people advocate unlicensed open saloons for the unrestricted sale of distilled liquor; and on the other hand no one would advocate a universal enforced dietary deemed by physicians most conducive to health. It is a question of degree; how far it is wise to go in restraining personal consumption for the benefit of the individual, or for the protection of the community . . .

CONSENT AND FORCE

Using "consent" in the broadest sense of "conformity," whether from conscious conviction or any other motive save fear of punishment, the two conjugate principles of consent and force are the cohesive elements in every political society. Men have written books to prove that either one or the other was the true basis of government, Hobbes at one extreme

---

[1] Findings of the court martial: "Fourthly — The Court strongly feels that, although it is much to be regretted that Rear Admiral Albert Hastings Markham did not carry out his first intention of semaphoring to the Commander-in-Chief his doubt as to the signal, it would be fatal to the best interests of the Service to say he was to blame for carrying out the directions of his Commander-in-Chief present in person." In short, they approved of delaying to obey, but not of disobedience even in view of obvious disaster.

and numberless modern treatises at the other; but in fact both are always present, although in greatly varying proportions. Quite apart from armed resistance to external foes, probably no government has ever existed that did not use force, or the threat of force, to prevent crimes against itself or its citizens on the part of internal violators of its laws and customs. No government, on the other hand, could endure, even for a brief period, without a large measure of consent, at least among those willing to maintain it by force. If well organized and determined, the ratio of such men to the subject population may be small, but without their consent a despotism would be quickly overthrown. Moreover we are apt to attribute to autocrats a greater reliance on force than is always the case. Despotic rule, especially in the East, has often been popular, and sometimes after a period of disorder a great public boon, requiring little force to maintain it. The true opposite of consent is not despotism but force. It may be argued that in despotic governments, as indeed in more popular ones, apathy in the mass of the people plays a large part, and that is true, but under the definition already given apathy is properly classed as consent, albeit of a negative kind.

Consent and force are not the less conjugate — that is opposite — principles because both may move a person at one time in the same direction. The principles of economic liberty and compulsion may in the case of an individual work in harmony. He may, and often does, find his personal interest promoted by the law he must obey, so that the two motives coincide; and in the same way every law-abiding citizen is usually more or less unconsciously affected by the principles of both consent and force. If he does not park his car contrary to the local regulations it is partly from a sense of propriety, and partly because he does not want to get into trouble by having it tagged. This is ordinarily true of matters not involving a grave moral wrong that shocks the conscience too much for thought of anything else.

While, therefore, consent and force may act conjointly in their impulse on an individual, yet from the standpoint of government, as means of obtaining compliance, they are conjugate or opposite; and hence comes the notable fact that as consent lessens the use of force normally increases. One may see this in all profound upheavals, like the French Revolution and the Bolshevist revolt in Russia, where social institutions are overturned, feelings are intense, consent far from universal, and therefore force is used to maintain the change. But here let us distinguish between things commonly called by the same name. We commonly speak of any forcible change in the form of a government as a revolution; but the throwing off of a foreign rule may not at once affect deeply the laws, customs or even the public life of a people, and hence may not change greatly the attitude of consent toward these things. In spite of the strain of a long war, this was in the main true of the American Revolution, and goes far to explain the comparative ease with which the Constitution was adopted, and normal orderly conditions restored. In Massachusetts, for example, where a great part of the rich were loyal and left with the British troops, new men took their place as a class, the public authorities went on much as before, and the deeper effects due to the penetration of democratic ideas did not come for another generation. It came slowly, by a gradual change of opinion, and thus there was at no time cause for internal violence. Shays' Rebellion in Massachusetts — an apparent exception — was a demonstration due to the pressure of debts, especially mortgages, and was a fiasco. One may observe the same sequence of events in comparing the overthrow in England of Charles the First and James the Second. The conflict with the former arose from deep-seated changes in the life and ideas of the community and was accompanied with much strife and force. That with James was on the whole conservative, a resistance to change, and was well-nigh pacific. In fact the reciprocal relations of consent and force are logically obvious, as well as historically manifest. The less the one the greater must be the other.

In all periods of political stress, when passions run high and consent is far from general, force, and terror which is a fear of force, become prominent. The amount varies from time to time as the sense of danger by those in power rises and falls. The more they fear plots against their rule the more ruthless they are in suppressing them, and hunting down all men suspected of connection with them. The Reign of Terror in France came at the period of disaffection and quarrels among the revolutionary leaders, the time when tenure of power was insecure, when consent was by no means universal. The same has been true of the Soviet government. Lack of confidence in its own stability has at times increased its severity in dealing with its foes. But that is only saying that when its confidence in the consent or submission of those who may be dangerous has lessened its resort to force has grown, and therefore the use of force or terrorism is in inverse ratio to its sense of security and may be taken as a rough measure thereof.

Naturally the relation between consent and force as conjugate principles is most readily observed in great national upheavals where events are spectacular, but it is not less true of efforts at other times to produce uniformity by law among people who do not consent to the object sought. Attempts to suppress religious dissent, for example, have always aroused intense, if numerically limited, opposition. There being entire absence of consent on the part of the recalcitrant, such attempts have involved persecution, that is the use of force in varying degrees of severity. We have a civic instance of the phenomenon to-day in national prohibition in the United States, which was enacted with far from universal consent, and hence the endeavor to execute the law has required enforcement at enormous cost. It is not irrelevant to observe that force, if not effective or ruthless enough to accomplish its object, is likely to engender a general disregard of law and a callousness to the use of violence.

In all cases of conjugate principles the problem is to discover the appropriate

mean; and one of the arts of government lies in finding the true mean between consent and force. Probably most people in a modern civilized state would agree that it is to be found in as large a measure of consent, and as little force, as is consistent with good order and social improvement. But such a formula merely states a doctrine without determining its application, which must depend upon the conditions. Russia is experimenting with the question how much force is needed to carry out the Soviet policy; Italy with the comparative value of liberty and force in promoting order and efficiency; the United States with the use of force to prevent the use of alcohol. Such efforts are as old as history. According to the wisdom with which the conditions have been perceived, they have at times succeeded and at others failed, and sometimes they have attained their immediate object, but brought subsequent evils on the people they were designed to benefit.

PATRIOTISM AND HUMANITARIANISM

This is another pair of conjugate principles for whose limits since the World War the nations have been groping. The question takes many forms, arouses strong emotions, and is extremely difficult; yet upon a rational solution depends the future of mankind, perhaps the very existence of our civilization. In fact the greatest danger to peace and good-will among men lies now less in individual than in collective selfishness.

"Deutschland über Alles," "My country right or wrong," express in an extreme form one of these principles. The duty of equal treatment for all men, without regard to race or nationality, of every nation to love its neighbour as itself, is an extreme statement of the other. Both are true within their proper spheres; both are capable of being carried to a disastrous excess; and when passion enters into an argument — as it does in matters of this kind — disputants, revolted by the attitude of their opponents, are often driven to assert opinions more drastic than they would hold if reflecting in tranquil solitude. For example, the idea of patriotism is easily associated with that of war, and a few people, in their intense hatred of war, profess the doctrine of national non-resistance; while their theories urge others to violent language on the opposite side; and thus we hear the terms "pacifist" and "militarist" unjustly hurled at opponents, whereas in fact all sensible men agree that the principles I have called humanitarianism and patriotism are both good, but each has limitations, although the proper line of demarkation is not easy to draw.

Very few men would blame, or fail to extol, Aetius and Theodoric for checking at Châlons the ravages of Attila; Charles Martel for driving back the invading Saracens at Tours; the Emperor Constantine Palaeologus for his last stand against Mahomet II in the gate of Constantinople; or John Sobieski for marching to save Vienna from the Turks. On the other hand few men believe in the right of a nation to use its military strength for reckless conquest. There is now a general conviction that no nation — certainly no nation but one's own — must conquer another civilized people in order to exploit it or make use of its resources. Public opinion is beginning to extend the same principle to races with an inferior civilization. Slavery and forced labor in backward countries shocks us to-day. Hence the sensitiveness to charges of abusing the negroes in African dependencies and the talk about the white man's burden, when in fact he, and his burden, are supported by others with a darker skin. Hence also the demand after the World War that colonies, instead of being simply transferred to new masters, should be assigned under the supervision of the League of Nations, by mandates designed to provide a benevolent tutelage for the natives until they are capable of governing themselves by European methods.

These simple instances suffice to show that, in respect to the use of force, the prevalent opinion of civilized men favors neither an extreme application of humanitarianism, that is considering injury to one's own country of no more consequence than harm to a foreign one; nor

an excessive patriotism, whereby national interests alone are regarded, with a callous indifference to the sufferings of others. So far have Western ideas advanced in the matter of force. It is interesting to inquire into their progress in other directions. Religion felt the humanitarian impulse first; the desire to save the souls of the heathen long preceded toleration at home, yet the growth of religious liberty has given it a wider scope. No doubt the missionaries have not always been wise, no doubt they have sometimes been used for political purposes, but their unselfish devotion to alien races, amid hardships, perils and sufferings, has been one of the finest chapters in modern altruism.

Of late years philanthropy has become international. When large gifts have been made by American foundations or individuals to promote education, hospitals or other charitable objects in Europe or in China we have heard no complaint that it would have been more patriotic to make them at home. On the contrary the benefactors have been praised, not only because they were believed to be fostering international good-will, but also from a kindly feeling toward the foreign recipients. In short men recognize that while a primary love of one's own country is a virtue, private generosity to other peoples is good also.

How about national generosity? The relinquishment of our Boxer Indemnity for education in China was certainly such a case, and seems to have met with general approbation in this country. President Hoover's moratorium likewise sprang in part from a desire to help Europe, although it was also proposed, and mainly vindicated, on the ground that it was a wise measure for ourselves. A generation ago the policy of unrestricted immigration was often defended by the argument that the United States was, and should be, an asylum for the oppressed of all nations; and that feeling would probably have continued in the case of Europeans had it not been for the excessive numbers, difficult to assimilate, who flocked here. The freedom of immigration was, of course, supported also by the desire for workmen in a rapidly developing country, but the existence of sympathy with the desire of the immigrant to improve his lot is evidence of a sentiment not purely self-regardant.

Although the course of events since the war has made men deeply conscious that the prosperity or distress of any great nation affects profoundly the rest of the world, most people would be astonished, if not shocked, at the idea that in its economic policy a country should pay any serious attention to the interests of outsiders. An altruistic tariff seems a contradiction in terms. People who accuse other countries of selfishness in the matter would hardly enact duties disadvantageous to themselves without a countervailing benefit in some form of reciprocity. Yet there may be limits even here. Would a nation to-day be justified for a small profit to itself in destroying by a tariff the chief occupation of a little neighbour, as Great Britain was accused long ago of doing with the linen industry of Ireland? Would such an object be frankly admitted? If not, there is a conceivable limit to the purely selfish patriotism of a nation's economic policy. General recognition of any such limit may be very distant, and finding where it lies will be no simple matter; but until some approach is made in the direction of an understanding that grave sudden changes which dislocate trade should not be made without opportunity for adjustment, hard feeling between nations will constantly recur. Treaties running for definite periods with notice of non-renewal a fixed time in advance can do much, and such agreements are a recognition of the principle of mutual regard for the interests of the parties thereto.

It will be said that national economic policy is an internal or domestic matter, quite different from a breach of the international rights of another country. This is very true. The difference is like that in personal relations between generosity and duty, between what conscience demands and the law compels; yet a good neighbour often does more than the law prescribes. Generosity must be left to the expansion of sympathy, the growth of mutual good-will, and the limits can never be precisely fixed. Duty can be determined by law, which is constantly adapting itself to changing conditions, seeking to prevent, not only downright injustice, but also attempts to balk the fair expectation of others. In international relations we may strive for some mutual consideration in subjects that are not capable of being reduced to legal rules, and for precise definition in those that can be formulated as rights.

If there be limits between the conjugate principles of patriotism and humanitarianism, finding them may be a matter of great consequence, for if those limits should be universally accepted and observed wars would cease; and so far as an approach is made thereto wars will be less frequent. We should therefore seek for such limits in the directions where they may be found. The chief of these is international law. Of course that is not positive law in the sense that it is enforced by an authority superior to the parties involved, but in times of peace, and to some extent even during hostilities, it is commonly observed between nations standing on the same plane of political maturity. In this way it has prevented conflicts, and still more the exasperation that causes conflicts, because nations have refrained from acts that would obviously violate its accepted principles. The very recognition that there is such a thing as international law has made possible the submission to arbitration, or to an international tribunal, of cases like the Alabama claims, where there was a difference of opinion upon the rights and duties in question. Like most other law, this has grown from custom, from the writings of jurists, from decisions in actual cases and from contract, the last taking the form of treaties; and it is noteworthy that all these may contribute to the body of international law even for nations not parties to the transaction that gave rise to the rule. A striking example may be found in the Treaty of Paris of 1856, by which the nations that signed it agreed to abolish the use of privateers in war. The United States refused to adhere because the conference would not go farther and give to private property at sea the same protection as that on land. But so strong was the feeling created against privateers that on the outbreak of the war with Spain our government declared that it would not use them; and no civilized power would now venture to do so, whether a party to the Treaty of Paris or not. The decision in the Geneva Arbitration on the fitting out of warships in a neutral port has probably become in the same way a rule for all nations. The advantage to any country with wide interests in taking part in all possible agencies that may crystallize the rules of international law is obvious, and it is one of the strongest arguments advanced by advocates of our joining the World Court and the League of Nations.

Since independent states are subject to no superior authority, international law is not created by statute; no command, or majority vote, settles where the line shall in future be drawn between conflicting rights, claims and interests. Acceptance of any rule of law purports to be voluntary on the part of each nation; but practically the growth of a general opinion on what is just, fair and honorable acquires a force that modifies the conduct of governments in their relations to one another. No nation to-day ventures to treat another harshly, however insignificant its actual power of resistance, without an attempt to show that its conduct is justified by the rules and conventions commonly approved. Such an admission of an obligation, although in particular cases sometimes more formal than sincere, has on the whole a distinctly restraining influence. The great increase of treaties of arbitration, the creation of the World Court, are steps toward bringing the relations of states into the domain of law and order. No doubt the line between what nations may, and may not, properly do is still imperfect; no doubt it will change from time to time as conditions alter; but the fact that there is such a line, or fragments of a line, tends to prevent arbitrary acts, allay friction and reduce the risk of war. Now to draw such a line

is in its essence to find the limit between patriotism, that is the exclusive regard for the interests of one's own country, and humanitarianism, a consideration for the welfare of mankind as a whole. It is again a search for the limit between conjugate principles, and one of the great needs of our time.

In this connection it may be of interest to observe the effect of trying to act on two opposite principles at once without being aware that they are inconsistent. It may be observed in the career of Napoleon. In the wars that followed immediately upon the Revolution the French believed that they were not only fighting in self-defence, but carrying to other peoples the light of freedom, a deliverance from outworn and blighting institutions. They had a gladsome gospel to spread over Europe, by the sword if necessary; and Napoleon inherited that spirit. In intent it was humanitarian; but with it was associated in his mind the aggrandizement and domination of France — an ultra-patriotic and nationally selfish motive. These two principles, which seemed to him compatible, were in fact contradictory, and their combination was one of the causes that led to his downfall. Had he pursued either one of them alone the result might have been different. Had he sought only to spread the doctrines of the French Revolution, without assuming to annex or control the lands overrun, he might not have aroused all Europe against him, at least to the degree that he did. Wars there surely would have been, but the deep patriotic sentiment stirred by fighting against him for independence could hardly have been so intense or universal. If, on the other hand, his aim had been solely to exalt France he would probably have perceived that he could not wisely annex, or subdue, an indefinite quantity of aliens, and would have set to conquest a bound that might have proved more stable. Nor would he have obtained in the lands liberated by his victories so much support, or the recruits that helped to fill his armies. The conjunction of the two motives helped his progress at first, but finally united all the nations against him until he fell under their combined weight.

PERSONAL CONDUCT

The limits between conjugate principles are displayed most clearly, or at any rate most constantly, in questions of personal conduct, and in the right decision of these lies the secret of wisdom. A catalogue of such conflicts, wholly or partially under voluntary control, would involve the whole map of life, but a few examples may serve to show their frequency and significance.

One pair of opposite principles, by no means entirely under direct voluntary control, is that of contentment and discontent. Each of these is a virtue within proper limits and an evil beyond them. Contentment with what can not be changed, in illness, for example, in irremediable personal or domestic handicaps, is certainly a great and rare virtue; but discontent with oneself and with the conditions of human life is the source of all improvement and all progress in civilization, while carried too far it is the cause of most crime and of vast suffering. The natural desire of the ruling classes in England to preserve their position was nowhere better shown than in the catechism of the Established Church, which made each child acknowledge the Christian duty of being content with the state in life to which it had pleased God to call him. Both principles are perfectly right when rightly applied; neither is absolute under all conditions; and both are wrong and harmful when pushed to extremes. Christianity teaches both. It came as a religion of revolt against the state of the world, and yet it taught that the world was in the hands of a just, merciful and loving God who desired the happiness of men. Hence it has been at times the driving power of the reformer and the revolutionist, at times the mainstay of established authority; sometimes it has been appealed to by one of these forces alone, sometimes by both of them on the same occasion, for the Christian religion inculcates general principles of morality and leaves men to discover the limits of their practical application . . .

Closely allied to the principles of contentment and discontent are those of ambition and modesty. "You should have," said the philosopher, "some latent ambition," and without it in some form a man would be an inert, useless being accomplishing nothing. An ambition to do well, as well as he can do it, anything he undertakes is the motive for all good work, and a desire to do something still better worth doing is the motive for the greatest achievements. On the other hand ill directed ambition on the part of a military despot, an unscrupulous statesman or a financial magnate has been the cause of incalculable misery. A Chapter of Erie, by the late Charles Francis Adams . . . shows to what extent insatiate ambition for wealth and power, coupled with unscrupulous methods, can be pushed when the public is apathetic.

Probably everyone who has passed middle life has known some men who from modesty have not accomplished as much, or filled as large a place, as they might have done; and others whose excessive ambition has led them into situations with which they could not cope. If anyone has not known men of the latter class in his own experience he can find them studded through the pages of history. It is another case of gauging the limits of conjugate principles, and involves for oneself a right estimate of one's own capacities — a gift which no fay can give us if we have it not within ourselves.

Another pair of such principles are thrift and liberality; but little need be said of these, with which everyone is familiar; for half mankind thinks the other half parsimonious, and the second half thinks the first extravagant, while most men feel that they are themselves following the golden mean.

A matter about which people think less, because its effects are less marked, or at least less universal, is the question of speech and silence. Many men talk too much for their own good and that of those who hear them; some express themselves too little; and a few have the art of speaking much and not saying what had better be left unsaid. We have heard of an English cabinet minister in the middle of the last century who would talk to an outsider with a confidential freedom that shocked the hearer, until in trying to remember the conversation afterwards he could recall nothing he did not read in the *Times*. A man entrusted with important affairs learns wisdom in these matters, and finds when he may, and when he will not, be quoted or misquoted. Through mistakes he becomes cautious. But we all tend to discuss other people in their public or private relations without adequate knowledge. Under such conditions we often say what we had better not; but sometimes we do not say what would tend toward a healthy opinion about conduct that is doing harm; and this I think is more common than it was formerly, when the conviction of the wickedness of sin was stronger than it is now. "Speech is silver but silence is gold," like most proverbs, is only a partial truth seen from one side of a question. Every word that is spoken, or left unsaid, contributes its particle, large or minute, to that body of thought, right or wrong, on which the fate of mankind depends. We are told that a man shall be held to account for every idle word, but also that if the watchman who sees danger coming blows not the trumpet the blood resulting shall be required at his hand; and to decide whether his words are idle or he is a watchman is a responsibility that, great or small, is laid on every man.

Many young men, not successful at the outset, are faced with the question of abandoning or persisting in the career on which they have entered. No general answer can be given, nor is there a presumption in favor of either course. Wise choice depends upon a multitude of conditions, the chance of ultimate success, the fitness of the individual for achieving it, the other paths in which he may direct his life. Many men who seemed to have met with a chilling defeat have afterwards risen high in the same field. Lemuel Shaw, the great Chief Justice of Massachusetts, was not, I believe, a suc-

cess at the bar. Robert Louis Stevenson had his first considerable book rejected by the publisher to whom it was offered. Captain Alfred T. Mahan's Influence of Sea Power in History was refused by one publisher after another until in despair he almost gave up the idea of printing it, when Mr. Parkman induced Little, Brown and Company to do so. For a time it did not sell, and then its significance was seen in England and his name became better known over the world than that of any other American author. On the other hand William James began by a discouraging attempt to paint, dropped it and went through the Medical School, drifted into psychology and finally into philosophy. Samuel Clemens began life as a pilot on the Mississippi River, — whence his pseudonym Mark Twain, — not, indeed, without success, but also not in the line of his later fame. Phillips Brooks made a pathetic failure as a teacher in the Boston Latin School and resigned half way through the first year. But it is needless to multiply instances of false starts followed by success in another line of work, for everyone is familiar with some of them. It would be interesting to know in what proportion it is true of the men whose names appear in a national biography, and how they compare with those who, after severe discouragement, have by persistence won distinction in their original field.

In all the conjugate principles mentioned in this chapter the practical question depends upon numberless complex conditions, and among them the personal capacity and temperament of the man himself. Mr. Justice Holmes once remarked to the writer that the art of life — mind, the art, not the philosophy — consists in making correct guesses on insufficient information; insufficient because we can never know all the elements that enter into a right decision. This is hard enough in one's own case, much more so in that of another, and hence as one grows older he becomes more weary in giving advice on personal questions of far-reaching import.

As a final example of conjugate principles in personal matters may be mentioned those of credulity and skepticism. As usual, the question of the limit between them is often begged by the use of epithets laudatory or opprobrious according to the standpoint of the speaker, such words as "conviction" and "cynicism" on the part of the believer, "bigotry" and "open-mindedness" on the other side. In fact the art of putting opponents in the wrong by using for one's own position the word for a quality good when properly applied and for theirs the name of a quality that has become bad by being carried to excess, is nowhere more common than in this case. For we must remember that in almost all conjugate principles there is a term of praise for each when within the right limit, and of blame when carried beyond that limit to a point where it becomes wrong. Such are "courage" and "rashness"; "caution" and "timidity"; "persistence" and "obstinacy"; "self-respect" and "vanity"; "self-confidence" and "conceit"; and the like through the whole gamut of contrasted qualities. So far as these are purely personal qualities we use them in criticism of others rather than of ourselves, for we are more prone to condemn the views of others than our own. Matters of opinion touch our sensibility. Our convictions are brought into emotional conflict with those of our opponents, and hence we are inclined to attribute the good word to the principle we hold and to the antagonist the bad one for excess in the conflicting principle. For mark again, the reason conjugate principles create contentions is that each side starts with a doctrine, substantially true in the conditions or assumptions of its origin, and carries it into other conditions where it is true only partially if at all, quite unconscious withal that he has done so.

Credulity and skepticism are both necessary for the well-being and progress of mankind. "Credulity" is a bad word because it is commonly used to indicate the quality carried beyond its proper limits. Let us therefore rather say "conviction." Both principles are essential for truth; conviction being the positive, constructive faculty, and skepticism the negative critical element. Both are evil when carried to an extreme; conviction or credulity obviously so. On the other hand, skepticism, if overdone, causes all resolution to be sicklied o'er with the pale cast of thought. Much of the moral basis of men's character rests on assumption rather than reason, and attempts to demonstrate its grounds often result in arguments of strange futility. The motive power of all right action is faith that what one is doing is worth while. Without it there is no vital impulse and the spring of action fails. The perfect man should have skepticism enough to insure by all the light he can obtain that his opinions are right, and faith enough to give them effect with all the force at his command.

MENTAL PATTERNS

Conjugate principles depend much in their application upon the pattern of life and its issues in one's mind. Everyone has such a pattern more or less fully developed and inclusive: the philosopher one that seeks to cover the whole range of knowledge; the less systematic thinker one sufficient for his ordinary needs, and often vaguely much more. The basic conceptions and the attitudes they produce vary greatly, not only between different racial cultures, but also between individuals of the same nation and habitat; and they often prevent mutual understanding. The futility of much discussion comes from approaching a subject from diverse preconceived views, for many conflicts of opinion arise in the fourth dimension — that is in assumptions unconsciously made and not mentioned, lying far back in the pattern of ideas. Sir Henry Maine told of an attempt by an Englishman to demonstrate to a Hindoo the utilitarian doctrine, with a lack of success that seemed strange until it appeared that the obstacle lay in the principle of the greatest good of the greatest number, the Hindoo believing that a Brahman was entitled to twenty times as much happiness as other people.

Let us take an example of difference in patterns due to occupation, that between the army and the navy. The army thinks primarily of land; its maps are those of land, with their routes, their contours, their obstacles, and their commanding points. The navy sails and thinks of the sea; its charts end where the maps of the army begin; and if the two arms do not understand one another's point of view so as to coöperate effectively there is danger of disaster. When Hannibal invaded Italy his best chance of success lay in keeping open communication with Carthage by sea, which for a nation with maritime supremacy should not have been difficult. But it was not done, and therefore European history followed a course wholly different from what it might otherwise have been. This was a case where the navy did not perceive the needs of the army. The opposite occurred in the Spanish Armada, which was fitted out to transport troops for fighting on land, but whose only battle was in the English Channel, where it was defeated by a force far inferior in numbers of ships and men.

Most variations in pattern are partly natural and partly acquired, but tend to become distinctly marked. The student of physical science thinks, as such, of natural forces operating under fixed laws. His ultimate data are observed phenomena, and in experimental science controlled ones. Hence his usual deficiency in investigating fraud in proponents of psychic marvels. The classical economists conceived of their subject as a science based upon rational, ascertainable laws, with too little regard for men's habits, prejudices and sentiments, and thus their foresight proved imperfect. Men of affairs, on the other hand, who deal with people, sometimes feel that the essential thing is their support or approval, to the comparative neglect of attaining certainty in the facts involved. Hence the need in all large matters of concerted action by the expert and the layman, each contributing what is lacking in the pattern of the other. When diverse points of view can be made to blend into a common product, without losing the momentum of the more constructive one, the result is excellent, but this can not always be done. The great and dramatic example

in our history is the contest between Jefferson and Hamilton in Washington's first cabinet. Hamilton's ideas focused on the nation as a whole, and his thoughts dwelt on collective, or urban, industry; while Jefferson's picture of life was distinctly rural, his ideas centring on the rights of the individual and of the smaller communities. Neither would have denied some merit to the principle of the other, but they drew the limits between them at such different points, and with such conviction, that an accord was impossible.

Patterns may be predominantly political, economic, moral, philanthropic, scholarly, artistic, or of any other nature where the mind of man can roam. When the opinions of people differ they are sometimes thinking of things wholly incommensurate, like the importance of a Titian and of the next election; sometimes of things that are comparable, but approached from such different standpoints that a common ground for discussion is lacking. One man sees chiefly, and has confidence in, the better impulses of human nature; another its defects which cause him distrust. One man perceives the advantages of change, and the benefits it will bring; another the complex relations in the organization of society and the danger of dislocating vital ones. This last is akin to the strength in individuals of Pareto's "instinct of combinations" and "persistence of aggregates." In all these cases the pattern is so closely woven into the fabric of men's minds that it is almost impossible to see it otherwise. Stronger or fainter, the impression on the mind is to some extent indelible. A second photograph can not be taken on the same plate; the ghost, at least, of the earlier one will appear.

Mental patterns are formed by heredity, by environment; through experience, through association; by reason, by suggestion; and so on through all the processes whereby ideas develop. They grow by accretion, for they direct attention to those things that harmonize therewith and absorb them into themselves. To most people that attraction is much stronger than the omnivorous curiosity that draws all things to observation and plants them in the memory. The prehensile nature of patterns in the mind, whereby they seize upon ideas and facts that fit into and complete their design, is a reason why specialized study, though enlarging knowledge, skill and acumen, may not by itself increase wisdom, that is mental balance, poise, sound judgment, in short the art of finding the right limit between conflicting principles. In the realm of thought there is an essential difference between the whole of a part and a part of the whole.

But the important matter for us in this connection is not how patterns arise, but that they differ, have a high degree of permanence, and furnish a large element in the personal attitude of the individual. Changes, no doubt, occur; sometimes by a sudden conversion which to the man himself is spectacular; more often by the infiltration of inconsistent ideas so gradual that one is only half conscious that the change has taken place, or how great it is. People, indeed, are by no means fully aware of the patterns in their own minds. Everyone naturally thinks his own opinions and views of life correct; if not he would not hold them so strongly. To be of force he must believe in them, for the cynic who pretends to doubt everything, including his own ideas, is either a poseur or is doomed to impotence. Yet men not seldom suppose their patterns to be different from what they really are, liking to think of themselves as belonging to one type of opinion when in fact naturally prone toward another, a condition that may lead to confusion in life. One sees this where people are complacent about qualities they have striven to acquire, as compared with those they possess by nature. The man who takes pride in being open-minded, and never losing his temper in argument, probably does so because he has made a conscious effort to control himself, while his success therein is not so fully recognized by others. He that is receptive by nature, and has little tendency to lose his temper, rarely thinks much about it.

.   .   .   .   .

So far as a pattern is conscious, and an incentive is consecutive action, it becomes an aspiration or a vision; and two of these that aim at distinct objectives may cut different diagonals through the tangle of human affairs, and thus not draw the line between conjugate principles at the same place. This is true of the man striving to construct something positive and his critics. The former includes all the facts that make up his picture; the latter often have an ideal, imperfect by embracing only a part of them, but ranging beyond into other matters. Each may err, but both are needful, and combined in mutual sympathy may create a nearer approach to a common objective. Unfortunately this does not always happen.

Patterns in the mind determine largely men's position in regard to conflicting principles. They are usually formed on one side or the other of the perfect limit between them, and when human affairs so frame themselves that a decision must be made they settle on which side a man shall take his stand and fix his loyalty. To be loyal a man may be, and usually is, free from strife, as a father, for example, or a teacher, a physician or a searcher for knowledge; and he can be loyal at once to his family, his friends, his school or college, his club, his trade or profession, his church, his town, state and country, without the slightest feeling that any of these attachments diminishes the strength of any other. Yet loyalties are sometimes contradictory, and in large bodies of men are as a rule most intense when they are so. Professor Royce was clearly right in insisting on the greatness and beneficence of loyalty. It is among the most admirable of qualities, the basis of all that is best, and the traitor for selfish motives has ever been regarded as the most despicable of malefactors. Yet its right object is by no means always obvious. Conflicting loyalties have torn men's souls from the sacrifice of their daughters by Jephthah and Agamemnon to the present day. During the police strike in Boston in 1919, the wife of one of the strikers was quoted as saying that they did not want to join the strike, but did so from loyalty to their comrades; while the community thought their loyalty should attach to their professional duty and to the government. Everyone is faced at times by occasions when he must decide between conflicting loyalties, but this is merely saying in another form that he must draw the line between conjugate principles. To an infinite intelligence every true principle must have its proper place in one all-inclusive pattern, but in finite minds proportions are imperfect, and the patterns that determine thought inevitably differ.

Procedure in a Science*

BY LAWRENCE J. HENDERSON

The subject of this book is "concrete sociology." "Sociology" will be here defined as the science that is conversant with a certain class of phenomena. This class of phenomena includes all events and processes in which interactions between two or more persons occur. In general, we shall limit our study to phenomena in which such interactions between persons seem to be important, or not conveniently negligible.

An example may help to fix our ideas and to illustrate the meaning of the above statement: A and B, two men previously inexperienced, had been engaged for about a month in sawing logs with a crosscut saw. One day B was replaced by C, an experienced sawyer and more powerful man. A, working with his new partner C, found his day's work more fatiguing and judged it less effective than his work with B. He said, "The boss is riding me."

The following comments are to the point and should be carefully noted: (1) By abstraction, the physical aspects only of the day's work may be considered, for instance the efficiency, in the thermodynamical sense, of the work of A and C. Such a study is physical and physiological, not sociological. (2) By another abstraction, the cost of the labor of A and C may be separated out for study. Such a study is economic (in the narrow sense of the term), not sociological. (3) Accordingly, for certain purposes the interactions between A and B, and those between A and C, may be disregarded. But for other purposes they cannot be conveniently disregarded. Thus, it may be desirable to know how far A's belief that his efficiency had diminished is due to an actual lack of physiological (neuromuscular) coördination between A and C, that is, to inadequate physiological interaction between the two individuals, and how far it is due to A's resentment at the change of partners, which may be a psychological interaction between A and X, Y, or Z — say the boss, B's wife, or B himself. This is a sociological problem. (4) It may then be well to know how far A is correct in thinking his work less effective. Then (1), (2), and (3) may all be involved. This is also a sociological problem. Accordingly, sociological studies may, and in general do, involve physical, physiological, psychological, and (even in the strict sense) economic factors. But in any event, conformably to our definition, they involve at least interactions between persons.

* This lecture is the first of a series of three given for several years (1937–1941) as the introduction to Henderson's course in Concrete Sociology in Harvard College. The next two lectures summarized Pareto's conceptual scheme for social organization. After these lectures had been delivered, a number of visiting lecturers (mostly "men of affairs") presented "cases" from their own experience. The students then discussed the cases, using Henderson's point of view for analysis.

The lectures were mimeographed in several editions. During the war years, Henderson decided to publish them (along with another article he then titled "Lecture IV"). His death prevented publication. Mr. Chester I. Barnard, a participant in the original course, has recently edited the lectures for eventual publication under the title "Introductory Lectures in Concrete Sociology." Mr. Barnard very kindly offered us his copy — the only one in existence — of Henderson's final revision.

A's remark is the expression of an attitude. It may or may not be a true or partly true assertion.

This illustration has been chosen because, among other reasons, it is a simple case that is likely to seem trivial. Note well, however, that nothing is trivial, but thinking (or feeling) makes it so, and that we must ever guard against coloring facts with our prejudices. There was a time not so very long ago when electromagnetic interactions, mosquitoes, and microorganisms seemed trivial. It is when we study the social sciences that the risk of mixing our prejudices and passions with the facts, and thus spoiling our analysis, is most likely to prevail.

For our present purposes all this is most important, and the considerations involved in the analysis of this simple case are the better grasped because the case is simple. Moreover, the very simplicity and familiarity of the case have helped to draw our attention to three general aspects of interaction between persons: First, such interaction often takes the form of mutual adaptation and skill in "teamwork"; secondly, it often involves strong sentiments; thirdly, words are often an expression of attitudes or sentiments. In such cases they often have no other "meaning" and may therefore be regarded as neither true nor false. Everyone knows these facts, though many are prone to forget them if it is convenient to do so; but for our present purpose they must be fixed in the mind and *invariably* applied when relevant. They have a deep physiological foundation in the establishment of conditioned reflexes.[1]

So we have already a definition and three theorems (or laws):

Definition: Sociology, *as we choose to say,* is conversant with the interactions between persons.

Theorems: *As experience shows,* (1) interactions between persons often take the form of mutual adaptation and skill, (2) they often involve strong sentiments,

(3) words often express sentiments or attitudes and sometimes approximately nothing else.

Note well that definitions are, within limits, arbitrary; but theorems or laws are not, because they depend upon inductions from experience and upon deductive reasoning. The test of a definition is its convenience; the test of a theorem is its accord with experience, that is, observation and experiment.

If I say "Infanticide is a crime," I may well be confusing a definition and a theorem. The confusion is resolved by stating a definition such as *A crime is what is so recognized by a court.* Then a theorem may follow to the effect that in many communities known to us all forms of infanticide are crimes. In doubtful cases a definition of "infanticide" may also be necessary; for example, the sacrifice of an infant at birth in order to save the mother's life may or may not be included in a definition of the term.

In general, a definition is convenient when clear, univocal, and frequently relevant. In general, a theorem is the more trustworthy the more widely it has been tested by observation and experiment. It should be relied on only within the limits of experience. Formerly, no swans were black and no chemical elements could be disintegrated. In observational and experimental science *we are concerned with probability, never with certainty, with approximations, never with absolute precision,* and I repeat: Scientific generalizations should be regarded as valid only within the limits of our experience of time, place, temperature, pressure, social structure, and so forth.

Some readers will think these theorems obvious and feel them accordingly unimportant. Well, the experience of all highly developed sciences shows that the clear, explicit formulation of "the obvious" and its incorporation in the systematic treatment of a subject is both necessary and very convenient. We are all apt to

---

[1] It is still an open question whether the term "conditioned reflex" is a convenient one, because, as C. S. Sherrington suggests, the differences between reflexes and conditioned reflexes may be more important than the resemblances, for the purposes of physiological research. Throughout this book, the term is used because it is today the usual label for a certain class of phenomena and without any other implications.

neglect, or overlook, or forget such things, especially when we wish to, and above all when we so wish unconsciously. The obvious has sometimes been defined as an important proposition that we wish to disregard. Voltaire has a phrase, "Le superflu, chose très nécessaire"; he might well have added, "L'évident, chose indispensable."

In order to fix this idea, it may be useful to consider two examples. (1) In medical practice there are many considerations leading to the rule that when you do not know what to do you should in general do nothing, or as little as possible beyond the immediate care of the patient. Under pressure to "do something," even physicians who are familiar with these considerations sometimes disregard them or do not think of them. This would probably happen more rarely if the rules of expectant treatment were today more clearly formulated and more systematically presented to medical students and young physicians by their teachers and masters. (2) Many liberals express contempt and disgust at the behavior of the masses in response to advertising and propaganda. The same persons often express unqualified confidence in the referendum as a means of reaching sound decisions about complex political and social problems. It is an induction from experience that people are more often than not emotional, irrational, or at least nonlogical in making decisions. If such liberals were as familiar with this theorem as they are with the multiplication table, some of them might form less absolute conclusions.

METHODS AND PROCEDURES

For the moment, we are concerned with a brief introduction to fix certain ideas, delimit our work, and provide a provisional scheme of analysis and procedure.

Near the end of the *Nicomachean Ethics*, Aristotle prepares the way for his transition to the study of politics with the following remarks:

Must we not admit that the Political Science plainly does not stand on a similar footing to that of other sciences and faculties? I mean, that while in all other cases those who impart the faculties and themselves exert them are identical (physicians and painters for instance) matters of Statesmanship the Sophists profess to teach, but not one of them practices it, that being left to those actually engaged in it: and these might really very well be thought to do it by some singular knack and by mere practice rather than by any intellectual process: for they neither write nor speak on these matters (though it might be more to their credit than composing speeches for the courts or the assembly), nor again have they made Statesmen of their own sons or their friends.

One can hardly suppose but that they would have done so if they could, seeing that they could have bequeathed no more precious legacy to their communities, nor would they have preferred, for themselves or their dearest friends, the possession of any faculty rather than this.

Practice, however, seems to contribute no little to its acquisition; merely breathing the atmosphere of politics would never have made Statesmen of them, and therefore we may conclude that they who would acquire a knowledge of Statesmanship must have in addition practice.

But of the Sophists they who profess to teach it are plainly a long way off from doing so: in fact, they have no knowledge at all of its nature and objects; if they had, they would never have put it on the same footing with Rhetoric or even on a lower: neither would they have conceived it to be an easy matter to legislate by simply collecting such laws as are famous because of course one could select the best, as though the selection were not a matter of skill, and the judging aright a very great matter, as in Music: for they alone, who have practical knowledge of a thing, can judge the performances rightly or understand with what means and in what way they are accomplished, and what harmonizes with what: the unlearned must be content with being able to discover whether the result is good or bad, as in painting.

Now laws may be called the performances or tangible results of Political Science; how then can a man acquire from these the faculty of Legislation, or choose the best? We do not see men made physicians by compilations: and yet in these treatises men endeavor to give not only the cases but also how they may be cured, and the proper treatment in each case, dividing the various bodily habits. Well, these are thought to be useful to professional men, but to the unprofessional useless. In like manner it may be that collections of laws and Constitutions would be exceedingly useful to such as are able to speculate on them, and judge what is well, and what ill, and what kind of things fit in with what others: but they who without this qualification should go through such matters cannot have right judgment, unless they have it by instinct, though they may become more intelligent in such matters.[2]

Elsewhere Aristotle says, "People who have spent their lives observing nature are best qualified to make hypotheses as to the principles that bring great numbers of facts together."[3]

The substance of what Aristotle said so long ago has been many times repeated. For example, Sainte-Beuve once wrote, "Commynes completely justifies for me the phrase of Vauvenargues: 'The real politicians know men better than those whose trade is philosophy: I mean that they are more truly philosophers.' "[4]

In another place Sainte-Beuve reports a similar judgment of Chesterfield's on Cardinal de Retz,[5] and only the other day Monsieur de Saint Aulaire, a former French ambassador to London, remarked of Richelieu, "One recognizes in him as in Lyautey a technician of general ideas."[6] During the French Revolution, Gouverneur Morris remarked, "None know how to govern but those who have been used to it and such Men have rarely either Time or Inclination to write about it. The Books, therefore, which are to be met with, contain mere Utopian Ideas."[7] Hazlitt expressed much the same opinion when he said, "The most sensible people to be met with in society are men of business and of the world, who argue from what they see and know, instead of spinning cobweb distinctions of what things ought to be."[8]

Some years ago a young Oxford don came to the conclusion that men who have missed the highest academic prizes and gone out into the world seem, thirty years after when they come back to Oxford, better men than their successful competitors who have stayed on to lead the academic life. He was so struck by this contrast that he resigned his fellowship and left Oxford. An English scholar who has become an administrator of public affairs, and therefore knows both the academic life and the life of affairs, told this tale. In reply, it was suggested that it is not merely experience of the world which changes and develops men in this way, but still more the practice of deciding and acting under the burden of responsibility for the consequences. This suggestion was unhesitatingly accepted. Indeed, observation and experience clearly indicate that nothing contributes more to the difference that Aristotle recognized between men of action and theorists than practice or lack of practice in deciding and acting under the burden of responsibility.

The man who has the habit of action under responsibility is deeply modified and differently oriented because of this experience. It is not too much to say that his whole organism is in a different state from that of a person who has not the habit of action under responsibility. This

---

[2] *Nicomachean Ethics* (Everyman's Edition), book X, pp. 260–261.
[3] *De generatione et corruptione*, 1, 2, 10.
[4] "Philippe de Commynes," last p. Causerie of 7 Mai 1850.
[5] "Mémoires du Cardinal de Retz," last p. Causerie of 20 Octobre 1851.
[6] *Richelieu* (Paris: Dunod, 1932), p. 40.
[7] Diary, 9 November 1790.
[8] *Table-Talk; Essays on Men and Manners* (London: Humphrey Milford, 1933), p. 101.

is not conceived, and can only with difficulty be imagined, by young, inexperienced students, or even in many cases by theorists who without practical experience have devoted much study to a subject. But unless a man, young or old, is aware of the importance of this psychophysiological adaptation, that is, of the nature and effect of certain kinds of conditioned reflexes and of the way in which both action and understanding are thereby modified, he can hardly understand many aspects of the interactions between men.

Accordingly, Aristotle's criticism may still be made, more than two thousand years after, of much of our current political science *and, in general, medicine only excepted, of the branches of science that are conversant with experiences and affairs of daily life,* that is to say, with events in which interactions between persons are important. Meanwhile, medicine has progressed. Why?

Aristotle's explanation may still be given. In the complex business of living, as in medicine, *both* theory and practice are necessary conditions of understanding, and the method of Hippocrates is the only method that has ever succeeded widely and generally. The first element of that method is hard, persistent, intelligent, responsible, unremitting labor in the sickroom, not in the library: the all-round adaptation of the doctor to his task, an adaptation that is far from being merely intellectual.[9] The second element of that method is accurate observation of things and events, selection, guided by judgment born of familiarity and experience, of the salient and recurrent phenomena, and their classification and methodical exploitation. The third element of that method is the judicious construction of a theory — not a philosophical theory, nor a grand effort of the imagination, nor a quasi-religious dogma, but a modest pedestrian affair, or perhaps I had better say, a useful walking stick to help on the way — and the use thereof.

All this may be summed up in a word: The physician must have, first, intimate, habitual, intuitive familiarity with things; secondly, systematic knowledge of things; and thirdly, an effective way of thinking about things. His intuitive familiarity must embrace his systematic knowledge and his way of thinking as well as the things he studies. Without these three qualifications, no man can be trusted to think scientifically. It is one of the broadest of inductions that competent men of science are no more logico-experimental than other men when they step outside the field in which they have acquired intuitive familiarity with things.

Discussions of scientific method are often more concerned with the publications of men of science — with their finished product — than with the habits, attitudes, and characteristic behavior of such men while they are at work and especially before they write their papers or books. It is partly for this reason that the importance of intuitive familiarity with things is often little appreciated. Note well that this intuitive familiarity includes not only intuitive familiarity with the objects of an investigation but also with the systematic knowledge and with the effective way of thinking. Such all-round intuitive familiarity is almost indispensable — indeed, it may be fairly said to be quite indispensable — for effective scientific work of every kind. One conspicuous result of it is the intuitive avoidance of pitfalls.

At each stage of his work before the final formulation and exposition, a skillful investigator is more often than not hardly aware of what he is doing, and much of his thinking is of the nature of reverie and free association. In early stages especially, his speculation is likely to be curiously untrammeled. There is an old tale of Faraday, the source of which I have been unable to recover, about a conversation of his with a colleague. After a time Faraday became silent, and his friend then asked him

[9] Cf. Galileo, *Dialogues concerning Two New Sciences* (New York: Macmillan, 1914), p. 1: "Indeed, I myself, being curious by nature, frequently visit [the arsenal of Venice] for the mere pleasure of observing the work of those who, on account of their superiority over other artisans, we call 'first rank men.' Conference with them has often helped me in the investigation of certain effects including not only those which are striking, but also those which are recondite and almost incredible."

what he was thinking about. He replied — as I remember the story — "If I were to tell you what I am thinking about, you would think me insane." Few have thought as successfully as Faraday, but many thousands of men of science could probably have given a similar answer on a similar occasion.

Your reveries run on what you are interested in. For effective scientific work it is necessary that your reveries should in large measure run on your work, for you must be interested in it, or rather, perhaps, you must be interested in order that your reveries may run on your work. But it is also necessary that these reveries should run — one cannot say skillfully — but in a way the result of which is equivalent to the result of skill in work. Now for this, intuitive familiarity is necessary.

Consider also the famous fifth postulate of Euclid: "If a straight line meet two straight lines, so as to make the interior angles on the same side of it taken together less than two right angles, these straight lines, being continually produced, will at length meet on that side on which are the angles which are less than two right angles." Few things in the whole range of science have been more discussed than this, and many attempts have been made to find a more convenient postulate. In general, few among those suggested as substitutes permit a successive development of theorems as simple as Euclid's, and, while others may be simpler in form, it is doubtful if they appeal so strongly to visual and kinesthetic intuition. Accordingly, one may at least conjecture that the special form of Euclid's postulate was as much determined by intuition as by reason.

Experience shows that the way of Hippocrates is the way to success. It has long been followed in studying sickness, but hardly at all in studying the other experiences of everyday life. The method of this book depends upon the conviction that there is much to be gained by cautiously following the procedure of Hippocrates in the study of the interactions between persons. Let us, therefore,

consider more carefully what Hippocrates did and what he did not do.

Hippocrates was in reaction chiefly against three things: first, against the ancient, traditional myths and superstitions which still prevailed among the physicians of his day; secondly, against the recent intrusion of philosophy into medical doctrine; thirdly, against the extravagant system of diagnosis of the Cnidian School, a body of contemporary physicians who seem to have suffered from a familiar form of professional pedantry. Here Hippocrates was opposing a pretentious systematization of knowledge that lacked solid objective foundation; the concealment of ignorance, probably more or less unconsciously, with a show of knowledge. Note well that such concealment is rarely altogether dishonest and that it may be performed in thorough good faith.

The social sciences today suffer from defects that are not unlike the defects of medicine to which Hippocrates was opposed. First, social and political myths are everywhere current, and if they involve forms of superstition that are less apparent to us than the medical superstitions of long ago, that may well be because we recognize the latter class of superstitions for what they are while still accepting or half accepting the former class. For instance, "the dictatorship of the proletariat" as used by Lenin, "race" as used by Hitler, "communism" as used by Stalin, and "majority rule" as used by Roosevelt are myths.[10] How many of us recognize all four for what they are? Secondly, there is at least as much philosophy mingled with our current social sciences as there was at any time in the medical doctrines of the Greeks. Thirdly, a great part of the social science of today consists of elaborate systematization on a very insufficient foundation of fact.

Hippocrates endeavored to avoid myths and traditional rules, the grand search for philosophical truth, the authority of philosophical beliefs, the concealment of ignorance with a show of systematic knowledge. He was concerned first of all

---

[10] See F. R. Kent, *The Great Game of Politics* (rev. ed.; New York: Doubleday, Doran, 1930), *passim*.

not to conceal his own ignorance from himself. When he thought abstractly, or in general terms, his thought was limited and constrained because he had wide intuitive knowledge based on the habit of responsible action in concrete situations. There is a test for this kind of thinking: the question, "for example?" Those who generalize from experience almost always pass this test; others do not. Indeed, the test is frequently destructive of unfounded generalization and is likely to lead to painful embarrassment. For this reason its use is often inexpedient.

Experience shows that there are two kinds of human behavior which it is ordinarily convenient and often essential to distinguish:

1. Thinking, talking, and writing, by those who are so familiar with relevant concrete experiences that they cannot ordinarily forget the facts, about two kinds of subjects. These are (a) concrete observations and experiences which are representable by means of sharply defined or otherwise unambiguous words; and (b) more general considerations, clearly and logically related to such concrete observations and experiences.

2. Thinking, talking, and writing about vague or general ideas or "concepts" which do not clearly relate to concrete observations and experiences and which are not designated by sharply defined words. On the whole, the works of Plato belong to this second class, the Hippocratic writings to the first class.

It is surprisingly easy even after twenty-three hundred years to imagine Hippocrates going about his work and to discern his methodical procedure. First of all, he was a practicing doctor. His life was spent in the treatment of patients. That was the milieu in which he lived and thought. It is more than possible that Aristotle had Hippocrates in mind when he wrote the lines above cited, and it seems safe to say that Hippocrates resembles Richelieu, or Lyautey,

or Robert Walpole, or Bismarck, or Cavour more than he does Hobbes, Hegel, Mill, or Marx.

The so-called genuine works of Hippocrates[11] reveal a method in the exploitation of everyday experience with the lives and deaths of men that can never be too carefully studied. But we must confine ourselves to a few important aspects of the Hippocratic method.

In the beginning are the cases. The very first of these is as follows:

Philiscus lived by the wall. He took to his bed with acute fever on the first day and sweating; night uncomfortable.

Second day. General exacerbation, later a small clyster moved the bowels well. A restful night.

Third day. Early and until mid-day he appeared to have lost the fever; but towards evening acute fever with sweating; thirst; dry tongue; black urine. An uncomfortable night, without sleep; completely out of his mind.

Fourth day. All symptoms exacerbated; black urine; a more comfortable night, and urine of a better colour.

Fifth day. About mid-day slight epistaxis [nosebleed] of unmixed blood. Urine varied, with scattered, round particles suspended in it, resembling semen; they did not settle. On the application of a suppository the patient passed, with flatulence, scanty excreta. A distressing night, snatches of sleep, irrational talk; extremities everywhere cold, and would not get warm again; black urine; snatches of sleep towards dawn; speechless; cold sweat; extremities livid. About midday on the sixth day the patient died. The breathing throughout, as though he were recollecting to do it, was rare and large. Spleen raised in a round swelling; cold sweats all the time. The exacerbations on even days.[12]

This case is fairly typical of the col-

---

[11] In speaking of Hippocrates, I mean the author or authors of these works and wish to express no opinion about the man of that name, whose life is little known. We need here feel no concern for the question whether this man wrote these works.

[12] "Epidemics I, Case 1," *Hippocrates*, 2 vols. (Loeb Classical Library, 1923), I, 187.

lection. The following points are important and should be carefully noted: (1) It consists of bare observations of bare facts, uncolored by theory or presupposition and condensed to the very limit of possible condensation. These are the practicing physician's data, freed so far as possible from everything that is not a datum. (2) The data are of two kinds: the first kind, contained in the first part, are single observations; the second kind, contained in the second part, are uniformities observed throughout this particular illness of this particular person. (3) The curious form of breathing referred to is the first mention now known of what is called Cheyne-Stokes breathing. Apart from one other reference to the phenomenon in another Hippocratic case, it is the only known reference before the eighteenth century of our era. This is one sign among many that Hippocrates was no casual and no ordinary observer. On the contrary, he was a constant observer with whom observation was a great part of the business of life, a skillful observer whose skill depended upon both native capacity and long practice. Such at least is the interpretation that all current medical experience forces upon us.

The next step, after the recognition of uniformities in a particular case, is the recognition of a wider kind of uniformity: the recurrence again and again in different cases, often otherwise very various, of single events or of the uniformity observed within a single case — for example, regularities in the duration of certain fevers, the frequent discharge of fluid through the nose in what we now call diphtheria, and in general the prognostic importance of a wide range of symptoms. The most famous of all the descriptions of such uniformities is that of the so-called "facies Hippocratica," the appearance of the face at the point of death in many acute diseases: "Nose sharp, eyes hollow, temples sunken, ears cold and contracted with their lobes turned outwards, the skin about the face hard and tense and parched, the colour of the face as a whole being yellow or black." [13]

Throughout a great part of his work Hippocrates is thus moving step by step toward the widest generalizations within his reach. In great part he is seeking a natural history of acute disease, or at least of those acute diseases that were prevalent among his patients. His success was great, and the whole history of science goes far to support the view that such a methodical procedure is a necessary step in the development of a science that deals with similarly complex and various phenomena.

Beyond this stage there is one even wider generalization that plays an important part in the writings and thought of Hippocrates. This is the principle that came to be known, and is still remembered, as the *vis medicatrix naturae*. For the purposes of sociological study it is an important principle, and we must now examine one or two aspects of it precisely.

Before Hippocrates, about 500 B.C., Alcmaeon of Croton had expressed the opinion that health is an isonomy or harmony (we may say equilibrium) between opposites, sickness a state of monarchy or disequilibrium. Now the widest of all generalizations in the work of Hippocrates is this, that as a rule sick people recover without treatment. The conclusion of Hippocrates was that the state of health is similar to that state defined by Pareto in his treatise on General Sociology, *The Mind and Society*,[14] as equilibrium: "A state such that if a small modification different from that which will otherwise occur is impressed upon a system, a reaction will at once appear tending toward the conditions that would have existed if the modification had not been impressed."

This definition applies to many phenomena and processes, both static and dynamic. It applies not only in the fields of pathology and sociology but very generally in the description of almost all

[13] "Prognostic, II, 6–11," *Hippocrates*, II, 9.
[14] New York: Harcourt, Brace, 1935, pp. 1435–1442. But I quote my own translation.

kinds of phenomena and processes. It is indeed a statement of one of the most general aspects of our experience, a recognition of one of the commonest aspects of things and events. For example: (1) a ball which is in a cup, and which is struck a blow that is not too hard, will return to its original position; (2) a candle flame which is deflected by a draft that is not too strong will resume its original form; (3) a trout brook that is "fished out" will, if carefully protected, regain its former population of fish; and (4), to take a Hippocratic instance, an infant after a disease that is not too severe will gain in weight until that weight is reached which is approximately what would have been reached if there had been no sickness. In statics, this definition is applicable only to what is there called stable equilibrium, and there are, of course, other kinds of phenomena which resemble those of unstable or neutral equilibrium in statics to which the definition does not apply, but since they have little "survival value" they are probably not very common.

Pareto's definition bears the marks of centuries of further work in science and logic; but the Hippocratic analysis comes to much the same thing as Pareto's definition. In both cases, there is the underlying theory that equilibrium is an equilibrium of forces, more or less like the equilibrium, for instance, in a box spring; that a small modification leaves the forces substantially intact; and that the forces tend to reëstablish the state that would have existed if no modification had occurred, just as a box spring which has been depressed when one lies down on it resumes its original form when one gets up. So in February 1937 the people of Louisville, driven away by a flood, returned to their homes when the flood receded; and a few weeks later life was going on with little change. So within a decade the traces of the earthquake and fire in San Francisco could hardly be seen, or the devastations of the war of 1914–1918 along the battlefront in northern France. In such cases the "forces" that tend to produce "the con-

ditions that would have existed if the modification had not been impressed" are what we describe as habits, sentiments, and economic interests.

It should now be evident that Hippocrates, perhaps under the influence of Alcmaeon, made use of his broadest generalization, that sick people usually recover without treatment, in order to construct a conceptual scheme or theory of the nature of sickness. It is herein that he differs from men like Richelieu, Lyautey, Robert Walpole, Bismarck, and Cavour. He differs from them in that he was both a practitioner and a theorist, while, so far as we know, they were practitioners who made use of no general all-embracing theory or conceptual scheme.

In order to construct a useful conceptual scheme, Hippocrates proceeded to analyze the phenomenon, as he abstractly conceived it, into elements. This analysis and the resulting elaboration of the theory need not detain us. To them we owe the survival of such words as "crisis" and "coction." But the theory, having served its purpose, is obsolete, like Ptolemy's astronomy.

We must, however, note carefully that this obsolete theory, like so many others, once served its purpose well. In particular, it was the firm support of the Hippocratic principle of expectant treatment and of the precept "Do no harm," a principle and a precept which still preserve their utility in the practice of medicine and even in government and the affairs of everyday life, and which are too often disregarded by physicians, surgeons, and politicians.

Bagehot clearly recognized the importance of this principle and often pointed it out, for example, in the following passage:

One may incline to hope that the balance of good over evil is in favor of benevolence; one can hardly bear to think that it is not so: but anyhow it is certain that there is a most heavy debit of evil, and that this burden might almost all have been spared us if philanthropists as well as others had not inherited from their barbarous forefathers a wild passion for instant action.[15]

The Hippocratic conceptual scheme suffers from one particular defect that should be carefully noted: It presents a view of the physiological system in a state of equilibrium, without giving a satisfactory picture of the constituent parts of the system or of the forces that operate between these parts. We now know that it is convenient and reasonably satisfactory to think of the constituent parts as chemical substances, fluids, cells, tissues, and organs; and of the forces as the forces with which theoretical physics and theoretical chemistry are concerned. Such a conception was not available to Hippocrates. Nevertheless, his conceptual scheme worked and for a long time worked well. This is, in fact, the test of a conceptual scheme and the only test: It must work well enough for the purpose of the moment. A conceptual scheme survives just so long and just in so far as it continues to be convenient to use it for the purpose of scientific work.

In a discussion of scientific hypotheses, Henri Poincaré once remarked: "These two propositions, 'the external world exists,' or 'it is more convenient to suppose that it exists,' have one and the same meaning." [16] The proof of this assertion is that in scientific work no use can be made of the proposition, "The external world exists," that cannot be made of the statement, "We assume for the present purpose that the external world exists." Moreover, all our conceptual schemes are in a state of flux. There is hardly one we now use that was used in precisely its present form fifty years ago. It is therefore dangerous to believe that a conceptual scheme is a description of some ultimate metaphysical reality. In other words, belief in the "truth" of a conceptual scheme is for scientific purposes not

only irrelevant but misleading. This confusion may or may not be important for a chemist or a physiologist to bear in mind, but students of the social sciences will neglect it at their peril, for the risk of the intrusion of their own sentiments into their work is serious and ever present.

For this reason, it is convenient to distinguish scientific theories from what we often speak of as ideologies. Today, clear-headed physicists no longer "believe" their theories; but Marxists, Freudians, Fascists, New Dealers, and disciples of "laissez faire" are in general believers in dogma rather than mere users of theory. Physicists use both the undulatory theory and the corpuscular theory of light in their modern forms, but it is hard to find anyone who uses both the Marxian and the Fascist theories of society, and perhaps impossible to find a single person who uses both and believes neither. Of course, this is partly owing to the fact that these theories are hardly suited to scientific use.

There is, however, another side to this question that may be mentioned here, because it involves an important sociological fact. Many investigators, especially when young, seem to be stimulated and encouraged by an emotional belief that they are about to solve a riddle of the universe or at least to contribute some permanent description of a bit of "ultimate reality." So long as they work in the scientific manner and keep their conviction that they are dealing with ultimate reality carefully segregated from their work, they may be helped and not hindered by this delusion.

In the preceding analysis I have tried to show how the works of Hippocrates illustrate the statement with which I began: "The physician must have, first, intimate, habitual, intuitive familiarity with things; secondly, systematic knowl-

[15] *The Works of Walter Bagehot* (Hartford, Connecticut, 1889), IV, 566. This quotation is from "Physics and Politics," a work in some respects unfortunately influenced by early "Darwinism," by the writings of Herbert Spencer and of contemporary anthropologists, to all of which Bagehot ascribed too much weight or intellectual authority. But, after errors of judgment and fact have been deleted, "Physics and Politics" remains an important and original work. Possibly his bad health while writing this book may explain the defects, for Bagehot had been of all the Victorians, one of the freest from the influences of intellectual authority.

[16] *La Valeur de la science* (Paris, no date), p. 272.

edge of things; and thirdly, an effective way of thinking about things." I now ask you to consider briefly a remark of Robert Hooke's which is particularly interesting because it states explicitly some of the most characteristic features of the work of a scientific investigator. In one respect, much more than Hippocrates, Hooke here himself gives us an account of his procedure:

So many are the *links,* upon which the true Philosophy depends, of which, if any one be *loose,* or *weak,* the whole *chain* is in danger of being dissolv'd; it is to *begin* with the Hands and Eyes, and to *proceed* on through the Memory, to be *continued* by the Reason; nor is it to stop there, but to *come about* to the Hands and Eyes again, and so, by a *continual passage round* from one Faculty to another, it is to be maintained in life and strength, as much as the body of man is by the *circulation* of the blood through the several parts of the body, the Arms, the Feet, the Lungs, the Heart, and the Head.[17]

This statement sums up a part of what has just been said of the Hippocratic method and adds further considerations.

We may note, to begin with, that it is a statement of what men do in scientific work rather than of the product of their works or of the "method of science." It is behavioristic rather than rational. Secondly, it emphasizes the importance of continuous, persistent occupation with a subject. Thirdly, it makes quite clear the need for both observation and experiment, on the one hand, and for theory, on the other hand. Again, it implies that the activity of the man of science is all one process, like the circulation of the blood; that in a sense we do violence in analyzing it into parts; and that all these parts are united in an organic whole, the activity of the investigator. So far, then, it confirms what has been said while putting the emphasis on another aspect of the subject.

Hooke's statement, however, gives a certain primacy to the hands and eyes, to observation and experiment. Here again his statement is a fair description of the Hippocratic procedure, and the whole long history of science clearly shows that observation and experiment are in one respect the primary features of scientific investigation, because when they give rise to well-established and thoroughly confirmed data and when these data are incompatible with theory or with previous conclusions, then the theory and the previous conclusions yield and suffer modification or destruction, as the case may be.

An interesting statement of Leonardo's expresses the same opinion: "It seems to me that those sciences which are not born of experience, the mother of all certainty, and which do not end in known experience — that is to say, those sciences whose origin or process or end does not pass through any of the five senses — are vain and full of error." [18]

There is one addition to Hooke's statement that we must now make. It is not enough to mention the hands and eyes. We must add the ears if we are to study the interactions of men, for in these phenomena our data come from what we hear as well as from what we see and do. Speech is our chief means of communication and therefore a primary factor in human interactions. Even this platitude has to be stated and restated.

There is a sect of psychologists that will have nothing to do with what men say (unless they are fellow behaviorists talking about behavior of members of another sect of psychologists quarreling with the behaviorists). I warn you against worrying about their inhibitions. There have been few psychologists in the history of the human race and many doctors, and the doctors have always found it necessary to take account of what patients tell them. If a doctor were to refuse to listen to his patients, he would cut himself off from information that experience shows to be indispensable for the skillful practice of the profession. It may be left to the reader's imagination to picture a sick and suffering behaviorist

---

[17] *Micrographia* (1665), preface.
[18] *Trattato della Pittura,* 33.

consulting a physician who refuses to listen to the report of symptoms. Let him also reflect on what Molière might have done with such a scene. Perhaps further reflection, with such a picture in mind, may suggest that certain dogmas of behaviorists are partly "rationalization."

Hippocrates says clearly that among the circumstances from which he framed his judgments were "talk, manner, silence, thoughts . . . the nature and time of dreams . . ." [19] Nevertheless, it is also necessary to distinguish between what you see for yourself and what you are told by another. This corresponds to the ancient distinction in medicine between signs and symptoms, signs being what the doctor himself observes, for instance, *rubor, tumor, calor*, in a patient with an abscess. Symptoms are what he cannot observe but is told, for instance, *dolor* in the same case. Note, however, that if a patient says to you that he feels pain, then it is your datum, your own observation, that the patient *says* he feels pain.

One of the greatest difficulties in medical practice arises from the fact that the patient's report of pain is, like most things that people say about their bodily sensations or their private affairs, often untrustworthy on two scores. In the first place, accurate description of such things is nearly, if not quite, impossible, and even moderately successful description is rare. And, in the second place, the patient may be trying to deceive you or, for any one of many reasons, conscious or unconscious, so phrasing his statements that there is a tendency to deceive.

The crude data of sociology may be roughly described as consisting of what men say, of what they do, and of what happens to them, in so far as these things are significantly related to their interactions.

The difficulty that hearsay, whether oral or printed, makes up a great part of the crude material out of which social science must be constructed can be neither gainsaid nor obviated. But it can be lessened, and, so far as we know, the best way to lessen it is to follow the practice of skillful physicians.

When a skillful physician tries to appraise the meaning and significance of what he is told, his interpretation is modified by long familiarity with facts such as these: The patient may be truthful or a liar, well-balanced or hypochrondriacal, courageous or fearful, calm or excited, hysterical or neurotic or stable, capable or incapable of self-analysis, and so on. He may be a person fully capable of reasoned, logical interpretations of his own experience, or he may be one in whom nearly all expression is emotional and unreasoned. He may or may not have something to conceal. There may well be certain guiding principles of his thought and conduct — such as a hypochondriac's unconscious assumption that everything not perfectly safe is dangerous, or a young man's that everything not perfectly successful is a failure — which prevent him from saying things because they never occur to him, and some of these things may be very important for the doctor's information. In accordance with his judgment of such things, his interpretation of the patient's utterances will vary.

With such things in mind, or so well known that they come to mind spontaneously at need, the physician listens, first, to what the patient wants to tell; secondly, for implications of what he doesn't want to tell; and thirdly, for implications of what he can't tell. Further, the physician avoids the intrusion of his own assumptions, beliefs, and feelings. He bewares of the expression of moral judgments and of bare statements of bare truth or bare logic. He avoids leading questions, but encourages the patient to talk freely and discursively. He does not argue.

So by degrees an experienced, skillful physician often obtains from a patient's own statements a good understanding of what it is important for him to know. Then after diagnosis, or rather apart from it, he has to consider the effect of his bearing and his utterances as a part of the treatment.

The procedure of a skillful lawyer is often somewhat similar to that of a doctor, and the law courts or still better the

---

[19] "Epidemics, I, xxiii," *Hippocrates* (Loeb ed.), I, 181.

lawyer's office, no less than the consultation room, afford material that will teach a wise man much about the interpretation of what men say. In his interesting book, *The Endless Adventure*, F. S. Oliver has a small chapter on "The Variety of Witnesses." A few quotations from this will be useful.

> The great majority . . . were mindful of their oath to this extent — they were resolved to tell "nothing but the truth." Few, however, were willing to tell "the whole truth." There was nearly always something that a passing honest witness was anxious to keep back . . . The transparently frank and open witness was much rarer . . . Then there was the loquacious egotist, whose testimony was a tissue not so much of lies as of illusions . . . There was the fly-away witness who darted zigzag like a woodcock . . . There was the cool and sophisticated witness, unwilling to tell a positive untruth if he could help it; but anxious at the same time to produce a general impression that was false . . . Then there was the witness . . . whose overmastering desire was to tell the whole truth without omitting a single circumstance that had ever come under his observation, or — if the judge would let him — that he had ever heard tell of.[20]

All this shows very clearly that the interpretation of hearsay is a difficult art, but it is a necessary part of the art of the physician and of the lawyer, and not less of the scientific student of the interactions between persons. One important feature of the skillful practice of this art is clearly illustrated and should be evident in the above quotation. Very often it is not the meaning of the uttered words that is important but the attitudes and sentiments that they reveal. I repeat; many things — in many circumstances, most things — that men say are neither true nor false; they are expressions of hopes and fears, of anxieties and obsessions, of likes and dislikes, of aspirations and discouragements.

Experience shows that, like other arts,

the art of interpreting or appraising what men say cannot be learned without practice, and unfortunately that practice is not enough, for not everyone can become a good diagnostician, like the good physician, of disease and of the private troubles of men; or, like the skillful lawyer and competent man of affairs, of the complex situations of everyday life and of the purposes that men try to hide. As Aristotle remarked, politicians rarely succeed in communicating their skill to their own sons. In like manner, even some of the best medical students turn out to be mediocre interns in a hospital. But the really good hospital intern goes through a change which is perhaps the most remarkable change that can be observed anywhere in our educational system.

More often than not, skillful diagnosticians reach a diagnosis before they are aware, or at any rate conscious, of the grounds that justify their decision. If asked to explain the reasons for the diagnosis, they often clearly show by their behavior that they are obliged to think them out and that to do so is an awkward task. This is true of doctors, of lawyers, and of men of affairs. It is here cited as one mark of a kind of skill, hardly ever learned except by long practice, that is indispensable in the interpretation of what men say.

One of my colleagues is a professor of medicine who has collaborated in the course "Concrete Sociology" upon which the present book is founded. Not long after he had for the first time read this statement about "snap" diagnoses, the report of a case in his clinic was presented to him by an assistant in the presence of some medical students. He heard the report of the "history" of the case, of the physical examination, of the symptoms, and so forth. When it was then suggested that the diagnosis was pulmonary tuberculosis, he at once replied, "No, it isn't; it's asthma of neurotic origin." Thereupon a student very properly asked, "Dr. X, why do you say that?" And Dr. X, as he later told me, was obliged to pause and think for what seemed to him not less than two minutes

---

[20] *The Endless Adventure* (Boston: Houghton Mifflin, 1931), pp. 20–21.

before he could give his reasons, because before he could give them he had first to find them.

The probability that a diagnosis is correct is less than the probability that a careful deduction from accurate measurements is correct. But when better ways do not avail, experience shows that the conclusions of the skilled diagnostician may be cautiously used with good results even for scientific purposes. Not less important is the fact that practice in diagnosis is a means of becoming thoroughly familiar with the material in which one works and that skill in diagnosis is an unmistakable sign of that familiarity.

One of the principal reasons why Aristotle's criticism of academic teachers of political and social science hits the mark is that those who lead the intellectual life rarely feel the need or the desire to practice the diagnosis of what men mean and wish from what they say. And few social scientists have learned that the relevant question is often not "What does this mean?" but "Why does he say it?" Now what men say makes up such a large part of the crude data of the social sciences that practice in the art of this kind of interpretation is all but an essential part of the professional formation of a social scientist, as it is of a doctor, lawyer, or businessman. To be sure, there are numerous specialties in the social sciences where the importance of this kind of skill is less than it is in general throughout the field. But any social scientist neglects this part of his training at his peril. Indeed, we are here concerned with one implication, in some respects the most important one, of the rule that the social scientist must avoid the intrusions of his own sentiments and skillfully interpret the role of the sentiments of others if he is to be a good workman.

The way in which sentiments and emotions play an important role in what men say may be clearly illustrated by an analysis of language in relation to thinking. Language is the vehicle of thought, and words are chiefly motor habits or symbols which carry the meaning of experiences. A child becomes so emotionally conditioned to the words used in describing experiences that it is exceedingly difficult for him upon reaching maturity to extricate himself from the emotional accompaniment of his words, whether they relate to religion, politics, the social system, or matters of everyday life. This adds materially to the difficulties confronting the social scientist in thinking objectively and interpreting what other men say.

This may be better understood by contrasting the function of words in everyday communication with their function in scientific writing. In science, words are arbitrary symbols and they are nothing more. Thus, for instance, few chemists remember the derivation of "oxygen," none attach any scientific importance to it. All this was long ago clearly understood by Galileo, who said:

Note by the way the nature of mathematical definitions which consist merely in the imposition of names or, if you prefer, abbreviations of speech established and introduced in order to avoid the tedious drudgery which you and I now experience simply because we have not agreed to call this surface a "circular band" and that sharp solid portion of the bowl a "round razor." Now call them by what name you please . . .[21]

It is a well-established induction from experience, thoroughly confirmed by general psychological, physiological, and biological considerations, that men are more often moved by passions and prejudices, wishes and strong sentiments, hopes and fears, than by reason. In some ways the most striking evidence that this is so may be found in the contrast between what they say and what they do. On this point, it is well to consult Bacon on idols, Pareto on derivations, and (with due skepticism) the psychoanalytical description of rationalization.

The great need for and primary importance of the interpretation of what men say is, then, the characteristic feature of work in the social sciences, at one

---

[21] *Dialogues concerning Two New Sciences*, p. 28.

stage of that work. I have here tried to present the necessary, if barely sufficient, outline of what you ought to bear in mind in studying cases. A word of comfort for those who are concerned with sociology rather than history may be added. General sociology has to do with uniformities; with recurrent phenomena, or, speaking more precisely, with the recurrent features of concrete phenomena; with collections of phenomena, rather than with single events. For this reason the diagnostic task of the general sociologist is less difficult in one respect than that of the historian or of the practitioner of medicine or law or business. For example, let us consider medical charlatans. If we study the practice of a supposed individual charlatan, interview him, and carefully find out all about what he says and does, we may well be at a loss after all to decide how far the man is a conscious hypocrite and how far he is a sincere crank, and whether he is in fact a charlatan. But if we study not merely one but one hundred supposed charlatans, it may be that the same amount of skill in diagnosis on our part will lead to a far more accurate estimate of the extent to which as a rule hypocrisy, deceit, or self-delusion prevails among such persons and the degree to which supposed charlatans are in fact properly so designated. It is often impossible to find out quickly by inspection whether a particular man is a hypocrite or an honest crank or is in advance of his fellows, but it is very easy to know that there are charlatans and that both hypocrisy and honest delusions are prevalent among them. Speaking generally, the first problem corresponds to the work of the historian, the second problem to that of the sociologist.

The reader must not be misled by this long discussion of what men say. It is necessary in scientific work to observe *all* kinds of things that can be observed. Among these are what men say and many other things. The principal features of an event are very often to be looked for among these other things. I have said less about them because methods and procedures for observing them

and for interpreting the observations are well known.

Finally, it may be useful to warn against anxiety about or anxious striving for high systematization and rigor. It is the fashion among many social scientists and psychologists to devote much attention to what is called "methodology." This may be in itself a blameless occupation, but I think such discussions are ordinarily a mere nuisance to those whose aim is to get on with scientific work. The position adopted in this book is that we may well judge from experience what procedures are likely to be effective in scientific work. I believe it is an induction that they are of the kind described in this chapter and that elaborate discussions of methods and of logic and the search for rigor are to be noted only in philosophical writings, in the pseudo-sciences, and in the sciences that have reached a high development. There is a fact that should be pondered by social scientists: Before the nineteenth century, the methods of the differential and integral calculus were not rigorously analyzed, and the treatment of this highly developed part of mathematics was known to be not rigorous. We now have a rigorous calculus, which is in itself an advance in science; yet it has had very little effect upon other things and has but little modified the methods of the calculus. It is ordinarily far more useful to get to work on the phenomena and so acquire familiarity with things than to spend time talking about "methodology" or even to pay too much attention to the analysis of actual methods.

SUMMARY

The principal material contained in this chapter is as follows:

The subject . . . is "concrete sociology."

Sociology treats of interactions between persons.

Concrete sociology is the study of cases.

Mutual adaptation and skill, and the involvement of strong sentiments, are frequent characteristics of interactions between persons.

The social sciences are still open to Aristotle's criticism that those who practice do not teach and that those who teach do not practice.

Lack of practice on the part of theorists often involves the defects that Aristotle noted in the Sophists.

In general, both theory and practice are necessary for the effective study of sociology.

The sociologist, like the physician, should have, first, intimate, habitual, intuitive familiarity with things; secondly, systematic knowledge of things; and thirdly, an effective way of thinking about things.

If he would be scientific, he must try to avoid traditional myths and superstitions, the intrusion of philosophy into his thought, and systematization on insufficient foundation of fact.

Among scientific workers he is one of those most exposed to the risk of self-deception.

Sciences that are concerned with very complex phenomena are most successful when concrete facts are carefully collected and recognized for what they are, viz., the primary features of scientific work, in one respect, because theory and previous conclusions invariably yield to the facts when the facts have been well established and thoroughly confirmed.

After the collection of facts, one proceeds to the discovery of uniformities in the facts. From less general uniformities, one proceeds to more and more general uniformities.

The most general uniformities have a peculiar importance because they are peculiarly useful in the formation of a conceptual scheme.

The preceding statements are in agreement with the opinions of Hippocrates, of Robert Hooke, and of a large proportion of the effective working men of science who have expressed their opinions about scientific method.

One uniformity which may be used in forming a conceptual scheme is that noted by Hippocrates and more sharply characterized by Pareto as a definition of equilibrium: The physiological system and the social system ordinarily exist in "a state such that if a small modification different from that which otherwise occur is impressed upon a system, a reaction will at once appear tending toward the conditions that would have existed if the modification had not been impressed."

Unlike most sciences, sociology is greatly concerned with what men say. The crude data of sociology, indeed, consist in large part of what men say.

This is also true of the crude data of medicine. The practicing physician has always found it necessary to study both signs *and* symptoms.

The best available means of study and interpretation of what men say are those that have been worked out by medical men, lawyers, and men of affairs.

Effective rules of procedure in interpreting what men say have not yet been developed and tested, as the effective rules of procedure have been developed and tested in dealing with the kind of data that are the concern of the physical sciences. Therefore, we are in respect of this kind of work still more or less in the master-apprentice stage. However, useful discussions of certain aspects of the phenomena abound, as in Bacon's treatment of idols, in the psychoanalytical description of rationalization, and especially in Pareto's classification of derivations.

In certain respects, the characteristic feature of the social sciences is the observation, study, and interpretation of what men say. That is why it has been brought forward in this chapter. It is especially difficult in the study of history, in so far as history is concerned merely with concrete events, somewhat less difficult in general sociology, where uniformities are in question.

The Psychology of Control*

BY MARY PARKER FOLLETT

Last summer in England I was interested in two letters on the coal strike sent to the London *Times* by two bishops. One said that we must not confuse economic and moral issues, that the coal strike was a purely economic issue and should be treated as such. A few weeks later another bishop wrote to *The Times,* not in answer to the first, but independently, and said that the coal strike would never be settled if it was not understood that the issues involved were not economic but moral issues.

Undepartmentalized Thinking — Emphasis on the Whole as a Unit of Study

I was interested in these letters because I am coming more and more to think that we cannot departmentalize our thinking in this way, that we cannot think of economic principles and ethical principles, but that underneath all our thinking there are certain fundamental principles to be applied to all our problems.

Let me give another illustration. A man, the owner of a store, marked a certain grade of women's stockings which he had been selling for $1 a pair down to 87 cents, because he thought the price had been too high. His son reported later that the reduction had spoiled the sale of that item, that customers felt that something must be the matter with it; they wanted a "dollar stocking" as they had always had. Now I do not know what the rest of that story was, but one can imagine the son, being modern, talking of the "psychology" of the customer, while one can imagine that the father, brought up in an age which did not talk psychology in season and out, and being an upright, conscientious business man, was thinking of something he called an

"economic" price. Here again I should like to ask: Could not that problem have been solved by some principle which was not wholly psychological or wholly economic? Here again, would it not be possible to undepartmentalize our thinking? I think we should do this — undepartmentalize our thinking — in regard to every problem that comes to us. I am going to say before the end of my talk how I think this could have been done in the stocking controversy. I do not think we have psychological and ethical and economic problems. We have human problems with psychological, ethical, and economic aspects, and as many more as you like, legal often. I know a lady who asked her maid to lift a large pot of ferns from one place to another in the room. The maid replied that the lady was stronger than she was and she thought she should do the lifting. Here you see was a problem with an economic aspect and a psychological and an ethical. It could not have been satisfactorily solved by any one of these disciplines alone.

If we have to undepartmentalize our thinking and get down to principles that are fundamental for all the social sciences, fundamental indeed for all the life processes, surely we have to do that especially for the subject of this paper. The aim of organization engineering is control through effective unity. If, therefore, we wish to understand control, we should begin by trying to understand the nature of unities. And as our thinking on this subject has of recent years been greatly enriched by the thinking in other fields, I want to speak briefly of what we are learning of unities from biologists, psychologists, philosophers. Professor Henderson, a biological chemist, tells us

* Reprinted by permission from *Dynamic Administration, The Collected Papers of Mary Parker Follett,* ed. Henry C. Metcalf and L. Urwick, Harper & Brothers, New York, 1942, pp. 183–209. This paper was presented to business executives in March 1927 at a conference of the Bureau of Personnel Administration in New York City.

that we have to study a whole as a whole, not only through an analysis of its constituents. He says: "The old physiologists described the circulation of the blood, the beating of the heart, or the properties of gastric juice, and could tell you separate facts, but could not connect these facts so as to make a satisfactory picture of the organism." Again he says: "Physiology is far from seeing the organism as a whole yet, but we can put together the carriage of oxygen, of carbonic acid, the alkalinity of the blood, and see how these three are parts of one process. We can study how this bit of integration is itself an adaptation." Professor Henderson is always looking on the functioning of a whole as the adapting and integrating of parts. (Is not that the chief job of the organization engineer?) And he goes so far as to say — after stating the fact that doctors used to study separate diseases but now tend to study man as a whole — that this may be the beginning of a new science, the science of human biology.

This emphasis on a whole as a unit of study we see in many places. Dr. Cannon's physiology is the physiology of the integrated organism rather than of analysed parts. J. B. S. Haldane points out that the metabolic activity within the organism is a "whole" activity, the different sides of which are indissolubly associated, instead of being, as was formerly thought, isolable physical or chemical processes. A very suggestive treatment of wholes has come from those who have been working at the integrative action of the nervous system. Sherrington has shown us convincingly that the simple reflex, which has been treated as an isolable and isolated mechanism, is an artificial abstraction, that the nervous system functions as a whole. Kempf, a psychobiologist, deals with what he calls "whole personalities." He tells us of an integrative unity, of a functional whole. Many psychologists today are taking the idea of "organization," "integration," "total activities of the individual," as the pivotal point in their psychology. (Here again are words and phrases with which we are coming to be familiar in business

management.) The *Gestalt* school gives us what is called explicitly the doctrine of wholes, which denies that physical, psychical, or social situations are made up of elements in a plus-plus relation. The whole, they tell us, is determined, not only by its constituents, but by their relation to one another. This is not new doctrine, but, being put forward as the cardinal feature of a whole school of psychology, it is having a large influence.

Moreover, those engaged in personality studies have been especially influenced by the *Gestalt* school, and they are having a direct influence on industry through personnel directors, employment managers, industrial psychologists. Their enlarged understanding of the nature of unities has affected hiring, promotion, and dismissal, for this view of wholes rather than of parts is what now guides us in our estimates of individuals. We used to describe people by naming a number of characteristics — he is selfish and he is so and so and so and so. But now we know that we do not get a very correct idea of a man thus described. We know that it is the way these characteristics are related that makes a man's personality. Aggressiveness in Roosevelt [Theodore Roosevelt] may mean something quite different from aggressiveness in someone else. It is certain that biographies of the future will be very different from those of the past because of the larger understanding of this point.

Again, consider the way we now use intelligence tests. Here is one list: "reasoning ability, imagination, verbal memory, incidental learning, judgment, learning in specific fields of knowledge." It used to be thought sufficient to get percentages for each of these. Now we ask how they modify one another. If a man is over-confident (or over-cautious, either) that may affect his reasoning ability so that his judgments may not be so good as one might expect from the way his reasoning ability was rated.

All this is reflected in placement or promotion in industry. The men who hire have discovered that skill is often overestimated in determining industrial value. They ask (if they are up to their job) what that man's interest in his job is and how that affects his skill. They ask also his ability to work in a group or get along with his foreman, and how that affects his skill. Of course, it is equally true the other way round, that his degree of skill may be affecting his other qualities. He may, for instance, take so much interest in doing his work well that any resentment he may have against foreman or fellow worker gets smoothed out.

The importance of noting the relative significance of the different factors concerned has been pointed out by Cyril Burt, in his *Study in Vocational Guidance*, and also by Dr. Yoakum when speaking at these Bureau of Personnel Administration Conferences. And I think it is Dr. Yoakum who has also told us of another unity which it is necessary to consider. The personnel manager has to think of the efficiency ratings of the man, of the job analysis, of the promotion policies of the company, and of production and sales figures; and it is recognized to-day by some of the best personnel managers that the crux of their job is to understand the relations between these factors.

Let me give one more illustration from the field of industrial psychology. Fatigue studies used to consider the monotony of the task and its effect on the individual. Now a study is made of the different modes of expenditure of energy natural to that individual. In other words, we are always studying the total situation. All industrial psychologists feel that Dr. Mayo has added a very valuable contribution to their work by his insistence on "the total situation." And we must remember that we should always mean by that not only trying to see every factor that influences the situation, but even more than that, the relation of these factors to one another.

This is the most important, far the most important, trend in the thinking of to-day. In a certain hospital there is a consultation clinic for the man of moderate means. For the sum of $10 he can be examined by specialist after specialist. But there is no one doctor who reads the opinions of all these specialists to see what they amount to all together. The reports of the neurologist, the radiologist, and the others are forwarded to the doctor who has sent the patient to the hospital, and he says, "What on earth does all this mean? What does it add up to?" But certain doctors are hoping to remedy this defect, and that is yet another indication of the growing appreciation of wholes.

We see this in almost every field of study. You will find it very explicitly stated in an article in *Science*, on "Emergent Evolution and the Social," written by Professor William Morton Wheeler, an eminent zoologist who has written on the social life of insects. I do not think he has sufficient grounds for his conclusions in that article, but the first part of the article is an interesting statement of the principle we are here considering.

Again, another illustration from zoology, an article on wild mice in the *Journal of Mammalogy*, shows that the local distribution of wild mice is not controlled by any single factor of the physical environment — by climatic conditions, or food and water supply, or antagonism between species, or nesting material — but is due to the relation of the mice to the biotic community as a whole of which they are members. This relating of the "behaviour of animals to the environmental complex" marks an interesting correspondence in the thinking in different fields. It has exactly the same significance as Dr. Mayo's "total situation."

In the field of anthropology, Malinowski says cultures are wholes, and you cannot alter any feature without producing repercussions which alter the whole.

In philosophy, our greatest thinkers have given us more than indications of this view of unity. Among living philosophers, I think Professor Whitehead is contributing most to our understanding of this truth.

To turn to the field of the social sciences, we find in our study of government the same truth — namely, that unities are determined not only by their constituents but by the relation of these constituents to one another. We see, for instance, how the realignments of nations change each nation. As the biologist tells us that every organism has a form or structure which is determined by the way the elements are placed in that structure, so we find on the social level, too, that rearrangement is always more than rearrangement; it changes the character of the things arranged. The regrouping of European nations has its effect on each nation.

In the study of government we find many examples which throw light on unities — genuine unities, pseudo-unities, attempted unities. We have not time for the many, but one may point to the League of Nations. One might point to the crop of autocrats which southern Europe seems to be reaping. I believe the cause of that lies in the fact that these nations find that unity is necessary and that they have not yet found out how to get it in a better way, or rather how to get nearer a genuine unity.

Some political scientists make the mistake of considering co-ordination and balance synonymous. Most of the political pluralists do this. The guild socialists tell us that their co-ordinating congress is an arbitrator, or court of appeal, to keep the balance between co-ordinate autonomies. According to the doctrine I am expressing, "co-ordinate autonomies" is an impossible expression. You cannot have co-ordinate autonomies because co-ordination is the building up of a functional total.

One of the most interesting indications in the field of government of the appreciation of the principle we are considering is the present effort in England to functionalize the departments of government and to provide for cross-relations between the departments which shall bring about a closer and more effective unity, not an arbitrary or artificial unity based on the dictum of constitution or law, but a functional unity.

To take another illustration from the field of government, many people think that democracy means all taking part. If it means only that, I do not believe in democracy. It is the fruitful relating, the interacting of parts, a co-functioning, that we want. We must provide the organiza-

tion necessary for such interactions and also recognize and control those which we now have. To deny that they exist is a basic error. Professor Dewey says that it is the role of the public in government (I am using his words) to intervene not continuously but at certain junctures. He explains the phrase "not continuously" by saying that the public has its own life to lead, it is preoccupied with its own work and amusements. I do not think that there is any possible way in which Professor Dewey can support this statement. We have our own work? As a Vermont farmer, I go out and shear my sheep, but at Washington they are putting a tariff on wool — I hope. My amusements? I go to the movies and at the same time the government is censoring them — I fear. But I must not go into such questions as this. I have taken a moment for this only because I want to show that the basis for understanding the problems of political science is the same as the basis for understanding business administration — it is the understanding of the nature of integrative unities.

In economics, too, we find this same development in thinking. Ten or fifteen years ago we heard a great deal from certain economists about instincts; one instinct was to be satisfied thus and so, another by some other means. To-day I do not know any economist who is thinking in this way. They see that instincts interact, that the result depends on the way in which they interact.

We hear also from both economists and psychologists of a "want-system," by which they mean that we cannot satisfy one want or desire after another, that my different desires act on each other, and that the total want-system is different from the addition of separate wants. Their use of the word "system" is significant. They are using it in the technical sense in which biologists use the word, in the sense of organized activity. We are all coming to see that our lives are controlled not so much by certain "drives" or wants as by their relation to one another.

I think the general recognition of want-systems would do away with a great deal of unnecessary discussion. Arthur Pugh, one of the ablest of the trade-union leaders in England — some people think the ablest — said to me this summer, "It isn't more pay the workers are usually after; it is improvement in status." I do not suppose he could have meant that literally, so I suppose he meant to emphasize a want-system in which status has an important place. We know that the worker wants a good many things — security in his job, work that interests him, congenial companions, recognition of his special ability, decent work conditions. Now, these wants have some relation to each other; they form, in the words we are using, a structure, a pattern, a whole, a unity.

In another field, psychiatrists look for a complex, not a single cause. There has been a marked advance in psychiatry in this respect.

Again, the probation officer, too, recognizes wholes, or the environmental complex, to use the expression of the zoologist. He sees not only that a number of things are influencing the boy's life, but he tries to understand the way in which they are influencing one another.

Take an instance of a social worker. She is dealing with a girl of a difficult temperament who has a nagging stepmother, a job for which she is not fitted, and evening recreations of not the most wholesome character. The most successful social worker is not the one who deals with these one by one merely, but who sees their relation to one another. A more suitable job may change all the others and therefore the total.

I am emphasizing this matter of relation because, while it is customary now to speak of "the total situation," that phrase means to many people merely that we must be sure to get all the factors into our problem. For instance, some of the industrial psychologists who are using this phrase tell us that when a workman is grossly rude to his foreman we must not jump too quickly to the conclusion that he has an habitually bad temper or an exasperating foreman; the cause may have been a quarrel with his wife at breakfast. That is, these psychologists are warning us that we must be sure to get all the factors in. What I am emphasizing is not merely the totalness of the situation, but the nature of the totalness.

I am taking some time to speak of the nature of unities because if unity is the key-word for biology, psychology, philosophy, the same thing, what we call co-ordination, is certainly the crux of almost every problem the organization engineer or the business manager has to deal with. In talking with organization engineers in both England and America, I am always told that co-ordination is their most important, as it is their most difficult problem. And they are coming to understand co-ordination as the making of an "integrative unity" (Kempf's expression). They know that the parts of a business should so move together in their reciprocally adjusting activities (almost Professor Henderson's phrase) that they make a working *unit*, not a congeries of separate pieces. They are coming to see also that you do not have co-ordination by two units existing harmoniously side by side, that these units have to make a unity before you can say that you have co-ordination. And they are also coming to know, as the biologist and psychologist and philosopher know, that we advance by progressively evolving unities.

The possible examples from business management of the working of this fundamental principle are innumerable. In considering any business problem, you always find that what you have to consider in a situation is not all the factors one by one, but also their relation to one another. This means, among other things, that when a factor is added to or subtracted from a situation, you have not that situation minus or plus that factor, for all the rest will be changed. You see it in a board of directors. One man leaves and all the rest become a little different. The influence of that board of directors as a total is not the same as it was minus that man's influence, because his withdrawal, by changing slightly every other man, has made the total different. Every business man knows that the president of a company in relation to one board of directors may be very different from that same president in relation to another board.

An organization consultant, called in to find why a certain department in a business was not keeping pace with the rest of the business, told me that he found the solution of the problem was not to change any one thing or any two or three things in that department, although that was what the board of directors had expected him to do. But what he suggested to the board was certain changes in the relation between the factors or sections of which the department was composed.

Take a situation made by credit conditions, customers' demand, output facilities, and workers' attitude. They all together make a certain situation, but they constitute that situation through their relation to one another. If you change one, usually some, if not all, of the others are changed.

I was very much interested in something the head of a large business said to me just the other day, since I began writing this paper. I will quote it, and while I am quoting please think of what the *Gestalt* school is telling us of a unity, that is not a plus-plus relation of parts. He said:

If my heads of departments tell me that Department D and Department E are co-ordinated, and then I find that Department D and Department E are exactly the same as they were before, then I know that what I have been told is not true; they are not co-ordinated. If they have been co-ordinated, then the parts will be changed, that is, the practice of Department D will differ in some respects from what it was before co-ordination.

This statement contains a very profound truth, but it was a practical business man who made this statement, not a philosopher.

One might think that this is a statement affirming that the whole determines the parts as well as that the parts determine the whole, but that would not be strictly accurate. The same activity determines both parts and whole.

My illustrations serve, I hope, to show that the same fundamental principle holds good in various fields of study, namely, that the reciprocal activity of the parts changes the parts while it is creating the unity. That is the first point of this paper.

The Nature of Reciprocal Activity in Creating Unities

My second point concerns the nature of the interacting. If we could discover that, I think we should have arrived at something very fundamental. Suppose you have two factors, or I should prefer to say two activities, A and B, reciprocally influencing each other. The key to our problem lies in what we mean by reciprocally influencing. Do we mean all the ways in which A influences B, and all the ways in which B influences A? Reciprocal influencing means more than this. It means that A influences B, and that B, made different by A's influence, influences A, which means that A's own activity enters into the stimulus which is causing his activity. This is something like what on the physiological level has been called circular response, the full significance of which was well shown by Bok, the Dutch physiologist. In every situation our own activity is part of the cause of our activity. We respond to stimuli which we have helped to make. Capitalism is not responding to trade unionism but to the relation between itself and trade unionism. As soon as we take any actual instance like that, we see how inadequate it would seem not to take this fact into consideration. It is the fact which is of the greatest importance for all consideration of conflict. I am never fighting you, but always you plus me, or, more accurately, the relation between you and me. France is not responding to Germany alone, because so much of Germany's activity has been brought about by the actions of France. The behaviour of France is not a function of the behaviour of Germany, but of the interweaving between France and Germany. We need an understanding of this law for any situation where human beings are concerned. I think it is the key to history, law, economics, and to business administration.

Let us note this, too — When we say that the behaviour of France is a function of the interweaving between France and Germany, we are speaking of a unity which is not the result of an interweaving, but *is* the interweaving. Unity is always a process, not a product. I suppose that is really the pivotal point of this paper. Unless we are thinking wholly in terms of process, the statements I am making will be meaningless. With this in mind we see that when we say that the behaviour of France is a function of the interweaving between France and Germany, we are saying much more than that the parts are altering each other; we are saying also that the whole a-making is altering the parts.

Please notice that we have now carried our argument a step further. I have been saying that the whole is determined not only by its constituents, but by their relation to one another. I now say that the whole is determined also by the relation of whole and parts. Nowhere do we see this principle more clearly at work than in business administration. Production policy, sales policy, financial policy, personnel policy, influence one another, but the general business policy which is being created by the interweaving of these policies is all the time, even while it is in the making, influencing production, sales, financial, and personnel policies. Or put it the other way round — the various departmental policies are being influenced by general policy *while* they are making general policy. This sounds like a paradox, but it is the truest thing I know. Business unifying must be understood as a process, not as a product. We have to become process-conscious. I believe that is the first essential to the understanding of business organization. We sometimes hear the question discussed whether general policy should dictate departmental policies or departmental policies contribute to general policy. There is a deeper truth than either of these, and that is this something which I am trying to express to you — namely, that it is the same activity which is mak-

ing the whole and parts simultaneously. We never "put parts together" even when we think we do. We watch parts behaving together, and the way they behave together *is* the whole. I say "parts," and people often speak of "factors" or "elements" in a total, but when we use any of these words we must remember that we are talking of activities.

I wish I had time to show how this fundamental principle works on the personal level, but just let me recall what you have often noticed, that while the different characteristics which make up a personality are all the time influencing one another (I am selfish, but my degree and my kind of selfishness are determined partly by my other characteristics), while the different characteristics, I say, are all the time influencing one another, at the same time they are being influenced by the whole personality as it is at any one moment. My personality as a whole is influencing my selfishness, my aggressiveness. Next year if my personality as a whole is different, it will have a different influence on the different characteristics which make up my personality.

It is the same with business unities. I have just given the example of the influence of general policy on departmental policies, but there is no point in an industrial plant where this is not seen. If two department heads form a good working team, the kind of team they make will influence the activities of each. At the same time, the activities of each are relating themselves to each other to form the whole. When you put it in terms of yourself and Jones in the next room, it seems easy enough to understand, and yet we have here one of the most profound truths of philosophy. However, while it may be easy enough to understand in the case of yourself and Jones, it is by no means so easy to understand when relations become more complex. When we do understand this more fully, it will be a big step forward for business organization.

But both in my illustrations from the social level and from the personal level, I have run the risk of presenting this idea to you in an over-simplified form. To

THE MARKETING CO-OPERATIVES WANT:	THE INDIVIDUAL FARMERS WANT:
1. To get enough cotton or tobacco or whatever the commodity may be to control the market.	1. Higher prices and a stabilized market.
2. To get enough money to pay overhead.	2. Easier credit.
3. To keep the goodwill of the farmers, so that they will not only fulfill their contracts this time because they must, but will sign up next time.	3. To avoid certain disastrous consequences of not selling independently this particular year.

avoid this danger, let me take some actual instance and run over it quickly. I am going to take the conflict which often occurs between a marketing co-operative association and its members over the question of violation of contract, and I am going to express this conflict in terms of desire [see table above].

My chief point in this illustration is that the process of forming a unity here is not that 1, 2, and 3 on the left-hand side interweave, and 1, 2, and 3 on the right-hand side interweave, and then these two unities join. Nothing could be further from life than this, for the interweaving between the left-hand and right-hand sides is going on at the same time that 1, 2, and 3 on each side are unifying, and, moreover, is influencing very greatly the unifying of 1, 2, and 3 on each side of the line. No study of any social situation will be adequate if it does not take this into account.

I have been speaking of the nature of the interacting which constitutes a unity. While we have not time to go very far into this process, I want to pause to note one feature of it, what I have called the evoking, that each calls out something from the other, releases something, frees something, opens the way for the expression of latent capacities and possibilities. This is a very important consideration for business management, for you have to call out all the capacities of everyone in your organization before you can unite these capacities. Evoking, releasing, is the foundation of co-ordination. In other words, you have to catch your hare before you cook him.

It is because of this necessity that we are now emphasizing education in the plant, education of both workmen and executives. It is not because of some vague idea that it is better for everyone to be educated, but, taking co-ordination as the central point of organization, we say to ourselves: What is the quality of that which we are going to unite? That is the initial step — to look first of all to that which is to be co-ordinated.

The Emergence of the Synthesis

We now come to the third point of this paper. Every social process has three aspects: the interacting, the unifying, and the emerging. But our consideration of the interacting has shown us that the interacting and unifying are one. Shall we now therefore consider the emerging? We have already done that. Because the emerging also is part of the same process. Still I am not expressing myself quite accurately when I speak of it as *part* of the process. These three — the interacting, the unifying, and the emerging — are not parts of a process in the sense of steps in a process. There is one simultaneous process, and these three are aspects of that process.

"Emerging" is the word which is being used more and more every day by scientists to denote the novelty wherever it appears in evolution. Morgan has told us of emergent evolution, Spaulding of creative synthesis, Broad of emergent vitalism. Emerging and the emergent seem to be the words most commonly used. They signify at once the something new, the progressive feature in the process. And these philosophers and scientists agree that the emergent pattern, the complex emergent whole, is formed by the interacting, the relating, of the constituent factors. This, too, we see every day in business administration. In situation after situation we find that when we have a progressive and successful policy it has resulted from what a scientist has called an "interactive accumulation," what I have called integration. Let me give an example.

I want to say first, however, that when I use these expressions of the scientists, like interactive accumulation, emerging, and the rest, I hope you understand that I am not trying to put everyday truths to you in a learned form. I am using these expressions because I am interested — more interested than in anything else in the world — in these correspondences in thinking between scientists, philosophers, and business managers, because such correspondences seem to me a pretty strong indication that we are on the right track. If people studying relations from such totally different angles come to the same conclusions, it seems to me of the greatest significance.

To return now to the example I was about to give you of integration. A purchasing agent suggests buying a material which is somewhat inferior which he says will do just as well for the purpose it is to be used for, and he can get it at a lower price than what he has been paying. The head of the production department says that he cannot get satisfactory results with this material. Which is to have his way? Perhaps this very difference of opinion may make the purchasing agent begin a more systematic search for a material which will cost less and at the same time give results satisfactory to the production manager. This would be an integration. And I want you to notice that we should have here the three results which often follow an integration: both parties would be satisfied; the situation would be improved — that is, costs would be reduced without deterioration in the quality of the product; and there might in time be a still wider, a community, value, in this material being used throughout the industry for this

particular purpose, and thus a reduction to the consumer eventually effected.

When I gave you the illustration of the dispute between father and son as to whether a certain grade of stockings should be sold for 87 cents or $1, I said we would speak of a possible solution later. This dispute reflects the whole irregularity, inconsistency, planlessness in price-fixing. Suppose father and son had recognized this, suppose this occurrence had led them to make some beginning toward getting retailers, wholesale merchants, and manufacturers to try to find some proper basis for price-fixing, and then some means to educate the public to understand the basis of price-fixing. In that case, the psychological aspirations of the son and the economic integrity of the father might eventually have been satisfied; and besides satisfying the two parties concerned, there would have been an emergent value, the emergent value being a better business policy, a better social policy.

To end my third point and to summarize thus far: My first point concerned the total situation; my second the nature of the interacting which determines the total situation; my third, the evolving situation. We have come to see that reciprocal adjustment is more than mere adjustment; that it is there we get what the psychologist has called the "something new," "the critical moment in evolution." Every one of us engaged in any form of constructive activity is looking for the plus values of our activity. As men who are interested in organisms, in unities (biologists, philosophers, social scientists, or whatever they may be) are interested in what is called by some the emerging, by some the overflow, by some the evolving, by some the appearance of new values — Professor Whitehead's philosophy is largely based on what he calls "the interplay of diverse values" and the "emergent values" — so in business management we find this same principle at work. We see that functional relating has always a value beyond the mere addition of the parts. A genuine interweaving or interpenetrating by changing both sides creates new situations. Recall what the president of the factory said in regard to the co-ordinating of his departments — that a genuine co-ordinating changed to some extent the two parts co-ordinated. *Functional relating is the continuing process of self-creating coherence.* Most of my philosophy is contained in that sentence. You can take that sentence, I believe, as a test for any part of business organization or business management. If you have the right kind of functional relating, you will have a process which will create a unity which will lead to further unities — a self-creating progression.

An understanding of this is of the utmost importance in settling labour disputes. If we want a settlement which will mean progress, greater success for our business, we shall try to include the values of both sides, which will give us more than the values of the two sides added together, will give us an emergent value. Our outlook is narrowed, our chances of success are largely diminished, when our thinking is constrained with the limits of an either-or situation. We should never allow ourselves to be bullied by an either-or. We want to learn how to make any human association most effective, most fruitful. The reciprocal influence, the interactive behaviour, which involves a developing situation, is fundamental for business administration as it is for politics, economics, jurisprudence, and ethics.

Before going on to the second part of my paper, to the question of control, let me take a moment to carry the correspondences I have been speaking of into still another field, for I cannot emphasize too strongly the significance of finding the same underlying principles in every field of human activity. We find in the arts — in architecture, in painting, in poetry, in music — that the fundamental principle is organization, is relatedness. I have been interested in that approach to the study of Greek art during the last decade which involves a mathematical analysis and hence rests on relations. In a recent book on poetry I read: "In so far as a poem is an organic unity, it changes its meaning, which is why it

lasts to ever succeeding generations." As to music, I was much struck by what a friend said to me only last week: that while we think of the players in an orchestra as each knowing his part and of the conductor as having an awareness of the total process as an integrative unity, we must remember also that the players play best when the conductor is able to make each share his inclusive awareness. This is a rather subtle point, I think.

Besides the interest and significance of seeing our principle at work in the arts, I am also very much interested in the different degrees of sensitiveness to relations shown by different people. A biologist who had, among his assistants, a Japanese who made drawings for him said that a fish under the hand of this Japanese took on certain curves indicating movement, suggesting water. He did not seem to be able to draw a fish as the other young men did — just a fish.

I sometimes think we are all more sensitive to relations aesthetically than we are in our everyday jobs. In taking a railway journey a succession of pictures, that is, of wholes, passes before your eyes all day. You see flowers by a stream, cows in a meadow, a boulder at the foot of a pine. At the end of the day you have this accumulation of *pictures,* you do not think merely of fields and rocks and streams and trees. I believe this same sensitiveness in regard to relations is going to be our greatest asset in business management.

The Nature of Control — Dependence upon an Understanding of Unities

What has all this to do with the title of my paper, *Control?* Why have I talked so long of the nature of unities? Because we cannot understand control without understanding unities. I said that the chief problem of the organization engineer was acknowledgedly co-ordination. That simply means he cannot get control without unity. Put this in the plainest language of your everyday job. In order to control a certain situation, you have to get the co-operation of those fellow executives who are also concerned in that situation. The degree of control will depend partly on how far you can successfully unite the ideas of these men and yourself.

I find this the law on every level I have studied. Those biologists, psychologists, and philosophers I have mentioned in this paper whose most fundamental thinking is concerned with integrative unities, tell us of the self-regulating, self-directing character of an organism as a whole. They mean that the organizing activity *is* the directing activity. The interacting *is* the control, it does not set up a control, that fatal expression of some writers on government and also some writers on business administration. I cannot get up in the morning, I cannot walk to my work, without that co-ordination of muscles which is control. The athlete has more of that co-ordination and therefore more control than I have. On the personal level, I gain more and more control over myself as I co-ordinate my various tendencies. This is interesting to us from two points of view, not only as showing the operation of the same law on different levels, but because we are more and more using this knowledge in dealing with individuals in industry as well as to obtain effective group action. In fact, the two are more closely connected than is always recognized. When we have conflicts, or differences of opinion, between two individuals — employer and employee, or two executives, or two members of a board of directors — it is not only our task to try to reconcile these two individuals. We have to study each individual to see if there are not, perhaps, diverse tendencies warring with each other within the individual, for this internal conflict may be the very thing which will prevent a satisfactory settling of the conflict between these individuals. We have, moreover, to see what measures we can take to reconcile these warring tendencies, to resolve the internal conflict, in order that these individuals can enter into effective relations with each other. But we must remember, what is sometimes forgotten, that this is not an antecedent process; the two integrations are simultaneous. The conflict between A and B, or the integrating between A and B, may help A to unify the diverse tendencies in himself, may help B to do the same. These are not really two processes, but one; the individual would not be integrating his personality if he lived in a world by himself. It is exactly the same kind of a double process as that which I gave you in my illustration from the marketing co-operatives.

Not all psychiatrists who go into industry pay enough attention to this. They are going to adjust the individual, they say, but the very word "adjust" implies that the man is to be adjusted *to* something, and the simultaneous processes of internal and external adjustment, and their influence on each other, should be fully recognized.

I have said that on the biological level, growth is by integration, by the continuous integration of simple, specific responses. I have said that we see the same law in operation on the personal level; diverse tendencies are united into new action patterns. I have said that in the case of two individuals, that is, on the social level, here, too, we get control through effective integration. Authority should arise within the unifying process. As every living process is subject to its own authority, that is, the authority evolved by or involved in the process itself, so social control is generated by the process itself. Or rather, the activity of self-creating coherence *is* the controlling activity. We see this clearly in international relations. We shall never be able to make an international settlement and erect some power to enforce it; the settlement must be such as to provide its own momentum. A political scientist says in a recent book that authority co-ordinates the experience of men. It does not. It is just the other way around. Legitimate authority flows from co-ordination, not co-ordination from authority. This is implied in everything I have said here. Legitimate authority is the interweaving of all the experience concerned.

The intellectuals of the English Labour Party are making, I think, a grave mistake in not accepting this fundamental principle. They see the whole labour question in the fight pattern. G. D. H. Cole, in a passionate article in the *Labour Magazine* advocating the acceptance of Easton Lodge, which Lady Warwick had offered for a Labour College, ended with these words: "And education . . . will create in the hearts of our young workers a will to power . . . that will carry us on to victory."

You see, Cole is thinking in terms of the fight; but as we have been trying that for several thousands, or millions, of years, and it does not seem to be very successful, why not try another method? And another is indicated to us, indicated in the idea that one part can never get any lasting power over another, but that you can have self-direction by forming integrative unities. When employers and employees are willing to sit down together to try to solve their problems rather than to bargain on the basis of who possesses the greater economic power of the moment, then we shall be on the road to settling "the labour question." That genuine authority arises spontaneously within the process of building up an integrative unity should be the argument for employee representation, not that it is the "right" of the workman nor because it will ease up things for the employer.

I speak of the English Labour Party. We see in many places this same disregard of the fundamental principle of control as part of the essential nature of a unity. Many in the Consumers' League over-emphasize the "fight" with the manufacturers; they do not see that they will get their full share in controlling the situation only when they and the manufacturers join. In the very last circular I received from the Consumers' League, it is stated, "With the consumer lies the balance of power." I hope I do not have to pause and say why I think this all wrong. "The balance of power" is the phrase we hear in international disputes, in industrial controversy, and here in the mouths of the consumers as against the manufacturers. What I think the doctrine of this paper shows us is that a jointly developing power means the possibility of creating new values, a wholly different process from the sterile one of balancing.

I have spoken of government, of international relations, of capital and labour, of producer and consumer. In the study of business organization we are saying that authority is not all at the top, that authority goes with function, that what we are seeking in business organization is the method of obtaining a cumulative authority as the interweaving experience of all those who are performing some functional part of the activity under consideration.

Let us note, too, that if control arises within the unifying process, then the more highly integrated unity you have, the more self-direction you get. When bankers, manufacturers, workers, and consumers learn how to form an integrative unity, then we shall have a large degree of social control.

I was much interested last summer in England in a small occurrence which yet seemed to me to have a good deal of significance. I dropped my watch, and it stopped. I was leaving London the next day and wished to get it repaired at once, as I had no other watch with me. I took it to the repair department of a jeweller in Bond Street, and they said it would take ten days to repair it. I understood that it would if the usual routine was followed of sending the watch to a repair shop and letting it wait its turn. So I explained to them the urgency of the case and asked if they would give me the address of someone who did repairing. They said they did not know of anyone. I then walked the length of Bond Street going into those shops that had watches in the windows and asking the same question. They all made the same reply, that they did not know of anyone, but all offered to get it done for me. Now I do not believe this could have happened in America. I think it is because there has not developed in England a group consciousness of sellers. And when I was told in England, as I was, that retail selling is done better in America than in England, I thought to myself that I knew one of the reasons why. These men selling watches in Bond Street were thinking of the immediate profit of the few shillings they would make from repairing my watch; they were not thinking that whatever arouses confidence on the part of the buying public in those who sell is in the long run to the greatest advantage of the selling group. Here was lacking a consciousness of unity, and in so far there was lacking control in retail selling. There are many other reasons why retail selling is more advanced in America, but I thought this was probably one reason.

To sum up what I have said of control thus far: Control is part of a process, a process which we see on biological, personal, and social levels. Conscious control is the self-regulation of the biologist rising to consciousness. And conscious control is the dominant thought of the twentieth century. More and more do we hear that phrase from economists, jurists, historians, and sociologists. It is the chief contribution which our generation is making to the world. And we get control through co-ordination.

I have not entered on the *methods* of obtaining control through effective unities, as that is the whole problem of management and would take a whole series of conferences instead of only one conference. Overselling, for instance, is a lack of control through lack of co-ordination of the departments concerned, and you could give me a hundred illustrations. And we should remember that we must unify policies before we can unify activities. Suppose a department in our business is studying customers' demands. We shall never be able to co-ordinate that department successfully with the selling department unless the underlying policies of these two departments are the same.

Summary: Steps in Attaining Control

If there is not time to consider the matter of control in detail, let us at least note in a general way the steps to be taken in attaining control, using the terms of this paper. I shall take this as a means of summarizing the whole paper. As a summary, there will be some repetition. The first step is to see the field of con-

trol. In any situation the total is complex, not single. Consider Italy at the present moment. While the most interesting thing about the situation is that one man is such a large factor in it, yet to understand the Italian situation we have to get together all that is influencing Italy, all that has gone to give Mussolini his power. But we have to go beyond finding the elements which constitute the field of control. We have to see the field of control as an integrative unity — that is, we have to realize that it is constituted not by certain elements alone, but by certain reciprocal activities.

If the first step in the understanding of a problem is an understanding of the field of control as an integrative unit, the second is the process of passing from one field of control to another. When we get to this point, we are so in the heart of the matter that I wish we were just beginning this discussion. If I elaborated this point, it would be along the line of what I have said of the emerging. I can only say here that when we understand this process, anticipation will not mean forecasting alone, it will mean more than predicting. It will mean more than meeting the next situation; it will mean making the next situation. One of the largest manufacturers in Milan said last July that he and a number of other Italian manufacturers were studying American methods of scientific management so that they would be ready to deal with the industrial situation when Mussolini's hand should be withdrawn. This means, in the language we are using this evening, that when that field of control is broken up, they are going to have a hand in making the next.

I cannot therefore wholly agree with those historians who say that the study of history should help us to predict situations; it should do more than this — it should help us to create situations.

This has enormous importance in business management. Many employers are being told that they should study the psychology of the workers so that in the next strike they will know how to win. I think their aim should be not to be able to *meet* a strike situation, but to *create* a strike-less situation. Again, consider the business cycle. It used to be thought that there was something fatalistic about the business cycle. Then business men began to study it in order to meet the demands made by these periodic fluctuations. The next step is to prevent the fluctuations. When, for instance, enough manufacturers see that times of peak prosperity are not the times to expand — to introduce new lines of goods, new equipment, and so on — then perhaps business will not follow an alternation of peaks and slumps. I spoke at Oxford this autumn at a conference on business management, and one of the papers was on forecasting, a very able and interesting paper, but in the discussion that followed I was much interested in the fact that few there had apparently got beyond the idea of forecasting as predicting. In America many of our business men are trying to do what Hoover has called flattening out the cycle.

How to pass from one situation to another is the point on which we most need light; it is to this that we should now direct our studies. We have been told a good deal by biologists, philosophers, and psychologists of how a unity, or total situation, is constructed; we do not know so much about passing from one unity to another or, to use the language of the *Gestalt* school of psychology, how to make productive configurations. A friend who is a political scientist has told me that he considers this one of the chief problems of the political scientist. For instance, shall the Social-Democratic Party in Germany join a coalition? Will that make a productive configuration? Will it make an effective total situation? We do not know and we do not know how to find out. But while the political scientists have not yet worked out any satisfactory tests or technique of thinking here, the fact that they are working at this problem, and the fact that it is the same problem in which many of us are most interested seems to me hopeful. There are two fundamental problems for business management: first, to define the essential nature of the total situation; secondly, how to pass from one total situation to another. I think we have answered the first fairly satisfactorily as being not inclusiveness alone, but also relatedness, a functional relating. We have not yet answered the second, but the mere fact of stating a problem is a long way toward its solution, and many of us are now trying to state the problem of control.

CHAPTER II

Difficulties in Clinical Observation

IN THE first chapter we considered the importance of developing an "effective way of looking at things" in human relations; we considered the advantages of the clinical approach to the unique situations we are dealing with in this field. We emphasized the complexity of concrete facts and the possibility of oversimplification of abstract concepts in relation to the concrete facts.

It is often noticed that when different people view the same situation (such as a "case"), each individual sees it differently; each is interested in different phases of the total situation. This is inevitably so. Each person's past experience makes him look at situations in ways that are meaningful to him. This statement may seem self-evident, yet even in the field of visual perception we apparently see similar things largely because our experience from childhood has been similar. We see what we are trained to see and what we want to see, as well as what is "really there." And yet somehow we must learn to see clearly what is "really there" if we are to act appropriately in the situations in which we find ourselves. Earl C. Kelley shows the importance of past training even in visual perception. Read

EARL C. KELLEY, *Education for What Is Real* (New York: Harper, 1947), pp. 24–56.

As our visual perception is trained and limited by our experience, so is our understanding of situations by our habits of thought and language. We think largely with words, and we tend to shape our raw perceptions into word-patterns as we think about them. The words carry with them connotations inexorably gained from our past experience which tend to mold perceptions into familiar forms. In this sense, words impose themselves upon the situation and modify our perception of it.

Since any other person's experiences are different from our own, so may the meaning be different that he attaches to the words he uses. Many of us live and work largely in a verbal environment, and we must be careful not to assume that the situation which another is discussing is necessarily identical with our understanding of it *merely* because he uses the same words about it that we would use.

The way in which words shape social observations may be clarified by considering the answers that might be given to a single question, "What kind of a man is this?" The answer can be at three wholly different levels, indicating the quite different connotations you may be considering when you reply.

You might reply, "He is the kind of a man I like" (or "don't like"). In this answer you are considering some characteristics of the man in relation to certain feelings (opinions) you yourself hold. If you expand this statement, you will describe the way he seems to differ from a standard within you. This discussion will not tell us more about the man himself, but rather more about your standard of likes and dislikes; we rapidly stop our consideration of the man and start considering your standards of judgment. In this way you answer a question which is searching for facts about a man with a "value judgment" which gives us details about yourself.

Another reply you might make would be, "Oh, he's a clubman" — or "fraternity man," or "grind," or "Irish," or "foreign." This might be considered a statement of fact classifying this man with others like him and conveying that information to your listener. However, an essential element of such a statement is the implied stereotype. By tone of voice or gesture or by further details you usually also convey your feeling about the man and the type. This answer is more subtle than the first because it appears to have a validity based on a broad classification that seems factual. The problem this reply raises is twofold. First, it is not an objective description of a man — it abstracts a few character-istics about him, which may or may not be descriptive, and merges them haphazardly with all other men who supposedly share them. Second, your listener, having had experience with "clubmen," "fraternity men," "grinds," "Irishmen," "foreigners" quite different from your experience with them, may assume that you mean something very different from what you intended.

Both these first two answers are "oversimplifications." They assume that pertinent characteristics of the man are described by a statement of *your* standard about the man (value judgment) or from *your* classification into a particular group (stereotype). Both these answers may be inadequate if you are dealing with a situation in which this man is involved.

It is possible to answer this question in a way that has much more "ob-jectivity" than either of the above answers. You might be careful to state the limits of your observation by saying, "He has been on the Dean's list for the past two years," or even, "I had dinner with him last night and he seems like a good guy." Some ideas of your values are implied here, but you were careful to qualify your statements; you have not implied that everyone will have a good time with him or even that you would every time you were together. Of course, if you had merely described him physically, your statement would have been more "objective" and more open to verification by anyone who saw him.

If we are to observe accurately and describe even to ourselves what we see, we must be conscious of our use of "value judgments" and too simple classi-fications into "types." Both ways of thinking lead to a defense of our own standards and take us away from the human situations we are observing. Particularly if we are trying to convey our observations to another, we must be careful to separate what "is" from what we think "ought to be."

Of course, we must not maintain that value judgments are "bad." All our actions are based on our values. We wouldn't cross the street unless we had, at the moment anyway, a feeling that it would be better to be on the other side. And in social dealings, we certainly must be able to recognize a man that we "don't want to have anything to do with."

But we tend to misuse our values in two ways: (1) Sometimes we apply them too soon — we decide that a man is "no good" before we really look at him. Such action is especially common when we think in stereotypes; if the man is a "grind" we often dismiss him without taking the trouble to observe that he has some special characteristics that might make him very pleasant in spite of his extreme devotion to books. (2) Sometimes we act in terms of our values in a situation where they are inappropriate. Lowell examined this tendency in his discussion of principles. For instance, a physician, like all other men, has preferences about the kind of people whose company he will enjoy. He may not like "foreigners." But when he is acting clinically in his professional capacity he cannot act on the basis of his tastes for social companions; instead, he must treat the "foreigner" as a "patient" and not let his social tastes interfere with his professional observations. We are all sometimes involved in situations where we will be able to act more effectively if we hold in abeyance the values appropriate to other situations.

We carry forward a large part of the values of our past experience through words. This is useful and inevitable. Yet the relevance of our past experience to present action is often distorted by some very common misunderstandings about the relation of words to reality. Words often represent reality in our thinking and in our talking about reality to other persons. We often feel that if we can express a thing clearly in words, it must be so. Although we know that words are only symbols that are convenient for us to use when referring to reality, we often behave as if they were reality itself. S. I. Hayakawa, in *Language in Thought and Action,* gives an interesting example of the way in which our thinking may become distorted through our use of words. Consider the word "churchgoer." Literally, it refers only to those people who attend divine services more or less regularly; it says nothing about the character of the churchgoer. It is a word that can be used about many people regardless of whether they are good or bad, rich or poor, happy or unhappy. However, there are other connotations to the term, as Hayakawa points out:

> "Churchgoer" *suggests* "good Christian"; "good Christian" *suggests* fidelity to wife and home, kindness to children, honesty in business, sobriety of living habits, and a whole range of admirable qualities. These suggestions further *suggest* . . . that non-churchgoers are likely not to have these qualities . . .
>
> . . . we can manufacture verbally a whole system of values — a whole system for the classification of mankind into sheep and goats — out of the connotations . . . of the term "churchgoer." That is to say, once the term is given, we can, by proceeding from connotation to connotation, keep going indefinitely. A map is independent of territory, so that we can keep on adding mountains and rivers after we have drawn in all the mountains and rivers that actually exist in the territory . . .
>
> [Let us consider] a certain Mr. William McDinsmore — the name is fictitious, of course — [who] has had the term "churchgoer" applied to him because of his habit of going to church. On examination, Mr. McDinsmore turns out to be, let us say, indifferent to his social obligations, unkind to his children, unfaithful to his wife, and dishonest in his trusteeship of other people's funds. If we have been habitually orientated towards Mr. McDinsmore [from the point of view] of the word "churchgoer," this proves to be a shocking case. "How can a man be a churchgoer and so dishonest at the same time?" The problem is completely incapable of solution for some people . . . they are forced into one of three conclusions, all absurd:
>
> 1. "This is an exceptional case" — meaning, "I'm not changing my mind about churchgoers, who are *always* nice people *no matter how many exceptions you can find.*"
>
> 2. "He isn't *really* that bad! He *can't* be!" — that is, *denying* the fact in order to escape the necessity of accounting for it.

3. "All my ideas are shattered! A man can't believe anything any more! My belief in human nature is destroyed!" [1]

Distortions of this sort — although perhaps not to this degree — are implicit in many discussions. It would be useful to look in more detail at the ways in which we use words, particularly to distinguish the ways in which words support our mental and physiological processes from those ways in which they hinder our observations.

It is not uncommon for us to feel that if we could only find more precise words for the things we are trying to say, others would understand us more clearly. Yet there are an infinite number of situations we try to describe with a necessarily limited number of words. In fact, if the search for precise words were carried to its logical extreme, the "best" word would be one that could describe adequately only one situation and could therefore be used only once. We limit the total number of words we need by using the same ones over again in similar situations. This process allows us to describe situations to people who have never experienced them — we use words covering similar areas of experience which they have encountered. Clear understanding is obtained by listening carefully to the context in which the words are used and to the concrete situations which are being discussed. Read

S. I. HAYAKAWA, *Language in Thought and Action* (New York: Harcourt, Brace, 1949), pp. 1–81, 165–247.[2]

This author makes several useful distinctions. He develops the relation of language and thinking to concrete events. He distinguishes two referents for the meaning of words: one "intensional," that is, the word-images inside our heads; the other "extensional," that is, the concrete things themselves which the words are used to describe. He demonstrates that in our ordinary conversations we often confuse these referents; we talk about our mental impressions rather than the concrete situations we are purporting to discuss. He illustrates the confusions that result when we think about events in terms of words whose referents are "verbal" rather than "situational."

In developing the concept of "extensional" thinking, Hayakawa emphasizes that words relate to things at several different levels of abstraction. He compares abstractions to "maps" — both are supposed to represent a "territory." To do so, they leave out some of the characteristics (facts) of the territory in order to picture others, and two maps of a territory may differ widely in the amount of detail included. The words "cows" and "farm assets" may both refer to a particular herd of cattle, but they are maps at very different levels of abstraction. If two men were talking about cattle, and one was thinking about his favorite cow, Bessie, and the other was thinking about the assets of the farm, they might differ violently on the desirability of having beef for Sunday dinner. We tend to forget the omissions and act on the assumption that the map is exactly like the territory. This gets us into trouble in two ways. First, we may overlook things in the territory that are not on the map. Second, we may get into meaningless arguments about a particular situation because another's map about that situation is different from ours. The discussion Hayakawa describes

[1] S. I. Hayakawa, *Language in Thought and Action* (New York: Harcourt, Brace, 1949), pp. 254–255.
[2] There is an earlier edition with different pagination: *Language in Action* (New York: Harcourt, Brace, 1939).

in "A Semantic Parable" at the beginning of his book is an eloquent example.

We are especially prone to carry over maps from old and familiar situations into new ones. This makes it hard to observe or handle adequately a new situation, which is always unique and sometimes critically so.

The difficulties in observing which we have been considering in this chapter — difficulties developed by our own past experiences — are among the facts of life, the givens, and cannot be removed. Our training in seeing, and in reacting with words to what we see, shapes the way in which each of us relates himself to the world around us.

Lowell J. Carr discusses this point:

As an ordinary person facing a social situation, you are a poor instrument to prepare a record for four reasons:

1. *You look at your social world through a set of colored spectacles.* Every one of us is the product of the culture in which he has been reared. Culture is the body of man-made things, symbols, relationships, ideas, beliefs, practices, and values peculiar to a population. That you bear your father's family name, that you believe every effect has a cause, that you eat with a knife and fork and pay for your food with money, that a man or woman is supposed to have only one mate at a time and then only after a certain binding ceremony called marriage — these are matters of culture. As we all know, culture has been evolving and accumulating for at least 500,000 years. You were born into a preexisting culture, you have as a matter of course assimilated the beliefs and presuppositions implicit in your family and community culture, and you tend, therefore, to see situations as your culture defines them for you, and to adopt the role, or set of behavior patterns, prescribed by your culture for each situation. This is what we mean by looking at situations through "colored spectacles." Culture defines your world for you. Before you can become a dependable observer you must learn to discount your culture — learn to make allowance for the fact that your culture tells you "Negroes are inferior"; "Capital must control labor"; "This is a man's world," and so on. You must learn, in other words, to become keenly aware of the relativity of your own point of view in every social situation and to make allowance for that relativity. If you cannot overcome your stereotypes, or dominant expectations, at least you can become aware that you have them.

2. You are also a poor instrument to prepare an objective record because you *have a habit of wanting practical results, rather than mere objective data in any given situation* — you want to catch a train, or win an argument, or get a job, or make a date, or advance some specific cause such as Communism or the reelection of a Democratic administration, and so on. In nearly every situation you want some one specific outcome rather than another. Even at the movies you identify yourself with the hero or heroine and hope the villain gets what's coming to him. That attitude of wanting one thing to happen rather than another is not scientific detachment. In any situation in which your real interests are involved you will find it very difficult indeed to discount the distorting effect of this tendency of yours to take sides. But the preparation of an objective record of any situation demands just that — your own wants and wishes must be kept out of the picture.

3. A third reason why you are a poor instrument for the preparation of an objective record is that *you do not want to be objective,* you do not want to dissociate yourself from the phenomena under observation. In any situation involving another race, another social class, the other sex, or some idea that vigorously challenges one of your own pet ideas, you will cling tenaciously to your own stereotype (expectation) or desire. You will resist objectivity with every subterfuge and rationalization that you can think of. And you will insist that the situation is what you say it is

because that is what you want it to be; any other kind of interpretation would make you too uncomfortable. "There just can't be another world war because civilization couldn't stand it."

4. Finally, you are a poor instrument for the preparation of an objective record of any situation bigger than your immediate presence for your contacts with such situations *are bound to be more or less haphazard, incomplete, and subject to all kinds of distortions implicit in the processes of distance communication in modern society*. What, for example, were your contacts with the coal miners or the railroad workers in the great strikes of 1946? What have been your contacts with the Russian government? And so on. Actually most of us have to take our definitions of beyond-the-horizon situations at second, fourth, or tenth hand, and we can never know just how much arbitrary selection and distortion have gone into the process before the product reaches us. After all, no picture can be any better than the man who points the camera.

Because of your cultural stereotypes, your practical desires, the pleasure principle in your intellectual life, and the inadequacy of your contacts with beyond-the-horizon situations, you are a poor risk as a situational observer at this moment.[3]

We have been stressing the pitfalls that face us because of the influence of our own pasts on the way we observe. But we should not overlook the advantages. We always share *some* experiences with the individual we are observing. Charles H. Cooley says that if it were not for those similar experiences we could not understand the other fellow at all. The more closely our past and his are similar, the closer the *potential* understanding. We observe through a complicated process of looking inward as well as outward. We see the other fellow in a certain situation; we imagine ourselves in his shoes and respond to the situation with our own emotions. How else could we have any idea of how he "feels"? Cooley calls this "sympathetic introspection" and describes it in the following article. Read

CHARLES H. COOLEY, "The Roots of Social Knowledge," below.

Cooley points out the way in which this process differs from the observation of physical objects. He shows how difficult it is, but nevertheless insists that it is possible to control the procedure so as to produce reliable knowledge.

ADDITIONAL READINGS

Ichheiser, Gustav, "Misunderstandings in Human Relations: A Study in False Social Perception," *American Journal of Sociology*, LV (September 1949), 1–70.
A systematic analysis of the mistakes we make in observing other people and of the false clues for action these mistakes give us.

Korzybski, Alfred, *Science and Sanity: An Introduction to Non-Aristotelian Systems and General Semantics* (Lancaster, Pennsylvania: The In-ternational Non-Aristotelian Library Publishing Company, 1933).
Korzybski was the philosophic leader of the semantics movement. His book is not easy reading but is worth the attention of the serious student of the use of words.

Redfield, Robert, "The Art of Social Science," *American Journal of Sociology*, LIV (November 1948), 181–190.
A defense of "sympathetic introspection" as a tool of social insight. Redfield admits its limitations, but insists on its utility.

---

[3] Lowell J. Carr, *Situational Analysis* (New York: Harper, 1948), pp. 5–7.

He shows how it can be nurtured through a study of great works in the humanities.

Whorf, Benjamin Lee, *Four Articles on Metalinguistics* (Washington, D.C.: Foreign Service Institute, Department of State, 1949).

Four essays on the intimate ties between language, cultural orientations, and the way we perceive the world.

The Roots of Social Knowledge*

BY CHARLES H. COOLEY

If we are to gain a large view of knowledge we should, it seems to me, consider it genetically by tracing it to its sources in human nature and human history. Knowledge is, after all, a phase of higher organic evolution, and has apparently been developed for the sake of its function in giving us adjustment to, and power over, the conditions under which we live. If these conditions present any fundamental division in kind we should expect that the capacities of the human mind and the knowledge based upon these capacities would show a corresponding division.

In fact, the conditions with which the mind has to deal, and has had to deal ever since life began to be human, divide themselves rather sharply into two kinds: the material, on the one hand, and the human or social, on the other. We have always needed to understand both things and persons, and the most primitive savage, though he may occasionally confuse them, is quite aware that they are different and must be understood in different ways.

This division lies as deep as anything in our experience, and it corresponds to a like division in our mental apparatus. For the external contacts we have our various senses, and also, in recent times, the extension and refinement of these through aptly named "instruments of precision" which have made the exact sciences possible. For the internal contacts we have a vast and obscure outfit of human susceptibilities, known as instincts, sentiments, emotions, drives, and the like, quite as firmly grounded in the evolutionary process as the senses, capable of extension and refinement in ways of their own, and giving rise to a kind of knowledge that we recognize as peculiarly human and social.

You will say, perhaps, that all knowledge, whether of things or of men, comes to us by the aid of the senses, and that the division I assert is therefore imaginary. It is true that all knowledge calls for sense activity of some sort or degree, but the function of this activity in material or spatial knowledge, on the one hand, and in human or social knowledge, on the other, is quite different. In dealing with things sensation is the main source of the raw material which the mind works up into knowledge; in dealing with men it serves chiefly as a means of communication, as an inlet for symbols which awaken a complex inner life not primarily sensuous at all. In the one case it is our principal instrument; in the other only ancillary. When I meet a stranger and judge by his face, bearing, and voice that he is a kindly and cultured man, and by his words perceive, in a measure, the working of his mind, the sensuous images are like the starting mechanism of an automobile; they set at work processes more complicated and potent than themselves, of which, mainly, the resulting knowledge consists.

For our present purpose we may, then, distinguish two sorts of knowledge: one, the development of sense contacts into knowledge of things, including its refinement into mensurative science. This I

* This paper was read as the presidential address before the Michigan Academy of Science, Arts, and Letters, March 31, 1926. Reprinted from the *American Journal of Sociology*, XXXII (July 1926), 59–65.

call spatial or material knowledge. The second is developed from contact with the minds of other men, through communication, which sets going a process of thought and sentiment similar to theirs and enables us to understand them by sharing their states of mind. This I call personal or social knowledge. It might also be described as sympathetic, or, in its more active forms, as dramatic, since it is apt to consist of a visualization of behavior accompanied by imagination of corresponding mental processes.

There is nothing mysterious or unfamiliar about social knowledge, except as we may be unaccustomed to recognize and think about it. It is quite as early to appear in the child and in the race as is material knowledge, quite as useful in the everyday affairs of life, and quite as universally accepted as real by common sense. If there are men of science who do not see that it is something distinct in kind, but are inclined to regard it as spatial knowledge in an imperfect state, destined in time to be perfected by more delicate measurements, this is doubtless because they approach the matter with the *a priori* conceptions appropriate to physical research. In relation to social phenomena the merely spatial conception of knowledge indicates an abstract way of thinking that does not envisage the facts. It is not, in this field, in accord with common sense. All of us know that the essential things in our relation to other men are not subject to numerical measurement.

I trust it will not be supposed that I am advocating any metaphysical dualism between mind and matter. It is not necessary, for my present purpose, to take a side on that question, but I have myself no doubt that all the phenomena connected with social knowledge, including introspection, have physical concomitants in the brain and nervous system. In theory these physical facts are capable of physical measurement, but when we consider their minuteness and inaccessibility, the likelihood of their being measured in a spatial sense seems quite remote. We must get at them, in practice, through consciousness and through overt behavior.

Spatial knowledge, we know, has been extended and refined by processes of measurement, calculation, and inference, and has given rise to exact science. It is generally agreed that knowledge of this sort is verifiable and cumulative, making possible that ever growing structure of ascertained fact which is among the proudest of human achievements. It may be worth while to consider for a moment to what this peculiarly verifiable character is owing.

It is owing, I take it, to the fact that this sort of knowledge consists essentially in the measurement of one material thing in terms of another, man, with his senses and his reason, serving only as a mediator between them. If, then, a group of investigators can agree upon a technique of measurement they may go ahead, achieving results and passing them on from man to man and from generation to generation, without concerning themselves with the vagaries of human nature and social life. This technical agreement is found possible, and the accumulation of knowledge goes on. But we must, of course, discriminate between the immediate results of measurement and the body of hypothesis and theory which is constantly arising out of them. Science gives us fact out of which the intellect endeavors to build truth. And what we judge to be true, even in the spatial sciences, is largely a social matter dependent upon the general movement of thought. A group of scientific men, familiar with previous investigation in a given field and armed with a sound technique, is the best instrument we have for the pursuit of truth, and is one of the most remarkable products of our social system; yet it is, of course, far from infallible. All groups have a body of beliefs which are taken for granted merely because no one disputes them, and which often turn out to be illusions. Assent is induced by conforming influences not wholly different from those operating in religion or politics. In short, no group is a trustworthy critic of its own conclusions, and only the test of time and of exacting criticism from wholly different points of view can determine the value of its contribution. There have been many groups, made up of very intelligent men working devotedly and in full assurance of being on the right track, who are now seen to have been astray. And although scientific methods are no doubt improved, it would be fatuous to suppose that they are a guaranty against group error. Some of the teachings of science are permanent truth, but only time reveals which they are.

The practical success of spatial science in enabling us to predict, and even to control, the behavior of the material world about us has given it vast prestige and brought about a feeling that the more all our mental processes are like it the more perfect they will become. A conception of what social science ought to be has accordingly grown up and gained wide vogue which is based rather upon analogy than upon scrutiny of the conditions with which we have to deal. Let us return, then, to the sources of our knowledge of mankind, and consider for a moment the development of this sort of knowledge in a child. He comes into the human world already provided with a vast complex of innate capacity for life peculiar to the human race and embracing in its potential content those processes of social emotion, sentiment, and intelligence in which men find their chief interests and motives. All this is an outcome of evolution, highly practical, the very stuff that has made man the most puissant of animals, and it has, no doubt, the same physical reality as any other nervous or mental processes. Regarding the exact content of this inborn raw material of personal and social life there has been much discussion, into which, fortunately, we need not enter. Some say that it includes quite definitely organized mechanisms, similar to the instincts of the lower animals; others, that the inborn mechanisms of man are small and indeterminate, taking on organization only under the stimulus of a particular kind of life. However this may be, no one can doubt that we are born with an inchoate world of mental capacity, existing physically as a mass of brain and nerve complexes, which requires as the main condition of its growth an interchange of stimulation with similar complexes existing in other personal organisms.

The process by which a distinctively human or social mind and a corresponding type of knowledge grows up within us was first expounded at some length in 1895 by James Mark Baldwin, who called it "the dialectic of personal growth." It resembles a game of tennis in that no one can play it alone; you must have another on the opposite side of the net to return the ball. From earliest infancy our life is passed in eager response to incitements that reach us through the expressive behavior of other people, through facial expression, gesture, spoken words, writing, printing, painting, sculpture, the symbols of science, and the mechanic arts. Every response we make is a step in our education, teaching us to act, to think, and to feel a little more humanly. Our brain and nerve complexes develop in the sense of our social surroundings. And at the same time our consciousness takes account of this inward experience and proceeds to ascribe it to other people in similar conditions. Thus by a single process we increase our understanding of persons, of society, and of ourselves. When you play golf you not only acquire spatial knowledge in the shape of a certain muscular skill, but also social knowledge through learning the pride one feels when he makes a long drive, or the humiliation when he tops the ball and gets into the creek. As you see another man do these things you repeat, sympathetically, your own inner response on former occasions and ascribe it to him. A new reach of human experience is opened to you and you enlarge your understanding of men. And you extend your knowledge of domestic life, of letters, arts, and sciences in much the same way. Consider scientific work in the laboratory and in the field. Does it give only material knowledge of the behavior of *things* in test tubes, of the look and feel of strata, of the habits of fishes, or does it also teach you to understand chemists, geologists, and zoologists as *men*, to participate in a phase of human life, share its ideals, and learn its social methods?

And is not the latter knowledge quite as important to the man of science as the former? Able men in every field excel, as a rule, in human as well as technical knowledge, because both are the fruit of a richly developed mind, and both must also be cultivated as instruments of success.

If the distinctive trait of spatial knowledge is that it is mensurative, that of social knowledge is, perhaps, that it is dramatic. As the former may be resolved into distinctions among our sensations, and hence among the material objects that condition those sensations, so the latter is based ultimately on perceptions of the inter-communicating behavior of men, and experience of the processes of mind that go with it. What you know about a man consists, in part, of flashes of vision as to what he would do in particular situations, how he would look, speak and move; it is by such flashes that you judge whether he is brave or a coward, hasty or deliberate, honest or false, kind or cruel, and so on. It also consists of inner sentiments which you yourself feel in some degree when you think of him in these situations, ascribing them to him. It is these latter sympathetic elements which make the difference between our knowledge of a man and our knowledge of a horse or a dog. The latter is almost wholly external or behavioristic, although those who associate intimately with them may acquire some measure of true sympathy. We know animals mostly as a peculiarly lively kind of thing. On the other hand, although our knowledge of people is likewise behavioristic, it has no penetration, no distinctively human insight, unless it is sympathetic also.

There is, no doubt, a way of knowing people with whom we do not sympathize which is essentially external or animal in character. An example of this is the practical but wholly behavioristic knowledge that men of much sexual experience sometimes have of women, or women of men — something that involves no true participation in thought and feeling. The more behavior in the other sex is instinc-tively sexual, the more our understanding of it is apt to be external rather than sympathetic. Or, to put it rather coarsely, a man sometimes understands a woman as he does a horse; not by sharing her psychic processes, but by watching what she does. There is, in fact, a complete series in our knowledge of persons, from the purely external, like our knowledge of babies, of idiots, of the wildly insane, up through all grades to the completely internal or sympathetic, as when, in reading a meditative writer like Marcus Aurelius, we know his consciousness and nothing else. For the most part, however, human knowledge is both behavioristic and sympathetic: the perception or imagination of the external trait is accompanied by sympathy with the feeling, sentiment, or idea that goes with it.

This is also the process by which we come to understand the meaning of a word, and through such understanding make ourselves at home in that vast realm of meanings to which words are the key. We may know words as mere behavior, as when a man speaks to us in a strange tongue, but in that case they do not admit us to the realm of meanings. To have human value the word and the inner experience that interprets it must go together.

In short, we learn to know human life outwardly and inwardly at the same time and by a single process continuous from infancy.

Adopting a convenient and popular term, I will call the individual human mind, including all these socially developed sentiments and understandings, the *mental-social complex*. I hope by the use of this colorless expression to escape from the traditional implications that obscure such terms as mind, consciousness, spirit, and soul.[1] About this, whatever we call it, the question of the nature and possibilities of social knowledge centers. It is our supreme gift; but for that very reason, because all the deep things of life are in it, it is the part of us about which we know least, and is least amenable to precise treatment. Can it be made avail-

---

[1] In a similar way the "group mind," that is, a collective view of individual complexes communicating with, and influencing, one another, might be called the social-mental complex.

able for science, or shall we try in some way to dodge it, or cancel it out, as the physical scientist does when he requires that the ideas about nature which come from it shall be verified by nature herself through physical measurement? The trouble with any such plan would seem to be that in human life the mental-social complex *is* nature. It is the very heart of what we seek to describe and make intelligible. It cannot be dodged without dodging life itself.

Suppose, for example, you secure, by a series of mental tests, detailed knowledge of what a certain person does in various situations. This may be of great value; I expect important results from such studies; but after all they cannot enable you to know the person as a living whole. The social man is something more than the sum of standardized acts, no matter how many or how well chosen. You can grasp him only by the understanding and synthetic power of your own mental complex, without which any knowledge you may gain from behavior tests must remain superficial and unintelligent. Is it not a somewhat equivocal use of terms when we talk of measuring intelligence or personality? What we measure is the performance of standardized operations. To pass from these to the organic whole of intelligence or personality is always a difficult and fallible work of the constructive imagination.

Many people, agreeing perhaps with what I have said about the ultimate difference in kind between spatial and social knowledge, will hold that just because of this difference anything like social science is impossible. While spatial knowledge is precise and communicable, and hence cumulative, the dramatic and intuitive perceptions that underlie social knowledge are so individual, so subjective, that we cannot expect that men will be able to agree upon them or to build them up into an increasing structure of ascertained truth.

This is, in fact, a formidable difficulty which enthusiasts for exact social science are apt to ignore. I may say at once that I do not look for any rapid growth of science that is profound, as regards its penetration into human life, and at the same time exact and indisputable. There is a difference in kind here which it would be fatuous to overlook.

Regarding subjectivity, I may say that all knowledge is subjective in one sense: in the sense, namely, that it is mental, not the external thing, but a construct of the mind. Even the simplest perceptions of form or extent, much more the exact perceptions of science, far from being mere physical data, are the outcome of an extended process of education, interpretation, and social evolution. Your so-called physical sciences are, after all, part of the social heritage and creatures of the mental-social complex. In so far, then, spatial knowledge and social knowledge are on the same footing.

The question of more or less subjectivity, as among different kinds of knowledge, I take to be one of more or less agreement in the elementary perceptions. If the phenomena can be observed and described in such a way as to command the assent of all intelligent men, without regard to theory or to bias of any sort, then the factual basis of knowledge acquires that independence of particular minds which we call objectivity. A yardstick is objective because it provides an undisputed method of reaching agreement as to certain spatial relations. Professor Einstein has shown, I believe, that this objectivity is not absolute, but it suffices for most purposes of spatial science. Strictly speaking, there are no yardsticks in social knowledge, no elementary perceptions of distinctively social facts that are so alike in all men, and can be so precisely communicated, that they supply an unquestionable means of description and measurement. I say distinctively social facts, because there are many facts commonly regarded as social which are also material events, like marriages, and as such can be precisely observed and enumerated. But the distinctively social phenomena connected with marriage are inward and mental, such as the affection and desire of the parties, pecuniary considerations, their plans for setting up a household, and so on. These also can be known and communicated, but not with such precise agreement among observers as to make decisive measurement possible.

You may say that while it is true that the mental-social phenomena cannot be observed directly with much precision, they express themselves in behavior, which is tangible and which we may hope eventually to record and measure with great exactness. Even our inmost thoughts and feelings take form in the symbols of communication, in gesture, voice, words, and the written symbols which are preserved unchanged for ages. All this is true and much to the point: I am a behaviorist as far as I think I can be without being a fanatic. But we must not forget, as behaviorists sometimes appear to do, that the symbol is nothing in itself, but only a convenient means of developing, imparting, and recording a meaning, and that meanings are a product of the mental-social complex and known to us only through consciousness. Reliance upon symbols, therefore, in no way releases us from the difficulty arising from the unmeasurable nature of our elementary social perceptions. We can record behavior and handle the record by statistics, but I see no way of avoiding the ultimate question, What does it mean?

And how about introspection? Does not the kind of perception which I inculcate involve this disreputable practice, and if so, is it not thereby hopelessly vitiated?

The word "introspection," as commonly used, suggests a philosopher exploring his inner consciousness in more or less complete abstraction from the ordinary functions of life. While this method may have its uses it is thought to have been more relied upon in the past than it deserves. Let us observe men under more normal conditions, and preferably, it is urged, through their actions rather than through their supposed thoughts.

But just what, after all, is introspection? It is not merely the philosophic introversion I have indicated, but takes various forms, some of which, in everyday use by all of us, are indispensable to any real knowledge of the minds of other men.

That whole process of the social growth of the mind which I have mentioned involves elements introspective in character. We come to know about other people and about ourselves by watching not only the interplay of action, but also that of thought and feeling. As we perceive and remember sensuous images of gesture, voice, and facial expression, so, at the same time, we record the movements of thought and feeling in our consciousness, ascribe similar movements to others, and so gain an insight into their minds. We are not, for the most part, reflectively aware of this, but we do it and the result is social knowledge. This process is stimulated and organized by language and — indirectly, through language — by the social heritage from the past. Under the leading of words we interpret our observation, both external and introspective, according to patterns that have been found helpful by our predecessors. When we have come to use understandingly such words as "kindly," "resolute," "proud," "humble," "angry," "fearful," "lonesome," "sad," and the like, words recalling motions of the mind as well as of the body, it shows that we have not only kept a record of our inner life, but have worked up the data into definite conceptions which we can pass on to others by aid of the common symbol.

Much of our social knowledge, especially that acquired from reading, involves a process more consciously introspective. One can hardly read a play or a novel intelligently, I should say, without recalling ideas and emotions from his own past for comparison with those of the people described. The hero, as we conceive him, is fashioned out of material from our own lives. Is it not rather absurd for scientific men to repudiate introspection? Does any one prepare a scientific report or article without first turning an inward eye upon the contents of his mind in order to see what he has to offer and how he can arrange and present it? In short, introspection, however abused by philosophers, is a normal and common process, without which we could know very little about life.

Introspection, if critical, is more objective than the usual practice of floating upon social currents without attempting to become aware of them. How can you be objective with regard to your motives unless you hold them off and look at them? I have in mind a recent book, a good book, too, in which the writer, who deprecates introspection, advances a series of opinions on social questions of the day so obviously those of his race, country, and social class that one can only smile at his naïveté. Surely a little introspection would not be out of place here: one's subjectivity needs to be understood, if only to avoid it.

It seems, then, that outside and inside in human life, consciousness and behavior, mutually complement and explain each other, and that the study of external behavior as a thing by itself must, in the human field, be as barren as mere introspection, and for much the same reason, namely, that it isolates one aspect of a natural process from another. Nature has joined these things together, and I do not think that we gain anything by putting them asunder. Records of behavior without introspective interpretation are like a library of books in a strange tongue. They came from minds, and mean nothing until they find their goal in other minds.

However, I see no reason for quarreling with those extreme behaviorists who hold that we should observe men merely from the outside, as we do other animals. Let them work on this theory, if they find it helpful, and show what they can do. Even if it is wrong it may give rise to a valuable technique, as wrong theories have done in the past. It is fair to judge behaviorists by their behavior. I suspect that they will be found in practice to make use of introspection when they need it, much like the rest of us.[2]

At the opposite pole, it would seem, from behaviorism we have the method, or rather various methods, of mental analysis through the probing of consciousness and memory. These all rest in great part upon sympathetic introspection, or the understanding of another's consciousness by the aid of your own, and give full play to the mental-social complex. They may be used in sociology as well as in psychiatry, and, in fact, do not differ in principle from the personal interviews widely employed in the study of social situations. Indeed, I take it that the psychoanalytic psychology owes its vogue to its boldness in disregarding the rather narrowly spatial methods within which laboratory psychologists were confining themselves, and venturing, by the light of clinical interviews and introspective interpretation, to explore the weird caverns of the human mind. Men saw that the sequent revelations resembled what they knew of their own egos. The method is quite separable from the extravagant theories associated with it and will no doubt be largely used.

I have conceded that social observation is, on the whole, less precise and verifiable, and hence less surely cumulative, than spatial observation, not only because the conditions can seldom be reproduced by experiment, but because the perceptions themselves are less alike in different persons, and so less easy to agree upon. Experience shows, however, that these difficulties are .by no means sufficient to prevent objective and cooperative study of social phenomena, and a cumulation of knowledge which, though not so tangible as in experimental science, is capable in time of yielding vast results.

The basis of common social perceptions, and hence of cumulation, is in the general similarity of mental-social complexes throughout the human race, and the much closer similarity among those formed by the common language and culture. We became aware of this similarity by watching the behavior of other men, including their language, and finding that this behavior can be interpreted successfully by ascribing to them thoughts

---

[2] I need hardly say that the scientific study of behavior has no necessary connection with the group of men who call themselves "behaviorists." Their extreme doctrine of the rejection of consciousness is best understood as a reaction against a former extreme, in psychology, of purely introspective study. Social studies have always been mainly behavioristic.

and sentiments similar to our own. The idea that they are like us is practically true; it works. It was generated in the experience of our earliest childhood, and we have gone upon it all our lives. This fundamental agreement upon meanings can be more precise by the careful use of language and other communicative signs, something as sense-perceptions are refined by the use of instruments of precision (though probably to nothing like the same degree), and thus allows a transmission and cumulation exact enough for practical use.

All history, all news, all social investigation, is a record of what men did — of such visible acts as are thought to be significant, and also of their symbolic acts, their speech, and their works of art. But what makes the record interesting is that through our likeness to them it becomes also a record of what they were, of their meanings, of their inner life, the semblance of which is awakened in us by the acts recorded.

I open Herodotus at random and find an account of how the Carthaginians, having captured many Phoceans from disabled ships, landed them and stoned them to death. But after this the sheep, oxen, or men who passed the spot were stricken with palsy. So they consulted the Delphic Oracle, who required them to institute a custom of honoring the dead Phoceans with funeral rites. Here is a record of behavior which we interpret by sympathy. We feel the cruelty of the Carthaginians, their wonder and alarm at the strange conduct of the stricken men and animals, their anxious resort to Delphi, their awed obedience to the oracle. Of the grounds for criticizing this narrative from the standpoint of a wider study of human ideas and human behavior I need not now speak. Like all social observation that comes down from the past, it must be interpreted in view of the difference in mental complexes between the men who made the records and us who read them. We must, as we say, get their background and point of view. But men are, after all, so much alike that an imagination trained by comparative study can usually make out fairly well what

the records mean. The true reason why we must, in sociology, rely mainly upon contemporary rather than historical facts is the inadequacy of the record. History does not tell what we want to know, and we must look in the world about us for answers to questions which the men of old never thought of putting.

At any rate we actually have accumulations of social knowledge. Aristotle and many other early writers collected facts which are still held to be trustworthy, and interpreted them by generalizations which still command respect. In modern times the process has gone on developing in volume, diversity, and precision, and has given rise to technical groups of specially trained men. We have many kinds of history, we have social anthropology, political science, law, economics, sociology, comparative religion, comparative literature and art, and other departments, each with its own archives of recorded fact.

Indeed, as regards cumulation the study of mankind has a great advantage in that its subject matter is uniquely self-recording. Even the records of geology and paleontology do not compare in richness with those that man hands down about himself through language and the several arts. And the more he approaches and enters a civilized state, the more extensive these records become. The dinosaur may leave his skeleton and even his (or her) eggs, but man deposits a fossil mind. We know infinitely more about him than we do about any other animal, and the difficulty of accumulating knowledge, so far as primary facts are concerned, is quite imaginary. Dispute, as in other fields, is mainly about interpretation. The selection and explanation of facts has heretofore proved provisional; it has to be done over again with every change in the general current of thought. But is not this true of all science? At this moment the whole theoretical trunk of physics has been torn up by the roots and seems likely to be thrown upon the rubbish pile. A lasting structure of knowledge is hardly to be expected, except as regards the primary facts and their simpler relations, and this much we may expect in social science as well as in spatial.

It is high time that I referred to that body of knowledge and practice known as statistics. Statistics is an exact method, and it is enabled to be such precisely because it is not in itself social but mathematical. It does not directly *perceive* social facts, or any other kind of facts, but it takes standard units of some sort, which may be perceived social facts, and compiles, arranges, manipulates, and presents them in a way intended to make them yield illumination. The statistician operates between the primary observer, on the one hand, and, on the other, the theorist who demands light on certain hypotheses. Perhaps I may without offense liken him to a cook, who neither supplies the food nor consumes it, but is a specialist upon the intervening processes.

Evidently it would not be good sense to assume any antagonism between the exact methods of statistics and the more fallible procedure of sympathetic observation and interpretation. They are complementary and do not or should not overlap. The only opposition likely to arise is one due to the bias of the practitioner. A statistician, if he lacks breadth of mind, is apt to be so fond of his exact processes that he avoids and depreciates anything else, while the sympathetic observer is apt to be impatient of statistics. This difference of tastes would not do much harm if the functions were kept separate, but when a man who is fit for only one assumes both the result is unfortunate. Much statistical work, especially that based upon questionnaires or interviews, is vitiated by a lack of dramatic insight into the states of mind of the people who supply the information. A questionnaire is an instrument of social perception, and if its use is to have any scientific character, the first duty of the user is to dramatize the play of thought and feeling that takes place between the person that puts the question and the person that answers it. What was the actual state of mind of the latter, and what the human significance of his reply? Not every investigator has the insight and the conscience to perceive and report this real fact, commonly so different from the apparent fact, upon which the value of his work depends.

And so with the questions or problems used in mental tests. If they aim only to test the power to perform standardized operations they are objective, but, socially speaking, superficial; if they go beyond this and attempt to discover social or moral attitudes they are subjective, and of no value for science without sympathetic interpretation.

It is not the case that social science is becoming exact through the substitution of statistics for social sympathy and imagination. What is taking place is, rather, that the use of sympathy and imagination is becoming more competent, while statistics is being substituted for guesswork in the manipulation of data.

Another impression which I take to be erroneous is that statistics is revealing uniformities or regularities in social phenomena which indicate that these phenomena may in time prove to be subject to exact prediction in quite the same way as those of physics. It is true that statistics is revealing sequence, order, and a remarkable degree of predictability in certain social processes. By analysis of what has taken place during the past ten years, especially in the economic field, where the facts are largely material, it may be possible to forecast what will take place in the next five; and no one can say how far we may go in this direction. The whole basis of this, however, seems to be the prevalence of inertia and the rarity and slowness of the more originative processes. The greater part of human phenomena are so far routinized as to be more or less subject to calculation. Wherever men, under the impetus of habit and suggestion, are moving ahead in a mechanical manner, or where their intelligence is merely repeating what is essentially an old synthesis of motives — as, for example, in deciding whether to marry or not — exact methods are in place. The complex of human events can, to a great extent, be resolved into currents of tendency moving on definite line~ at ascertainable speeds. If we can meas ure these lines and speeds it may be possible to predict their combined operation, much as the motion of a comet is predicted by calculating the resultant of the gravity, tangential momentum, and other forces acting upon it. The whole basis of prediction in such fields as that of the business cycle is the belief that the underlying motivation is essentially standardized or repetitive.

Probably no exact science could have foreseen the sudden rise of the automotive industry and the genius of Henry Ford, although now that this industry is developed and institutionized we may perhaps calculate with some precision what it will bring forth in the near future.

There is no good reason to think that such statistical methods can anticipate that which, after all, chiefly distinguishes human life from physical processes, namely, originative mental synthesis, whether by outstanding individuals or by groups. The kind of mechanistic theory which would exclude the unique function of human consciousness and will is not only highly speculative and unverifiable, but seems, as a speculation, to be losing ground. Recent philosophic writers (for example, our colleague Professor Sellars[3]), in so far as they accept mechanism or determinism, interpret them in such a way as to leave intact our human power of reorganizing and redirecting life in a manner that no exact science can hope to foresee.

There is indeed one way in which physical and social science may be assimilated. We may find that atoms and electrons are not so uniform and reliable as has been believed, that the supposed physical laws are only statistical, covering diversity in the phenomena somewhat as social statistics cover the diversities of individual men. Indeed, we are told by men apparently competent that "the present state of physics lends no support whatever to the belief that there is a causality in physical nature which is founded on rigorously exact laws." [4] In some such way as this the gulf may be bridged, but never, I think, by reducing the human will to zero.

Having dealt so far with observation, either direct or mediated by technique, I come now to the interpretive use of the data, to the attempt to build a structure of social truth. This is, in all sciences, a work of the imagination, and a work which has always in the past proved to be provisional and to require renewal to meet the general advance of thought. I see no reason to expect anything else in the future.

At the present time all the sciences of life are, I suppose, controlled by the idea of organic development. Darwin gave these studies their orientation by making them studies of process rather than state, of what is going on rather than what is, of a drama rather than a picture. For many years, however, evolutionary ideas were applied to social phenomena chiefly in an external and analogical way; they were imposed artificially, not allowed to grow naturally out of the social processes themselves. The result was a vast body of social theory and propaganda, all claiming to be evolutionary and scientific, but none of it the work of a technical group devoted primarily and disinterestedly to the study of social facts. Even at the present time specialists in contiguous evolutionary fields contribute profusely to social literature and by no means hide their belief that they know more about what is important to society than do the so-called "sociologists." Whether they do or not, it is a fact that some of these extraneous doctrines, like the pseudo-Darwinism of Nietzsche or the hereditary determinism of the more extreme followers of Galton, have had, and still have, a wide influence.

I shall assume, however, that, after all, social phenomena are most likely to be understood by those who make the study of them their main business, and that the application of evolutionary ideas in this sphere is the task mainly of history, anthropology, ethnology, political science, economics, social psychology, sociology, and kindred disciplines. All of these stud-

[3] R. W. Sellars, *Evolutionary Naturalism*, passim.
[4] Hermann Weyl, quoted by J. W. N. Sullivan, *Aspects of Science*, p. 158.

ies have, in fact, a decidedly evolutionary trend, and several of them may be said to have been created by the evolutionary movement. All of them aim at the understanding of personal and social wholes in the actual process of living. All make increasing use of social psychology. They do not aim to resolve social phenomena into elements which are not social, but rather to investigate the simpler and more general social processes and use the knowledge thus gained in synthetic interpretation of larger social wholes. This may be done by the use of well-chosen samples, as in studies of individual persons, of typical local or institutional conditions, and the like.

In general, the insights of sociology, if I may take that subject as representative, are imaginative reconstructions of life whose truth depends upon the competence of the mind that makes them to embrace the chief factors of the process studied and reproduce or anticipate their operation. This requires native ability, factual knowledge, social culture, and training in a particular technique.

It is sometimes supposed that pre-Darwinian studies in history, literature, art, and social theory were essentially unscientific and futile; in fact, mere rubbish needing to be swept aside by the advancing forces of science. On the contrary, many of these studies were based on common sense, had a sound empirical basis, and are even now of more value than hurried, dogmatical, and mostly analogical efforts to supplant them by something having the appearance of natural science. Such efforts have given rise to a variety of pseudo-sciences, some of which are flourishing at the present time, but they have not broken the real continuity of contemporary social knowledge with the solid work of earlier generations. Sociology, at least, recognizes wholeheartedly the value of pre-evolutionary research, and expects that its students shall know something of the great currents of historical, literary, and artistic tradition; shall have, indeed, as broad a culture in the humanities as possible. This culture affords the only access to great stores of facts with which we cannot

dispense. It also affords a perspective of the development of social interpretation. Most of the generalizations now being defined, explored, tested, and developed into systematic knowledge were foreshadowed by penetrating minds of the past. How much of modern social psychology is implicit in the maxims of La Rochefoucauld, what insight into social processes had Gibbon! Sainte-Beuve, who saw literature as an organic human whole, observing the individual writer and the current of literary tendency with equal understanding, was a real sociologist in the field of criticism. Goethe was one in an even larger sense. An honest and competent student will be deferent to the achievements of the past and will lend no countenance to those shallow spirits who see scientific method as a sort of trick of laboratories and schedules by which they may avoid the slow approaches of actual social knowledge.

As to prediction, I have already pointed out that in the more mechanized processes of the social system it may be remarkably exact. We have no ground, however, to expect any such exactness in foretelling the multitudinous fluctuations of human life in general. Prediction, in any science, requires that the mind embrace the process, as the physicist, in his formula, embraces the process of a falling body, and so, through participation, foresee the outcome. Even in natural science this can usually be done with precision only when the process is artificially simplified, as in the laboratory. The social processes of actual life can be embraced only by a mind working at large, participating through intellect and sympathy with many currents of human force, and bringing them to an imaginative synthesis. This can hardly be done with much precision, nor done at all except by infusing technical methods with a total and creative spirit.

The human mind participates in social processes in a way that it does not in any other processes. It is itself a sample, a phase, of those processes, and is capable, under favorable circumstances, of so far identifying itself with the general movement of a group as to achieve a remarkably just anticipation of what the group will do. Prediction of this sort is largely intuitive rather than intellectual; it is like that of the man with a genius for business as contrasted with that of the statistician; it is not science, but it is the very process by which many of the great generalizations of science have first been perceived.

Predictions of any sort, however, are most likely to be sound when they are made by those who have the most precise familiarity with the observable processes, and it is the increase of this familiarity on the part of social observers, along with their greater insight into principles, that should make them better guessers of what is to happen than they have been in the past.

What, then, is there new in contemporary social science, what, if anything, that promises a more rapid and secure accumulation of knowledge than in the past? Mainly, I should say, the following:

1. Liberation from outworn theological and metaphysical assumptions and reorganization on the basis of factual study and an evolutionary outlook.

2. The rise of a technical group of adequately trained scholars with those traditions and standards, that expert criticism and exacting group atmosphere, indispensable to all higher achievement.

3. The development, since 1860, and especially since 1900, of a network of factual theory, by which I mean theory springing from observation and capable of being verified or refuted by the closer study of fact. Such theory is to be distinguished from much of the older speculation, which was largely metaphysical, unverifiable, and for that reason of no use in stimulating research.

There is nothing startling in the present movement. It shows no break with the past, does not promise any phenomenal power of prediction, and is, in fact, chiefly occupied with the ascertainment of what is actually going on and with the development of technique. We are trying to describe and interpret human life in the same spirit that the life of animals and plants has been described and interpreted, but with due regard to the different character of the problem. The human material is peculiar not only in its enormous abundance and variety, but in requiring, to deal with it, a radically different theoretical and technical equipment.

CHAPTER III

Cultural Values and Social Roles

IN DEALING with face-to-face human interactions we often patiently study the "obvious" and find that back of the obvious are more significant and fundamental matters. We cannot readily separate the relationships of people in everyday affairs from our observations of them. The ways in which we observe and think about these relationships influence our reactions to them, and the reactions in turn influence the relationships. We find it is particularly difficult to avoid confusing our thinking about things with the nature of things themselves.

The complexity of the problem says to us, in effect, *stop* and *look;* stop moving so rapidly through the "obvious" world and look at it more carefully. The earlier reading has indicated some of the limitations of "looking." For example, Kelley suggests that individuals see largely what their experience has trained them to see. Because our experience is different from someone else's, so our observations are different. If we broaden our experience, if we take into consideration many divergent points of view, our observations are likely to be more closely related to the unique situation with which we are always dealing. We broaden our experience in many ways — by reacting to new situations and observing the consequences of our actions, by listening to the descriptions of situations in which others have been involved and to their conclusions about them, by reading the opinions of others about their experience. In so far as we can relate any of these to our own experience in a meaningful way, they become useful to us. They permit us to make new assumptions, or modify old assumptions, and then test them in later situations as the opportunities arise. If by these tests the new assumptions seem useful, we incorporate them into our behavior.

Discussions are one way of broadening experience. Even when we are considering exactly the same material, such as a written case read by all, our discussions indicate that we do not always perceive the material in the same way. Each of us reacts in terms of his own personal interests and enthusiasms. The teacher in "Jinny Stover," [1] for example, reminds one of us of his eighth-grade teacher — "she couldn't control a class either." The adviser in "Robert Kelly" [2] reminds another of his college adviser — "and they never really care." We look at not only the material before us but our own experiences as well. As we discuss, we may also take some cognizance of the points of view of others, and from this comes a major value of discussion. A pooling of different perspectives provides a chance for new insights for each of us.

This diversity of past experience, although at times interesting, also leads to

---

[1] See Vol. II, Case 4.
[2] See Vol. II, Case 1.

arguments and confusion. We may want to believe that our own views of the situation are adequate; yet our experiences are personal and private — different in some respects from those of any others. It is thus difficult to communicate our views to others and even more difficult to apply them systematically in response to the views of others. In so far as we have or can develop joint past experiences, communication with others is simplified; they seem to understand "what we are talking about." Discussions with others over a period of time help build just such a joint past.

But our interactions with the ideas of others need not be entirely limited to those with whom we talk directly. Sometimes our experiences seem to us too limited to provide desirable insights into situations that interest us. We may then wonder what others might see in these situations, particularly those whom we consider trained and experienced observers. Such men have presented their ideas in their writings. By each of us being familiar with such writings, we can to some extent build a useful joint past. We can read about these ideas, consider them reflectively in relation to our own ideas about similar matters, and even adopt them as our own. We can also, if we read carefully, retain these ideas of certain others and use them "for the sake of argument" in discussion when they seem pertinent.

The readings in this book present the ideas of social scientists about matters that seem important to them and often include some description of the concrete situations on which they have based their conclusions. In Hayakawa's terms, the writers describe "maps" they have drawn about particular "territories." It is important for us to keep in mind that these are only "maps" and that they are drawn to clarify particular facets of the "territories" observed. We will not find them all equally useful, and ones that are useful to some of us will not be useful to others. Like all maps, they will be significant to us as they are related to our own interests — a geologist would be little interested in a map showing the population density of a country district.

Although the experiences of each man are always different from those of other men and the meanings he attaches to them are personal and private, yet some elements of these experiences are common to all. Man's biological equipment has much similarity and responds in similar ways — men are classifiable as belonging to the same species. All live in a world surrounded by other people where things grow and disintegrate, where night follows day. Out of such fundamental life experiences men build assumptions. If they live together in the same society, they share further experiences. They have had a similar type of childhood dependence; they have a similar relationship with their parents and their contemporaries; they have been trained to consider similar ideas as important. In this way they build a common set of assumptions about the world which is called their "culture." Each society has a somewhat different slant on life reflected in its special culture; yet all have *some* common elements and arrive at *some* common assumptions.

Each man's personal desires and goals are the result of his own experiences. It is often believed that these desires are unique and clearly the product of his own thinking; surely each man knows what he wants. The desires of others around him often seem just a block to the fulfillment of his private wishes. Emile Durkheim, in the following selection, takes a look at this common approach and finds it inadequate. He insists that even man's desires are culturally and socially formed; without group norms, man would *not* know what he wants. And when the group conditions change radically and no longer guide his wishes, man becomes isolated and confused. Then his basic assumptions about the world no longer fit the world he sees, and that is a frightening experience. Durkheim's work suggests the depth to which group influences on man may go. Read

EMILE DURKHEIM, "Anomie," below.

Durkheim discusses the relation of the individual to Western European society. He finds that man's desires are oriented toward the future. The desire for something "better" than the present seems to him innate, unlimited, and controllable only by strong group norms. More recent studies of other cultures have suggested that these desires for the future, which seem "natural" to Europeans and Americans, are not universal. All cultures do not emphasize continual expansion and improvement.

Florence R. Kluckhohn, in the reading below, compares cultures and observes that there are a limited number of basic questions, the answers to which all men in all societies seek. Among the basic questions are these: whether the forces of nature are to be accepted or overcome; whether man is basically good or evil; whether past, present, or future time is the most important; what are considered the most valued relationships with other men. Cultures can be compared by noting the answers expressed by the behavior of men in each society. Broad cultural values seem to grow out of these answers. The values then become trained into the behavior of individuals, so that they are often accepted as assumptions hardly to be questioned. They determine what things are more important than others, what things seem desirable and what do not. Even totally new experiences are evaluated in terms of the old assumptions.

Apparently no culture can decide these questions so surely or transmit them so exactly that every person will apply cultural values in the same way to his own life. In every society value assumptions will be considered as more or less true, and alternative assumptions are often available. Thus Kluckhohn sees both "dominant" and "variant" cultural orientations. But regardless of variation, there are always some cultural restraints on the individual — a control that Durkheim found so important to the life and happiness of the individual. Read

FLORENCE R. KLUCKHOHN, "Dominant and Variant Cultural Value Orientations," below.

In dealing with individual desires and with the cultural values of large groups, we are considering concepts that social scientists have constructed to help them see society more clearly. They are not saying: "The world *is* as I describe it." Rather they are saying: "With these concepts, I am able to develop a point of view, a map, that makes discriminations about society that seem to me useful for the reasons that I give. They seem to me important in varying degrees in many situations." The extent to which the concepts are important to us depends not only on our understanding of them but also on their utility to us in observing particular situations.[3]

Durkheim and Kluckhohn considered, implicitly and explicitly, questions of

---

[3] See Lowell, "Conflicts of Principle," above, Chapter I.

"status" and "role" — concepts that have been very fruitful. Social scientists have seen that within all societies, primitive and civilized, men make distinctions between one another. The observers have noted that various status positions are assigned different degrees of worth by the groups concerned and that the groups expect varying "roles" to be played by the people in the different status positions.

Ralph Linton defines these concepts and indicates that they describe one part of the interactions of people with each other. He introduces a significant distinction between "ascribed" and "achieved" statuses. The former we have without effort, the latter we must work for. In societies where, for example, a dominant value (to use Kluckhohn's term) is the great importance of the past, "ascribed" statuses are widespread and individual initiative within the roles is limited to the skills with which they are played. In other societies, such as our own, a high premium is placed on "achieved" statuses, and major changes in status are often acquired through individual initiative.

Linton considers the question of how one gets appropriate training for the roles one is required to play and the importance of the fact that one must continually adopt new roles as one grows older and accepts new responsibilities.[4] The emphasis our present society places on achieved statuses and the lack of clear role expectations to accompany them often puts a very different sort of pressure on our personalities from that which was formerly active. Read

RALPH LINTON, "Status and Role," below.

Linton's concept of "role" seems more specific than Kluckhohn's idea of "value orientation." By definition, when two people interact in terms of reciprocal roles, they each behave *differently* but in ways that mesh together. The boss gives orders; the subordinate follows them. The housewife role may emphasize care of home and children; the husband role stresses earning a living outside the home. It seems likely that different roles will be based on somewhat different value orientations; indeed, Kluckhohn briefly suggests just that. But apparently all the roles that are part of a given culture (or subculture) will have some values in common. Kluckhohn tends to stress the common values that unite a given society, that allow us to say "That is typically American" or "typically French." Linton stresses the variation of roles within a culture that permits division of labor.

The meshing together of individual roles that complement each other produces social institutions — families, factories, governments. It is through these institutions that society is enabled to get its basic work done — to feed, protect, and perpetuate itself. But smoothly functioning institutions do much more: they give "meaning" and "purpose" to the activities of their individual members. This meaning or purpose is the exact opposite of the *anomie* or aimlessness which Durkheim discusses. It gives man's life zest and vitality through providing the ends or goals of his activity.

Such meaning comes to a society when the various roles that man plays all express common ideals or values; Edward Sapir calls this situation a "genuine culture." For example, when work activities are infused with religious purpose,

---

[4] It might be helpful when reading Linton's article to keep in mind the interactions of the various members of "The Michaelson Family" (Vol. II, Case 3). Was Mrs. Michaelson's own concept of a "good mother" influencing her behavior in the role of "grandmother"? Was Carl's idea of the responsibilities of a "son" important to the situation?

they lose the character of necessary but drab chores and take on that of exciting opportunities to give vent to one's deepest emotions about the nature of the world. As Sapir has put it:

> The genuine culture is not of necessity either high or low; it is merely inherently harmonious, balanced, self-satisfactory. It is the expression of a richly varied and yet somehow unified and consistent attitude toward life, an attitude which sees the significance of any element of civilization in its relation to all others. It is, ideally speaking, a culture in which nothing is spiritually meaningless, in which no important part of the general functioning brings with it a sense of frustration, of misdirected or unsympathetic effort. It is not a spiritual hybrid of contradictory patches, of watertight compartments of consciousness that avoid participation in a harmonious synthesis.[5]

The point of view of Durkheim, Kluckhohn, and Linton is that culture creates goals and desires in man, then gives him a means of fulfilling them through recognized social roles. A concept of man abstracted from culture and society would show an aimless, distracted wanderer with no place to go and no means of transport.

Durkheim, Kluckhohn, and Linton present certain abstract concepts that they find useful in the analysis of human interaction. The readings below present two books which use these concepts to describe actual societies. Extensive data are included to help us determine for ourselves the degree to which the concepts are useful. The authors tell us about a "primitive" tribe and a "civilized" American community, and contrast the ways of life of these two societies in terms of general values and specific roles.

Ruth Benedict, in *Patterns of Culture,* dramatizes cultural diversity. She contrasts three cultures that vary widely from each other and from our own. Each of them has existed for a long period of time, and the values of each are well integrated into a composite whole; each produces satisfactions for the individuals in it. These satisfactions in some ways seem to us ridiculous, yet they are apparently as meaningful to others as our own are to us.

Benedict's discussion of the Zuni Indians of New Mexico offers a description of a culture with many values in striking contrast to those of urban America. For one thing, Zuni family structure is matrilineal: descent is followed through the mother's line, and a man goes to live in a large household with his wife's mother's family. For another, the emphasis is more on smooth group functioning than on individual initiative (which Benedict describes by comparing the Zuni to other Indian groups who lived on the Great Plains).

Benedict believes that many crucial aspects of Zuni life can be summed up by saying that they express a key value orientation which she calls "Apollonian"; she contrasts this with the "Dionysian" orientation of the Plains Indians. Many people have criticized her for oversimplifying; Kluckhohn, for instance, believes that we need at least five variables to characterize, even in the most abstract way, the central tendencies of any culture. Whatever its adequacy as a scientific construct, Benedict's notion of a core idea at the root of many different aspects of a culture is a useful descriptive tool. We get from her material on the Zuni a feeling of understanding of a people who view the world quite

---

[5] Edward Sapir, "Culture, Genuine and Spurious," *American Journal of Sociology,* XXIX (January 1924), 401.

differently from the way in which we view it. We can see how different parts of their society fit together meaningfully. And perhaps we can get a new perspective which will allow us to view our own society more clearly. Read

RUTH BENEDICT, *Patterns of Culture* (Boston: Houghton Mifflin, 1934),[6] Chapter IV.

In contrast to Benedict, the work of W. Lloyd Warner and Paul S. Lunt is based on direct observation of our own society. They studied a small city in New England which they called "Yankee City" and found that the values of the people were not all the same, even though a few general values did seem to claim the allegiance of most of the people. They concluded that the most significant differences in values were those between "social classes." They did not start out with the concept of class structure, but found that their clinical data could be organized only through the adoption of some such conceptual scheme. In fact, they started their study with the hypothesis that "the fundamental structure of our society, that which ultimately controls and dominates the thinking and actions of our people, is economic, and that the most vital and far-reaching value systems which motivate Americans are to be ultimately traced to an economic order."[7]

However, as they talked with people in the community, Warner and Lunt found that people were assigned statuses by criteria which were not solely economic — other values were clearly considered.

> Great wealth did not guarantee the highest social position. Something more was necessary. In our efforts to find out what this "something more" was, we finally developed a class hypothesis which withstood the later test of a vast collection of data and of subsequent rigorous analysis. By class is meant two or more orders of people who are believed to be, and are accordingly ranked by the members of the community, in socially superior and inferior positions. Members of a class tend to marry within their own order, but the values of the society permit marriage up and down. A class system also provides that children are born into the same status as their parents. A class society distributes rights and privileges, duties and obligations, unequally among its inferior and superior grades. A system of classes, unlike a system of castes, provides by its own values for movement up and down the social ladder. In common parlance, this is social climbing, or in technical terms, social mobility. The social system of Yankee City, we found, was dominated by a class order.[8]

In the first chapter listed below, Warner and Lunt discuss the hypothesis of six relatively distinct class divisions which they felt was necessary to understand the data they had observed. The following chapter of their book, entitled "Class and Social Structure," analyzes this hypothesis and shows in class terms how the interactions of people maintain the social structure. Although this chapter is not included in the reading, it shows in detail the use to which this concept can be put and the corollary hypotheses that develop therefrom. The balance of the reading illustrates the hypothesis by the use of case material. This latter chapter, entitled "Profiles from Yankee City," is a series of sketches about various people and institutions. It indicates by the pictures it

---

[6] Also available as a "Mentor Book" (New York: New American Library, 1948).

[7] W. Lloyd Warner and Paul S. Lunt, *The Social Life of a Modern Community* (New Haven: Yale University Press, 1941), p. 81.

[8] *Social Life of a Modern Community*, p. 82.

draws the ways in which people evaluate each other and through their interactions support and enhance these values.

These concepts may at first seem self-evident; certainly ideas of class and
status positions have been widely discussed. Warner and Lunt, however, employ these ideas in a more narrowly defined way to make certain discriminations about our own society. The work is significant, not because the broad
concepts are new or startling, but because they were developed from observed,
clinical data and, as used by Warner and Lunt, produce some interesting conclusions. Although we often say we consider ours to be a "classless" society, our
behavior seems to belie our words.

As you read the case material in the "Profiles," compare it with similar experiences you have had. Observe the different values about things, ideas, or
organizations that people in different statuses seem to hold. To what extent
are "right" evaluations of any particular behavior more than indications of the
status an individual holds in his society; are some things that seem right to one
group entirely wrong to another? Consider whether or not such points of view
add new meaning to some of your own experiences.[9] Warner and Lunt say
that this chapter of "Profiles"

> relates some of the more critical or revealing happenings in the lives of typical
> Yankee City people. Successful and unsuccessful upward mobility within several
> classes is illustrated. The methods of including and excluding people from signifi-
> cant groupings are portrayed. The outward symbols of class are given; and the
> negative and positive evaluations of the several classes are expressed in the actions
> and words of the participants.[10]

Read

W. LLOYD WARNER and PAUL S. LUNT, *The Social Life of a Modern Community* (New Haven: Yale University Press, 1941), pp. 81–91, 127–201.

Status, role, and value orientation are concepts helpful in viewing the actions of people in a community. They offer a way of "adding up" the parts of
social behavior into a "whole" — classes, communities, societies. However, this
social behavior remains in some sense individual, for it is only the similarity
of training that individual people have had which creates group uniformities.
These concepts are, therefore, as useful in observing behavior from the point
of view of the individual himself as from the point of view of the total system.

Each individual is apparently able to play a sequence of different roles during a lifetime. In fact, with the high emphasis that our culture places on individualism and future time, it is perhaps more important for us than for many
others that we develop "new" ways of doing things. We must learn to change
our role behavior to fit new situations. The person who does learn to adjust
easily is able to behave "appropriately" in a wide variety of situations. He can
feel "comfortable" with different sorts of people and is considered to be "flexible" in his relationships.

Two sorts of difficulties often arise out of role definitions. In some situations
the people who are interacting do not share reciprocal role expectations. If two

---

[9] See also, for example, the following cases in Vol. II: "Robert Kelly," Case 1; "Mu Nu Fraternity,"
Case 5; and "Ida Geneva," Case 6.
[10] *Social Life of a Modern Community*, pp. 127–128.

How most of us behave from day to day often comes as a shock

We grow up thinking our ways are natural to all mankind

parties to an interaction both want to be "boss," they are bound for trouble. In new marriages, we often hear of the time it takes for the husband and wife to become "adjusted." We might say instead that they must learn to behave in terms of compatible roles that complement instead of conflict with each other. Smooth interaction grows as they learn their new complementary roles.

Another difficulty can arise from the fact that our roles change as we grow older. Some people do not easily unlearn old roles when the situation calls upon them to play new ones. An individual trying to play incompatible roles simultaneously can cause as much havoc in human relations as several people playing roles that do not mesh. For example, consider the man who wishes to be a "good son" and to do what "the family wants" at the same time that he is trying to be an "independent college man." [11]

In the article below, Benedict points out some of the problems involved in learning new roles as we grow older. She believes that certain aspects of our child-training methods make these problems more acute than is necessary. To make her point, she presents contrasts from some primitive societies that use different training methods. She does not conclude, of course, that primitive societies lack role conflicts. She simply takes the best primitive examples she can find to highlight, by contrast, certain deficiencies in our training methods that she believes can be improved. Indeed, no society can avoid role conflict; as long as men must play several roles either simultaneously or in sequence, they will sometimes have difficulty in finding the right role at the right time. All of us can handle our own problems of role more easily if we realize their source in cultural standards and do not assume that we are unique in having such problems.

Benedict selects for discussion three contrasts "that occur in our culture between the individual's role as child and as father: 1. responsible — nonresponsible status role; 2. dominance — submission; 3. contrasted sexual role. It is largely upon our cultural commitments to these three contrasts that the discontinuity in the life cycle of an individual in our culture depends." A son must later be a father, and "these roles in our society are strongly differentiated; a good son is tractable, and does not assume adult responsibilities; a good father provides for his children and should not allow his authority to be flouted . . . The individual in one role must revise his behavior from almost all points of view when he assumes the second role." [12] Comparing our practices with those of other societies, Benedict is able to show that these discontinuities are cultural and do not automatically reflect innate biological characteristics.

In the next article, Talcott Parsons considers questions of status and role as they apply to certain facets of the American "middle-class" family. Here also we can observe the ways in which these concepts are useful in making discriminations about the relation of the individual to a group immediately around him. The middle-class values on which Parsons focuses our attention have been historically very important in American life. Indeed, these values are found to such a large degree throughout our society that they describe the dominant American pattern. Yet, as the Warner and Lunt material indicates, variant values are also present, and neither dominant nor variant values are fully descriptive of the behavior of any particular family.

---

[11] Consider "James Alton Johnson," Vol. II, Case 12.

[12] Ruth Benedict, "Continuities and Discontinuities in Cultural Conditioning," by permission from *A Study of Interpersonal Relations*, edited by Patrick Mullahy. Copyright, 1949, by Hermitage Press, Inc. Published by Hermitage Press, Inc., New York. See also reading below.

Parsons uses Linton's idea that the primary criteria for differentiation between roles are those of age, sex, and family relationship. He then analyzes the behavior that is expected of American middle-class men and women as adolescents, mature adults, and elderly people. He extends Benedict's discussion by considering a number of role components beyond the three that especially concern her. In particular, he focuses on strains in each of the roles — on contradictory expectations, on difficulties in transition from one role to another through time. He concludes that "youth culture" is an expression of these strains, as are feelings of alienation and isolation that often appear after retirement. In terms of the particular value orientations of our culture, for example, the grandparents' role has little meaning as compared with the parents' role.[18] Read

RUTH BENEDICT, "Continuities and Discontinuities in Cultural Conditioning," below.

TALCOTT PARSONS, "Age and Sex in the Social Structure of the United States," below.

ADDITIONAL READINGS

Hollingshead, August B., *Elmtown's Youth* (New York: Wiley, 1949).
The author studied the importance of the social-class system in shaping the life of adolescents in a small midwestern city. He shows the way it influences their choice of courses in high school, their job aspirations, their sex life, their whole set of basic assumptions about their environment.

Kluckhohn, Clyde, and others, "Values and Value-Orientations in the Theory of Action," *Toward a General Theory of Action*, ed. Talcott Parsons and Edward A. Shils (Cambridge: Harvard University Press, 1951).
Kluckhohn reviews the anthropological and philosophical literature, then offers a definition of "value" along with specific suggestions for its use in research operations.

Malinowski, Bronislaw, *Argonauts of the Western Pacific* (London: George Routledge, 1932).

An excellent description of "primitive" life by one of the keenest anthropological observers.

Mead, Margaret, *And Keep Your Powder Dry* (New York: William Morrow, 1942).
This book is an anthropologist's attempt to find certain crucial patterns in the "typical" American personality that could be utilized in furthering the war effort. Given this somewhat restricted aim, the author has achieved in the first nine chapters a remarkable description of American society and its effects on the American personality. She focuses on the class system, on our peculiarities as an immigrant nation, and on certain values of competition and success in life that are inculcated into us as children.

Williams, Tennessee, *A Streetcar Named Desire* (Norfolk, Connecticut: New Directions, 1947).
A play which offers a striking portrayal of roles in conflict.

---

[18] Reconsider in this connection "The Michaelson Family," Vol. II, Case 3; and "James Alton Johnson," Vol. II, Case 12.

Anomie*

BY EMILE DURKHEIM

No man can be happy nor can he go on living at all if the demands he makes of life exceed any possibility of fulfillment. If a man aspires to the impossible, he will be hurt constantly and will not be able to function without pain. Now, any action which can be accomplished only with pain tends not to be accomplished at all. Desires which are not satisfied atrophy, and, since the inclination to live is simply the accumulative result of all desires, its tenacity is weakened along with the others.

For the normal animal, there is an automatic and spontaneous equilibrium which depends solely on material factors. The animal organism demands simply that restitution make up for deterioration; that the amount of matter and energy used in living be regularly replaced. When his hungers are satisfied, the animal is content and asks for nothing more. His powers of reflection are not sufficiently developed to enable him to dream of goals beyond those implicit in his physical being. Equilibrium in the animal also is self-produced, since the work demanded of each organ depends on the general condition of the vital forces and on the needs of physical balance, with deterioration well regulated by the possibilities for restitution. The limits of both are well defined and are a part of the very constitution of the animal which has no means of exceeding them.

This is not true for man, because his needs are not — or not to the same degree — dependent on his body. At the most, one could consider as measurable the amount of material sustenance needed for the sustaining of human life. Even this would be far less certain if allowance were made for the element of choice and desire involved; for beyond the indispensable minimum with which nature is instinctively satisfied, a more developed thought imagines far better conditions as desirable goals. Nevertheless, desires of this sort sooner or later meet unsurpassable boundaries.

How can the amount of ease, of comfort, of luxury be determined which a human being can legitimately seek? Neither in the physical nor the psychological make-up of man is there a fixed limit for such desires. The functioning of no individual life demands that a man stop here rather than there; proof of this lies in that the average health has not been lowered, although since the beginning of history desires have continued to develop with increasing satisfactions. Especially, how can the manner be determined in which desires should vary according to social levels, professions, the relative importance of work? In no society are they equally satisfied at the different levels of the social hierarchy. In its essential characteristics, human nature is perceptibly the same in all people. Human nature cannot set up the variable limits essential to these desires; insofar as they depend on the individual alone, they are without limits. Without any outside force to control them, our emotions create a bottomless pit which nothing can fill.

If nothing controls them from without, emotions can be nothing but a source of torment, because uncontrolled desires are insatiable by definition. It is not without reason that this insatiability is looked upon as a sign of morbidity. Since nothing imposes limits upon them, desires forever surpass the hope of any satisfaction and nothing can appease them. An

---

* Book II, chapter 5, sections ii and iii, of Emile Durkheim, *Le Suicide*. First published by Librairie Félix Alcan, Paris, 1897; reprinted in 1930. Translated from the French by Natalie Harris Cabot, and copyrighted, 1948, by the President and Fellows of Harvard College, as HP292.

unquenchable thirst is a torture perpetually renewed.

It has been stated that it is proper human activity to push forward ceaselessly, to attempt goals that are unattainable. But it is impossible to perceive how such a state of uncertainty can be satisfactory either to the conditions of mental life or the exigencies of physical life. Whatever pleasure a man may feel in doing, in moving, in making an effort, he still needs to feel that his efforts are not in vain and that in walking, he is moving forward. A man does not move forward when he is walking toward no goal, or, what amounts to the same thing, when the goal toward which he is walking is unreachable. With the remaining distance always the same, no matter which road he may have taken, it is as if he had gone through futile motions without having left the starting point. Even the looks he might cast over his shoulder and the feelings of pride that he might feel in seeing the distance already covered could create no more than an illusory satisfaction, since the distance to be covered has not diminished at all.

By hypothesis, therefore, man in attempting to reach an inaccessible goal is condemning himself to a constant state of discontent. Without doubt, man can hope against all reason, and, however unreasonable, hope has its joys. Indeed, it can sustain for a time; but it can never survive the repeated disillusionments of experience. In effect, what more has the future to offer than the past, since it is never possible to achieve a state which remains constant and since one cannot even draw near to the envisaged ideal? Thus the more a man has, the more he wishes to have, and the satisfactions received excite rather than appease the desires. Can this be called pleasant? Only if there is sufficient self-deception so that the futility of it is not apparent. In order for the pleasure to continue and to conceal the painful anxiety which accompanies it, nothing must interfere. Let it meet any obstacle and only the anxiety remains, together with the accompanying discomfort. It would, however, be a miracle if an insurmountable obstacle

were never to appear. Under these conditions, a man holds to life only by a tenuous thread which can be snapped at any moment.

In order for the situation to be different, the emotions must be controlled. Only then can emotions be in accord with the experience of the senses and, therefore, satisfied. Since there is nothing within the individual which can set the limits, they must come from a force outside the individual. There must be a regulating power which serves the same function for emotional desires as the organism does for physical desires. The regulating power must be moral. Only the conscience can reëstablish balance, since the awakening of the conscience first disturbed the state of equilibrium in which the animal slumbered. In this instance, material constraint would be without effect; it is not by physio-chemical forces that hearts can be changed. Insofar as appetites are not automatically contained in physiological mechanisms, they can be controlled only by rules which they consider just. Men would not consent to limit their desires if they believed themselves privileged to go beyond the rules laid down for them. Men do not, however, know how to set up any just rules for themselves, for reasons that have already been stated. Therefore, they must receive them from an authority which they respect and before which they bow spontaneously. Society alone, either directly and in its full strength, or through the intermediary of one of its groups, is capable of playing the part of moderator; because society is the only moral force whose superiority the individual will recognize. Society alone has the necessary authority to establish rules and to define the point beyond which the passions must not go. Society alone can appraise what comparative rewards should be offered each occupational group for the best common good.

In effect, at every moment of history, there has existed in the moral conscience of society a latent evaluation of the respective worth of the various occupations in the community, of the relative remuneration due to each, and, consequently, of the measure of ease which is suitable for every level of worker. It is as if there were a hierarchy by which public opinion sets up each level, and a certain coefficient of well-being is accorded each level depending upon its place in the hierarchy. There is, for example, a certain manner of living which is considered the best that a laborer can hope to attain in his effort to improve his condition, and a low point beneath which society does not tolerate his living unless he has given serious offense. Both the high and the low points vary for the city and the country worker, for the journalist and the domestic, for the business employee and for the public servant. Society also frowns upon the rich man who lives like the poor, and he is blamed equally if he surrounds himself with excessive luxury. In vain do the economists protest; public sentiment will always be scandalized by the fact that one man can have a superfluous amount of riches, and this intolerance seems to lessen only in times of moral perturbation.[1]

Despite its lack of legal form, there is a regulation which sets the maximum of ease which each class of society can legitimately seek to attain. Moreover, the scale of values has nothing static about it. It changes with the earning power of the group and with the changes brought about in the society's moral ideas. Thus, what seemed to be luxury in one era no longer appears so in another; the well-being once granted only to the privileged class eventually seems to be completely necessary and equitable for all.

Under this constraint, everyone recognizes vaguely the outside limits for his ambitions and does not aspire beyond them. If he respects the rules and submits to group authority — that is, if he is of sound moral constitution — a man feels that it is not good to demand more of life. A goal and a limit are thus determined for the emotions. This determination is neither rigid nor absolute. The economic ideal assigned to each category is bounded by certain limits within which

desires can move with freedom. But there are limits. These relative limits and the resulting moderation make men content with their lot while stimulating them to improve it; and it is this average contentment which gives birth to a feeling of both quiet and active happiness, to an enjoyment of being and living which is for societies and for individuals the true characteristic of health. At least generally, everyone is then in harmony with his position and desires no more than he can legitimately expect as the normal reward for his endeavors. This does not mean that man is therefore condemned to a sort of immobility. He can attempt to improve his existence; but the attempts which he makes in this connection can be unsuccessful without leaving him hopeless. For, since he likes what he has and does not put his whole heart into seeking what he has not, his hopes and aspirations for new things can fail without everything failing at once. The essential things are left him. His balance of happiness is good because it is definite and a few miscalculations cannot upset it.

It would be useless to consider the hierarchal status determined by public sentiment as fair, unless one also considered equally just the manner in which the work status is established. The worker is not in good harmony with his social situation unless he is convinced that it is the one in which he must necessarily find himself. If he believes himself privileged to aspire to another social level, he will not be content.

It is not enough that the average level of needs for each status be determined by public sentiment; there must be another and more exact set of rules which determines the manner in which different social levels are open to particular individuals. In effect, such a set of rules exists for every society. They vary with time and place. Once, birth was the only determining factor for social classification; today, there is no inequality except that which inevitably results from inherited wealth or from merit. In all their various forms, these sets of rules have

---

[1] This is actually a moral judgment and does not lend itself to legal sanction. We do not believe that any kind of restraining legal laws are desirable or even possible.

the same objective. They cannot be effective unless they are imposed on individuals by an authority higher than themselves, that is, by group authority. They must demand from all people, sometimes unequally, concessions and sacrifices for the common good.

To be sure, certain people have felt that this moral pressure would become useless from the moment that economic status ceased to be transmitted through heredity. If, it has been said, the heritage were done away with and everyone began life with the same resources; if the struggle between competitors were under conditions of perfect equality; surely no one could find the results unfair. Everyone in the world would then think that things are as they should be.

Without doubt, the more one approached this ideal of equality, the less However, this is only a question of degree, since the ideal of equality cannot would social constraint be necessary. be attained. There is a heredity of natural endowment which will always exist. Intelligence; taste; a talent for science, the arts, literature, or business; courage; manual skills — all these are gifts with which we are born, just as an heir is born to wealth or the nobleman of former times was born to his title and position. Therefore, there must be a moral discipline which makes those who are the least favored by nature accept the lesser birthright which they owe to blind chance. Can the claim be made that everything should be equally divided among all and that no advantage be given to the more useful and the more deserving? Then a strong discipline indeed would be needed to make these latter willing to abide by a treatment equal to that given the useless and the mediocre.

However, this discipline, like the foregoing, can be effective only if it is considered fair by the people who must submit to it. When it is maintained only through habit or through force, peace and harmony reign only superficially; feelings of unrest and discontent are latent; barely controlled appetites are quickly unleashed. This is what happened in Rome and in Greece, when the beliefs on which the old order was founded were disrupted; and in our modern societies when the preconceived opinions of the aristocracy began to lose their strength. But this state of disruption is the exception; it happens only when a society is in the throes of an unhealthy crisis. Normally, group authority is recognized as just by the majority. Therefore, when we state that authority must be imposed upon men, we certainly do not mean that violence is the only means by which it can be imposed. Because this set of rules is intended to constrain individual passions, it must emanate from a power which dominates people; but this power must be obeyed through respect and not through fear.

Thus, it is not true that human endeavor can be liberated from all constraint. There is nothing in this world that can benefit from any such privilege. Every being, as a part of the universe, lives in relation to it; his nature and the manner in which he manifests it depend not on him alone but on others who consequently constrain and rule him. In this respect, there is only a difference of degree and form between inert matter and the thinking being. The very characteristic of man is that the constraint to which he is submitted is not physical but moral; that is, social.

He does not obey a brute physical law, but rather a superior conscience which he recognizes as such. Since during the greatest and best part of his life, he rises above his corporeal body, he escapes its yoke but submits to the one imposed by society.

However, when society is upset either by painful crises or by happy but too sudden changes, it is temporarily incapable of exercising any authority and thus causes the sharp rise in the curve of suicides, as we shall show below.

During periods of economic disaster, there is a sudden loss of status which throws certain people into a position inferior to the one previously held. They must lower their sights, limit their needs, and learn to get along with less than before. All the benefits of social forces in their daily life are gone, and their moral education must begin again. This is not a time when society can bend them to this new life or teach them to cope with a manner of life to which they are not accustomed. The result is that they neither adjust to it nor is the prospect of continuing it even bearable; instead, before they have so much as experienced this inferior existence, their sufferings remove them from it.

It is no different if the economic crisis is inflationary and produces a sudden rise in power and fortune. In this case, as living conditions are changed, so is the scale by which needs were measured; for the scale varies with the social resources, since it determines for the most part what each occupational group should earn. The yardstick no longer measures accurately, yet it is impossible to establish a new one. It takes time for men and things to be reclassified by the social conscience. So long as social forces, thus liberated, have not recovered their equilibrium, their relative value remains indeterminate, and consequently all order is lost for a time. People no longer know what is possible and what is not, what is fair or unfair, which are proper claims and hopes and which go beyond the limit. Consequently, there is nothing which people will not attempt.

The disturbance may be so far-reaching that it affects the reclassification of people in their jobs. For since the relationships between the various classes of society are necessarily modified, the ideas which express these relationships cannot remain the same. The class which has benefited the most by the inflationary crisis accepts things as they are more reluctantly than heretofore; and obviously, the spectacle of this newly acquired wealth awakens envy on every side. No longer restrained by public judgment, appetites know no bounds. Moreover, desires are naturally in a state of great exaltation, if only because the general vitality is more intense. The richer prey excites them, makes them more demanding, impatient of all restraint, at the very time when established rules have lost their authority. This state

of disorder or *anomie* is reinforced by the fact that the emotions are the least disciplined at the very moment when a stronger discipline is needed.

Emotional demands become such that it is impossible to satisfy them. Overstimulated ambition always expects results impossible to achieve, since there is no warning that this is false expectation. Nothing brings contentment, and this disturbance keeps itself perpetually alive without finding any appeasement. Moreover, since the only possible pleasure in the pursuit of an unattainable goal is the pursuit itself, interference of any sort is serious. In a time of greater competition and less restraint the struggle becomes more violent and painful. No class is exempt since there are no established class levels. At the very moment that it is least likely to succeed, the effort made is greater. How could the will to live fail to weaken under such conditions?

The above explanation is confirmed by the unusual immunity to suicide enjoyed by poor countries. Poverty protects against suicide because it acts as a restraint in itself. Desires must reckon to a certain degree with financial means; what a man has serves as a point of departure in determining what he would like to have. Consequently, the less he has, the less he is led into widening without limit the areas of his requirements. Lack of power, in subjecting us to moderation, accustoms us to it. Where mediocrity is the general rule, nothing comes along to excite envy.

Wealth, on the other hand, through the power that it confers, gives us the illusion that we get ahead only by our own efforts. In diminishing the resistance that things give us, wealth leads us to believe that all obstacles can be overcome indefinitely. Now the less we feel limited, the more any kind of limitation seems unbearable. It is not without reason that so many religions have proclaimed the benefits and moral worth of poverty, since it is the best school for teaching men to restrain themselves. In obliging us to exercise a constant self-discipline, it prepares us to accept with docility collective discipline. Wealth, however, in exalting the individual, always risks awakening a spirit of rebellion which is the very source of immorality. Beyond doubt, this is no reason to stop humanity from improving its material conditions. However, even if there is no remedy for it, the moral danger brought about by any increase in ease should not be overlooked.

If, as is discussed above, *anomie* appeared only in intermittent spurts and under crises, it might well produce occasional variation in the total number of suicides; it would not be a regular and constant factor. However, there is an area of social life where *anomie* actually is chronic: the areas of business and industry.

During the past century, economic progress has consisted chiefly of removing all regulations from industrial relations. Until recently, a whole system of moral and social forces served as disciplinary measures. First, there was religion, the influence of which was felt alike by workers and employers — by poor and rich. It consoled the poor by teaching them that they must be content with their lot; that the social order was providential; that the portion for each class was allotted by God himself; and that the rewards of the world to come would make up for the inequalities of this one. It influenced the rich by reminding them that for man there are other than worldly interests; that these worldly interests must be subordinate to other higher interests; and that, consequently, they cannot be pursued without rule or limitation. Second, governmental power held business in check through the supremacy it exercised over economic forces and the relatively subordinate state in which it held them. Finally, at the very heart of the business world, professional bodies, by regulating salaries, the price of products, and production itself, determined indirectly the average income level, which, in turn, was a factor in determining average requirements.

In describing this structure, it is not our intent to cite it as a model. It is clear that without great changes, it would not be suitable for actual societies today. We are stating only that it existed, that it had useful effects, and that today nothing remains of it.

Religion has lost most of its influence. Governmental power, instead of regulating economic life, has become its instrument and servant. Entirely opposing schools consisting of both orthodox economists and extreme socialists are agreed that the role of government should be that of an intermediary, more or less passive, between various occupational groups. Some wish to make of it simply the guardian of individual contracts. Others assign it the task of maintaining understanding between different groups, by registering consumer demands, transmitting these to manufacturers, making an inventory of total income, and distributing this according to an established formula. All of them refuse government the right to stand in authority to the remainder of society or to determine for it a common goal. Everywhere it is declared that nations should have industrial prosperity as their chief and only objective; that is what is implied in the dogma of economic materialism which serves as the basis for apparently opposing systems. Since these theories do no more than express the weight of opinion, industrial prosperity has become the supreme goal of individuals and societies, instead of continuing to be regarded as a means to a higher end. Thus, the appetites which it unbridles have become free of any limiting authority.

This apotheosis of well-being in sanctifying these desires has put them above any human law. It is as though there were some sort of sacrilege in any attempt at restraint. That is why even the purely utilitarian regulations imposed by the industrial world, through the intermediary of corporations, have not managed to survive. Finally, this unleashing of desires has been further aggravated by the industrial development itself and by the almost endless expansion of the market. As long as a manufacturer could sell his goods only in the immediate vicinity, the moderate potential profit did not overstimulate his ambition. Now that he can claim almost the whole world as his market, now that his horizons are limitless, how can he accept the emotional limitations of an outmoded past?

Thus in industry we find an agitation, an excitement, which extends into other spheres. The state of crisis and *anomie* is constant and, so to speak, normal. From top to bottom of the social ladder, immoderate desires are in revolt without knowing where to stop. There is no way of appeasing them, since their goal is forever beyond attainment. Reality seems without worth as compared with the possibilities envisaged by a fevered imagination; detached from reality in order to pursue an imaginary goal, a man detaches himself once again when this goal has been attained. There is nothing but desire for new things, unknown joys, unnamed sensations, all of which lose their flavor the minute they have been experienced. From then on, there is no strength left to bear the slightest reversal. The fever dies down and it becomes clear that the tumult was sterile; there all the new sensations have not created a solid reservoir of happiness which might have served in good stead during days of trouble. The wise man knows how to enjoy his achievements without perpetually feeling the need of replacing them with others, and so he has something that holds him to life when the hour of trouble strikes. The man who has always lived for the future, with his eyes fixed on tomorrow, has nothing in his past which protects him from the bitterness of the present; because the past was for him nothing but a series of stages impatiently traversed. He deceived himself because he always counted on finding later the happiness which he had not yet found. When his forward progress stops, he has nothing either ahead of or behind him on which he can count. Furthermore, fatigue in itself is sufficient to produce the disenchantment. It is difficult, in the end, not to realize the futility of endless pursuit.

This state of mind might be sufficient in itself to produce the crop of suicides which occur during economic catastrophe. In societies where man is subject to a healthy discipline, he submits more easily to the blows of circumstance. Accustomed to inconvenience and restraint, the effort necessary for a little more inconvenience costs him relatively little. On the other hand, when all restraint is odious, how can even greater restraint appear to be anything short of unbearable? Feverish impatience scarcely produces resignation. If the only goal is that of surpassing the point already attained, how painful it is to have a setback! The lack of organization which characterizes our economic system paves the way for all types of experiences. Since unrestrained imagination produces eagerness for novelty, and no discipline is imposed, there is constant groping. Greater risks are necessarily accompanied by defeat, and so crises are more frequent at the very moment when they are the most destructive.

These tendencies are so usual that society considers them normal. Over and over again it is stated that man is forever discontent, that he must constantly pursue an indeterminate goal. This pursuit is presented daily as desirable, whereas actually it is the creation of disordered minds which set up as a pattern the very disorder from which they suffer. The doctrine of the most rapid conceivable progress at any cost has become a tenet of faith. Parallel with these theories which glorify the benefits of instability are others generalizing on the conditions which have created them, declaring, namely, that life is bad, filled with more pain than pleasure, luring man only by its false attractions. Since this disorder is at its height in the economic world, it is there that it takes its heaviest toll.

Business and industrial occupations are among those which contribute the greatest number of suicides. These suicides nearly equal those of the professions, sometimes even outnumbering them; they are notably more numerous than those of agriculture. In agriculture the established regulating forces still make their influence felt, since the fever of business has penetrated here the least. Agriculture is the most reminiscent of the general economic conditions of an earlier period. The differentiation between suicides in industry and other fields would be more noticeable if it were possible to differentiate between owners and workers, because it is probably the former who are most subject to *anomie*. The enormous toll among the land-owning population (720 out of a million) demonstrates adequately that it is the wealthiest who suffer the most. Everything which compels subordination lessens the effects of *anomie*. The lower classes have their horizons limited by their superiors, and owing to that fact alone their desires are more definite. On the other hand, those in the upper classes, who have no superiors, necessarily lose themselves in the void above them, since there is no power to restrain them.

To summarize, in modern societies, *anomie* is a regular and specific factor in suicide; it is one of the contributing sources to the annual toll. Consequently, we are faced with a new type of suicide which should be distinguished from the others. It differs in that it depends not on the manner in which individuals are related to society, but rather on the manner in which society controls them. In the egoist suicide, men no longer find a reason for living; in the altruist suicide, the reason for life seems to be in the life

hereafter; and in the third type, the existence of which we have just established, suicide takes place because all activities are disordered and men suffer thereby. Because of its origin, we have given the name anomic suicide to this last type.

Obviously, this type of suicide and the egoist suicide are not without relationship. Both result from the fact that society is not sufficiently in the individual's consciousness. But the way in which it is absent is different in each case. In the egoist suicide, society is imperfect in its group activity, supplying neither purpose nor significance. In the anomic suicide, society does not control individual emotions and leaves them without any restraints. Thus, despite their interrelationship, the two types remain independent of each other. We can be socially well related without knowing how to limit our desires; without being an agoist, we can live in a state of *anomie* and inversely. Furthermore, the two types of suicides are drawn chiefly from the same social backgrounds; but the egoist type, on the one hand, from the world of thought and intellectual pursuits; the anomic, on the other hand, from the industrial and business world.

Dominant and Variant Cultural Value Orientations[*]

BY FLORENCE ROCKWOOD KLUCKHOHN

That culture greatly influences both individual personalities and all types of social processes is no longer a debatable question for most persons interested in the study of human behavior. The following statement made by Kluckhohn and Murray in *Personality in Nature, Society and Culture*, and many others similar to it, are today readily accepted:

The similarities of character within a group are traceable less to constitu-

tional factors than to formative influences of the environment to which all members of the group have been subjected. Of these group-membership determinants, culture is with little doubt the most significant. To say that "culture determines" is, of course, a highly abstract way of speaking. What one actually observes is the interaction of people. One never sees "culture" any more than one sees "gravity."

[*] Rewritten especially for this volume by the author from her paper of the same title published in *The Social Welfare Forum* (New York: Columbia University Press, 1951). Originally delivered as a lecture to the National Conference of Social Work, 78th annual meeting. Copyright, 1951, National Conference of Social Work.

But "culture" is a very convenient construct which helps in understanding certain regularities in human events, just as "gravity" represents one type of regularity in physical events. Those who have been trained in childhood along traditional lines, and even those who have as adults adopted some new design for living, will be apt to behave predictably in many contexts because of a prevailing tendency to conform to group standards . . .

Not only the action patterns but also the motivational systems of individuals are influenced by culture. Certain needs are biologically given, but many others are not. All human beings get hungry, but no gene in any chromosome predisposes a person to work for a radio or a new car or a shell necklace or "success." Sometimes biologically-given drives, such as sex, are for longer or shorter periods subordinated to culturally acquired drives, such as the pursuit of money or religious asceticism. And the means by which needs are satisfied are ordinarily defined by cultural habits and fashions.[1] The studies of various anthropologists and the collaborative work many of them have done with psychologists, psychiatrists, and sociologists have gone far in demonstrating many of the relationships between individual desires and group experiences — between culture and personality.[2] Yet, for all of the valuable insights produced and the considerable progress thus far achieved, there have been some severe and — in the opinion of the writer — justified criticisms of many of the facile conclusions drawn by some anthropologists. Especially in some of the recent interpretations of so-called national character structure, one notes a repeated tendency to derive highly generalized and far-sweeping conclusions from a few specific items of culture con-

tent. Sociologists and psychologists alike have cavilled at the apparent ignoring of interaction processes and the too deterministic effects often claimed for cultural factors.

Much of the difficulty in all attempts to use the cultural anthropologists' concepts and data arises from an absence of a systematic theory of cultural variation and from the tendency of most anthropologists to rely too much upon mere empirical generalizations. The most casual observer is aware that the customs of different societies vary. He knows, too, that the behavior patterns of individuals within a given society are often markedly different. Indeed, when dealing with variation at this level, one cannot but be acutely conscious of the wide range of "individual differences." But it is not this plethora of specific content which is of the most critical importance if the aim is to understand better the relationship of cultural factors to either the structuring of social groups or the personalities of the individuals who comprise the social groups. It is rather the generalized meanings or values which should be the major or at least the first concern. *Specific patterns of behavior in so far as they are influenced by cultural factors (and few are not so influenced) are the concrete expressions reflecting generalized meanings or values. And to the extent that the individual personality is a product of training in a particular cultural tradition, it is also at the generalized value level that one finds the most significant differences.*

As Gregory Bateson has remarked: "The human individual is endlessly simplifying and generalizing his own view of his own environment . . . he constantly imposes upon this environment his own constructions and meanings . . . these constructions and meanings . . . are regarded as characteristic of one culture, as over against another."[3] Or, as

---

[1] Clyde Kluckhohn and Henry A. Murray, *Personality in Nature, Society and Culture* (New York: Alfred A. Knopf, 1950), pp. 40–41.

[2] An excellent brief sketch of what has been done in this field is given by Ralph Linton in his introduction to Abram Kardiner's *The Psychological Frontiers of Society* (New York: Columbia University Press, 1945).

[3] "Cultural Determinants of Personality," *Personality and the Behavior Disorders*, ed. J. McV. Hunt (New York: Ronald Press, 1944), p. 723.

Clyde Kluckhohn has stated, "There is a 'philosophy' behind the way of life of every individual and of every relatively homogeneous group at any given point in their histories." [4]

The writer agrees with these and many similar statements made by other anthropologists which emphasize the importance of "value orientations" in the lives of individuals and groups of individuals.[5] There is in many of them, however, too much stress — implied when not actually stated — upon the unitary character of value orientations. Variation for the same individual when he is playing different roles and variation between whole groups of persons within a single society are not adequately accounted for. More important still, the emphasis upon the uniqueness of the variable value systems of different societies ignores the fact of the universality of human problems and the correlate fact that human societies have found for some problems approximately the same answers. Yet certainly it is only within a frame of reference which deals with universals that variation can be understood. Without it, it is not possible to deal systematically with either the problem of similarity and difference as between the value systems of different societies or the question of variant values within societies.

Human behavior mirrors at all times an intricate blend of the universal and the variable. The universals and variations are of many kinds. All human beings have many and significant biological similarities as members of a particular species — *Homo sapiens* — yet variability within the species is great. We frequently note both the similarities and differences which are psychological. We all recognize that men are alike in that they all live in some kind of social group — are, as Aristotle called them, political animals — yet different in the kinds of groups they develop.

The universal and variable in cultural values have not been so clearly distinguished. Some persons have tended, as did the evolutionists, to view all culture as a single whole, unfolding through time; others have held too rigidly to analyses within the comparative-culture frame of reference and as a result have overstressed differences.

The problem of the invariant and variant in culture patterning can, of course, be approached in different ways. Precisely which way will depend upon the specific type of investigation being made. We are here interested in a conceptual approach which will permit a systematic analysis of differences in cultural value orientations as these are held within a framework of common human — or universal — problems.

In a paper already published,[6] the author has presented a classification of cultural orientations (value orientations) and the beginnings of a theory of variant culture. I shall now hastily sketch and illustrate the main ideas presented in that paper.

The postulate fundamental to the classification and theory of cultural value orientations is simply this: *That there are a limited number of basic human problems for which all peoples at all times and in all places must find some solution.* The second stated assumption is that *while variability is certainly to be noted in the solutions which are found, it is variability within limits — within a range of possible variations.*

The five common human problems tentatively singled out as those of key importance can be stated in the form of questions:

1. What are the innate predispositions of men?
2. What is the relation of man to nature?
3. What is the significant time dimension?

---

[4] "Values and Value-Orientations in the Theory of Action," *Toward a General Theory of Action,* ed. Talcott Parsons and Edward A. Shils (Cambridge: Harvard University Press, 1951), p. 409.

[5] Clyde Kluckhohn, *ibid.,* p. 411, defines value orientation as "a generalized and organized conception, influencing behavior, of nature, of man's place in it, of man's relation to man, and of the desirable and nondesirable as they may relate to man-environment and interhuman relations."

[6] "Dominant and Substitute Profiles of Cultural Orientations: Their Significance for the Analysis of Social Stratification," *Social Forces,* XXVIII (May 1950), 376–393.

Innate Predispositions	Evil (mutable or immutable)	Neither good nor bad (mutable or immutable)	Good (mutable or immutable)
Man's Relation to Nature	Man subjugated to nature	Man in nature	Man over nature
Time Dimension	Past	Present	Future
Valued Personality Type	Being	Being-in-Becoming	Doing
Modality of Relationship	Lineal	Collateral	Individualistic

4. What personality type is to be most valued?

5. What is the dominant modality of man's relations to other men?

The limits of variability in the solutions found for these common human problems suggested as at least a testable conceptualization are presented in the table above.

That the definition of the *innate predispositions* of human nature has differed from society to society is — or should be — obvious. We have only to look about us to recognize that there is considerable variability in our present-day American conception of human nature. The orientation we inherited from Puritan ancestors, and still strong in many of us, is that human nature is basically evil but perfectible. Constant control and discipline of the self are essential if any real goodness is to be achieved and maintained, and the danger of regression is always present. But some in our society today — perhaps a growing number — are inclined to the more tolerant view that human nature is a mixture of the good and the bad. They would say that control and effort are certainly needed, but lapses can be understood and need not always be severely condemned. Such a definition of basic human nature would appear to be a somewhat more common one among the peoples of the world — both literate and nonliterate — than the view we have held in our own historical past. Whether there are any total socie-

ties given to the definition of human nature as immutably good is to be doubted. The position is, however, a possible one and should be found ever present as an alternative definition within societies.

The range of variation in the *man-nature* relationship is also fairly obvious. There are whole societies where the dominant tendency is to view man as subjugated to nature — where he is seen to be the victim of his environment. Spanish-American culture as I have known it in the American Southwest illustrates well this interpretation of the man-nature relationship.[7] To the typical Spanish-American sheep raiser in that region there is little or nothing which can be done if a storm comes to damage his range lands or destroy his flocks. He simply accepts the inevitable as the inevitable. His attitude toward illness and death is the same fatalistic attitude. "If it is the Lord's will that I die, I shall die," is the way he expresses it. Many a Spanish-American has been known to refuse the help of any doctor because of this attitude.

Another way of phrasing the man-nature relationship is to regard all natural forces and man himself as one harmonious whole. One is but an extension of the other, and both are needed to make the whole. Such was the attitude frequently found as the dominant one in China in the past centuries.

A third way of viewing this relationship is that of man against or over nature. According to this view, which is clearly

[7] See *Los Atarqueños*, my unpublished Ph.D. thesis, Radcliffe College, 1941. Considerable material on Spanish-American culture is contained in my article "The American Family and the Feminine Role," below, Chapter IX.

the one characteristic of Americans, natural forces are something to be overcome and put to the use of human beings. We span our rivers with bridges, blast through our mountains to make tunnels, make lakes where none existed, and do a thousand and one other things to exploit nature and make it serve our human needs. In general, this means that we have an orientation to life which is that of overcoming obstacles. And it is difficult for us to understand the kind of people who accept the obstacle and give in to it or even the people who stress the harmonious oneness of man and nature.

Concerning the definition of the human being's place in *time,* it should be apparent that there is always a past to be reckoned with, a present in which we live, and a future which lies ahead. No society ever does, or can, completely ignore any of the three time periods. Yet how greatly societies differ as to which of the three dimensions they stress or make dominant!

Spanish-Americans, whom we have described as having the attitude that man is a victim of natural forces, are also a people who emphasize present time. They pay little attention to what has happened in the past, and regard the future as a vague and most unpredictable period. Planning for the future or hoping that the future will be better than either present or past simply is not their way of life. In dealing with Spanish-Americans one must always take into account the fact that they have quite a different time sense from our own. Too often, we, who are in the habit of making definite appointments for two or five o'clock and expect to keep and have them kept, are baffled by the Spanish-American to whom two or five o'clock means little or nothing. For an appointment made for two o'clock he may arrive at any time between one and five o'clock, or, most likely, he will not arrive at all. Something else which interests him more may well have turned up to absorb his attention.

China of past generations, and to some extent still, was a society which put its main emphasis upon past time. Ancestor worship and a strong family tradition were both expressions of this past-time orientation. So also was the Chinese attitude that nothing new ever happened in the present or would happen in the future. It had all happened before in the far distant past. Thus it was that the proud American who thought he was showing some Chinese a steamboat for the first time was quickly put in his place by the remark, "Our ancestors had such a boat two thousand years ago." Many modern European countries also tended to stress the past. Even England — in so far as it has been dominated by an aristocracy and traditionalism — has voiced this emphasis. Indeed, one of the chief differences between ourselves and the English is to be found in our somewhat varying attitudes toward time. We have difficulty in understanding the respect the English have for tradition, and they do not appreciate our disregard for it.

Americans, more than most people of the world, place emphasis upon the future — a future which we anticipate to be "bigger and better." This does not mean we have no regard for the past or fail to give thought to the present. But it certainly is true that no current generation of Americans ever wants to be called "old-fashioned." We do not consider the ways of the past to be good just because they are past, and we are seldom content with the present.

The fourth of the common human problems is called the *valued personality type.* The range of variation in this case yields the being, the being-in-becoming, and the doing orientations. Since it is assumed that all the orientations are an aspect of the action and motivational systems of the individual personalities, "valued personality type" is perhaps not the happiest of terms for designating this particular range of them; for the time being, however, we shall retain it.

This range of orientations has been derived for the most part from the distinction long made by philosophers between "being" and "becoming." The accordance is, however, far from complete. As used in this schema the polar terms being and becoming, now made into the three-point range of being, being-in-becoming and doing, are much more narrowly defined than has been the custom of philosophers. Furthermore, the view here is that these orientations vary independently relative to those which deal with the relation of man to nature, to time, and innate predispositions. The tendency of the philosophers, writing with different aims, has been to treat these several types of orientations as relatively undifferentiated clusters.

The essence of the being orientation is that it stresses the spontaneous expression of what is conceived to be "given" in the personality. The orientation is, as compared with the being-in-becoming or doing, essentially *non*-developmental. It might even be phrased as a spontaneous expression of impulses and desires; yet care must be taken not to make this interpretation a too literal one. In no society, as Clyde Kluckhohn has commented, does one ever find a one-to-one relationship between the desired and the desirable. The concrete behavior of individuals in complex situations, and the moral codes governing that behavior, usually reflects all the orientations simultaneously. A stress upon the "isness" of the personality and a spontaneous expression of it is not pure license, as we can easily see if we turn our attention to a society or segments of a society in which the being orientation is dominant. Spanish-American society, for example, is clearly one in which the being orientation is dominant. Their wide-range patterning of *Fiesta* activities alone shows this. Yet never in the *Fiesta* or other patterns of spontaneity is there pure impulse gratification. The value demands of other of the orientations — the relational orientation, the conception of human nature as being good and evil and in need of control, and others — all make for codes which restrain individuals in very definite ways.

The being-in-becoming orientation shares with the being a great concern with what the person is rather than what he can accomplish, but here the similarity ends. In the being-in-becoming orientation the idea of development, which is so little stressed in the being orientation, is paramount.

Erich Fromm's conception of "the spontaneous activity of the total integrated personality" is close to the being-in-becoming type. "By activity," he states, "we do not mean 'doing something' but rather the quality of the creative activity which can operate in one's emotional, intellectual and sensuous experiences and in one's will as well. One premise of this spontaneity is the acceptance of the total personality and the elimination of the split between 'reason' and 'nature.' " [8] A less favorably prejudiced and, for our purposes, a more accurately limited statement would be: The being-in-becoming orientation emphasizes self-realization — self-development — of all aspects of the self as an integrated whole.

The doing orientation is so characteristically the one dominantly stressed in American society that there is little need for an extensive definition. Its most distinguishing feature is its demand for action in the sense of accomplishment and in accord with standards which are conceived as being external to the acting individual. Self-judgment as well as the judgment of others is largely by means of measurable accomplishment through action. What does the individual do, what can he or will he accomplish, are almost always primary questions in our scale of appraisal of persons. "Getting things done" and finding ways "to do something" about any and all situations are stock American phrases. Erich Fromm also recognizes this orientation as separable from that which he defines in his concept of spontaneity and which we have called the being-in-becoming, but he seems to view it as mainly compulsive. With this I cannot agree. Many persons in our society who follow patterns in accord with the doing orientation are compulsive; many are not. Conformity, which is essential in all societies whatever the arrangement of their orientations, should not be so much and so often confounded with compulsiveness.

The fifth and last of the common hu-

---

[8] Erich Fromm, *Escape from Freedom* (New York: Farrar and Rinehart, 1941), pp. 258–259.

man problems treated in this conceptual scheme is the definition of *man's relation to other men*. This orientation, the relational, has three subdivisions: the lineal, the collateral, and the individualistic.

Sociologists have long used various types of dichotomies to differentiate homogeneous folk societies from the more complex urban societies. *Gemeinschaft — gesellschaft;* traditionalistic — rational-legal; mechanical solidarity — organic solidarity; or simply rural — urban are the most familiar of the several paired terms. Anthropologists, who have for the most part studied *gemeinschaft* or folk peoples, have frequently in their analyses of kinship structure or social organization made much of the difference between a lineage and a lateral extension of relationships.

The distinctions being made here obviously owe much to the concepts used in both these fields, but they are not identical with those of either field. The lineal, collateral, and individualistic relational principles are analytical elements in total relational systems and are not to be confused with categories descriptive of concrete systems.

It is in the nature of the case that all societies — all groups — must give some attention to all three principles. Individual autonomy cannot be and is not ignored by the most extreme type of *gemeinschaft* society. Collaterality is found in all societies. The individual is not a human being outside a group, and one kind of group emphasis is that put upon laterally extended relationships. These are the immediate relationships in time and place. All societies must also pay some attention to the fact that individuals are biologically and culturally related to each other through time. This is to say that there is always a lineal principle in relationships which is derived from age and generational differences and cultural tradition. The fundamental question is always that of emphasis.

There will always be variability in the primacy and nature of goals according to which of the three principles is stressed. If the individualistic principle is domi-

nant and the other two interpreted in terms of it — as is the case in the United States — individual goals will have primacy over the goals of either the collateral or lineal group. When the collateral principle is dominant the goals — or welfare — of the laterally extended group have primacy for all individuals. The group in this case is viewed as being moderately independent of other similar groups, and the question of continuity through time is not critical. Where the lineal principle is most heavily stressed, it is again group goals which are of primary concern to individuals, but there is the additional factor that an important one of those goals is continuity through time. Both continuity and ordered positional succession are of great importance when lineality dominates the relational system. Spanish-American society has been, until recently, one with a relatively strong lineal stress combined with a strong second-order collaterality.

How continuity and ordered positional succession are achieved in a lineal relational system is separate from the principle as such. It does in fact seem to be the case that the most successful way of maintaining a stress on lineality is through mechanisms which are either actual hereditary ones based upon biological relatedness or ones which are assimilated to a kinship system. The English, for example, maintained such an emphasis into the present time by consistently moving successful members of its more individualistic middle class into the established peerage system. Other societies have found other, but similar, mechanisms.

Thus far in the discussion of the major orientations the aim has been to show that different societies make different selections among possible solutions of common human problems. They raise to dominant position some *one* of the alternative principles. However, at no time has it been stated or implied that any society will or can ignore any of the dimensions. On the contrary, it is a fundamental proposition of this conceptual approach that all dimensions of all orientations *not only are but must be* present at all times in the pattern structure of every society.

However important it is to know what is dominant in a society at a given time, we shall not go far in understanding the dynamics of that society without paying careful heed to the variant orientations. That there be individuals and whole groups of individuals who live in accordance with patterns which express variant rather than the dominantly stressed orientations is, it is maintained, essential to the maintenance of the society. *Variant values, are, therefore, not only permitted but actually required.* It has been the mistake of many in the social sciences, and of many in the field of practical affairs as well, to treat all behavior and certain aspects of motivation which do not accord with the dominant values as some kind of deviance. It is urged that we cease to confuse the deviant who by his behavior calls down the sanctions of his group with the variant who is accepted and frequently required as far as the total social system is concerned. This is especially true in a society such as ours, where, beneath the surface of what has so often been called our compulsive conformity, there lies a wide range of variation. The dynamic interplay of the dominant and the variant is one of the outstanding features of American society, but as yet it has been little analyzed or understood.

Illustrations of variant value orientations, whether of individuals or whole groups, are numerous. Let us look at these three kinds: *ethnic differences,* of which the United States has had, and still has, so many; *class differences;* and *role differences,* as they are seen, for example, in the role of the American woman.

The usual tendency of most observers has been either to view all ethnic groups as one undifferentiated whole or, with a concern for understanding better the problems of particular groups, to seek out the quite specific ways in which they differ. Attention is given to the kind of parental authority a given people prefer, the attitude they have toward women, or, perhaps, the type of child-training

patterns they follow. These specific patterns are, of course, important; but it is obvious that knowing them all is in most cases impossible. Furthermore, when there is no general framework within which to consider the specific differences noted, there develops so frequently a tendency to attribute too much to single items of cultural content.

We could know many such concrete patterns followed by the Spanish-Americans in the Southwest and still not know why after one hundred years within the borders of the United States their way of life has changed so little until very recently. We can know, and have known, many such patterns and yet are forced to admit that understanding between Anglo-Americans and Spanish-Americans is not even now very great.

When, however, we look to fundamental differences in value orientations, we are led quickly to this proposition: The slow rate of assimilation of Spanish-Americans (and more recent Mexican immigrants also) and the low level of understanding as well are in large part attributable to a wide disparity in *all* the major orientations of Anglo-Americans and Spanish-Americans.

Illustrations of most of the Spanish-American orientations have already been given singly. Let us now take them as a whole system and again quickly compare them with the system of orientations dominantly stressed in American society. Where the Anglo-American stresses individualism, the Spanish-American puts his primary emphasis upon a combination of the lineal and the collateral. The semifeudal *patrón-peón* system of Mexicans, both in the United States and in Mexico, has neither permitted nor required very much independent behavior of most people. Or, to phrase this another way, whereas the Anglo-American is quite systematically trained for independent behavior, the Spanish-American or Mexican is trained for dependence.

The American dominant time orientation has been noted to be future, that of the Spanish-Americans, present. We show a vague awareness of this difference when we so often refer to Mexicans in general as being a *mañana* people. Yet how very much bound by our own cultural values we are when we interpret *mañana* to mean that a Mexican will always put off until tomorrow what should be done today. Tomorrow in a highly specific sense is meaningless to the Spanish-American or Mexican. He lives in a timeless present, and as one Mexican scholar phrased it: "The Mexican never puts off until tomorrow what can be done *only* today."

Consider, too, the vast difference between the Spanish-American being orientation and the American emphasis upon doing or accomplishing. Doing things in the name of accomplishment is not usual Spanish-American behavior. That which "is" is in large part taken for granted and considered as something to be enjoyed rather than altered.

Our own and the Spanish-Americans' definitions of the man-nature relationship are likewise poles apart. We set out to conquer, overcome, and exploit nature; they accept the environment with a philosophical calm bordering on the fatalistic. And seldom in Spanish-American culture does one find evidence of our own historical view of human nature as evil but perfectible. Their view would appear to be much more that of human nature as a mixture of the good and bad.

With such differences as these it is not a cause for wonder that Anglo-American educators, social workers, politicians, and a host of others have been both deeply frustrated and quite unsuccessful in their many attempts either to alter rapidly the Spanish-American way of life or adjust Anglo-American values to it. Nor is it strange that the understanding between Anglo- and Spanish-Americans in an area (New Mexico and Arizona) where each group constitutes approximately half of the total population has been inadequate throughout a whole century.

This highly dramatic and most extreme illustration of cultural variation within our own borders tells us a great deal if only we look at it in terms of major value orientations instead of always considering particular and specific bits of behavior.

To be meaningful the specific, we repeat, must be viewed as an item in the wider context of value orientations.

Generalizing this conception to all such groups as the Spanish-American, we would first hypothesize that *the rate and degree of assimilation of any ethnic group into general dominant American culture will in large part depend upon the degree of goodness of fit of the group's own basic value orientations with those of dominant American culture.*

Turning our attention to our second example of variant values, we note that class differences have greatly concerned American social scientists in the last two decades. The best-known studies of the class structure of the United States are those of W. Lloyd Warner and his associates,[9] but there are also many others with different points of view and in which conclusions different from those of the Warner group are reached. From all the studies we have learned much that Americans have been unwilling to admit or discuss in past years. We know that there are great differences between the classes in attitudes toward education and politics, in association memberships, in family life, in occupational interests and opportunities, in reading habits, in recreational interests, and a host of other things.

Yet in spite of all the differences observed and recorded, there is a tendency in all the studies to assume that all the variation is variation on the same value theme — the so-called American Creed. What is remarked is that the behavior and attitudes of some classes are harmoniously in tune with the generalized creed, whereas those of other classes are off in pitch and limited in range. That the value themes themselves might be different is seldom suggested.

But according to the conceptual scheme of the dominant and variant in cultural orientations, it is assumed at the start that there is a dominant class — in the case of the United States, the middle class — in which adherence to dominant values is marked, but also that there are other classes which hold to variant val-

---

[9] W. Lloyd Warner, *et al.*, *Social Class in America* (Chicago: Science Research Associates, 1949).

ues in much of what they do and believe. As I have suggested elsewhere, the observed behavior of an upper class in an old and declining community shows an adherence to lineality rather than individualism, to past time more than future, and to being or being-in-becoming rather than doing personalities. Also, in some parts of the lower class — a class so heterogeneous and diffuse that it should be "classes" and not just "class" — present-time and being orientations are often combined with either individualism or collaterality.

There has not been sufficient work done to date to state with certainty that this different approach will provide a more accurate knowledge and appraisal of class differences. One study now in progress — a study of the occupational aspirations of a large group of high-school boys in a metropolitan community — shows some promise of demonstrating the existence of value-orientation differences between classes and segments of classes.[10] In another study just completed by Dr. Charles McArthur, it has been shown that on the average public and private school boys give predictably different responses to the pictures in the Murray and Morgan Thematic Apperception Test.[11] For example, on the assumption that public school boys are predominantly middle class and hence future-time and doing oriented, while private school boys — especially those of certain selected schools — are predominantly upper class with past-time and either a being or being-in-becoming orientation, these two predictions were made regarding the variability of responses to the first picture of the test (a small boy is seated before a table on which there lies a violin; the subject is asked to invent a story about him):

1. That more public school boys (now students in a large university) will tell stories to the violin picture in which the parent demands work from the child.

2. That more private school boys will tell violin stories in which the music les-

son is seen by the child as a way to create beauty and/or express or develop himself.

These predictions, as well as many others similar in type but different in content, were borne out by McArthur's data. And, as he himself said: "They constituted a neat demonstration that the attitudes of individuals, as measured by one of the psychologist's best projective tests of personality, can be predicted from a knowledge of the person's subcultural orientations profile."

The variant value orientations which lie behind the structuring of the feminine role in American culture have been as little recognized as those of the different classes. It is pointed out that the woman's role is poorly defined and contradictory in its demands. There is also considerable discussion of the many expectations for women which are markedly different from those for men. But once again the tendency is to view the different patterns of expectations as complementary counterparts which are simply expressing the *same* values in varying ways. Such seems not to be the case. In many respects the feminine role is structured in accord with variant values. In much of the behavior which is expected of wives and mothers the relational orientation emphasized is collaterality rather than individualism, and ideally the being-in-becoming personality orientation is substituted for the doing one. Furthermore, a married woman's participation in the patterns which express a future-time emphasis is mainly a vicarious one. A man in his main role — his occupational one — is autonomous and individualistic, and he is also ideally an action-oriented person. A wife and mother, on the contrary, is supposed always to put the goals of the family group ahead of any of her own individualistic ones. She should also be the one who takes care of the refinements of life — all things intellectual and aesthetic — and leisure-time amusements figure much more prominently in her role — ideally

---

[10] This project is sponsored by the Harvard University Laboratory of Social Relations and is under the direction of Professors Samuel A. Stouffer and Talcott Parsons and the writer.

[11] Charles McArthur, "Cultural Values as Determinants of Imaginal Productions," unpublished Ph.D. thesis, Harvard University, 1952.

at least — than in man's role. She is, in other words, a "culture bearer" and a "status symbol."

There are strains for women in this definition of the feminine role. There is first the problem of the relatively low evaluation of her various activities — motherhood excepted, of course — as compared to the economic pursuits of men who are getting really "important" things done. A still more critical problem is that which results from a woman's having to assume this total role after having been trained as a child and young girl in quite other ways. For training in independence, in accomplishment, and in future-mindedness is given to young girls in almost the same measure as to boys.

Both of these problems and additional ones are treated in some detail in another chapter of this book.[12] They are noted here simply as an illustration of a role which is in large part a variant one. The variation in this case has proved troublesome. In other instances of variant roles the strains are fewer. The man who chooses to be a withdrawn scholar or an artist may often be made to feel that he is outside the main stream of life, but

it is doubtful that he is subject to as many doubts about the value of what he does as are many women. In the main this is because he is creative, whereas the intellectual and aesthetic interests of women have been, to date, chiefly appreciative.

There is much more value variation within our own or any other social system than these few illustrations indicate. The varying roles any individual plays at different times and places may be, and often are, different in the value orientations they express. No individual any more than any whole society can live always in all situations in accord with patterns which allow for expression of only a single dimension of the orientations. One can also note many shifts of emphasis in the range of one orientation or another as between the different historical time periods of a social system. Thus we repeat: If a knowledge of major cultural value orientations is essential to the understanding of social situations and individual personalities (and I would say it certainly is), it is also necessary to know the variant value orientations and their relation to the dominant ones.

Status and Role*

BY RALPH LINTON

In the preceding chapter we discussed the nature of society and pointed out that the functioning of societies depends upon the presence of patterns for reciprocal behavior between individuals or groups of individuals. The polar positions in such patterns of reciprocal behavior are technically known as *statuses*. The term *status*, like the term *culture*, has come to be used with a double significance. A *status*, in the abstract, is a position in a particular pattern. It is thus

quite correct to speak of each individual as having many statuses, since each individual participates in the expression of a number of patterns. However, unless the term is qualified in some way, *the status* of any individual means the sum total of all the statuses which he occupies. It represents his position with relation to the total society. Thus the status of Mr. Jones as a member of his community derives from a combination of all the statuses which he holds as a citizen,

---

[12] See my article, "The American Family and the Feminine Role," below, Chapter IX.

* Pages 98–108 reprinted with permission from Ralph Linton, *The Study of Man* (New York: Appleton-Century-Crofts, Inc., 1936), pp. 113–131; pages 109–110 reprinted with permission from Ralph Linton, *The Cultural Background of Personality* (New York: Appleton-Century-Crofts, Inc., 1945), pp. 77–82.

as an attorney, as a Mason, as a Methodist, as Mrs. Jones's husband, and so on.

A status, as distinct from the individual who may occupy it, is simply a collection of rights and duties. Since these rights and duties can find expression only through the medium of individuals, it is extremely hard for us to maintain a distinction in our thinking between statuses and the people who hold them and exercise the rights and duties which constitute them. The relation between any individual and any status he holds is somewhat like that between the driver of an automobile and the driver's place in the machine. The driver's seat with its steering wheel, accelerator, and other controls is a constant with ever-present potentialities for action and control, while the driver may be any member of the family and may exercise these potentialities very well or very badly.

A *role* represents the dynamic aspect of a status. The individual is socially assigned to a status and occupies it with relation to other statuses. When he puts the rights and duties which constitute the status into effect, he is performing a role. Role and status are quite inseparable, and the distinction between them is of only academic interest. There are no roles without statuses or statuses without roles. Just as in the case of *status,* the term *role* is used with a double significance. Every individual has a series of roles deriving from the various patterns in which he participates and at the same time *a role,* general, which represents the sum total of these roles and determines what he does for his society and what he can expect from it.

Although all statuses and roles derive from social patterns and are integral parts of patterns, they have an independent function with relation to the individuals who occupy particular statuses and exercise their roles. To such individuals the combined status and role represent the minimum of attitudes and behavior which he must assume if he is to participate in the overt expression of the pattern. Status and role serve to reduce the ideal patterns for social life to individual terms. They become models for organizing the attitudes and behavior of the individual so that these will be congruous with those of the other individuals participating in the expression of the pattern. Thus if we are studying football teams in the abstract, the position of quarter-back is meaningless except in relation to the other positions. From the point of view of the quarter-back himself it is a distinct and important entity. It determines where he shall take his place in the line-up and what he shall do in various plays. His assignment to this position at once limits and defines his activities and establishes a minimum of things which he must learn. Similarly, in a social pattern such as that for the employer-employee relationship the statuses of employer and employee define what each has to know and do to put the pattern into operation. The employer does not need to know the techniques involved in the employee's labor, and the employee does not need to know the techniques for marketing or accounting.

It is obvious that, as long as there is no interference from external sources, the more perfectly the members of any society are adjusted to their statuses and roles the more smoothly the society will function. In its attempts to bring about such adjustments every society finds itself caught on the horns of a dilemma. The individual's formation of habits and attitudes begins at birth, and, other things being equal, the earlier his training for a status can begin the more successful it is likely to be. At the same time, no two individuals are alike, and a status which will be congenial to one may be quite uncongenial to another. Also, there are in all social systems certain roles which require more than training for their successful performance. Perfect technique does not make a great violinist, nor a thorough book knowledge of tactics an efficient general. The utilization of the special gifts of individuals may be highly important to society, as in the case of the general, yet these gifts usually show themselves rather late, and to wait upon their manifestation for the assignment of statuses would be to forfeit the advantages to be derived from commencing training early.

Fortunately, human beings are so mutable that almost any normal individual can be trained to the adequate performance of almost any role. Most of the business of living can be conducted on a basis of habit, with little need for intelligence and none for special gifts. Societies have met the dilemma by developing two types of statuses, the *ascribed* and the *achieved*. *Ascribed* statuses are those which are assigned to individuals without reference to their innate differences or abilities. They can be predicted and trained for from the moment of birth. The *achieved* statuses are, as a minimum, those requiring special qualities, although they are not necessarily limited to these. They are not assigned to individuals from birth but are left open to be filled through competition and individual effort. The majority of the statuses in all social systems are of the ascribed type and those which take care of the ordinary day-to-day business of living are practically always of this type.

In all societies certain things are selected as reference points for the ascription of status. The things chosen for this purpose are always of such a nature that they are ascertainable at birth, making it possible to begin the training of the individual for his potential statuses and roles at once. The simplest and most universally used of these reference points is sex. Age is used with nearly equal frequency, since all individuals pass through the same cycle of growth, maturity, and decline, and the statuses whose occupation will be determined by age can be forecast and trained for with accuracy. Family relationships, the simplest and most obvious being that of the child to its mother, are all so used in all societies as reference points for the establishment of a whole series of statuses. Lastly, there is the matter of birth into a particular socially established group, such as a class or caste. The use of this type of reference is common but not universal. In all societies the actual ascription of statuses to the individual is controlled by a series of these reference points which together serve to delimit the field of his future participation in the life of the group.

The division and ascription of statuses with relation to sex seems to be basic in all social systems. All societies prescribe different attitudes and activities to men and to women. Most of them try to rationalize these prescriptions in terms of the physiological differences between the sexes or their different roles in reproduction. However, a comparative study of the statuses ascribed to women and men in different cultures seems to show that while such factors may have served as a starting point for the development of a division the actual ascriptions are almost entirely determined by culture. Even the psychological characteristics ascribed to men and women in different societies vary so much that they can have little physiological basis. Our own idea of women as ministering angels contrasts sharply with the ingenuity of women as torturers among the Iroquois and the sadistic delight they took in the process. Even the last two generations have seen a sharp change in the psychological patterns for women in our own society. The delicate, fainting lady of the middle eighteen-hundreds is as extinct as the dodo.

When it comes to the ascription of occupations, which is after all an integral part of status, we find the differences in various societies even more marked. Arapesh women regularly carry heavier loads than men "because their heads are so much harder and stronger." In some societies women do most of the manual labor; in others, as in the Marquesas, even cooking, housekeeping, and baby-tending are proper male occupations, and women spend most of their time primping. Even the general rule that women's handicap through pregnancy and nursing indicates the more active occupations as male and the less active ones as female has many exceptions. Thus among the Tasmanians seal-hunting was women's work. They swam out to the seal rocks, stalked the animals, and clubbed them.

Tasmanian women also hunted opossums, which required the climbing of large trees.

Although the actual ascription of occupations along sex lines is highly variable, the pattern of sex division is constant. There are very few societies in which every important activity has not been definitely assigned to men or to women. Even when the two sexes coöperate in a particular occupation, the field of each is usually clearly delimited. Thus in Madagascar rice culture the men make the seed beds and terraces and prepare the fields for transplanting. The women do the work of transplanting, which is hard and back-breaking. The women weed the crop, but the men harvest it. The women then carry it to the threshing floors, where the men thresh it while the women winnow it. Lastly, the women pound the grain in mortars and cook it.

When a society takes over a new industry, there is often a period of uncertainty during which the work may be done by either sex, but it soon falls into the province of one or the other. In Madagascar, pottery is made by men in some tribes and by women in others. The only tribe in which it is made by both men and women is one into which the art has been introduced within the last sixty years. I was told that during the fifteen years preceding my visit there had been a marked decrease in the number of male potters, many men who had once practised the art having given it up. The factor of lowered wages, usually advanced as the reason for men leaving one of our occupations when women enter it in force, certainly was not operative here. The field was not overcrowded, and the prices for men's and women's products were the same. Most of the men who had given up the trade were vague as to their reasons, but a few said frankly that they did not like to compete with women. Apparently the entry of women into the occupation had robbed it of a certain amount of prestige. It was no longer quite the thing for a man to be a potter, even though he was a very good one.

The use of age as a reference point for establishing status is as universal as the use of sex. All societies recognize three age groupings as a minimum: child, adult, and old. Certain societies have emphasized age as a basis for assigning status and have greatly amplified the divisions. Thus in certain African tribes the whole male population is divided into units composed of those born in the same years or within two- or three-year intervals. However, such extreme attention to age is unusual, and we need not discuss it here.

The physical differences between child and adult are easily recognizable, and the passage from childhood to maturity is marked by physiological events which make it possible to date it exactly for girls and within a few weeks or months for boys. However, the physical passage from childhood to maturity does not necessarily coincide with the social transfer of the individual from one category to the other. Thus in our own society both men and women remain legally children until long after they are physically adult. In most societies this difference between the physical and social transfer is more clearly marked than in our own. The child becomes a man not when he is physically mature but when he is formally recognized as a man by his society. This recognition is almost always given ceremonial expression in what are technically known as puberty rites. The most important element in these rites is not the determination of physical maturity but that of social maturity. Whether a boy is able to breed is less vital to his society than whether he is able to do a man's work and has a man's knowledge. Actually, most puberty ceremonies include tests of the boy's learning and fortitude, and if the aspirants are unable to pass these they are left in the child status until they can. For those who pass the tests, the ceremonies usually culminate in the transfer to them of certain secrets which the men guard from women and children.

The passage of individuals from adult to aged is harder to perceive. There is no clear physiological line for men, while even women may retain their full physical vigor and their ability to carry on the activities of the adult status for several years after the menopause. The social transfer of men from the adult to the aged group is given ceremonial recognition in a few cultures, as when a father formally surrenders his official position and titles to his son, but such recognition is rare. As for women, there appears to be no society in which the menopause is given ceremonial recognition, although there are a few societies in which it does alter the individual's status. Thus Comanche women, after the menopause, were released from their disabilities with regard to the supernatural. They could handle sacred objects, obtain power through dreams and practise as shamans, all things forbidden to women of bearing age.

The general tendency for societies to emphasize the individual's first change in age status and largely ignore the second is no doubt due in part to the difficulty of determining the onset of old age. However, there are also psychological factors involved. The boy or girl is usually anxious to grow up, and this eagerness is heightened by the exclusion of children from certain activities and knowledge. Also, society welcomes new additions to the most active division of the group, that which contributes most to its perpetuation and well-being. Conversely, the individual who enjoys the thought of growing old is atypical in all societies. Even when age brings respect and a new measure of influence, it means the relinquishment of much that is pleasant. We can see among ourselves that the aging usually refuse to recognize the change until long after it has happened.

In the case of age, as in that of sex, the biological factors involved appear to be secondary to the cultural ones in determining the content of status. There are certain activities which cannot be ascribed to children because children either lack the necessary strength or have not had time to acquire the necessary technical skills. However, the attitudes between parent and child and the importance given to the child in the family structure vary enormously from one culture to another. The status of the child among our Puritan ancestors, where he was seen and not heard and ate at the second table, represents one extreme. At the other might be placed the status of the eldest son of a Polynesian chief. All the *mana* (supernatural power) of the royal line converged upon such a child. He was socially superior to his own father and mother, and any attempt to discipline him would have been little short of sacrilege. I once visited the hereditary chief of a Marquesan tribe and found the whole family camping uncomfortably in their own front yard, although they had a good house built on European lines. Their eldest son, aged nine, had had a dispute with his father a few days before and had tabooed the house by naming it after his head. The family had thus been compelled to move out and could not use it again until he relented and lifted the taboo. As he could use the house himself and eat anywhere in the village, he was getting along quite well and seemed to enjoy the situation thoroughly.

The statuses ascribed to the old in various societies vary even more than those ascribed to children. In some cases they are relieved of all heavy labor and can settle back comfortably to live off their children. In others they perform most of the hard and monotonous tasks which do not require great physical strength, such as the gathering of firewood. In many societies the old women, in particular, take over most of the care of the younger children, leaving the younger women free to enjoy themselves. In some places the old are treated with consideration and respect; in others they are considered a useless incumbrance and removed as soon as they are incapable of heavy labor. In most societies their advice is sought even when little attention is paid to their wishes. This custom has a sound practical basis, for the individual who contrives to live to old age in an uncivilized group has usually been a person of ability and his memory constitutes a sort of reference library to which one can turn for help under all sorts of circumstances.

In certain societies the change from the adult to the old status is made more difficult for the individual by the fact that the patterns for these statuses ascribe different types of personality to each. This was the case among the Comanche, as it seems to have been among most of the Plains tribes. The adult male was a warrior, vigorous, self-reliant, and pushing. Most of his social relationships were phrased in terms of competition. He took what he could get and held what he had without regard to any abstract rights of those weaker than himself. Any willingness to arbitrate differences or to ignore slights was a sign of weakness resulting in loss of prestige. The old man, on the other hand, was expected to be wise and gentle, willing to overlook slights and, if need be, to endure abuse. It was his task to work for the welfare of the tribe, giving sound advice, settling feuds between the warriors, and even preventing his tribe from making new enemies. Young men strove for war and honor, old men strove for peace and tranquillity. There is abundant evidence that among the Comanche the transition was often a difficult one for the individual. Warriors did not prepare for old age, thinking it a better fate to be killed in action. When waning physical powers forced them to assume the new role, many of them did so grudgingly, and those who had strong magic would go on trying to enforce the rights which belonged to the younger status. Such bad old men were a peril to young ones beginning their careers, for they were jealous of them simply because they were young and strong and admired by the women. The medicine power of these young men was still weak, and the old men could and did kill them by malevolent magic. It is significant that although benevolent medicine men might be of any age in Comanche folklore, malevolent ones were always old.

Before passing on, it might be well to mention still another social status which is closely related to the foregoing. This is the status of the dead. We do not think of the dead as still members of the community, and many societies follow us in this, but there are others in which death is simply another transfer, comparable to that from child to adult. When a man dies, he does not leave his society; he merely surrenders one set of rights and duties and assumes another. Thus a Tanala clan has two sections which are equally real to its members, the living and the dead. In spite of rather half-hearted attempts by the living to explain to the dead that they are dead and to discourage their return, they remain an integral part of the clan. They must be informed of all important events, invited to all clan ceremonies, and remembered at every meal. In return they allow themselves to be consulted, take an active and helpful interest in the affairs of the community, and act as highly efficient guardians of the group's mores. They carry over into their new status the conservatism characteristic of the aged, and their invisible presence and constant watchfulness does more than anything else to ensure the good behavior of the living and to discourage innovations. In a neighboring tribe there are even individual statuses among the dead which are open to achievement. Old Betsileo men and women will often promise that, after their deaths, they will give the living specific forms of help in return for specified offerings. After the death of one of these individuals, a monument will be erected and people will come to pray and make offerings there. If the new ghost performs his functions successfully, his worship may grow into a cult and may even have a priest. If he fails in their performance, he is soon forgotten.

Biological relationships are used to determine some statuses in all societies. The mere fact of birth immediately brings the individual within the scope of a whole series of social patterns which relate him to his parents, either real or ascribed, his brothers and sisters, and his parents' relatives. The biological basis for the ascription of these family statuses is likely to blind us to the fact that the physiological factors which may influence their content are almost exactly the same as those affecting the content of sex and age statuses. While there is a special relationship between the young child and its mother, based on the child's dependence on nursing, even this is soon broken off. After the second year any adult woman can do anything for the child that its mother can do, while any adult male can assume the complete role of the father at any time after the child is conceived. Similarly, the physiological factors which might affect the statuses of uncle and nephew, uncle and niece, or brother and sister are identical with those affecting the relations of persons in different age or sex groupings. This lack of physiological determinants may be responsible in part for the extraordinarily wide range of variation in the contents of the statuses ascribed on the basis of biological relationships in various societies.

Actually, the statuses associated with even such a close biological relationship as that of brother and sister are surprisingly varied. In some societies the two are close intimates. In others they avoid each other carefully and cannot even speak to each other except in the presence of a third party who relays the questions and answers. In some systems the eldest child ranks the others regardless of sex and must be respected and obeyed by them. In others the question of dominance is left to be settled by the children themselves, while in still others the youngest child ranks all those who preceded him. Practically every possible arrangement is represented in one society or another, suggesting that we have here a free field for variation, one in which one arrangement will work quite as well as another. The same sort of wide variation is found in the content of all the other statuses based on blood relationship with the exception of those relating to mother and child, and even here there is a fair degree of variation. There are a number of societies in which there is a more or less conscious attempt to break up the child's habits of dependence upon the mother and to alienate the child from her in order to bring it into closer association with its father's relatives. The child is taught that its mother really is

not a member of the family, and hostility between mother and child is encouraged.

Not only do the statuses assigned by different societies to persons standing in the same blood relationships vary markedly, but there is also a high degree of variation in the sorts of blood relationship which are recognized and used as reference points for the assignment of status. Some societies, like our own, tend to recognize only close relatives and to be vague as to the reciprocal rights and duties of any relationship more remote than first cousin. Others select the line of the mother or the father and utilize relationships in this line to remote degrees while ignoring all but the closest relationships in the other line. In a very few cases, relationship in both lines is recognized to remote degrees, with a consequent assignment of status. Where this is the case the statuses based on relationship may actually include a whole tribe and determine the mutual rights and duties of all its members. Thus in certain Australian groups recognized blood relationships are extended to include not only the whole tribe but numerous individuals in other tribes as well. It is said that when a stranger visits such a tribe the old men investigate his genealogy until they find some point in common with one of the genealogies within their own group. When such a point of contact has been established, they can determine the relationship of the newcomer to all the various members of their own group and assign him a series of statuses which immediately fit him into the social body. If they are unable to find such a common point of relationship, they usually kill the stranger simply because they do not know what else to do with him. They have no reference points other than blood relationships by which statuses might be assigned to him.

There is another type of biologically conditioned relationship which is recognized in practically all societies. This is the relationship arising from the more or less continuous sexual association of individuals, i.e., marriage. The real importance of such associations lies in their continuity, in social recognition, and in the new series of blood relationships to which they give rise through the offspring which they produce. Casual or temporary sexual associations usually receive only a negative recognition from society, being ignored when not actually reprehended. Patterns may be developed to govern the behavior of individuals in such casual associations, but these patterns are usually extremely limited in their scope. They only affect the individuals who are directly involved and do not establish new statuses for the members of the families to which the contracting parties belong. Marriage, on the other hand, always establishes a series of such statuses. Thus the parents of a man and his mistress do not become parties to any reciprocal pattern of rights and duties, while the parents of a man and his wife always do become parties to such a pattern.

While relationships arising from sexual association are intrinsically different from those deriving from blood relationships, the two types have become interrelated in all societies. Blood relationships are everywhere used as reference points for delimiting the group of individuals within which marriage relationships may be contracted. This regulation is usually of a negative sort, certain blood relatives being prohibited from marrying but at the same time permitted freedom of choice among individuals not standing in these relationships. However, there are a fair number of societies in which such regulations assume a positive aspect. In such societies a man is not only forbidden to marry certain female relatives, such as his mother or sister, but is also enjoined to marry within a particular group of female relatives, as his mother's brother's or father's sister's daughters. In some cases these prescriptions are so strong that a man may have no alternatives except to marry a particular woman or remain a bachelor.

The causes which underlie such limitations on marriage, technically known as incest regulations, are very imperfectly understood. Since these regulations are of universal occurrence, it seems safe to assume that their causes are everywhere present, but biological factors can be ruled out at once. Close inbreeding is not necessarily injurious. Even when hereditary defects in the strain may make it so, its deleterious results require a long time to manifest themselves. Moreover, the average uncivilized group is small and rarely marries with outsiders. Within a few generations the heredity of its members becomes so uniform that there is little if any biological difference between marriage with a first cousin and marriage with a fourth cousin. Neither are purely social explanations of incest regulations altogether satisfactory, since the forms which these regulations assume are extremely varied. The prohibition of marriage between mother and son is the only one universally present. Marriage between father and daughter is permitted in at least one society, the Azande, while several societies have recognized or even required marriage between brother and sister. This last seems to occur mainly in small ruling groups and seems to be designed to keep privilege and rank rigidly within the group. Thus in Hawaiian royal families brother and sister were required to marry and to cohabit until an heir had been born, although after this they might separate. It seems possible that there are certain psychological factors involved, but these can hardly be strong enough or constant enough to account for the institutionalization of incest regulations. This is proved by the fact that cases of incest between all the prohibited degrees do occur in all societies and that all societies have certain preventive regulations which would be unnecessary if the rules were self-enforcing. Incest regulations, once developed, are a valuable tool for preventing conflicts in the statuses held by individuals, but it is a little hard to imagine their invention for this purpose. They have probably originated from a combination of all these factors.

The bulk of the ascribed statuses in all social systems are parceled out to individuals on the basis of sex, age, and family relationships. However, there are many societies in which purely social factors are also used as a basis of ascription.

There seems to be a general tendency for societies to divide their component individuals into a series of groups or categories and to ascribe to such categories differing degrees of social importance. Such divisions may originate in many different ways. They may grow out of individual differences in technical skill or other abilities, as in the case of craft groups or the aristocracies of certain Indian tribes, membership in which was determined by the individual's war record. They may also originate through the conscious formation of some social unit, such as the first college fraternity or the first business men's club, which is usually followed by the formation of a series of similar units organized upon nearly the same lines. Lastly, such divisions may originate through the subjugation of one society by another society, with the subsequent fusion of both into a single functional unit, as in the case of Old World aristocracies deriving from conquest. Even when the social divisions originate in individual differences of ability, there seems to be a strong tendency for such divisions to become hereditary. The members of a socially favored division try to transmit the advantages they have gained to their offspring and at the same time to prevent the entry into the division of individuals from lower divisions. In many cases these tendencies result in the organization of the society into a series of hereditary classes or castes. Such hereditary units are always used as reference points for the ascription of status.

The factor of social class or caste rarely if ever replaces the factors of sex, age, and biological relationship in the determination of status. Rather, it supplements these, defining the roles of individuals still more clearly. Where the class system is strong, each class becomes almost a society in itself. It will have a series of sex, age, and relationship statuses which are peculiar to its members. These will differ from the statuses of other classes even when both are determined by the same biological factors. Not only is the commoner debarred from the occupation of aristocratic statuses, but the aristocrat is similarly debarred

from the occupation of common statuses. It may be mentioned in passing that this arrangement is not always entirely to the advantage of the members of the upper class. During the nineteenth century the aristocratic prohibition against engaging in trade condemned many aristocrats to genteel poverty.

Feudal Europe offers an excellent example of the ascription of statuses on the basis of social class. A man born into the noble class could look forward to being a bachelor, in the technical sense of a boy beginning his training for knighthood, a squire, and lastly a knight and lord of a manor. The performance of the roles connected with the final status required a long and arduous training both in the use of arms and in administration. The woman born into the same class could also look forward to being lady of a manor, a task which entailed special knowledge and administrative ability fully on a par with that of her husband. A man born into the peasant class could look forward only to becoming a tiller of the soil. He would pass through no statuses corresponding to those of bachelor or squire, and although he might be trained to the use of weapons, these would be different weapons from those used by the knight. The woman born in this class could only look forward to becoming a simple housewife, and her necessary training for this status was limited to a knowledge of housekeeping and baby-tending. The third class in medieval society, the burghers, also had its own series of statuses, the boy looking forward to becoming first an apprentice and then a master training apprentices in turn. All these divergent, class-determined statuses were mutually interdependent, and all contributed to the successful functioning of medieval society. The noble provided protection and direction, the peasant provided food, and the burgher took care of trade and manufactures.

Ascribed statuses, whether assigned according to biological or to social factors, compose the bulk of all social systems. However, all these systems also include a varying number of statuses which are open to individual achievement. It seems as though many statuses of this type were primarily designed to serve as baits for socially acceptable behavior or as escapes for the individual. All societies rely mainly on their ascribed statuses to take care of the ordinary business of living. Most of the statuses which are thrown open to achievement do not touch this business very deeply. The honored ones are extremely satisfying to the individuals who achieve them, but many of them are no more vital to the ordinary functioning of the society than are honorary degrees or inclusions in "Who's Who" among ourselves.

Most societies make only a grudging admission of the fact that a limited number of statuses do require special gifts for their successful performance. Since such gifts rarely manifest themselves in early childhood, these statuses are, of necessity, thrown open to competition. At the same time, the pattern of ascribing all vital statuses is so strong that all societies limit this competition with reference to sex, age, and social affiliations. Even in our own society, where the field open to individual achievement is theoretically unlimited, it is strictly limited in fact. No woman can become President of the United States. Neither could a Negro or an Indian, although there is no formal rule on this point, while a Jew or even a Catholic entering the presidential race would be very seriously handicapped from the outset. Even with regard to achievable statuses which are of much less social importance and which, perhaps, require more specific gifts, the same sort of limited competition is evident. It would be nearly if not quite impossible for either a woman or a Negro to become conductor of our best symphony orchestra, even if better able to perform the duties involved than any one else in America. At the same time, no man could become president of the D. A. R., and it is doubtful whether any man, unless he adopted a feminine *nom de plume,* could even conduct a syndicated column on advice to the lovelorn, a field in which our society assumes, *a priori,* that women have greater skill.

These limitations upon the competition for achieved statuses no doubt entail a certain loss to society. Persons with special talents appear to be mutants and as such are likely to appear in either sex and in any social class. At the same time, the actual loss to societies through this failure to use their members' gifts to the full is probably a good deal less than persons reared in the American tradition would like to believe. Individual talent is too sporadic and too unpredictable to be allowed any important part in the organization of society. Social systems have to be built upon the potentialities of the average individual, the person who has no special gifts or disabilities. Such individuals can be trained to occupy almost any status and to perform the associated role adequately if not brilliantly. The social ascription of a particular status, with the intensive training that such ascription makes possible, is a guarantee that the role will be performed even if the performance is mediocre. If a society waited to have its statuses filled by individuals with special gifts, certain statuses might not be filled at all. The ascription of status sacrifices the possibility of having certain roles performed superlatively well to the certainty of having them performed passably well.

When a social system has achieved a good adjustment to the other sectors of the group's culture and, through these, to the group's environment, it can get along very well without utilizing special gifts. However, as soon as changes within the culture or in the external environment produce maladjustments, it has to recognize and utilize these gifts. The development of new social patterns calls for the individual qualities of thought and initiative, and the freer the rein given to these the more quickly new adjustments can be arrived at. For this reason, societies living under new or changing conditions are usually characterized by a wealth of achievable statuses and by very broad delimitations of the competition for them. Our own now extinct frontier offered an excellent example of this. Here the class lines of the European societies from which the frontier population had been drawn were completely discarded and individuals were given an unprecedented opportunity to find their place in the new society by their own abilities.

As social systems achieve adjustment to their settings, the social value of individual thought and initiative decreases. Thorough training of the component individuals becomes more necessary to the survival and successful functioning of society than the free expression of their individual abilities. Even leadership, which calls for marked ability under conditions of change, becomes largely a matter of routine activities. To ensure successful training, more and more statuses are transferred from the achieved to the ascribed group, and the competition for those which remain is more and more rigidly delimited. To put the same thing in different terms, individual opportunities decrease. There is not an absolute correlation between the degree of adjustment of a social system to its setting and the limitation of individual opportunity. Thus if the group attaches a high value to individual initiative and individual rights, certain statuses may be left open to competition when their ascription would result in greater social efficiency. However, well-adjusted societies are, in general, characterized by a high preponderance of ascribed over achieved statuses, and increasing perfection of adjustment usually goes hand in hand with increasing rigidity of the social system.

Americans have been trained to attach such high values to individual initiative and achievement that they tend to look down upon societies which are rigidly organized and to pity the persons who live in them. However, the members of a society whose statuses are mainly prescribed are no less happy than ourselves and considerably more at peace. It would never occur to an orthodox Hindu that he was to be pitied because he could not change his caste. His whole life is arranged and oriented in terms of caste, and if he ever envies the members of other castes the emotion is on a par with our own envy of some animal's obvious comfort or satisfaction. His religion provides him with rationalizations of the whole system and with an explanation of his presence in the caste as a result of his soul's evolutionary status. It also holds out the hope of a better position in his next incarnation if his work in this is properly done. As a caste member his social and even emotional needs are amply provided for. There are even a small series of achievable statuses open to him if he is ambitious. He may become a member of the caste's governing body or the best goldsmith in a group of goldsmiths, admired by those whose admiration is based on a thorough knowledge of the work. In any struggle for advancement he knows exactly who his competitors are and what it is he wants to attain. He is much less likely to be disappointed than a man living under our own system, where every other man may be a rival and where the limits for ambition are not socially defined.

In India the idea of ceremonial pollution makes social intercourse between the castes difficult; but in societies which have strong class lines, without this idea, the presence of classes actually makes for ease of social intercourse. Here also, classes serve to delimit fields of competition. Where there can be no rivalry in vital matters and no social climbing, snubbing becomes unnecessary and indeed meaningless. Social status is something fixed and understood by both parties, so it can be ignored under circumstances where it has no direct bearing. Members of different classes can form friendships which are the stronger because their interests can never clash and they can evaluate each other as human beings with a clarity unclouded by fear of rivalry. Membership in a rigidly organized society may deprive the individual of opportunities to exercise his particular gifts, but it gives him an emotional security which is almost unknown among ourselves. Which of these is best or which makes for the greatest happiness to the greatest number the reader must decide for himself.

A particular status within a social system can be occupied, and its associated role known and exercised, by a number of individuals simultaneously. In fact, this is the normal condition. Thus every society ordinarily includes several persons who occupy the status of adult male and adhere to the adult male role. It similarly includes a number of persons who occupy the status of father in the organizations of the particular family groups to which they belong. Conversely, the same individual can and does occupy simultaneously a series of statuses each of which derives from one of the systems of organization in which he participates. He not only occupies these statuses, but he also knows the roles pertaining to them. However, he can never exercise all these roles simultaneously. Such roles are a constant element in his participation in the covert culture of his society, but function intermittently with respect to his participation in its overt culture. In other words, although he occupies statuses and knows roles at all times, he operates sometimes in terms of one status and its role, sometimes in those of another. The status in terms of which an individual is operating is his *active status* at that particular point in time. His other statuses are, for the time being, *latent statuses*. The roles associated with such latent statuses are temporarily held in abeyance, but they are integral parts of the individual's culture equipment.

This formulation can be made clearer by an example. Let us suppose that a man spends the day working as clerk in a store. While he is behind the counter, his active status is that of a clerk, established by his position in our society's system of specialized occupations. The role associated with this status provides him with patterns for his relations with customers. These patterns will be well known both to him and to the customers and will enable them to transact business with a minimum of delay or misunderstanding. When he retires to the rest room for a smoke and meets other employees there, his clerk status becomes latent and he assumes another active status based upon his position in the association group composed of the store's employees as a whole. In this status his

relations with other employees will be governed by a different set of culture patterns from those employed in his relations with customers. Moreover, since he probably knows most of the other employees, his exercise of these culture patterns will be modified by his personal likes and dislikes of certain individuals and by considerations of their and his own relative positions in the prestige series of the store association's members. When closing time comes, he lays aside both his clerk and store association statuses and, while on the way home, operates simply in terms of his status with respect to the society's age-sex system. Thus if he is a young man he will at least feel that he ought to get up and give his seat to a lady, while if he is an old one he will be quite comfortable about keeping it. As soon as he arrives at his house, a new set of statuses will be activated. These statuses derive from the kinship ties which relate him to various members of the family group. In pursuance of the roles associated with these family statuses he will try to be cordial to his mother-in-law, affectionate to his wife and a stern disciplinarian to Junior, whose report card marks a new low. If it happens to be lodge night, all his familial statuses will become latent at about eight o'clock. As soon as he enters the lodge room and puts on his uniform as Grand Imperial Lizard, in the Ancient Order of Dinosaurs, he assumes a new status, one which has been latent since the last lodge meeting, and performs in terms of its role until it is time for him to take off his uniform and go home.

The fact that the individual's various statuses are activated at different times prevents a head-on collision between the roles associated with them. At most, the overt behavior which is part of the role connected with one status may negate the results of the overt behavior which is part of another role. The behaviors themselves will not conflict because of the time differential. Moreover, the roles associated with the statuses within a single system are usually fairly well adjusted to one another and produce no conflicts as long as the individual is operating within this system. This also holds for statuses within different systems whenever these statuses are of such a sort that they normally converge upon the same individuals. Thus in any society the roles of adult male, of father, of craft specialist, of friend, and so on, will normally be adjusted to one another in spite of the different systems from which they derive. Such adjustments, of course, are not the result of conscious planning. They are developed through the experience of individuals who have occupied such series of statuses simultaneously and have gradually eliminated most of the conflicts through a process of trial and error. Thus if patterns of formal friendship are borrowed from some other society, such patterns will soon be modified in such ways that there will be no conflict between them and the patterns already established by the local system of family organization.

In the rare cases in which, through some accident, statuses whose roles are fundamentally incompatible converge upon the same individual, we have the material of high tragedy. While most societies feel little sympathy for the individual who is trying to escape the performance of certain of his roles, all can sympathize with the dilemma of a person who must choose between statuses and roles which are equally valid. Such dilemmas are a favorite theme in the literature of the more sophisticated or introspective societies. The tragedy of the House of Oedipus and the closing episodes of the Niebelungenlied are classical examples, while at the level of simpler folklore we have the Scottish story of the man who finds himself host to his brother's murderer. In each of these cases the individual upon whom the incompatible roles converge meets the problem by the familiar pattern of operating in terms of different statuses at different times, even though recognizing that the associated roles will, in their performance, negate each other's results. Thus in the Scottish story the brother, as host, conducts the murderer safely beyond clan territory then, as brother to the victim, engages him in combat to the death.

Such conflicts rarely arise in primary societies or even within larger social groupings which have persisted for some time and developed well-integrated cultures. However, they may become fairly frequent under the conditions existing in our current society. Under the necessity of reorganizing our social structure to meet the needs of a new technology and of a spatial mobility unparalleled in human history, our inherited system of statuses and roles is breaking down; while a new system, compatible with the actual conditions of modern life, has not yet emerged. The individual thus finds himself frequently confronted by situations in which he is uncertain both of his own statuses and roles and of those of others. He is not only compelled to make choices but also can feel no certainty that he has chosen correctly and that the reciprocal behavior of others will be that which he anticipates on the basis of the statuses which he has assumed that they occupy. This results in numerous disappointments and frustrations.

Continuities and Discontinuities in Cultural Conditioning*

BY RUTH BENEDICT

All cultures must deal in one way or another with the cycle of growth from infancy to adulthood. Nature has posed the situation dramatically: on the one hand, the new born baby, physiologically vulnerable, unable to fend for itself, or to participate of its own initiative in the life of the group, and, on the other, the

* By permission from *A Study of Interpersonal Relations*, edited by Patrick Mullahy. Copyright, 1949, by Hermitage Press, Inc. Published by Hermitage Press, Inc., New York.

adult man or woman. Every man who rounds out his human potentialities must have been a son first and a father later and the two roles are physiologically in great contrast; he must first have been dependent upon others for his very existence and later he must provide such security for others. This discontinuity in the life cycle is a fact of nature and is inescapable. Facts of nature, however, in any discussion of human problems, are ordinarily read off not at their bare minimal but surrounded by all the local accretions of behavior to which the student of human affairs has become accustomed in his own culture. For that reason it is illuminating to examine comparative material from other societies in order to get a wider perspective on our own special accretions. The anthropologist's role is not to question the facts of nature, but to insist upon the interposition of a middle term between "nature" and "human behavior"; his role is to analyse that term, to document local man-made doctorings of nature and to insist that these doctorings should not be read off in any one culture as nature itself. Although it is a fact of nature that the child becomes a man, the way in which this transition is effected varies from one society to another, and no one of these particular cultural bridges should be regarded as the "natural" path to maturity.

From a comparative point of view our culture goes to great extremes in emphasizing contrasts between the child and the adult. The child is sexless, the adult estimates his virility by his sexual activities; the child must be protected from the ugly facts of life, the adult must meet them without psychic catastrophe; the child must obey, the adult must command this obedience. These are all dogmas of our culture, dogmas which in spite of the facts of nature, other cultures commonly do not share. In spite of the physiological contrasts between child and adult these are cultural accretions.

It will make the point clearer if we consider one habit in our own culture in regard to which there is not this discontinuity of conditioning. With the greatest clarity of purpose and economy of training, we achieve our goal of conditioning everyone to eat three meals a day. The baby's training in regular food periods begin at birth and no crying of the child and no inconvenience to the mother is allowed to interfere. We gauge the child's physiological make-up and at first allow it food oftener than adults, but, because our goal is firmly set and our training consistent, before the child is two years old it has achieved the adult schedule. From the point of view of other cultures this is as startling as the fact of three-year-old babies perfectly at home in deep water is to us. Modesty is another sphere in which our child training is consistent and economical; we waste no time in clothing the baby and in contrast to many societies where the child runs naked till it is ceremonially given its skirt or its public sheath at adolescence, the child's training fits it precisely for adult conventions.

In neither of these aspects of behavior is there need for an individual in our culture to embark before puberty, at puberty or at some later date upon a course of action which all his previous training has tabued. He is spared the unsureness inevitable in such a transition.

The illustration I have chosen may appear trivial, but in larger and more important aspects of behavior, our methods are obviously different. Because of the great variety of child training in different families in our society, I might illustrate continuity of conditioning from individual life histories in our culture, but even these, from a comparative point of view, stop far short of consistency and I shall therefore confine myself to describing arrangements in other cultures in which training which with us is idiosyncratic, is accepted and traditional and does not therefore involve the same possibility of conflict. I shall choose childhood rather than infant and nursing situations not because the latter do not vary strikingly in different cultures but because they are nevertheless more circumscribed by the baby's physiological needs than is its later training. Childhood situations provide an excellent field in which to illustrate the range of cultural adjustments which are possible within a universally given, but not so drastic, set of physiological facts.

The major discontinuity in the life cycle is of course that the child who is at one point a son must later be a father. These roles in our society are strongly differentiated; a good son is tractable, and does not assume adult responsibilities; a good father provides for his children and should not allow his authority to be flouted. In addition the child must be sexless so far as his family is concerned, whereas the father's sexual role is primary in the family. The individual in one role must revise his behavior from almost all points of view when he assumes the second role.

I shall select for discussion three such contrasts that occur in our culture between the individual's role as child and as father: 1. responsible — non-responsible status role; 2. dominance — submission; 3. contrasted sexual role. It is largely upon our cultural commitments to these three contrasts that the discontinuity in the life cycle of an individual in our culture depends.

1. RESPONSIBLE — NON-RESPONSIBLE STATUS ROLE

The techniques adopted by societies which achieve continuity during the life cycle in this sphere in no way differ from those we employ in our uniform conditioning to three meals a day. They are merely applied to other areas of life. We think of the child as wanting to play and the adult as having to work, but in many societies the mother takes the baby daily in her shawl or carrying net to the garden or to gather roots, and adult labor is seen even in infancy from the pleasant security of its position in close contact with its mother. When the child can run about it accompanies its parents still, doing tasks which are essential and yet suited to its powers, and its dichotomy between work and play is not different from that its parents recognize, namely the distinction between the busy day and the free evening. The tasks it is asked to perform are graded to its powers and its elders wait quietly by, not offering to do the task in

the child's place. Everyone who is familiar with such societies has been struck by the contrast with our child training. Dr. Ruth Underhill tells me of sitting with a group of Papago elders in Arizona when the man of the house turned to his little three-year-old granddaughter and asked her to close the door. The door was heavy and hard to shut. The child tried, but it did not move. Several times the grandfather repeated, "Yes, close the door." No one jumped to the child's assistance. No one took the responsibility away from her. On the other hand there was no impatience, for after all the child was small. They sat gravely waiting till the child succeeded and her grandfather gravely thanked her. It was assumed that the task would not be asked of her unless she could perform it, and having been asked the responsibility was hers alone just as if she were a grown woman.

The essential point of such child training is that the child is from infancy continuously conditioned to responsible social participation while at the same time the tasks that are expected of it are adapted to its capacity. The contrast with our society is very great. A child does not make any labor contribution to our industrial society except as it competes with an adult; its work is not measured against its own strength and skill but against high-geared industrial requirements. Even when we praise a child's achievement in the home we are outraged if such praise is interpreted as being of the same order as praise of adults. The child is praised because the parent feels well disposed, regardless of whether the task is well done by adult standards, and the child acquires no sensible standard by which to measure its achievement. The gravity of a Cheyenne Indian family ceremoniously making a feast out of the little boy's first snowbird is at the furthest remove from our behavior. At birth the little boy was presented with a toy bow, and from the time he could run about serviceable bows suited to his stature were specially made for him by the man of the family. Animals and birds were taught him in a graded series beginning with those most easily taken, and as he brought in his first of each species his family duly made a feast of it, accepting his contribution as gravely as the buffalo his father brought. When he finally killed a buffalo, it was only the final step of his childhood conditioning, not a new adult role with which his childhood experience had been at variance.

The Canadian Ojibwa show clearly what results can be achieved. This tribe gains its livelihood by winter trapping and the small family of father, mother and children live during the long winter alone on their great frozen hunting grounds. The boy accompanies his father and brings in his catch to his sister as his father does to his mother; the girl prepares the meat and skins for him just as his mother does for her husband. By the time the boy is 12, he may have set his own line of traps on a hunting territory of his own and return to his parents' house only once in several months — still bringing the meat and skins to his sister. The young child is taught consistently that it has only itself to rely upon in life, and this is as true in the dealings it will have with the supernatural as in the business of getting a livelihood. This attitude he will accept as a successful adult just as he accepted it as a child.[1]

2. DOMINANCE — SUBMISSION

Dominance — submission is the most striking of those categories of behavior where like does not respond to like but where one type of behavior stimulates the opposite response. It is one of the most prominent ways in which behavior is patterned in our culture. When it obtains between classes, it may be nourished by continuous experience; the difficulty in its use between children and adults lies in the fact that an individual conditioned to one set of behavior in childhood must adopt the opposite as an adult. Its opposite is a pattern of approximately identical reciprocal behavior, and societies which rely upon continuous conditioning characteristically invoke this pattern. In some primitive cultures the very terminology of address between

father and son, and more commonly, between grandfather and grandson or uncle and nephew, reflects this attitude. In such kinship terminologies one reciprocal expresses each of these relationships so that son and father, for instance, exchange the same term with one another, just as we exchange the same term with a cousin. The child later will exchange it with his son. "Father — son," therefore, is a continuous relationship he enjoys throughout life. The same continuity, backed up by verbal reciprocity, occurs far oftener in the grandfather-grandson relationship or that of mother's brother-sister's son. When these are "joking" relationships, as they often are, travellers report wonderingly upon the liberties and pretensions of tiny toddlers in their dealings with these family elders. In place of our dogma of respect to elders such societies employ in these cases a reciprocity as nearly identical as may be. The teasing and practical joking the grandfather visits upon his grandchild, the grandchild returns in like coin; he would be led to believe that he failed in propriety if he did not give like for like. If the sister's son has right of access without leave to his mother's brother's possessions, the mother's brother has such rights also to the child's possessions. They share reciprocal privileges and obligations which in our society can develop only between age mates.

From the point of view of our present discussion, such kinship conventions allow the child to put in practice from infancy the same forms of behavior which it will rely upon as an adult; behavior is not polarized into a general requirement of submission for the child and dominance for the adult.

It is clear from the techniques described above by which the child is conditioned to a responsible status role that these depend chiefly upon arousing in the child the desire to share responsibility in adult life. To achieve this little stress is laid upon obedience but much stress upon approval and praise. Punishment is very commonly regarded as quite outside the realm of possibility, and na-

---

[1] Landes, Ruth, *The Ojibwa Woman*, Part 1, Youth — Columbia University Contributions to Anthropology, Volume **XXXI**.

tives in many parts of the world have drawn the conclusion from our usual disciplinary methods that white parents do not love their children. If the child is not required to be submissive however, many occasions for punishment melt away; a variety of situations which call for it do not occur. Many American Indian tribes are especially explicit in rejecting the ideal of a child's submissive or obedient behavior. Prince Maximilian von Wied who visited the Crow Indians over a hundred years ago describes a father's boasting about his young son's intractability even when it was the father himself who was flouted; "He will be a man," his father said. He would have been baffled at the idea that his child should show behavior which would obviously make him appear a poor creature in the eyes of his fellows if he used it as an adult. Dr. George Devereaux tells me of a special case of such an attitude among the Mohave at the present time. The child's mother was white and protested to its father that he must take action when the child disobeyed and struck him. "But why?" the father said, "he is little. He cannot possibly injure me." He did not know of any dichotomy according to which an adult expects obedience and a child must accord it. If his child had been docile he would simply have judged that it would become a docile adult — an eventuality of which he would not have approved.

Child training which brings about the same result is common also in other areas of life than that of reciprocal kinship obligations between child and adult. There is a tendency in our culture to regard every situation as having in it the seeds of a dominance-submission relationship. Even where dominance-submission is patently irrelevant we read in the dichotomy, assuming that in every situation there must be one person dominating another. On the other hand some cultures, even when the situation calls for leadership do not see it in terms of dominance-submission. To do justice to this attitude it would be necessary to describe their political and especially their economic arrangements, for such an attitude to per-

sist must certainly be supported by economic mechanisms that are congruent with it. But it must also be supported by — or what comes to the same thing, express itself in — child training and familial situations.

3. CONTRASTED SEXUAL ROLE

Continuity of conditioning in training the child to assume responsibility and to behave no more submissively than adults is quite possible in terms of the child's physiological endowment if his participation is suited to his strength. Because of the late development of the child's reproductive organs continuity of conditioning in sex experience presents a difficult problem. So far as their belief that the child is anything but a sexless being is concerned, they are probably more nearly right than we are with an opposite dogma. But the great break is presented by the universally sterile unions before puberty and the presumably fertile ones after maturation. This physiological fact no amount of cultural manipulation can minimize or alter, and societies therefore which stress continuous conditioning most strongly sometimes do not expect children to be interested in sex experience until they have matured physically. This is striking among American Indian tribes like the Dakota; adults observe great privacy in sex acts and in no way stimulate children's sexual activity. There need be no discontinuity, in the sense in which I have used the term, in such a program if the child is taught nothing it does not have to unlearn later. In such cultures adults view children's experimentation as in no way wicked or dangerous but merely as innocuous play which can have no serious consequences. In some societies such play is minimal and the children manifest little interest in it. But the same attitude may be taken by adults in societies where such play is encouraged and forms a major activity among small children. This is true among most of the Melanesian cultures of Southwest New Guinea; adults go as far as to laugh off sexual affairs within the prohibited class if the children are not mature, saying that since they cannot marry there can be no harm done.

It is this physiological fact of the difference between children's sterile unions and adults' presumably fertile sex relations which must be kept in mind in order to understand the different mores which almost always govern sex expression in children and in adults in the same culture. A great many cultures with pre-adolescent sexual license require marital fidelity and a great many which value pre-marital virginity in either male or female arrange their marital life with great license. Continuity in sex experience is complicated by factors which it was unnecessary to consider in the problems previously discussed. The essential problem is not whether or not the child's sexuality is consistently exploited — for even where such exploitation is favored in the majority of cases the child must seriously modify his behavior at puberty or at marriage. Continuity in sex expression means rather that the child is taught nothing it must unlearn later. If the cultural emphasis is upon sexual pleasure the child who is continuously conditioned will be encouraged to experiment freely and pleasurably, as among the Marquesans;[2] if emphasis is upon reproduction, as among the Zuni of New Mexico, childish sex proclivities will not be exploited for the only important use which sex is thought to serve in his culture is not yet possible to him. The important contrast with our child training is that although a Zuni child is impressed with the wickedness of premature sex experimentation he does not run the risk as in our culture of associating this wickedness with sex itself rather than with sex at his age. The adult in our culture has often failed to unlearn the wickedness or the dangerousness of sex, a lesson which was impressed upon him strongly in his most formative years.

DISCONTINUITY IN CONDITIONING

Even from this very summary statement of continuous conditioning the economy of such mores is evident. In spite of the obvious advantages, however, there are difficulties in its way. Many primitive societies expect as different behavior from an individual as child and as adult as we do, and such discontinuity involves a presumption of strain.

Many societies of this type however minimize strain by the techniques they employ, and some techniques are more successful than others in ensuring the individual's functioning without conflict. It is from this point of view that age-grade societies reveal their fundamental significance. Age-graded cultures characteristically demand different behavior of the individual at different times of his life and persons of a like age-grade are grouped into a society whose activities are all oriented toward the behavior desired at that age. Individuals "graduate" publicly and with honor from one of these groups to another. Where age society members are enjoined to loyalty and mutual support, and are drawn not only from the local group but from the whole tribe as among the Arapaho, or even from other tribes as among the Waga-waga of Southeast New Guinea, such an institution has many advantages in eliminating conflicts among local groups and fostering intratribal peace. This seems to be also a factor in the tribal military solidarity of the similarly organized Masai of East Africa. The point that is of chief interest for our present discussion however is that by this means an individual who at any time takes on a new set of duties and virtues is supported not only by a solid phalanx of age mates but by the traditional prestige of the organized "secret" society into which he has now graduated. Fortified in this way, individuals in such cultures often swing between remarkable extremes of opposite behavior without apparent psychic threat. For example, the great majority exhibit prideful and nonconflicted behavior at each stage in the life cycle even when a prime of life devoted to passionate and aggressive head hunting must be followed by a later life dedicated to ritual and to mild and peaceable civic virtues.[3]

---

[2] Ralph Linton, class notes on the Marquesans.
[3] Henry Elkin, manuscript on the Arapaho.

Our chief interest here, however, is in discontinuity which primarily affects the child. In many primitive societies such discontinuity has been fostered not because of economic or political necessity or because such discontinuity provides for a socially valuable division of labor, but because of some conceptual dogma. The most striking of these are the Australian and Papuan cultures where the ceremony of the "Making of Man" flourishes. In such societies it is believed that men and women have opposite and conflicting powers, and male children, who are of undefined status, must be initiated into the male role. In Central Australia the boy child is of the woman's side and women are tabu in the final adult stages of tribal ritual. The elaborate and protracted initiation ceremonies of the Arunta therefore snatch the boy from the mother, dramatize his gradual repudiation of her. In a final ceremony he is reborn as a man out of the men's ceremonial "baby pouch." The men's ceremonies are ritual statements of a masculine solidarity, carried out by fondling one another's *churingas*, the material symbol of each man's life, and by letting out over one another blood drawn from their veins. After this warm bond among men has been established through the ceremonies, the boy joins the men in the men's house and participates in tribal rites.[4] The enjoined discontinuity has been tribally bridged.

West of the Fly River in southern New Guinea there is a striking development of this Making of Men cult which involves a childhood period of passive homosexuality. Among the Keraki[5] it is thought that no boy can grow to full stature without playing the role for some years. Men slightly older take the active role, and the older man is a jealous partner. The life cycle of the Keraki Indians includes, therefore, in succession, passive homosexuality, active homosexuality and heterosexuality. The Keraki believe that pregnancy will result from post-pubertal passive homosexuality and see evidences of such practices in any fat man whom even as an old man, they may kill or drive out of the tribe because of their fear. The ceremony that is of interest in connection with the present discussion takes place at the end of the period of passive homosexuality. This ceremony consists in burning out the possibility of pregnancy from the boy by pouring lye down his throat, after which he has no further protection if he gives way to the practice. There is no technique for ending active homosexuality, but this is not explicitly tabu for older men; heterosexuality and children however are highly valued. Unlike the neighboring Marindanim who share their homosexual practices, Keraki husband and wife share the same house and work together in the gardens.

I have chosen illustrations of discontinuous conditioning where it is not too much to say that the cultural institutions furnish adequate support to the individual as he progresses from role to role or interdicts the previous behavior in a summary fashion. The contrast with arrangements in our culture is very striking, and against this background of social arrangements in other cultures the adolescent period of *Sturm und Drang* with which we are so familiar becomes intelligible in terms of our discontinuous cultural institutions and dogmas rather than in terms of physiological necessity. It is even more pertinent to consider these comparative facts in relation to maladjusted persons in our culture who are said to be fixated at one or another pre-adult level. It is clear that if we were to look at our social arrangements as an outsider, we should infer directly from our family institutions and habits of child training that many individuals would not "put off childish things"; we should have to say that our adult activity demands traits that are interdicted in children, and that far from redoubling efforts to help children bridge this gap, adults in our culture put all the blame on the child when he fails to manifest spontaneously the new behavior or,

[4] Spencer, B., and Gillen, F. J., *The Arunta*; N. Y., Macmillan, 1927 (2 vols.). Róheim, Géza, Psycho-Analysis of Primitive Cultural Types. *Internat. J. Psychoanal.* (1932) 13:1–224 — in particular, Chapter III, on the Aranda, The Children of the Desert.

[5] Williams, Francis E., *Papuans of the Trans-Fly*; Oxford, 1936.

overstepping the mark, manifests it with untoward belligerence. It is not surprising that in such a society many individuals fear to use behavior which has up to that time been under a ban and trust instead, though at great psychic cost, to attitudes that have been exercised with approval during their formative years.

Insofar as we invoke a physiological scheme to account for these neurotic adjustments we are led to overlook the possibility of developing social institutions which would lessen the social cost we now pay; instead we elaborate a set of dogmas which prove inapplicable under other social conditions.

Age and Sex in the Social Structure of the United States*

BY TALCOTT PARSONS

In our society age grading does not to any great extent, except for the educational system, involve formal age categorization, but is interwoven with other structural elements. In relation to these, however, it constitutes an important connecting link and organizing point of reference in many respects. The most important of these for present purposes are kinship structure, formal education, occupation and community participation. In most cases the age lines are not rigidly specific, but approximate; this does not, however, necessarily lessen their structural significance.

In all societies the initial status of every normal individual is that of child in a given kinship unit. In our society, however, this universal starting point is used in distinctive ways. Although in early childhood the sexes are not usually sharply differentiated, in many kinship systems a relatively sharp segregation of children begins very early. Our own society is conspicuous for the extent to which children of both sexes are in many fundamental respects treated alike. This is particularly true of both privileges and responsibilities. The primary distinctions within the group of dependent siblings are those of age. Birth order as such is notably neglected as a basis of discrimination; a child of eight and a child of five have essentially the privileges and responsibilities appropriate to their re-

spective age levels without regard to what older, intermediate, or younger siblings there may be. The preferential treatment of an older child is not to any significant extent differentiated if and because he happens to be the first born.

There are, of course, important sex differences in dress and in approved play interest and the like, but if anything, it may be surmised that in the urban upper middle classes these are tending to diminish. Thus, for instance, play overalls are essentially similar for both sexes. What is perhaps the most important sex discrimination is more than anything else a reflection of the differentiation of adult sex roles. It seems to be a definite fact that girls are more apt to be relatively docile, to conform in general according to adult expectations, to be "good," whereas boys are more apt to be recalcitrant to discipline and defiant of adult authority and expectations. There is really no feminine equivalent of the expression "bad boy." It may be suggested that this is at least partially explained by the fact that it is possible from an early age to initiate girls directly into many important aspects of the adult feminine role. Their mothers are continually about the house and the meaning of many of the things they are doing is relatively tangible and easily understandable to a child. It is also possible for the daughter to participate actively and use-

---

* Reprinted from *American Sociological Review*, VII (October 1942), 604–616.

fully in many of these activities. Especially in the urban middle classes, however, the father does not work in the home and his son is not able to observe his work or to participate in it from an early age. Furthermore many of the masculine functions are of a relatively abstract and intangible character, such that their meaning must remain almost wholly inaccessible to a child. This leaves the boy without a tangible meaningful model to emulate and without the possibility of a gradual initiation into the activities of the adult male role. An important verification of this analysis could be provided through the study in our own society of the rural situation. It is my impression that farm boys tend to be "good" in a sense in which that is not typical of their urban brothers.

The equality of privileges and responsibilities, graded only by age but not by birth order, is extended to a certain degree throughout the whole range of the life cycle. In full adult status, however, it is seriously modified by the asymmetrical relation of the sexes to the occupational structure. One of the most conspicuous expressions and symbols of the underlying equality, however, is the lack of sex differentiation in the process of formal education, so far, at least, as it is not explicitly vocational. Up through college differentiation seems to be primarily a matter on the one hand of individual ability, on the other hand of class status, and only to a secondary degree of sex differentiation. One can certainly speak of a strongly established pattern that all children of the family have a "right" to a good education, rights which are graduated according to the class status of the family but also to individual ability. It is only in post-graduate professional education, with its direct connection with future occupational careers, that sex discrimination becomes conspicuous. It is particularly important that this equality of treatment exists in the sphere of liberal education since throughout the social structure of our society there is a strong tendency to segregate the occupational sphere from one in which certain more generally human patterns and values are dominant, particularly in informal social life and the realm of what will here be called community participation.

Although this pattern of equality of treatment is present in certain fundamental respects at all age levels, at the transition from childhood to adolescence new features appear which disturb the symmetry of sex roles while still a second set of factors appears with marriage and the acquisition of full adult status and responsibilities.

An indication of the change is the practice of chaperonage, through which girls are given a kind of protection and supervision by adults to which boys of the same age group are not subjected. Boys, that is, are chaperoned only in their relations with girls of their own class. This modification of equality of treatment has been extended to the control of the private lives of women students in boarding schools and colleges. Of undoubted significance is the fact that it has been rapidly declining not only in actual effectiveness but as an ideal pattern. Its prominence in our recent past, however, is an important manifestation of the importance of sex role differentiation. Important light might be thrown upon its functions by systematic comparison with the related phenomena in Latin countries where this type of asymmetry has been far more sharply accentuated than in this country in the more modern period.

It is at the point of emergence into adolescence that there first begins to develop a set of patterns and behavior phenomena which involve a highly complex combination of age grading and sex role elements. These may be referred to together as the phenomena of the "youth culture." Certain of its elements are present in pre-adolescence and others in the adult culture. But the peculiar combination in connection with this particular age level is unique and highly distinctive for American society.

Perhaps the best single point of reference for characterizing the youth culture lies in its contrast with the dominant pattern of the adult male role. By contrast with the emphasis on responsibility in this role, the orientation of the youth culture is more or less specifically irresponsible. One of its dominant notes is "having a good time" in relation to which there is a particularly strong emphasis on social activities in company with the opposite sex. A second predominant characteristic on the male side lies in the prominence of athletics, which is an avenue of achievement and competition which stands in sharp contrast to the primary standards of adult achievement in professional and executive capacities. Negatively, there is a strong tendency to repudiate interest in adult things and to feel at least a certain recalcitrance to the pressure of adult expectations and discipline. In addition to, but including, athletic prowess the typical pattern of the male youth culture seems to lay emphasis on the value of certain qualities of attractiveness, especially in relation to the opposite sex. It is very definitely a rounded humanistic pattern rather than one of competence in the performance of specified functions. Such stereotypes as the "swell guy" are significant of this. On the feminine side there is correspondingly a strong tendency to accentuate sexual attractiveness in terms of various versions of what may be called the "glamor girl" pattern.[1] Although these patterns defining roles tend to polarize sexually — for instance, as between star athlete and socially popular girl — yet on a certain level they are complementary, both em-

phasizing certain features of a total personality in terms of the direct expression of certain values rather than of instrumental significance.

One further feature of this situation is the extent to which it is crystallized about the system of formal education.[2] One might say that the principal centers of prestige dissemination are the colleges, but that many of the most distinctive phenomena are to be found in high schools throughout the country. It is of course of great importance that liberal education is not primarily a matter of vocational training in the United States. The individual status on the curricular side of formal education is, however, in fundamental ways linked up with adult expectations, and doing "good work" is one of the most important sources of parental approval. Because of secondary institutionalization this approval is extended into various spheres distinctive of the youth culture. But it is notable that the youth culture has a strong tendency to develop in directions which are either on the borderline of parental approval or beyond the pale, in such matters as sex behavior, drinking and various forms of frivolous and irresponsible behavior. The fact that adults have attitudes to these things which are often deeply ambivalent and that on such occasions as college reunions they may outdo the younger generation, as, for instance, in drinking, is of great significance, but probably structurally secondary to the youth-versus-adult

---

[1] Perhaps the most dramatic manifestation of this tendency lies in the prominence of the patterns of "dating," for instance among college women. As shown by an unpublished participant-observer study made at one of the Eastern Women's colleges, perhaps the most important single basis of informal prestige rating among the residents of a dormitory lies in their relative dating success — though this is by no means the only basis. One of the most striking features of the pattern is the high publicity given to the "achievements" of the individual in a sphere where traditionally in the culture a rather high level of privacy is sanctioned — it is interesting that once an engagement has occurred a far greater amount of privacy is granted. The standards of rating cannot be said to be well integrated, though there is an underlying consistency in that being in demand by what the group regards as desirable men is perhaps the main standard.

It is true that the "dating" complex need not be exclusively bound up with the "glamor girl" stereotype of ideal feminine personality — the "good companion" type may also have a place. Precisely, however, where the competitive aspect of dating is most prominent the glamor pattern seems heavily to predominate, as does, on the masculine side, a somewhat comparable glamorous type. On each side at the same time there is room for considerable difference as to just where the emphasis is placed — for example as between "voluptuous" sexuality and more decorous "charm."

[2] A central aspect of this focus of crystallization lies in the element of tension, sometimes of direct conflict, between the youth culture patterns of college and school life, and the "serious" interests in and obligations toward curricular work. It is of course the latter which defines some at least of the most important foci of adult expectations of doing "good" work and justifying the privileges granted. It is not possible here to attempt to analyze the interesting, ambivalent attitudes of youth toward curricular work and achievement.

differential aspect. Thus the youth culture is not only, as is true of the curricular aspect of formal education, a matter of age status as such but also shows strong signs of being a product of tensions in the relationship of younger people and adults.

From the point of view of age grading perhaps the most notable fact about this situation is the existence of definite pattern distinctions from the periods coming both before and after. At the line between childhood and adolescence "growing up" consists precisely in ability to participate in youth culture patterns, which are not for either sex, the same as the adult patterns practiced by the parental generation. In both sexes the transition to full adulthood means loss of a certain "glamorous" element. From being the athletic hero or the lion of college dances, the young man becomes a prosaic business executive or lawyer. The more successful adults participate in an important order of prestige symbols but these are of a very different order from those of the youth culture. The contrast in the case of the feminine role is perhaps equally sharp, with at least a strong tendency to take on a "domestic" pattern with marriage and the arrival of young children.

The symmetry in this respect must, however, not be exaggerated. It is of fundamental significance to the sex role structure of the adult age levels that the normal man has a "job" which is fundamental to his social status in general. It is perhaps not too much to say that only in very exceptional cases can an adult man be genuinely self-respecting and enjoy a respected status in the eyes of others if he does not "earn a living" in an approved occupational role. Not only is this a matter of his own economic support but, generally speaking, his occupational status is the primary source of the income and class status of his wife and children.

In the case of the feminine role the situation is radically different. The majority of married women, of course, are not employed, but even of those that are a very large proportion do not have jobs which are in basic competition for status with those of their husbands.[3] The majority of "career" women whose occupational status is comparable with that of men in their own class, at least in the upper middle and upper classes, are unmarried, and in the small proportion of cases where they are married the result is a profound alteration in family structure.

This pattern, which is central to the urban middle classes, should not be misunderstood. In rural society, for instance, the operation of the farm and the attendant status in the community may be said to be a matter of the joint status of both parties to a marriage. Whereas a farm is operated by a family, an urban job is held by an individual and does not involve other members of the family in a comparable sense. One convenient expression of the difference lies in the question of what would happen in case of death. In the case of a farm it would at least be not at all unusual for the widow to continue operating the farm with the help of a son or even of hired men. In the urban situation the widow would cease to have any connection with the organization which had employed her husband and he would be replaced by another man without reference to family affiliations.

In this urban situation the primary status-carrying role is in a sense that of housewife. The woman's fundamental status is that of her husband's wife, the mother of his children, and traditionally the person responsible for a complex of activities in connection with the manage-

---

[3] The above statement, even more than most in the present paper, needs to be qualified in relation to the problem of class. It is above all to the upper middle class that it applies. Here probably the great majority of "working wives" are engaged in some form of secretarial work which would, on an independent basis, generally be classed as a lower middle class occupation. The situation at lower levels of the class structure is quite different since the prestige of the jobs of husband and wife is then much more likely to be nearly equivalent. It is quite possible that this fact is closely related to the relative instability of marriage which Davis and Gardner (Deep South) find, at least for the community they studied, to be typical of lower class groups. The relation is one which deserves careful study.

ment of the household, care of children, etc.

For the structuring of sex roles in the adult phase the most fundamental considerations seem to be those involved in the interrelations of the occupational system and the conjugal family. In a certain sense the most fundamental basis of the family's status is the occupational status of the husband and father. As has been pointed out, this is a status occupied by an individual by virtue of his individual qualities and achievements. But both directly and indirectly, more than any other single factor, it determines the status of the family in the social structure, directly because of the symbolic significance of the office or occupation as a symbol of prestige, indirectly because as the principal source of family income it determines the standard of living of the family. From one point of view the emergence of occupational status into this primary position can be regarded as the principal source of strain in the sex role structure of our society since it deprives the wife of her role as a partner in a common enterprise. The common enterprise is reduced to the life of the family itself and to the informal social activities in which husband and wife participate together. This leaves the wife a set of utilitarian functions in the management of the household which may be considered a kind of "pseudo-" occupation. Since the present interest is primarily in the middle classes, the relatively unstable character of the role of housewife as the principal content of the feminine role is strongly illustrated by the tendency to employ domestic servants wherever financially possible. It is true that there is an American tendency to accept tasks of drudgery with relative willingness, but it is notable that in middle class families there tends to be a dissociation of the essential personality from the performance of these tasks. Thus, advertising continually appeals to such desires as to have hands which one could never tell had washed dishes or scrubbed floors.[4] Organization about the function of housewife, however, with the addition of strong affectional devotion to husband and children, is the primary focus of one of the principal patterns governing the adult feminine role — what may be called the "domestic" pattern. It is, however, a conspicuous fact, that strict adherence to this pattern has become progressively less common and has a strong tendency to a residual status — that is, to be followed most closely by those who are unsuccessful in competition for prestige in other directions.

It is, of course, possible for the adult woman to follow the masculine pattern and seek a career in fields of occupational achievement in direct competition with men of her own class. It is, however, notable that in spite of the very great progress of the emancipation of women from the traditional domestic pattern only a very small fraction have gone very far in this direction. It is also clear that its generalization would only be possible with profound alterations in the structure of the family.

Hence it seems that concomitant with the alteration in the basic masculine role in the direction of occupation there have appeared two important tendencies in the feminine role which are alternative to that of simple domesticity on the one hand, and to a full-fledged career on the other. In the older situation there tended to be a very rigid distinction between respectable married women and those who were "no better than they should be." The rigidity of this line has progressively broken down through the infiltration into the respectable sphere of elements of what may be called again the glamor pattern, with the emphasis on a specifically feminine form of attractiveness which on occasion involves directly sexual patterns of appeal. One important expression of this trend lies in the fact

---

[4] This type of advertising appeal undoubtedly contains an element of "snob appeal" in the sense of an invitation to the individual by her appearance and ways to identify herself with a higher social class than that of her actual status. But it is almost certainly not wholly explained by this element. A glamorously feminine appearance which is specifically dissociated from physical work is undoubtedly a genuine part of an authentic personality ideal of the middle class, and not only evidence of a desire to belong to the upper class.

that many of the symbols of feminine attractiveness have been taken over directly from the practices of social types previously beyond the pale of respectable society. This would seem to be substantially true of the practice of women smoking and of at least the modern version of the use of cosmetics. The same would seem to be true of many of the modern versions of women's dress. "Emancipation" in this connection means primarily emancipation from traditional and conventional restrictions on the free expression of sexual attraction and impulses, but in a direction which tends to segregate the element of sexual interest and attraction from the total personality and in so doing tends to emphasize the segregation of sex roles. It is particularly notable that there has been no corresponding tendency to emphasize masculine attraction in terms of dress and other such aids. One might perhaps say that in a situation which strongly inhibits competition between the sexes on the same plane the feminine glamor pattern has appeared as an offset to masculine occupational status and to its attendant symbols of prestige. It is perhaps significant that there is a common stereotype of the association of physically beautiful, expensively and elaborately dressed women with physically unattractive but rich and powerful men.

The other principal direction of emancipation from domesticity seems to lie in emphasis on what has been called the common humanistic element. This takes a wide variety of forms. One of them lies in a relatively mature appreciation and systematic cultivation of cultural interests and educated tastes, extending all the way from the intellectual sphere to matters of art, music and house furnishings. A second consists in cultivation of serious interests and humanitarian obligations in community welfare situations and the like. It is understandable that many of these orientations are most conspicuous in fields where through some kind of tradition there is an element of particular suitability for feminine participation. Thus, a woman who takes obligations to social welfare particularly seri-

ously will find opportunities in various forms of activity which traditionally tie up with women's relation to children, to sickness and so on. But this may be regarded as secondary to the underlying orientation which would seek an outlet in work useful to the community following the most favorable opportunities which happen to be available.

This pattern, which with reference to the character of relationship to men may be called that of the "good companion," is distinguished from the others in that it lays far less stress on the exploitation of sex role as such and more on that which is essentially common to both sexes. There are reasons, however, why cultural interests, interest in social welfare and community activities are particularly prominent in the activities of women in our urban communities. On the one side the masculine occupational role tends to absorb a very large proportion of the man's time and energy and to leave him relatively little for other interests. Furthermore, unless his position is such as to make him particularly prominent his primary orientation is to those elements of the social structure which divide the community into occupational groups rather than those which unite it in common interests and activities. The utilitarian aspect of the role of housewife, on the other hand, has declined in importance to the point where it scarcely approaches a full-time occupation for a vigorous person. Hence the resort to other interests to fill up the gap. In addition, women, being more closely tied to the local residential community are more apt to be involved in matters of common concern to the members of that community. This peculiar role of women becomes particularly conspicuous in middle age. The younger married woman is apt to be relatively highly absorbed in the care of young children. With their growing up, however, her absorption in the household is greatly lessened, often just at the time when the husband is approaching the apex of his career and is most heavily involved in its obligations. Since to a high degree this humanistic aspect of the feminine role is only partially institutionalized it is not surprising that its patterns often bear the marks of strain and insecurity, as perhaps has been classically depicted by Helen Hokinson's cartoons of women's clubs.

The adult roles of both sexes involve important elements of strain which are involved in certain dynamic relationships, especially to the youth culture. In the case of the feminine role marriage is the single event toward which a selective process, in which personal qualities and effort can play a decisive role, has pointed up. That determines a woman's fundamental status, and after that her role patterning is not so much status determining as a matter of living up to expectations and finding satisfying interests and activities. In a society where such strong emphasis is placed upon individual achievement it is not surprising that there should be a certain romantic nostalgia for the time when the fundamental choices were still open. This element of strain is added to by the lack of clear-cut definition of the adult feminine role. Once the possibility of a career has been eliminated there still tends to be a rather unstable oscillation between emphasis in the direction of domesticity or glamor or good companionship. According to situational pressures and individual character the tendency will be to emphasize one or another of these more strongly. But it is a situation likely to produce a rather high level of insecurity. In this state the pattern of domesticity must be ranked lowest in terms of prestige but also, because of the strong emphasis in community sentiment on the virtues of fidelity and devotion to husband and children, it offers perhaps the highest level of a certain kind of security. It is no wonder that such an important symbol as Whistler's mother concentrates primarily on this pattern.

The glamor pattern has certain obvious attractions since to the woman who is excluded from the struggle for power and prestige in the occupational sphere it is the most direct path to a sense of superiority and importance. It has, however, two obvious limitations. In the first place, many of its manifestations encoun-

ter the resistance of patterns of moral conduct and engender conflicts not only with community opinion but also with the individual's own moral standards. In the second place, it is a pattern the highest manifestations of which are inevitably associated with a rather early age level — in fact, overwhelmingly with the courtship period. Hence, if strongly entered upon serious strains result from the problem of adaptation to increasing age.

The one pattern which would seem to offer the greatest possibilities for able, intelligent, and emotionally mature women is the third — the good companion pattern. This, however, suffers from a lack of fully institutionalized status and from the multiplicity of choices of channels of expression. It is only those with the strongest initiative and intelligence who achieve fully satisfactory adaptations in this direction. It is quite clear that in the adult feminine role there is quite sufficient strain and insecurity so that widespread manifestations are to be expected in the form of neurotic behavior.

The masculine role at the same time is itself by no means devoid of corresponding elements of strain. It carries with it to be sure the primary prestige of achievement, responsibility and authority. By comparison with the role of the youth culture, however, there are at least two important types of limitations. In the first place, the modern occupational system has led to increasing specialization of role. The job absorbs an extraordinarily large proportion of the individual's energy and emotional interests in a role the content of which is often relatively narrow. This in particular restricts the area within which he can share common interests and experiences with others not in the same occupational specialty. It is perhaps of considerable significance that so many of the highest prestige statuses of our society are of this specialized character. There is in the definition of roles little to bind the individual to others in his community on a comparable status level. By contrast with this situation, it is notable that in the youth culture common human elements are far more strongly emphasized. Leadership and eminence are more in the role of total individuals and less of competent specialists. This perhaps has something to do with the significant tendency in our society for all age levels to idealize youth and for the older age groups to attempt to imitate the patterns of youth behavior.

It is perhaps as one phase of this situation that the relation of the adult man to persons of the opposite sex should be treated. The effect of the specialization of occupational role is to narrow the range in which the sharing of common human interests can play a large part. In relation to his wife the tendency of this narrowness would seem to be to encourage on her part either the domestic or the glamorous role, or community participation somewhat unrelated to the marriage relationship. This relationship between sex roles presumably introduces a certain amount of strain into the marriage relationship itself since this is of such overwhelming importance to the family and hence to a woman's status and yet so relatively difficult to maintain on a level of human companionship. Outside the marriage relationship, however, there seems to be a notable inhibition against easy social intercourse, particularly in mixed company.[5] The man's close personal intimacy with other women is checked by the danger of the situation being defined as one of rivalry with the wife, and easy friendship without sexual-emotional involvement seems to be inhibited by the specialization of interests in the occupational sphere. It is notable that brillance of conversation of the "salon" type seems to be associated with aristocratic society and is not prominent in ours.

Along with all this goes a certain tendency for middle-aged men, as symbolized by the "bald-headed row," to be interested in the physical aspect of sex — that is, in women precisely as dissociated from those personal considerations which are important to relationships of companionship or friendship, to say nothing of marriage. In so far as it does not take this physical form, however, there seems to be a strong tendency for middle-aged men to idealize youth patterns — that is, to think of the ideal inter-sex friendship as that of their pre-marital period.[6]

In so far as the idealization of the youth culture by adults is an expression of elements of strain and insecurity in the adult roles it would be expected that the patterns thus idealized would contain an element of romantic unrealism. The patterns of youthful behavior thus idealized are not those of actual youth so much as those which older people wish their own youth might have been. This romantic element seems to coalesce with a similar element derived from certain strains in the situation of young people themselves.

The period of youth in our society is one of considerable strain and insecurity. Above all, it means turning one's back on the security both of status and of emotional attachment which is engaged in the family of orientation. It is structurally essential to transfer one's primary emotional attachment to a marriage partner who is entirely unrelated to the previous family situation. In a system of free marriage choice this applies to women as well as men. For the man there is in addition the necessity to face the hazards of occupational competition in the determination of a career. There is reason to believe that the youth culture has important positive functions in easing the transition from the security of childhood in the family of orientation to that of full adult in marriage and occupational status. But precisely because the transition is a period of strain it is to be expected that it involves elements of unrealistic romanticism. Thus significant features in the status of youth patterns in our society would seem to derive from the coinci-

---

[5] In the informal social life of academic circles with which the writer is familiar there seems to be a strong tendency in mixed gatherings — as after dinner — for the sexes to segregate. In such groups the men are apt to talk either shop subjects or politics whereas the women are apt to talk about domestic affairs, schools, their children etc., or personalities. It is perhaps on personalities that mixed conversation is apt to flow most freely.

[6] This, to be sure, often contains an element of romantization. It is more nearly what he wishes these relations had been than what they actually were.

dence of the emotional needs of adolescents with those derived from the strains of the situation of adults.

A tendency to the romantic idealization of youth patterns seems in different ways to be characteristic of modern western society as a whole.[7] It is not possible in the present context to enter into any extended comparative analysis, but it may be illuminating to call attention to a striking difference between the patterns associated with this phenomenon in Germany and in the United States. The German "youth movement," starting before the first World War, has occasioned a great deal of comment and has in various respects been treated as the most notable instance of the revolt of youth. It is generally believed that the youth movement has an important relation to the background of National Socialism, and this fact as much as any suggests the important difference. While in Germany as everywhere there has been a generalized revolt against convention and restrictions on individual freedom as embodied in the traditional adult culture, in Germany particular emphasis has appeared on the community of male youth. "Comradeship" in a sense which strongly suggests that of soldiers in the field has from the beginning been strongly emphasized as the ideal social relationship. By contrast with this, in the American youth culture and its adult romantization a much stronger emphasis has been placed on the cross-sex relationship. It would seem that this fact, with the structural factors which underlie it, have much to do with the failure of the youth culture to develop any considerable political significance in this country. Its predominant pattern has been that of the idealization of the isolated couple in romantic love. There have, to be sure, been certain tendencies among radical youth to a political orientation but in this case there has been a notable absence of emphasis on the solidarity of the members of one sex. The tendency has been rather to ignore the relevance of sex difference in the interest of common ideals.

The importance of youth patterns in contemporary American culture throws into particularly strong relief the status in our social structure of the most advanced age groups. By comparison with other societies the United States assumes an extreme position in the isolation of old age from participation in the most important social structures and interests. Structurally speaking, there seem to be two primary bases of this situation. In the first place, the most important single distinctive feature of our family structure is the isolation of the individual conjugal family. It is impossible to say that with us it is "natural" for any other group than husband and wife and their dependent children to maintain a common household. Hence, when the children of a couple have become independent through marriage and occupational status the parental couple is left without attachment to any continuous kinship group. It is, of course, common for other relatives to share a household with the conjugal family but this scarcely ever occurs without some important elements of strain. For independence is certainly the preferred pattern for an elderly couple, particularly from the point of view of the children.

The second basis of the situation lies in the occupational structure. In such fields as farming and the maintenance of small independent enterprises there is frequently no such thing as abrupt "retirement," rather a gradual relinquishment of the main responsibilities and functions with advancing age. So far, however, as an individual's occupational status centers in a specific "job," he either holds the job or does not, and the tendency is to maintain the full level of functions up to a given point and then abruptly to retire. In view of the very great significance of occupational status and its psychological correlates, retirement leaves the older man in a peculiarly functionless situation, cut off from participation in the most important interests and activities of the society. There is a further important aspect of this situation. Not only

---

[7] *Cf.* E. Y. Hartshorne, "German Youth and the Nazi Dream of Victory," *America in a World at War, Pamphlet,* No. 12, New York, 1941.

status in the community but actual place of residence is to a very high degree a function of the specific job held. Retirement not only cuts the ties to the job itself but also greatly loosens those to the community of residence. Perhaps in no other society is there observable a phenomenon corresponding to the accumulation of retired elderly people in such areas as Florida and Southern California in the winter. It may be surmised that this structural isolation from kinship, occupational, and community ties is the fundamental basis of the recent political agitation for help to the old. It is suggested that it is far less the financial hardship[8] of the position of elderly people than their social isolation which makes old age a "problem." As in other connections we are here very prone to rationalize generalized insecurity in financial and economic terms. The problem is obviously of particularly great significance in view of the changing age distribution of the population with the prospect of a far greater proportion in the older age groups than in previous generations. It may also be suggested, that through well-known psychosomatic mechanisms, the increased incidence of the disabilities of older people, such as heart disease, cancer, etc. may be at least in part attributed to this structural situation.

---

[8] That the financial difficulties of older people are in a very large proportion of cases real is not to be doubted. This, however, is at least to a very large extent a consequence rather than a determinant of the structural situation. Except where it is fully taken care of by pension schemes, the income of older people is apt to be seriously reduced, but, even more important, the younger conjugal family usually does not feel an obligation to contribute to the support of aged parents. Where as a matter of course both generations shared a common household, this problem did not exist.

CHAPTER IV

The Responsibility of Decision

IN THE preceding chapter, we considered the importance of basic cultural values in a society and some concepts of use in observing these values. We saw that values are in the nature of assumptions. Man — alone and in groups — apparently needs and develops in this way a method of synthesizing his observations over long periods of time into some sort of a meaningful whole. New observations then support and explain things that happen in terms of the basic assumptions and therefore tend to confirm them. The process is circular and does not modify the assumptions until a large body of new, unexplained phenomena forces a modification.

If, for example, a primitive man regularly sat on a rock and later became ill, he might have had no trouble explaining what had happened. If his culture assumed the existence of spirits in rocks, he would have "known" that an evil spirit had harmed him, and he would have had available acceptable ways of exorcising it. But if this occurrence had happened to a man in our society even as recently as a hundred years ago, he would have had no way of understanding this particular phenomenon. For a cold, "inanimate" rock to do such damage would have been inexplicable. The tendency then would have been to deny the observation altogether — to say the man was crazy to connect the rock with his illness, and to forget about it. Only when we have postulated new concepts based on a large number of such observations can we begin to understand what happened. Nowadays we "know" that a rock such as pitchblende is "radioactive" and in sufficient concentration can injure men. We explain the event with as much assurance as primitive people.

Similar events that are inexplicable in terms of existing concepts are undoubtedly still common. Our present general concepts do not explain or even permit the observation of all things that happen. Particular events will continue to be observed and understood for the first time as accumulated evidence forces the development of new hypotheses about the world.

These considerations are as significant for our individual development as for the development of group ideas. As we grow, we seem to evolve our own concepts and assumptions to help us observe and understand our world. These individual assumptions are culturally trained but are based on personal observations. They change only slowly and by the same process that forces change in group ideas.

The concept of basic cultural values was developed to help describe the assumptions held by very large groups of people. It seems clear that even here some modification is continually taking place. Dominant and variant cultural values are observed to exist within a society at all times. As individuals, we can then find confirmation in the thinking of others for many different private assumptions. We may assume that this world is the best of all possible worlds, or that every man has to take care of himself, or that economic factors are the most important ones in our lives, or that in this competitive world every man's hand is against another's. We can always find adequate evidence that any such evaluation is "true" and rest secure in holding it.

Such personal assumptions are, furthermore, so woven into the fabric of our thinking that a change in one "idea" requires the modification of many others. If circumstances arise which we feel require us to question any of our fundamental beliefs, they seem to upset us severely; we become anxious and afraid. Most of us are not usually afraid of darkness, yet unexplained "night" in the middle of the day would be very frightening. The anger we feel when we cannot find something where we *know* we left it may have some of this element in it. The strength with which we deny ideas that are difficult to understand — which involve the problem of fitting new information into our thoughts about the world — may rest on this foundation.

Underlying all such values there seems to be one assumption that no large group of people have seriously questioned. Man must relate himself directly or indirectly to other men; the very threat of isolation is intolerable. Durkheim observes man's need to be related and indicates why he considers it to be fundamental; Fromm, in the reading below, gives further reasons. The specific ways in which man relates himself to others may vary widely. The relationships may remain relatively stable for a long period of years, or they may be modified frequently. But if change is impending and no similar relationships seem to be available to replace them, man becomes upset.[1] Some sort of relationship with others appears to be a basic necessity if personal integration is to be maintained.

Erich Fromm says:

> To feel completely alone and isolated leads to mental disintegration just as physical starvation leads to death. This relatedness to others is not identical with physical contact. An individual may be alone in a physical sense for many years and yet he may be related to ideas, values, or at least social patterns that give him a feeling of communion and "belonging." On the other hand, he may live among people and yet be overcome with an utter feeling of isolation, the outcome of which, if it transcends a certain limit, is the state of insanity which schizophrenic disturbances represent. This lack of relatedness to values, symbols, patterns, we may call moral aloneness and state that moral aloneness is as intolerable as the physical aloneness, or rather that physical aloneness becomes unbearable only if it implies also moral aloneness. The spiritual relatedness to the world can assume many forms; the monk in his cell who believes in God and the political prisoner kept in isolation who feels one with his fellow fighters are not alone morally. Neither is the English gentleman who wears his dinner jacket in the most exotic surroundings nor the petty bourgeois who, though being deeply isolated from his fellow men, feels one with his nation or its symbols. The kind of relatedness to the world may be noble or trivial, but even being related to the basest kind of pattern is immensely preferable to being alone. Religion and nationalism, as well as any custom and any belief however absurd and degrading, if it only connects the individual with others, are refuges from what man most dreads: isolation.[2]

---

[1] Consider "Jinny Stover," Vol. II, Case 4.
[2] Erich Fromm, *Escape from Freedom* (New York: Rinehart, 1941), pp. 19–20. This book is published in England by Routledge and Kegan Paul under the title *Fear of Freedom*.

On this foundation, Fromm examines some of the consequences of modern social conditions that force man into situations where he feels alone. Fromm finds that the increasing emphasis on individualism puts a burden of personal decision on each of us that at times frightens us. We seem to be free to make many decisions for ourselves — to make our own choices among various ways of conduct or action — but we also feel the isolation of such decisions and may struggle valiantly to escape from the very freedom we have been seeking. Read

ERICH FROMM, *Escape from Freedom* (New York: Rinehart, 1941), pp. 3–206.

In chapters 1 and 2, he shows how the basic problem of aloneness appears in the natural process of growing up. "The child becomes more free *to* develop and express its own individual self unhampered by those ties which were limiting it. But the child also becomes more free *from* a world which gave it security and reassurance." These first two chapters are crucial to Fromm's thesis.

In chapters 3 and 4, he gives detailed historical evidence that a way of thinking which poses a dilemma has been built into our society. If man "stands on his own feet" and makes his individual decisions, he tends to feel less closely related to other men, and the fear of this isolation becomes unbearable. If, on the other hand, he tries to maintain the type of close relationships in which he grew up, which gave him such reassurance and security, he feels the loss of the individuality that our culture has taught him to desire.

In chapter 5, Fromm examines the mechanisms through which the individual escapes (or tries to escape) from the dilemma thus posed. He finds three general techniques. The first method he calls authoritarianism. By this method the individual places himself in a position where some "authority" is available to take the responsibility for those decisions (choices) that seem too great. Authority is not used here in the organizational sense of a division of responsibilities, one above the other, but rather in the sense of a crutch or "magic helper" on which one leans when faced with difficult personal problems. "Someone must know what is right." There are many ways in which this authority relationship can be maintained that seem satisfactory to the individual. All of them are escapes from the main dilemma and give up a large measure of the freedom of personal choice.

The second method he calls destructiveness. When such a method is used, the basic problem is assumed to be an outside force which is seeking to overwhelm the individual. "Everyone is forcing me to make decisions I don't want to make." Destructiveness is viewed as the only means by which this force can be handled. It is true that if it were accomplished, isolation would be complete. But it is felt that the isolation would be in a world free from the crushing outside forces. "Then I would be free to do as I please."

The third method he calls automaton conformity. He feels this is the solution that the majority of normal individuals find in modern society; here the individual adopts the kind of personality offered to him by cultural patterns. In this way he becomes exactly as all others are and as they expect him to be. His own choices become the choices he feels others expect of him, and his oneness with them is complete.[3]

---

[3] Fromm asserts that the need to escape in some such ways as these from the dilemmas posed by the culture of our times has had its effects on the institutions we are trying to build. He examines these effects in chapters 6 and 7, "The Psychology of Nazism" and "Freedom and Democracy." These chapters go somewhat beyond the considerations of this book and are not included in pages 3–206, referred to above.

The basic problems Fromm is dealing with have direct application to every individual. As the individual grows and develops within a family group, he must find ways of living up to its expectations and thereby avoiding isolation from it. He learns how to be a "good boy" and how to avoid (when he wishes) being a "bad boy." This often involves largely "doing as he is told," permitting others to take the responsibility, and submitting willingly (often anxiously) to their decisions. Practically all of an individual's wants as a small child can thus be anticipated by parents or other adults. For the individual, therefore, this is a comfortable period in which the expression of wants often brings immediate satisfaction; the memory of this period is extraordinarily persistent.

As the child grows older, he attempts to satisfy many of his basic wants in a similar way. Reinforced by the need for strong emotional ties with his family (and often other "grown-ups"), he tries to anticipate their wishes and *thereby lets them take responsibility for his actions*. If he does as "They" want, if he is a "good" boy, if he is submissive and non-responsible — to use Benedict's terms — then everything will be all right.

However, he conforms at the price of his sense of individuality, and he can often see clearly that this is not the way he will learn to grow up. As Linton would say, he must try to prepare himself for the role he will ultimately have to fill. He may see this more clearly than his parents or other authority figures around him. He observes that adults are dominant and do take responsibility, largely, it appears, on the basis of their own individual desires at the moment. As long as he merely does what "They" want, there is somehow a feeling of loss of individuality, of "Me-ness." So he tends at times to do the opposite of what They want just to confirm his individuality: he makes his own "decisions."

This course of action also has its serious problems. First, it is vaguely felt by the individual to be merely a negative response to a situation defined by Them. The positive action that They would want must be clearly in mind if a negative response is to be developed. Second, this negative decision brings with it the feeling of always being wrong, since the assumption that They are right is confirmed by the consequences of such indiscriminate negativism. So this response brings with it a fear of taking the very responsibility that the individual feels so necessary if he is to be himself.

It is difficult for us to see that these problems are a result of the way we respond. Rather, they usually appear attributable to some outside force which we feel is trying to make us do something. Jacques Barzun, in discussing the teacher-pupil relationship, says:

> Even under the best conditions of fair play and deliberate spontaneity, the pupil, while needing and wanting knowledge, will hate and resist it. This resistance often makes one feel that the human mind is made of some wonderfully tough rubber, which you can stretch a little by pulling hard, but which snaps back into shape the moment you let it go.
>
> Consider how the student feels, subjected to daily and hourly stretching. "Here am I," he thinks, "with my brains nicely organized — with everything, if not in its place, at least in a place where I can find it — and you come along with a new and strange item that you want to force into my previous arrangement. Naturally I resist. You persist. I begin to dislike you. But at the same time, you show me aspects of this new fact or idea which in spite of myself mesh in with my existing desires. You seem to know the contents of my mind. You show me the proper place

for your contribution to my stock of knowledge. Finally, there is brooding over us a vague threat of disgrace for me if I do not accept your offering and keep it and show you that I still have it when you — dreadful thought! — examine me. So I give in, I shut my eyes and swallow. I write little notes about it to myself, and with luck the burr sticks: I have learned something. Thanks to you? Well, not exactly. Thanks to you and thanks to me. I shall always be grateful for your efforts, but do not expect me to love you, at least not for a long, long time."

At any stage in learning, this inner dialogue between opposite feelings goes on. It should go on. Teaching is possible only because there is a dialogue and one part of the mind can be used to rearrange the other.[4]

This struggle *within* the individual between the desire for "independence" and the desire to "belong" is exaggerated in our childhood and adolescence because we perceive it oversimply. The problem is to discover the more complex process through which we can adopt and use other people's ideas, can maintain close contact with them and yet retain and embrace our sensed individuality. We must "grow up"; we must become "adult." Yet many people who certainly have been around enough years don't seem to behave "grown-up." They don't seem to have progressed much beyond the level of "I'll believe what you say if you are nice to me," or its corresponding negative response, "I don't like you or anyone like you, and I wouldn't believe anything you say on a bet." Somehow we have to do better than that.

William G. Perry, Jr. also considers these matters within the context of the student-teacher relationship. In his terms an individual in growing up changes his notions of the essential nature of his individuality, growing from a "Me" to a "Self." The integrity of Me is considered by the child to reside in his personal wants and wishes — the unrestricted, the pleasant. The Theys of the environment then seem to stand against the Me and represent all the necessary, unpleasant things that *should* or *must* be done. Reality — cause and effect as applied to behavior and its consequences — then seems nothing but an aspect of authority, nothing but what They say will happen if one does this or doesn't do that. The feeling is that when one grows up one will run things differently. "Self-ness" is approached first through the discovery that freedom from authority does not result in freedom from fact. Then it is attained through the assumption of responsibility for *choice* among conflicting values in a real and limited world. This responsibility makes real freedom less unlimited than what was dreamed of, but despite its shortcoming it is experienced as a greater freedom than the trap of negativistic revolt. In it the individual may express his independence through his choice of purposes (what he will act for and against) and replace the relatedness of dependency with the relatedness of dependability and coöperative effort. Read

WILLIAM G. PERRY, JR., "The Student's Response to Teaching," below.

Perry suggests, then, that people find a resolution of the dilemma we have been discussing in the awareness that the separateness implied by individuality need not mean intolerable loneliness and isolation, but may be used instead as the basis of productive relationships. In this article addressed to teachers, he suggests that "selfhood" may be best fostered in the young by showing them

---

[4] Jacques Barzun, *The Teacher in America* (Boston: Little, Brown — Atlantic Monthly Press, 1945), pp. 19–20.

that adults too have wishes and feelings similar to their own and that maturity consists not in the denial of emotional life but in its skillful furtherance within the limits imposed by a real world.[5]

ADDITIONAL READINGS

Horney, Karen, *The Neurotic Personality of Our Time* (New York: W. W. Norton, 1937).

Dr. Horney is a psychoanalyst who is interested in the cultural factors that influence personality. Her thesis is simple: neurotic conflicts are merely exaggerations of contradictions in cultural norms that face everyone. She examines modern culture with that in mind and shows how individuals react to its dilemmas. By concentrating on the extreme reactions leading to neuroses, she is able to describe many psychic processes that are of interest to the student of the "normal."

Koestler, Arthur, "In Memory of Richard Hillary," *The Yogi and the Commissar and Other Essays* (New York: Macmillan, 1946).

The true story of an English student who joined the R.A.F. during the war, was shot down and seriously injured, then sought a new group of pilots with whom he could overcome his moral aloneness.

It is a case study which dramatizes some of the general ideas of Fromm.

Leighton, Dorothea, and Clyde Kluckhohn, *Children of the People* (Cambridge: Harvard University Press, 1947).

This book describes how Navaho children are taught the values of their culture.

Miller, Arthur, *Death of a Salesman* (New York: Viking Press, 1949).

A play that gives a penetrating picture of a man who is slowly isolated from his fellows.

Zorbaugh, Harvey W., "The World of Furnished Rooms," chapter 4 of *The Gold Coast and the Slum* (Chicago: University of Chicago Press, 1929).

A study of Chicago which shows that moral aloneness or *anomie* is unrelated to the number of people surrounding a person. A crowded rooming house can be the most lonely place in the world.

The Student's Response to Teaching[*]

BY WILLIAM G. PERRY, JR.

Education has been defined, and quite helpfully, as the transmission of the culture from one generation to another. Of course this gets us into a definition of culture and so forth, and things get a little complicated. But nonetheless we can suppose that culture is a term which must be applied not only to those things which are the rewards and benefits of the society and those things that we can all get from knowledge — understanding and the richness of life — but it must also refer to the "do's" and the "don'ts,"

the "this-way's" and the "not-that-way's" of the society. Now since the teacher is someone who has been hired by the community to engage full-time in this transmission of the culture, you will find that you are not just a Ganymede or a Hebe standing at the fountain of knowledge with a little cup, but rather you will find that your students are quite properly responding to you as if your other hand, the one you have behind your back, had brass knuckles on it. They will be responding to you as if you were saying,

---

[5] Consider "Dave Campbell," Vol. II, Case 15.

[*] An excerpt from a lecture to prospective teachers, reprinted from William G. Perry, Jr., "Conflicts in the Learning Process: The Student's Response to Teaching," in *A Handbook for College Teachers*, ed. Bernice Brown Cronkhite (Cambridge: Harvard University Press, 1950), pp. 20–35.

as you must say — as you cannot escape saying whether you put it into words or not — not only, "Come and drink from the fountain of knowledge," but also, "And while you are at it, bud, you do it our way *on time;* if you don't, you will not only get these lovely things, but you will be sent shamefully home, a *failure.*"

Now what do people do under stresses and threats like that? They resist, just as Sally resists eating those beans, not because she doesn't like beans, but because she is afraid that by liking them, now that you have told her to eat them, she will somehow be losing something. She doesn't know quite what, but she feels that something dreadfully important will be lost. So what students do in their resistance is to conform to the letter of what you say. They will eat two spoonfuls of beans, with one bean on each. They will say the letter of what you require them to repeat, but they will reject the spirit, even if they think it will be good for them. I remember saying to my boy the other day, "You forgot to pick up your shoes." He replied, "Well, you didn't tell me to pick up my shoes, you told me to pick up my clothes." So when you make an assignment from page such-and-such to page such-an-such, and when you ask some questions about it, you may say, "Look at these papers; no one has thought about this." And the response will be, verbalized or not, "You didn't tell us to think about it, you just told us to read it."

What I should like to do, therefore, is to abandon for a while all thoughts of the teaching process, of the giving end of education, and to examine the receiving end. What I am going to do is to try to explore how the educational world looks to the student — perhaps, indeed, how the world itself looks. By this I don't mean what he will or can tell you about it; I mean, rather, what his assumptions are and what his frame of reference is, the more or less unconscious basis of his behavior. Here I am launching those tentative suppositions in which one must explore the sea of one's ignorance. I am going to draw a kind of chart in the hope

that it may keep us from becoming utterly lost.

When we as children first come into the world and look around to see what the world is made of, we see soon enough that the world is made of They. And what are They like? They tell us, do they not, what we *ought* to do? They tell us our *duty.* They tell us what is *necessary.* And it is necessary to do a lot of things that we don't like in the world, so They say. It is necessary to do a lot of things that are unpleasant. So that this business that They tell us about is by their own account *unpleasant.* So this is the world and its demands.

But now, as I look at this world, I begin to think of my own individuality and separateness, and I say to myself, "Who's Me?" Well, I am little and I am helpless, but I obviously have to be something quite different from all this if I am going to have any differentness, any individuality, which seems so precious to me. And what is the opposite to all that They stand for? Why, it is obviously what I *want.* So it follows that my individuality and my integrity, for which I will fight to the death, consists of what I want — that is, of my *wishes* — all of which I associate with the *pleasant:*

ME
*integrity conceived
as residing in:*

|

wants

|

wishes

|

the unrestricted

|

the pleasant

THEY
*perceived as
representing:*

|

oughts

|

duties

|

the necessary

|

the unpleasant

Clearly, now, I am faced at once with a number of serious difficulties. In the first place my integrity demands that I get what I want. If I do not, I am not only frustrated, I am much worse than that: I am somehow less Me. On the other hand, a lot of things that I want can be attained only through They, and They disapprove of other things that I want. If I do not give up these tabooed wants and do a certain amount of the unpleasant, then They will not love me any more, and that would be fatal to all my wishes. Furthermore, I may feel in part genuinely fond of They in that They do give me some things I want. Another difficulty is still more confusing. I soon discover, let us say at the age of three or four, or five, that They got me so young, when I was unable to defend myself, that They went and put a little bit of They in Me and I can't get away from it; it keeps nagging me all the time.

The dilemma is very serious indeed, and is made worse by the conflicting nature of my wishes. I wish to be dominant and independent; I wish also to be dependent and loved. However, I blind myself to this internal source of difficulty and concentrate on what seems the external problem of getting what I want and placating They. There are all sorts of attempted solutions to this almost insoluble problem. The most obvious one is the Social Contract of Rousseau — that is, the compromise. In this solution I simply do a number of the things that They say I ought to do, and then I hope that They will leave me alone to go forth and do some of the things that I want. The trouble with this solution is that the compromise never really seems to be accepted by either side; both sides seem to be trying to beat the game and to ask for more. It is a very uneasy situation. I do some of the things that I want to do for a while; then I get a guilty conscience and do some of the things that I ought to do for a while; then I feel frustrated and so I go and do what I want to do, and then I get conscience-stricken again, and back and forth, back and forth, I go. And all this time the sensation keeps piling up that somebody is wasting time.

We might digress for a moment here and look at a curious application of this Social Contract in the educational world. It is perfectly clear to Me, in the educational world, that what They want is for me to be good; what They want is for me to do my duty, which is to sit down and do this studying that I have been given to do. If I do that, their part of the bargain is that They will give me the good grade that I want, so we get the curious formula which you find running throughout education, namely: work through time equals grades. This is a kind of basic moral law. It does not matter what I say on an examination; if I have done the work I should get the grade, and if my roommate, who has done none of the work, reads my notes before the examination and goes in and gets a higher grade than I do, that shows that They are unfair.

We might digress a little further. My integrity, my sense of Me-ness is bound up with my wishes, and since They invade my integrity with all these "don'ts" and "ought's," and since the Social Contract is not working very well and I am getting a little resentful, it is very natural for me to decide that I really could have everything that I wanted if it were not for They; given half a chance I would prove as omnipotent as I secretly believe myself to be. This feeling, which we have all shared, is exemplified by a student who once said: "I really could cut loose from everything; I could cut loose from my parents and my wife and from everything, just as a friend of mine has done who is now down in Ceylon. I could do that, only I don't think I ought to. I could be really perfectly independent and get everything that I wanted. I just don't do it because I don't think I *should*. Besides that, of course, I gain such satisfactions from my family." I said, "You mean that if you went to Ceylon you wouldn't have those satisfactions that you want?" He replied, "No." He was still blind to his contradiction. Then suddenly it struck him, and he said, "This is the first time I've ever realized that I couldn't really have everything I wanted if it wasn't for them."

If it is natural and easy for us to engage in this kind of thinking about our omnipotence, we can carry it one step further. I shall bethink me of the future; I shall conjure up an ideal picture of what I shall become. I shall be a doctor, a really great doctor; I shall be so clever that everyone will admire me, and I shall know so much that I can do anything I want. Now it is a highly commendable thing to be a good doctor and to make discoveries that will ease the lot of the human race, and here, you see, is where I satisfy They, especially the They of my own conscience. So here I have an ideal which seems to satisfy both my need for independence or power and my conscience. There is only one trouble with it — the minute that I try to put it into action, They get in my way again; They require that I study German and various aspects of physics and literature which will be really of no use to me. Naturally, it is an invasion of my integrity to study these requirements and somehow I have a terrible time with them. "I won't eat those beans if They tell me to; no matter how good they may be, no matter how fine the dessert, it is not worth the price of my integrity, and I won't do it." Or if my revolt is not as conscious as this, I will simply relegate doing them until "tomorrow."

We had better not digress any more, for we could probably digress forever and still have an over-simple picture of the matter. It is my opinion, anyway, that from the particular point of view of which we have been speaking — that is, the child's point of view — the problems of life are actually insoluble. It has always been my suspicion that Rousseau never quite grew up. Let us go back to the point where we felt that in the midst of all these attempted solutions somebody was wasting time.

It is this very notion of time that is crucial. Until now we have made no mention of time. Time is an aspect of reality, and we have made no mention whatever of reality. To the child there is no such thing as reality directly; there is only what They say is necessary, and even when what They say is necessary or real

actually happens, even that appears to be just an "I-told-you-so" of grown-ups. Time, as one aspect of reality, does not apply to Me. In fact Me is at its most omnipotent in the timelessness of tomorrow. One of the most obvious solutions to the dilemma of the Me is to do what I want to do today and do what I ought to do tomorrow. Perhaps it is in large part through this sensation of wasting time that reality first comes into awareness — that I get my first glimpse of just plain fact. It is this stunning revelation of the factual, the notion that I cannot go to Ceylon and have everything that I want, that breaks down utterly the dichotomy of the They and the Me. And here we are on the brink of maturity. For now that this dichotomy is broken down, we can have a look at the frame of reference from which the sensation that I have been wasting time arises. The whole sensation implies a new value system, some wholly different frame of reference in which defending the integrity of my wishes is not what I really want to be doing. Here it is that I discover that the person who has been wasting time is my Self.

It is upon the difference between the Me and the Self that everything that I have to say hinges. The difference is one of essential personal identity; it is a felt difference that concerns who I am — that concerns what makes up, for me, my personal individuality. We have already seen that for the child identity is conceived as consisting of wishes, especially those wishes which the child holds in contradistinction to They. No internal conflict or contradiction is accepted among these wishes; all conflict is projected and seems to be externally imposed. But for the Self wishes suddenly lose their distinctive and individual character. I suddenly perceive that everyone has much the same wishes, and furthermore I see these wishes as an aspect of fact and reality. They then lose their glorious simplicity and can be seen in all the conflict and complexity which is really theirs. For the first time, therefore, I am confronted with the real issue of *choice*. The individuality and integrity of the Self is therefore conceived to reside not in my wishes, but in the act of choosing in the midst of the complexity of reality. This reality consists not only of my wishes, but also of society and of physical limitations, including that of time. Up until now I had confused freedom with independence, now I realize that freedom is not the independence to follow one's wishes, but the act of choice among personal values. And personal values for my Self include not only wishes in the narrow sense of impulses, but also objective purposes in a real world *and* many of those responsibilities and obligations and duties which I have previously seen only as the demands of They. In this new frame of reference it is no longer either a loss of integrity, or an act of masochism, to do something unpleasant; it may be simply useful or productive. And though I still have both my wishes and my "ought's," my integrity is not at issue between them; it is, in fact, expressed in my act of choice whichever way I choose in relation to a particular set of circumstances in reality.

reality — SELF — others
*integrity conceived
as residing in:*
|
choices
|
purposes
|
facts — action — facts

As an illustration we might consider the matter of the language requirement. Almost all colleges and graduate schools have a language requirement, and as students we buck it. It is a great symbol, the language requirement; it is the last great apotheosis of Their incredible and unreasonable demands. When it comes time to sit down and do that German, we read the newspaper, we read *Life,* we sharpen our pencils, we do anything to delay the awful moment. When finally we do get to work, we do just what we feel we are "required" to do: we turn the word-cards over, we translate word by word from this or that, and if nothing comes from all our labors, it is not our fault, it is Theirs; and the fact that nothing ever seems to come out of it just goes to show

how right we are. The language requirement appears as a price we are forced to pay for a degree which They withhold. It obviously is not the business of a Me, it is just a requirement of They, and I spend a great deal of time expanding upon its archaism and injustice. From the point of view of the Self, however, the matter looks very different indeed. You have come to this store of your own choice, to buy a certain article, an A.B. or a Ph.D. And how in this store does this article come packaged; in what form does it appear on the counter? It always includes the language requirement. It is not, if you please, a price that you pay, but rather part of the product that you buy. You may not want this accessory, you understand, you may not consider it reasonable, and you may wish that the product came packaged without it; but if the management is not disposed to change the package, you have, in fact, a choice of taking the article or leaving it. If you choose to take it, it is not an invasion of your integrity to fulfill the language requirement, it is, in fact, an expression of your own choice in regard to reality; and because the Self is primarily the chooser, it is an act of Self-expression. Certainly it may be unpleasant or dull, and even frustrating of other purposes that you would like to substitute for it; but for the Self, frustration is not purely an imposition from the outside and a threat to integrity, rather it is one of the conditions of life, because even my own wishes are often incompatible. Hence, dull or not, it can be done with a will.

In the event that you have been subscribing at all to this, you have probably been looking at yourself, if not with alarm, at least with some concern, with the question, "Am I a Me or am I a Self? Am I a child or am I an adult?" I doubt that you will find a ready answer. The question would have been prompted by the way I have been presenting this. I have seemed to imply that a person is either a child or an adult, but this is because such things as authority, necessity, and the unpleasant are so sharply different in quality when looked at from the two points of view that there are really no in-betweens; it is an all-or-none proposition. The two frames of reference are separate, distinct, and self-contained, but what makes growth into maturity look like a gradual thing is, I think, first that we take the point of view of Self in one area of life at a time and, second, that even in those areas in which we have attained it, it is notoriously unstable. A student, for instance, may attain a mature frame of reference in his social relationships and remain a child in his school work. He may feel and act as an adult in his summer job and in the fall drag his feet, as a pupil, reluctantly to school. He may feel and act as an adult away from home, but when he returns to the family that treats him as a child, he will feel like one. It is this jumping back and forth from one frame of reference to another that is the basis, I believe, of the instability of adolescence. Of course it stays with us, to a degree, all our lives.

So far I have painted the frame of reference of the Self as so much more comfortable and desirable that this critical instability may seem strange. Let us have a look at a few of its discomforts. Being a Self is a very risky and frightening business. As a Me I still have claims on that day when things go wrong in life. When I fail, when I am disappointed, when I am hurt, I can call on Them for comfort, for love, for reassurance, for protection. If I am a Self, I no longer have these claims in anything like the same degree. In fact I am alone, and I have not yet learned that to be alone, as all human beings are, is not necessarily to be lonely. Hardest of all, I must, to be a Self, allow my wishes, my omnipotence, and my fantasies to suffer real defeats in the face of reality. I may never be a really great doctor, and to be even a mediocre one, or even a failure, I must sweat. Even if I turn out to have ability and have worked hard, just plain circumstances may defeat me. Can I stand this without the compensation of Their sympathy and support, without being able to demand that They play fair? And deeper down than any of this, can I really trust my Self? If I try to rely on choice instead of upon the compulsions of "ought's" and

"must's," will I ever get anything done?

We might take this last question and see how the fear operates to tip us out of the mature frame of reference. Suppose that I am approaching my academic work, and the language requirement too, with all kinds of maturity. I have kept in mind my own choice; I have come to this institution because I chose to; I accept the language requirement as an aspect of reality; I accept the notion that time applies to me; and I choose, therefore, to do the language requirement now rather than tomorrow. I am doing my German, and my roommate comes in and asks me to make a fourth at bridge. Now I enjoy bridge; furthermore I haven't played for quite some time; furthermore I have been working very hard. I deserve (what frame of reference does that word come from?) a bit of change, a little relaxation. I am sorely tempted. Suddenly I am afraid. I am afraid that I will go and play bridge and not get that language requirement done. I suddenly lose confidence in the Self to choose wisely. I cannot say to my roommate or to myself, "That sounds nice, but I want to get this German done." I cannot voice a simple preference. Instead, I say, "No, I really *ought* to do my German, I really *must* get it done." Now understand me, it looks as if I have not capitulated. I have not said to myself that I can do the German "tomorrow" and I have not gone off to play bridge. But I have capitulated. I have lost confidence in my own capacity to choose, and I have called upon the "ought's" and the "should's" and the "must's" to compel me, to do the deciding for me; and in the next hour, how I will resent it! I have set They up again as my masters, and how I will buck them! I will feel frustrated, I will think about the bridge, and somehow I will defeat my efforts to learn anything. Of course I may be able to get something done for a while by glorying in a kind of masochistic righteousness, but I won't keep it up for long. My spell of self-righteousness will only give me the excuse for taking the whole week end off. From the mature point of view it would have been better had my Self actually chosen to play bridge and to deal with the consequences. I am not arguing against the value of a conscience; I am saying that if we set up the conscience as our compulsive authority instead of as our guide, then we may react as children toward it. To rely entirely upon its compulsion is to surrender the integrity of the Self, to abnegate the function of choice. Until one has had a little experience with the Self, it is hard to believe that we, as people, could really *prefer* to do our work. We say, "I have to drive myself to work." Who is driving whom here? Self-expression is the act of doing what we as *whole* people prefer.

Perhaps we can turn now to the subject of education. I was talking with a student the other day who relied so heavily upon his conscience and upon his parents that though he had the intentions of doing college work, he could not see them as his own. Whenever he told himself that he ought to get to work, he sounded to himself so much like his parents that he resisted his own statements. There was a constant strife between the parent in him, who was trying to make him do things, and the child in him, who was in revolt. Things had gotten a little pressing just before examinations, and he had begun to do a little work. He had decided, he said, that the only trouble with him was that he had no incentive. "But recently," he said, "I've had a lot of incentive; in fact I can't remember being so incensed in all my life."

What I am trying to say is that being incensed may be the normal and appropriate state of mind of the young while being educated. Education is the way that we get at them. We force the culture upon them, the "do's" and the "don'ts" and the "ought's" and the "must's," and when they start doing these, can they eagerly espouse them and keep their integrity, or must they resist to live? Watch them. They go on slow-down strikes and become slow readers. They bewilder themselves by their "laziness." They appeal to you, in conscience-stricken despair. And when they do their work, is their main purpose to learn something or to placate you? It is very profitable and enlightening to look at the act of studying as the process of placating authority in the educational world.

Does this sound extreme? I remember when I first went into the business of helping students to study better, more efficiently and all that. I assumed, of course, that everybody wants to be efficient — that is to get the same results with the least effort — and for all I know this still may be a perfectly reasonable assumption. When a student came to me, I would try to show him how to be efficient. He would say, "Here are my notes. I take lots of notes. I don't really know what is the matter, I'm not getting anywhere, that's all. I've been working and working and working, but I don't get the grades." Well, he would have plenty of notes, all right, stacks of them, all very neatly arranged, and most of them copied right out of the book; so I would show him, as kindly as possible, how inefficient all this was, how he had written and written but hadn't learned a thing. And I would show him how to learn much more and to do about one-fourth of all that copy work, and then he would say, "I don't know why I didn't think of that before; why that's marvelous! Thank you so much, sir." And he would run off. In a few weeks I'd see him again and say, "How are you getting on these days?" And there would be that same mass of verbatim notes. And while I sat there, feeling that wave of the teacher's despair, the student would say, "I tried your method, sir, really I did [whose method?], but I don't know, really, sir, it just seems *better* this way."

Now the student was right. I had been trying to give him an efficient way of learning something, whereas he already had a very efficient way of satisfying his conscience, which was what he was mainly trying to do. You cannot imagine a more efficient way to satisfy your conscience than sitting for hours and writing out those notes. The note goes from the book up one finger and one arm, and across the shoulders, and down the other arm onto the paper, and your mind and heart and soul can be off on something else more pleasant. No extra effort at all. Such a method for such a student is admirably designed to fit his purposes. Do you suppose, as a teacher, that your main problem will be your students' stupidity? Or does it begin to seem as if your main problem might be the extraordinary wisdom of their resistance?

No wonder, then, that you will suffer moments of dark despair.

At this point I hesitate to remind you that this is an excursion into my ignorance and that I have no more idea of what to do about these things than you have. I may have offered you the sorry consolation that when you fail to educate a student it may not be wholly your own fault. But surely I am not going to leave you with this, and surely there must be something that you can do about the situation, in addition to the big job of accepting it. Nobody knows the answer to this one, but it may help a little if we look back over the implications of what we have been saying.

From what we have said, it seems to follow that the good teacher's greatest responsibilities and greatest skills lie not in his love for the subject or in the clarity of his exposition, or in his enthusiasm, but in his handling of the problems of resistance. That is to say he will accept the fact that his students will react to him not in terms of who he is, but as a They, and he will, in the face of this, attempt to create a situation in which his students may more readily become Selves in the educational world.

We might expand on the first of these a little. You will be told by another lecturer, "Naturally you never will pull your rank on your students." Now I don't think you will either, not if you have acknowledged that you have a rank and are willing to accept the consequences. The only teacher who pulls his rank is the person who refuses to accept either the rank itself or the adolescents' reaction to it. If you refuse to accept your disciplinary function as an educator, either in kindergarten or in graduate school, and pose, in your own mind, simply as the students' guide and friend, you will be very vulnerable indeed. For when a student turns the hostility which he has accumulated for those who do not let him have what he wants (and he could have it if it were not for Them), when he turns that full blast on you, with an accuracy which he has learned from long experience, and hurts right on the sore spot, what will you do then? If you take it personally, you will pull your rank on him out of your own self-preservation. But if you see it in its context, it will not look like a personal affront, and you will deal with it educationally in its own terms. But more important, if you acknowledge to yourself what your role is and how your students view you, then you will be able to handle your authority productively instead of denying it. That is, you will be able to use it in ways in which it will do the least harm by exciting resistance. Denying it does not do away with it; it simply leaves it out of control. We have all been taught by the teacher who stands between his subject and his students, so that he seems to represent his subject in such a way that the subject matter is inextricable from our reaction to his authority. The admonition which you received earlier not to stand between your students and what you had written on the blackboard referred to something much deeper than the interference caused by your bodily opacity. The good teacher stands to one side of the direct line between his students and his subject. Then his authority can be perceived as a separate matter, and his teaching can be interpreted as assistance rather than imposition.

The job of helping students to discover their Selves in the educational world follows directly from this sort of thing, but it is so complex, so subtle, and so obscure, that I dare not venture far upon it. Certainly it must have something to do with the complicated job of acknowledging one's authoritative position and still treating one's students as persons with integrity and freedom of choice. It would be easy to say that if we want our students to act and think of themselves as mature, we must treat them as mature. It is correspondingly easy to suppose that any teacher who fails to do so fails because of the limitations of his own character. But this is a very harsh judgment indeed, because once more it leaves the students' response out of the picture. The adolescent's desire to be treated as an adult is a highly ambivalent desire. With being an adult come all the difficulties and handicaps which we mentioned. For most of his life, too, the student has developed his skills and his sense of security in dealing with an authoritarian They. He has learned that the way to deal with teachers is to get them to commit themselves, to find out what they think and hand it back to them on examinations. Suppose, then, that you start encouraging your students to think for themselves, and you withhold your own convictions as stultifying to this process. The anxiety and the panic and the hostility will be indescribable. How much of it can you stand? Can you permit the organized conspiracy to promote a whispering campaign on the campus to the effect that your course is vague and indeterminant? Can you let your students complain to the dean that you do not tell them what to expect? Can you allow the head of your department to learn that the students "aren't getting anything" out of your section meetings? Experience with this sort of thing has shown that the students will eventually reverse themselves, but it takes a full academic year for them to do it. Do not judge your colleagues too harshly should they fail to carry through the experiment.

I should like to venture one idea from the counseling process itself, even though I am not very sure how generally it may apply. It sometimes seems to me that the greatest source of anxiety among college students is their sense of personal isolation from their teachers. By personal isolation I do not refer to the lack of teas and social gatherings and bull sessions, or to any specific item of academic paraphernalia. What I mean is the sense that the only connection one has with the professor and the institution at large resides in one's academic record. As one student said, "I feel like a B-minus walking around on two legs." The anxiety of this personal isolation is the breeding ground of infantile defensiveness and resistance. A large part of it is doubtless inevitable and only an indirect expression

of homesickness, but much more of it seems to be a vicious by-product of the fixity of student-teacher roles in our education. When a student comes to you after class with a question about a mathematical problem, what he may really want to say is, "I'm scared to death, I don't think anybody knows I'm here, and nobody cares. Please, teacher, acknowledge that I count, that I am a person, and that you are paying attention." But he cannot say this. He cannot say that in mathematics he is lonely; so he asks a question about a problem, and what are you to do? Can you do anything but answer the question? I do not know. I only know that in the counseling clinic where such things are, after all, infinitely easier to do, more difficulties with mathematics are resolved by accepting and acknowledging how the student feels than by demonstrating some difficult point in a proof.

Now one cannot engage in a Rogerian non-directive interview while erasing the blackboard at the end of a lecture, but in the briefest of these student contacts there can be an enormous difference in quality. The difference resides in the implied topic of the conversation. It can be perfectly clear that the topic of conversation is the subject matter and nothing more, or it can be equally clear that the topic of conversation is the student in his emotional relation to his work. If this is important in the brief moments after class, it should be infinitely more so in the longer office hours. It is extraordinary how simple a matter it really is to give a student a sense of personal relatedness to the community of scholars. All one really has to do is to try to see how he himself at this particular moment sees things and feels things and to show him that one somehow understands. It is in the student's sense of the warmth of being understood, of being therefore personally related, that he is set free from his anxiety so that he can do his academic work productively.

And it is not impossible that it is through the warmth that you may convey this way that the student may come to feel that it may be worth while to grow up. If grown-ups are impersonal, authoritative, and intellectual, then it is perfectly clear that being mature means to give up having fun. It means to the student that to grow up and be a Self must carry with it an absolutely intolerable loss, the discard of *all* his impulses and desires, and that to be a Self will not only mean to be alone, but to be lonely indeed. But if you are warm and attentive to your students' feelings, then they will realize that you, too, put some value on feelings, and that maybe it would be possible to grow up and still have feelings and still have fun. In that case, since you eat beans, maybe they will try them, too.

CHAPTER V

Our Developing Social Interactions

WE HAVE been considering from various points of view how our need to be related to others in a meaningful way is expressed in our behavior, thoughts, and social institutions. Inextricably bound together with this need is a corresponding need for a sense of personal integrity through which to express our individuality. We cannot be satisfied with only an automatic interdependence with others in the way the cells of our bodies are related and necessary to each other; such a relationship is clearly not the nature of our social world. We play a creative part in our interactions with others and we need to feel the special significance of our individual actions.

Perry, when he considers in the article in the preceding chapter the Me and the Self as two "separate, distinct, and self-contained" frames of reference for the developing sense of individuality, describes the Me as a point of view which emphasizes the immediate response to personal wishes and to pleasant-unpleasant feelings. In our development as children our experiences thoroughly train this point of view into our thought and behavior. As infants we apparently first respond to the world without distinguishing between ourselves and others. Our responses seem to be limited to responses to our own feelings. We behave as if both the social and physical environment were simply an extension of ourselves. We are either hungry or not hungry, but we have no conception of food or mother as external objects which relieve our hunger.

During our first or second year we observe as a new experience that the world includes others outside ourselves. The divergent actions of others, which prior to that time we had not noticed, are forced upon our attention. The things we want to do and the things They want us to do are different: our feelings and Theirs are separate. Others seem to be able to make us do things and to limit our actions. Often They seem largely to oppose the things we want; we feel needs which we can satisfy only if They will let us. Further, when They stop some action of ours, They are also sometimes angry with us — They don't seem to like us as much as They did. Yet we may want to be liked by Them as much as or more than we want anything else. We are caught in a conflict: we want to act as They want us to act and at the same time we want to act on some opposing desire of our own.

Often the choice of action in the situations which we meet during these early years is in fact confined largely to a decision whether or not we shall oppose Their limitations. Although we experiment widely with this limited area of choice, it is frequently found to be unsatisfactory. Our decisions do not — as indeed they cannot — satisfy the opposing needs. We may feel that we can behave *either* as They expect *or* as we want, but not both — and neither choice is wholly pleasant. The situations in which we find ourselves then

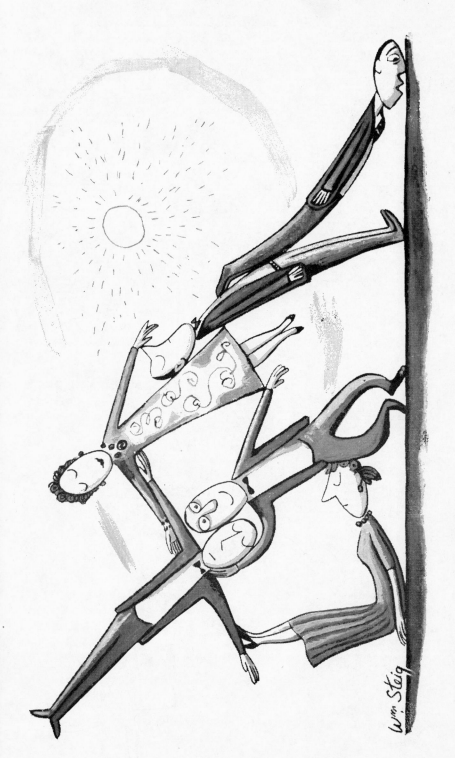

Life is just one human relation after another

Like everybody else, we prefer winning an argument to improving our knowledge

do not strengthen our belief in our own ability to make satisfactory choices.

As our experience accumulates, however, we begin to observe that other areas of choice are open to us. Certainly we wish to retain our own individuality by behaving as we want, and of course we want to behave frequently as others behave. But They are behaving in many different ways. Our father and mother do not behave alike or even consistently; our brothers and sisters are behaving differently from the way we felt we should; others outside the home are behaving still differently. We then experiment with many different roles — we "try them on for size" — we behave like father or mother or brother or sister or maybe a little like several of them, until we find a way of behaving that seems fairly satisfactory to us.

These roles are not a consistent series of acts logically tied together, but rather a set of responses that seem to us to be effective. We learn as children to respond appropriately to social situations long before we "understand" either the situation or our response. We learn to behave in ways that others in observing our actions describe as "good" or "bad" at home, a "good sport" or an "athlete" or a "grind" among our friends. If these responses seem to us to result in behavior that is more "successful" than not, then we begin to have some faith in "ourselves"; *we develop some confidence in our own ability to choose between alternative ways of behaving.* This confidence, as Perry observes, is the foundation of the integrity of Self, and on it rests the ability to handle skillfully the more complex situations of later life.

Skill in responding to many different situations is difficult to develop. There is never any general agreement on how we should *always* act; we must choose a way of our own in each instance. We want to find ways of relating ourselves to all others who are important to us. Yet to please one group we run the risk of antagonizing others. The very act of choice separates us from some of them. Thus the feeling of possible isolation from some group is inherent in the choice, and anxiety may be aroused that will delay our subsequent development toward the integrity of Self. This anxiety tends to force us back to a dependency on the choices of others — with all the contradictions that this involves — so that we can maintain a "satisfactory" relationship with them. Our need for personal integrity may then limit us so that we react solely to the immediate feelings of pleasure in our relations with others. In addition, any "growing up" which demands choices that involve immediate displeasure, even for the sake of later pleasure, may seem intolerable.

Ruth Benedict, in her article "Continuities and Discontinuities in Cultural Conditioning," observes that we do not always emphasize in the training of children the attainment of a degree of responsibility that we must exert as adults. Our very training, then, may stand in the way of our acquisition of a feeling of personal integrity through successful accomplishment. A different type of training is suggested in her example of the Papago child. She says:

> Dr. Ruth Underhill tells me of sitting with a group of Papago elders in Arizona when the man of the house turned to his little three-year-old granddaughter and asked her to close the door. The door was heavy and hard to shut. The child tried, but it did not move. Several times the grandfather repeated, "Yes, close the door." No one jumped to the child's assistance. No one took the responsibility away from her. On the other hand there was no impatience, for after all the child was small. They sat gravely waiting till the child succeeded and her grandfather gravely

thanked her. It was assumed that the task would not be asked of her unless she could perform it, and having been asked the responsibility was hers alone just as if she were a grown woman.[1]

The training of the Papagos may have helped the child to learn that being oneself might mean being able to overcome obstacles that one meets as well as doing what one wants. As the child struggled with the door, she may well have felt her inadequacy to the task, but she also found she could accomplish it. Her family's behavior contrasts vividly with the "conscientious" parent in our culture who is always trying to "help" the child long after such help is necessary or even useful. As Benedict suggests in her article, a degree of responsibility is retained by the parent that prevents the child from acting responsibly. Consider the father who says to his college son after Sunday supper, "Well, it's eight o'clock. I suppose you will have to study now." Or consider the mother who on returning from shopping with her teen-age daughter says, "Put the groceries on the table, dear, and go clean up for lunch." There may have been many "good reasons" for such remarks — the father may have merely wanted to be alone or the mother may have been in a hurry — but both of them took the responsibility for simple decisions out of the hands of their children. In our culture parents may decide most of the routines we shall follow, teachers may decide in detail what we shall learn, bosses may decide even the small things we shall do at our jobs, all making it difficult for us to develop the confidence necessary for responsible behavior.

There seem to be three general stages of the development of our interactions with others. At first we seem to be merely responding by motor schema developed from sensations themselves. We do not yet distinguish between the feelings that spontaneously arise within us and those which are responses to others: between hunger and anger. In the second stage we begin to differentiate more fully, and we observe that there are many people and things outside ourselves that are doing things to us. In this second stage our responses seem to be closely tied to our feelings about what They are doing to us. We may then make further distinctions about our interactions with others and enter a third stage where we observe the possibilities of choosing between many different types of responses. Jean Piaget and his associates, in their clinical studies of children in Switzerland which are considered below, observe these three stages of development in considerable detail.

The underlying experiences on which these hypotheses are based are familiar in a general way to all of us; we have lived through them. We have all learned as we grew up that our early view of the world was too limited to satisfy us and from time to time have modified these earlier views with more complex observations. At no time, however, do these limited views prevent us from arriving at some sort of conclusions. We do the best we can with such observations as are available to us at the time. Although we arrive at many conclusions we later find to be inadequate, nevertheless the earlier observations form — for better or worse — a matrix through which later observations are screened, excluded, or interpreted.

At the earliest stage children seem to be observing almost exclusively their sensations about the things that happen to them; they seem to be responding

[1] Ruth Benedict, "Continuities and Discontinuities in Cultural Conditioning," by permission from *A Study of Interpersonal Relations*, edited by Patrick Mullahy. Copyright, 1949, by Hermitage Press, Inc. Published by Hermitage Press, Inc., New York. See also reading above, Chapter III.

to the physical sensations developed by the activities in which they engage. Through the satisfaction of these sensations the infant learns to respond purposefully to the world in terms of his own needs and desires. The ways these needs are met set up expectations; the infant learns that he can satisfy these needs if he behaves in certain ways defined by the group around him. What started, for example, as an undifferentiated feeling (later recognized as hunger) is narrowed rapidly to a specific demand for milk. From the very beginning a dynamic process is developed in which the child's needs and the group's demands are related.

In this process the child's feelings seem to play a major unifying part, constantly modifying and being modified by group definitions. Since feelings are of central importance during these early years, the problems that arise for children involve comparatively simple elements of choice. Even as late as four or five years old the choices seem to remain largely two-valued: "I would or would not like to go to sleep; I want to play or I don't; I feel hungry or I don't." Similarly, most of the problems that children bring to adults for help during these early years are ones that can be settled on an either-or, yes-or-no basis. Many of them involve relations with parents, their abilities, and their standards. "Will you tie my shoes? Do I have to wash? I want to go out, will you let me? John won't let me play with his ball, will you make him let me? I'm hungry, can I have some milk? I like reading, will you read to me now?" Adults can and do help children of these ages solve most of their problems on the basis of the simple two-valued orientation discussed by Hayakawa. The solutions may or may not satisfy the children, but in either case the response tends to confirm for them the importance of the feelings themselves. Later experiences and observations may indicate that our immediate feelings are not the only significant elements of choice in many problems. Yet early conclusions about the *exclusive* importance of feelings have been useful and important to us for so many years that it is doubtful if any of us ever completely forget them.

Although children respond appropriately to situations without fully understanding them, they also try consistently to improve both their responses and their understanding. Children are omnivorous in the acquisition of data, and they put together the new data as received into some sort of sensible system in their minds. Feelings are the earliest unifying force — a sensible system at this stage means one that makes sense to the child's feelings. But soon other relationships between data become apparent. Things are observed to occur that involve feelings to only a minor extent. These things children accept as related to each other merely because they have occurred together. Children prior to seven or eight years old feel no necessity to look further for any explanation. Many things are observed as together in time or space, but logical or causal relations are complexities that have not yet entered their heads. Many ideas and ways of behaving are thoroughly fixed in our minds during this period and turn up as "illogical" thoughts or actions in later years.

Adults in primitive cultures and children in all cultures observe, for example, that a man and his shadow appear together. They both believe that the shadow is part of the man, and they both know that the sun exists and gives light. Yet they both fail to observe the relationship between the sun and the shadow. This is not a failure of mental activity in the sense that it indicates a weak or inadequate mind, but rather a failure to develop a concept of sufficient complexity to include sun-man-shadow as related terms. Although the adults of many primitive cultures never observe the sun as the source of the shadow, they do elaborate extensively in a highly logical way the consequences of their limited observation. The shadow as part of the man must be treated as one would treat the man's hand or foot; one must walk around it carefully — it would be insulting to step on it. It is considered that man can and does make his shadow grow and shrink, and theories are developed about why this is so. Although our children may develop such theories, they soon abandon them. They, in our culture, obtain a concept ready-made from adults that permits eventual observation of the sun as a related datum.

Jean Piaget and his associates have been particularly interested in the relationship between children's development and their thinking. There is voluminous evidence in this research of the ways we put our observations together into "wholes" at various stages of our development.[2] In the years before six or seven, children in the second stage observe as irrevocably bound together those things that occur together, and any one part of the observation can be used to "explain" another part. Thus, Piaget says,

> When children 5–6 are asked "Why do the sun and moon not fall down?" the answer does no more than to invoke the other features appertaining to the sun and moon, because these features, having been perceived *en-bloc* and within the same whole as the feature requiring explanation, seem to the child sufficient reason for the latter. Leo (age 6) says, "The sun does not fall down *because it is hot. The sun stops there.* How? *Because it is yellow.* And the moon, how does it stop there? *The same as the sun, because it is lying down on the sky.*" Bea (age 5) says, *"Because it is very high up, because there is no* (no more) *sun, because it is very high up."* Or again, if one shows the child a glass of water and if, after putting a small pebble into it so as to make the level of the water rise, one asks the child why the water has risen, the only explanation given will often be a simple description of what has happened; but this description will possess explanatory value for the child. In Tor's opinion (age 7½) the water rises when a pebble is dropped in the glass because the pebble is heavy. When wood is used the water rises because the wood is light.[3]

It is of no consequence to the child whether he says the water rises because the wood is light or the wood is light and the water rises. When "because" is used by the child it does not as yet denote any clear relation of "cause and effect" but something vaguer and more undifferentiated, indicating only that those things in fact are occurring simultaneously. It apparently takes many years for even an elementary understanding of "causal" relations to develop. A child in the second stage will observe, for example, the details about his tricycle with considerable clarity — he will be able to describe the frame and the scratches and dents on it, the pedals and the way they are worn, the wheels and even the fact that they revolve together — but he will not observe the tricycle as a collection of parts put together in a *particular* way, nor will he observe that the wheels turn *because* of force applied to the pedals.

This lack of relatedness is particularly clear when a child is asked to describe some event in which he has just participated. He will describe a movie, for example, with a vivid recollection of its separate parts, but will feel no need to put the parts together in the same way as they were related in the movie.

---

[2] For specific references, see the Additional Readings in this chapter.
[3] Jean Piaget, *Judgment and Reasoning in the Child* (New York: Harcourt, Brace, 1928), pp. 229–230.

During their early development children are dealing with distinctions between things that are much simpler than seem reasonable to us as adults. An adequate answer to a child's question, "Why is that building high?" is often, "Yes, it is high" — a mere confirmation of the fact. A father was surprised recently by the annoyance he received from his seven-year-old son when he tried to answer the question, "Why do the cars in a freight train have numbers on them?" by a simple explanation of the transportation system. He might have found that the child would have been satisfied with an answer such as, "Well, they are sort of like names, so that they can tell the cars apart." A child at this stage considers a name to be one of the characteristics of the object itself; like all other characteristics, it came into existence with the object and cannot be changed. It is like height, breadth, color, and so forth, and is of equal importance.

Piaget in his studies emphasizes that the child in the second stage does not yet observe logical or causal relations between things. He calls the thinking of the second stage *syncretistic*. Often in such thinking the child's feelings are tied together with his observations so that they become an inseparable part of the whole. Not all of our early thinking involves feelings, but when it does, the syncretisms involved in that thinking persist much more strongly in later life. The very feelings themselves seem to possess a "logical" quality that makes it difficult for us to discriminate further. All of us are familiar with our unreasoning dislike of some food and with the facile explanation, "Perhaps I ate it sometime and it made me sick." We feel that this explanation is entirely adequate without any evidence that sickness for us is in fact inseparable from that particular food. Again, many people say, "I don't like the name Pearl" — or Mary Jane, or Agnes — "I knew an awful girl by that name once" — as if the name were inseparable from the girl. At the time the original impression was formed the distinction was about as precise as our experience had indicated the need of making. This type of explanation — which might be called a *syncretism* — was useful to us for a long time and, unless some later development requires that we rethink it, frequently remains satisfactory.

Syncretisms express a phase of our thinking that seems inappropriate only after more useful distinctions have been made. The primitive person's observation that the shadow is part of the man is syncretistic, but it is wholly appropriate to the thinking of the primitive culture. When our thinking is characterized by an insufficient complexity about the concrete situation with which it deals, it has many features in common with the syncretistic thinking of the child that we have been discussing. Consider the following description of the Polish peasant's thinking about his social environment (circa 1910):

> His ideas about other people are . . . schematic, either appropriated from the traditional store or independently elaborated at some moment of intense thinking and afterward used without any new reflection. The peasant's general prepossession about people is that everybody is moved only either by his egotistic interest or by solidarity with his group; if neither can be detected, then evidently the man is clever enough to keep his motives hidden . . . The willingness of the peasant to do business with a given person and particularly to be persuaded by him depends upon the degree to which he understands or thinks that he understands the motives of this person. He will show confidence more readily in a man whose motives he knows to be not only interested but even dishonest than in one whom he does not understand, because in the first case he can take the motives into account,

while in the second he does not know how to limit the possibilities and does not know what to expect. Accordingly he has a summary and egocentric classification ready and applies it in any given case. Those of the first class are the members of his family, whose behavior ought to be determined by the familial relations themselves and from whom solidarity can be expected. Then come the members of the community, classified again according to their nearer or more remote neighborhood, their fortune, character, etc. Then come all the other, unknown peasants, whose interests are supposed to be the same as those of the known ones. The priest, the noble, the Jew, are people of different classes, but still supposedly known. The priest's official character has already been determined, and of course the peasant understands the usual weaknesses of the country priest — money, wine and his housekeeper. Every noble is supposed to desire in his heart the reintroduction of serfdom; but besides this he is a farmer, a man who has innumerable common traditions with the peasant. There may be hostility between him and his peasant neighbors, but there is always more or less of reciprocal understanding. The Jew is classed once and forever as a merchant and cheater, and no other motive than money is ascribed to him; but this makes his schematization relatively easy in spite of the fact that the peasant knows little, if anything, about his familial and religious life.[4]

We might say that neither peasants, nor primitives, nor children have had sufficient interaction with others whose thinking is more precise to force them to observe any inadequacy in their schematic thought. This way of thinking does not appear to result so much from a fundamental difference in the thinking process as from a difference in experience with others — a difference in the material available in the mind to think about.

Children, as their interactions with others in our culture increase, may become aware of differences between their thinking and that of others. If this awareness develops, they then may be forced to make more precise discriminations between the relations of different things in order to retain a necessary unity in their thinking.

Children in their early years, however, lack just this close association between their thoughts and the thoughts of others; in fact, children apparently do not observe for years that their thoughts are in any way different from the thoughts of others around them. Piaget observes that children up to the age of about six often behave as if they believed that all their thoughts were also in other's minds and that there was no need of any verbal communication between them. They will talk extensively with other children and adults without waiting for answers or even hearing what others say. "Collective monologues" of this sort are typical when young children play together. For example, Piaget observes that nearly a quarter of the entire conversation of Lev (age 6) consisted of collective monologues. Piaget illustrates with a few of Lev's remarks "which show how little the child is concerned with speaking to anyone in particular, or even with making himself heard":

> Mlle L. tells a group of children that owls cannot see by day. Lev: "Well, I know quite well that it can't." Lev (at a table where a group is at work): "I've already done *moon* so I'll have to change it." Lev picks up some barley-sugar crumbs: "I say, I am the captain on horseback. I say, I've got a horse and a gun as well."

---

4 William I. Thomas and Florian Znaniecki, *The Polish Peasant in Europe and America* (New York: Knopf, 1918, 1927), I, 291–292.

The opening phrase, "I say, I" which occurs in most of these sentences is significant. Everyone is supposed to be listening. This is what distinguishes this type of remark from pure monologue. But with regard to its contents it is the exact equivalent of the monologue. The child is simply thinking out his actions aloud, with no desire to give anyone any information about it . . .

[The following is a further example] of collective monologue . . . although the remarks are all addressed to someone.

Den (girl, aged 4 years and 5 months) is talking volubly as she works. Bea (girl; 5 years, 10 months) comes into the work room. Den: "You've got a sweater on, I haven't, Mummy said it wasn't cold." Den goes on working. Bea does not answer.

Den to Geo (boy, 6 years): "I know how to, you'll see how well I know. You don't know how. (No answer, Den goes back to her place.) I know how."

Den to Bea: "What do you want? (No answer.) I shall want some little holes." . . .

Why does [Den] speak to Bea? Not for the sake of telling her anything, still less for the sake of getting an answer, but simply as an excuse for talking. Similarly, Den's question to Bea is purely rhetorical, it is a pseudo-question which simply serves as an introduction to the remark which immediately follows. The social attitude is there only in form, not in substance.[5]

This type of playing together where children seem to be responding to little more than an enjoyment of each other's company is not confined to any one culture. A dramatic illustration of this in the British culture is found in the following short story by Joyce Cary.

A SPECIAL OCCASION [6]

The nursery door opened and Nurse's voice said, in the sugary tone which she used to little girl guests, "Here you are, darling, and Tommy will show you all his toys." A little brown-haired girl in a silk party frock, sticking out all round her legs like a lampshade, came in at the door, stopped, and stared at her host. Tom, a dark little boy aged five, also in a party suit, blue linen knickers and a silk shirt, stared back at the girl. Nurse had gone into the night nursery, next door, on her private affairs.

Tom, having stared at the girl for a long time as one would study a curiosity, rare and valuable, but extremely surprising, put his feet together, made three jumps forward and said, "Hullo."

The little girl turned her head over one shoulder and slowly revolved on one heel, as if trying to examine the back of her own frock. She then stooped suddenly, brushed the hem with her hand, and said, "Hullo."

Tom made another jump, turned round, pointed out of the window, and said in a loud voice something like "twanky tweedle." Both knew that neither the gesture nor the phrase was meant to convey a meaning. They simply expressed the fact that for Tom this was an important and exciting, a very special occasion.

The little girl took a step forward, caught her frock in both hands as if about to make a curtsy, rose upon her toes, and said in a prim voice, "I beg your pardon."

They both gazed at each other for some minutes with sparkling eyes. Neither smiled, but it seemed that both were about to smile.

Tom then gave another incomprehensible shout, ran around the table, sat down on the floor and began to play with a clockwork engine on a circular track. The

---

[5] Jean Piaget, *The Language and Thought of the Child* (New York: Harcourt, Brace, 1932), pp. 18–19, 57.

[6] Originally printed in *Harper's Magazine*, vol. 203, no. 1216 (September 1951), pp. 97–98. Copyright, 1951, by Harper and Brothers. Reprinted by permission of the author.

little girl climbed on a tricycle and pedaled round the floor. "I can ride your bike," she said.

Tom paid no attention. He was trying how fast the engine could go without falling off the track.

The little girl took a picture book, sat down under the table with her back to Tom, and slowly, carefully, examined each page. "It's got a crooked wheel," Tom said, "that's what it is." The little girl made no answer. She was staring at the book with round eyes and a small pursed mouth — the expression of a nervous child at the zoo when the lions are just going to roar. Slowly and carefully she turned the next page. As it opened, her eyes became larger, her mouth more tightly pursed, as if she expected some creature to jump out at her.

"Tom." Nurse, having completed her private business, came bustling in with the air of one restored to life after a dangerous illness. "Tom, you naughty boy, is this the way you entertain your guests? Poor little Jenny, all by herself under the table." The nurse was plump and middle-aged; an old-fashioned nanny.

"She's not by herself," Tom said.

"Oh Tom, that really is naughty of you. Where are all your nice manners? Get up, my dear, and play with her like a good boy."

"I am playing with her," Tom said, in a surly tone, and he gave Nurse a sidelong glance of anger.

"Now Tom, if you go on telling such stories, I shall know you are trying to be naughty. Get up now when I ask you." She stooped, took Tom by the arm, and lifted him up. "Come now, you must be polite, after you've asked her yourself and pestered for her all the week."

At this public disclosure, Tom instantly lost his temper and yelled, "I didn't — I didn't — I won't — I won't!"

"Then I'll have to take poor little Jenny downstairs again to her mummy."

"No — no — no."

"Will you play with her, then?"

"No, I hate her — I never wanted her."

At this the little girl rose and said, in precise, indignant tones, "He *is* naughty, isn't he?"

Tom flew at her and seized her by the hair; the little girl at once uttered a loud scream, kicked him on the leg, and bit his arm. She was carried screaming to the door by Nurse, who, from there, issued sentence on Tom, "I'm going straight to your father, as soon as he comes in." Then she went out, banging the door.

Tom ran at the door and kicked it, rushed at the engine, picked it up and flung it against the wall. Then he howled at the top of his voice for five minutes. He intended to howl all day. He was suffering from a large and complicated grievance.

All at once the door opened and the little girl walked in. She had an air of immense self-satisfaction, as if she had just done something very clever. She said, in a tone demanding congratulation, "I've come back."

Tom gazed at her through his tears and gave a loud sob. Then he picked up the engine, sat down by the track. But the engine fell off at the first push. He gave another sob, looked at the wheels, and bent one of them straight.

The little girl lifted her party frock behind in order not to crush it, sat down under the table, and drew the book onto her knee.

Tom tried the engine at high speed. His face was still set in the form of anger and bitterness, but he forgot to sob. He exclaimed with surprise and pleased excitement, "It's the lines too — where I trod on 'em."

The little girl did not reply. Slowly, carefully, she opened the book in the middle and gazed at an elephant. Her eyes became immense, her lips minute. But suddenly, and, as it were, accidentally, she gave an enormous sigh of relief, of happiness.

During their sixth and seventh years the children in Piaget's studies begin to collaborate more frequently with each other. Then conversation often occurs where one child is paying some attention to the others. At this point each speaker is talking only about himself and from his own point of view, but he is heard and understood by the other children. There is as yet no collaboration in a common activity, but there is some response. In the following example the children are busy drawing, and each one tells the story which his drawing illustrates. "Yet," Piaget says, "at the same time they are talking about the same subject and pay some attention to each other":

> Lev (5; 11): "It begins with Goldylocks. I'm writing the story of the three bears. The daddy bear is dead. Only the daddy was too ill." Gen (5; 11): "I used to live at Saleve. I lived in a little house and you had to take the funicular railway to go and buy things." Geo (6; 0): "I can't do the bear." Li (6; 10): "That's not Goldylocks." Lev: "I haven't got curls." [7]

Such conversations and common activities indicate the beginning of a third stage of development, where genuine interaction between contemporaries can first be observed. In the first stage of the process of developing social interactions the child does not observe any distinction between himself and others; he is concerned almost exclusively with his own feelings and sensations. In the second stage he starts to observe that there are things and people outside himself that behave differently from himself. He then develops a certain capacity for observation and description. Early in this second stage, for example, the child learns to avoid a chair in running around the room because he feels that the chair might bump and hurt him; later in this stage he distinguishes between animate and inanimate objects, and he is "good" or "bad" because he feels They make him behave this way. In both the first and second stages his thinking and behavior are essentially egocentric or self-centered, and although he becomes aware of the distinction between the animate and inanimate objects that surround him, he is not yet aware of the individuality of others. Early in the third stage of development there emerges, in addition, a desire to respond more closely to the different views of other people, and consequently the child starts to observe their individuality more fully. An important part of the development from the second stage to the third is the distinction the child draws between a response that he feels is forced upon him and one that he makes because he wants to do it. So, in this third stage, he may learn to respond to others because he wants to do certain things with them.

It might be said that in a child's development he learns appropriate "rules" of behavior that guide him so that his relations with both things and people seem reasonably satisfactory. He builds up a "morality" by which he judges and responds to the behavior of others and himself. During early development the child is dealing, in Piaget's words, with a "morality of constraint." Either things or people *make* him act in certain ways. In the third stage he may learn a "morality of coöperation": he may expand his outlook to include the points of view of others and develop a feeling of integrity from his very skills in deciding upon behavior for himself that will unite his activities with theirs.

These developments are by no means mutually exclusive. In fact, they all seem at times to operate simultaneously. The "morality of coöperation" devel-

---

[7] *The Language and Thought of the Child,* p. 58.

ops in those situations where the authority of others is felt to be less omnipresent. It operates alongside the "morality of constraint" as the situation permits. In a specific situation the child will use either of these ways — or parts of each of them — whichever seems appropriate.

The changes in the child's responses and in his thoughts about them may become clearer if we consider them in relation to a single activity over a period of years. Piaget and his associates have studied the development of children in respect to the game of marbles as it is played in Switzerland. There this game forms an important part of the child's total activities; he first learns the rules of marbles from parents and other "older" people in the same ways that he becomes aware of other cultural rules. As he grows older the importance of the authority figures may change in respect to the rules of marbles — the child may learn that he knows the rules as well as or better than the older people. A group force is eventually added which gives the child needed strength to modify the authoritarian rules. The child may learn the strength of "all the boys play that way." Then the attitude toward rules may change. The rules are no longer felt to be external; they are no longer felt through syncretistic thinking to be one of the unchangeable characteristics of the game of marbles as heat is of fire. They become subject to change through group decision. Freed from the pressures of external authorities, rules no longer have to be imposed from above. The child can and does develop rules as a mutually accepted method of ordering an activity between contemporaries for the benefit of all. In respect to these particular rules the child may go through a complete "life-cycle," from which some interesting general concepts can be drawn. Read

JEAN PIAGET, "The Rules of the Game," below.

As children reach the ages of seven or eight they seem to find more need to interact with others of their own age. They continue to behave almost at random, but the behavior is more in response to the other children around them. They now start to play marbles together rather than as an individualized activity; they now try to "win." In this behavior they find the earlier, rigid rules learned individually from their elders less useful. Endless arguments and disputes ensue. Although their ideas about rules remain vague for several years and they can rarely agree about any single set of rules for longer than one game, they discuss them at length. They seem to find eventually that only through mutual consent can they resolve the inadequacies that are inherent in the rules learned individually at the earlier stages. Conflicts and disagreements are the methods through which the mutually agreeable codes of behavior are evolved. They find that they must often reconcile nearly opposing points of view if a game is to be played. These views cannot be successfully modified by the earlier type of consideration of "right and wrong" in respect to an externally imposed set of standards. They find that they must weigh, modify, or choose between the opinions of many others and then act on the final result. The basic objective becomes a group objective rather than solely an individual one. A decision as to what is "fair" becomes more important than what is "right." A feeling of loyalty to a contemporary group and the personal importance of a sense of belonging to that group becomes predominant. A system of mutual regulation is developed that is particularly valuable to them because they feel that they need it and can modify it whenever desirable. Such coöperative activity does not mean freedom from conflict or disagreement, but rather the freedom to conflict and disagree in ways that will produce mutually desirable results in a particular situation.

The skills that children develop in this coöperative stage are not skills in observing the exact nature of their own feelings or the results of any particular choice of action on these feelings. Rather they are skills in observing the thoughts and feelings of others *and* unifying them into a mutually satisfactory code of behavior for a specific situation. Earlier the feelings of others are considered important, but only as something to be accepted or rejected — and children do not always "want" the things the others feel "should" be wanted. In the coöperative stage of development children find ways of making their wants a part of the group objectives and feel that their personal integrity is assured if they are skillful in choices which integrate the group around specific activities.

Many things happen to prevent children from going through the third stage of development or from responding to it as the children did in Piaget's study of the game of marbles. Piaget did not report observations of the children who did not play marbles and consequently did not have this experience. A particular child may have found the conflict of the initial interactions too unpleasant, and he may have avoided as much as possible thereafter any such interactions with his contemporaries. Or he may have continued playing with the group but may have felt "forced" to submit to the group rules in a way very similar to that in which he submitted to parental authorities. He thus may have merely reinforced his understanding of a "morality of constraint," though shifting the locus of authority from adults to contemporaries.

Piaget's studies suggest that if the child did not experience the developments of the coöperative stage, then he may not have learned any techniques for building the codes of behavior that are so important in dealing with others on a non-authoritarian basis. All of us learned thoroughly at one time a "morality of constraint" to which we both submitted and objected. Not all of us, however, interacted sufficiently with our contemporaries after the ages of seven or eight under conditions of comparative freedom from authority pressures to have experienced equally thoroughly a "morality of coöperation."

The behavior that is learned in response to the morality of coöperation is of particular importance to the attainment of the Self orientation which Perry describes. In the second stage of development, we feel secure and protected by Their benevolence and power. To lose this security would force us to face an intolerable isolation in the fact of our real separateness as individuals — unless we can find security in another way. Such security can develop in the coöperative context of We-ness — of group belonging — and may help us accept the responsibilities attendant upon our developing capacities to choose. Only in coöperative effort can we learn that to be as we are, biologically alone, is not to be intolerably lonely. In this coöperative stage the elements of choice are found to be many and complex, *but* a technique of dealing with the conflicting choices may be developed for use in particular situations. The success of this behavior may then form the foundation of an orientation where the integrity of Self with its skill of individual choices can exist.[8]

---

[8] Consider "Mu Nu Fraternity," Vol. II, Case 5.

ADDITIONAL READINGS

Durkheim, Emile, *The Division of Labor in Society,* trans. George Simpson (Glencoe, Illinois: The Free Press, 1947; first published in French in 1893).

Durkheim discusses two types of social organization that parallel Piaget's two types of morality: mechanical solidarity (based on a morality of constraint) and organic solidarity (based on a morality of coöperation). The book further elucidates the close connection between modes of individual thought and types of social interaction.

Mead, George H., *Mind, Self, and Society* (Chicago: University of Chicago Press, 1934).

Mead develops a theory of the growth of the conception of self through role playing. He believes that we only become conscious of ourselves as entities when we take the roles of others and view ourselves through their eyes. He shows how the self slowly grows through social interaction.

Piaget, Jean, *The Language and Thought of the Child* (London: Routledge and Kegan Paul, 1926); *Judgment and Reasoning in the Child* (London: Routledge and Kegan Paul, 1928); *The Child's Conception of the World* (London: Routledge and Kegan Paul, 1929); *The Child's Conception of Physical Causality* (London: Routledge and Kegan Paul, 1930); *The Moral Judgment of the Child* (London: Routledge and Kegan Paul, 1932; Glencoe, Illinois: The Free Press, 1948).

In these books, Piaget and his associates report their clinical studies of children and build a theory of interpretation around the observations. They observe particularly the relation of the child's behavior to his thought and its implications for adult behavior.

Riesman, David, *et al.,* *The Lonely Crowd: A Study of the Changing American Character* (New Haven: Yale University Press, 1950).

A new interpretation of the "typical" American as a man who has become "other-directed" — a man whose central purpose is adjustment to the demands of his peers. Riesman contrasts this new American with his grandfather, who was "inner-directed" — a man with strong moral values which gave him direction regardless of the demands of others. In a sense, Riesman is examining the logical extreme of Piaget's "stage of coöperation."

The Rules of the Game*

BY JEAN PIAGET

Children's games constitute the most admirable social institutions. The game of marbles, for instance, as played by boys, contains an extremely complex system of rules, that is to say, a code of laws, a jurisprudence of its own. Only the psychologist, whose profession obliges him to become familiar with this instance of common law, and to get at the implicit morality underlying it, is in a position to estimate the extraordinary wealth of these rules by the difficulty he experiences in mastering their details.

If we wish to gain any understanding of child morality, it is obviously with the analysis of such facts as these that we must begin. All morality consists in a system of rules, and the essence of all

* Reprinted with permission from the first chapter of *The Moral Judgment of the Child,* translated by Marjorie Gabain (London: Routledge and Kegan Paul Ltd., 1932). This chapter was written with the collaboration of Mme. V. J. Piaget, MM M. Lambercier and L. Martinez.

morality is to be sought for in the respect which the individual acquires for these rules. The reflective analysis of Kant, the sociology of Durkheim, or the individualistic psychology of Bovet all meet on this point. The doctrines begin to diverge only from the moment that it has to be explained how the mind comes to respect these rules. For our part, it will be in the domain of child psychology that we shall undertake the analysis of this "how."

Now, most of the moral rules which the child learns to respect he receives from adults, which means that he receives them after they have been fully elaborated, and often elaborated, not in relation to him and as they are needed, but once and for all and through an uninterrupted succession of earlier adult generations.

In the case of the very simplest social games, on the contrary, we are in the presence of rules which have been elaborated by the children alone. It is of no moment whether these games strike us as "moral" or not in their contents. As psychologists we must ourselves adopt the point of view, not of the adult conscience, but of child morality. Now, the rules of the game of marbles are handed down, just like so-called moral realities, from one generation to another, and are preserved solely by the respect that is felt for them by individuals. The sole difference is that the relations in this case are only those that exist between children. The little boys who are beginning to play are gradually trained by the older ones in respect for the law; and in any case they aspire from their hearts to the virtue, supremely characteristic of human dignity, which consists in making a correct use of the customary practices of a game. As to the older ones, it is in their power to alter the rules. If this is not "morality," then where does morality begin? At least, it is respect for rules, and it appertains to an enquiry like ours to begin with the study of facts of this order. Of course the phenomena relating to the game of marbles are not among the most primitive. Before playing with his equals, the child is influenced by his parents. He is subjected from his cradle to a multiplicity

of regulations, and even before language he becomes conscious of certain obligations. These circumstances even exercise, as we shall see, an undeniable influence upon the way in which the rules of games are elaborated. But in the case of play institutions, adult intervention is at any rate reduced to the minimum. We are therefore in the presence here of realities which, if not amongst the most elementary, should be classed nevertheless amongst the most spontaneous and the most instructive.

With regard to game rules there are two phenomena which it is particularly easy to study: first the *practice* of rules, *i.e.* the way in which children of different ages effectively apply rules: second the *consciousness* of rules, *i.e.* the idea which children of different ages form of the character of these game rules, whether of something obligatory and sacred or of something subject to their own choice, whether of heteronomy or autonomy.

It is the comparison of these two groups of data which constitutes the real aim of this chapter. For the relations which exist between the practice and the consciousness of rules are those which will best enable us to define the psychological nature of moral realities.

One word more. Before embarking upon an analysis of the practice or of the consciousness of rules, we must first give some account of the actual content of these rules. We must therefore establish the social data of the problem. But we shall confine ourselves only to what is indispensable. We have not attempted to establish the sociology of the game of marbles; this would have meant finding out how this game was played in the past and how it is now played in different parts of the world . . . Even confining ourselves to French Switzerland, we believe it would need several years of research to discover all the local variants of the game and, above all, to outline the history of these variants throughout the last few generations. Such an enquiry, which might be useful to the sociologist, is superfluous for the psychologist. All the latter needs in order to study how rules are learned is a thorough knowledge of a given custom in actual use, just as in order to study child language, all he needs is to know a given dialect, however localized, without troubling to reconstruct all its semantic and phonetic changes in time and space. We shall therefore confine ourselves to a short analysis of the content of the game as it is played in Geneva and Neuchâtel, in the districts where we conducted our work.

1. The Rules of the Game of Marbles

Three essential facts must be noted if we wish to analyse simultaneously the practice and the consciousness of rules.

The first is that among children of a given generation and in a given locality, however small, there is never one single way of playing marbles, there are quantities of ways. There is the "square game" with which we shall occupy ourselves more especially. A square is drawn on the ground and a number of marbles placed within it; the game consists in aiming at these from a distance and driving them out of the enclosure. There is the game of "courate" where two players aim at each other's marble in indefinite pursuit. There is the game of "troyat" from "trou" (= hole) or "creux" (= hollow), where the marbles are piled into a hole and have to be dislodged by means of a heavier marble, and so on. Every child is familiar with several games, a fact that may help according to his age to reinforce or to weaken his belief in the sacred character of rules.

In the second place, one and the same game, such as the Square game, admits of fairly important variations according to when and where it is played. As we had occasion to verify, the rules of the Square game are not the same in four of the communes of Neuchâtel [1] situated at 2–3 kilometers from each other. They are not the same in Geneva and in Neuchâtel. They differ, on certain points, from one district to another, from one school to another in the same town. In addition to this, as through our collaborators' kindness we were able to establish, variations occur from one generation to another. A student of twenty assured us that in his village the game is no longer played as it was "in his days." These variations according to time and place are important, because children are often aware of their existence. A child who has moved from one town, or merely from one school building to another will often explain to us that such and such a rule is in force in one place but not in the other. Very often, too, a child will tell us that his father played differently from him. Last of all, there is the boy of 14 who has given up playing because he is beginning to feel superior to the little ones, and who, according to his temperament, laughs or mourns over the fact that the customs of his generation are going by the board instead of being piously preserved by the rising generation.

Finally, and clearly as a result of the convergence of these local or historical currents, it will happen that one and the same game (like the Square game) played in the playground of one and the same school admits on certain points of several different rules. Children of 11 to 13 are familiar with these variants, and they generally agree before or during the game to choose a given usage to the exclusion of others. These facts must therefore be borne in mind, for they undoubtedly condition the judgment which the child will make on the value of rules.

Having mentioned these points, we shall give a brief exposition of the rules of the Square game, which will serve as a prototype, and we shall begin by fixing the child's language so as to be able to understand the reports of the conversations which will be quoted later on. Besides, as is so often the case in child psychology, some aspects of this language are in themselves highly instructive.

A marble is called "un marbre" in Neuchâtel and "un cœillu" or "un mapis" in Geneva. There are marbles of different value. The cement marble has the place of honour. The "carron" which is smaller and made of the more brittle clay is of less value because it costs less. The

---

[1] Neuchâtel, La Coudre, Hauterive and Saint-Blaise.

marbles that are used for throwing[2] and are not placed inside the square are called according to their consistency "corna" (if in carnelian), "ago," or "agathe," "cassine" (glass ball with coloured veins), "plomb" (large marble containing lead), etc. Each is worth so many marbles or so many "carrons." To throw a marble is to "tirer" (shoot) and to touch another marble with one's own is to "tanner" (hit).

Then comes a set of terms of ritual *consecration,* that is, of expressions which the player uses in order to announce that he is going to perform such-and-such an operation and which thus consecrate it ritually as an accomplished fact. For, once these words have been uttered, the opponent is powerless against his partner's decision; whereas if he takes the initiative by means of the terms of ritual *interdiction,* which we shall examine in a moment, he will in this way prevent the operation which he fears. For example, in order to play first in circumstances when it is possible to do so, the child will say (at Neuchâtel) "prems" — obviously a corruption of the word "premier" (first). If he wants to go back to the line that all the players start from at their first turn and which is called the "coche," [3] he simply says "coche." If he wishes to advance or retreat to a distance twice as great, he says "deux coches," or if to a distance of one, two, or three hand-breadths he says "one (or two, or three) empans" (spans). If he wishes to place himself in relation to the square at a distance equal to that at which he finds himself at a given moment, but in another direction (so as to avoid the probable attacks of his opponent) he says "du mien" (mine), and if he wishes to prevent his opponent from doing the same thing he says "du tien" (yours). This applies to Neuchâtel. In Geneva these displacements are expressed by the terms "faire une entasse" or "entorse" (to make a twist). If you wish to give up your turn and be "dead" until your op-

ponent has moved, you say "coup passé" (my turn passed).

As soon as these terms have been uttered in circumstances which of course are carefully regulated by a whole juridical system, the opponent has to submit. But if the opponent wishes to anticipate these operations, it is sufficient for him to pronounce the terms of ritual *interdiction,* which at Neuchâtel are simply the same terms but preceded by the prefix "fan," from "défendu" (forbidden). For example, "fan-du-mien," "fan-du-tien," "fan-coche," "fan-coup-passé," etc. Some children, not having understood this prefix, which does not, after all, correspond with anything in the speech they hear around them, say "femme-du-tien," "femme-coche," etc.

Two more particularly suggestive terms of consecration should be noted, which are current among the little Genevans: "glaine" and "toumiké." When a player places a marble of superior value in the square, thinking that he has put down an ordinary marble (say an "ago" instead of a "cœillu") he is naturally allowed, if he has noticed his mistake, to pick up his "ago" and put an ordinary marble in its place. Only a dishonest opponent would take advantage of his partner's absent-mindedness and pocket this "ago" after having hit it. The children we questioned on this point were unanimous in pronouncing such procedure equivalent to stealing. But if, on the other hand, the opponent spots his partner's mistake in time and utters the word "toumiké" or (by doubling the last syllable) "toumikémik," then the absent-minded player no longer has the right to pick up his "ago"; he must leave it on the ground like a common-or-garden "cœillu," and if one of the players succeeds in hitting it, this player will be allowed in all fairness to take possession of it. This shows us a very interesting example of a word consecrating a mistake and by doing so changing a dishonest action into one that is legitimate and recognized as

---

[2] The English technical equivalent is the generic term "shooter," which we shall use in the interrogatories given below. For the rest we have generally retained the French words as one cannot be sure that the English terms mean exactly the same. [Trans.]

[3] English, pitch-line (sometimes). [Trans.]

such by all. We have here for the first time an example of that formalism which belongs to certain aspects of childish morality, and into whose nature we shall go more deeply in the sequel in connection with objective responsibility.

In the same way, the word "glaine" legitimatizes piracy in certain well-defined conditions. When one of the players has succeeded, either by luck or by skill, in winning all his partners' marbles, it is a point of honour similar to that which sociologists designate with the term "potlatch" that he should offer to play a fresh set and should himself place in the square the necessary marbles, so as to give his less fortunate playmates the chance of recovering a portion of their possessions. If he refuses, of course no law can force him to do this; he has won and there is the end of it. If, however, one of the players pronounces the word "glaine" then the whole gang falls upon the miser, throws him down, empties his pockets and shares the booty. This act of piracy which in normal times is profoundly contrary to morality (since the marbles collected by the winner constitute his lawfully acquired possession) is thus changed into a legitimate act and even into an act of retributive justice approved by the general conscience when the word "glaine" has been pronounced.[4]

At Neuchâtel we noticed neither "glaine" nor "toumiké," but, on the other hand, we found "cougac." When one of the players has won too much (therefore in the situation just described) his defeated partner can force him to offer to play another set by uttering the word "cougac" (probably derived from coupgagné just as "prems" was from premier). If the winner wishes to evade the obligation laid upon him by the fateful word, he has only to anticipate the blow by saying "fan-cougac."

Our reason for emphasizing these linguistic peculiarities is only to show from the first the juridical complexity of game rules. It is obvious that these facts could be analysed more fundamentally from other points of view. One could, for example, work out the whole psychology of consecration and interdiction in connection with the child and, above all, the psychology of social games. But these questions are really outside our scope.[5] Let us therefore return to what is the essential point so far as we are concerned, namely, the rules themselves.

The Square game thus consists, in a word, in putting a few marbles in a square, and in taking possession of them by dislodging them with a special marble, bigger than the rest. But when it comes to details this simple schema contains an indefinite series of complications. Let us take them in order, so as to get some idea of their richness.

First of all, there is the "pose" or outlay. One of the players draws a square and then each places his "pose." If there are two players, each one puts down two, three, or four marbles. If there are three players, each puts down two marbles. If there are four or more players, it is customary to put down only one marble each. The main thing is equality: each one puts down what the others do. But in order to reach equality the relative value of the marbles must be taken into account. For an ordinary marble, you must put down eight "carrons." A little "corna" is worth eight "marbres," sixteen "carrons," and so on. The values are carefully regulated and correspond roughly to the price paid at the shop round the corner. But alongside of financial operations proper, there are between children various exchanges in kind which appreciably alter current values.

Then the game begins. A certain distance is agreed upon where the "coche" is drawn; this is the line from which the players start. It is drawn parallel to and generally one or two metres away from one of the sides of the square, and from it each player will fire his first shot.

---

[4] This word "glaine" really has a wider sense. According to several children it entitles whoever pronounces it simply to pick up all the marbles that are on the ground when a discussion arises about them, or if a player forgets to take possession of what is his due. It is in this sense that the word is taken, for instance, in Philippe Monnier's, *Le Livre de Blaise* (3rd ed., p. 135).

[5] With regard to social games we are awaiting the publication of R. Cousinet's book which will incorporate all the valuable material which this author has been accumulating for so many years.

(To "fire" is to throw one's shooter — "agathe" or "cornaline" — into the square.)

All, therefore, start from the coche. In some games you return to the coche at each fresh turn, but it is more usual after the first shot to play from the place that your marble has rolled to. Sometimes this rule is limited by saying that the marble must not be further removed from the square than the coche. Thus if your marble has rolled two metres away from the square in any direction whatsoever, you bring it back to a distance of 1m. 50 if this is the distance at which the coche itself stands.

But before the game begins you must settle who is to play first. For the first player has the advantage of "firing" into a square full of marbles, whereas those who follow are faced only with what is left after the gains of the preceding players. In order to know who is to begin, a series of well-known rites are put in action. Two children walk towards each other stepping heel to toe, and whichever steps on the other's toe has the right to begin. Or else rhymed formulæ or even syllables devoid of any meaning are recited in sacramental order. Each syllable corresponds to a player, and he on whom the last syllable falls is the lucky one. In addition to these customary usages there is a method of procedure peculiar to the game of marbles. Each boy throws his "shooter" in the direction of the coche or of a line specially traced for the purpose. Whoever comes nearest up to the line begins. The others follow in order of their nearness up to the line. The last to play is the boy who has gone beyond the coche, and if several have gone beyond it, the last to play will be the boy whose marble has gone furthest.

The order of the players having been settled in this way, the game begins. Each player in turn stands behind the coche and "fires" into the square. There are three ways of throwing one's marble: "Piquette" (Eng., "shooting") which consists in projecting the marble by a jerk of the thumb, the marble being placed against the thumb-nail and kept in place by the first finger; "Roulette" (Eng., "bowling") which consists simply in rolling your marble along the ground, and "Poussette" (Eng., "hunching") which consists in addition in carrying your hand along with it over a sufficient distance to correct the initial direction. Poussette is always banned and may in this connection be compared to the push stroke of a bad billiard player. At Neuchâtel it is customary to say "fan-poussette" or again "femme-poussette." In Geneva, the simpler expression "défendu de trainer" (dragging forbidden) is in use. Roulette ("bowling") is also generally banned ("fan-roulette") but is at times tolerated, in which case everyone will of course have the right to play in this way, and absolute equality before the law will even be agreed upon at the beginning of the game.

The players are therefore throwing in the manner that has been agreed upon. Suppose one of the marbles included in the square has been hit. If it has gone outside the square it becomes the property of the boy who has dislodged it. If it remains inside the enclosure it cannot be taken. If, finally, it remains on the line the case is judged by the partners: a marble which is half outside is regarded as out, not otherwise. Here, naturally, a whole lot of subsidiary rules will establish the procedure in disputed cases. There remains the case of the marble with which one shoots (the shooter, or taw, etc.) remaining in the square or failing to lie beyond one of the lines of the square by at least half of its diameter: its owner is "cuit" (dished), i.e. he cannot play any more. If this marble is projected outside the square by that of another player, it becomes, like the others, the latter's property, except in the case of special conventions generally agreed upon at the beginning of the game. Finally, there are the possible complications arising from cases of rebounding marbles. A marble that bounces out of the square off another is sometimes not held to be won, and a fortiori in the case of a marble of value.[6] In other cases, everything that goes outside the enclo-

---

[6] This is expressed by saying that the "revenette" does not count.

sure belongs to the player who has expelled it. The particular cases that arise in this way are settled in conformity with principles that are established either before or during the game by mutual agreement between all the participants.

Then comes the question of the number of "shots" to be allowed to each. The player who has succeeded in winning one or more marbles has the right to play again, and so on, for as long as he wins. But sometimes the following reservation is made: for the first round in each game every player plays once in turn, independently of gains or losses. Here again, therefore, it is a matter of previous arrangement.

In addition — and this is an essential rule — everyone has the right not only to "fire" at the marbles in the square, but also to "tanner" (hit) his neighbour's shooter, even outside the enclosure and indeed wherever it may happen to be in the course of the game. And of course the great difficulty is to shoot at the square without placing yourself within reach of your partners. This is why, when a shot would involve too many risks, you are allowed to say "coup-passé" and to remain where you are, provided, of course, that no one has foreseen this decision and said "fan-coup-passé." And this, really, is why you are allowed to change your position provided you place yourself at the same distance from the square as before, and provided you first say "du mien" (mine), unless, once again, your opponent has anticipated your move by saying "du tien" (yours).

Finally, a series of special rules deserves mention, the observance of which depends upon the particular town or school in question. The first player who says "place-pour-moi" (place for me) is not obliged to take up his position at one of the corners of the square. Any player who has succeeded in winning the equivalent of his "pose" (*i.e.* two marbles if he has placed two in the square, and so on) can say "queue-de-pose" which will allow him to have the first shot from the coche in the next game, and so on.

The game, regulated in this way by an indefinite number of rules, is carried on until the square is empty. The boy who has pocketed the largest number of marbles has won.

2. The Interrogatory and Its General Results

The rules that we have outlined above constitute a well-marked social reality, "independent of individuals" (in Durkheim's sense) and transmitted, like a language, from one generation to another. This set of customs is obviously more or less plastic. But individual innovations, just as in the case of language, succeed only when they meet a general need and when they are collectively sanctioned as being in conformity with the "spirit of the game." But while fully recognizing the interest attaching to this sociological aspect of the problem, it was from a different standpoint that we raised the questions which we are now going to study. We simply asked ourselves (1) how the individuals adapt themselves to these rules, *i.e.* how they observe rules at each age and level of mental development; (2) how far they become conscious of rules, in other words, what types of obligation result (always according to the children's ages) from the increasing ascendancy exercised by rules.

The interrogatory is therefore easy to carry out. During the first part, it is sufficient to ask the children (we questioned about 20 boys ranging from 4 to 12–13) how one plays marbles. The experimenter speaks more or less as follows. "Here are some marbles." (The marbles are placed on a large baize-covered table beside a piece of chalk.) "You must show me how to play. When I was little I used to play a lot, but now I've quite forgotten how to. I'd like to play again. Let's play together. You'll teach me the rules and I'll play with you." The child then draws a square, takes half the marbles, puts down his "pose," and the game begins. It is important to bear in mind all possible contingencies of the game and to ask the child about each. This means that you must avoid making any sort of suggestions. All you need do is to appear completely ignorant, and even to make intentional mistakes so that the child may each time point out clearly what the rule is. Naturally, you must take the whole thing very seriously, all through the game. Then you ask who has won and why, and if everything is not quite clear, you begin a new set.

It is of paramount importance during this first half of the interrogatory to play your part in a simple spirit and to let the child feel a certain superiority at the game (while not omitting to show by an occasional good shot that you are not a complete duffer). In this way the child is put at his ease, and the information he gives as to how he plays is all the more conclusive. Many of our children became absorbed in the game to the extent of treating me completely as one of them. "You are dished!" cries Ben (10 years) when my marble stops inside the square.

In the case of the little ones, who find difficulty in formulating the rules which they observe in practice, the best way is to make them play in pairs. You begin by playing with one of them in the manner described above, and ask him to tell you all the rules he knows. Then you make the same request of the second boy (the first being no longer present), and finally you bring the two together and ask them to have a game. This control experiment is not needed for older children, except in doubtful cases.

Then comes the second part of the interrogatory, that, namely, which bears upon the consciousness of rules. You begin by asking the child if he could invent a new rule. He generally does this easily enough, but it is advisable to make sure that it really is a new rule and not one of the many existing variants of which this particular child may already have knowledge. "I want a rule that is only by you, a rule that you've made up yourself and that no one else knows — the rule of N—— [the child's name]." Once the new rule has been formulated, you ask the child whether it could give rise to a new game: "Would it be all right to play like that with your pals? Would they want to play that way? etc." The child either agrees to the suggestion or disputes it. If he agrees, you immediately ask him

whether the new rule is a "fair" rule, a "real" rule, one "like the others," and try to get at the various motives that enter into the answers. If, on the other hand, the child disagrees with all this, you ask him whether the new rule could not by being generalized become a real rule. "When you are a big boy, suppose you tell your new rule to a lot of children, then perhaps they'll all play that way and everyone will forget the old rules. Then which rule will be fairest — yours that everyone knows, or the old one that everyone has forgotten?" The formula can naturally be altered in accordance with the turn which the conversation is taking, but the main point is to find out whether one may legitimately alter rules and whether a rule is fair or just because it conforms to general usage (even newly introduced), or because it is endowed with an intrinsic and eternal value.

Having cleared up this point it will be easy enough to ask the two following questions. (1) Have people always played as they do to-day: "Did your daddy play this way when he was little, and your grand-dad, and children in the time of William Tell, Noah, and Adam and Eve, etc., did they all play the way you showed me, or differently?" (2) What is the origin of rules: Are they invented by children or laid down by parents and grown-ups in general?

Sometimes it is best to begin by these last two questions before asking whether rules can be changed; this avoids perseveration, or rather reverses its direction, and so facilitates the interpretation of the answers. All this part of the interrogatory, moreover, requires extremely delicate handling; suggestion is always ready to occur, and the danger of romancing is ever present. But it goes without saying that the main thing is simply to grasp the child's mental orientation. Does he believe in the mystical virtue of rules or in their finality? Does he subscribe to a heteronomy of divine law, or is he conscious of his own autonomy? This is the only question that interests us. The child has naturally got no ready-made beliefs on the origin and endurance of the rules of his games; the ideas which he invents then and there are only indices of his fundamental attitude, and this must be steadily borne in mind throughout the whole of the interrogatory.

The results which we obtained from this double interrogatory, and which we shall examine in greater detail later on, are roughly the following.

From the point of view of the practice or application of rules four successive stages can be distinguished.

A first stage of a purely *motor* and *individual* character, during which the child handles the marbles at the dictation of his desires and motor habits. This leads to the formation of more or less ritualized schemas, but since play is still purely individual, one can only talk of motor rules and not of truly collective rules.

The second may be called *egocentric* for the following reasons. This stage begins at the moment when the child receives from outside the example of codified rules, that is to say, some time between the ages of two and five. But though the child imitates this example, he continues to play either by himself without bothering to find play-fellows, or with others, but without trying to win, and therefore without attempting to unify the different ways of playing. In other words, children of this stage, even when they are playing together, play each one "on his own" (everyone can win at once) and without regard for any codification of rules. This dual character, combining imitation of others with a purely individual use of the examples received, we have designated by the term Egocentrism.

A third stage appears between 7 and 8, which we shall call the stage of incipient *cooperation*. Each player now tries to win, and all, therefore, begin to concern themselves with the question of mutual control and of unification of the rules. But while a certain agreement may be reached in the course of one game, ideas about the rules in general are still rather vague. In other words, children of 7–8, who belong to the same class at school and are therefore constantly playing with each other, give, when they are questioned separately, disparate and often en-

tirely contradictory accounts of the rules observed in playing marbles.

Finally, between the years of 11 and 12, appears a fourth stage, which is that of the *codification of rules*. Not only is every detail of procedure in the game fixed, but the actual code of rules to be observed is known to the whole society. There is remarkable concordance in the information given by children of 10–12 belonging to the same class at school, when they are questioned on the rules of the game and their possible variations.

These stages must of course be taken only for what they are worth. It is convenient for the purposes of exposition to divide the children up in age-classes or stages, but the facts present themselves as a continuum which cannot be cut up into sections. This continuum, moreover, is not linear in character, and its general direction can only be observed by schematizing the material and ignoring the minor oscillations which render it infinitely complicated in detail. So that ten children chosen at random will perhaps not give the impression of a steady advance which gradually emerges from the interrogatory put to the hundred odd subjects examined by us at Geneva and Neuchâtel.

If, now, we turn to the consciousness of rules we shall find a progression that is even more elusive in detail, but no less clearly marked if taken on a big scale. We may express this by saying that the progression runs through three stages, of which the second begins during the egocentric stage and ends towards the middle of the stage of cooperation (9–10), and of which the third covers the remainder of this cooperating stage and the whole of the stage marked by the codification of rules.

During the first stage rules are not yet coercive in character, either because they are purely motor, or else (at the beginning of the egocentric stage) because they are received, as it were, unconsciously, and as interesting examples rather than as obligatory realities.

During the second stage (apogee of egocentric and first half of cooperating stage) rules are regarded as sacred and untouchable, emanating from adults and lasting forever. Every suggested alteration strikes the child as a transgression.

Finally, during the third stage, a rule is looked upon as a law due to mutual consent, which you must respect if you want to be loyal but which it is permissible to alter on the condition of enlisting general opinion on your side.

The correlation between the three stages in the development of the consciousness of rules and the four stages relating to their practical observance is of course only a statistical correlation and therefore very crude. But broadly speaking the relation seems to us indisputable. The collective rule is at first something external to the individual and consequently sacred to him; then, as he gradually makes it his own, it comes to that extent to be felt as the free product of mutual agreement and an autonomous conscience. And with regard to practical use, it is only natural that a mystical respect for laws should be accompanied by a rudimentary knowledge and application of their contents, while a rational and well-founded respect is accompanied by an effective application of each rule in detail.

There would therefore seem to be two types of respect for rules corresponding to two types of social behaviour. This conclusion deserves to be closely examined, for if it holds good, it should be of the greatest value to the analysis of child morality. One can see at once all that it suggests in regard to the relation between child and adult. Take the insubordination of the child towards its parents and teachers, joined to its sincere respect for the commands it receives and its extraordinary mental docility. Could not this be due to that complex of attitudes which we can observe during the egocentric stage and which combines so paradoxically an unstable practice of the law with a mystical attitude towards it? And will not cooperation between adult and child, in so far as it can be realized and in so far as it is facilitated by cooperation between children themselves, supply the key to the interiorization of commands and to the autonomy of the moral con-

sciousness? Let us therefore not be afraid of devoting a certain amount of time to the patient analysis of the rules of a game, for we are here in possession of a method infinitely more supple, and consequently more sure, than that of merely questioning children about little stories, a method which we shall be obliged to adopt in the latter part of this book.

3. *The Practice of Rules: I. The First Two Stages*

We need not dwell at any length upon the first stage, as it is not directly connected with our subject. At the same time, it is important that we should know whether the rules which come into being previous to any collaboration between children are of the same type as collective rules.

Let us give a handful of ten marbles to a child of three years and four months and take note of its reactions:

Jacqueline has the marbles in her hands and looks at them with curiosity (it is the first time she has seen any); then she lets them drop on to the carpet. After this she puts them in the hollow of an arm-chair. "*Aren't they animals?* — Oh, no. — *Are they balls?* — Yes.*" She puts them back on the carpet and lets them drop from a certain height. She sits on the carpet with her legs apart and throws the marbles a few inches in front of her. She then picks them up and puts them on the arm-chair and in the same hole as before. (The arm-chair is studded with buttons which create depressions in the material.) Then she collects the lot and lets them drop, first all together, then one by one. After this she replaces them in the arm-chair, first in the same place and then in the other holes. Then she piles them up in a pyramid: "*What are marbles?* — What do you think? — . . ." She puts them on the floor, then back on to the arm-chair, in the same holes. — We both go out on to the balcony: she lets the marbles drop from a height to make them bounce.

The following days, Jacqueline again places the marbles on the chairs and arm-chairs, or puts them into her little sauce-pan to cook dinner. Or else she simply repeats the behaviour described above.

Three points should be noted with regard to facts such as these. In the first place, the lack of continuity and direction in the sequence of behaviour. The child is undoubtedly trying first and foremost to understand the nature of marbles and to adapt its motor schemas to this novel reality. This is why it tries one experiment after another: throwing them, heaping them into pyramids or nests, letting them drop, making them bounce, etc. But once it has got over the first moments of astonishment, the game still remains incoherent, or rather still subject to the whim of the moment. On days when the child plays at cooking dinner, the marbles serve as food to be stewed in a pot. On days when it is interested in classifying and arranging, the marbles are put in heaps in the holes of arm-chairs, and so on. In the general manner in which the game is carried on there are therefore no rules.

The second thing to note is that there are certain regularities of detail, for it is remarkable how quickly certain particular acts in the child's behaviour become schematized and even ritualized. The act of collecting the marbles in the hollow of an arm-chair is at first simply an experiment, but it immediately becomes a motor schema bound up with the perception of the marbles. After a few days it is merely a rite, still performed with interest, but without any fresh effort of adaptation.

In the third place, it is important to note the symbolism[7] that immediately becomes grafted upon the child's motor schemas. These symbols are undoubtedly enacted in play rather than thought out, but they imply a certain amount of imagination: the marbles are food to be cooked, eggs in a nest, etc.

This being so, the rules of games might be thought to derive either from rites

analogous to those we have just examined or from a symbolism that has become collective. Let us briefly examine the genesis and ultimate destiny of these modes of behaviour.

Genetically speaking, the explanation both of rites and of symbols would seem to lie in the conditions of pre-verbal motor intelligence. When it is presented with any new thing, a baby of 5 to 8 months will respond with a dual reaction; it will accommodate itself to the new object and it will assimilate the object to earlier motor schemas. Give the baby a marble, and it will explore its surface and consistency, but will at the same time use it as something to grasp, to suck, to rub against the sides of its cradle, and so on. This assimilation of every fresh object to already existing motor schemas may be conceived of as the starting point of ritual acts and symbols, at any rate from the moment that assimilation becomes stronger than actual accommodation itself. With regard to ritual acts, indeed, one is struck by the fact that from the age of about 8 to 10 months all the child's motor schemas, apart from moments of adaptation in the real sense, give rise to a sort of functioning in the void, in which the child takes pleasure as in a game. Thus, after having contracted the habit of pressing her face against her parents' cheeks, crumpling up her nose and breathing deeply the while, Jacqueline began to perform this rite as a joke, crumpling up her nose and breathing deeply in advance, merely suggesting contact with another person's face, but without, as before, expressing any particular affection by the act. Thus from being actual, and incorporated in an effective adaptation, this schema has become ritualized and serves only as a game.[8] Or again, Jacqueline in her bath is engaged in rubbing her hair; she lets go of it to splash the water. Immediately, she repeats the movement, touching her hair and the water alternately, and during the next few days the schema has

---

[7] We use the term "symbol" in the sense given to it in the linguistic school of Saussure, as the contrary of sign. A sign is arbitrary, a symbol is motivated. It is in this sense, too, that Freud speaks of symbolic thought.

[8] Age: 10 months.

become ritualized to such an extent that she cannot strike the surface of the water without first outlining the movement of smoothing her hair.[9] In no way automatic, this rite is a game that amuses her by its very regularity. Anyone observing a baby of 10 to 12 months will notice a number of these rites which undoubtedly anticipate the rules of future games.

As for symbols, they appear towards the end of the first year and in consequence of the ritual acts. For the habit of repeating a given gesture ritually gradually leads to the consciousness of "pretending." The ritual of going to bed, for instance (laying down one's head and arranging the corner of the pillow with the hundred and one complications which every baby invents), is sooner or later utilized "in the void," and the smile of the child as it shuts its eyes in carrying out this rite is enough to show that it is perfectly conscious of "pretending" to go to sleep. Here already we have a symbol, but a "played" symbol. Finally, when language and imagery come to be added to motor intelligence, the symbol becomes an object of thought. The child who pushes a box along saying "tuff-tuff" is assimilating in imagination the box's movement to that of a motor-car: the play symbol has definitely come into being.

This being so, can one seek among rites and symbols for the origin of the actual rules of games? Can the game of marbles, with its infinite complexity both with regard to the actual rules and to all that relates to the verbo-motor system of signs in use — can the game of marbles, then, be conceived simply as the result of an accumulation of individual rites and symbols? We do not think that it can. We believe that the individual rite and the individual symbol constitute the substructure for the development of rules and collective signs, its necessary, but not its sufficient, condition. There is something more in the collective rule than in the motor rule or the individual ritual,

just as there is something more in the sign than in the symbol.

With regard to motor or ritualistic rules, there can be no doubt that they have something in common with rules in the ordinary sense, namely the consciousness of regularity. When we see the delight taken by a baby of 10 to 12 months or a child of 2–3 in reproducing a given behaviour in all its details, and the scrupulous attention with which it observes the right order in these operations, we cannot help recognizing the *Regelbewusstsein* of which Bühler speaks. But we must distinguish carefully between the behaviour into which there enters only the pleasure of regularity, and that into which there enters an element of obligation. It is this consciousness of obligation which seems to us, as to Durkheim[10] and Bovet,[11] to distinguish a rule in the true sense from mere regularity.

Now this element of obligation, or, to confine ourselves to the question of the practice of rules, this element of obedience, intervenes as soon as there is a society, *i.e.* a relation between at least two individuals. As soon as a ritual is imposed upon a child by adults or seniors for whom he has respect (Bovet), or as soon, we would add, as a ritual comes into being as the result of the collaboration of two children, it acquires in the subject's mind a new character which is precisely that of a rule. This character may vary according to the type of respect which predominates (respect for the senior or mutual respect) but in all cases there enters an element of submission which was not contained in the rite pure and simple.

In actual fact, of course, there is every degree of variety between the simple regularity discovered by the individual and the rule to which a whole social group submits itself. Thus during the egocentric stage we can observe a whole series of cases in which the child will use a rule as a mere rite, to be bent and modified at will, while at the same time he already tries to submit to the common

---

[9] Age: 12 months.
[10] *L'Education Morale.*
[11] "Les Conditions de l'Obligation de la Conscience," *Année Psychol.*, 1912.

laws. Just as the child very soon acquires the use of language and of the abstract and general concepts while retaining in his attitude to these much that still belongs to egocentric modes of thought and even to the methods peculiar to symbolic and play thought, so, under the rules that are imposed upon him, he will for a long time contrive (in all good faith, needless to say) to maintain his own fantasy in the matter of personal decisions. But this factual continuity between ritual and rule does not exclude a qualitative difference between the two types of behaviour.

Let us not, however, anticipate what will be said in our analysis of the consciousness of rules, but return to the matter of ritual. The individual rite develops quite naturally, as we have just shown, into a more or less complex symbolism. Can this symbolism be regarded as the starting point of that system of obligatory verbo-motor signs which are connected with the rules of every collective game? As with the previous problem, we believe that the symbol is a necessary, but not a sufficient, condition of the appearance of signs. The sign is general and abstract (arbitrary), the symbol is individual and motivated. If the sign is to follow upon the symbol, a group must therefore strip the individual's imagination of all its personal fantasy and then elaborate a common and obligatory imagery which will go hand in hand with the code of rules itself.

Here is an observation showing how far removed are individual rites and symbols from rules and signs, though moving towards these realities in so far as collaboration between children becomes established.

Jacqueline (after the observations given above) is playing with Jacques (2 years, 11 months and 15 days), who sees marbles for the first time. I. Jacques takes the marbles and lets them drop from a height one after another. After which he picks them up and goes away. II. Jacques arranges them on the ground, in a hollow, and says, "*I'm making a little nest.*" Jacqueline takes one and sticks it in the ground in imitation. III. Jacques also takes one, buries it and makes a mud-pie above it. He digs it up and begins over again. Then he takes 2 at a time which he buries. Then 3, 4, 5 and up to 6 at a time, increasing the number of marbles systematically each time by one. Jacqueline imitates him: she first puts one marble down and makes a mud-pie over it, then two or three at random and without adopting a fixed system of progression. IV. Jacques puts all the marbles on a pile, then he places an india-rubber ball beside them and says: "*That's the Mummy ball and the baby balls.*" V. He piles them together again and covers them up with earth which he levels down. Jacqueline imitates him but with only one marble, which she covers up without levelling the earth. She adds: "*It's lost*," then digs it up and begins over again.

This example shows very clearly how all the elements of individual fantasy or symbolism remain uncommunicated; as soon as the game takes on an imaginative turn each child evokes its favourite images without paying any attention to anyone else's. It will also be observed how totally devoid of any general direction are the ritualized schemas successively tried. But as soon as there is reciprocal imitation (end of II and whole of III) we have the beginnings of a rule: each child tries to bury the marbles in the same way as the other, in a common order only more or less successfully adhered to. In bringing out this aspect, the observation leads us to the stage of egocentrism during which the child learns other peoples' rules but practices them in accordance with his own fantasy.

We shall conclude this analysis of the first stage by repeating that before games are played in common, no rules in the proper sense can come into existence. Regularities and ritualized schemas are already there, but these rites, being the work of the individual, cannot call forth that submission to something superior to the self which characterizes the appearance of any rule.

The second stage is the stage of *ego-*

centrism. In studying the practice of rules we shall make use of a notion which has served on earlier occasions in the descriptions we have given of the child's intellectual behaviour; and, in both cases, indeed, the phenomenon is of exactly the same order. Egocentrism appears to us as a form of behaviour intermediate between purely individual and socialized behaviour. Through imitation and language, as also through the whole content of adult thought which exercises pressure on the child's mind as soon as verbal intercourse has become possible, the child begins in a sense, to be socialized from the end of its first year. But the very nature of the relations which the child sustains with the adults around him prevents this socialization for the moment from reaching that state of equilibrium which is propitious to the development of reason. We mean, of course, the state of cooperation, in which the individuals, regarding each other as equals, can exercise a mutual control and thus attain to objectivity. In other words, the very nature of the relation between child and adult places the child apart, so that his thought is isolated, and while he believes himself to be sharing the point of view of the world at large he is really still shut up in his own point of view. The social bond itself, by which the child is held, close as it may seem when viewed from outside, thus implies an unconscious intellectual egocentrism which is further promoted by the spontaneous egocentrism peculiar to all primitive mentality.

Similarly, with regard to the rules of games, it is easy to see, and greater authorities than ourselves[12] have already pointed out, that the beginnings of children's games are characterized by long periods of egocentrism. The child is dominated on the one hand by a whole set of rules and examples that are imposed upon him from outside. But unable as he is, on the other hand, to place himself on a level of equality with regard to his seniors, he utilizes for his own ends, unaware even of his own isolation, all that he has succeeded in grasping of the social realities that surround him.

To confine ourselves to the game of marbles, the child of 3 to 5 years old will discover, according to what other children he may happen to come across, that in order to play this game one must trace a square, put the marbles inside it, try to expel the marbles from the square by hitting them with another marble, start from a line that has been drawn beforehand, and so on. But though he imitates what he observes, and believes in perfect good faith that he is playing like the others, the child thinks of nothing at first but of utilizing these new acquisitions for himself. He plays in an individualistic manner with material that is social. Such is egocentrism.

Let us analyse the facts of the case.

MAR (6)[13] seizes hold of the marbles we offer him, and without bothering to make a square he heaps them up together and begins to hit the pile. He removes the marbles he has displaced and puts them aside or replaces them immediately without any method. "Do you always play like that? — *In the street you make a square.* — Well, you do the same as they do in the street. — *I'm making a square, I am.*" (He draws the square, places the marbles inside it and begins to play again.) I play with him, imitating each of his movements. "Who has won? — *We've both won.* — But who has won most? . . ." — (Mar does not understand.)

BAUM (6½) begins by making a square and puts down three marbles, adding: "*Sometimes you put 4, or 3, or 2.* — Or 5? — *No, not 5, but sometimes 6 or 8.* — Who begins when you play with the boys? — *Sometimes me, sometimes the other one.* — Isn't there a dodge for knowing who is to begin? — *No.* — Do you know what a coche

---

[12] Stern in his *Psychology of Early Childhood* notes the identity of the stages we have established in children's conversations with those he has himself established with regard to play, pp. 177 and 332.

[13] The numbers in parentheses give the child's age. The words of the child are in italics, those of the examiner in Roman lettering. Quotation marks mark the beginning and end of a conversation reported *verbatim*. All the subjects are boys unless the letter G. is added, indicating that the subject is a girl.

is? — *Rather!*" But the sequel shows that he knows nothing about the coche and thinks of this word as designating another game. "And which of us will begin? — *You.* — Why? — *I want to see how you do it.*" We play for a while and I ask who has won: "*The one who has hit a mib,*[14] *well, he has won.* — Well! who has won? — *I have, and then you.*" I then arrange things so as to take 4 while he takes 2: "Who has won? — *I have, and then you.*" We begin again. He takes two, I none. "Who has won? — *I have.* — And I? — *You've lost.*"

LOEFF (6) often pretends to be playing with Mae, of whom we shall speak later. He knows neither how to make a square nor to draw a coche. He immediately begins to "fire" at the marbles assembled in a heap and plays without either stopping or paying any attention to us. "Have you won? — *I don't know. I think I have.* — Why? — *Yes, because I threw the mibs.* — And I? — *Yes, because you threw the mibs.*"

DESARZ (6): "Do you play often? — *Yes, rather!* — With whom? — *All by myself.* — Do you like playing alone best? — *You don't need two. You can play only one.*" He gathers the marbles together without a square and "fires" into the heap.

Let us now see how two children, who have grown accustomed to playing together, set about it when they are left alone. They are two boys of whom one (Mae) is a very representative example of the present stage, while the other (Wid) stands at the border line between the present stage and the next. The analyses of these cases will be all the more conclusive as the children in question are no mere beginners at the game.

MAE (6) and WID (7) declare that they are always playing together. Mae tells us that they both "*played again, yesterday.*" I first examine Mae by himself. He piles his marbles in a corner without counting them and throws his shooter into the pile. He then places 4 marbles close together and puts a fifth on top (in a pyramid). Mae denies that a square is ever drawn. Then he corrects himself and affirms that he always does so: "How do you and Wid know which is to begin? — *One of the two throws his shooter and the other tries to hit it. If he hits it, he begins.*" Mae then shows us what the game consists in: he throws his shooter without taking into account the distances or the manner of playing ("piquette"), and when he succeeds in driving a marble out of the square he immediately puts it back. Thus the game has no end. "Does it go on like that all the time? — *You take one away to make a change.*" (He takes a marble out of the square, but not the one that he has touched.) "*It'll only be finished when there's only one left.*" (He "fires" again twice.) "*One more shot, and then you take one away.*" Then he affirms: "*Every third shot you take one away.*" He does so. Mae removes a marble every third shot independently of whether he has hit or missed, which is completely irregular and corresponds to nothing in the game as habitually played, or as we have seen it played in Neuchâtel or Geneva. It is therefore a rule which he has invented then and there but which he has the impression of remembering because it presents a vague analogy with what really happens when the player removes the marble he has just "hit" (touched). This game of Mae's is therefore a characteristic game of the second stage, an egocentric game in which "to win" does not mean getting the better of the others, but simply playing on one's own.

Wid, whom I now prepare to question and who has not assisted at Mae's interrogatory, begins by making a square. He places 4 marbles at the 4 corners and one in the middle (the same disposition as Mae's, which was probably a deformation of it). Wid

---

[14] English equivalent for "marbre." [Trans.]

does not know what to do to decide which is to begin, and declares that he understands nothing of the method which Mae had shewn me as being familiar to both of them (trying to hit one's partner's shooter). Wid then throws his shooter in the direction of the square, knocking out one marble which he puts in his pocket. Then I take my turn, but fail to touch anything. He plays again and wins all the marbles, one after the other, keeping them each time. He also declares that when you have knocked a marble out, you have the right to play another shot straight away. After having taken everything he says: *"I've won."* Wid therefore belongs to the third stage if this explanation is taken as a whole, but the sequel will show that he takes no notice of Mae's doings when they are playing together. Wid stands therefore at the boundary line which separates the stage of egocentrism from the stage of cooperation.

I then tell Mae to come into the room and the two children begin to play with each other. Mae draws a square and Wid disposes the marbles in accordance with his habitual schema. Mae begins (he plays "Roulette" whereas Wid most of the time plays "Piquette") and dislodges four marbles. *"I can play four times, now,"* adds Mae. This is contrary to all the rules, but Wid finds the statement quite natural. So one game succeeds another. But the marbles are placed in the square by one child or the other as the spirit moves them (according to the rules each must put his "pose") and the dislodged marbles are sometimes put straight back into the square, sometimes retained by the boy who has won them. Each plays from whatever place he chooses, unchecked by his partner, and each "fires" as many times as he likes (it thus often happens that Mae and Wid are playing at the same time).

I now send Wid out of the room and ask Mae to explain the game to us for a last time. Mae places 16 marbles in the middle of the square. "Why so many as that? — *So as to win.* — How many do you put down at home with Wid? — *I put five, but when I'm alone, I put lots."* Mae then begins to play and dislodges a marble which he puts on one side. I do the same. The game continues in this way, each playing one shot at a time without taking the dislodged marbles into account (which is contrary to what Mae was doing a moment ago). Mae then places five marbles in the square, like Wid. This time I arrange the five marbles as Mae himself had done at the beginning of the interrogatory (four close together and one on top) but Mae seems to have forgotten this way of doing things. In the end Mae plays by taking away a marble every three shots, as before, and says to us: *"It's so that it should stop."*

We have quoted the whole of this example in order to show how little two children from the same class at school, living in the same house, and accustomed to playing with each other, are able to understand each other at this age. Not only do they tell us of totally different rules (this still occurs throughout the third stage), but when they play together they do not watch each other and do not unify their respective rules even for the duration of one game. The fact of the matter is that neither is trying to get the better of the other: each is merely having a game on his own, trying to hit the marbles in the square, *i.e.* trying to "win" from his own point of view.

This shows the characteristics of the stage. The child plays for himself. His interest does not in any way consist in competing with his companions and in binding himself by common rules so as to see who will get the better of the others. His aims are different. They are indeed dual, and it is this mixed behaviour that really defines egocentrism. On the one hand, the child feels very strongly the desire to play like the other boys, and especially like those older than himself; he longs, that is to say, to feel himself a member of the very honourable fraternity of those who know how to play marbles correctly. But quickly persuading himself, on the other hand, that his playing is "right" (he can convince himself as easily on this point as in all his attempts to imitate adult behaviour) the child thinks only of utilizing these acquisitions for himself: his pleasure still consists in the mere development of skill, in carrying out the strokes he sets himself to play. It is, as in the previous stage, essentially a motor pleasure, not a social one. The true "socius" of the player who has reached this stage is not the flesh and blood partner but the ideal and abstract elder whom one inwardly strives to imitate and who sums up all the examples one has ever received.

It little matters, therefore, what one's companion is doing, since one is not trying to contend against him. It little matters what the details of the rules may be, since there is no real contact between the players. This is why the child, as soon as he can schematically copy the big boys' game, believes himself to be in possession of the whole truth. Each for himself, and all in communion with the "Elder": such might be the formula of egocentric play.

It is striking to note the affinity between this attitude of children of 4 to 6 in the game of marbles and the attitude of those same children in their conversations with each other. For alongside of the rare cases of true conversation where there is a genuine interchange of opinions or commands, one can observe in children between 2 and 6 a characteristic type of pseudo-conversation or "collective monologue," during which the children speak only for themselves, although they wish to be in the presence of interlocutors who will serve as a stimulus. Now here again, each feels himself to be in communion with the group because he is inwardly addressing the Adult who knows and understands everything, but here again, each is only concerned with himself, for lack of having dissociated the "ego" from the "socius."

These features of the egocentric stage will not, however, appear in their full light until we come to analyse the consciousness of rules which accompanies this type of conduct.

4. The Practice of Rules: II. Third and Fourth Stages

Towards the age of 7–8 appears the desire for mutual understanding in the sphere of play (as also, indeed, in the conversations between children). This felt need for understanding is what defines the third stage. As a criterion of the appearance of this stage we shall take the moment when by "winning" the child refers to the fact of getting the better of the others, therefore of gaining more marbles than the others, and when he no longer says he has won when he has done no more than to knock a marble out of the square, regardless of what his partners have done. As a matter of fact, no child, even from among the older ones, ever attributes very great importance to the fact of knocking out a few more marbles than his opponents. Mere competition is therefore not what constitutes the affective motive-power of the game. In seeking to win the child is trying above all to contend with his partners *while observing common rules*. The specific pleasure of the game thus ceases to be muscular and egocentric, and becomes social. Henceforth, a game of marbles constitutes the equivalent in action of what takes place in discussion in words: a mutual evaluation of the competing powers which leads, thanks to the observation of common rules, to a conclusion that is accepted by all.

As to the difference between the third and fourth stages, it is only one of degree. The children of about 7 to 10 (third stage) do not yet know the rules in detail. They try to learn them owing to their increasing interest in the game played in common, but when different children of the same class at school are questioned on the subject the discrepancies are still considerable in the information obtained. It is only when they are at play that these same children succeed in understanding each other, either by copying the boy who seems to know most about it, or, more frequently, by omitting any usage that might be disputed. In this way they play a sort of simplified game. Children of the fourth stage, on the contrary, have thoroughly mastered their code and even take pleasure in juridical discussions, whether of principle or merely of procedure, which may at times arise out of the points in dispute.

Let us examine some examples of the third stage, and, in order to point more clearly to the differentiating characters of this stage, let us begin by setting side by side the answers of two little boys attending the same class at school and accustomed to playing together. (The children were naturally questioned separately in order to avoid any suggestion between them, but we afterwards compared their answers with one another.)

BEN (10) and NUS (11, backward, one year below the school standard) are both in the fourth year of the lower school and both play marbles a great deal. They agree in regarding the square as necessary. Nus declares that you always place 4 marbles in the square, either at the corners or else 3 in the centre with one on top (in a pyramid). Ben, however, tells us that you place 2 to 10 marbles in the enclosure (not less than 2, not more than 10).

To know who is to begin you draw, according to Nus, a line called the "coche" and everyone tries to get near it: whoever gets nearest plays first, and whoever goes beyond it plays last. Ben, however, knows nothing about the coche: you begin *"as you like. —* Isn't there a dodge for knowing who is to play first? *— No. —* Don't you try with the coche? *— Yes, sometimes.* — What is the coche? *— . . ."* (He cannot explain.) On the other hand, Ben affirms that you "fire" the first shot at a distance of 2 to 3 steps from the square. A single step is not enough, and *"four isn't any good either."* Nus is ignorant of this law and considers the distance to be a matter of convention.

With regard to the manner of "firing," Nus is equally tolerant. According to him you can play "piquette" or "roulette," but *"when you play piquette everyone must play the same. When one boy says that you must play roulette, everyone plays that way."* Nus prefers roulette because *"That is the best way"*: piquette is more difficult. Ben, however, regards piquette as obligatory in all cases. He is ignorant, moreover, of the term roulette and when we show him what it is he says: *"That is bowled piquette!* [Fr., Piquette roulée] *That's cheating!"*

According to Nus everyone must play from the coche, and all through the game. When, after having shot at the square you land anywhere, you must therefore come back to the coche to "fire" the next shot. Ben, on the contrary, who on this point represents the more general usage, is of the opinion that only the first shot should be fired from the coche: after that *"You must play from where you are."*

Nus and Ben thus agree in stating that the marbles that have gone out of the square remain in the possession of the boy who dislodged them. This is the only point, this and the actual drawing of the square, on which the children give us results that are in agreement.

When we begin to play, I arrange to stay in the square (to leave my shooter inside the enclosure). *"You are dished* (Fr., cuit), cries Ben, delighted, *you can't play again until I get you out!"* Nus knows nothing of this rule. Again, when I play carelessly and let the shooter drop out of my hand, Ben exclaims *"Fan-coup"* to prevent me from saying "coup-passé" and having another shot. Nus is ignorant of this rule.

At one point Ben succeeds in hitting my shooter. He concludes from this that he can have another shot, just as though he had hit one of the marbles placed in the square. Nus, in the same circumstances, does not draw the same conclusions (each must play in turn according to him) but deduces that he will be able to play the first shot in the next game.

In the same way, Ben thinks that everyone plays from the place the last shot has led him to and knows the rule that authorizes the player to change places, saying *"du mien"* or *"un em-pan,"* whereas Nus, who has certainly heard those words, does not know what they mean.

These two cases, chosen at random out of a class of 10-year-old pupils, show straight away what are the two differential features of the second stage. 1. There is a general will to discover the rules that are fixed and common to all players (cf. the way Nus explains to us that if one of the partners plays piquette *"everyone must play the same"*). 2. In spite of this there is considerable discrepancy in the children's information. Lest the reader should think the above examples exceptional here are, on the same point, the answers of another child from the same class:

Ross (11; 1): *"First, every one puts two marbles on the square. You can make the square bigger when there are more playing."* Ross knows the method of the coche for knowing who is to begin. Like Nus, he allows both roulette and piquette. He also allows what is not only contrary to all established usages but also to the sense of the words, a way of playing which he calls *"femme-poussette"* which consists in carrying one's hand along with the marble as one throws it (push stroke in billiards). Now this is always forbidden, and the very word that Ross has deformed says so — "fan-poussette." According to Ross, you play from the place you have reached with the last shot, and when you have won a marble you have the right to another shot straight away. To change your place you must say "du mien." *"If a stone gets in our way, you say 'coup-passé' and have another shot. If it slips* [if the marble slips out of your hand] *you say 'laché'* [Eng., 'gone']. *If you don't say that, you can't have another turn. It's the rules!"* Ross here stands mid-way between Nus and Ben. Finally, Ross knows of a rather peculiar custom which is unknown to Nus and Ben. *"If you stay in the square you can be hit and then he picks up the marbles* [= If your shooter stays inside the square and is

touched by your opponent's shooter, he is entitled to all the marbles in the square]. *He* [the opponent] *can have two shots* [to try and hit the shooter in question] *and if he misses the first he can take* [at the second shot] *the shooter from anywhere* [though of course only from the outside of the square] *and make the marbles go out* [= take them]." This rule has generally only been described to us by children of the fourth stage, but the rest of Ross's interrogatory is typically third stage.

Such then is the third stage. The child's chief interest is no longer psycho-motor, it is social. In other words, to dislodge a marble from a square by manual dexterity is no longer an aim in itself. The thing now is not only to fight the other boys but also and primarily to regulate the game with a whole set of systematic rules which will ensure the most complete reciprocity in the methods used. The game has therefore become social. We say "become" because it is only after this stage that any real cooperation exists between the players. Before this, each played for himself. Each sought, it is true, to imitate the play of older boys and of the initiated, but more for the satisfaction, still purely personal, of feeling himself to be a member of a mystical community whose sacred institutions are handed down by the elders out of the remote past, than from any real desire to cooperate with his playmates or with anyone else. If cooperation be regarded as more social than this mixture of egocentrism and respect for one's seniors which characterizes the beginnings of collective life among children, then we may say that it is from the third stage onwards that the game of marbles begins to be a truly social game.

As yet, however, this cooperation exists to a great extent only in intention. Being an honest man is not enough to make one to know the law. It is not even enough to enable us to solve all the problems that may arise in our concrete "moral experience." The child fares in the same way during the present stage, and succeeds, at best, in creating for himself a "provisional morality," putting off till a later date the task of setting up a code of laws and a system of jurisprudence. Nor do boys of 7 to 10 ever succeed in agreeing amongst themselves for longer than the duration of one and the same game; they are still incapable of legislating on all possible cases that may arise, for each still has a purely personal opinion about the rules of the game.

To use an apter comparison, we may say that the child of 7 to 10 plays as he reasons. We have already[15] tried to establish the fact that about the age of 7 or 8, precisely, that is to say, at the moment when our third stage appears, in the very poor districts where we conducted our work,[16] discussion and reflection gain an increasing ascendency over unproved affirmation and intellectual egocentrism. Now, these new habits of thought lead to genuine deductions (as opposed to primitive "transductions") and to deductions in which the child grapples with a given fact of experience, either present or past. But something is still lacking if deduction is to be generalized and made completely rational: the child must be able to reason formally, *i.e.* he must have a conscious realization of the rules of reasoning which will enable him to apply them to any case whatsoever, including purely hypothetical cases (mere assumptions). In the same way, a child who, with regard to the rules of games, has reached the third stage, will achieve momentary coordinations of a collective order (a well-ordered game may be compared on this point to a good discussion), but feels no interest as yet in the actual legislation of the game, in the discussions of principle which alone will give him complete mastery of the game in all its strictness. (From this point of view the juridico-moral discussions of the fourth stage may be compared to formal reasoning in general.)

It is, on an average, towards the age of 11 or 12 that these interests develop. In order to understand what is the practice of rules among children of this fourth stage let us question separately several children from the same class at school, and we shall see how subtle are their answers, and how well they agree with one another.

RIT (12), GROS (13) and VUA (13) often play marbles. We questioned them each separately and took steps to prevent them from communicating to each other during our absence the contents of our interrogatory.

With regard to the square, the "pose," the manner of throwing, and generally speaking all the rules we have already examined, these three children are naturally in full agreement with each other. To know who is to play first, Rit, who has lived in two neighbouring villages before coming to town, tells us that various customs are in usage. You draw a line, the coche, and whoever gets nearest to it plays first. If you go beyond the line, either, according to some, it does not matter, or else *"there is another game: when you go beyond the line, you play last."* Gros and Vua know only of this custom, the only one that is really put into practice by the boys of the neighbourhood.

But there are complications about which the younger boys left us in the dark. *"Whoever,* according to Gros, *says 'queue' plays second. It's easier because he doesn't get 'hit'* [= if a player's shooter lands near the square, it is exposed to hits from the other players]." In the same way, Vua tells us that *"whoever says 'queue de deux' plays last."* And he adds the following rule, also recognized by Gros: *"When you are all at the same distance from the coche whoever cries 'egaux-queue' plays second."* (The problem is therefore to play sufficiently soon still to find marbles in the square, but not first, for fear of being hit.)

On the other hand, Gros tells us: *"Whoever takes out two* [two of the

---

[15] *Judgment and Reasoning in the Child,* chap. IV.

[16] We take this opportunity of reminding the reader of what has not been sufficiently emphasized in our earlier books, viz. that most of our research has been carried out on children from the poorer parts of Geneva. In different surroundings the age averages would certainly have been different.

marbles placed inside the square, *i.e.* the equivalent of the player's 'pose'] *can say 'queue-de-pose.' In that way he can play second from the coche in the next game."* And Vua: *"When there are two outside* [when two marbles have been knocked out of the square] *you can dare to say 'queue-de-pose,' and you can play second from the coche again in the second game."* Rit gives us the same information.

This is not all. According to Rit, *"If you say 'deux-coups-de-coche' you can have two shots from the line. If you say 'deux-coups-d'empan' you play the second shot from where you are. You can only say that when the other* [= the opponent] *has made up his pose* [= has won back as many marbles as he had originally deposited in the square]." This rule is observed in the same way by the other two children.

In addition, there is a whole set of rules, unknown to the younger boys, which bear upon the position of the marbles in the square. According to Gros, *"The first boy who says 'place-pour-moi'* [Eng., place-for-me] *does not have to place himself at one of the corners of the square,"* and *"The one who has said 'places-des-marbres'* [Eng., place for the marbles] *can put them down as he likes, in a 'troyat'* [all in a heap] *or at the four corners."* Vua is of the same opinion and adds: *"If you say 'place-pour-toi-pour-tout-le-jeu* [Eng., your-place-for-the-whole-game] *the other chap* [the opponent] *must stay at the same place."* Rit, who knows both these rules, adds the further detail that *"you can't say 'place-pour-moi' if you have already said 'place-pour-toi.'"* This gives some idea of the complications of procedure!

Our three legal experts also point the measures of clemency in use for the protection of the weak. According to Vua *"If you knock out three at one shot and there's only one left* [one marble in the square] *the other chap* [the opponent] *has the right to play from half-way* [half-way between the coche and the square] *because the first boy has made more than his 'pose.'"*

Also: *"The boy who has been beaten is allowed to begin."* According to Gros, *"If there is one marble left at the end, the boy who has won, instead of taking it, can give to the other chap."* And again, *"When there's one boy who has won too much, the others say 'coujac,' and he is bound to play another game."*

The number of shots at the disposal of each player also gives rise to a whole series of regulations on which the three boys lay stress, as before, in full agreement with each other. For the sake of brevity we refer the reader on this point to the general rules outlined in Section I.

There is only one point on which we saw our subjects differ. Rit, who, it will be remembered, has known the game in three different districts, tells us that the boy whose shooter stays inside the square may generally come out of it. He added, it is true, that in some games the player in such a plight is "dished" (Fr., *brulé*), but this rule does not seem to him obligatory. Vua and Gros, on the contrary, are of opinion that in all cases *"when you stay inside the square you are dished."* We think we may confuse Vua by saying: "Rit didn't say that! — *The fact is,"* answers Vua, *"that sometimes people play differently. Then you ask each other what you want to do.* — And if you can't agree? — *We scrap for a bit and then we fix things up."*

These answers show what the fourth stage is. Interest seems to have shifted its ground since the last stage. Not only do these children seek to cooperate, to "fix things up," as Vua puts it, rather than to play for themselves alone, but also — and this undoubtedly is something new — they seem to take a peculiar pleasure in anticipating all possible cases and in codifying them. Considering that the square game is only one of the five or ten varieties of the game of marbles, it is almost alarming in face of the complexity of rules and procedure in the square game, to think of what a child of twelve has to store away in his memory.

These rules, with their overlapping and their exceptions, are at least as complex as the current rules of spelling. It is somewhat humiliating, in this connection, to see how heavily traditional education sets about the task of making spelling enter into brains that assimilate with such ease the mnemonic contents of the game of marbles. But then, memory is dependent upon activity, and a real activity presupposes interest.

Throughout this fourth stage, then, the dominating interest seems to be interest in the rules themselves. For mere co-operation would not require such subtleties as those attending the disposition of the marbles in the square ("place-pour-moi," "place-des-marbres," "place-pour-toi-pour-tout-le-jeu," etc.). The fact that the child enjoys complicating things at will proves that what he is after is rules for their own sake. We have described elsewhere[17] the extraordinary behaviour of eight boys of 10 to 11 who, in order to throw snow-balls at each other, began by wasting a good quarter-of-an-hour in electing a president, fixing the rules of voting, then in dividing themselves into two camps, in deciding upon the distances of the shots, and finally in foreseeing what would be the sanctions to be applied in cases of infringement of these laws. Many other facts analogous to this could be culled from studies that have been made on children's societies.

In conclusion, the acquisition and practice of the rules of a game follow very simple and very natural laws, the stages of which may be defined as follows: 1. Simple individual regularity. 2. Imitation of seniors with egocentrism. 3. Cooperation. 4. Interest in rules for their own sake. Let us now see whether the consciousness of rules describes in its evolution an equally uncomplicated curve.

5. Consciousness of Rules: 1. The First Two Stages

As all our results have shown, consciousness of rules cannot be isolated from the moral life of the child as a whole. We might, at the most, study the practical applications of rules without bothering about obedience in general, *i.e.* about the child's whole social and moral behaviour. But as soon as we try, as in the present case, to analyse a child's feelings and thoughts about rules, we shall find that he assimilates them unconsciously along with the commands to which he is subjected taken as a whole. This comes out particularly clearly in the case of the little ones, for whom the constraint exercised by older children evokes adult authority itself in an attenuated form.

Thus the great difficulty here, even more than with the practice of rules, is to establish the exact significance of the primitive facts. Do the simple individual regularities that precede the rules imposed by a group of players give rise to the consciousness of rules, or do they not? And if they do, is this consciousness directly influenced by the commands of adults? This very delicate point must be settled before we can embark upon the analysis of the more transparent data furnished by the interrogatory of older children. With regard to consciousness of rules, we shall designate as the first stage that which corresponds to the purely individualistic stage studied above. During this stage the child, as we noted, plays at marbles in its own way, seeking merely to satisfy its motor interests or its symbolic fantasy. Only, it very soon contracts habits which constitute individual rules of a sort. This phenomenon, far from being unique, is the counterpart of that sort of ritualization of behaviour which can be observed in any baby before it can speak or have experienced any specifically moral adult pressure. Not only does every act of adaptation extend beyond its content of intellectual effort into a ritual kept up for its own sake, but the baby will often invent such rituals for its own pleasure; hence the primitive reactions of very young children in the presence of marbles.

But in order to know to what consciousness of rules these individual schemas correspond it should be remem-

---

17 *Judgment and Reasoning in the Child*, p. 96.

bered that from its tenderest years everything conspires to impress upon the baby the notion of regularity. Certain physical events (alternation of day and night, sameness of scenery during walks, etc.) are repeated with sufficient accuracy to produce an awareness of "law," or at any rate to favour the appearance of motor schemas of prevision. The parents, moreover, impose upon the baby a certain number of moral obligations, the source of further regularities (meals, bed-time, cleanliness, etc.) which are completely (and to the child indissociably) connected with the external regularities. From its earliest months the child is therefore bathed in an atmosphere of rules, so that the task of discerning what comes from itself in the rites that it respects and what results from the pressure of things or the constraint of the social environment is one of extreme difficulty. In the content of each ritual act it is certainly possible to know what has been invented by the child, what discovered in nature, and what imposed by the adult. But in the consciousness of rules, taken as a formal structure, these differentiations are non-existent from the point of view of the subject himself.[18]

An analysis of the rites practised by older children, however, will allow us to introduce a fundamental distinction at this point. On the one hand, certain forms of behaviour are, as it were, ritualized by the child himself (e.g. not to walk on the lines that separate the paving stones from the kerb of the pavement). Now, so long as no other factor intervenes, these motor rules never give rise to the feeling of obligation proper. (This is true even of the example we selected intentionally just now — that of a simple game which only becomes obligatory when it becomes connected later on with a pact, i.e. with a social operation, for the pact with oneself is undoubtedly a derivative of the pact with others.) On the other hand, certain rules — it matters not whether they were previously invented by the child, imitated, or received

from outside — are at a given moment sanctioned by the environment, i.e. approved of or enjoined. Only in such a case as this are rules accompanied by a feeling of obligation. Now, although it is always difficult to know to what extent an obligatory rule covers up in the mind of a child of one or two years a motor ritual, it is at any rate obvious that the two things are psychologically distinct. And this distinction should be borne in mind when we come to the study of the rules of the game.

The reader will recognize in the way in which we have stated the problem the striking thesis of M. Bovet on the genesis of the feeling of moral obligation in man's conscience: the feeling of obligation only appears when the child accepts a command emanating from someone whom he respects. All the material analysed in the present work, beginning with the facts relating to consciousness of the rules of the game, confirm this thesis, which is parallel rather than contradictory to Durkheim's doctrine of the social genesis of respect and morality. The only change we wish to effect in Bovet's theory is to extend it and to introduce alongside of the unilateral respect of the younger child for the grown-up, the mutual respect that is entertained among equals. Consequently, a collective rule will appear to us as much the product of the reciprocal approbation of two individuals as of the authority of one individual over another.

What then does consciousness of rules amount to during our first stage? In so far as the child has never seen anyone else play, we can allow that it is engaged here upon purely personal and individual ritual acts. The child, enjoying as it does any form of repetition, gives itself schemas of action, but there is nothing in this that implies an obligatory rule. At the same time, and this is where the analysis becomes so difficult, it is obvious that by the time a child can speak, even if it has never seen marbles before, it is already permeated with rules and regu-

---

[18] E.g. Heat burns (physical law), it is forbidden to touch the fire (moral law) and the child playing about in the kitchen will amuse himself by touching every piece of furniture except the stove (individual ritual). How can the subject's mind distinguish at first between these three types of regularity?

lations due to the environment, and this in the most varied spheres. It knows that some things are allowed and others forbidden. Even in the most modern form of training one cannot avoid imposing certain obligations with regard to sleeping, eating, and even in connection with certain details of no apparent importance (not to touch a pile of plates, daddy's desk, etc., etc.). It is therefore quite possible that when the child comes across marbles for the first time, it is already convinced that certain rules apply to these new objects. And this is why the origins of consciousness of rules even in so restricted a field as that of the game of marbles are conditioned by the child's moral life as a whole.

This becomes clear in the second stage, the most interesting for our thesis. This second stage sets in from the moment when the child, either through imitation or as the result of verbal exchange, begins to want to play in conformity with certain rules received from outside. What idea does he form of these rules? This is the point that we must now try to establish.

We made use of three groups of questions for the purpose of analysing the consciousness of rules in this second stage. Can rules be changed? Have rules always been the same as they are to-day? How did rules begin? Obviously the first of these questions is the best. It is the least verbal of the three. Instead of making the child think about a problem that has never occurred to him (as do the other two), it confronts the subject with a new fact, a rule invented by himself, and it is relatively easy to note the child's resulting reactions, however clumsy he may be in formulating them. The other two questions, on the contrary, incur all the objections that can be made against questioning pure and simple — the possibility of suggestion, of perseveration, etc. We are of the opinion, nevertheless, that these questions have their use, if only as indices of the respect felt for rules and as complementary to the first.

Now, as soon as the second stage begins, *i.e.* from the moment that the child begins to imitate the rules of others, no matter how egocentric in practice his play may be, he regards the rules of the game as sacred and untouchable; he refuses to alter these rules and claims that any modification, even if accepted by general opinion, would be wrong.

Actually, it is not until about the age of 6 that this attitude appears quite clearly and explicitly. Children of 4–5 seem, therefore, to form an exception and to take rules rather casually, a feature which, if judged purely externally, recalls the liberalism of older children. In reality, we believe that this analogy is superficial, and that little children, even when they seem not to be so, are always conservative in the matter of rules. If they accept innovations that are proposed to them, it is because they do not realize that there was any innovation.

Let us begin by one of the more difficult cases, the difficulty being all the greater because the child is very young and consequently very much inclined to romance.

FAL (5) is at the second stage with regard to the practice of rules. "Long ago when people were beginning to build the town of Neuchâtel, did little children play at marbles the way you showed me? — *Yes.* — Always that way? — *Yes.* — How did you get to know the rules? — *When I was quite little my brother showed me. My Daddy showed my brother.* — And how did your daddy know? — *My Daddy just knew. No one told him.* — How did he know? — *No one showed him!*" "Am I older than your Daddy? — *No, you're young. My Daddy had been born when we came to Neuchâtel. My Daddy was born before me.* — Tell me some people older than your daddy. — *My grand-dad.* — Did he play marbles? — *Yes.* — Then he played before your daddy? — *Yes, but not with rules!* [said with great conviction]. — What do you mean by rules? — . . ." (Fal does not know this word, which he has just heard from our lips for the first time. But he realizes that it means an essential property of the game of marbles; that is why he asserts so emphatically that his grand-dad did not play with rules so as to show how superior his daddy is to everyone else in the world.) "Was it a long time ago when people played for the first time? — *Oh, yes.* — How did they find out how to play? — *Well, they took some marbles, and then they made a square, and then they put the marbles inside it . . .*" etc. (He enumerates the rules that he knows.) "Was it little children who found out or grown-up gentlemen? — *Grown-up gentlemen.* — Tell me who was born first, your daddy or your grand-dad? — *My Daddy was born before my grand-dad.* — Who invented the game of marbles? — *My Daddy did.* — Who is the oldest person in Neuchâtel? — *I dunno.* — Who do you think? — *God.* — Did people know how to play marbles before your daddy? — *Other gentlemen played* [before? at the same time?]. — In the same way as your daddy? — *Yes.* — How did they know how to? — *They made it up.* — Where is God? — *In the sky.* — Is he older than your daddy? — *Not so old."* "Could one find a new way of playing? — *I can't play any other way.* — Try . . . [Fal does not move]. Couldn't you put them like this [we place the marbles in a circle without a square]? — *Oh, yes.* — Would it be fair? — *Oh, yes.* — As fair as the square? — *Yes.* — Did your daddy use to play that way or not? — *Oh, yes.* — Could one play still other ways? — *Oh, yes."* We then arrange the marbles in the shape of a T, we put them on a matchbox, etc. Fal says he has never seen this done before, but that it is all quite fair and that you can change things as much as you like. Only his daddy knows all this!

Fal is typical of the cases we were discussing above. He is ready to change all the established rules. A circle, a T, anything will do just as well as the square. It looks, at first, as though Fal were near those older children who, as we shall see, no longer believe in the sacred character

of rules and adopt any convention so long as it is received by all. But in reality this is not the case. However great a romancer Fal may be, the text of which we have quoted the greater part seems to show that he has a great respect for rules. He attributes them to his father, which amounts to saying that he regards them as endowed with divine right. Fal's curious ideas about his father's age are worth noting in this connection; his daddy was born before his grand-dad, and is older than God! These remarks, which fully coincide with those collected by M. Bovet,[19] would seem to indicate that in attributing the rules to his father, Fal makes them more or less contemporaneous with what is for him the beginning of the world. Characteristic, too, is the manner in which the child conceives this invention of rules on the part of his father: this gentleman thought of them without having been told or shown anything, but other gentlemen may equally have thought of the same thing. This is not, in our opinion, mere psittacism. One should be careful, of course, not to read into these remarks more logic than they contain: they simply mean that rules are sacred and unchangeable because they partake of paternal authority. But this affective postulate can be translated into a sort of infantile theory of invention, and of the eternity of essences. To the child who attaches no precise meaning to the terms "before" and "after" and who measures time in terms of his immediate or deeper feelings, to invent means almost the same thing as to discover an eternal and pre-existing reality in oneself. Or to put it more simply, the child cannot differentiate as we do between the activity which consists in inventing something new and that which consists in remembering the past. (Hence the mixture of romancing and exact reproduction which characterizes his stories or his memory.) For the child, as for Plato, intellectual creation merges into reminiscence.[20] What, then, is the meaning of Fal's tolerance with regard to the new laws we

---

[19] P. Bovet, *The Child's Religion*, London, 1930.
[20] Cf. *The Child's Conception of the World*, p. 52, the case of Kauf (8; 8): this child believes that the stories she tells were written in her brain by God. *"Before I was born, he put them there."*

suggested to him? Simply this, that confident of the unlimited wealth of rules in the game of marbles, he imagines, as soon as he is in possession of a new rule, that he has merely rediscovered a rule that was already in existence.

In order to understand the attitude of the children of the early part of the second stage — they all answer more or less like Fal — we must remember that up till the age of 6–7 the child has great difficulty in knowing what comes from himself and what from others in his own fund of knowledge. This comes primarily from his difficulty in retrospection (see *Judgment and Reasoning in the Child*, Chap. IV, § 1), and secondly from the lack of organization in memory itself. In this way the child is led to think that he has always known something which in fact he has only just learned. We have often had the experience of telling a child something which immediately afterwards he will imagine himself to have known for months. This indifference to distinctions of before and after, old and new, explains the inability of which we spoke just now to differentiate between invention and reminiscence. The child very often feels that what he makes up, even on the spur of the moment, expresses, in some way, an eternal truth. This being so, one cannot say that very young children have no respect for rules because they allow these to be changed; innovations are not real innovations to them.

Added to this there is a curious attitude which appears throughout the whole of the egocentric stage, and which may be compared to the mental states characteristic of inspiration. The child more or less pleases himself in his application of the rules. At the same time, Fal and others like him will allow any sort of change in the established usage. And yet they one and all insist upon the point that rules have always been the same as they are at present, and that they are due to adult authority, particularly the authority of the father. Is this contradictory? It is so only in appearance. If we call to mind the peculiar mentality of children of this age, for whom society is not so much a successful cooperation between equals as a feeling of continuous communion between the ego and the Word of the Elder or Adult, then the contradiction ceases. Just as the mystic can no longer dissociate his own wishes from the will of his God, so the little child cannot differentiate between the impulses of his personal fancy and the rules imposed on him from above.

Let us now pass on to the typical cases of this stage, *i.e.* to children who out of respect to rules are hostile to any innovation whatsoever.

We must begin by quoting a child of 5½ years, LEH, whose reaction was among the most spontaneous that we had occasion to note. Leh was telling us about the rules of the game before we had questioned him about consciousness of rules. He had just begun to speak and was showing us how to play from the coche (which was about the only thing in the game that he knew) when the following dialogue took place. We asked Leh quite simply if everyone played from the coche or whether one could not (as is actually done) put the older ones at the coche and let the little ones play closer up. "No," answered Leh, "*that wouldn't be fair.* — Why not? — *Because God would make the little boy's shot not reach the marbles and the big boy's shot would reach them.*" In other words, divine justice is opposed to any change in the rules of marbles, and if one player, even a very young one were favoured in any way, God Himself would prevent him from reaching the square.

PHA (5½): "Do people always play like that? — *Yes, always like that.* — Why? — *'Cos you couldn't play any other way.* — Couldn't you play like this [we arrange the marbles in a circle, then in a triangle]? — *Yes, but the others wouldn't want to.* — Why? — *'Cos squares is better.* — Why better? — . . ." We are less successful, however, with regard to the origins of the game: "Did your daddy play at marbles before you were born? — *No, never, because I wasn't there yet!* — But he was a child like you before you

were born. — *I was there already
when he was like me. He was bigger.*"
"When did people begin to play marbles? — *When the others began, I began too.*" It would be impossible to
outdo Pha in placing oneself at the
centre of the universe, in time as well
as in space! And yet Pha feels very
strongly that rules stand above him:
they cannot be changed.

GEO (6) tells us that the game of
marbles began with *"people, with
the Gentlemen of the Commune* [the
Town Council whom he has probably
heard mentioned in connection with
road-mending and the police]. — How
was that? — *It came into the gentlemen's heads and they made some marbles.* — How did they know how to
play? — *In their head. They taught
people. Daddies show little boys how
to.* — Can one play differently from
how you showed me? Can you change
the game? — *I think you can, but I
don't know how* [Geo is alluding here
to the variants already in existence].
— Anyhow? — *No there are no games
you play anyhow.* — Why? — *Because
God didn't teach them* [the Town
Council]. — Try and change the
game." (Geo then invents an arrangement which he regards as quite new
and which consists in making a big
square with three rows of three marbles
each.) "Is that one fair, like the other
one? — *No, because there are only
three lines of three.* — Could people
always play that way and stop playing
the old way? — *Yes, M'sieu.* — How
did you find this game? — *In my head.*
— Can we say, then, that the other
games don't count and this is the
one people must take? — *Yes, M'sieu.
There's others too that the Gentlemen
of the Commune know.* — Do they
know this one that you have made
up? — *Yes* [*!*]. — But it was you who
found it out. Did you find that game
in your head? — *Yes.* — How? — *All
of a sudden. God told it to me.* — You
know, I have spoken to the gentlemen
of the Commune, and I don't think
they know your new game. — *Oh!*
[Geo is very much taken aback]. —

But I know some children who don't
know how to play yet. Which game
shall I teach them, yours, or the other
one? — *The one of the Gentlemen of
the Commune.* — Why? — *Because it
is prettier.*" "Later on when you are a
big man and have got moustaches perhaps there won't be many children left
who play the game of the Gentlemen
of the Commune. But there may be
lots of boys who play at your game.
Then which game will be fairest,
yours, which will be played most, or
the game of the Gentlemen of the
Commune, which will be nearly forgotten? — *The game of the Gentlemen
of the Commune.*"

The case of Geo comes as a beautiful
confirmation of what we said in connection with Fal, viz. that for little children
inventing a game comes to the same
thing as finding in one's head a game that
has already been anticipated and classified by the most competent authorities.
Geo attributes the game he has invented
to divine inspiration, and supposes it to
be already known to the "Gentlemen of
the Commune." As soon as we undeceive
him he undervalues his own invention
and refuses to regard it as right even if
ratified by general usage.

MAR (6), whose behaviour in the
practice of rules we have already examined in § 3, declares that in the
time of his daddy and of Jesus, people
played as they do now. He refuses to
invent a new game. *"I've never invented games."* We then suggest a
new game which consists of putting
marbles on a box and making them
fall off by hitting the box: "Can one
play like this? — *Yes* [He does so, and
seems to enjoy it]. — Could this game
ever become a fair game? — *No, because its not the same.*" Another
attempt calls forth the same reaction.

STOR (7) tells us that children
played at marbles before Noah's ark:
"How did they play? — *Like we
played.* — How did it begin? — *They
bought some marbles.* — But how did
they learn? — *His daddy taught
them.*" Stor invents a new game in
the shape of a triangle. He admits that

his friends would be glad to play at it, *"But not all of them. Not the big ones, the quite big ones. —* Why? *— Because it isn't a game for the big ones. —* Is it as fair a game as the one you showed me? *— No. —* Why? *— Because it isn't a square. —* And if everyone played that way, even the big ones, would it be fair? *— No. —* Why not? *— Because it isn't a square."*

With regard to the practical application of rules all these children therefore belong to the stage of egocentrism. The result is clearly paradoxical. Here are children playing more or less as they choose; they are influenced, it is true, by a few examples that have been set before them and observe roughly the general schema of the game; but they do so without troubling to obey in detail the rules they know or could know with a little attention, and without attributing the least importance to the most serious infringements of which they may be guilty. Besides all this, each child plays for himself, he pays no attention to his neighbour, does not seek to control him and is not controlled by him, does not even try to beat him — "to win" simply means to succeed in hitting the marbles one has aimed at. And yet these same children harbour an almost mystical respect for rules: rules are eternal, due to the authority of parents, of the Gentlemen of the Commune, and even of an almighty God. It is forbidden to change them, and even if the whole of general opinion supported such a change, general opinion would be in the wrong: the unanimous consent of all the children would be powerless against the truth of Tradition. As to any apparent changes, these are only complementary additions to the initial Revelation: thus Geo (the most primitive of the above cases, and therefore nearest to those represented by Fal and so confirming what we said about the latter) believes the rule invented by him to be directly due to a divine inspiration analogous to the inspiration of which the Gentlemen of the Commune were the first recipients.

In reality, however, this paradox is general in child behaviour and consti-

tutes, as we shall show towards the end of the book, the most significant feature of the morality belonging to the egocentric stage. Childish egocentrism, far from being asocial, always goes hand in hand with adult constraint. It is presocial only in relation to cooperation. In all spheres, two types of social relations must be distinguished: constraint and cooperation. The first implies an element of unilateral respect, of authority and prestige; the second is simply the intercourse between two individuals on an equal footing. Now egocentrism is contradictory only to cooperation, for the latter alone is really able to socialize the individual. Constraint, on the other hand, is always the ally of childish egocentrism. Indeed it is because the child cannot establish a genuinely mutual contact with the adult that he remains shut up in his own ego. The child is, on the one hand, too apt to have the illusion of agreement where actually he is only following his own fantasy; the adult, on the other, takes advantage of his situation instead of seeking equality. With regard to moral rules, the child submits more or less completely in intention to the rules laid down for him, but these, remaining, as it were, external to the subject's conscience, do not really transform his conduct. This is why the child looks upon rules as sacred though he does not really put them into practice.

As far as the game of marbles is concerned, there is therefore no contradiction between the egocentric practice of games and the mystical respect entertained for rules. This respect is the mark of a mentality fashioned, not by free cooperation between equals, but by adult constraint. When the child imitates the rules practised by his older companions he feels that he is submitting to an unalterable law, due, therefore, to his parents themselves. Thus the pressure exercised by older on younger children is assimilated here, as so often, to adult pressure. This action of the older children is still constraint, for cooperation can only arise between equals. Nor does the submission of the younger children to the rules of the older ones lead to any sort of cooperation in action; it simply produces a sort of mysticism, a diffused feeling of collective participation, which, as in the case of many mystics, fits in perfectly well with egocentrism. For we shall see eventually that cooperation between equals not only brings about a gradual change in the child's practical attitude, but that it also does away with the mystical feeling towards authority.

In the meantime let us examine the subjects of the final period of the present stage. We found only three stages with regard to consciousness of rules, whereas there seemed to be four with regard to the practice of the game. In other words, the cooperation that sets in from the age of 7–8 is not sufficient at first to repress the mystical attitude to authority, and the last part of the present stage (in the consciousness of rules) really coincides with the first half of the cooperative stage (in the practice of the game).

BEN (10 yrs.), whose answers we have given with regard to the practice of rules (third stage) is still at the second stage from the point of view that is occupying us just now: "Can one invent new rules? — *Some boys do, so as to win more marbles, but it doesn't always come off. One chap* [quite recently, in his class] *thought of saying 'Deux Empans'* [two spans] *so as to get nearer* [actually this is a rule already known to the older boys]. *It didn't come off.* — And with the little ones? — *Yes, it came off all right with them.* — Invent a rule. — *I couldn't invent one straight away like that.* — Yes you could. I can see that you are cleverer than you make yourself out to be. — *Well, let's say that you're not caught when you are in the square.* — Good. Would that come off with the others? — *Oh, yes, they'd like to do that.* — Then people could play that way? — *Oh, no, because it would be cheating.* — But all your pals would like to, wouldn't they? — *Yes, they all would.* — Then why would it be cheating? — *Because I invented it: it isn't a rule! It's a wrong rule because it's outside of the rules. A fair rule is one that is in the game.* — How does one know if it is fair? — *The good*

players know it. — And suppose the good players wanted to play with your rule? — *It wouldn't work. Besides they would say it was cheating.* — And if they all said that the rule was right, would it work? — *Oh, yes, it would. . . . But it's a wrong rule!* — But if they all said it was right how would anyone know that it was wrong? — *Because when you are in the square it's like a garden with a fence, you're shut in* [so that if the shooter stays inside the square, you are 'dished']. — And suppose we draw a square like this [we draw a square with a break in one of the sides like a fence broken by a door]? — *Some boys do that. But it isn't fair. It's just for fun for passing the time.* — Why? — *Because the square ought to be closed.* — But if some boys do it, is it fair or not? — *It's both fair and not fair.* — Why is it fair? — *It is fair for waiting* [for fun]. — And why is it not fair? — *Because the square ought to be closed.* — When you are big, suppose everyone plays that way, will it be right or not? — *It will be right then because there will be new children who will learn the rule.* — And for you? — *It will be wrong.* — And what will it be 'really and truly'? — *It will really be wrong.*" Later on, however, Ben admits that his father and grandfather played differently from him, and that rules can therefore be changed by children. But this does not prevent him from sticking to the view that rules contain an intrinsic truth which is independent of usage.

Borderline cases like these are particularly interesting. Ben stands midway between the second and third stages. On the one hand, he has already learned, thanks to cooperation, the existence of possible variations in the use of rules, and he knows, therefore, that the actual rules are recent and have been made by children. But on the other hand, he believes in the absolute and intrinsic truth of rules. Does cooperation, then, impose upon this child a mystical attitude to law similar to the respect felt by little children for the commands given them by adults?

Or is Ben's respect for the rules of the game inherited from the constraint that has not yet been eliminated by cooperation? The sequel will show that the latter interpretation is the right one. Older children cease to believe in the intrinsic value of rules, and they do so in the exact measure that they learn to put them into practice. Ben's attitude should therefore be regarded as a survival of the features due to constraint.

Generally speaking, it is a perfectly normal thing that in its beginnings cooperation — on the plane of action — should not immediately abolish the mental states created — on the plane of thought — by the complexus: egocentricity and constraint. Thought always lags behind action and cooperation has to be practised for a very long time before its consequences can be brought fully to light by reflective thought. This is a fresh example of the law of *prise de conscience* or conscious realization formulated by Claparède[21] and of the time-lag[22] or "shifting" which we have observed in so many other spheres (see *Judgment and Reasoning in the Child*, Chap. V, § 2 and *The Child's Conception of Causality*, 2nd part). A phenomenon such as this is, moreover, well fitted to simplify the problem of egocentrism in general since it explains why intellectual egocentrism is so much more stubborn than egocentrism in action.

6. Consciousness of Rules: II. Third Stage

After the age of 10 on the average, *i.e.* from the second half of the cooperative stage and during the whole of the stage when the rules are codified, consciousness of rules undergoes a complete transformation. Autonomy follows upon heteronomy: the rule of a game appears to the child no longer as an external law, sacred in so far as it has been laid down by adults; but as the outcome of a free decision and worthy of respect in the

measure that it has enlisted mutual consent.

This change can be seen by three concordant symptoms. In the first place, the child allows a change in the rules so long as it enlists the votes of all. Anything is possible, so long as, and to the extent that, you undertake to respect the new decisions. Thus democracy follows on theocracy and gerontocracy: there are no more crimes of opinion, but only breaches in procedure. All opinions are tolerated so long as their protagonists urge their acceptance by legal methods. Of course some opinions are more reasonable than others. Among the new rules that may be proposed, there are innovations worthy of acceptance because they will add to the interest of the game (pleasure in risks, art for art's sake, etc.). And there are new rules that are worthless because they give precedence to easy winning as against work and skill. But the child counts on the agreement among the players to eliminate these immoral innovations. He no longer relies, as do the little ones, upon an all-wise tradition. He no longer thinks that everything has been arranged for the best in the past and that the only way of avoiding trouble is by religiously respecting the established order. He believes in the value of experiment in so far as it is sanctioned by collective opinion.

In the second place, the child ceases *ipso facto* to look upon rules as eternal and as having been handed down unchanged from one generation to another. Thirdly and finally, his ideas on the origin of the rules and of the game do not differ from ours: originally, marbles must simply have been rounded pebbles which children threw about to amuse themselves, and rules, far from having been imposed as such by adults, must have become gradually fixed on the initiative of the children themselves.

Here are examples:

Ross (11) belongs to the third stage in regard to the practice of rules. He

---

[21] This term (Claparède's *prise de conscience*) simply means "coming into consciousness," and has nothing to do with intellectual formulation. [Trans.]

[22] This is the term that has been selected by the author for the French *décalage*, a somewhat more complex notion which in previous volumes, cf. *Language and Thought of the Child*, pp. 208 ff., has been rendered as a process of "shifting." [Trans.]

claims that he often invents new rules with his playmates: "*We make them [up] sometimes. We go up to 200. We play about and then hit each other, and then he says to me: 'If you go up to 100 I'll give you a marble.'* Is this new rule fair like the old ones, or not? — *Perhaps it isn't quite fair, because it isn't very hard to take four marbles that way!* — If everyone does it, will it be a real rule, or not? — *If they do it often, it will become a real rule.* — Did your father play the way you showed me, or differently? — *Oh, I don't know. It may have been a different game. It changes. It still changes quite often.* — Have people been playing for long? — *At least fifty years.* — Did people play marbles in the days of the 'Old Swiss'? — *Oh, I don't think so.* — How did it begin? — *Some boys took some motor balls* [ball bearings] *and then they played. And after that there were marbles in shops.* — Why are there rules in the game of marbles? — *So as not to be always quarrelling you must have rules, and then play properly.* — How did these rules begin? — *Some boys came to an agreement amongst themselves and made them.* — Could you invent a new rule? — *Perhaps . . .* [he thinks] *You put three marbles together and you drop another from above on to the middle one.* — Could one play that way? — *Oh, yes.* — Is that a fair rule like the others? — *The chaps might say it wasn't very fair because it's luck. To be a good rule, it has to be skill.* — But if everyone played that way, would it be a fair rule or not? — *Oh, yes, you could play just as well with that rule as with the others.*"

MALB (12) belongs to the fourth stage in the practice of rules: "Does everyone play the way you showed me? — *Yes.* — And did they play like that long ago? — *No.* — Why not? — *They used different words.* — And how about the rules? — *They didn't use them either, because my father told me he didn't play that way.* — But long ago did people play with the same rules? — *Not quite the same.* —

How about the rule not hitting for one? — *I think that must have come later.* — Did they play marbles when your grandfather was little? — *Yes.* — Like they do now? — *Oh, no, different kinds of games.* — And at the time of the battle of Morat? — *No, I don't think they played then.* — How do you think the game of marbles began? — *At first, children looked for round pebbles.* — And the rules? — *I expect they played from the coche. Later on, boys wanted to play differently and they invented other rules.* — And how did the coche begin? — *I expect they had fun hitting the pebbles. And then they invented the coche.* — Could one change the rules? — *Yes.* — Could you? — *Yes, I could make up another game. We were playing at home one evening and we found out a new one* [he shows it to us]. — Are these new rules as fair as the others? — *Yes.* — Which is the fairest, the game you showed me first or the one you invented? — *Both the same.* — If you show this new game to the little ones what will they do? — *Perhaps they will play at it.* — And if they forget the square game and only play this one, which will be the true game, the new one that will be better known, or the old one? — *The best known one will be the fairest.*"

GROS (13 yrs. at the fourth stage in the practice of the rules) has shown us the rules as we saw above. "Did your father play that way when he was little? — *No, they had other rules. They didn't play with a square.* — And did the other boys of your father's time play with a square? — *There must have been one who knew, since we know it now.* — And how did that one know about the square? — *They thought they would see if it was nicer than the other game.* — How old was the boy who invented the square? — *I expect thirteen* [his own age]. — Did the children of the Swiss who lived at the time of the battle of Morat play at marbles? — *They may have played with a hole, and then later on with a square.* — And in the time of David de Purry [a perriwigged gentleman whose statue on one of the public squares of Neuchâtel is known to all]? — *I expect they had a bit of a lark too!* — Have rules changed since the square was invented? — *There may have been little changes.* — And do the rules still change? — *No. You always play the same way.* — Are you allowed to change the rules at all? — *Oh, yes. Some want to, and some don't. If the boys play that way* [changing something] *you have to play like they do.* — Do you think you could invent a new rule? — *Oh, yes . . .* [he thinks]; *you could play with your feet.* — Would it be fair? — *I don't know. It's just my idea.* — And if you showed it to the others would it work? — *It would work all right. Some other boys would want to try. Some wouldn't, by Jove! They would stick to the old rules. They'd think they'd have less of a chance with this new game.* — And if everyone played your way? — *Then it would be a rule like the others.* — Which is the fairest now, yours or the old one? — *The old one.* — Why? — *Because they can't cheat."* (Note this excellent justification of rules: the old rule is better than the innovation, not yet sanctioned by usage, because only the old rule has the force of a law and can thus prevent cheating.) "And if nearly everyone played with their feet, then which would be fairest? — *If nearly everyone played with their feet, then that would be the fairest."* — Finally we ask Gros, "Suppose there are two games, an easy one where you win often, and a difficult one where you win seldom, which would you like best? — *The most difficult. You end by winning that way."*

VUA (13), whose answers about the practice of rules we have already examined (4th stage) tells us that his father and his grandfather played differently from him. "In the days of the 'Three Swiss' did boys play at marbles? — *No. They had to work at home. They played other games.* — Did they play marbles in the days of the battle of Morat? — *Perhaps, after the war.*

— Who invented this game? — *Some kids. They saw their parents playing at bowls, and they thought they might do the same thing.* — Could other rules be invented? — *Yes."* (He shows us one he has invented and which he calls "the line" because the marbles are arranged in a row and not in a square.) "Which is the real game, yours or the square? — *The square, because it is the one that is always used.* Which do you like best, an easy game or a difficult one? — *The more difficult, because it is more interesting.* The 'Troyat' [a game that consists in heaping the balls into piles] *is not quite the real game. Some boys invented it. They wanted to win all the marbles."* On this point Vua seems to be answering like a child of the preceding stage who will invoke the "real game" that conforms to tradition as against contemporary innovations. But Vua seems to us rather to be contrasting a demagogic procedure (the "Troyat," which by allowing too great a part to chance gives rise to illicit and immoral gains) with practices that are in keeping with the spirit of the game, whether they are ancient, like the square, or recent like his own game. The proof of this would seem to lie in the following remarks relating to his own playing: "Is the game you invented as fair as the square, or less fair? — *It is just as fair because the marbles are far apart* [therefore the game is difficult]. — If in a few years' time everyone played your line game and only one or two boys played the square game, which would be the fairest, the line or the square? — *The line would be fairest."*

BLAS (12, 4th stage in the practice of rules) thinks that the game of marbles must have begun round about 1500 at the time of the Reformation. "*Children invented the game. They made little balls with earth and water and then they amused themselves by rolling them about. They found it was rather fun making them hit, and then they had the idea of inventing a game, and they said that when you hit any-*

one else's marble with your own you could have the marble you hit. After that I expect they invented the square, so that you should have to make the marbles go out of the square. They invented the line, so that all the marbles should be at the same distance. They only invented it later. When cement was discovered, marbles were made like they are to-day. The marbles of earth weren't strong enough, so the children asked the manufacturers to make some in cement." We ask Blas to make up a new rule, and this is what he thinks of. First there must be a competition, and whoever makes his marbles go furthest can play first. But the rule seems *"bad because you'd have to run too far back to fetch the marbles."* He then thinks of another which consists in playing in two squares one inside the other. "Would everyone want to play that way? — *Those who invented it would.* — Later on, if your game is played just as much as the square, which will be the fairest? — *Both the same."*

The psychological and educational interest of all this stands out very clearly. We are now definitely in the presence of a social reality that has rational and moral organization and is yet peculiar to childhood. Also we can actually put our finger upon the conjunction of cooperation and autonomy, which follows upon the conjunction of egocentrism and constraint.

Up to the present, rules have been imposed upon the younger children by the older ones. As such they had been assimilated by the former to the commands given by adults. They therefore appeared to the child as sacred and untouchable, the guarantee of their truth being precisely this immutability. Actually this conformity, like all conformity, remained external to the individual. In appearance docile, in his own eyes submissive and constantly imbued as it were with the spirit of the Elders or the Gods, the child could in actual fact achieve little more than a simulation of sociality, to say nothing of morality. External constraint does not destroy egocentrism. It covers and

conceals when it does not actually strengthen it.

But from henceforward a rule is conceived as the free pronouncement of the actual individual minds themselves. It is no longer external and coercive: it can be modified and adapted to the tendencies of the group. It constitutes no revealed truth whose sacred character derives from its divine origin and historical permanence; it is something that is built up progressively and autonomously. But does this not make it cease to be a real rule? Is it perhaps not a mark of decadence rather than of progress in relation to the earlier stage? That is the problem. The facts, however, seem definitely to authorize the opposite conclusion: it is from the moment that it replaces the rule of constraint that the rule of cooperation becomes an effective moral law.

In the first place, one is struck by the synchronism between the appearance of this new type of consciousness of rules and a genuine observation of the rules. This third stage of rule consciousness appears towards the age of 10–11. And it is at this same age that the simple cooperation characteristic of the third stage in the practice of rules begins to be complicated by a desire for codification and complete application of the law. The two phenomena are therefore related to each other. But is it the consciousness of autonomy that leads to the practical respect for the law, or does this respect for the law lead to the feeling of autonomy? These are simply two aspects of the same reality: when a rule ceases to be external to children and depends only on their free collective will, it becomes incorporated in the mind of each, and individual obedience is henceforth purely spontaneous. True, the difficulty reappears each time that the child, while still remaining faithful to a rule that favours him, is tempted to slur over some article of the law or some point of procedure that favours his opponent. But the peculiar function of cooperation is to lead the child to the practice of reciprocity, hence of moral universality and generosity in his relations with his playmates.

This last point introduces us to yet another sign of the bond between autonomy and true respect for the law. By modifying rules, *i.e.* by becoming a sovereign and legislator in the democracy which towards the age of 10–11 follows upon the earlier gerontocracy, the child takes cognizance of the *raison d'être* of laws. A rule becomes the necessary condition for agreement. "*So as not to be always quarrelling,*" says Ross, "*you must have rules and then play properly* [= stick to them]." The fairest rule, Gros maintains, is that which unites the opinion of the players, "*because* [then] *they can't cheat.*"

Thirdly, what shows most clearly that the autonomy achieved during this stage leads more surely to respect for rules than the heteronomy of the preceding stage is the truly political and democratic way in which children of 12–13 distinguish lawless whims from constitutional innovation. Everything is allowed, every individual proposition is, by rights, worthy of attention. There are no more breaches of opinion, in the sense that to desire to change the laws is no longer to sin against them. Only — and each of our subjects was perfectly clear on this point — no one has the right to introduce an innovation except by legal channels, *i.e.* by previously persuading the other players and by submitting in advance to the verdict of the majority. There may therefore be breaches but they are of procedure only: procedure alone is obligatory, opinions can always be subjected to discussion. Thus Gros tells us that if a change is proposed "*Some want to and some don't. If boys play that way* [allow an alteration] *you have to play like they do.*" As Vua said in connection with the practice of rules (§ 4), "*Sometimes people play differently. Then you ask each other what you want to do. . . . We scrap for a bit and then we fix things up.*"

In short, law now emanates from the sovereign people and no longer from the tradition laid down by the Elders. And correlatively with this change, the respective values attaching to custom and the rights of reason come to be practically reversed.

In the past, custom had always prevailed over rights. Only, as in all cases where a human being is enslaved to a custom that is not part of his inner life, the child regarded this Custom imposed by his elders as a sort of Decalogue revealed by divine beings (*i.e.* adults, including God, who is, according to Fal, the oldest gentleman in Neuchâtel after his own father). With the result that, in the eyes of a little child, no alteration of usage will dispense the individual from remaining faithful to the eternal law. Even if people forget the square game, says Ben, and adopt another, this new game "*will really be wrong.*" The child therefore distinguishes between a rule that is true in itself and mere custom, present or future. And yet he is all the time enslaved to custom and not to any juridico-moral reason or reality distinct from this custom and superior to it. Nor indeed is this way of thinking very different from that of many conservative adults who delude themselves into thinking that they are assisting the triumph of eternal reason over present fashion, when they are really the slaves of past custom at the expense of the permanent laws of rational cooperation.

But from now on, by the mere fact of tying himself down to certain rules of discussion and collaboration, and thus cooperating with his neighbours in full reciprocity (without any false respect for tradition nor for the will of any one individual) the child will be enabled to dissociate custom from the rational ideal. For it is of the essence of cooperation as opposed to social constraint that, side by side with the body of provisional opinion which exists in fact, it also allows for an ideal of what is right functionally implied in the very mechanism of discussion and reciprocity. The constraint of tradition imposes opinions or customs, and there is an end of it. Cooperation imposes nothing except the actual methods of intellectual or moral interchange (Baldwin's[23] synnomic as opposed to his syndoxic).

---

[23] J. M. Baldwin, *Genetic Theory of Reality.*

Consequently we must distinguish alongside of the actual agreement that exists between minds, an ideal agreement defined by the more and more intensive application of the processes of mental interchange.[24] As far as our children are concerned, this simply means that in addition to the rules agreed upon in a given group and at a given moment (constituted morality or rights in the sense in which M. Lalande speaks of "raison constituée" [25]) the child has in mind a sort of ideal or spirit of the game which cannot be formulated in terms of rules (constitutive morality or rights in the sense of "raison constituante"). For if there is to be any reciprocity between players in the application of established rules or in the elaboration of new rules, everything must be eliminated that would compromise this reciprocity (inequalities due to chance, excessive individual differences in skill or muscular power, etc.). Thus usages are gradually purified in virtue of an ideal that is superior to custom since it arises from the very functioning of cooperation.

This is why, when innovations are proposed to the child, he regards them as fair or unfair not only according as they are likely or not to rally the majority of players in their favour, but also according as they are in keeping with that spirit of the game itself, which is nothing more or less than the spirit of reciprocity. Ross tells us, for instance, concerning his own proposition, *"Perhaps it isn't quite fair, because it isn't very hard to take four marbles that way,"* and again, *"The chaps might say it wasn't very fair because it's luck. To be a good rule, it has to be skill."* The Troyat, Vua informs us, is less fair than the square (though equally widespread and equally well known to former generations), because it was invented *"to win all the marbles."* In this way, Vua draws a distinction between demagogy and a sane democracy. In the same way, Gros and Vua prefer difficult games because they are more "interesting": cleverness and skill now matter more than winning. Art for art's sake is far more disinterested than playing for gain.

In a word, as soon as we have cooperation, the rational notions of the just and the unjust become regulative of custom, because they are implied in the actual functioning of social life among equals — a point which will be developed in the third chapter of this book. During the preceding stages, on the contrary, custom overbore the issue of right, precisely in so far as it was deified and remained external to the minds of individuals.

Let us now see what sort of philosophy of history the child will adopt in consequence of having discovered democracy. It is very interesting, in this connection, to note the following synchronism. The moment a child decides that rules can be changed, he ceases to believe in their endless past and in their adult origin. In other words, he regards rules as having constantly changed and as having been invented and modified by children themselves. External events may of course play a certain part in bringing this about. Sooner or later, for example, the child may learn from his father that the game was different for previous generations. But so unmistakable is the correlation (on the average, of course) between the appearance of this new type of consciousness of rules and the disappearance of the belief in the adult origin of the game that the connection must be founded on reality. Is it, then, the loss of belief in the divine or adult origin of rules that allows the child to think of innovations, or is it the consciousness of autonomy that dispels the myth of revelation?

Only someone completely ignorant of the character of childish beliefs could imagine that a change in the child's ideas about the origin of rules could be of a nature to exercise so profound an influence on his social conduct. On the contrary, here as in so many cases, belief merely reflects behaviour. There can be no doubt that children very rarely reflect upon the original institution of the game of marbles. There are even very strong reasons for assuming that as far as the children we examined are concerned such a problem never even entered their heads

---

[24] See our article, "Logique génétique et sociologie," *Revue Philosophique,* 1928.
[25] Lalande, A., "Raison constituante et raison constituée," *Revue des Cours et Conférences.*

until the day when a psychologist had the ridiculous idea of asking them how marbles were played in the days of the Old Swiss and of the Old Testament. Even if the question of the origin of rules did pass through the minds of some of these children during the spontaneous interrogatories that so often deal with rules in general (*Language and Thought of the Child,* Chap. V, §§ 5 and 10), the answer which the child would give himself would probably be found without very much reflection. In most cases the questions we asked were entirely new to the subject, and the answers were dictated by the feelings which the game had aroused in them in varying intensity. Thus, when the little ones tell us that rules have an adult origin and have never changed, one should beware of taking this as the expression of a systematic belief; all they mean is that the laws of the game must be left alone. And when, conversely, the older ones tell us that rules have varied and were invented by children, this belief is perhaps more thought out since it is held by more developed subjects, but it is still only valuable as an indication: the child simply means that he is free to make the law.

We may well ask ourselves, then, whether it is legitimate to question the child about such very verbal beliefs, since these beliefs do not correspond to thought properly so called, and since the child's true thought lies much deeper, somewhere below the level of formulation. But in our opinion these beliefs have their interest because the same phenomena reappear in adult mental life and because the psychological facts lead by a series of intermediate steps to metaphysical systems themselves. What Pareto,[26] basing his relatively simple conclusions on such a wealth of erudition, has called "derivations" are really present in germ in our children's remarks about the origin of games. These remarks have no intellectual value, but they contain a very resistant, affective and social element — the "residuum" to quote Pareto again. To the residuum peculiar to the conforming attitude of the little ones correspond the

derivations "divine or adult origin" and "permanence in history." To the residuum peculiar to the more democratic attitude of the older children correspond the derivations "natural [childish] origin" and "progress."

One more fundamental question must still be discussed. How is it that democratic practice is so developed in the games of marbles played by boys of 11 to 13, whereas it is still so unfamiliar to the adult in many spheres of life? Of course it is easier to agree upon some subjects than on others, and feeling will not run so high on the subject of the rules of the "Square" as in an argument about the laws of property or the legitimacy of war. But apart from these questions (and after all, is it so obvious that social questions are more important to us than are the rules of a game to the child of 12?) there are others of greater psychological and sociological interest. For it must not be forgotten that the game of marbles is dropped towards the age of 14–15 at the latest. With regard to this game, therefore, children of 11–13 have no seniors. The following circumstance is important. Since they no longer have to endure the pressure of play-mates who impose their views by virtue of their prestige, the children whose reactions we have been studying are clearly able to become conscious of their autonomy much sooner than if the game of marbles lasted till the age of 18. In the same way, most of the phenomena which characterize adult societies would be quite other than they are if the average length of human life were appreciably different from what it is. Sociologists have tended to overlook this fact, though Auguste Comte pointed out that the pressure of one generation upon the other was the most important phenomenon of social life.

We shall have occasion to see, moreover, that towards the age of 11 the consciousness of autonomy appears in a large number of different spheres. Whether this is the repercussion of collective games on the whole moral life of the child is a question which will be taken up later.

---

[26] *Traité de Sociologie générale.*

CHAPTER VI

Thought Processes

THE PATTERN of our thinking results from the meanings we have assigned to our experiences — the aspects we have abstracted for special attention — reaching back even to our childhood. These meanings have been derived from particular experiences and are attached to specific situations. When we find ourselves again in similar situations, we tend to respond with behavior that we found appropriate previously. If our experiences have been limited largely to relations with authority figures, then the discriminations we will make about the social world around us may be phrased in dominance-submission terms. We may learn early or late the behavior and thinking appropriate to relations with others where authoritarian pressures are minimal (as is often true with contemporaries), but when we do, we also learn to observe the people around us from a different point of view.

In the article below, Elton Mayo considers some aspects of the process by which we learn to make satisfactory discriminations about our own observations. The things to which we pay attention and which we retain in conscious thought for further consideration determine much — though not all — of our picture of the world. These thoughts are modified by our interactions with others and in turn modify the interactions themselves. Our learning is conditioned by the things to which we do in fact pay attention. Read

ELTON MAYO, "Notes on Consciousness and Attention," below.

The recognition of totalities and a response of some sort, Mayo states elsewhere, is of vital importance, and it must precede the development of careful reflection and depth of response. The way in which our thinking constructs "wholes" determines our effectiveness in life situations. These "wholes" cannot include every detail of the situation but *must include all pertinent details* if our understanding of the situation is to be adequate for skilled action. The effectiveness of the result then depends on the pertinence to the situation of the parts abstracted for special attention.

This pertinence necessarily reflects an individual view of the situation. When we learn from experience, *what* we learn depends upon the way in which we interpret the experience. For example, if a boy is using a chisel which slips and cuts his thumb, he might evaluate the risks in such a way that he would consider chisels "dangerous" for him; he might feel he had so little carpentering skill that it would not be worth his while to practice further. This conclusion would fit well into a view of the world as a dangerous place and a basic assumption about his own unworthiness; it might be entirely pertinent to his own feelings and confirm them. Yet it would limit the areas in which future choice would be possible. He would feel that he could *either* continue working with such tools and be cut again — a painful thought — *or* give up the idea altogether. In this way any further development of his carpentering skills might be considered clearly impossible.

On the other hand, his way of thinking might construct a "whole" which would view as pertinent other aspects of the situation. He might assess what had happened not only in terms of subjective, individual feelings, but also in terms of other factors that were operating on the chisel, wood, hands, and so forth, at that time. In this way his "mistake" might help him determine the relevance of these other factors, and he might learn more from it than from anything else that could have happened to him. Following such a process of thought he might go on to develop a high skill.

We can view the world only from some point of view based on a collection of concepts. We continually try to construct systems, "wholes," which will pull together our observations more effectively. Still, in this process, we are more or less conscious that we leave out many observations which might be important. We often compensate for this in our behavior. Systems previously developed to clarify our thinking survive *in our thoughts* beyond their usefulness to us because we take into consideration *in our behavior* factors we have left out of the system. These factors were necessarily omitted from the system because they were not pertinent to our view of the situation at that time. They are not, however, necessarily forgotten and are often used when we are acting in respect to a situation. The boy with the chisel might have sufficient pressures on him to make him work with carpentering tools in spite of a conclusion of poor skill. He might continue to cut himself, thus supporting his original system, but still learn through trial and error a certain degree of skill. Much of our early learning, and in fact a good deal of our later learning, is of this order. Many considerations of the social scientists which have been presented in these readings may not seem useful to some of us — may not fit into the systems we have constructed — but we still may behave experimentally in response to them when faced with concrete situations. Our ability to use "irrelevant" data when necessary in specific situations both permits the original systems to continue unchanged in conscious thought and allows us to operate in situations where the systems are only partially adequate. Read

LEWIS MUMFORD, "The Fallacy of Systems," below.

We frequently seem to act in response to factors omitted from the conscious, systematic processes of our minds. From Mayo's discussion of consciousness, it is clear that all factors cannot be equally present in our minds — we do not pay much attention to some; others are constantly before us. Some factors we can bring to our attention as we wish; others seem steadily to elude us. Our discriminations about our environment often do not seem to have been made at any present, conscious level. We can observe later that we *have* arrived at these conclusions, yet cannot determine readily the process by which we got there. Some sort of earlier conclusion retained in the back of our mind seems to have helped us on our way.

Syncretistic thinking,[1] for example, which formed such a large part of our

---

[1] F. K. Berrien, in *Comments and Cases on Human Relations* (New York: Harper, 1951) pp. 48ff, uses the word "syncretistic" to identify the mental processes by which we balance, nearly automatically as we act, contradictory observations which might affect our behavior. In this process we weigh the importance of the probable relationships between the various factors as indicated by our accumulated past

mental processes during formative years, remains always with us. It is never, perhaps, at the apex of our focused attention but remains as an associative process; it pulls together factors that do not fit together in any logical system but which nevertheless seem to us to be related in some way. The fundamental relation may be only the occurrence together of these factors in the past, but this relatedness may be elaborated extensively through the *feeling* of similarity with later events. Memory of events that have occurred in the past with the emotional meanings we have attached to them is extraordinarily persistent. We often say this or that occurrence is "just like" something that happened to us earlier, although the similarity may be only a common feeling that we now observe as present in both.[2]

In many situations careful, precise thinking and talking would inhibit, not assist, communication. For certain purposes the type of thinking that leaps from one aspect of a subject to another without pausing to consider the how and why, is entirely effective. Examples stare at us from the pages of any magazine which carries national advertising: a car that is better because it has glamour, drinks compared to daisies or named after roses, athletic prowess and smoking cigarettes, weddings and soap, popularity and toothpaste; all suggest "wholes" that have no logical validity. Perhaps the most common American example of this form of thinking is the equating of bigness in size with preeminence in quality: the tallest building, the largest stadium, the man with the biggest salary, the biggest business, and so forth. Such thinking is a powerful determinant of human behavior. Unsystematic though it may seem, it performs an important function in our dealings with others.

Some of this syncretistic material never becomes conscious at all in the sense that we can specifically state it. We can recognize that we behave as if we were making some particular assumption even when we do not know the source of the assumption. We can frequently observe, for example, that in arguments where people are angry they shout louder and louder at each other as if the noise of their voices would add to the conviction of their words or in some way force the opponents into agreement. The basic assumptions seem to be that force must be met with equal or greater force, that the words themselves are inadequate to the task, and that submission and agreement are similar. Perhaps the frequency with which the assumption is made that force of some sort must be used is itself syncretistic. It may be a survival of the thinking of the egocentric stage of our development, when we may have realistically observed our own inadequacies to handle many situations. The presence of anxiety and doubts about our skills in dealing with situations often seems to lead us to use greater force — a force out of all proportion to the demands of the immediate

---

experience and arrive rapidly at a decision on how to behave in this concrete situation. This process permits us to act almost instantaneously, but with a "minimum of rational analysis of discrete elements." Berrien discusses the important process by which we understand, without much conscious thought, the significance of certain factors for a particular judgment which we are about to make.

The "syncretistic" process, as the word has been used in our discussion, refers to a very different mental activity whose foundation is a lack of understanding, either conscious or unconscious, of the complex relationship between the various factors of an observed "whole." These "syncretistic schemas" as they form in the child's mind from his as yet limited observation *do* assist him in his understanding of the world and *do* assist his behavior responses to it. They *do not*, however, according to Piaget (*Language and Thought of the Child*, p. 159), "lead the child on to a progressive adaptation. There is nothing unintelligent about these schemas; they are simply too ingenuous and too facile for purposes of accuracy. Sooner or later they will be submitted to rigorous selection and to a mutual reduction, which will sharpen them into first rate instruments of invention in spheres of thought where hypotheses are of use."

[2] Consider in this connection the thinking of Mrs. Stanislaus about her throat operation, in the "Osler Memorial Hospital," Vol. II, Case 16, Part C.

situation. It seems at times as if our sense of security is in inverse ratio to the strength which we exert in meeting a situation. We can speculate about the source of such widespread nonlogical assumptions, but probably can never recollect exactly how they developed in our own minds.

Dramatic illustrations of the ways in which data will control our behavior even though they are irrelevant to our basic ideas can be found in hypnosis experiments. In one experiment the subject, a graduate student, was instructed under profound hypnosis that he (a) wanted to give up smoking, (b) felt the habit was too strong to break, (c) would be very reluctant to smoke and would give anything not to smoke, and (d) would experience all these feelings after he was awakened. The student had no prior knowledge of the conditions of the experiment, and there is no evidence that any of these ideas formed a basic part of his regular thinking. Yet he responded without conscious thought to all of them.

After he was awakened the subject was drawn into a casual conversation with the hypnotist who, lighting one himself, offered him a cigarette. The subject waved it aside with the explanation that he had his own and that he preferred Camels, and promptly began to reach for his own pack. Instead of looking in his customary pocket however, he seemed to forget where he carried his cigarettes and searched fruitlessly through all of his other pockets with a gradually increasing concern. Finally, after having sought them repeatedly in all other pockets, he located his cigarettes in their usual place.

He took them out, engaged in a brief conversation as he dallied with the pack, and then began to search for matches, which he failed to find. During his search for matches he replaced the cigarettes in his pocket and began using both hands, finally locating the matches too in their usual pocket. Having done this, he now began using both hands to search for his cigarettes. He finally located them but then found that he had once more misplaced his matches. This time, however, he kept his cigarettes in hand while attempting to relocate the matches.

He then placed a cigarette in his mouth and struck a match. As he struck it, however, he began a conversation which so engrossed him that he forgot the match and allowed it to burn his finger tips, whereupon, with a grimace of pain, he tossed it in the ash tray. Immediately he took another match, but again introduced a diverting topic by asking the audience in a humorous fashion if they knew the "Scotch" way of lighting a cigarette. As interest was shown, he carefully split the match through the middle. One half of the match he replaced in his pocket in a time-consuming manner and tried to light his cigarette with the other half. When it gave too feeble a flame he discarded it and had to search for the second half. After striking this another interesting topic of conversation developed and again he burned his fingers before he made use of it.

He apologized for his failure to demonstrate the "Scotch" light successfully and repeated the performance, this time holding the flame in such a way as to ignite only a small corner of the cigarette from which he succeeded in getting only one satisfactory puff. Then he tossed the match away and tipped the cigarette up so that he could see the lighted end. He started to explain that that was how the "Scotch" light was obtained and noted that only one small corner of the cigarette was lit. He smiled in a semi-apologetic manner and explained that he had really given a "Jewish" light to the cigarette, whereupon the lighted corner expired. He made a few more humorous comments, and as he talked and gesticulated appropriately he rolled the cigarette between his fingers in such a fashion that he broke it, whereupon he put it aside and took another.

This time a member of the audience stepped up and proffered him a light, but as the lighted match drew near to the tip of his cigarette the subject sneezed and blew it out. He apologized again and said he thought he would light his own cigarette. While taking out his matches he commented on the vaudeville trick of rolling cigars from one corner of the mouth to the other and proceeded to demonstrate how he could roll a cigarette in that fashion, which he did fairly successfully. However, in doing so he macerated the tip of the cigarette and had to discard it.

He took another, holding it in his mouth while he reached for his matches, started a conversation, and took the cigarette out so that he could talk more freely. It was observed that he took the cigarette out with his hand held in the reverse position to that which he usually used, and after completing his remarks he put the dry end of the cigarette in his mouth, exposing the wet end. He then tried to light this, held the match to the tip in the proper fashion, puffed vigorously, finally got a puff of smoke and then blew out the match. Naturally the wet end of the cigarette did not burn satisfactorily and quickly went out. He looked at it in amazement and in a semi-embarrassed manner mumbled that he had lit the wrong end of the cigarette; he then commented that now both ends of the cigarette were wet, and discarded it for another. After several similar trials he finally succeeded in lighting the cigarette. It was observed that although he took deep puffs he tended to let his cigarette burn undisturbed, and that instead of smoking it down to a reasonable butt he quickly discarded it.

A little later while smoking the subject attempted to demonstrate the violent gestures of a patient and in doing so knocked off the burning tip. Then while lighting another cigarette he became so interested in talking that he lit the cigarette in the middle rather than at the tip and had to discard it. As usual he showed profound embarrassment at seeming so awkward.

On other occasions when the subject had demonstrated this phenomenon, he would finally complete the demonstration by selecting a cigarette in a strained and laborious fashion and then, obviously centering all of his attention upon the procedure of lighting it, would hold his hand tensely as he lit the match, applying it with noticeable rigidity to the cigarette and holding it there so long and puffing so repeatedly that all doubt was removed concerning the actual lighting of the cigarette, whereupon his whole manner and attitude would relax and he would appear to be physically comfortable.[3]

The basic concept that we frequently respond in our behavior to "unconscious" thoughts is now widely accepted. It even forms a basis for cocktail conversation and humor. Guesses are common about what might have been in the background of our minds as motivation for some illogical behavior or slip of the tongue. But when Sigmund Freud first started about 1890 to study these phenomena in his patients, he was a pioneer in a new field. Perhaps the most productive use of the concept of dynamic unconscious thought has been made in therapeutic assistance to people whose basic assumptions have tended to prevent them from adjusting adequately to the world. Nevertheless, such "unconscious memories" operate in us at all times, and the concept can be fruitful in improving our observations of all social activities.

Freud demonstrated through extensive clinical data not only the existence of mental material we do not recognize but showed ways in which it interacts with our conscious thoughts. In the reading below he discusses first the slips and errors in speech and behavior which seem to have no "logical" foundation.

---

[3] Milton H. Erickson, "Experimental Demonstrations of the Psychopathology of Everyday Life," *The Psychoanalytic Quarterly*, vol. VIII, no. 3 (July 1939), pp. 338–353.

He shows that these slips are frequently more than mere accidents; they are often related to feelings we have about some current situation, and these feelings may be significant in determining the nature of our response to the situation. Freud then discusses the content of dream material and indicates that it offers a source of knowledge about unconscious processes. The unconscious material seems to consist largely of conclusions we have drawn from earlier experiences — the meanings to us of events in terms of both thoughts and feelings — but conclusions that do not fit into our conscious thoughts. Our critical faculties which select the material proper for our systematic thought reject certain observations as "illogical" and force them into the unconscious. In dreams, however, the pressure of external events to which we must respond with critical care is less omnipresent, and the rejected conclusions may reappear. Aspects of impulse life, too — those hopes and aspirations, those loves and hates which we "know" to be "unrealistic" — seem to be active here. Still, even in dreams our critical attention does not appear to be entirely absent and the material is forced into disguises. It appears in symbolic and condensed or distorted forms which tend to hide its basic meaning from our conscious thought. The dreams are usually built around incidents that have occurred recently, but also include reflections of thoughts and feelings that may have been buried in the unconscious for many years. Read

SIGMUND FREUD, *A General Introduction to Psycho-analysis*, trans. Joan Riviere (New York: Liveright, 1935),[4] Lectures 1–15.

Although our logical systems of thought reject the unconscious material, it remains important to us. We need it when we act in specific situations. The unconscious processes are the way we make use of rejected observations "behind our own backs." These rejected observations are not only those we made early in our development; we continue to make similar new observations and to reaffirm or modify old ones. By its very nature such mental activity can only with difficulty be brought to the focus of our attention. We deny vehemently the ability of others to interpret correctly our slips of the tongue, and our dreams tend to vanish as we awake. Much of this unconscious material is wholly incompatible with important conscious thoughts and would produce serious dilemmas if fully expressed, even to ourselves. Yet it cannot be neglected altogether; we use it, we respond to it, but we cannot think precisely about it. The inadequacies of many of our observations may be concealed from us and yet form a foundation for some of our favorite systems of logical behavior.

ADDITIONAL READINGS

Freud, Sigmund, "The Origin and Development of Psychoanalysis," *An Outline of Psychoanalysis*, ed. J. S. Van Teslaar (New York: Modern Library, 1925).

A series of five nontechnical lectures delivered at Clark University in 1910. In them Freud tells of his early discoveries about the unconscious and shows through the story of his first patient how he utilized his observations to effect a cure. A good introduction to the therapeutic theories of psychoanalysis.

Lecky, Prescott, *Self-Consistency — A Theory of Personality* (New York: Island Press, 1945). Chapter 3, "The Structure of the Personality," and chapter 4, "The Personality."

[4] Reprint edition: Garden City, New York: Garden City Publishing Co., 1943.

A development of the theory that we learn those things that seem to fit into our ideas about ourselves and avoid learning those things that seem inconsistent therewith. Learning is fundamentally a unifying process which strenuously resists ideas that create contradictions within us; as soon as "the response has been unified and conflicts eliminated, attention must be turned elsewhere."

Snygg, Donald, and Arthur W. Combs, *Individual Behavior* (New York: Harper, 1949).

A psychological text which considers human behavior "not from an outsider's point of view but from the point of view of the behaver himself." The authors' language system is clear and uses a minimum of specialized words. The following chapters might be found useful: chapter 2, "The Personal Frame of Reference"; chapter 3, "How Behavior Changes"; chapter 4, "What People Strive For"; and chapter 5, "The Way We See Ourselves."

Notes on Consciousness and Attention*

BY ELTON MAYO

A vivid awareness of context is the primary condition of effective attention. The skilled person ignores what is not immediately relevant to action, not because it is meaningless, but rather because it is in fact fulfilling the meaning he is actively assigning it. At the present moment the reader is either attentive to this chapter or the chapter is conducive to relaxation or thought of tomorrow's activities. The reader is nevertheless actively aware that the room in which he reads has windows, and for so long as they behave as mere windows he will not regard them with special interest or curiosity. But if, for example, a giraffe were suddenly to intrude its head through one of them, the effect would be instantaneous and startling. Every activity — reading, or thought of next day's occupations — would be interrupted; he would turn to inspect the astonishing phenomenon. This, because the appearance of a giraffe is not ordinarily included in the back-

ground of the room in which he reads. In other words, the window would have ceased to carry the function he implicitly assigns to it. It is because we do actively assign meaning to the items of a context that they do not attract our attention. It is not because we are unaware or unconscious of them.[1]

I. CONSCIOUSNESS

William James in his first published book[2] restates the question with which psychology begins: What is the fact of consciousness? He points out that, "Most psychologists start with sensations, as the simplest mental facts, and proceed synthetically, constructing each higher stage from those below it";[3] and he immediately adds, "But this is abandoning the empirical method of investigation." He proceeds to show that, although we know consciousness directly, we do not know in the same way what sensations are. "No one ever had a simple sensation by itself.

---

* Excerpted and edited by Hugh Cabot from Mayo's lectures in psychology, delivered at the University of Queensland, Australia, 1919–20, and mimeographed as Case HP 243, Graduate School of Business Administration, Harvard University. Mayo himself felt that these lectures represented only certain aspects of the relationship between attention and learning and did not intend them to be an adequate description of the learning process.

Two paragraphs have been inserted as indicated from Mayo's *Some Notes on the Psychology of Pierre Janet* (Cambridge: Harvard University Press, 1948).

[1] Mayo, *Some Notes on the Psychology of Pierre Janet*, pp. 60–61.

[2] *Principles of Psychology* (1890).

[3] *Ibid.*, I, 224.

Consciousness, from our natal day, is of a teeming multiplicity of objects and relations, and what we call simple sensations are results of discriminative attention, pushed often to a very high degree."

This leads James to his admirable statement of the central problem of psychology: "The only thing which psychology has a right to postulate at the outset is the fact of thinking itself, and that must first be taken up and analysed." In other words, the fact with which psychological investigation begins is a total fact of consciousness.

James then asks if we are ever "wholly unconscious"; and he points out that consciousness of some kind persists even during sleep. During sleep, for example, we are able to discriminate between one sound and another; the capacity of a sound to disturb us is determined, not by its mere intensity, but by its *meaning* for the sleeper. So, if a countryman visits the city, the noise made by the passage of an electric tram is apt to disturb him at first; very soon, however, he grows accustomed to the noise (i.e., he comes to know its meaning) and it disturbs him no more. The dweller in the city, similarly, is not disturbed; for him the *intensity* of the sound does not matter, provided he knows its significance. Sounds which are much less intense, on the other hand, do possess a capacity for disturbing our slumbers, provided that their meaning for us makes it desirable that we should wake. Thus the cry of a baby will immediately rouse its mother, James points out; the movement of a patient will rouse a nurse.[4]

Ideas, feelings, and so on are not primary mental states directly known by us, but are rather elements in terms of which we learn to state a total momentary consciousness or experience. We do not know the nature of a particular idea unless we know something of the nature of the consciousness of the individual whose idea it is. An instance will serve to illustrate the truth of this. If a vinegrower and a temperance reformer look simultaneously at a glass of wine, the object from the point of view of the sensations may be considered to be the same for both; yet the idea in the mind of one (i.e., the meaning which he gives the object) is quite different from the idea in the mind of the other. To the one, the glass of wine is an ordinary commodity of trade, an object of special interest to him since he makes his living by it, but beyond this it is not an object which calls for any special comment or remark. With the temperance reformer, the case is quite otherwise. For him the glass of wine summarizes and expresses the chief ill of civilization; to it he traces the failure of humanity to achieve a higher condition, and he regards it therefore with a peculiar scorn and loathing. To what is this difference due? Certainly not to the mere sensations (color, shape, odor, and so on) which constitute the object; it is due rather to the fact that each individual sees the glass of wine as part of a context and assigns to it a meaning which describes its functions with relation to that context. To the vinegrower, the glass of wine is a commodity of trade; to the temperance reformer, it is the outstanding cause of social misery and destitution. Similarly, the meaning of every lesser object is determined in the main not so much by the sensations which constitute the object, but rather by the general meaning which we give the world and the function which we assign in the world to the object under consideration.

Though each object and observation can be defined only in terms of its relation to some particular meaning for us, consciousness is more than a sum of such elements. At any given moment we may be conscious of very many objects; but we are attending to, and learning something about, one only. Consciousness is a more or less orderly arrangement of ideas, and the essential of this arrangement is that during our waking lives one such thought dominates consciousness, and the remaining thoughts are subordinate. This dominant thought is a mental process in a sense which cannot be applied in explaining subordinate thoughts; the latter are not mental processes in the sense though they are undoubtedly ele-

---

[4] *Ibid.*, chapter 9.

ments in consciousness. We employ the term "mental process" to denote the manner in which we learn as the result of attending directly to some object or problem. We must first be able to give some kind of general meaning to the object of our study: accepting this, we look at the object in detail; by examining the detail carefully we become possessed of a new conception of the object, of a better understanding of the manner in which the various parts work together in fulfillment of their functions.

If we are to understand mental process, then, we cannot remain content with conceiving it as something which goes on haphazardly, something which merely accompanies the passage of time. As time passes, we turn our attention to one or other detail, one or other part, of an object; and by this means we learn to know it better. The attentive process, the thought which dominates consciousness, the topic we are thinking about — this particular part of consciousness differs from all the other parts. It is at this point only that learning is taking place, and it is at this point only that there is a mental process as we have been using the term.

II. OBJECTS IN CONTEXT

Analysis is easier if in the preliminary stages we consider, not consciousness merely, but the object of consciousness, the world as we see it. A student working at his desk is not conscious of a chaotic multiplicity of objects; neither is he conscious of a mere collection of individual things. Beyond the textbook there lies for him a single total world; and the various things he is capable of discriminating are for him not things separately real, each on its own account, but *aspects of a total world*. Objects ultimately can only be defined by the individual in terms of the part they play in his universe. If we take the name of any common thing (chair, table, window, or any other object), we find that we have named, not a separately existent reality, but a human purpose; put briefly, we may say that we have defined the thing in terms of its utility to man.

The objective universe around us does not alter its dimensions during our lives. As we learn, however, the significance we are capable of giving it and its utility to us alter materially. We do not assume, for example, that the principle of gravity first came into operation at the moment when Newton first understood it. As an active principle gravity had always characterized physical reaction; Newton did not alter the universe — he enabled us to understand it better.

The first mental activities that are analogous to attentive experience are the "instinctive" activities in which learning begins. On the first experience of an instinctive activity, no meaning (properly so called) can be assigned by the individual to the particular thing which stimulates the reaction; but, although no meaning can yet be assigned, the inherited dispositions of the creature give the object a special interest. This means that the factor of significance, even though the significance is yet unknown, is nevertheless determining the direction and interest of the course of experience. The interest begins with the instinctive course of activity, awareness of what is happening accompanies the course, and the course ends in some kind of satisfaction; but for this factor of significance, the course of instinctive activity would not occur, nor would it run its appointed course to satisfaction. This significance of meaning as an instinctive course of action applies also, and more strongly, to the thoughts of an adult individual.

III. SELECTIVE FORGETTING

We tend to forget experiences so far as they are merely psychical events. This forgetting is indeed active; that is to say, we do not merely lose our memory of the successive events which make up an experience, we actively repress them. But the meaning we derive from such experiences remains with us. It remains with us not because we make a deliberate effort to remember, but because when we have learnt some new meaning we immediately *attribute it directly to the world*, and therefore *do not need to remember it* (in the ordinary sense of that term) at all. A familiar thing or situation is understood by us in the very act of recognition; we do not have to turn our attention away from it, or to "think back," in order to remember what it is; we see it in the world; we perceive it as playing a certain part in the world as we understand it; every object we know derives its significance from the world in which we see it. Understanding is therefore conditioned by meaning — we understand the world so far as it possesses meaning for us; *the world holds this meaning, we do not need to recollect it. As we learn, we reinterpret the significance of the world* from day to day; we do not need to recollect explicitly all the various meanings we have learned to assign to different aspects of the world; such meanings are nevertheless "there" in consciousness, even at such moments as we are attending to some other aspect of reality.

Normally we tend to repress recollection of the event and to retain the meaning. The mathematician, for example, does not need to recollect the circumstances under which he was instructed in the leading principles of algebra in order to solve some problem. It is quite likely, indeed, that he cannot bring to mind the exact circumstances under which his understanding of algebraic problems began; but he retains the meaning of the events, the capacity to solve difficulties for himself.

It can be said then that the mind carries forward into consciousness the results of experience in two ways: as events and as the significance to us of these events. As soon as the meaning of events becomes logically clear and the recollection of events no longer necessary for their understanding, we find that the events themselves tend to pass out of consciousness.

We all know individuals whose memory of past events is extraordinarily clear. For example, the elderly man whose reminiscences go on from one thing to another until he has forgotten the original purpose of his speech. The details are important not because they further something he was trying to illustrate but because they were part of the original events as they

occurred. There is no distinction at all between the relevant and irrelevant, no light and shade, no emphasis; everything that occurred is brought back to the mind simply because it occurred, and not because it is of interest or relevant to the topic under discussion. In such a thinker we find a minimum of relevance in a confusion of irrelevance; such thinking is not clear thinking, but confused thinking; the individual himself is totally unable to sift or discriminate his reminiscences. In such individuals who have failed to cultivate their understanding we find always an extraordinary capacity for the memory of the smallest details of passing events. This is not a sign of mental development, but the reverse; it shows the existence in such individuals of a very considerable incapacity to understand, a failure to appreciate meaning. In such individuals the selective character of attention is at its lowest; the emphasis is equal; all happenings are remembered, whether relevant or not to the problem under consideration.

IV. EFFECTIVE REMEMBERING

This is not to underestimate the importance of the memory of events as such. We must retain the memory of an event while we consider its meaning, and through the recollection of events we can reassign meaning to events in the light of later experience. However, it should be emphasized again that this retention in consciousness of the events themselves is useful in thinking only as they enable us to understand more fully their meaning.

The manner in which the recollection of events and understanding work together to help the individual in the task of learning may be illustrated by considering the development of habit. We are always told that "practice makes perfect"; but very rarely is the manner in which practice helps us to perfect an action pointed out. We develop a habit in two ways:

1. In the first place, by practice we make it easier for ourselves to repeat a former course of thought or action. We all recognize the fact that, especially in

matters of practical activity (e.g., walk-ing, running, driving a car), a certain amount of practice is necessary before the individual is able to master the mere routine and make the action habitual. In other words, we might say that the individual must develop a capacity for the performance of a number of detailed actions without needing to attend to or think about them at all. So far, then, prac-tice operates by strengthening the associ-ative bonds between the successive ex-periences and actions which constitute the course.

2. But this is not all that practice does; if this were all we should not practice games and other activities as assiduously as we do. We practice not merely in order to reinstate or to repeat a course of ac-tivity as it formerly was, but rather in order *to avoid repeating* certain parts of it. Practice would not make perfect if on every occasion we repeated our original awkwardness, clumsiness, or mistakes; it is because we are able gradually to elimi-nate errors such as these that we practice. Considered from this point of view, prac-tice makes perfect, not because we repeat, but because we avoid repetition. We are attending closely to the *significance* of such successive actions and find that some detailed actions are unnecessary, useless, or irrelevant. We eliminate these, and so learn to do better.

Practice therefore really implies *not merely the mechanical* standardization of a former course of activity, *but rather its gradual reconstruction:* the elimination of unnecessary or useless actions and the addition of others which are demanded by the purpose or significance of the course. Whatever be the direction in which we give our attention, whether we specialize in practical activities or in relatively abstract intellectual interest, it is always true that the attention given (i.e., the significance of the meaning of the course) determines what we shall remember, what actions we shall retain, and more generally the knowledge which is the result.

Briefly, then, our attention is always given to the acquisition of meaning, to an improvement of our understanding of the world about us and our relation to it. Our memory of psychical events as such is evanescent; the meaning we derive from a course of experience remains. On the one hand, consciousness has as its object a total world, which remains per-manently before us and forms the back-ground of every attentive act; on the other hand, there is in consciousness the meaning which we give this world, a meaning which is derived from the vari-ous acts of attention which have made up the mental life of the individual. These two — the meaning or significance of the world, and the world, or total object, which hold this meaning for the indi-vidual — tend to remain in the conscious-ness of the first level, while the memory of successive attentive experiences as such is repressed into the lower levels of consciousness.

V. REFLECTION

Continually we discover that some one or other of our customary perceptions or ideas is inadequate. The development of skill therefore demands additional experi-ence and reconsideration of the inade-quacy. This moreover affects not only our mental life of active effort, it affects also those moments of relative passivity that we characterize as reflective thinking . . . . It is *by reflection* . . . that *we give unity to our experience*. In moments of reflective thinking, our attention is with-drawn from the outer world, and we are preoccupied with some problem that we may, if asked, find difficult to define. But this at least can be said, that at such mo-ments some recent experience has caused us to doubt the adequacy of one of our conceptual schemes, or systems of ideas that we have been accustomed to use. And at such moments we are, whether we know it clearly or not, occupied with an endeavor to reconcile the contradiction or to decide upon a direction of inquiry that will throw new light on the apparent inconsistency. Reflective thinking, there-fore, may be described as an inner act of attention, demanded by experience, inti-mately concerned with the systematic arrangement or rearrangement of our knowledge.[5]

An act of learning in giving meaning to events implies a concentration of available energy to a particular task at hand; this in turn implies that other conscious activities not conducive to the particular task must be suppressed. To the extent that this is successful the degree of concentration increases. We can then devote our "whole" attention to the particular task, to analyzing the object (or event) and making a synthetic constitution of the qualities we thus notice. Whether we are looking at a concrete object or thinking out an abstract problem, the process is essentially the same; we notice one or other aspect of the object, and simultaneously in noticing such qualities we put them together, as it were, to represent our experience of the object as a whole. So the word "orange" may suggest to us immediately a multiplicity of visual, touch, and taste qualities: roundness, color, touch-sensations of shape and weight, taste-sensation of sweetness, and the like. All these things may easily be suggested by the word; but they are not suggested simply as though each quality were real upon its own account; they are implied in the very notion of an orange as representing its various attributes.

Attention is therefore at once analytic and synthetic. We analyze the object of our experience; we take it to pieces, as it were, but only in order to construct a representation of it in our minds. It does not, of course, follow that the representation which we construct is an adequate or a true picture of the object itself. The whole process of learning serves to show that we begin by noticing certain outstanding features of things: we begin by describing things to ourselves in terms of these most noticeable qualities. But we soon discover that these qualities are not all, that we cannot describe the world as a whole, nor anything in it, merely in terms of such qualities; and we learn to take notice of aspects of the world which in our former attentive acts we tended to disregard.

VI. THE SELECTIVE CHARACTER OF ATTENTION

An individual tends to remember what he observes; failure to remember is often due to failure to observe. This selective character of attention is of considerable importance.

The world, the total object of consciousness, is constantly before the mind. At any moment, however, the individual is observing only one part or aspect of this world. As three people look at the same scene, therefore, the object of which each is thinking may differ considerably from that of the other two. The landscape, considered as a whole, may be approximately the same for all three; but whereas one may pay especial attention to the sunset, and another to a river in the foreground, the third may be a botanist, and his attention may be specially drawn to a particular tree. The memory which each person has of the particular scene will be dominated for each by the attentive thought of the moment. Each will possess a certain generalized remembrance of the scene; but whereas one will particularly see the sunset, and another the river, the third will especially remember the botanical specimen that caught his interest. Each of the three selected something amongst the material which was offered for special consideration: and the choice which each made was determined for him by past acts of attention, i.e., the special knowledge and skill, or the particular attitude to life in general, which he had already developed.

Selection affects and controls his observation of not merely that part of the total object which possesses most interest for the individual, but also his observation of the whole object. A single book will have different meaning for two readers. To one it may be highly useful, to another boring. The type of question that one reader is asking of the book is very different from the other. One is asking questions that the writer also thought significant, and the reader making a similar

[5] Mayo, *Some Notes on the Psychology of Pierre Janet*, pp. 105–106.

discrimination about the subject finds the book useful.

It is this fact of purpose or intuition in thinking and the consequent discriminations which are responsible for much of what we know as skills in thought. The mental dispositions, the knowledge and skill we have acquired, reflect the questions we have asked ourselves as we looked at the world. The student who fails to remember or who finds his work difficult is the student who has asked himself the wrong question or who has failed to comprehend the question which his particular study asks with regard to the universe. We cannot hope to master or understand any science or study until we know something, first, of the general question which it asks with regard to the subject matter of the study, and second, something also of the particular questions which form the special investigations under the general question.

Every act of attention begins with an expressed or implied question which governs the selection of the parts which will "interest" us and which we will observe. A first duty in careful attention, therefore, is to be as clear as possible about the question which one is asking about the objects of attention. Once the basic questions are clear the problem then re-

solves itself into a discrimination between facts which are relevant and irrelevant to the questions asked. The superior capacity for understanding and reproducing is due to a superior capacity for discriminating the relevant from the irrelevant, for selecting amongst the material offered for observation. The possession of knowledge and skill enables the individual to *emphasize* his experiences rightly; knowing which aspects of the object are more important, he confines his attention mainly to these. The person who can read a book once and understand most of it cannot be said to remember more of it than most people. In fact he probably remembers less. He is, however, better able to distinguish the relevant from the irrelevant or illustrative material, and he confines his attention to these. Thus he may remember only small but highly significant parts of the book and from these he is able to reconstruct in his mind much of what the author was saying. Unless he is able to make this selection of the essential he cannot distinguish the thesis from the exposition and is compelled to take every part of the book as of equal value. If any of it is to be remembered, then all of it must be, and even the author himself could not do that.

The Fallacy of Systems*

BY LEWIS MUMFORD

There is a tendency in every culture to reduce the complicated order that serves life, an order that penetrates many different levels of experience, that includes "material" and "spiritual" attributes, to a single uniform system; and to make that system the sole repository of meaning and value. In order to take in life intellectually, a system must reject many of the factors that belong to life organically, by reason of its varied needs and ever-developing purposes; and to have faith in a system is, therefore, a form of idol-

worship, a pursuit of a false god, and a rejection of the manifold unity which alone can hold the meaning of life and preside fully over all its occasions.

The fallacy of systems is best exposed, perhaps, in education; and we can draw the moral equally from fictional or autobiographical accounts of it. One thinks, for example, of Sir Austin Feverel's system in Meredith's "The Ordeal of Richard Feverel." Full of reasoned contempt for the ordinary processes of his culture, Sir Austin contrived a watchful system of

* First printed in *The Saturday Review of Literature*, XXXII (October 1, 1949), pp. 8–9, and later incorporated in *The Conduct of Life*, copyright, 1951, by Lewis Mumford. Reprinted by permission of Harcourt, Brace and Company, Inc.

education, designed to avoid current errors and to produce a spirited, intellectually sound, thoroughly awakened young man. But the system has not reckoned upon the fact that a young man so trained might as the very proof of his education fall in love with a young girl not duly accounted for in the system, and elope with her in marriage; and that when the system intervened in this marriage, it would contrive a far worse tragedy than any purely conventional mode of education, less confident of its intentions, would have produced.

Or take an even better case: the childhood of Mary Everest, that woman of genius who eventually became the wife and helpmate of the great logician George Boole. Mary's father was the devoted disciple of Hahnemann, the philosopher of homeopathic medicine, and he applied Dr. Hahnemann's principles, not merely to medicine, but to the whole regimen of life. Following strictly the master's belief in long walks before breakfast and cold baths, the system-bound father practiced upon his children a form of torture that drove Mary Everest into a stoical unfeelingness: she hated every item in the routine, and her whole affectional and sentimental life as a young girl in relation to her parents was warped by it: the resentment she felt against this arbitrary disregard of natural feeling is still evident in the account the redoubtable woman wrote at the end of her life. Believing in the system, Mrs. Boole's father never observed what was actually happening in practice: for the sake of testing out a doctrine he was ready to ruin a life.

Every intellectually awakened parent who applied one or another of the rival systems in psychology and education that became fashionable during the last thirty years can testify out of his own experience, if he reflects upon it — at least his children could testify — to the fallacy of oversimplification, which is involved in the application of system. Life cannot be reduced to a system; the best wisdom, when so simplified, becomes an error. Actual historic institutions have been modified by anomalies, discrepancies, contradictions, compromises, which are regarded with high scorn by the believer in a system: but it is precisely these weaknesses that constitute their strength. Czarism, as practised in Russia during the midnineteenth century, was a hideous system: capricious, tyrannical, all-pervading, inwardly unified. But, as Alexander Herzen showed in his memoirs, the system was made tolerable by two things which had no lawful part in it: bribery and corruption on one hand, which made it possible to get around regulations and to soften punishments, and skepticism from within, on the other, which made many of its officers incapable of carrying out with conviction and therefore with rigor the task imposed on them.

This tendency toward laxity, corruption, disorder is the only thing that enables a system to escape self-asphyxiation; for a system is in effect an attempt to make mankind breathe nitrogen and oxygen alone: with effects that are temporarily either exhilarating or soporific, but in the end are lethal; since the air that keeps men alive is composed of all these things in due proportion with carbon dioxide and other gases.

So, too, with the Christian Church: as a system it could not have survived, since if its counsel to espouse virginity as the highest good had been taken seriously by the greater part of its early followers, the Christian Church would have disappeared as completely as the Shaker sect, which took the injunction not to marry and reproduce in all strictness. And it is not the purity of Roman Catholic doctrine that has kept that Church alive, and enabled it to flourish even in a scientific age, but just the opposite: the non-systematic elements, seeping in from other systems of thought and other cultures, not least the vast increment of Greek thought incorporated through Thomas Aquinas, that has given it a vital buoyancy that seemingly tighter systems of thought have lacked.

The fallacy of system has become particularly open to exposure during the last two centuries: never have its errors, in fact, proved more vicious than in our own time. Since the seventeenth century we have lived in an age of system-makers:

divided first of all into two general systems, the party of order and the party of progress, as if both order and change, stability and variation, were not equally fundamental attributes of all manifestations of life. People sought to live their lives on the Romantic system or the Utilitarian system: to be conservatives or radicals, capitalists or Communists; and to organize their existence and attempt to organize the community as a whole as if such wholesale simplifications could do justice to the actual situation. Actually, by the middle of the nineteenth century, it was plain that capitalism, which originally had come in as a beneficent countercurrent to spiritual disorder and feudal lethargy, would, if unmodified by social considerations, strangle life: maiming the young and innocent, starving adults wholesale, in obedience to the blind law of market competition.

Similarly, it has become equally apparent in our own time that Communism, starting from an opposite series of premises, and indifferent to human elements not taken into its system, is ready with equal brutality to sacrifice all the variety and initiative needed for life to its own single-minded effort to liquidate the capitalist class and to concentrate all its powers into a much more compact and arbitrary master-bureaucracy. In the effort to make life work in obedience to its simplified premises, Communism originally sought to break up the institution of monogamous marriage, as a bourgeois relic, and turn the relationship into a temporary matter of convenience, which could be abandoned at will at any time. Those who take systems seriously have therefore looked upon the return to stricter forms of marriage, with less casual attitudes toward family solidarity and child-bearing, as a betrayal of Communism: where it was, in fact, a recognition of life-needs that had been left out of the purely systematic formulation of sexual relations Engels had originally conceived.

Now a system is a theoretic scheme; and it has a pragmatic usefulness, in that the formulation of a system leads to intellectual clarification. The pre-scientific age of abstraction, as Comte originally characterized it, was a great period of disentanglement: the numerous threads which formed the warp and woof of the whole social system were then separated and isolated. When the red threads were united on one skein, when the white were united on another, when the green, the blue, the purple were united on still others, their true texture and color stood out much more clearly than they had done when they were woven together in a complex organic pattern. But the attempt to organize any social organization, indeed any set of living relations, on the basis of making the whole community and every sector of life wholly red, wholly blue, wholly green, stems from a radical fallacy. A community where everyone lived according to the romantic philosophy would have no stability, no continuity, no way of economically doing the thousand things that must be repeated every day of its life: a community that lived on the radical principle of divorcing itself from the past and being concerned wholly with the future would leave out as much of the richness of life as John Stuart Mill's father left out of his education: by cutting off memory it would even undermine hope. A Marxian community where everyone had no life except that provided for the state, on the terms set down by the state, would sacrifice the very possibility of creating whole human beings, which was the generous core of all of Marx's most revolutionary dreams. To take a single system and to attempt to follow this thread through all of life's occasions is to mistake the very nature of such a thread: which is to add to the richness of the complex pattern woven by life itself. The fallacy of "either or" dogs us everywhere: whereas it is in the nature of life to embrace and surmount its manifold contradictions, not by reducing them to units and pulling them apart, but by weaving them together in a more inclusive unity.

CHAPTER VII

The Individual's Response to Stress

M ANY THINGS in our environment are relatively stable, and in time we learn to deal with them. A table remains a table throughout our lifetime, and its meaning in the context of our lives remains little changed. A "Model A" Ford, except for a deterioration that we can readily appraise, is not radically different from what it was when it was built in 1930. A single model of a bomber remains much the same, and pilots can learn in time to deal with the hundreds of variables necessary for its successful operation.

But our relations with people have no such stability. No sooner do we work out one way of dealing with them than we find a new situation developing in which the variables are put together in a different way. Billy Jones today is not the same Billy Jones of ten years ago. Nor are we the same as we were. The certainty of important change seems to be inherent in human relationships.

Coping with people involves skill in observing changes and in responding appropriately. But this process of dealing with change makes thinking and acting so difficult that we steadily deny the changes which are occurring. Once we "thoroughly understand" a situation, we tend thereafter to exclude observations that would force us to admit any further change. It seems simpler to assume that the situation is as we always knew it to be.

George F. F. Lombard, in the article below, observes some of the problems of handling a changing situation by considering the example of a returning soldier readjusting to civilian life. An important part of the veteran's problem is a relearning of the relation between physiological processes and effective action. One of the difficulties of dealing with change is the fear or anxiety that may be aroused by it. These feelings are based on certain physiological responses that are useful in different ways to the soldier and the civilian.

Under certain conditions of danger, such as battle, physiological changes are essential if the body is to be ready to act effectively. Internal readjustments are necessary to increase bodily strength and endurance. These changes operate largely without conscious control: they are automatic reactions to stress situations. Fear and rage are conscious feelings that often accompany these bodily changes. In such a context, fear is useful — it helps the body act. Walter B. Cannon describes the physiological processes which accompany fear and rage:

> Respiration deepens, the heart beats more rapidly, the arterial pressure rises, the blood is shifted away from the stomach and intestines to the heart and central nervous system and the muscles, the processes in the alimentary canal cease, the spleen contracts and discharges its content of concentrated corpuscles, and adrenin is secreted from the adrenal medulla. The key to these marvelous transformations in the body is found in relating them to the natural accompaniments of fear and

rage — running away in order to escape from danger, and attacking in order to be dominant. Whichever the action, a life-or-death struggle may ensue.

The emotional responses just listed may reasonably be regarded as preparatory for struggle. They are adjustments which, so far as possible, put the organism in readiness for meeting the demands which will be made upon it. The secreted adrenin cooperates with sympathetic nerve impulses in calling forth stored glycogen from the liver, thus flooding the blood with sugar for the use of laboring muscles; it helps in distributing the blood in abundance to the heart, the brain and the limbs (i.e., to the parts essential for intense physical effort) while taking it away from the inhibited organs of the abdomen; it quickly abolishes the effects of muscular fatigue so that the organism which can muster adrenin in the blood can restore to its tired muscles the same readiness to act which they had when fresh; and it renders the blood more rapidly coagulable. The increased respiration, the redistributed blood running at high pressure, and the more numerous red corpuscles set free from the spleen provide for essential oxygen and for the riddance of acid waste, and make a setting for instantaneous and supreme action. In short, all these changes are directly serviceable in rendering the organism more effective in the violent display of energy which fear or rage may involve.[1]

Intellectually we are able to make many distinctions about these emotions that we are not able to follow physiologically. The same mechanisms which prepare us for the violent exertions of battle also operate in any other situation where fear, anger, or anxiety is present. Violent action may not be necessary, but the body prepares for it. The physiological changes are extensive, and the body will remain prepared to act vigorously for some time after the original stimulus has disappeared. We may then continue to *feel* afraid or angry long after there is any "reason" for it. A friend may say to us, "Why are you still upset? I've admitted I was wrong, haven't I?" If we reply, "That doesn't matter. I still feel angry," we may be responding inappropriately, but we probably are observing the physiological facts accurately. We can stop ourselves from acting on these feelings if we wish — we do not have to fight or run away — but we cannot stop the internal control of the body from keeping us prepared for a time to run or fight. Further, this physiological preparation, in reinforcing our feelings of fear and anger, may make a situation that we know intellectually is not dangerous at all *seem* similar to one that is. Our "feelings" about the two situations are the same. Significant differences in them that we might ordinarily observe do not under these circumstances come easily to our attention.

Training as a soldier involves acting rapidly and decisively on these "feelings" and in itself makes the return to civilian life more difficult. The stresses of civilian life will create feelings that to a veteran seem the same as those he felt in battle. Although these strains call for different behavior, they create similar feelings of anxiety and fear, and the differences are not evident to him. The interaction between physiological process and behavior may be clarified through a discussion of the readjustments that the veteran has to make. Read

GEORGE F. F. LOMBARD, "The Veteran Himself," below.

It is a characteristic of our early development to respond as we feel; it is typical of Piaget's first two stages of development and is often effective there. To meet rage with rage and fear with contempt are common reactions. For example, when an angry worker faces his foreman, the latter's response is fre-

---

[1] Reprinted from *The Wisdom of the Body* by Walter B. Cannon. By permission of W. W. Norton and Company, Inc. Copyright, 1939, by Walter B. Cannon.

quently anger. The foreman's anger may reinforce the worker's original rage, and so the worker's emotional response is prolonged or even built up. Similarly, contempt, by increasing a person's insecurity, may often increase fear and the physiological reactions which are a part of it.

Although often inappropriate, these physiological responses to fear frequently take place in modern culture:

> Crile gives the picture of the business man who sits at his desk and reads on his tape machine how his stocks are falling, so that he is faced with financial ruin. This man is afraid, and he is thrown into this physical state because it is the only way in which he can have fear. It is of no use to him that these changes should take place. His heart may bleed, in a figurative sense, but decreased clotting time will not help him. He may want to be up and doing, but his muscles will not need the extra sugar for their labour.[2]

Feelings of anxiety — with accompanying fears and angers — are especially likely to occur in situations that seem new or unusually difficult for us. Where there is unfamiliarity with the situation, such as results from rapid change or the uniqueness of an experience, or where our observations seem to throw some of our basic assumptions into question, then such feelings develop. If we also consider the situation one we *must* handle well, where the consequences of failure seem disastrous, then the anxiety itself may become the most important factor in the situation. Mayo, in an article entitled "Civilization — The Perilous Adventure," illustrates how, in his belief, anxiety develops in the early stages of our learning. He questions:

> Do we ever ask ourselves what we should think of events of the day if they occurred against a background or in a setting which was largely unrecognizable by us? Yet this, or something resembling this, is the situation of the child. The child looks out at a wide world which he does not understand; he feels his impotence and is afraid. The world may hold the thrill of splendid possibility; it certainly holds the threat of unanticipated disaster. The roads by which success or disaster may come are alike unknown. But something must be done; life has to be lived. The child has to reassure himself somehow or other before he can give attention to the affairs of the day. Magic is one means he employs. The pretence of control by words and ceremonies where no real control exists has the effect of setting at ease the unstable or fearful mind; it makes possible attention to play or domestic duties.
>
> I do not mean that the child clearly understands this need of reassurance or that magic is in any sense "make-believe." What I mean is rather that such practices originate in a human need of something to act as a set-off against ignorance and impotence: magic makes life livable. There is the closest possible relation between generalized fear and magical practices. Ignorance implies fear or, it may be, a combination of desire and fear. This is overcome by a magical fulfillment of the desired end, by the substitute of magical for real control. This "night-mind" of the child survives in the civilized adult; few, if any, are wholly free.
>
> Between the ages of three and eight the daily routine of speech and play does not altogether express the essential child; it is rather a species of civilized scaffolding behind which the essential child is forming himself by revery upon which he sees and hears.
>
> The child's reveries, his secret or behind-the-scene reactions to the events of the day, specially concern us. His habits of routine may be largely determined by

---

[2] N. H. M. Burke, "Some Aspects of the Inter-Relation Between Bodily and Mental Disease," *The British Journal of Medical Psychology*, vol. VI, pt. ii (1926), p. 114.

other, and adult, minds. Externally and to all seeming he may do exactly what parents or nurses require; but his interpretation is very different.

In this respect his attitude resembles that of primitive man. The briefest examination will suffice to show the immense importance in his secret life of magic, ceremonial, and taboo. He invents ceremonies which are designed to protect him from evil chance. A small boy of ten years was sent to school for the first time; previously he had been taught at home. Though backward at games, his mental development and aptitude for study were beyond his years. In spite of this he used to take minute precautions, as he walked to and from the school, that no one who passed him should tread upon his shadow. If someone by chance did so, the boy indulged in a peculiar three-step shuffle and another shuffle of four steps if he failed to step over the shadow of another person. These were supposed to act as antidotes. All of this happened without the knowledge of his parents or school-mates. Only later, when fighting down this magic practice in adolescence, did he make it known.[3]

Although such responses may seem entirely inappropriate to an adult in our society, and in fact seemed inappropriate to this boy in later years, never-theless they were very helpful to him at one time. By some means or other anxiety must be handled, and we tend to accept any means that seem to us useful. Our adult techniques do not always differ materially from those used by the boy; Fromm's discussion of how adults develop a "magic helper" when difficult problems arise is an indication of how early responses persist.

Mayo feels that anxiety is more widespread than we usually recognize. We often assume that it must be controlled by each individual himself; yet this assumption contains a potential threat of isolation which may increase the anxiety. In the reading below, Mayo considers the importance of dealing with anxiety as it appears in people threatened with illness. In an address delivered to doctors, he shows the patient's need of reassurance and its relation both to body disease and to the social environment of the patient. Read

ELTON MAYO, "Frightened People," below.

The patients Mayo describes are struggling anxiously to bring new situa-tions under control. As was said, anxiety is to some extent inherent in any new and difficult situation. The physiological processes discussed above prepare our bodies to act; these physiological changes produce a feeling of tension which we may recognize and describe as anxiety. In this way anxiety may be said to help us or free us to act, that is, to adjust to a situation or change it.

Although there may be situations in which we would not act at all without some anxiety, it is also apparent that we often do not act well because of it. We may concentrate on the anxiety itself rather than on the factors in the situation which are causing it. Observation of the relevant details of a situation may be hampered by the anxiety it arouses. As Harry Stack Sullivan puts it:

> One of the characteristics of anxiety is that it interferes with observation and analysis, with the acquisition of information and understanding and with recall and foresight. It interferes with alertness to the factors in a situation that are relevant to its occurrence. Therefore it interferes with effective action.[4]

---

[3] Elton Mayo, "Civilization — The Perilous Adventure," *Harper's*, October 1924, pp. 593–596.
[4] "The Theories of Harry Stack Sullivan," chapter 10 of Patrick Mullahy, *Oedipus Myth and Complex* (New York: Hermitage Press, 1948), p. 293.

By late adolescence we have had, directly or indirectly, so much experience that we recognize innumerable dilemmas in any concrete situation. It is perhaps surprising that when we feel something must be done quickly to relieve the anxiety induced by the dilemmas, we are able to find a way. The child faced with situations difficult for him uses magic to help him; in later life we develop more subtle techniques.

When faced with a new situation, we abstract by some process "pertinent" data from it before we can act effectively. Involved in the procedure are all our previous experiences and the meanings we have attached to them; the thoughts and dreams we have had about our experiences, the concepts we have created or accepted, the behavior we have found effective — all are used. Limitations arising either from lack of experience or lack of adequate observation of the experience will affect the utility of the result. Still, through a maze of conflicting possibilities, we do find data that *seem* pertinent. We simplify our view of the situation before us until it becomes "understandable," until we find some way to "control" it.

Simplification or abstraction is, therefore, an essential aspect of skillful adaptation. However, if the limitations of our experience or observation are great enough and our anxieties are sufficiently aroused, we tend to *oversimplify* the situation. We become satisfied with an insufficient observation of the specific situation before us; we avoid dilemmas inherent in the situation by not recognizing them, and may observe what we want to observe rather than what is really there. Until the dilemmas force themselves upon us, we hold tenaciously to our oversimplified view. Then we become involved in consequences we had not expected; our views are proved to have been ineffective, and our anxieties are reaffirmed.

If we have grown up, for example, under conditions of relative isolation from our contemporaries, we may be able to relate ourselves well only to the authority figures around us. We feel that we need the help of authority to handle most situations as they arise. We try to prove that we are better, stronger, or more skillful than others. We tend to react to change, as Fromm suggests, by relying on the orders of superiors or by issuing arbitrary orders to subordinates. Either action reassures us.

The underlying assumptions which seem to be developed and supported by this experience are that new situations are difficult to handle and that only firm authority can provide the necessary control or prevent the change. We have not had and do not get any experience with the subtle adjustments and flexibility of behavior necessary to meet change through coöperative action with others. But such coöperative action is sometimes the only effective response to the situation, and if we always behave as if authorities were needed, our actions will not bring satisfying results. Anxiety will develop, conditions will grow more divergent from our expectations and demands, our behavior will become less coöperative, our feelings of isolation and thus our anxiety will increase.[5] Such a point of view stands squarely in the way of coöperative behavior, since it assumes that coöperation is useless, that only authority can control the developing situation. We feel that our contemporaries, if left to their own desires, will act against us; that in one way or another people must be *forced* to behave as we want them to behave.

---

[5] It might be useful in this connection to consider "William Fay," Vol. II, Case 7.

Such oversimplifications are very common. Social scientists have made many careful distinctions between the methods through which we strengthen and affirm simplified views of situations.

One of the most common techniques has been called *regression*. This behavior involves abandoning a complicated but appropriate response to a situation in favor of a more simple response found useful at an earlier age. The wife who as a child found tears an effective way of modifying parental behavior may resort to tears when her husband complains, even though this has brought only impatience from him in the more immediate past. Such behavior involves an oversimplified view of the situation which brings a response to the new situation as if it were identical with the old, simply because of some similar elements. Under the pressure of anxiety the distinguishing elements are ignored. The instability between the Me and Self orientations which Perry notes in his article may involve regressions to the behavior of an earlier age where the responsibilities for choice did not seem so threatening.

Identification is another concept used to describe a pattern of behavior in respect to others. We find at an early age that we can imitate others, we can observe closely with considerable detail the things others do and then behave similarly ourselves. We behave as if we assumed a close relation between thought, feeling, and action and assumed that similar behavior means similar thoughts and feelings. These assumptions may well be fundamental to an early period of our lives during which we do not distinguish at all between an external or "objective" world and a "subjective" world. Some of this inability to distinguish between ourselves and others is carried over in the process of identification.

This process seems to be a basic part of our early learning and in some respects remains with us always as a learning tool. It is a particularly important technique in relieving us of anxiety in situations that seem difficult for us. As children we may be able to deal with situations that are too big for us by pretending to be father or mother or older brother and behaving as we observe they would behave. Admonitions of elders frequently encourage such behavior. We are told at various ages to "behave like a big boy" — "a gentleman," "a hero" — regardless of how we feel. We may also in this way learn a "role" acceptable to many social interactions which will permit us to behave appropriately in situations we know little about. Observation and understanding of the behavior of others may be assisted by this ability to identify with them. Cooley's statement of "sympathetic introspection" recognizes the importance of this process.

Although identification may be a useful technique in learning about ourselves and others, it may also lead to oversimplifications that prevent us from learning. This limitation is particularly true under conditions of stress. If, for example, we are anxious about our own popularity, we may identify with a popular friend, behave in a way that seems to us similar, and then assume that our friends *should* feel the same way about us as they apparently do about him. "Bill acting this way is doing O.K., so I must be doing all right, too." Or perhaps even, "I'm behaving just like Father. He is important, so I must be important, too." In this way we can maintain a way of behaving even though it is entirely inappropriate and avoid learning new and more appropriate behavior. We can, in situations that are extremely difficult for us, identify so fully with someone else that we appear to have no individuality of our own.

In considering the ways in which we oversimplify our observations of the interactions between ourselves and others, it is important to keep in mind that interactions always involve two terms and that it is easy to observe either term — ourselves or others — as the *most* significant factor in any particular interaction. The responsibility for the behavior may be either ours or others, but is more likely to be a complex mixture of both difficult to understand. Since we are personally involved and since our anxieties may be aroused by our observations, the ordinary difficulties of observing any dynamic process are greatly increased. To assist our understanding we simplify our observations. One simplification we frequently use is to decide that the situation must be *either* entirely our responsibility *or* entirely theirs. If we decide that the responsibility for any inadequacies belongs to others, we may feel our understanding to be adequate and our anxieties relieved. Then we, of course, are not forced to observe any inadequacy in our own behavior. If in a slightly different way we identify with a popular friend and behave "like" him, and others do not respond to us adequately, we can feel that it is their fault rather than our own and thus be relieved of any need for modifying our own behavior.

Another simplification of the relationship between the thoughts, feelings, and behavior of ourselves and others is the process known as *projection*. We observe that we have been behaving like others and assume without any further evidence that they have thoughts and feelings identical to our own. We can in this way attribute to others our own thoughts and feelings and then even deny them in ourselves. If a social situation makes us angry, we can attribute the anger to others, thereby justifying an angry response from us and permitting us to behave in a way that will make them angry. Then we can feel that "it was really his fault. He ought to control his anger better."

This process of projection can be used at many different levels of complexity. In ordinary social interactions projection frequently appears in minor ways; we can project our feelings about a situation on others and thus assume a particular set of feelings in them to which we can respond. In the absence of any evidence to the contrary this may often be a useful way of initiating a social interaction. If we then observe their actual feelings as expressed by their response to us and modify our responses accordingly, it may be entirely effective. However, we can also project our feelings on others and refuse to observe any differences in their feelings; we can say, "You can't feel that way. It's idiotic." If our anxieties are aroused, we may maintain this projection with considerable tenacity. Furthermore, if the situation is sufficiently important to us, we can feel free to criticize others for these projected feelings of our own, can bring social pressures on them — "They should know better than to behave that way" — and be relieved of the social pressures that might otherwise be levied against ourselves. We can deny that these are our feelings at all.

Rationalization is another process which is fundamental to the support of such oversimplifications. Here we select and support verbally those aspects of a situation which affirm the behavior we feel is desirable and omit from consideration those aspects which do not affirm such behavior. We find "good" reasons to substitute for our "real" reasons.[6] Rationalization is such a common phenomenon and seems so useful to us that it is difficult to recognize it as a technique that sustains an oversimplification of our observations.

---

[6] Many of the cases in Vol. II provide illustrations; consider "James Alton Johnson," Case 12; "The Fentons," Case 8; or "Grosvenor House," Case 32.

It should not be concluded that the sort of behavior outlined here is always ineffective or inadequate. It may be less effective than a more accurate observation of the total situation around us, but it is often useful as a step in the direction of better observation. It follows, for example, from Sullivan's statement quoted above that insofar as these techniques reduce anxiety, they may also improve observation. The more fully we observe the relevant factors of a situation, the more fully we can appraise the probability of getting satisfactory results from any particular action we wish to undertake.

Perhaps the social value of these ways of oversimplifying problems will be more clearly evident in the technique of *compensation.* Here we simplify the problem before us by refusing to recognize the importance to us of factors that would prevent us from acting in the way we want to act. We deny that these limiting factors exist, behave as if they were not part of the situation, and compensate for them by inordinate effort. The one-armed golfer, the "weakling" who becomes a great athlete, the man of moderate intellect who finds ways to get high grades, all may be involved in compensation. In our culture we put a high premium on such behavior, perhaps because we confuse it with deliberate effort consciously applied to overcome limiting factors which are taken into full account.

We are employing compensation of an indirect form when we seek success in one area for the purposes of demonstrating the unimportance to us of limiting factors in another area. Thus the child who finds difficulties in relating himself to his classmates in social activities may seek to become the brightest child in the school or the worst behaved. He seeks behavior that will bring him some admiration from his classmates. The original inadequacies remain but are buried under the admiration for the compensatory accomplishments.

Both types of compensation hold within them a necessity for their continuance, since otherwise the feelings of inadequacy that always accompany such oversimplifications would become overwhelming. Only so long as this compensatory behavior continues can these people operate at all. They put forth, therefore, tremendous efforts and are often very helpful or very damaging to society.

These concepts and many other similar ones are used by social scientists to make much more precise discriminations than are necessary here. But the fact that we do make many different types of oversimplifications and maintain them with considerable skill is of the utmost significance. Without some recognition of this activity, an expansion of our observation of the "total situation" in which we act is difficult. Such activity is very rigid and assists in its own defense; it leads to the growth of the original oversimplifications and reaffirms its utility to us by limiting observations that might undermine them.

Limitations to our thinking of this sort are widespread. The boy learning to use a chisel mentioned in the last chapter was thinking in terms of fixed entities such as "worthiness" or "unworthiness" of self, of "goodness" or "badness," rather than in terms of the concrete situation with which he was confronted.[7] Any of us may do this when we are faced with situations where we feel the limits of our abilities are being tested. It is not an uncommon way of thinking about grades and studies, about beginning attempts in athletics, and about the first efforts of an adolescent to develop new social skills. In these attempts to

---

[7] Danny Keith in "Mu Nu Fraternity" (Vol. II, Case 5) reduced his thinking to terms of "friend or enemy."

limit the factors of the situation that must be considered, we may fall into false dichotomies that are not adequately related to the situation. In Hayakawa's terms, we may make insufficient "maps" of the "territories" and fall into a two-valued orientation when we are in fact dealing with a multi-valued situation.

There is an important next step in the process we have been considering. We first limit the areas in which choices must be made, and then in Mayo's terms we "over-elaborate the over-simplifications." We develop logically in our minds the consequences of our conclusions. If, for example, we decide that we cannot learn economics or French, we *then* elaborate that we cannot graduate from college (or Father will stop the allowance, or we will be drafted), and we cannot earn a living, cannot get married, and so may eventually conclude that we are generally worthless. This thinking proceeds by logical steps from an observed premise felt to be irrefutable. But only the premise is at all related to the situation — and partially so at that. The thinking elaborates logically the consequences of this premise and the anxiety which surrounds the basic problem, and thus leads to further anxiety. Such thinking, characterized by the presence of anxiety *and* by an overelaboration of the disastrous consequences of a given premise, is called "obsessive thinking" by Mayo. It is not unusual; as Mayo puts it:

> Every one of us who has the remotest claim to intelligence has at one time or other experienced something of obsessive disability . . . We may banish the disadvantages of unfamiliarity . . . for I shall be discussing the problems of the office, the street, and the home. Obsessive thinking is the inevitable variation from the norm that upon occasion afflicts you — and me . . . [It] will be reproduced accurately, if not permanently, in any situation where, by reason either of external social constraint or of fatigue, an individual is prevented from following the line of development that his own interest dictates. Especially in situations where such constraint prevents the individual from *complicating* his thinking in the manner such thinking demands, he will begin to display the usual symptoms of irritability, indecision, and loss of interest in his work.[8]

In the following reading, Mayo discusses the importance of such thinking in our society, indicates his opinions about its source in our social development, and suggests the ways in which we can handle it in our behavior with others. Read

ELTON MAYO, *Some Notes on the Psychology of Pierre Janet* (Cambridge: Harvard University Press, 1948), pp. 3–23, 66–109.

Examples of an extreme nature indicate dramatically the type of problems we are concerned with and are useful to us, because in such extremes we can observe more clearly the mechanisms involved. When any of us find ourselves in a position which arouses serious anxiety, we tend to behave in ways similar to people with whom this anxiety is always present. We also may then tend to make inadequate discrimination between those factors in the situation that are hostile to us and those that are not. We may behave *at times* as if we felt that the hostility is inevitable and continuing.

Karen Horney, in the reading below, discusses the basic conflicts which she considers face all of us and which we all resolve or learn to live with in our own ways. In considering the neurotics as an extreme example of the failure to han-

---

[8] *Some Notes on the Psychology of Pierre Janet,* pp. 6, 108.

dle these conflicts effectively, we can see some of the elements of the problem more clearly. Horney discusses people who have decided that the world is always hostile to them. They develop, she suggests, three alternative ways of defending themselves against such an anticipation of hostility. First are those who *always* move toward people, who try to win the affection of others and lean on them. Second are those who *always* move against people and are determined to fight them. Third are those who *always* move away from people and keep apart. Each of these attitudes is common with all of us at certain times, but the neurotic people she considers always overemphasize one reaction to anxiety: the first group overemphasizes helplessness, the second aggression, and the third isolation. Horney says:

> From the point of view of the normal person there is no reason why the three attitudes should be mutually exclusive. One should be capable of giving in to others, of fighting, and of keeping to oneself. The three can complement each other and make for a harmonious whole. If one predominates, it merely indicates an over-development along one line.
>
> But in neurosis there are several reasons why these attitudes are inconceivable. The neurotic is not flexible; he is driven to comply, to fight, to be aloof, regardless of whether the move is appropriate in the particular circumstance, and he is thrown into a panic if he behaves otherwise . . . Also these attitudes do not remain restricted to the area of human relationships but gradually pervade the entire personality . . . the person's relation . . . to himself and to life in general.[9]

Read

KAREN HORNEY, *Our Inner Conflicts* (New York: W. W. Norton, 1945), pp. 40–95.

We have been considering the consequences of an inadequate relation to a particular situation in which we are involved. Possibly the situation is sufficiently new for us so that our training has not fitted us to make the discriminations that are most useful; possibly the situation is not unusual but still our learning has been inadequate. In any event, anxiety and fear are often present. Such feelings, reinforced by physiological processes and by the thinking mechanisms we may have developed to "control" these feelings, limit our ability to observe fully and to respond effectively.

ADDITIONAL READINGS

Cannon, Walter B., *The Wisdom of the Body* (New York: W. W. Norton, 1932).
Cannon developed the "equilibrium hypothesis" to show how the various bodily processes achieve a state of balance between internal mechanisms and external pressures. The interdependence of the various processes is dramatically illustrated.

Cantril, Hadley, Hazel Gaudet, and Herta Hertzog, *The Invasion from Mars* (Princeton: Princeton University Press, 1940).
A study of a panic reaction to a radio broadcast, showing that people have varying susceptibilities to fright according to their social integration and psychic make-up.

Freud, Anna, *The Ego and the Mechanisms of Defense* (New York: International Universities Press, 1946).
An analysis of the relationship between ego, id, and super-ego at different ages,

pointing out the dynamic equilibrium between them. Special emphasis is placed on the ego in its active process of defending itself against anxiety from various sources.

Grinker, R. R., and J. P. Spiegal, *Men under Stress* (Philadelphia: Blakiston, 1945).
A series of case studies of the reactions of soldiers to the stress of combat, analyzed from a psychiatric point of view.

May, Rollo, *The Meaning of Anxiety* (New York: The Ronald Press, 1950).
A discussion of the current psychological and cultural theories of anxiety, together with case studies.

Merton, Robert K., "Social Structure and Anomie," *The Family*, ed. Ruth Anshen (New York: Harper, 1949).

In this paper Merton develops a conceptual scheme for "deviance." He maintains that antisocial behavior is not merely the result of the obstreperousness of strange people but often emerges from a kind of social disorganization which keeps many people from obtaining the goals which they were taught by their culture to seek. He offers a sociological framework for such concepts as Horney's.

White, Robert W., *The Abnormal Personality* (New York: Ronald Press, 1948).
A description of the varieties of abnormal behavior dealing extensively with the dynamics of mental disorder. White integrates psychological and sociological concepts with unusual success. The book contains ample case material.

The Veteran Himself[*]

BY GEORGE F. F. LOMBARD

For any veteran a job is more than a chance to practice technical skills and earn a living. It is his opportunity to relate himself actively and functionally to a world in which he has a new part to play. What problems other than the vocational ones already discussed does he face?

READJUSTMENT OF NERVOUS SYSTEM

In the first place, the veteran returning to civilian life directly from active combat will be a man whose nervous system is conditioned to active and alert response to any unexpected happening. In helping him to react quickly to such occurrences, however slight, and to become actively alert to their every implication, his nervous system will have been superbly conditioned to back up the reactions which his thought processes have decided. Among other things, it will be prepared

to make the bodily changes which enable the human organism to prepare itself to handle any objects in the outside world which arouse fear, anger, hate, or rage. For example, it will be prepared to lessen the supply of blood going to his internal organs and to furnish additional amounts to his extremities for their use in dealing actively with the objects in the environment. Then it will be prepared to release adrenin into his blood stream to serve its several functions in maintaining and preserving his body in physical action. In fact, a soldier's return from front-line duty in good physical condition presupposes the effective functioning of such mechanisms. If his nervous system had not allowed him to make responses adequate to battle conditions over long periods of fatiguing work, he would have been a casualty.

The same unexpectedness of occur-

[*] A chapter from *Rehabilitation: The Man and the Job*, report of the Subcommittee on Rehabilitation of the Committee on Work in Industry, National Research Council (Baltimore: Lord Baltimore Press, 1945).

rences in industrial or other civilian life, however, calls for totally different responses from those necessary in combat. No longer do a man's reflexes need to convert him so completely and so quickly into a fighting organism. The veteran who threw an ax at the dog who was stealing his lunch,[1] the veterans who promised to smash up the night club where they had telephoned for reservations, only to be told on arrival while tables in plain view were still empty that no reservations had been made,[2] were responding to the unexpected as they had been trained to respond in ways appropriate to the battlefield. They had not yet developed, ready for their instant control, ways of handling such events appropriate to the new situations in which they occurred. Since in man responses to changes in the environment are subject to conscious control, the period of readjustment need not be long, even though it cannot be avoided. There has to be, as Colonel Rusk called it, a "period of decompression" to allow the superbly conditioned nervous system of the returned soldier to adjust to its new functions, its new rate of activity.

Until a veteran develops new responses appropriate to the demands of his new situations, he is bound to experience a kind of frustration. The results of the bodily changes already described, which occur to allow an organism to handle emergencies, if they are not expended in physical action, lead to an unreasonable irritability. If this irritability is misunderstood by others to be simply a reaction to them, their response to it will prolong a veteran's total problems of readjustment by re-enforcing any tendency which he may have to interpret happenings in the outside world as hostile. Furthermore, although time on furlough, on vacation, or in a hospital may be an important part of a "decompression" period (in this respect a man who has been wounded and through a period of hospitalization may be better prepared to return to civilian life than one who has not), it cannot always accomplish the whole of this readjustment. Experience in the successful handling of unexpected occurrences on the job cannot be gained on vacation. The atmosphere of relaxation in the total situation of a vacation contrasts too strongly with the atmosphere of strain in many work situations to accomplish such an easy transition. Yet a period of recreation, of completely following one's own desires, may well be an important part of the total transition from military to industrial life.

These problems of physiological adjustment will not be peculiar to veterans who have seen combat duty. Every veteran will face them in some degree, since in the Services an educational period, part of whose purpose from its beginning is to prepare the nervous system for combat duty starts with basic training.

READJUSTMENT OF WAYS OF THINKING

In the second place, the effects of military service on a man's way of thinking are no less striking. As Carl Rogers of Ohio State University, Director of Counseling Services for the United Service Organizations, Inc., has put it:

One of . . . [the] problems is that of the pent-up resentment and hostility, which is so frequently manifested by the returned man, and which has been an aftermath of every war for centuries . . .

Whether we regard these hostile reactions as due to the continued frustrations of military life, or to a lowered self-control due to combat fatigue, or to the release of repressed aggression in the battle situation, or to the basic injustice which sends one man into danger and keeps another safe, or to the many thwartings which are experienced upon re-entering the civilian world, they are an important present problem with which we must learn to deal . . .

[Another] major group of psychological adjustments are those in which a disturbance of the man's sense of adequacy is involved. There is, for

---

[1] A. Soutar, "Home Coming Isn't Easy," *Saturday Evening Post*, Vol. 217, December 16, 1944, p. 38.
[2] An incident mentioned at the Week-End Conferences at the Harvard Business School.

nearly all returning men and women, a sense of strangeness about civil life, even to the extent that men feel incapable of handling jobs at which they worked competently for years before the war. There is the feeling of those who return to college that the world of books and intellectual things is fearful and beyond their grasp. There is, above all, a sense of loss of status. Servicemen and women have been part of a struggle upon which the attention of the world was focussed. To drop out of this, to become one citizen among millions, unsupported by a widespread social purpose and a far-flung social group, is a difficult loss to assimilate. With some, the drop in status will be much more sharp, as in the case of air force majors and colonels, whose peacetime tasks will be sharply reduced in prestige and pay. The blow to self-esteem is very great, and the psychological reaction correspondingly deep . . .

There is another significant cluster of adjustments which the serviceman is called upon to make, and these have to do with purposes and goals. Both experimental data and common sense point out that a clearcut purpose is one of the basic elements of morale, individual or group. Yet present facts indicate that millions of men will leave the services with no clear or realistic goal . . .

In the field of family and marital relationships, the outstanding problem is the tendency to grow apart. This is probably most marked in the man's tie to his own parents. So different have been the experiences, the values, and the standards of parent and son during the war years that in many instances, unless parents are unusually flexible, the basis of common understanding will have almost completely disappeared. To a somewhat lesser extent this will be true of the man's relationship to his wife, and his own

family. The community of interests which existed before the war is likely to be sharply reduced.[3]

Consequently, the average veteran will have to make adjustments in his patterns of thinking that will not be automatic on his securing a job for which he is trained.

READJUSTMENT TO WORKING GROUPS

Finally, during the war men will have become accustomed to activity as a member of a team in a way which is a new and meaningful experience to them. Many authorities[4] place the satisfaction that an individual gets from such activities as among the most enduring of all satisfactions and as particularly characteristic of military life. Through this quality of military experience, many veterans will return to civilian life accustomed to group experience, and one of their greatest demands of it will be to find the close-knit feeling of comradeship that is such an important part of military operations. Whether they will find it or whether through the lack of finding it, they are driven, as someone has said, to make the most of such satisfactions as they can obtain from reliving in the present their past wartime experiences will depend upon the skills with which the administration of civilian activities is handled in the postwar period. But such satisfactions are at best a poor substitute for those that come from association with others in an activity that has a function in the present.

Furthermore, military organizations by requiring group leaders to take responsibility for men's lives promote on a scale found in no other type of organization the growth of a sense of responsibility, of initiative, of understanding, and of the other qualities that make up the complex of leadership. Once acquired, these skills of leadership are not easily laid aside, and if they cannot be used within the framework of activities in which a returned veteran finds himself, they can

[3] C. R. Rogers, "Psychological Adjustments of Discharged Service Personnel"; *Psychological Bulletin*, Vol. 41, No. 10; December, 1944, pp. 690–693.

[4] For instance, C. I. Barnard, *The Functions of the Executive*, Harvard University Press, Cambridge, 1938, p. 148, and the references there given; W. Waller, *The Veteran Comes Back*, The Dryden Press, New York, 1944, Part I, Chapter 3.

only be used to lead to suspicion of or hostility to those activities.

THE VETERAN'S TOTAL ADJUSTMENT

In summary, four aspects of a veteran's total adjustment, his vocational skills, his nervous system, his patterns of thinking, and his skills of getting on with and leading fellow workers can be distinguished as requiring attention in his transition to civilian life. These aspects of every individual's being function as a whole of course in all the activities in which he participates, though explicit attention does not have to be given to all of them on every occasion. For example, in a group whose membership and work routines are well established and operating smoothly many problems can be handled without going beyond the vocational level. In such a situation an individual's nervous system as well as his thinking and his relations with other people adjust to the transition without explicit attention. In other situations where a group's way of working is constantly revised, its members' points of view, as represented by their patterns of thinking and their relations with each other, have to be considered when technical or other changes are introduced; otherwise the effectiveness of the group's way of working will not be maintained. In these situations the condition of an individual's nervous system only infrequently has to be taken into account explicitly. Even when the demands that industrial jobs make of an individual's nervous system are extreme, as when a worker transfers from heavy manual labor to desk work, the adaptability of most individuals' nervous systems is adequate to the occasion. But success in responding to combat conditions requires an alertness to occurrences not demanded by industrial jobs. A veteran's nervous system cannot be expected to respond to the changed requirements of an industrial job without receiving explicit attention. Thus the manner of a veteran's response to what happens to him is no different than that of any individual, though the range of factors that may need explicit attention in handling him will often be greater.

A VETERAN'S EXPERIENCE

The following account of a veteran's own experiences clearly illustrates the way in which a purely vocational approach to this veteran's problems of adjustment was ineffective and how his readjustment was not completed until he had worked out for himself new patterns of thinking, attained membership in a group of workers, and reestablished the condition of his nervous system. The Subcommittee wishes to emphasize that it is using this account, *not* because it is typical of the way a veteran's problems of readjustment are handled — which it is not — but because it clearly illustrates the point at issue: the impossibility of disregarding a man's problems as a whole in placing him on a job.

Next I went to my rehabilitation board. . . . Kind as they were, I wanted only to be left alone for a while to think things out, to absorb again, a little at a time, this bewildering thing called America, home. . .

.   .   .   .   .

I resented the telephone calls from the rehabilitation board, solicitous in the beginning, then more insistent. I didn't feel prepared, mentally, to tackle work; couldn't make a decision, because for more than a year the Army had made all my decisions for me. I was frightened by mounting confusion and indecision.

So, in desperation, I signed with a government agency to pick potatoes. Radio, press and our Governor had been screaming loudly for volunteers to save the threatened potato crop, and I knew that many of those spuds would be dehydrated for the Army. Besides, I wanted to see what my repaired arm would do.

Yet, after a group of us had been accepted, there came a curt call of cancellation, stating that the government had all the help needed. For weeks afterward, then, the same frantic appeals continued, while we returned men sat at home and wondered what sort of fool country we'd been fighting for.

That's when I definitely decided not to be stampeded. And every returned man I know has reached this same decision sooner or later. Despite what authorities believe about delay in adjustment being dangerous, we feel that it is a mistake to hurry us.

The newspaper I had worked for offered me a reporting job. I was under agreement with the Army and the draft board to go into defense work, but it was "arranged" that this would suffice. As a naive veteran, this didn't seem valid to me and I said so. The board then agreed that I could go to a friend's farm, where I did work off some of the shock and resentment of the government potato fiasco by helping harvest a fine crop. When this ended, I felt more confused and restless than ever, unable to come to any sensible decision, and I stalled some more. This time, state rehabilitation authorities began to apply pressure.

At the next interview I blew up, and, in so doing realized soberly that I was in grave danger of becoming a "problem boy." I compromised by taking a temporary job delivering Christmas mail in subzero weather. This was better. At least I had some contact with reality in the V-mail coming from boys still across, whom I now frankly envied.[5]

To repeat, the Subcommittee refers to this veteran's experiences solely for purposes of illustration. It makes no claim that they are typical. His experiences make several points. No system for referring people to jobs can operate without such incidents as this veteran records; and it can be no criticism of his board that it has to report "the government had all the help needed." In those days of rapid change, such happenings are usual. They cannot be avoided, but the unwanted effects of their occurrence on a veteran's feelings will be minimized if the approach to aiding him is to his total problem rather than by directing him in regard to its vocational aspect alone.

Indeed a vocational approach to this veteran's problems could in the beginning get nowhere. Based on his training, and leaving aside for the moment the priorities of wartime industries, advice from a vocational point of view would have routed him back to newspaper work; but consider the path which he had to take by the trial-and-error methods of his own efforts before he successfully accomplished the transition to his former work.

He had first to secure for himself a "decompression" period of active physical work, less demanding than the conditions of combat but more demanding than the work for which he was heading. This period had effects both on the condition of his nervous system and his ways of thinking. His account goes on:

This experience convinced me that physical work under harsh, trying conditions was the quickest way to bridge the gulf between sanguinary battle conditions and comfortable professional life, and I customarily enjoy soft living as well as the next fellow. So I immediately took another job — in a bleachery this time.

The trucks that I pushed around all day were loaded with G. I. herringbone twill for fatigue clothes that would soon be stinking with blood and grime. Or they had linings for G. I. boots, the same old clodhoppers worn in the long trek across Africa to Bizerte. They felt good in my hands. You see, we can't make a clean break from old habits and associations too abruptly.

My pay was only twenty-six dollars, before taxes, but I began to get a grip on myself.

At the same time his own program achieved for him the feeling that he again belonged to a group with a function in the world:

I felt a warm kinship with, and admiration for, these men and women in the bleachery, who worked long,

---

[5] A. Soutar, "Home Coming Isn't Easy," *op. cit.*, pp. 35–36.

hard hours at wages the near-by ship-yard workers sneered at. They were the first outsiders to understand my feelings. They represented more what my soldier pals had been, and I was happy.

And finally he was ready to return to the vocation in which he was experienced.

I was making progress, but common sense told me I would have to start into my own line of work eventually, and when the newspaper called again that spring, I signed up. . . .

Perhaps the most important point of this veteran's experience is his clear, but unexpressed, feeling that it was he himself who was accomplishing his total rehabilitation. But he did it without understand-ing help from, and indeed by at times struggling against the vocationally oriented efforts of, the agencies which existed to help him.

The question for business and industry therefore is not whether a veteran's rehabilitation will be limited to his vocational problems. Inevitably his whole readjustment will occur. The question, rather, is whether his total rehabilitation will be planned for and organized for in ways that will help it in an orderly fashion, or whether the programs that are organized to handle it will be so centered on the vocational aspect alone that they will impede the total process. If the latter occurs, the veteran's willingness to contribute his best efforts on the job selected for him will be affected.

Frightened People*

BY ELTON MAYO

I shall begin by limiting my topic in two directions. I have no intention, for example, of quoting cases of a psychiatric type. I hope that such instances as I cite will be nearer the facts. This somewhat ambiguous phrase must not be taken to imply any aspersion upon a modern and most valuable development in medicine. I owe too much to psychiatry and psychiatrists to be guilty of such ingratitude. My meaning is merely that when I cite a case, I hope that it will be immediately possible for every member of the audience instantly to translate it into terms of his own experience — into terms of a similar situation with which he is directly acquainted.

The other limitation is that no question of the organic or mental origin of a disorder will be raised — as if these were alternate possibilities. I have no thesis, overt or implied, that the origin of any ill is "all mental." On the contrary, I assume in every instance an organic dis-ability of some kind — unbalance, infection, defect, pathology: but I assume also the existence of other factors of varying importance. These two limitations make it evident that I am confining my attention to the simple and the obvious. My comfort in this admission must be that the simple and the obvious are perhaps not often enough or not clearly enough stated.

A patient is a case — a case of something that can be looked up in a medical dictionary (B for botulism, T for typhoid); he is also a human being. Both aspects are important to the physician. In the medical schools of thirty or forty years ago the most elaborate care and attention were given to study of the former, the ailment, in clinic, hospital, and laboratory; no attempt was made to develop any systematic study of the human being. I shall later claim that this neglect was not altogether unjustifiable in the social circumstance of that time. But for the moment I wish merely to

* An address given on January 18, 1938, at the Harvard Medical School. First printed in the *Harvard Medical Alumni Bulletin*, January, 1939. Included as an appendix in Elton Mayo, *Some Notes on the Psychology of Pierre Janet* (Cambridge: Harvard University Press, 1948).

point out that the neglect carried curious consequences for the practice of medicine. For example, it was very generally believed in those days that the student who did best in his studies was very rarely the man who did best in professional practice afterwards. I am not interested in the truth or falsity of this belief; its interest here is merely as evidence that in some inarticulate way the physicians of that time were already aware of an omission in their general training.

Now when a patient walks into a consulting room he requires two kinds of aid from the physician. The first is medical attention, the second is assurance: in the ordinary consultation the second is as important as the first. The need of assurance is not adequately met by a hearty manner — nor by dogmatism or breezy self-confidence. The world is less suggestible than it used to be, and more obsessive. Especially in these days of universal education the assurance offered must be discriminating; it must be pointed at a particular item in the particular mental context — an item that has been discovered to be there. This differs in different patients, and is almost always left to the physician to discover. By this I mean that the physician is never told directly what the need is; sometimes, usually indeed, the patient cannot tell him, sometimes he does not want to. But in very many instances the physician's success will depend upon discovery of the exact locus of the need for assurance. The physician must therefore make two diagnoses: one of the organic ill, the other of the need of assurance. The latter is often simple, rather easily discovered. But it is unwise to ignore it because it is simple.

Almost twenty-five years ago in Queensland a young doctor came to me at the University and made a statement to the effect that his patients always suffered a "functional complication" — in the phrase of that time — of an organic ill. His practice, which was large, was in a good residential district and the average case was not very serious. He claimed that in the majority of these instances it was not difficult to mitigate, or to get rid of, the organic condition. "And then I

find," he added, "that the patient is no better. I have done nothing to get rid of the functional complication." This young man had taken a very good degree at a famous British university; he was very keenly interested in his work. In addition to this he was a high-minded and sympathetic human being. He had always attempted to make an approach to the person in a consultation. The method he had adopted was to assume in the patient an interest equal to and like his own. He would draw diagrams, take down a textbook, explain the nature of the disorder. And this method had no success at all. His patients had no desire to become amateurs of science or medicine; each one wanted reassurance as a person. The more the doctor enlarged upon "the case," the more the patient felt it as annihilation of the person. The physician was defeating his own admirable intention.

After some discussion he realized his error and determined to change his method. From this time on, he attempted to discover the fear and to reassure. The sequel was interesting: in a few months his practice had greatly increased; in a few years he had given up general medicine and become a specialist.

A person in need of assurance is a frightened person; but it is evident that the nature and degree of the fear will differ in different people. If the assurance is to be of the right kind and addressed to the appropriate locus in every individual instance, then the physician is in need of an approximate classification that will help him to identify, and be sufficiently adequate to, the situation set before him. With this in mind, and for purposes of ordered discussion, I have devised a classification of three types of personal situations. The classification is arbitrary and empirical; it is based upon an approximate estimate of the kind of fear and its distribution in the individual's thinking. In the simpler cases there is not much fear and what there is tends to attach itself to the actual organic disorder. In the more difficult cases there is a great deal of what has been termed "free anxiety," distributed widely through almost all the patient's thinking. In such a situation as this latter there is not necessarily any immediate or obvious relation between the organic dysfunction and the fear.

I. The first type of case may be described as illness under conditions such that the necessary assurance is almost automatic in the situation. In three continents I have happened across country districts in which the local physician was a first-class medical man practicing there because he liked the life of the countryside and disliked cities or crowded industrial centers. The chief local occupation was farming of various types, the social interrelation of the various family groups was complex and strong. Add to this an immense, and justified, confidence in the competence of the physician and my picture is complete. Even in these days of crowded city life one can discover a few instances of somewhat similar situations; for instance, if a child falls ill of mumps or measles in a well-ordered house in a well-ordered residential district, if a member of an athletic team or a soldier in wartime is injured, there is immediately available a competent physician who is known to the patient.

In instances such as these the need of assurance is in the charge of a closely united social group. The physician is an active member of the group and must know how to identify himself with the social reassurance function as he proceeds to technical examination. But everything in the surrounding is saying to the patient, "Here is the doctor. Now you will be all right." Since the patient usually knows the doctor personally and has known him for years, he is also saying this to himself. There is what one might call a total conspiracy of reassurance. Everyone takes the ailment as obvious; no one is frightened. This is almost a social ritual, and is automatic.

II. This almost automatic social assurance was at one time more general than it is now; it may indeed have been universal in the earlier stages of our history. Here may perhaps be found the historic justification of that seeming neglect of medical schools to study the human being as well as the ailment — the neglect of which I spoke earlier. But the physician of these days can no longer assume social collaboration of this extensive and adequate type in his ordinary consultations. The second type of case I specify must therefore be regarded as representing the usual or average medical consultation of today. The patient knows little or nothing of the doctor; he has been "sent" by someone, friend or physician. And the physician knows little or nothing of the patient — his family, his daily work, his social affiliations. In this situation the second diagnosis, the localization of the need of assurance, suddenly becomes more important. Little or no assistance, explicit or implied, can be expected from the patient's immediate and social background. The instances I cite under this general heading develop from the simple to the less simple.

(a) The most simple instance is that in which the assurance needed relates itself directly to the ailment or to a symptom. A patient with abdominal pain, for example, has given much thinking to identification of the pain with gastric ulcer or malignancy. Success in treating the organic disorder depends in part on discovering what the patient is frightened of as a result of "overthinking." An eminent physician, now in retirement, tells himself that in later middle age while still active he noticed that he was becoming breathless after mounting stairs. He reflected uneasily that he should perhaps consult a specialist colleague. Then one day as he came out of the subway he noticed that he was more breathless than usual. Suddenly he remembered that he had ascended on the escalator and had not mounted steps at all. He laughed and lost both the fear and the symptom. The physician being a skilled person could thus reassure himself or, rather, could be directly reassured by the obvious absurdity of the situation. The average patient without technical knowledge requires skilled assistance, and assurance, before he can develop such a point of view.

(b) The next instance cited is a situation in which the assurance demanded may have no direct relevance to the ailment protested. The assurance demanded is nevertheless particular and not necessarily evidence of a general anxiety. An industrial nurse, whose mornings were occupied in the conduct of a small clinic in a factory, made some interesting observations of this type of case. After two years of work in the factory, she came to know a considerable number of workers rather intimately. Being a good interviewer and observer, she noticed that it was rarely the minor casualty, for example, a cut or splinter, that brought a worker to her. Frequently, the worker would dress such an injury himself in a rough manner and without leaving his job. On the mornings that he brought such an injury to her for attention, there was some other matter he wished to discuss. And it was always a problem with respect to which he needed assurance. It might be medical — his own health or that of some member of his family — or it might be social — a son, daughter, or wife. The nurse became very alert to, or it might be said expectant of, the second consultation. A patient may bring a minor ill to a physician when he really wishes to consult him on another problem. This is the more characteristic the better he knows his physician.

(c) The reassurance must be addressed to the appropriate person, who is not always the patient himself. A girl does very well in her studies at college but does not find herself at ease with her associates. She does not go to dances as they do; she does not know any young men. She is apt to feel the social disability most acutely during the general chatter at mealtime; she develops globus hystericus. This does not trouble her greatly until she returns home for the holidays. Her father — sensitive, intelligent, educated — becomes alarmed and takes her to a throat specialist. The specialist sees the girl alone and speedily loses interest; he pushes her off with a vague assurance that she will be all right. He does not see the father except to say farewell. The father, still dissatisfied, goes to his phy-

sician. The latter, realizing that assurance is needed, explains the condition at length, and the father finally is comforted. When the father is reassured, the daughter's symptom begins to abate.

Two comments suggest themselves. The first is obvious, namely, that in such a case effective assurance is the most important part of the treatment. Further, the assurance must not be addressed to the patient only but to any person in her immediate social context whose affection and alarm provoke a consequent increase of alarm in her.

The second comment is an observation on the effect of diminished social contacts upon family life. In a small and ordered society the closely organized family operates, like the social group itself, to support the doctor and reassure the patient. In a situation where social contacts are weakened or diminished, the highly organized family operates in a contrary manner. Its isolation reinforces its anxiety; it tends therefore to alarm and to exaggeration of the ill rather than to reassurance.

III. The third type of case includes the really frightened people, those people who suffer a general alarm about themselves, their health, their position in the world. In such cases the ailment may itself be organic only in a minor fashion: it may in a sense be provoked, and it will surely be exaggerated, by the terror and general need of assurance. These cases are the exact contrary of the first type: in the first type the social system conspires to reassure; in this third type the lack of assured functional relation to the social system is conspiring to produce a sense of insecurity and terror.

(a) The simplest cases are instances of what Durkheim has called *anomie*.[1] A woman of seventy enters the outpatient department of a hospital complaining of pain in her legs. The hospital records show that she has periodically entered herself with this complaint over a number of years. The medical examiners have tended to refer her to the psychiatrists and the psychiatrists to send her back to

---

[1] Emile Durkheim, *Le Suicide* (Paris: Librarie Felix Alcan, 1897), p. 281.

the medical clinic. Encouraged to talk, she explained that for most of her life she had been a working housekeeper in hotels and successful in that function. Having saved money, she determined to "retire" when the economic depression diminished the amount of such work required. She acquired a room and furnished it; she developed a routine of living. The effect of this newly acquired routine of living was to shut her off from all active or effective human contacts. If she talked to women they "talked only of their troubles"; there was no other person with whom she could talk. It was after some months of this isolation that she presented herself at the hospital. For a person who has been continually active, who is still amazingly serene in the circumstances, this functionless style of living constitutes a major dysfunction. While this aspect of her situation was being made clear, she dropped all reference to and apparently forgot the pain in her legs. The hospital attempted to develop new and satisfactory human relationships for her.

This case relates itself to the experiences, quoted above, of the industrial nurse. It is a more complicated development of the same type of situation. The individual is unable herself to make articulate the nature of the dysfunction; but she is aware of an exaggeration of the organic condition, and her limited capacity for thought and expression lights upon this, the organic condition, for complaint to the physician. The physician naturally is unable to confirm this expression.

(b) A chance phrase dropped inadvertently by a physician may seem in such cases actually to provoke a disorder. This is not suggestion or suggestibility; there is no imitation of the appropriate organic symptoms as in hysteria. In one of the three well-ordered country districts of which I spoke above, the authorities decided to institute a high school. The newly appointed headmaster came from a large city; and, some six months after his arrival, he presented himself in the physician's consulting rooms and asked for a medical examination. A short conversa-

tion showed that he was not a candidate for life insurance, that he had suffered no accident, that he complained of no particular symptoms. The physician found himself somewhat puzzled by a consultation quite outside the ordinary run of his practice; however, he proceeded to subject his patient to an extremely careful examination. He found nothing that could be reported as variant from what might be expected in a normal person of the patient's age, other than a certain suggestion of apprehension. As the patient left him, he said more by way of conversation than diagnosis, "Your heart's a bit sluggish; don't get influenza." The patient left him, and a week or so later — in 1918 — the alarm of "Spanish Influenza" began. The patient lapsed into a condition of extreme anxiety and had to be sent to the city for medical care.

In this instance study of the individual showed that he had never in any real or human sense "belonged" to a group of people. It was this, rather than any mere city-bred character, which made him so utterly foreign to the country district. A solitary boyhood with few companions had been followed by an adolescence in which he had worked desperately for distinction in the educational system and had in some measure succeeded. Then an unfortunate incident — while staying in the house of an acquaintance he had seduced a maidservant and had felt it his duty to marry her. His wife was a pleasant, uneducated creature, utterly unfitted to be the comrade of an educator. This fact still further separated him from his fellows, and he became a prey to a heavy conviction of sin and to forebodings of calamity. His foreboding took the form of hypochondriacal alarms about his health. It was these alarms, and his general feeling that he was a social outcast, that took him into the consulting rooms of the physician.

Instances such as this may be multiplied almost indefinitely in any modern industrial or business center. They may seem to approximate or to shade into those cases that demand the special care and attention of the psychiatrist. Nevertheless it must be said that it is not intelligent or sensible for medicine to seek to unload all the personal problems it encounters upon the already overburdened shoulders of the psychiatrist. Furthermore, while many of these cases do not benefit greatly by prolonged "analysis," it is invariably necessary that something should be done to alter and amend effectively their social situation.

At this point I must pause to call attention to an interesting development in the theme of this address. I began by observing that a patient requires of his physician not only medical diagnosis but also personal assurance. I attempted to devise an arbitrary and empirical classification of three types of personal situation — the classification based upon an approximate estimate of the kind of fear an individual suffers and its distribution in his thinking. It is now apparent that observation of the type and extent of assurance needed has become observation also of the kind of social situation in which the patient habitually finds himself, the kind of social conditioning that has produced him. The individual who lives in a small and ordered community requires small assurance; the whole social situation, of which the physician is an essential part, conspires to reassure him. In a larger society an individual assured of his place and function may as a patient require assurance. But in this instance the assurance is probably more or less particular, more or less easily discovered — it is something left over, as it were, by the social order. At the extreme end of the scale is the individual who gets no assurance from this surrounding: on the contrary, his lack of continuous and intimate relationship with others inspires in him a fund of free anxiety, which attaches itself to all he thinks. In brief, one may claim that the need of assurance is an index not only of personal but of social well-being. The large-scale modern society very easily develops patches of social disintegration, of diminished human association. Within such patches is found great human unhappiness, which cannot be explained by the usual economic, psychological, or political studies.

This observation has importance not only for medical practice but for every human activity. The administrator in business or industry is already aware of increasing difficulty in the task of securing continuous and wholehearted coöperation from large associations of people. Diminished faith in the society shows itself in medicine as an increased need for assurance: it shows itself in industry as disquiet, unrest, disorder. Diminished social order — frightened people.

In these days it is characteristic that the small, well-ordered society is becoming less common, the large industrial and populous centers more common. Especially in these days then the physician in his ordinary practice must address himself to two diagnoses — the one a diagnosis of the medical ill in the strict sense; the other a diagnosis of the need of assurance. This latter involves careful investigation of the present situation of the individual, and of his personal and social history. It is no doubt possible sometimes to mitigate or banish an organic ill without the second diagnosis: but it is not possible so to *cure* the patient. The patient is not fully cured until he is himself certain of his restoration to health. Confidence in his medical attendant is established when the relevant personal situation has been brought to light. This is evidenced by a sudden disposition in the patient to "unload" everything upon the doctor. The capacity for assurance that a physician develops in such a context is astonishing — unnecessary pains and other symptoms will disappear almost at a word.

The physician who follows such a method has the satisfaction of knowing that he has been of immense aid to a fellow human being. I hope I have made it clear that he has the further satisfaction of knowing that he has contributed some small item of knowledge to the difficult problems — personal, social, political — of our difficult age.

CHAPTER VIII

Group Membership

WE ARE apparently always trying to respond in our behavior to situations as we perceive them in ways that produce results satisfactory to us. As children we seem to respond at random and in a sense experimentally with many types of activity. Quite rapidly we limit this random behavior to a relatively few ways; we try to simplify our responses as much as possible. But the situation before us is constantly changing and in a not wholly consistent manner; behavior that seemed satisfactory yesterday does not seem to be working in the "same" situation today. We are forced to observe some of the changes that are taking place and to deal with an increasingly complex situation. As we observe, consciously and unconsciously, that there are more variables to which we want to react effectively, we are forced to adopt more complex methods of response.

It is a basic hypothesis of much of the earlier reading that we respond in any situation with our total learned experience up to that time, and that we have to satisfy ourselves "as a whole" as well as meet the situation before us. In accomplishing this, we may select the more complex ways of behaving used by others immediately around us and imitate them to the best of our observation and ability. They then respond to our behavior, and we in turn react with further changes. In such a manner, we may learn to obtain satisfactions from our skill and flexibility in relating ourselves easily to the behavior of others.

As has been indicated in the earlier reading, however, many things stand in the way of our learning that satisfactions can be obtained from such social skills. We may observe the failure of others to respond to us in expected ways, but be unable to modify our own behavior. We may then develop techniques which protect us from feeling too upset as a result of our "failure." We may learn to oversimplify the situation in various ways that protect us from the necessity of observing the complexity of the changing situation before us.

We may, for example, assume as the result of our experiences some static point of view, such as that the world is *always* hostile to us, and develop a consistent set of responses based on that assumption. Since we are involved in interactions with others, they will often respond to this assumption of *ours*. We will behave aggressively because of our feeling that our objectives can be attained only by the use of force, and others may withstand our force with force of their own. This response will, as it occurs, confirm our view of the necessity of force; as we develop skills in the use of force, it may seem to work reasonably satisfactory in *all* situations.

This whole interactive process produces a net result which can be described as a feeling of well-being from our associations with others. We sense in a partly conscious way that we are acting appropriately and feel, in each experience where this occurs, a "value" that we want to repeat. This feeling may be the result of acts that some would describe as "good" or others as "bad," but for us these acts have an aspect of value in the feeling of satisfaction they create. Hadley Cantril calls this feeling the "value attribute" of each experience. He maintains that this very personal aspect of each experience is the unifying force of our lives and is a creative process through which we sense the nature of our interactions with others. He says:

> An outstanding characteristic of man is his capacity to sense the value in the quality of his experience. The value man is able to sense in the quality of his experience we will call "the value attribute" of experience. This experienced value attribute is a pervasive and inseparable aspect of every experience. All human wants, urges, desires, and aspirations are permeated with some value attribute . . .

> Man's unusual capacity to sense the value of experience in so many diverse ways provides the possibility of working out a plausible explanation for the many divergent types of activity men seek to repeat. Man tries to recapture qualities he has experienced on previous occasions: in his social gatherings, his ways of satisfying physical needs, his esthetic experiences, his work or his play. He wants to recapture these experiences simply because he enjoys experiencing the value attribute related to them . . .

> We remember the values experienced in life and we store them up, building out of them a standard or pattern of values which we inevitably, though generally unconsciously, use for later reference. Against this pattern of values derived from past experiences, we sense the quality of our present experience. It is the only value standard we know. On the basis of our acquired system of values we characterize our present experiences variously as "worthwhile," "satisfying," "pleasant," "fruitless," "disappointing," and the like.

> It is in terms of the values of experience that the "worthwhileness" of an action is tested. The value of the quality in experience comes into being only in concrete situations. In general it is not subject to recall as are conceptual abstractions.[1]

Through a process that can be described in some such terms as this concept of the value attribute of each experience, man can appraise the emergent value of each particular experience within which he is interacting. New situations are always developing, unlike in detail anything that has ever happened before, and from these man selects particular experiences as important to him in particular ways.

> The supposition of the enhancement of the value attributes in experience accounts for the aspect of growth. It is dependent on the capacity of man to look into the future as he takes part in and becomes part of emerging situations. What is experienced as an increment of value today becomes part of the value standard tomorrow if experiences can be repeated on similar future occasions. The process of development in the individual is a constant pyramiding of the set of value standards necessarily used as the test of the next experiences. Participation in any occasion of living alters for good or evil the standard of value built up which provides the only stepping-stone for the next participation.[2]

> The net result of our purposive actions is that we create for ourselves a set of assumptions which serve as guides and bases for future actions. These assumptions are standards which we have "taken up, or into" ourselves as the dictionary definition of "assume" implies. From this point of view, action is the process

---

[1] Hadley Cantril, *The "Why" of Man's Experience* (New York: Macmillan, 1950), pp. 22ff.
[2] *Ibid.*, p. 31.

involved in building up assumptions or in checking those we have. On each specific occasion of life we draw upon certain patterns of the total set of assumptions we have stored up.

The only world we know is created in terms of and by means of our assumptions. It is the world which provides what constancy there is in our environment; the world which gives our experience its consistency. And it *is* a world of assumptions — a world which we could not have at all except for our past experience in acting for the purpose of enhancing the quality of life.[3]

With these concepts, Cantril examines some of the transactions of living and makes general observations about the "why" of man's experience that may assist us in relating some of the ideas presented in previous chapters. Read

HADLEY CANTRIL, *The "Why" of Man's Experience* (New York: Macmillan, 1950), pp. 1–104.

Our assumptive worlds might be said to be the result of our own experiences selected and remembered by us as experiences that produced value attributes for us. Since both our experiences and our measures of the values of these experiences differ in many subtle ways from those of anyone else, each of our assumptive worlds in its entirety is unique. Still, within limits, we need to feel that we are like others and particularly like those who are close to us. If we constantly emphasized our uniqueness, anxiety about our isolation would stand in the way of meaningful participation with others. Generally, then, we seem to feel that our own assumptive worlds must not be permitted to appear so unique as to isolate us completely from our fellow men. Many facets of our experiences are sufficiently close to those of others that we can readily observe them as similar and feel them to be identical. To support this need to be related to others, we often consider experiences as similar where little similarity exists and neglect critical differences that may be present.

Basic orientations such as the authoritarian, the coöperative, the Me, or the Self, are patterns of behavior which emphasize certain characteristics that our private assumptive worlds share with those of others. Such orientations are useful in relating our private assumptive worlds to those of others. The superior utility of one or the other orientation will depend on the entire social setting in which we are establishing our relationships.

We work well within groups and enjoy most fully our associations with others when our assumptive words fit most closely with theirs. If our experiences, for example, are such that they lead us to believe that a world with rigid rules of behavior is the most satisfactory world, we will try to find or create situations where this view is common among our associates. Erich Fromm, in *Escape from Freedom*,[4] has indicated that something of this nature may be important in our culture as a whole. Something very similar may be observed in small groups.

We seem to be constantly seeking to affirm in group interactions the assumptive worlds our experiences have taught us to expect. This endless process is apparently fundamental in group interactions. We view the situations in ways that help us seem not too different from others; we join with others in situations — when we can — where our own view is not too difficult to maintain in

---

[3] *Ibid.,* p. 87.
[4] New York: Rinehart, 1941. See Chapter IV, above.

our interactions; we associate and interact most often with those individuals in the group who help us most in maintaining our own assumptive worlds; we "do well" in the group, if our views of the world are in close accord with those of many others in the group; we withdraw entirely from the group if possible or become isolated within it if our views depart too radically. Our feeling of "belonging" to a group may be no more than a realization of the important similarity that exists between our assumptive world and theirs. The strength with which we argue — the degree of upset we feel when a friend does not "understand" what we are driving at or does not want to do something we want to do — may be the result of a basic fear that our own assumptive world may have *too many* unique aspects.[5]

But since no group can satisfy *all* our own values in their exact degree of importance to us, we must and do accept in every particular situation some values as more important and satisfy those at the expense of lesser values. In our culture, for example, a high value is placed on some financial "success"; this is a common, although not universal, value. Another value, also widely held, is that we should work with people we like. Sometimes, however, in order to achieve financial success, we may feel we have to work with people we do not especially like. We hold in abeyance the lesser value of working with people we like in so far as it interferes with the attainment of the greater value of success.

In reacting together in a current situation we may find our private values coming closer to those of others. Our joint experiences, in creating a joint past that was previously unknown, may modify our individual assumptive worlds so that we learn to work together *and* like each other.[6]

Since each individual's past experience has led him to some unique assumptions about those around him and how he "should" respond to them, each individual will inevitably respond somewhat differently to the values of his face-to-face group and will be able to modify the group values in different ways. Those individuals who represent the group values most fully and respond to them most successfully will seem most important to the group and have a higher status in it. In this complex process, then, through which individuals obtain satisfactions from their associations with others in group activities, hierarchical relationships develop.

Economic organizations — one of the major segments of our modern society — indicate the nature of the processes we have been discussing. Much clinical material has been obtained in recent years in the study of business organizations. These studies have been largely oriented from the point of view of "What's wrong here?" or "How can this situation be improved?" Perhaps because of the economic pressure for "improvement," and perhaps because "conflict" and "disagreement" have seemed so abundantly evident, dissatisfactions seem to have been the focus around which a great deal of the work has been done.

In much of this work it seems to have been assumed that conflict and disagreement are "bad" at all stages of group activity and "should" always be

---

[5] The ways in which our private worlds interact and the importance of this to us as individuals is further considered in Kurt Lewin, *Resolving Social Conflicts* (New York: Harper, 1948). In his chapter entitled "Background of Social Conflict in Marriage," he uses similar concepts to view the smallest social group — the family.

[6] The reactions of Joseph Longman (see Vol. II, Case 18) to the changing situations in which he found himself are interesting in this connection.

avoided. Yet Piaget, in the work we considered in Chapter V, above, indicates that there is a basic desire of children to associate together in some common activity; that they in fact develop for themselves codes of behavior which assist them in obtaining satisfactions from this common activity; and that conflict and disagreement are inherent in the processes by which they develop these codes of behavior. There seems to be no evidence to make these observations of Piaget inapplicable to the adult groups in economic organizations. If viewed as a part of a total process that involves the constant harmonizing of individual and group purposes, disagreement and conflict are not necessarily "bad." New codes of behavior must frequently be formed to meet constantly changing situations and must take into consideration many different points of view. Only through interactions involving some disagreement can new agreement emerge.

The first major industrial research in this country that made clinical studies of groups was conducted at the Western Electric Company in the late 1920's. It was organized jointly by the company and the Graduate School of Business Administration of Harvard University. One of the research directors, Elton Mayo, describes the research and evaluates its general significance for our understanding of social life in his book, *The Human Problems of an Industrial Civilization.*[7]

The research at first was concerned with the effects of the physical conditions of work on the output of employees. The investigators were testing the hypothesis that there was a direct causal relationship between lighting conditions and output. After some time the clinical data gathered forced them to conclude that no such simple hypothesis was valid; the social conditions as well as the physical ones influenced output, and it seemed impossible to change one without changing the other in ways that were not understood. Consequently, a new study was designed to keep track of social as well as physical changes.

A group of six girls was put into a special observation room; their job was to assemble telephone relays. An observer stayed in the room at all times and attempted to record everything that was going on — changes in physical conditions, in methods of pay, in supervision, in social cohesiveness among the workers, in their home conditions, and so forth. All of these proved related to changes in attitude and output. The results are reported by Mayo in his third chapter, "The Hawthorne Experiment, Western Electric Company." [8]

The next step was to broaden the research to the whole plant. It was obviously impossible to study each work team as closely as the relay-assembly team was studied. Instead, a plant-wide interviewing program was established. During the next two years over 21,000 employees (half of those in the plant) were interviewed in sessions lasting from 30 to 90 minutes. As the research progressed, the complexity of the factors causing worker attitudes became more clear. As Mayo puts it:

Interviewers had noticed that an individual who is not very capable, or not very well adjusted socially, may behave capably and normally when he works in a human surrounding that suits and sustains him. And, on the contrary, an exceedingly capable and normal human being will behave as if he were neither when

---

[7] New York: Macmillan, 1933.

[8] The first two chapters, which are not included in the page references below, tell of the earlier lighting experiments and some related studies on industrial fatigue and monotony which were only partially successful because one factor was studied at a time instead of the total situation.

he works in inappropriate surroundings. [Thus it seemed evident that the locus of maladjustment was] somewhere in the relation between person-work-Company rather than in any individual or individuals.[9]

Because the research group observed that there was widespread evidence of a maladjustment of some sort, it was led to formulate two questions which continued to preoccupy those in charge of the research until the end of the inquiry. Mayo says these were:

(1) Is some experience which might be described as an experience of personal futility a common incident of industrial organization for work?
(2) Does life in a modern industrial city in some unrealized way predispose workers to obsessive response? [10]

In the balance of the reading, Mayo considers both the theoretical and clinical observations that assisted the research group in viewing these questions. Throughout the discussion he relates a number of the concepts we have discussed in previous chapters to the industrial situation as he observed it. Read

ELTON MAYO, *The Human Problems of an Industrial Civilization* (New York: Macmillan, 1933), pp. 55–143.[11]

This research team brought to light many forces hitherto only partially observed that were controlling group interactions within this industrial organization. Since the purpose of the organization was considered to be largely production for profit, the continued existence of the business depended on skills in economic activities. From this it had also been widely assumed that an individual's motivation for remaining with the organization either was or should be "making money." The research, however, indicated that although economic motivation formed a primary demand, it was not the only important demand made by individuals. The reasons for an individual's association in any group within an organization was found to be much more complex than the expressed logical purpose of the organization. Business, from the point of view of the individuals involved, exists for more than economic purposes, just as a religious organization exists for more than worship.

A business organization is made up of a number of interlocking groups, from the team working at the machines to the executive staff. We can study the process of an organization by studying the activities and interactions within each group. The face-to-face work group is the link between individual motivation and organizational function. The values of any particular group in an organization are related to the logical purposes of the total organization, but they are *also* related to the personal values of the individuals within that group. The individuals in any particular group are concerned with handling these various values in ways that bring maximum satisfaction to themselves. They are concerned with questions of their relationships with others around them, with the ways in which others view these relationships, with the ways they are able to handle the changes they observe.

Burleigh B. Gardner, in the first article below, considers how such personal values, only indirectly related to the formal objectives of the organization, cre-

---

[9] *Human Problems*, p. 116.
[10] *Ibid.*, p. 114.
[11] Second edition: Boston, Division of Research, Harvard Graduate School of Business Administration, 1946, pp. 53–137.

ate a *system* of social interactions of extreme importance to the functioning of the business. This social system of operation, although often rigidly adhered to by the individuals through a consistent feeling that "this is the way we do things here," is only partially related to the formal structure of the business as expressed in its "organizational chart."

Since no economic organization occupies the entire life of any individual, the values to which the individual is responding also include the constantly changing values of the community in which he lives. W. Lloyd Warner and J. O. Low, in the second article below, describe the ways in which the social forces of the community interact with and modify the values of the groups in a particular business organization.

The existence of a hierarchy within an organization implies that those with lower status in the organization will not completely share the values of those with higher status. Hence lower-status individuals and groups are "underprivileged" in terms of the values of those with higher status, since these latter values are most closely related to the over-all purposes of the organization. If it is true that individuals continue their association with a group only in so far as they obtain some kinds of satisfactions from this association, then it seems equally true that these "underprivileged" workers must have learned to obtain satisfaction very different from those obtained by the most privileged members.

It has been widely assumed that the underprivileged groups form the lowest level of the economic hierarchy solely because of their inability to attain a higher level, that they would not remain at the bottom if they could avoid it, and that their values call for rising in the hierarchy where possible. Allison Davis, however, in the third article below, considers the "motivation" of this group and suggests that such a conclusion is inadequate. He observes that underprivileged workers accept as norms of existence standards that bear little relation to a dominant American value of "making money." Their standards seem to be steadily reinforced by their associations with others of similar standards. His observations suggest that the difference is not one of the degree of economic satisfactions obtainable by this group but rather a difference in the *kind* of satisfactions for which this group is searching. The workers do not seem to be in this group only because of an inability to perform the tasks required by the business organization, but rather because of a basic difference in motivation and attitude which permits them to obtain adequate satisfactions in other ways.

The ways in which the activities of a *specific* work situation enter into the interactions of the individuals in it are studied in the article by William F. Whyte entitled "When Workers and Customers Meet." He deals with group relations in the restaurant industry and the problems that the workers in these groups must face if they are to establish relationships which will be productive of continuing satisfactions for them from this activity. He finds that although many of the individual objectives are wholly "illogical" to the economic purposes of the organization, they seem "reasonable" to the individuals in their associations with others. Read

WILLIAM F. WHYTE, ed., *Industry and Society* (New York: McGraw-Hill, 1946):

Burleigh B. Gardner, "The Factory as a Social System," chapter 2, pp. 4–20.

W. Lloyd Warner and J. O. Low, "The Factory in the Community," chapter 3, pp. 21–45.

Allison Davis, "The Motivation of the Underprivileged Worker," chapter 5, pp. 84–106.

William F. Whyte, "When Workers and Customers Meet," chapter 7, pp. 123–147.

This chapter has been concerned in an introductory way with the views of a number of social scientists about group functioning based both on their observations and their theoretical conclusions from these observations. These views indicate that the interactions of individuals within the relationships of an organization form a highly complex process. Many businessmen, for example, make the fundamental assumption that individuals remain within an organization because they wish for economic reasons to assist in the attainment of the organizational purpose as effectively as their "skills" permit. From this assumption it follows that the necessary technical skills must be carefully taught. Then failure of individuals to rise to the highest level of the organization is assumed to be due to their inherent inability to learn the necessary skills.

The work of the social scientists considered in this chapter suggests the possibility that such assumptions are based on an oversimplified view of the situation. If an individual is constantly seeking a very personalized objective from his interactions with others — which Cantril calls the "value attribute" of each experience — then the degree of skill in attaining the organizational objectives is partly a result of this personalized attitude, as well as any inherent ability. In his association with others the individual finds values important which *include* the acquisition of a certain degree of technical skills. The extent to which these skills will be acquired, however, depends partly on the value placed on these skills by the interaction of the group values with the personalized values of the individual. This view of the situation suggests that the way to teach the technical skills "necessary" to our society lies not only in more skillful training of innate technical abilities but also in modifying personal and group values so that these values harmonize.

In order to understand the ways in which these personalized values modify group behavior, it will be necessary to consider more carefully the complex processes which exist in the total activities of small face-to-face groups. The next few chapters will present material on the behavior of such groups and some concepts that social scientists have developed to assist them in understanding their observations of that behavior.

ADDITIONAL READINGS

Barnard, Chester I., "Functions and Pathology of Status Systems in Formal Organizations," *Industry and Society*, ed. William F. Whyte (New York: McGraw-Hill, 1946).
Barnard analyzes formal status systems and shows how they can further or obtruct coöperation. This is a continuation of the line of argument in Gardner's article in *Industry and Society*.

Halliday, James L., *Psychosocial Medicine* (New York: W. W. Norton, 1948).
This study of "sick" communities in Britain shows the connection between group disorganization and individual psychological disorder.

Moreno, Jacob L., *Who Shall Survive?* (Washington, D. C.: Nervous and

Mental Diseases Publishing Company, 1934).

A study of clique relationships which introduced important new techniques for discovering the friendship ties among people in large organizations.

Roethlisberger, F. J., and W. J. Dickson, *Management and the Worker* (Cambridge: Harvard University Press, 1939).

This book describes fully the Hawthorne experiment which Mayo summarizes. The book is classic material in its field and describes the clinical observations on which many of the conclusions of this chapter are based.

Whyte, William F., *Street Corner Society* (Chicago: University of Chicago Press, 1943).

Whyte gives a vivid description of the day-to-day interactions within a small clique of young men. The circular relationship between personal motives and group function is well portrayed. This is one of the best clinical studies of small groups that is available.

CHAPTER IX

Group Processes

Change is universal. Permanent elements may appear to challenge it, but they have no lasting substance. Yet change is not arbitrary. The future unfolds continuously out of the present. Earlier and later states do not confront each other as the senseless juxtaposition of one chaos beside another, but are linked by similarities which pervade change. This meaningful order underlying change is realized by a continuity in the sequence of change. In so far as change reveals this continuity and is not arbitrary, it is called process.

Moreover this continuity is universal and constitutes the unifying order which can be recognized throughout the diversity of all particular changes . . . Form is the recognizable continuity of any process . . . Some forms may appear to be static, but they none the less partake in the process of the whole. A process is fully identified when its form is recognized.[1]

M ANY OF the concepts we have been considering have dealt with some aspects of the process through which the form of the individual or the group becomes recognizable. For example, Mary Parker Follett, in the reading in Chapter I, deals with the problem of how observable control, both in the individual and group, could develop from an also observable process of constant change. At a fairly high level of generality, she concludes that the control lies in the nature of the process itself. She discusses the concept of process as it is applied in a number of scientific fields. In emphasizing the importance of the "nature of the totalness" of any situation under consideration, she observes that "when a factor is added or subtracted from a situation, you have not that situation plus or minus that factor, for all the rest will be changed." You then have a new total situation which you will have to consider. The addition or subtraction of an individual in a group has an effect on the entire group and on the individual as well. "Affirming that the whole determines the parts as well as the parts determine the whole . . . would not be strictly accurate. The same activity determines both parts and whole." [2] The new situation represents a unity that is always "a process, not a product."

She observes that the interacting and the unifying aspects of any situation are parts of the same process, as are the modifications and changes that take place as the situation develops. New things emerge that are inherent in the nature of the process that has been taking place. Follett says that "as every living process is subject to its own authority, that is, the authority evolved by or involved in the process itself, so social control is generated by the process

---

[1] L. L. Whyte, *The Next Development in Man* (New York: Mentor Edition, New American Library, 1950), p. 15. By permission of Henry Holt and Company, Inc., and Pearn, Pollinger and Higham Ltd.
[2] Mary Parker Follett, "The Psychology of Control," *Dynamic Administration: The Collected Papers of Mary Parker Follett*, eds. H. C. Metcalf and L. Urwick (New York: Harper, 1941), p. 193; and reading above, **Chapter I.**

itself. Or rather, the activity of self-creating coherence is the controlling activity." [3]

In studying individuals or groups, we are searching for clues that give a meaningful order to the sequence of change, that is, for uniformities out of which we can build concepts that will help us clarify and understand process. We have considered numerous concepts that apply to the human personality in its interrelations with others, such concepts as the "learning of cultural values," "attention and consciousness," "dynamics of the unconscious," "status and role," and "value attributes." In our shift of emphasis to the factors observable in group interactions, we stated that individuals are willing to lend their services to groups only if they obtain sufficient satisfactions from the group activity. We read a number of papers that described small groups in detail and related group process to individual satisfactions. Since individual values are the result of all of an individual's past experience and its meaning to him, it may seem surprising that such group satisfactions are ever adequate. Nevertheless, the individual process in its interaction with the group process often seems to adjust in a reasonably satisfactory way. As Follett observes that group controls are inherent in the process of group activity, so Cantril indicates that an ordering of experience is inherent in the individual process. These are complex interrelated processes that we separate for purposes of discussion but that in the world itself are inseparable.

Inherent in the various concepts discussed in these chapters is the notion that each of them describes only aspects of some total situation; each of them is interdependent with other concepts in ways that are but dimly understood. The attempt to clarify this connection often brings the discussion to a higher level of abstraction without adding much clarity; at this higher level it may be evident that there is an interconnection between the concepts, but the nature of the interconnection may not be more precise. Perhaps it is necessary in the present state of knowledge of social science that many discussions of its concepts should constantly return on themselves like a puppy chasing its tail. In any event, such discussions cannot be avoided for that reason alone; even the puppy covers some ground.

If we are to understand the context within which our personal value decisions are made, we must understand in some detail the operations of the small groups to which we belong. For this purpose we need a "way of looking at things" which will focus our attention on crucial variables and which will allow us to observe the continuity of process that occurs when group behavior changes. Such a scheme will give us a language with which to relate different groups to each other as well as compare different periods of time in the life of the same group.

George C. Homans, in the reading below, offers such a conceptual scheme. It grows out of his examination of clinical material about a number of small, face-to-face, "primary" groups. His book might be characterized as several detailed case discussions within the framework of a single language system. His variables are meticulously defined and cannot be torn out of the context of his total scheme. He has systematized many general ideas that we have already considered. Consequently, his scheme can be helpful in tying together many of the previous readings. Read

---

[3] *Ibid.*, p. 204, and reading above, Chapter I.

GEORGE C. HOMANS, *The Human Group* (New York: Harcourt, Brace, 1950), pp. 1–280.

In chapters 1 and 2 Homans discusses the limits within which he will operate and the basic factors in his conceptual scheme. He says that in considering the small, "primary" group in action he is dealing with a vision of "unity that is at the same time a process, the unity where parts taken separately slip out between our fingers. And yet the vision is not enough. It is one thing to see where we are going and quite another to get there; to build up, piece by piece, a picture of the dynamic unity of a group when, in taking the pieces out of the whole, we may falsify them and it." [4] He observes that he is dealing with persons and with "three elements of their behavior: *activity, interaction* and *sentiment.*"

In chapter 3 he reports the first case material that he uses, the Bank Wiring Observation Room studied at the Western Electric Company's Hawthorne Works in Chicago.[5] In the next three chapters Homans analyzes this case material thoroughly. Using the elements of behavior (activity, interaction, and sentiment) developed in chapter 2, and adding one more element, *norms,* in chapter 5, he discusses the nature of the process that is called the human group. He first discusses the group in relation to its external environment, then the group itself, and finally the subgroups within it. He develops hypotheses relating his variables in each of these areas.

In chapter 7 Homans reports his second case, the Norton Street Gang. He uses it in chapter 8 to add further hypotheses about the nature of groups, particularly in relation to their leaders.

> We are interested in establishing the similarities between groups that underlie the surface facts. The similarities, we believe, can only become clear to us if we have a single way of analyzing group behavior and apply it regularly to every new group we encounter . . .
>
> Although we shall apply our method in the same way to every new group, we shall not expect to emphasize the same points every time. That would only lead to dreary repetition, whereas we want to introduce one or two new ideas in each chapter. The same features tend to reappear in every group, but not all elaborated to the same degree. The most conspicuous feature of the Bank Wiring Observation Room was the development of the cliques and its relation to the organization of work. Leadership was only rudimentary. In the Norton Street Gang leadership was well developed, and we shall, in our analysis, pay most attention to its characteristics.[6]

In chapter 9 Homans reports his third case, the family in Tikopia, on the following grounds:

> Any book that pretends, as this one does, to study the general characteristics of the small group cannot afford to leave out of consideration this most nearly universal of human groups.
>
> We hold also that mankind is a unity. This does not mean we subscribe to the

---

[4] George C. Homans, *The Human Group* (New York: Harcourt, Brace, 1950), p. 9.

[5] The Bank Wiring Room was part of the research discussed in Elton Mayo's book, *The Human Problems of an Industrial Civilization* (see Chapter VIII, above). In that book, Mayo describes the Relay Assembly Test Room experiment; the Bank Wiring Room was set up in order to study more minutely the social organization of a work team which proved to be so important in that first experiment.

[6] *The Human Group*, p. 173.

theory that "human nature is the same the world over" in the sense of actual behavior being everywhere the same . . . Instead, mankind is a unity in the sense that men the world over placed in the same situations, or as a psychologist might say in the same "fields," will behave in the same way — and we must always include as a part of the field the traditions handed down in a society from past generations . . .

The "fields" are complex and may vary widely, partly because the behavior of individuals, which is determined by the fields, itself helps determine them. This is the great fact that an organic philosophy must face. But one theory is that if we applied the same kind of analysis to all the societies of men, we should find that they were different because they possessed in different degrees characteristics that are present in all. So far in this book we have analyzed groups within our own society. If our theory is correct, and if we are interested in the general characteristics of the small group, we should try to apply our method of analysis to at least one group in a society different from our own.[7]

In chapter 10 he considers from his conceptual frame of reference the system of interpersonal relations that he observes in the case material about the Tikopia family; he says it "must be treated as a web of relations between individuals or, better, between social personalities." [8] At the end of this chapter he compares this family briefly with the "modern American, middle-class urban family." Then he makes some pertinent observations that would be well to keep in mind when reading the selection by Florence Kluckhohn below.

Homans points out ways in which the familial activities, interactions, sentiments, and norms have altered during the process of change, particularly economic change, in modern times. He does not consider that the changes which have taken place necessarily forecast disintegration. Perhaps because he is observing in all his data what L. L. Whyte calls a continuity in the sequence of change and a unifying order in this sequence, Homans considers that a new balance of forces will develop. In the family "a new equilibrium will be reached, supported by new norms . . . The family may no longer be what it used to be — after all it used to be everything — but this will not prevent its being an essential, successful, and perhaps more flexible instrument. In the work of attaining that new equilibrium, we are helped, if intellect helps at all, not by denunciation but by understanding, and here, for the family of low integration, as for the family of high integration, the same patient analysis of the relations of mutual dependence in the internal and external systems, in which we have been drilling ourselves, will always be found useful." [9]

Kluckhohn takes a much more detailed look at the American family than does Homans. Her material emphasizes changes in the recent past which have been influential in shaping the contemporary urban family of the "middle-class" variety, and then focuses particularly on the role of women. She considers the continuity of change in "process" terms. Read

FLORENCE R. KLUCKHOHN, "The American Family and the Feminine Role," below.

Using Homans' concepts to describe Kluckhohn's work, we might say that she examines aspects of the "external system" that impinge upon the "internal system" of the family. She is interested both in changes in the economic order

---

[7] Ibid., p. 191. [8] Ibid., p. 231. [9] Ibid., p. 280.

of the external system that alter interaction patterns and in changes in the norms or values of the external system that impinge directly on the norms or values of the family. It is in this latter respect particularly that her emphasis is different from that of Homans.

It is Kluckhohn's central thesis that the behavior of family members cannot be understood without the wider perspective of the total society and its values. From this perspective, she maintains that our present family is not as "bad" as many reformers suggest, but in fact is fairly well adjusted to the total system of which it is a part:

> It has not been the intent of this discussion . . . to . . . insist upon the perfection of American economic, political, educational, and other institutions. Nor is our aim to argue that our American basic values, which all these institutions express, are those of final and ultimate validity. It is, however, assumed that a majority do hold to these values. This being the case, we must maintain our perspective and admit that, for all of the strains which may be created by our having small and independent families, we have a family type well suited to our society as a whole. Such a family is *potentially*, if not actually, the best training ground for the kind of individuals needed to maintain the basic values.[10]

In order to illustrate her thesis, she contrasts the middle-class American family with the Spanish-American family of the rural southwest. She does so in "value-orientation" terms, using her scheme which we considered above in Chapter III.

Once she has described the family as a unit and its place within the total society, she turns her attention to certain key internal relationships, especially the feminine role. Here she is less satisfied and concedes that strains do exist, but believes that adjustments can be made that will bring that role more into harmony with the values of the external system.

It is interesting to note the differences in the procedures followed by Homans and Kluckhohn. Homans has purposely limited himself to the forces operating in the particular group under consideration at the moment. By contrast, Kluckhohn offers observations about a multitude of groups (the millions of American middle-class families) and emphasizes similarities in them that permit her to speak of a whole class of individuals at once — America's women. Homans' view is a detailed examination of small, specific situations; Kluckhohn's is of general, widespread phenomena.

ADDITIONAL READINGS

Anshen, Ruth, ed., *The Family* (New York: Harper, 1949).
This book is a collection of articles comparing the family systems of different cultures and examining the internal dynamics of the American family.

Davis, Allison, Burleigh B. and Mary R. Gardner, *Deep South: A Social Anthropological Study of Caste and*
Class (Chicago: University of Chicago Press, 1941).
Chapters 4, 5, and 6 describe the family system of a southern city and show the differences between the classes. Chapters 7 and 9 are excellent studies of the clique behavior found in that city.

Frazier, E. Franklin, *The Negro Family in the United States* (Chicago: University of Chicago Press, 1939).

---

[10] Florence R. Kluckhohn, "The American Family and the Feminine Role," below.

This is an excellent book, both as a study of the family in America from the Civil War to the present and as an example of an analysis of a group which shows a continuity of process through time.

Mead, Margaret, *Male and Female* (New York: William Morrow, 1949).
Part Four, "The Two Sexes in Contemporary America," gives Mead's ideas about the American family, set in the framework of cross-cultural comparisons.

Merton, Robert K., and Paul F. Lazarsfeld, eds., *Continuities in Social Research* (Glencoe, Illinois: The Free Press, 1950). Edward A. Shils, "Primary Groups in the American Army." Robert K. Merton and Alice S. Kitt, "Contributions to the Theory of Reference Group Behavior."
Shils and Merton and Kitt examine the vast materials about the attitudes of soldiers contained in the first two volumes of S. A. Stouffer, *et al.*, *The American Soldier*, Studies in Social Psychology in World War II, 4 vols. (Princeton: Princeton University Press, 1949), in terms of the concept of group behavior. The second article pays special attention to the loyalties of men who belong to different (and, sometimes, conflicting) groups.

The American Family and the Feminine Role*

BY FLORENCE ROCKWOOD KLUCKHOHN

I. PROBLEMS IN FAMILY LIFE

Everywhere today — in magazines, books, and newspapers, on the radio, from the pulpits, and in the classrooms — one sees and hears discussions of American family life. An all too frequent phrasing of the situation is that the family has become demoralized and is disintegrating. Divorce, delinquency, and crime statistics are freely used to bolster the argument of decay. It is also pointed out, from the evidence of clinics and counseling agencies, that a vast percentage of individuals are maladjusted and hampered by anxieties of many kinds. The United States has become, it is sometimes said, a nation of neurotics, and the family system is to blame. Alarmists maintain that the structure of the whole society is being weakened and actually threatened with destruction because of the instability of the family institutions.

Americans have always been sentimental about their family system, have always believed it to be the most basic and important unit of their social life.

Hence the alarm as the evidence mounts to show that marriages are neither permanent nor stable and that family relationships in general are strained or shattered by conflict.

There is no denying that problems in American family life exist. There certainly seems to be much room for improvement in both the husband-wife and the parent-child relationships. But before entering the ranks of the alarmists, we should take time to learn from the history of past generations that the problems are not all new. Indeed, when one reads such a book as Arthur W. Calhoun's *A Social History of the American Family*,[1] one wonders if the family of today is in a much more critically acute state of distress than the families of other years.

Writers of the past, especially in the eighteenth and nineteenth centuries, frequently railed at American children and termed them impudent and unruly creatures. For describing American women a variety of terms were used, many of which were anything but laudatory. Men,

---

* Especially revised for this volume by the author from her chapters "The American Family — Past and Present" and "America's Women," *Psychological Patterns*, ed. O. H. Mowrer (Chicago: The Delphian Society, 1952).

[1] Three vols. (New York: Barnes and Noble, 1945; first published, 1917).

too, came in for their share of blame. Of course, the comments were not usually phrased in the language of today. America, being the change-worshiping nation she is, cannot even treat her problems in a traditionalistic way. Each generation must have its new version of the old problems and its new solutions too.

Yet some of the criticisms made in the past were not so very differently phrased. We can easily find similar ones today. Consider this one from an article written by an American in the nineteenth century:

The signs of the want of family discipline appear in the waywardness of the children while yet they are young. Given up to idleness, knowing no restraint but such as they are wont to defy, having no domestic exercise for entertainment and profit, and nothing to keep them home but their bed and board, and dreading their home for their leisure hours as a place of confinement; familiar with drunkenness, profaneness, and all the captivating forms of youthful dissipation; what have parents or the community to hope from such children? [2]

Another statement which appeared in the *Presbyterian Magazine* of the 1950's also has a familiar ring:

That the deficiencies which disclose themselves in the marriage relation must be ascribed mainly to an inadequate and improper training . . . It can excite no wonder, that young persons who have grown up without restraint — allowed to treat their parents with disrespect — indulged in all their whims and caprices — accustomed only to flattery and adulation — should be found very troublesome inmates in another household. [3]

An amusing comment, toward which some today would be sympathetic, was made in 1834 in a "modern catechism adapted to the times":

Who is the oldest man? The lad of fourteen who struts and swaggers and

smokes his cigar, and drinks rum; treads on the toes of his grandfather, swears at his mother and sister, and vows that he will run away and leave "the old man" if he will not let him have more cash. In what families is there the best government? Those in which the children govern the parents . . . Who brings up his children in the way they should go? He that teaches them to spend money without earning it; mixes sling whenever he thinks it will do him good, and always saves the bottom of the glass for little Frank. [4]

Comments on the status of women and criticisms of our women were frequent indeed. As the following quotations will show, the problem of the proper role of women was just as much a matter of concern, and at least somewhat in the same terms, generations ago as it is today.

Maternity, which we will here confine to the single idea of taking care of children, brings woman more within the precincts of the home . . . Authority must be vested somewhere . . . This authority in the human race is vested in man, as the divinely appointed head of creation. "Wives submit yourselves unto your husbands as unto the Lord." . . . Woman has a mission to perform, which dignifies her even among angels . . . To light up the household with joy and love, to nourish and train the immortal children within its precincts, to minister to the good government of the little family kingdom, to cheer the husband who is the "head" amidst the sorrows and trials of life, to be an example of faith and righteousness. [5]

Many of our females in their ambition to be considered "ladies" refuse to aid their toiling mothers, lest their fair hands should lose their softness and delicacy, and while using these useless appendages in playing with their ringlets, or touching the piano or guitar,

---

[2] *Presbyterian Magazine*, quoted in Calhoun, *A Social History of the American Family*, II, 69.
[3] *Ibid.*
[4] *The Man*, a New York labor newspaper, March 21, 1834, quoted, *ibid.*, p. 66.
[5] *Presbyterian Magazine*, 1852, quoted, *ibid.*, p. 97.

they will speak with contempt of the household drudge, and boast of their lady-like ignorance of domestic employments. Many a woman of intellect, on becoming a housekeeper, finds herself . . . unprepared . . . Want of practical knowledge and the unskillfulness of inexperience cause what little strength she possesses to be ineffectually expanded . . . Our women are generally less fitted for active household duties than in some countries are those even of the higher classes who are never placed under the necessity of performing them . . . [Few mothers teach their daughters how to be happy and useful at home.] [6]

Of the father and his role in the family of a hundred years ago Calhoun himself gives this description, which again with only slight change might well be a modern description.

The strenuous life of a society whose prime business was production rather than consumption lessened family endearment. Paternal preoccupation left wife and children a larger scope. Men were too busy to know their little ones, to enjoy much of their wives' society, or to lavish affection . . . Suppose a man to marry a woman with tastes, disposition, and character essentially different from his. The points of contact are so few that he might become the father of a large family and die without discovering his mistake. He has no time to be unhappy. Women are left all day to themselves: the life is monotonous. Hence they love their offspring passionately, "while for their husbands they feel a sort of half distant respect." [7]

Clearly, the problems of family life being discussed today do not belong to our generation alone. To be sure, the rapid urbanizing of the nation, the changed technology, and the development of a host of new non-family institutions and agencies have created some new and different causes for concern. Yet, for the most part, the difficulties we see are but an aggravation and extension of the issues of the past. To point this out is not to deny the importance or critical nature of many of the current trends. Rather, it is to urge a more cautious and careful approach both in making criticisms and in proposing reforms or alterations.

Even a study of historical facts is not sufficient. One needs, in the analysis of the family of either the present or the past, to go beneath the surface of the specific and apparent patterns of behavior to discover the basic values — or value orientations — which are reflected in those patterns. Family patterns as well as the patterns in all other aspects of the social life of a nation are the concrete expressions of deeply rooted value orientations.[8] And, unless a society is in a truly serious state of disintegration, the patterns in all the sectors of the social system are interrelated in such a way that they support the total system.

Thus, it may well be the case that certain of the changes which some persons today would choose to make in family life would be seriously detrimental to the system as a whole. For example, it has been shown that the American family with its loose generational ties, its high degree of individuation, and other characteristics which we shall describe shortly, is extremely well suited to the particular kind of occupational system which almost all persons would recognize to be the very keystone of American life.[9] To change radically the character of the family would mean radical changes in the occupational system as well. Both of these sectors of life reflect in differing ways the same value orientations, and

---

[6] Mrs. A. J. Graves, *Woman in America* (New York, 1855), quoted, *ibid.*, p. 225.

[7] *Ibid.*, p. 133.

[8] "A value-orientation [is] a generalized and organized conception, influencing behavior, of nature, of man's place in it, of man's relation to man, and of the desirable and nondesirable as they may relate to man-environment and interhuman relations" — Clyde Kluckhohn and others, "Values and Value-Orientations in the Theory of Action," *Toward a General Theory of Action,* ed. Talcott Parsons and Edward A. Shils (Cambridge: Harvard University Press, 1951), p. 411.

[9] See Talcott Parsons, "The Kinship System of the Contemporary United States," *Essays in Sociological Theory, Pure and Applied* (Glencoe, Illinois: The Free Press, 1949), and "Age and Sex in the Social Structure of the United States," above, Chapter III.

Innate Predispositions	Evil (mutable or immutable)	Neither good nor bad (mutable or immutable)	Good (mutable or immutable)
Man's Relation to Nature	Man subjugated to nature	Man in nature	Man over nature
Time Dimension	Past	Present	Future
Valued Personality Type	Being	Being-in-Becoming	Doing
Modality of Relationship	Lineal	Collateral	Individualistic

both are geared to each other — and other sectors as well — to create the social system as a whole. Thus, we see the importance of knowing what the value orientations of a people are.

II. DOMINANT AND VARIANT VALUE ORIENTATIONS

Cultural value orientations and the particular conceptualization of them which we shall use as the frame of reference for describing and analyzing family patterns are discussed elsewhere in this volume.[10] We shall, therefore, repeat only in brief outline the main points in the conceptual scheme and the major assumptions upon which it is based, and then proceed directly to a comparative analysis of two radically different family systems which give expression to two very different kinds of value orientations. The Spanish-American family of the Southwest will be used as our contrast to the more or less typical present-day American family.

It will be recalled that the value-orientation conceptual scheme is based upon these two major assumptions: (1) There is a limited number of basic and common human problems for which all societies at all times and in all places must find some solution. (2) That while variability in

solutions is certainly found, it is variation within a limited range of possible solutions.

The five common human problems set forth as the most basic and at the same time the most separable (this is to say that no one of them is considered as being a derivative of any of the others) are:

1. The definition of the innate predispositions of man (basic human nature).
2. The definition of the relationship of man to nature.
3. The definition of the most significant time dimension.
4. The definition of the most valued personality type.
5. The definition of the modality of man's relation to other men.

The ranges in solutions for these five types of problems proposed as at least a testable classification system of orientation difference is shown in the table.[11]

In the original presentation of the schema a comparison was made between the typical American value-orientation emphases and those of the Spanish-Americans (Mexicans) of the Southwest, especially New Mexico and Arizona.[12] It was noted that the two cultures preferred the following values:[13]

---

[10] Florence R. Kluckhohn, "Dominant and Variant Cultural Value Orientations," above, Chapter III.

[11] For definitions of these concepts, see "Dominant and Variant Cultural Orientations," above, Chapter III.

[12] The Spanish-speaking population in New Mexico and Arizona is sometimes referred to as a Mexican group. The people themselves tend to resent this term and greatly prefer either Spanish-American or *Hispano*. They call the English-speaking people *Anglo*-Americans, a term we use here for clarity of reference.

[13] The existence of these differences between the two groups was verified by a research project conducted in the summers of 1950 and 1951 by the writer, Professor Fred Strodtbeck of Yale University, and

Spanish-Americans

Innate predispositions, good and evil
   mixed
Man subjugated to nature
Present time
Being personality
Lineal-collateral relationships

Anglo-Americans

Innate predispositions, evil but per-
   fectible
Man over nature
Future time
Doing personality
Individualistic relationships

These contrasts are not, to be sure,
rigidly absolute. It is also to be remembered that a third fundamental assumption of the theory of value orientations is
that all the orientations on all the five
ranges are always present in all societies.
It is only the relative stressing or emphasis which is so different. Hence, as we
describe and analyze the family systems
of these two quite different peoples, it is
always to be kept in mind that we speak
of the dominant emphasis only. One
could easily find some Spanish-American
families whose patterns of living reflect
much more the dominant Anglo-American orientations than the Spanish-American ones. And certainly not all Anglo-
American families give expression to
dominant American value orientations.
There is always variation — always the
variant as well as the dominant. In general, however, there is a remarkably
sharp contrast between these two family
systems and the value orientations expressed in them.

III. THE SPANISH-AMERICAN FAMILY

The Spanish-Americans in New Mexico
and Arizona have been a part of the
greater United States society for over a
hundred years. Yet only very recently
have these people begun to change in the

value orientations they hold to. Even
today the change is not great, as has been
shown by the research project mentioned
above. I shall not, therefore, deal with
these changes, but will instead describe
the typically rural or village Spanish-
American family as I knew it some fifteen
years ago.[14]

Most of the Spanish-Americans of New
Mexico — a total group which constitutes
approximately one half of the population
of that state — have until quite recently
lived in small village units. Many of
them are still village people. In these
villages almost all persons were related to
each other by either blood or marriage.
In fact, the little towns — usually called
placitas — were really nothing but a
group of closely interrelated families. In
one well-known village, every family had
the same surname.

Within this network of family relationships the unrelated person was apt to
have none too easy a time. He was, until
he could establish some kind of relationship, an outsider about whom there was
always some concern and even suspicion. There has been a good and valid
reason for this. The social control, which
in the average American community is
exercised through such agencies as
courts, police organizations, and other
local government offices, has been a matter for families to handle in Spanish-
American towns. Families — one's own
and all others related to it — were the
primary means of keeping individuals in
line. In such a society the persons with
the most relatives are those most controlled, while those with few or no relatives are least controlled. The person with
no relatives is, therefore, not a very safe
person to have about. In the village where
I lived so long, the outsider would be
accepted fairly well just so long as he
behaved in strict accordance with community customs. Once let him fail in
this, and complete ostracism was the result. I recall well the case of a woman
(she had come to the village from Old

Dr. John M. Roberts and Mr. Kimball Romney of Harvard University. The research was under the aus-
pices of Harvard's Laboratory of Social Relations; results will be published in late 1952 or early 1953.
   [14] See my unpublished Ph.D. thesis, *Los Atarqueños*, Radcliffe College, 1941.

Mexico) whose behavior with men became suspect. Practically overnight she became an outcast. Only one woman continued to have anything to do with her, and the sister of this woman threatened to "witch" her if she did not bring an end to the friendship.

This extensive interrelatedness is achieved first by a wide-range recognition of kinship ties up and down the generations (vertically) and laterally to fifth- and sixth-degree cousins, and then further increased by a general acceptance as family members of everyone who is related in any way. The village Spanish-Americans were not different from Anglo-Americans or others in *having* grandparents, grandchildren, sisters, brothers, cousins, and so forth (except that they seemed to have more of most of them), but they did differ in the strength of the ties which bind all these together. The whole social system was — as has been the case in many other areas of the world — a familistic one.

The basic family relationships were those universal to all family systems — the husband-wife and the parent-child. Yet a good Spanish-American villager would have felt extremely impoverished if all the relatives he had about him were parents and children. His nieces and nephews were almost the same to him as his children, and his cousins were not greatly different from his own brothers and sisters. Everyone disciplined nieces and nephews as readily and as well as he did his own sons and daughters, and fed and cared for them too.

There was even a sharing of children which certainly has struck most Anglo-Americans as strange. It was felt that a number of children — preferably four to eight of them — were necessary to make a family. The unfortunate family with no children would usually take one, two, or three of those belonging to sisters, brothers, or even other people who it seemed had a few too many. I remember being truly baffled for a long time by the numerous children of varying names in a single family. When once I learned the pattern, I made lists of all the family exchanges and discovered that some 12

per cent of all children in the village were living with persons other than their biological parents. As can be imagined from such a figure, the Spanish-Americans have not had the typically Anglo-American attitudes toward adoption.

The combination of a lineal and collateral relational emphasis is easily seen in all these patterns. The lineal stress is even more evident in the authority lines of the Spanish-American family. These lines were, and to a marked extent still are, definite and firm: the old persons were the rulers, and the male sex was clearly dominant. Respect for and obedience to age were bred into the Spanish-American child early and were supposed never to be forgotten. Sons did not become independent upon reaching maturity. Only one son — the eldest (*hermano mayor*) — has been permitted by custom to have any kind of authority and responsibility. Even he is supposedly required to remain under the father's control until death or real infirmity of the father make it necessary for him to take over family affairs.

This special training of the eldest son — and it was usually so special that younger brothers and sisters treated him more as a father figure than one of themselves — was a way of insuring continuity of authority by age — a way of insuring "ordered positional succession." With families as large as most Spanish-Americans had, it often happened that a father died before all children had reached maturity. The eldest son simply moved into the father's position and all went on much as before. (The situation was not without strains, of course. In fact, were I to cite the one most critical area in the Spanish-American family system, it would be this relationship between the eldest and younger brothers. To it I would attribute a good deal of the impetus of the current shift in some families to the individualistic orientation of Anglo-American culture.)

The authority of family and age was extended even beyond the larger family units to a kind of feudal system which has commonly been called the *patrón-peón* system. There was usually in the villages one powerful and dominant family, the head of which was the village *patrón*. He ruled the whole community much as a father ruled within the single family. All those under the control of the *patrón* were called *peones*. The relationship between *patrón* and *peones* resembled the relationship which existed between the lord and serfs in the manorial system of feudal Europe.

Beyond even the *patrón* there was, and still is, in Spanish-American culture, another powerful "father figure." This is the village saint — the *Santo*. Almost all Spanish-Americans are good Catholics, but unlike most Catholics of today their interest in their own particular patron saint is far greater than any interest in the more abstract aspects of the religion. It is the *Santo* for whom the big annual fiesta is given. He, also, is the one whom everyone considers to be most responsible for the welfare of the whole village.

These attitudes toward lineal authority have been too well entrenched in the minds of Spanish-Americans to pass quickly or easily, even though currently some changes are certainly to be noted. It was only a year ago that a research student from one of the eastern universities tried in vain to convince a Spanish-American farmer that the office of the presidency of the United States was not, as he thought, simply passed down from father to eldest son. The Spanish-Americans in the Southwest have been voting citizens of the United States for many years, yet still today many of them cast the votes that they do not understand as their *patrones* tell them to.

Male dominance was as marked in the typical village as the lineal authority. Many Spanish-American women in towns and cities today take jobs and do many of the other things that Anglo-American women do, but in the villages women had only one career to look forward to — that of wife and mother. There was a clear-cut division of work, obligations, and rights between the sexes, and the equality made so much of by Anglo-Americans was not even a matter of much concern. The lives of all the women in the village I studied were so circumscribed that they were not even permitted to market in the village store. The store was a meeting place for men, hence neither a safe nor proper place for women. Men and small children bought all the supplies.

To a majority of Anglo-Americans all these patterns, as well as many others we have no space to describe, have seemed repressive. But, given Spanish-American values, such has not been the case. Or, at least, let us say that there were real advantages in them. Without such an emphasis upon dependence rather than independence and a stressing of the responsibility of all for all, it would not have been possible — and will not be possible — for Spanish-Americans to give full expression to all the other value orientations we have mentioned — the present-time, being, and man-subjugated-to-nature orientations.

The women, for example, always expected that their marriages would be permanent, and they were. Too, almost every village girl was well trained for her future job of housewife by the time she was twelve, and she moved into her adult role easily without ever having to face such vexatious questions as "Am I going to have an opportunity to marry?" or "Should I work at an outside job instead of marrying?" And all persons, men and women alike, could, as long as the dependent relationships were maintained, take the time for a spontaneous enjoyment of life from day to day. Note only this one of many cases. In 1936, the year I lived in one of these villages, I knew three related families — the families of a father and his two married sons. Years before, this family had been a landholding and livestock-owning family in which all male members worked at a common task. By 1936 all property was gone, but the old patterns persisted even though each of the men was a wage earner on a different kind of job. All three families maintained a common larder, and all contributed to the support of everyone without question. And never in all the time I observed these families was it the case that all three wage earners were working at the same time. At any time that two of them had fairly good jobs the third was certain to be on a trip or a vacation or just resting at home. Two could make all that any of them required or needed, since the conception of the standard of living was not oriented to an expanding future.

The *patrón,* too, was always there to help out in times of trouble or distress. Domineering as many of the *patrones* have been, it was seldom that they did not assume a host of obligations for all the families under their control. Anglo-Americans have seen only the blacker side of the picture — the side that produced a debt peonage which the United States government tried, not too successfully, to put out of existence by legal rules. What has not been so obvious to Anglos has been the real reluctance of many — even most — Spanish-Americans to fret much about the future and their willing acceptance of the dominance of a *patrón* who would see them through a bad period.

In even so brief a description as this, it must be apparent how all the family patterns — those defining relationships, those relating to work or to recreation or religion — have expressed the totality of the Spanish-American value orientations. It is also easy to see how the patterns expressive of the several orientations are, or have been, interlocked and supportive of each other. Today, under the pressure of Anglo-American culture, the lineal-collateral relationships are giving way to more individualistic ones. Yet so far none of the other value orientations seems to have been much changed. This presents great problems and is producing serious disruptions in the formerly tightly knit social life. One can only predict that either the Spanish-Americans must move further still in their acceptance of Anglo-American value orientations or suffer a real disintegration in their social life. There is some evidence of the former, but more of the latter.

IV. THE MODERN AMERICAN FAMILY

As we turn to the treatment of the modern American family and point out the ways in which it differs from the family just described, there will be those who will say that the chief dissimilarities are simply those which arise inevitably in an urban as contrasted to a rural area. Indeed, there are many today who like to picture the present-day family itself as a family fallen from "rural grace." Admittedly there are differences — significant ones — which must be attributed in some large part to the varying types of demands and opportunities afforded in rural and urban communities, but it is a mistake to attribute too much to them. Actually, the American family, even in the days when the country had an economy largely agricultural, was never a familistic unit as the Spanish-American and many others have been.

Space does not permit our discussing much of that which belongs to the history of the American family, but because it is one of our main arguments that the family expresses the value orientations which in embryo at least have been American since colonial days, we need to mention a few facts. Generational ties have always been weak in most parts of the United States. Family units on the farm were what have been called strong "solidary" units, but there was seldom much stress upon the preservation of family continuity in time and place. The mechanisms which would have insured ordered positional succession — primogeniture, for example — have never been established, not even in the South. There has also been a consistent trend through time toward an equalizing of the rights and opportunities of the two sexes. Since colonial days children have never been taught the kind of respect and obedience to age that Spanish-American and many other children of the world have instilled in them from birth. No, for all of the fact that families were once more stable and unified than many are today, familistic relationships as an end in themselves have never been a primary goal of our ideals. Mobile, ambitious, and forward-looking Americans have been expressing throughout their historical past something of the individualistic relational orientation, the future-time orientation, the man-over-nature conception, the doing type of personality, and the idea of self-control of a somewhat evil but perfectible human nature.

Of course, when we speak of *the* modern American family we are generalizing for a purpose. There really is no such thing as a single family type which can be said to be representative of all the United States. There is the kind of variation in families which results from there being large groups of people with quite different cultural backgrounds — groups with still recent memories of other countries. After all, the Spanish-American people we have described are a part of the United States, and they are only one of many partially assimilated peoples. Differences of another kind can be distinguished in the families of the several economic levels. Upper-class Boston families are not so-called typical American families. And aside from all these differences, there is considerable diversity in individual families. No two American families are ever found to be exactly alike.

Perhaps it is precisely this diversity which makes Americans put so much stress upon the dominant or ideal family. To hold all the differences together, a strong sense of conformity or oneness is needed — at least the norm of it is needed. Everyone is aware to one degree or another of the kinds of relationships and types of behavior which should be present in the "Good Family." There is, in other words, a model family according to which all others tend to be judged and like which most other families are striving to become. This model — the more or less typical middle-class family — is what we are referring to when we speak of *the* American family.

We cannot describe everything about this family. Our intention is to limit the discussion to the relations of family units to each other — and to the whole society — and to a brief analysis of the relationships *within* individual families. It is especially the latter analysis which will give us the most essential background facts for the subsequent treatment of the role women play in the American family and society.

The typical middle-class family of today is small. A father, a mother, and two or three children has been the numerical pattern in recent years. Very recently, to be sure, the birth rate in such families has shown something of an increase. As yet, however, there is no certain way of telling whether the fluctuation upward is to be permanent or is merely the result of a wartime situation. Whatever the case, it certainly seems doubtful that the typical family size will be greatly enlarged in the near future.

In addition to being small, this family is what sociologists term "isolated." This is to say that it is an independent unit both economically and socially. Even though its members always recognize the fact of relatives — grandparents, uncles, aunts, and cousins — the relational bonds with these relatives are not, in most cases, strong ones. Although personal preference may make them strong, there are no binding rules — such as there are in Spanish-American society — which make it necessary always to accept and get along with one's relatives whether one personally likes them or not.

Almost everyone grows up with brothers and sisters — one or two anyway — whom he likes in varying degrees. Perhaps a majority of persons also assume that the attachments to siblings will endure throughout a lifetime. Yet, if people would be thoroughly honest they would have to admit that many persons, by the time they reach the age of thirty-five or forty years, have associates and friends to whom they feel closer than they do to brothers or sisters. This is certainly apt to be the case when, as so often happens, brothers and sisters become geographically separated by hundreds or even thousands of miles. Or, it may be that the separation is social rather than geographical. One sister's husband is successful, another's is not. As a result they live in different social orbits and seldom meet. Even if the two sisters maintain their relationship, it is unlikely that their children will have much in common or many contacts with each other. Perhaps, in other cases, it is only that the interests of the family of one brother or sister are professionally oriented and those of another concentrated in the business world. Whatever the particular situation may be, the fact of the separation is evident in a very large number of families.

Even parent-child bonds are frequently more sentimental than real. The son or daughter who moves away from parents both geographically and occupationally comes, in time, to sense a chasm in the relationship over which the only possible bridge is sentiment. There has even been an institutionalization of one such sentimental bridge called "Mother's Day." A "rite of atonement" is what one anthropological analyst of American life has labeled the Mother's Day customs.

Because almost all Americans are deeply sentimental about family relationships, it probably is a trifle shocking to admit such facts as these. In some ways the shock is justified. For it is true that family patterns of this kind put quite severe strains upon individuals. There are often great anxieties among older people who feel they have no right to ask support from their children. The size to which insurance companies have grown is one indication of the extent of this anxiety. Present-day concern with old-age pensions is another. Whereas the Spanish-American or Chinese father or mother — of the past at any rate — would expect to live with his or her children and be supported by them, American parents usually have only fears that they might be forced to accept such a solution to their economic or health problems. Comic strips, stories, and everyday jokes all play upon the theme of the difficulties which arise when the generations — and especially in-laws — are placed together in the same household.

The great responsibility placed upon fathers of families is another of the strains inherent in these family patterns. In many societies, no man is made to feel that he, and he alone, is solely responsible for the welfare of his family. There are parents, brothers, even uncles and cousins to be called on in times of crisis or need. The American belief in independence permits little of such reliance upon family members without there being cen-

sure or shame attached. Many a man has been heard to say that he would far rather borrow from a stranger or friend than a relative. For most middle-class men the solution here, too, is insurance or savings of some kind. For families of lower economic status there is the less satisfactory solution of the application to some welfare agency.

It should be obvious that it is in this situation that we find one of the reasons why the American middle-class man is so "work-minded" and so absorbed in his own highly specialized business interests. It is not the only reason but an important one. And it is doubtful that American men will develop into men of broader interests as long as the situation remains as it is.

The independence of the small family unit also creates some problems for women. In this age of too little and poor household help it might be a real advantage to some women to have relatives upon whom they could depend for help with house and children. But seldom does one feel free to make the demand or even want to make it. Instead, there has been created the new pattern of "baby sitting," and there is a trend toward a still more highly organized system of household services. Other problems of a different order exist for women — especially those which have to do with domestic training in an ever-changing society. These, however, are better left for the later discussion of woman's role as a whole.

There may even be something to the argument advanced by some family critics that delinquency and other evidences of disturbances in children would be less were there stronger and more widely extended family controls over them. That delinquencies and other disturbances are effects of weak ties between families seems much less certain than the other effects we have pointed out. In so far as they are a result of family life, the source would seem to be more in the relationships of parents to each other — this is to say, in the quality rather than the quantitative inclusiveness of the ties. However, it is well to mention the possibility of the relationship, for our aim is to put into the picture of family life all the dark tones which realistically belong there. We do not claim that the American family type is a perfect one even for American society.

But neither is it an imperfect one. In spite of the strains and problems created for individuals by the independence and isolation of family units, the total effect for the whole society is anything but deleterious. Given American value orientations to which the vast majority still adhere, it is virtually the only kind of family possible. As was suggested earlier, if the aim is to produce achievement-minded, future-oriented, and independent persons, it is essential to have a family system which allows much individualistic expression and permits the members to go free of the bonds which would tie them to particular persons and places. Strong ties between family units and a widespread recognition of relatives just because they are relatives inevitably make for a society similar to the Spanish-American one. They make for societies which are traditionalistic and either indifferent or resistant to change. Americans are, and have long been, a fundamentally anti-traditionalistic people who want change in the areas of most concern to them — chiefly the occupational world. The marked fluidity of American society and its relative lack of a rigid class system depend more than anything else upon a weakness in family bonds. If ever those bonds are greatly strengthened, if ever a majority of occupational, political, and other positions are made hereditary ones to be passed down from generation to generation, the United States will have ceased to be the nation she now is. The basic values will have changed.

This is not to deny that in parts of the country in both the past and present there have been segments which stress family lines and past traditions. There is indeed, and always has been, some semblance of an upper class. There are other variations as well. Yet, basically, the middle-class patterns of belief and behavior do prevail. The road to success is a road into the future; it is a middle-class road upon which even the most advantaged must learn to travel. The best training for that road is to be found in the middle-class family type we have been describing.

The truth of the matter — whether one likes to believe it or not — is that this family, along with all other kinds of organizations and groups, is actually of less importance in the dominant American way of life than either the individual himself or the total society. Most persons are thoroughly committed to the idea of a highly productive society in which all members as independent individuals participate and from which all benefit. This commitment to a creative productivity of all for all makes the occupational world — the work and job world — much more important than family lines and traditions. In many, even most, societies of the world, family or other hereditary traditions govern occupations. Types of occupations, even actual positions in them, are inherited and not won on merit. To a very marked degree we in America have reversed this order of affairs. Although some American sons do take over the position of their fathers, there is, in general, resentfulness and even suspicion of such a pattern. In order to justify it there is often a resorting to the ruse of starting the boy "in at the bottom," even though all know his journey from bottom to top will not be the customarily long one. Another fact to be noted is how much more a particular family's class or social position is a result of the father's occupation than is that father's occupation a result of his having been born in a particular family. The main rewards, social and otherwise, go to successful producers. An English historian phrased all this well when he wrote:

The first and almost the last rule is that the rulers must deliver the goods, that they must share some of the winnings of the game with the clients, with the great mass of the American people, and that these winnings must be absolutely more than any rival system can plausibly promise . . . The American does not admire wealth as such . . . What the American admires in wealth is achievement, success in a game in which all are playing and whose rules are reasonably fair . . . The admirers of the American rich have not been tenants, but clients, economic dependents who are not disposed to go farther in the way of devotion than the economic bond suggests is advisable.[15]

This fervent belief in productivity requires a continuous progressiveness and change that is the antithesis of traditionalism. One certain way of insuring progressiveness is to make the choice of persons for jobs on the bases of ability, initiative, drive or ambition, and special training. Choice of this kind can only be a choice between individuals as independent competitors, and it is the American middle-class type of family with its disregard of tradition for tradition's sake and its loose ties which produces the independent competitors. Indeed, we can say, and say emphatically, that it is in the United States more than anywhere else that there has been produced the family system that can best meet the demands of a modern rationalized industrial and business economy. Were there space, we could also point to the ways in which this type of family is likewise suited to our educational, political, or other spheres of life. The "goodness of fit" is marked if often far from perfect. And it is this positive side of the family patterns which so many today are overlooking.

Perhaps those who are guilty of the overlooking are in reality challenging our total system rather than our family patterns as such. It has not been the intent of this discussion either to make such a challenge or insist upon the perfection of American economic, political, educational, and other institutions. Nor is our aim to argue that our American basic values, which all these institutions express, are those of final and ultimate validity. It is, however, assumed that a majority do hold to these values. This being the case, we must maintain our perspective and admit that, for all of the strains which may be created by our having small and independent families,

we have a family type well suited to our society as a whole. Such a family is *potentially*, if not actually, the best training ground for the kind of individuals needed to maintain the basic values.

If this contention be true, one may rightly ask why then it is that we have so many problems and difficulties in modern family life. Even if these problems are not all new, they are far too many and too serious to ignore. As we ourselves have just indicated, the American family seems potentially better than it actually is.

The realization of its potentialities would, however, seem to require much more of a reordering of relationships *within* family units than a strengthening of bonds *between* them. Our primary cause for concern is, we believe, in the nature of the husband-wife relationship and the parent-child relationships. There are many defects in both of a kind that a mere change from "rigid routine" to "self-demand" child-training practices will not overcome.

To state the situation quite bluntly: Many, if not most, American wives are chronically discontented or frustrated; a majority of American men retain in their characters too many adolescent traits of thought and behavior; very few husband-wife relationships are really mature man-woman relationships. Marriage instability and conflict, as well as personal dissatisfactions, are the inevitable results. Girls growing up in such a family environment become the discontented wives of the future; boys become but another crop of mother-dominated adolescents who too often doubt, yet feel compelled to prove, their masculinity.

These are extreme statements yet not nearly as bald as some that have been made. In 1946, David Cohn entitled a caustic article "Do American Men Like Women?" His answer to the title question was a categorical "No." A part of his argument for the negative answer ran as follows:

In this country, where marriage, two times in five, is a stylized detour to arrive at a divorce (statisticians esti-

---

[15] D. W. Brogan, *American Themes* (New York: Harper, 1947), pp. 37–38.

mate that by 1965 more than one half of all marriages will end in divorce), the relationship between millions of couples is not a man-woman relationship. Shortly after Herbert and Azadia have married, he comes to regard her not as a woman but as the Little Woman, while she looks upon him not as a man but as a Boy. To her he is a dear, sweet boy, helpless and in need of mothering; the poor thing can never find his brief case and forgets his galoshes on rainy days. And if he cannot call her Mama instead of Azadia two years after marrying, he is likely to look upon the whole thing as a failure.

The maternal love of Azadia for Herbert may be all to the good so far as he is concerned. It permits him to remain spiritually in a state of suspended animation. A man-woman relationship would consume more of his time and energy than he is willing to devote to it. It might reduce some of the emotional content he pours into his work as assistant display manager for northwestern Minnesota for the International Tweezers Corporation. His full duty toward his wife — and proof of the fact in his mind that he is essentially a decent man — is discharged by regarding his wife as a lady in the sense that he regards his mother as a lady. In this way he continues to remember Mama without ever discovering Azadia, and the fact that she may secretly feel he is overdoing the lady business never enters his mind.

The Boys of this country are simply retarded adolescents whose ideal of femininity remains a girl in a bathing suit, and who are incapable of developing a mature feminine ideal through a synthesis of spiritual and physical values. Men of this kind are neither adult nor adequate in their relations with women. They are the oafs who make "propositions" to every woman in sight and then fly in panic to Mama's protecting skirts, when they fear the proposition is about to be accepted. They are the brave lads who spoil the evening slippers of ladies by playing footsie with them under the dinner table; who think it manly ("sophisticated") to get drunk at the Country Club on Saturday nights and tell off-color stories to uninterested women on the theory that this is virile and the stories are fatally aphrodisiac. They care nothing for an interchange of ideas with women, or for any wit more subtle than the barnyard joke. And the country is filled with them. Yet, mice tailored to look like men, they want to be mothered by their wives — a process that freezes their already arrested development and renders impossible any relationship on a mature man-woman basis.

Every day, therefore, is Mother's Day in the lives of many women and without benefit even of a potted begonia.[16]

Most persons are, of course, reluctant to admit the truth in accusations such as these. They strike much too close to the central core of that which is fairly sacred to all. Yet is there much hope of evidence for denying them? The divorce statistics alone can tell us how unstable American marriages of today are. Indisputable evidence from doctors, from clinics and guidance centers, and from welfare agencies indicate widespread psychological frustrations and disturbances in both men and women — and children too. Teachers see the effects upon children. The evidence is considerable. Whether the situation is of the magnitude of seriousness either we or Mr. Cohn have claimed, it is certainly serious enough in scope and depth to affect the lives of everyone, either directly or indirectly.

Thus, rather than waste time in disputing the degree, is it not better to seek out the roots of the problems and try to find the ways of effecting some change within the system as it is? For unlike many today, we do not see family problems black enough to urge a different kind of family. Alteration and not radical change, evolution rather than revolution, would seem the better solution.

---

[16] David L. Cohn, "Do American Men Like Women?" *Atlantic Monthly*, vol. 178 (August 1946), p. 72.

The roots of the current maladjustments are deeply embedded in the very trends we have been analyzing. They are the same roots which have produced a family type that suits so well our kind of society. The same trends and events which produced the independence of families from each other have also brought about the individualizing of relationships within the family. And both effects were, as was pointed out above, more or less inevitable. That the one effect of keeping families fairly separate and independent has seemed to have been a better one for the whole society than the individualizing of the particular family's internal relationships is admittedly true. But is it true only as of today? Or to phrase this question another way: Can it not be that the evolutionary process has not yet gone far enough or has not gone evenly in its several directions?

Some of the results of the individualizing process have long been evident. The status of women has been greatly altered. In principle at least there is equality between the sexes. Children, once supposed to be seen rather than heard, are now quite often full-fledged members of family councils. Indeed, one sometimes wonders, as did one nineteenth-century writer quoted earlier, who really rules the family — the "old man" or the "strutting youth." In quite recent years there has appeared a greater and greater independence of interests among family members. It is not the family as a whole which participates in these outside affairs and events. Each member participates independently. More and more it is expected that individuals will seek out friends and activities of all kinds as autonomous persons rather than as representatives of the family group.

Participation patterns of this kind do, in general, fit in with the American way of life. The child who makes his own friends and seeks his own level in some group about which his father or mother knows very little is actually getting good preparation for what he will face when grown up. The man who works overtime in a factory or office far from wife and children is also behaving in accord with the demands of our economic-oriented and production-minded society. But for family living, problems are created by these and other types of independent behavior.

It would appear that the several family roles have not been evolved equally enough in independence to permit of successful mutual adjustments. The father's role is plainly too autonomous; the mother's too little so. In very important respects the equality between the sexes is more apparent than real. Most men are forced to concentrate too much attention on providing the family income for them to participate widely in other aspects of family life. Women are too much in the family and too little drawn into the main currents of the national life in ways that are satisfying to them as individuals. One result is a marked segregation (separation) of masculine and feminine interests. Another is that much-discussed mother-domination of children. For many women, loath to see their main life's work accomplished while they themselves are still very young, cling to children and deny them the right to the early independence our society favors and demands.

With relationships skewed this way it is not difficult to see why many husband-wife relationships are less satisfactory than they might be, or why our men must strive so hard to overcome too much feminine domination, or why women themselves are often so restless.

There are several points at which change might be effected in these relationships. Those today who advocate greater "permissiveness" in the training of children are making efforts in one direction. More leisure-time activities, often planned for full family participation, are a trial effort of another kind. There may be many ways. But the effects produced will depend upon whether what is planned and done strikes deeply and squarely at the roots of the problems or merely lops off a symptomatic branch here and there.

Although the judgment may be erroneous, the firm conviction derived from all that we have tried to analyze is that the most vital spot for attack is the feminine role. It is the role about which all people, men and women alike, are most in doubt. The strains in it are by far the most numerous and the most varied. And when we consider the extent of the influence of the American woman in American family life, it is safe to predict that some change in the role she plays will soon bring changes in all family relationships. With this judgment we leave our consideration of the general characteristics of family life in the United States and turn to the more specific problems of the social role of American women.

V. THE FEMININE CHARACTER AND THE FEMININE ROLE

Although there are obvious biological differences between the sexes, the *meaning* of the differences for the lives of individual men and women and for whole societies is not obvious at all. Few problems, other than that of the creation or fact of life itself, have so plagued the minds of men and women of all periods of history as this one of the differences between the male and the female. Not infrequently the question has been argued on the basis of inferiority and superiority. More often it becomes a disagreement over sex-determined attributes of mind and character. But let that disagreement become sufficiently bitter, and the competitive issue of superiority and inferiority again emerges. In fact, something of the issue is almost always present whether explicitly stated or not.

Without denying in the least that significant differences — psychological and other — between the male and female may, and probably do, exist, nothing can seem more certain than the lack of agreement as to what they are. Dr. Viola Klein in an excellent and recent book, *The Feminine Character*,[17] has surveyed and compared enough of the many ideologies concerning what is feminine to convince us that no agreement exists. Some analysts of the feminine charac-

ter start with what is viewed as a biologically determined passive role in sexual relations and from it derive a host of psychological traits. Dr. Klein points out, for example, that Sigmund Freud associates with woman's biological constitution, especially her lack of the male sex organs, the following (among other) psychological characteristics: a weak moral sense of right and wrong, little social conscience, modesty with which vanity and jealousy are combined, masochism, a predisposition to neurosis, and a general antagonism toward civilization and cultural pursuits.[18]

Havelock Ellis, another of those whose views Dr. Klein discusses, found in a combination of sexual passivity and social conditions the origin of these traits of the feminine character: receptivity, variability, submissiveness, modesty, a capacity to resist major disturbances while yet succumbing to minor ones, suggestibility, emotionality, and practical realism.[19]

Dr. Klein gives this summary of the views of a German philosopher:

In Otto Weininger's view woman has one purpose in life and only one essential interest: sexuality. Both in the type of mother and in that of courtesan she is either indirectly or directly concerned with matters of sex. She has no moral standards of her own, and the constant compliance with extraneous standards has produced in her mendacity, hypocrisy, and the disposition to hysteria. She has no capacity for clear thought, no memory other than the ability to repeat memorized matter. Her judgment is uncertain and her sensibility poor except for tactile sensations. She is sentimental, but incapable of deep emotions. She has no desire for individual immortality, and no appreciation for permanent values; she has no intellectual conscience, no relation to logic, and she lacks individuality and an independent will.[20]

Weininger's views, although written in

---

[17] New York: International Universities Press, 1949.
[18] *The Feminine Character*, p. 165.
[19] *Ibid.*, p. 164.
[20] *Ibid.*, p. 165.

the early part of our own century, will strike most of us as being extreme and strongly biased. Yet Dr. Klein is correct in warning us against too strong a reaction against them. As she states, they were probably not too inaccurate a description of a certain class of women of his time. Furthermore, she maintains, with good reason, that what he wrote provides us with an excellent example of the way in which attitudes toward women in the western world have always been "intertwined with a whole system of attitudes — toward Life in general and Sex in particular." [21]

In the whole of the Judaeo-Christian tradition sin and sex have been firmly linked. The legend of Eve has been very slow to die. How could it die easily when we had centuries of Church Fathers who could write as Tertullian did?

And do you not know that you are (each) an Eve? The sentence of God on this sex of yours lives in this age: the guilt must of necessity live too. *You* are the devil's gateway: *you* are the unsealer of that (forbidden) tree: *you* are the first deserter of that divine law: *you* are she who persuaded him whom the devil was not valiant enough to attack. *You* destroyed so easily God's image, man. On account of *your* desert — that is, death — even the Son of God had to die. And do you think about adorning yourself over and above your tunics of skins?" [22]

American Puritanism, of which there is still more than a memory, contained strong echoes of these harsh attitudes. All of European thought has been influenced by them. Hence it is not strange that we find their traces in the theories of a Weininger, an Ellis, or even in the ideas of Freud. Moral inferiority has been attributed to the women of the western world for too long for the attitude to fade quickly.

There have been, to be sure, counter-strains of thought. And some studies, starting with a different viewpoint, have certainly produced conclusions of an-

other kind. Dr. Helen B. Thompson, a psychologist of the same period as Weininger and Freud, for example, found that her experiments disclosed only the slightest of differences in masculine and feminine aptitudes and abilities. They did not show "any marked differences in intellectual interests, methods of work, in type of mental activity or average capacity, in the intensity of emotions or in the degree of impulsiveness of action." [23] The only significant difference was a greater tendency to inhibit the expression of emotions, and this, Dr. Klein says, Dr. Thompson attributed to social conditions rather than any innate predispositions.

It must also be remembered that there has always been in western thought a recurring idealization of women. In the Middle Ages and again in later periods women — *some* women, at least — were so completely idealized that they were regarded as the very symbols of purity. But whenever this happened, there was a separation of the Feminine from Sex. The most notable example of this idealization is, of course, the Madonna. But she is not the only one. We shall soon discuss the effect of this attitude upon the role of women in the United States in the nineteenth century — and even today. For is it not true that the woman most Americans idealize is the mother and not the wife?

Considering this variety of views and analyses we are rightfully doubtful about what is the truth regarding the feminine character and its differences from the masculine. Certainly it will not be until we have factored out both that which is a part of a long western tradition and the many attitudes specific to particular societies that we can state with any certainty that marked differences exist or have real significance.

Anthropologists and sociologists, in their recent studies of many different kinds of peoples, are now able to prove quite conclusively that societies vary greatly both in what they expect of the

[21] *Ibid.*, p. 69.
[22] Quoted in Ernest Groves, *The American Woman* (New York: Emerson Books, 1944), p. 22.
[23] Quoted in Klein, *The Feminine Character*, p. 166.

two sexes and in their judgments of their separate qualities. Of all the anthropologists none has been so interested in this particular question as Dr. Margaret Mead. One of her conclusions is as follows:

The differences between the two sexes is one of the important conditions upon which we have built the many varieties of human culture that give human beings dignity and stature. In every known society, mankind has elaborated the biological division of labour into forms often very remotely related to the original biological differences that provided the original clues. Upon the contrast in bodily form and function, men have built analogies between sun and moon, night and day, goodness and evil, strength and tenderness, steadfastness and fickleness, endurance and vulnerability. Sometimes one quality has been assigned to one sex, sometimes to the other. Now it is boys who are thought of as infinitely vulnerable and in need of special cherishing care, now it is girls. In some societies it is girls for whom parents must collect a dowry or make husband-catching magic, in others the parental worry is over the difficulty of marrying off the boys. Some peoples think of women as too weak to work out of doors, others regard women as the appropriate bearers of heavy burdens, "because their heads are stronger than men's." The periodicities of female reproductive functions have appealed to some peoples as making women the natural sources of magical or religious power, to others as directly antithetical to those powers; some religions, including our European traditional religions, have assigned women an inferior role in the religious hierarchy, others have built their whole symbolic relationship with the supernatural world upon male imitations of the natural functions of women. In some cultures women are regarded as sieves through whom the best-guarded secrets will sift; in others it is the men who are the gossips. Whether we deal with small matters or with large, with the frivolities of ornament and cosmetics or the sanctities of man's place in the universe, we find this great variety of ways, often flatly contradictory one to the other, in which the roles of the two sexes have been patterned.

But we always find the patterning. We know of no culture that has said, articulately, that there is no difference between men and women except in the way they contribute to the creation of the next generation; that otherwise in all respects they are simply human beings with varying gifts, no one of which can be exclusively assigned to either sex." [24]

Yet even Dr. Mead, who — because of her stressing so much the variety of interpretation of sex roles — has sometimes been accused of trying to dismiss the fact of difference altogether, is the first to urge that we find out what the real differences are. It is only when we know them, she states, that we can synthesize them into the kind of harmonious whole which will permit each sex to contribute fully to social life.

Dr. Klein in her analysis of the feminine character comes to a similar conclusion. At least, she indicates a belief that after all the factors of social conditioning are removed, we shall find remaining a residue of "typically feminine traits." [25] It is only that to date — and for the reasons we have been discussing — no validity can be claimed for what have been called the traits of the feminine character.

Even though it cannot be said with certainty what aspects of the feminine role are or have been a result of "typically feminine traits," it is possible to point to some universals which have demanded and still demand differentiation. We know, for example, that the sexual instinct is one of life's basic and most powerful ones. It can be a force which brings disruption in social life. In periods of war, such disruption often

---

[24] Margaret Mead, *Male and Female* (New York: William Morrow, 1949), p. 7.
[25] *The Feminine Character*, p. 182.

occurs. We have only to examine the records to see that every society has felt the need of controlling sexuality with regulations of some kind. Marriage and family life have been, to date, one of the universal solutions of this social need. Some societies permit polygamy as well as monogamy; some allow much more leeway than others for sexual relations both before marriage and outside the marriage relationship; yet all have some kind of family system in which there are rules regulating the sexual access of individuals to each other.

Of course, it is not only some control of the sexual instinct which is needed. Human children must have long years of care before they are mature enough to fend for themselves. Theoretically, they could be reared by other means than family life. Plato proposed different means; the Russians for a brief period attempted other ways; and new proposals continue to appear. As yet there has been no successful attempt at a substitute for the family which has achieved any magnitude. Thus far in human history family life has been the universal solution to the two universal needs of a control of the sexual instinct and the rearing of children. There may be, and probably are, other universal needs which the family also meets, but of these two there is real certainty.

Within family organization it is the women who bear the children, and it is *probably* true that they are better suited to care for children in a personal way in early years. We are not postulating a "mother instinct," for there is some disagreement that it exists. Nor are we saying that every woman must bear and care for children just because she is a woman. It is, however, true that the survival of the human species depends upon a majority of women bearing children and also upon there being some kind of organized group life which insures the rearing of them to maturity.

These facts of human existence are too well known to be in need of elaboration. We refer to them only for the special purpose of focusing attention upon the *social necessity* and *social value*

of the domestic aspect of the woman's role. There is, as we shall soon see, some danger of Americans irreparably warping this aspect of the role by a continuous demeaning of its significance.

But granted that American women are women, it is also true that they are Americans. They are as much imbued — from birth on — with American values as are American men. And, as has been contended previously, it is not possible to create and maintain powerful values and then deny to half of the society's population a full right to participate in the behavioral expressions of them. Thus far in the history of the United States it has been the fate of women to be given more the right for *indirect* than *direct* participation. This is not an adequate solution.

The profound and enormously difficult question is, then, this: How can the feminine role be so redefined that it both retains the needed emphasis upon the domestic aspect and also allows for a more direct participation of women in those aspects of American life which offer many, if not most, of the most sought-after rewards for achievement and the greatest opportunity for shared interests?

Any proper or final answer to a question of this magnitude probably lies far in the future. Later we shall indicate some few changes which might conceivably provide a partial answer — the beginnings of a solution. But no answer is apt to be a very meaningful one unless it is based upon a knowledge of what the present situation is and how it came to be. Diagnosis should always precede a recommendation of therapy. Our chief aim, therefore, is that of giving a diagnostic analysis of the American woman's role. It will not be perfect or complete. But if it challenges further thought and serves, even partially, to disentangle that which is feminine from that which is more particularly American we shall, for the present, be content.

VI. COMPONENTS OF THE FEMININE ROLE; THEIR ORIGIN AND EVOLUTION

There are today four distinguishable aspects — *components* as Professor Parsons of Harvard University has called them[26] — in the American woman's total feminine role. The first of these is the domestic component, which now is split into the two parts of *mother-wife* (most especially mother) and the *housewife* roles. Second in importance for many women is the *career* or job component. Third is that aspect which we shall call the *glamour girl* component. The *culture bearer* or *humanistic* component is the fourth. Cross-cutting all of these, hence not as clearly distinguishable, is a fifth important aspect of the role — woman as the husband's *status symbol*.

Most of these components are self-explanatory as stated. The meaning of the one or two not so obvious ones will become clear in our subsequent discussion. It will also, it is hoped, become evident why such a breakdown of the total role is essential to an understanding of the problems which the women of today, and the whole society with them, face. Two of our main tasks will be those of demonstrating the conflict between the several components and delineating the satisfactions or dissatisfactions each creates for American women. However, before engaging our attention in either task, we must look into the historical background of these components.

The domestic component of woman's role — in both its aspects — is the oldest of any. For a long period it was the only role which custom decreed to be the right and proper one. Colonial women in that role had little authority and small recognition as individuals either legally or politically. Their social status in general was low by today's standards. The descriptions of the household activities of that time easily convince us that women worked long and hard at a thousand tasks which no housewife of today would deign to undertake. It is easy, in other words, to paint the picture of their lives quite black. But was it so absolutely black? There is always a bright side to any position or any work if it provides the rewards of prestige and approval. To a marked degree colonial

women had such rewards and had them precisely for the reason that domesticity was considered a first-order virtue.

There is no need to enumerate all the activities then encompassed by the term domestic. They were too many and are too well known. The point of importance is that the women of that time were economically indispensable and knew it. All their many tasks were essential for production itself. Practical, thrifty, energetic — in fact, filled with all the qualities extolled in the Puritan "work ideology" — they went into early training for their job, labored hard at it, and through successful accomplishment won for themselves real prestige in the wider social community.

This concept of woman's work retained much of its content as long as America was predominantly a rural nation. It lingers still as a concept, but what a hollow and contentless one it is for many women — especially middle-class women! Except for the mother aspect, the domestic role of today carries few meaningful rewards.

To be sure, there was some pressure for change from so narrow a definition of women's role (narrow in scope if not content) even in colonial times. Although the expected and approved pattern was as we have pictured it, there were countless women who took an active part in a variety of business enterprises. Elisabeth A. Dexter in *Colonial Women of Affairs*[27] gives vivid accounts of women who ran farms, plantations, taverns, mills, export-import, and many another kind of business. In a majority of the cases, to be sure, the women were more or less forced into such positions by the death of a husband or father. Yet it cannot be denied that their successes had some effect upon the then current attitudes toward women.

The type of family situation which permitted or forced the entrance of women into such work was, however, more important than the actual successes some women achieved. Even in those days families tended to be, in most areas,

---

[26] Talcott Parsons, "Age and Sex in the Social Structure of the United States," above, Chapter III.
[27] Boston: Houghton Mifflin, 1924.

independent units of husband, wife, and children. Although it was often the case that unattached relatives — many spinster aunts for example — lived with these families, there were not the kind of extended family ties which would always insure a new male head for the family. As we have noted previously, Americans have never subscribed to the kind of family institutions which provide, as do the Spanish-American or Chinese institutions, for family continuity and an unbroken chain of patriarchal authority. And it has been a marked characteristic of Americans to expect women to "take over" in times of emergency whether of family or nation. The effect of this expectation for producing changes in the feminine role has been considerable.

The beginnings of change — the beginnings of a trend toward the individualizing of the feminine role — were present very early. They were there primarily because there was rapidly evolving in the whole society the value orientations which demanded the change. Significant concrete changes were, however, slow in materializing. The eighteenth century, important in so many other respects, did not produce many noticeable alterations in the attitudes toward the woman's social position. Seeds were being planted, but little of what took root and grew from them became easily obvious until the nineteenth century.

It is in the history of the nineteenth century that we can see so clearly the results for the feminine role of these events and trends: growing industrialization; the feminist movement; a romantic movement borrowed from Europe; the development of a definite middle-class character in the total society; a shattering war. Each had its marked but different effect on the role of the American woman, and it was from these frequently contradictory nineteenth-century alterations that most of our present-day confusion has stemmed.

A rapidly developing industrialization produced changes of different kinds. For the first time an appreciably large number of women were working outside the home for wages. This fact proved, in the long run, to be important, but the immediate effects of the large-scale employment of women in factories were very sorry ones. Work conditions in general were miserable, and wages were low. Very often women and children were hired solely or chiefly because their services could be obtained at lower wage rates than those of men. The legal rights of women were too few for them to make many demands in their own behalf. Furthermore, in many cases women had no control over their own earnings. Although the laws in the several states varied and were changing at different rates, it was chiefly in the industrial states that changes of benefit to women came late. It was not, for example, until 1860 that New York State granted to married women the right of control over their own wages. Massachusetts — the state in which so many women were employed in textile mills — was likewise slow to alter wage and property laws in favor of women. Thus, on the whole, the working women of this period were badly exploited by employers, fathers, husbands, and even brothers and sons. One young millworker has left us this statement of her own and other girls' reasons for working:

The most prevailing incentive to our labor was to secure the means of education for some male member of the family. To make a gentleman of a brother or a son, to give him a college education, was the dominant thought in the minds of a great many of these provident mill girls.[28]

It was partly because of a rapidly developing counter-trend — that which brought about an idealization of women in more fortunate economic circumstances — that the entrance of women in the occupations at this time was slow to affect the status of women. Care must be taken, however, not to play down too much the influence. For one thing, the poor conditions under which women worked, and the laws which denied them

[28] Harriet H. Robinson, *Loom and Spindle* (New York, 1898), quoted in Calhoun, *A Social History of the American Family*, II, 175.

property and wage-control rights, were avidly seized upon by feminists as grist for their mill of protest. A further weakening of family bonds was another definite result. And, as Calhoun points out, a new and different kind of unity was being forged between the sexes. While the working conditions, especially wage rates, for men were better than those for women, they were not appreciably so. In protesting for themselves men came also to protest for women who lacked the right of political self-expression. There was both a kind of chivalry in this and a recognition of a nondomestic unity between the sexes.[29]

There were other effects upon family patterns and the feminine role which followed on a growing concern with economic productivity. The men of the nation were fast dedicating themselves to the "affairs of the market place" and the Business Man was emerging as the ideal American man. In other societies it is so often the scholar, the statesman, or even the gentleman of leisure who represents the ideal. But not here! Scholars have usually been "long hairs" and statesmen mere "politicians," because neither the abstract affairs of the mind nor matters of government have a significance or prestige comparable to that which can be found in the business world. This is the American middle-class way which demands that all men work and work hard in order that they — and the whole nation with them — may "get ahead as fast as possible." The getting ahead, of course, is to be defined primarily in economic production terms. No other nation has ever been so definitely committed to mass production.

Yet for all of the strength of the commitment, there came, as contacts with other nations increased, an uncomfortable awareness that many were beginning to label Americans intellectual barbarians. Even morals in the United States have been declared to be solely those of the market place. It was recognized all too clearly that whereas other peoples took time for the arts and had an ap-

preciation for them, there was, among Americans, both a small aesthetic development and little nurture of it. It was also obvious that the "well-to-do" in other societies — those which had real aristocracies — were a relatively leisured class of people. There were people who had time not only for cultural pursuits but also for a display of the symbols of their position and wealth. Not to be completely outdone or too much ridiculed by peoples of greater tradition, the people of the United States found their own way to include leisure-time pursuits, display of wealth, and cultural interests in their scheme of life. That way was to make all this mainly the responsibility of women. Morality too — or at least the guarding of it — was largely left to women.

Thorstein Veblen in *The Theory of the Leisure Class*[30] analyzed a part of all this long ago. It was he who labeled American women — those of the economically successful groups — the "symbols of their husbands' ability to pay" and further described them as being themselves "items of conspicuous consumption." The success of men was to be judged not by what the men themselves were, or did, but rather by what their wives and daughters could display through personal adornment, an interest in the arts, and even mere idleness.

There is no intent to imply that developments such as these were deliberately planned by anyone in particular. They simply grew out of processes which were flowing naturally from an adherence to particular value orientations and a certain juxtaposition of historical factors. It was, for example, fairly easy, once the conception of woman as a status symbol had begun to evolve, to adjust nineteenth-century romanticism to it. The result was that idealization of women (of only certain classes, to be sure) which was so extreme that it caused Pearl Buck to call it the era of the "angel on the pedestal." Gentility, Piety, and actual physical fragility were the prevailing standards for all those "good women" who had hus-

---

[29] Calhoun, II, 185.
[30] New York: Macmillan, 1899.

bands or fathers economically capable of supporting them in such a way of life. These were the women who were thought to be too delicate and too pure to have any knowledge of the industrial and business world that was growing ever noisier and dirtier. They were the women who were too pure to have much knowledge of, or pleasure in, bodily things and most especially in sexual relations. There were women, many of them, who had both, but these were the nineteenth century's "bad women." The line between "good" and "bad" women was firmly drawn in that century and remained in evidence for a long time.

The importance of the idealized woman for the society as a whole was more in the fact of her being a model for all women than in the numbers she represented. These women, many of whom were parasites in the true sense of the word, were the arbiters of both fashion and morality straight across the country. Their moral power derived in large part from the conception of them as being fragile and pure and devoid of sexual interests, other than those absolutely necessary for the conceiving of children. "Prudish" is what most persons today would call these "angels" of another time. Women themselves eventually rebelled against much that was contained in this way of life, but the impression of it remains firmly printed upon the feminine role.

Nineteenth-century women of quite another kind than either these or those who labored in factories were making history in a different way. They were the feminists who militantly agitated for women's rights. The feminist movement did not, of course, originate in the nineteenth century. It owed a great deal to such English women as Mary Wollstonecraft and much even to colonial American women like Anne Hutchinson. Yet as a social movement it is usually considered to be both American and nineteenth century.

Initially the women's rights movement, however militant some of the agitators for it may have been, had only the aim of obtaining for women, and especially married women, greater legal, political, and educational rights. Note the specific kind of charges which were made against men in the famous Seneca Falls declaration of 1848, which was so influential in the whole feminist movement.

He has made her, if married, in the eye of the law, civilly dead.

He has taken from her all right in property, even to the wages she earns.

He has made her, morally, an irresponsible being, as she can commit many crimes with impunity, provided they be done in the presence of her husband. In the covenant of marriage, she is compelled to promise obedience to her husband, he becoming to all intents and purposes her master — the law giving him power to deprive her of her liberty and to administer chastisement.

He has so framed the laws of divorce, as to what shall be the proper causes, and, in case of separation, to whom the guardianship of the children shall be given, as to be wholly regardless of the happiness of woman — the law in all cases going upon a false supposition of the supremacy of man, and giving all power into his hands.[31]

But that which started as a married woman's plea for a more equitable distribution of rights soon veered off into a rampant feminism. The more vocal proponents — persons like Margaret Fuller, Elizabeth Cady Stanton, and Lucy Stone — began to present arguments and make demands that greatly obscured, when they did not obliterate altogether, the fact of sex differences. Women were declared to be the equals of men in all ways, hence deserving of the same rights and opportunities. Much discussion was centered on woman's right to enter the occupations and her rights to control property and wages. It was in these demands that full use was made of the descriptions of the conditions women faced in factory work.

---

[31] Quoted in Calhoun, *A Social History of the American Family*, II, 119.

Another central issue was that of the training and education of women. The differential training of even young boys and girls was distasteful to most — though certainly not all — of the feminists. One of Elizabeth Stanton's statements runs as follows:

> The girl must be allowed to romp and play, climb, skate, and swim; her clothing must be more like that of the boy . . . that she may be out at all times, and enter freely into all kinds of sport. Teach her to go alone, by night and day, if need be, on the lonely highway, or through the busy streets of the crowded metropolis. The manner in which all courage and self reliance is educated out of the girl, her path portrayed with dangers and difficulties that never exist, is melancholy indeed.[32]

One result of all this agitation was some real advance in the legal and political status of women. The steps were slow and had behind them the force of more than the feminist movement, yet none can deny the influence of that movement in providing for American women a political and legal status far greater than most women of the world enjoy. Indeed, to many women of other countries, American women would appear to be far in advance of all women. That the situation is not so simple as legal rules and political rights would make it seem, we shall soon see.

Other effects of the feminist movement were not so beneficial. In fact, some of the issues raised by it seem only to have muddied the waters in the stream of progress. It has been, for example, chiefly the feminist agitators who have created and kept alive the vicious alternative — marriage or career. It is frequently pointed out by psychologists, and most especially by psychoanalysts, that many feminists were, and are, strongly motivated by both a hatred of men and a great envy of them. Marriage for such women could only be an admission of defeat. Although it is difficult to concur completely with this analysis (there was too much else involved in the protests

being made), it certainly is a fact that the feminists' tendency was to pose marriage and career as mutually exclusive alternatives. The problems which many educators today are finding in the training of women derive in large part from this alternative phrasing of the woman's role.

Frontier life was still another of the important influences on the status of women, and in some few respects it had an effect in the same direction as feminism. The scarcity of women in frontier regions was a chief factor. Men, absorbed with the tasks of breaking and clearing new lands and the warding off of hostile Indian populations, needed women both to care for their personal needs and to aid in the developing of new lands. And women were few. Even very unattractive women, if only they would venture out upon the frontier, were assured of a wide range of choice in marriage partners. Once having become a part of frontier life, they gained an authority both within the home and on the outside which few colonial women ever achieved. The dangers and hardships that confronted the families and the isolation in which most of them lived gave to those women who survived many new kinds of responsibilities and rights. The best evidence of the liberalizing influence provided by this rigorous life is found in the fact that it was the western states which often took the lead in granting to women equal rights. The first seven of the states to vote for women's suffrage were Washington (1910), California (1911), Arizona, Kansas, and Oregon (1912), Montana and Nevada (1914). It was mainly the opposition in the older and more settled eastern states which delayed suffrage on a national scale for six more years.

In other ways, however, the influences of frontier life did not accord at all with feminism. The efforts to make women the equals of men in occupational opportunities were only faintly echoed in the family life of the West, where the spheres of the sexes were, in general, still viewed as separate. Indeed, the greatest contri-

---

[32] *History of Woman Suffrage,* 4 vols. (Rochester, 1889), quoted in Calhoun, II, 114.

bution of this rugged family of the West to the evolution of the feminine role would seem to have been an enormous strengthening of the authority of the woman *within* the home. From it emerged the powerful mother-child relationship about which there is today good reason to be concerned.

Thus we see that several major trends sometimes pulled together in one direction and sometimes went their separate and opposite ways. Some of the effects of the feminist movement were supported and reinforced by the effects of both industrialization and our westward rural expansion. Others did not accord with them at all. And certainly there was little or no agreement between what the feminists were urging and the kind of gentility, fragility, and parasitism which resulted from the two congruent trends which on the one hand idealized or romanticized women and on the other made of them pampered status symbols. Nor was there much in these latter two trends which fitted well with what factory employers or frontier husbands expected of women. Yet neither factory employers nor frontier husbands could prevent women from making the man's "angel on the pedestal" their own idol and model. All trends interlocked at some points.

Three wars, one in the nineteenth century and two in the twentieth century, proved to be catalysts in this test tube of confusion. While they were not good enough catalytic agents to bring forth a clearly crystallized feminine role, they did have the effect of stressing some trends and retarding others.

The War between the States was in some ways the most disrupting war the United States has yet known. It was a war on American soil and in one way or another involved almost everyone. As far as women were concerned, it was the first time that they were called on to help meet a truly large-scale national emergency. In both the North and the South, women were thrust into every conceivable kind of task which fighting

men had had to forsake. In most cases they not only took on the tasks but also displayed in the doing of them a courage and level of ability which was astonishing both to themselves and others.

To the nation as a whole this may have been just the meeting of an emergency. For many women the significance was of quite a different order. Many had found in the tasks they performed a sense of usefulness and a kind of prestige hitherto unknown to them. They viewed a return to their former kind of life with anxious reluctance. Calhoun phrased their feelings well when he said: "Thousands of women learned contempt for frivolity, gossip, fashion, and idleness; learned to consider seriously and fairly the capacities of their sex; and thus laid a strong and practical basis for the advancement of the rights of women." [33]

Some of the women thus affected found new satisfactions by pushing their way into business and the professions. The census of 1870 was the first in history to list employed persons by sex. It was also only after the Civil War that nursing was recognized as a profession. For this development much of the credit belongs to the two women who had so successfully organized and trained corps of nurses during the war — Clara Barton and Dorothea Dix.[34] Yet the numbers of women who entered any of these fields at that time were small. Resistances and antagonisms were still too great to permit a large-scale entrance of women into the occupations at this middle-class level.

For a majority of the women made restless by the war, another answer was found. Organized women's clubs, the first two of which were founded in 1868, were one of the most important byproducts of the Civil War. For the most part the early clubs only gave organization to activities which had already been defined as belonging to woman's realm. They were either study clubs devoted to the advancement of broader culture (those humanistic interests for which men either had, or thought they had, so little time) or philanthropic ones with

---

[33] *A Social History of the American Family*, II, 360.
[34] Una B. Sait, *New Horizons for the Family* (New York: Macmillan, 1948), p. 422.

aims of social betterment. Later, of course, other things became the concern of some of the organizations. Not infrequently even leisure-time pursuits supplanted a concern with either educational or social problems.

The next two wars — World Wars I and II — brought women out of their homes in vast numbers. This time they were to prove less willing to find a substitute for their desire for recognition in the occupational system. There had already been a slow but steady increase in the number of women who were employed in gainful occupations. After World War I the demand for a still greater participation became fairly insistent. By 1930 approximately one fourth of all women over sixteen years of age were in the American labor force. Four million of the total number were married women.[35]

Everyone knows of the range and variety of tasks which American women performed in World War II. They were so many that newspapers did not hesitate to use captions declaring, "It is a woman's war too." The praise heaped upon women for doing what they did at home and abroad was great. Yet always there were some who questioned whether women had not at last lost their willingness to accept an emergency definition of their jobs. It is reported that one of our widely known politicians was heartily booed when in a speech to a group of women he suggested that they would welcome the war's end in order that they might then return to their domestic life. Mary Beard has drawn attention to the fact that one of the manuals issued to soldiers was "sharpened as if by a razor's edge to invite a pointed argument: 'Do you want your wife to work after the war?' "[36]

The issue was rapidly being crystallized. It is, however, a long way from being settled. A deep-seated ambivalence regarding woman's proper role remains.

Women in the labor force now represent 30 per cent of the total working population. More surprising than this figure is the percentage of it represented by women who either now have, or have had, marital status. A 1947 United States Women's Bureau report stated that some 60 per cent of all gainfully employed women either were married at the time or had previously been married. The issue of job *versus* marriage or job *and* marriage is now clear-cut and must be faced as one of the country's major problems.

Before discussing it and the countless other problems facing women today, we must mention one other important phase of the feminine revolt which followed upon the First World War. Although, once again, signs of a trend had been in evidence for many years, it was not until the 1920's — the decade following the war — that there came a definite blurring of the nineteenth-century line between "good women" and "bad women." This was the era of the "flapper."

Interestingly enough, the flapper went in two directions at once, and while in each of the ways there was something new — something added — neither was entirely new. Looking back upon all her efforts to flatten breasts, streamline hips, and shorten hair, and her striving to prove that she could compete successfully with men on playing fields and in classrooms, one often calls the flapper radical. But was she so radical in this emulation of the masculine? There was a very great deal in these aspects of her behavior which was clearly reminiscent of feminism.

Perhaps the frequent failure to recognize the similarity is because of her other ways of behaving which so definitely tended toward a maximizing rather than a minimizing of sex differences. It was in the twenties that "sex appeal" became a phrase of common usage. In the use of it was the idea that glamour was a practical if not entirely proper road to feminine success. This idea, which is certainly still current and perhaps somewhat more proper now that it has been tempered by time, is one which empha-

---

[35] Sait, pp. 436, 437.
[36] *Woman as a Force in History* (New York: Macmillan, 1946), p. 16.

sizes very well a difference between the sexes and a separation of their interests. It differs from the nineteenth-century dichotomy of masculine and feminine chiefly in that it includes and openly recognizes sexuality as an aspect of the feminine. The decorative and pampered "doll" of nineteenth-century fame may have had sex appeal, but she dared not flaunt it openly or use it obviously as a means of success.

The flapper died, of course, after a brief day in a brief period of ostentation of many another kind than hers. She probably was doomed to die young even had there not been a depression to turn American minds to problems of living more serious than any she had. The truth of the matter was that she was just a bit too brazen for American moralists — and who in the country is not a bit of one? — to accept without real qualms of conscience. However, she, too, has left her mark on the feminine role. It is plain to see in what we have labeled the "glamour girl" component of woman's current role.

VII. MODERN WOMEN WITHIN THE HOME; THE HOUSEWIFE-MOTHER ROLE

We have declared the domestic component of woman's role — except in its mother aspect — to be a quite hollow one for many of today's women. What evidence is there for the statement? Actually, it is to be found about us everywhere. One only has to pick up any current magazine to realize that the home is pictured constantly as a mild variety of penal institution. Work in it must be reduced to a minimum, or so, at least, say all the advertisements for every kind of household equipment and gadget — washing machines, egg beaters, dishwashers, vacuum cleaners, and the thousands of others. If dishes must be washed by hand, one must certainly take care to use the kind of soap which will insure against "dishpan hands." For feminine glamour must be preserved! If meals must be cooked, they should properly be cooked on an *automatic* cook stove which has a mechanical sense ade-

quate for the cooking of meals by itself in an empty house. But better still, one may pick fully prepared meals out of the grocer's deep freeze and have only the trouble of a thorough heating.

There certainly is nothing wrong, morally or otherwise, with either the gadgets themselves or the saving of time. We cannot agree at all with the two writers who have recently suggested as one solution of woman's plight a removal of modern household aids.[37] One might as well expect a farmer to store his tractor and buy back his old team of horses. It is not possible to have a technological era and confine a use of the conveniences it produces to the masculine half of the population. Such a procedure would provide only one more example of women's partial participation in this kind of society.

It is something far more significant than mere gadgetry that the advertisements of gadgets are expressing. Almost every one of them, whether for soaps or cook stoves, is tacitly asserting a now widely accepted assumption that household tasks are menial and lacking in prestige. This is the basic difference between the attitude toward the tractor and the automatic stove or dishwasher. It is still a "good thing" to get the fields of the farm ploughed; it is only a "necessity" that dishes must be washed.

Even the feeling of pride and usefulness women once had in the cooking of meals has been turning into indifference. This is certainly true in urban areas. Though there may be still many women in small towns and rural areas who have a pride in the culinary arts, the trend toward indifference is noticeable there too.

A comment which illustrates well this indifference was one made to me several years ago by a suburban housewife. The occasion was a lecture on the subject of today's women. This particular woman, who already knew some of my views on American domesticity, approached me before the lecture with this remark: "I understand you think we women should

---

[37] Ferdinand Lundberg and Marynia F. Farnham, *Modern Woman: The Lost Sex* (New York: Harper, 1947).

pay more attention to cooking and other things around the house than we usually do. I certainly agree with you, and I have been trying so hard to get my sixteen-year-old daughter into the kitchen sometimes. I always tell her that *I myself hate it,* of course, but that *we do have to eat,* and it is better to learn a little about cooking now than to have to struggle so hard later on." The woman was so earnest, yet simply could not understand why her daughter was completely resistant to her suggestion.

That daughter is only one of so many who are to be tomorrow's indifferent housewives. Brought up by mothers who find little or nothing of interest in household tasks, further trained by schools and colleges which have even less concern with them, they have small chance of turning out otherwise. Often in the past, while teaching in a woman's college, I would ask whole groups of girls what they knew about cooking, the rearing of children, marketing, or household management. Their variously phrased replies could — with an exception here and there — be nicely summed into a single and very telling answer: "I will do all that when I have to." Economics, music, history, sociology, physics, or other of the academic subjects — and dates — were much too absorbing to permit time for a consideration of such matters.

Nor is it just cooking, dishwashing, or the household accounts for which most American women have little feeling. Japanese women often devote two or more years to training in the art of arranging flowers (it is, of course, a ceremonial activity in Japan). Some American women today take an interest in this kind of creativity, but usually flowers — bought in even and uninteresting dozens — are merely dropped into bowls or vases to create their own haphazard arrangements. Interior decoration is too often the handiwork of some commercial shop or a copy of a magazine's pictures. Individuality is lacking and, where existent, seldom produces truly aesthetic effects. There is comfort in the average

American home but very little of true beauty which has in it the housewife's own well-developed creativity and imagination. This kind of beauty is not to be purchased in shops and is not achieved by a mere reading of current magazines. It must come from long training of fundamental creative urges, a training which few American women either have or seem to want. There are exceptions, of course — we hope a growing number of them.

Neither is the average American housewife of today a good organizer and manager. In spite of having the best equipment in the world to work with, in spite of commercial services of a number and kind that women in other countries scarcely dream of, many American homes are a chaos of confusion. Several years ago, in an article written for the *Atlantic Monthly,* Della Cyrus painted a picture of this confusion in most dreary tones.[38] The reader himself becomes weary following her account of women being distracted by telephone bells, late deliveries, tardy plumbers, crying babies, delayed husbands, and many another "annoyance." Miss Cyrus' own aim in writing as she did was that of showing just how difficult woman's life in the home really is. But certainly, a justified query of reply might be: "Why is it so difficult?" A part of the answer we might also suggest.

Without in the least minimizing the range and seriousness of the problems housewives face, there can be little doubt that poor management accounts for a great deal of the confusion in the meeting of them. Grocers, plumbers, and service persons of every kind victimize housewives both because they know they can and because they themselves are victimized by housewives.

The hours American women spend in marketing alone is uneconomical for everyone. Observation has proved that it is not unusual for women in cities to stand (clutching in their hands a call-number) an hour or more in a bake shop just to buy a cake and six rolls for one evening's meal. This is but one illustration

---

[38] Della Cyrus, "What's Wrong with the Family?" *Atlantic Monthly,* vol. 178 (November 1946), pp. 67–73.

of the hundreds which might be given. In this day of refrigerators, freezers, aluminum foil, hydrators, and a host of other inventions for storage, marketing time can and should be cut by many hours. A few woman, but all too few, have proved that it can be done. Many will meet the argument with a retort that modern homes are not built with the storage space requisite to such long-range planning. But whose fault is it that kitchens and storage space get smaller with each year's building — the architect's or the housewife's?

We freely admit these criticisms lean to the side of the severe. We know they do not apply to *all* women. The number to whom they can be applied is, however, very large and the trend toward its increase is moving rapidly. *Modern women themselves will not do everything, or even very much, to stay the trend. The reason they will not is that the responsibility for it is not really theirs — certainly not solely theirs.*

In the history we have traced, we saw the trend coming. In the values Americans hold to so firmly we found some of the origins of its evolution. The emphasis upon the occupational system as the main avenue to success; the stress upon the autonomy of individuals; the use of women as status symbols; even the idealization of women — all these and much more that we have previously discussed have served to tear away the rewards and prestige attached to domestic tasks. These tasks, with the exception of those specifically defined as being in the mother role, are generally viewed as second-rate activities which women do "when they have to." The truly interesting activities lie *outside* the home, hence the women who are still held *within* it speak of isolation and show resentment at being cut off from what they have been taught in books, in classrooms, in jobs, and in travel to value most highly.

For the most part, the women of today are trained according to the patterns which were originally evolved for a training of men. Girls sit with boys in the same classrooms, read the same books, and very often play the same games.

Even the patterns of adolescence which push girls — at least some girls — to a use of glamour techniques are only superficially different. For, as we have said before, glamour is a means to success. Furthermore, it is a highly individualistic kind of success in which the competition is often keen enough to be labeled cruel. There is in a use of it, and in all else for which girls are trained, virtually the same stress upon independence and autonomy that maturing boys are made to feel. It is even expected that most women will be capable of supporting themselves in case they do not marry or in those times when emergencies demand that they work. It is a *contingency education* that is being given at present to most women. It is as if everyone were saying that women should be trained as men are trained *just in case* they must compete with them while still hoping that they will not have occasion to use the training.

The hope is firmly rooted in a widely shared expectation that the vast majority of women will marry and become wives and mothers — and housewives too. Even though the schooling in the art of being wives, mothers, and housewives is meager to an extreme, no one — not even a majority of the women themselves — considers other alternatives very seriously. Married women simply are, or should be, housewives. They are a source of trouble and arouse anxieties when and if they become something else — as of course many today are.

The reasons for the attitudes are plain enough. They are mainly to be found in that deep and sentimental reverence everyone has for family life even though the family unit is really more of a training ground for individualistic and independent persons than it is an end in itself. Few in this country ever have or are likely to suggest a substitute for the family system as the Russians once did. In spite of the lack of strength in generational ties and the other characteristics we described earlier, love for family life is great indeed, and many of the very deepest sentiments are centered on it.

Of all the sentiments, those attached to the mother are probably the strongest.

Lincoln expressed them well long ago when he said: "All I am I owe to my angel mother." But Lincoln's mother was a frontier woman whose housewifely duties were as highly valued as her mother role. In contrast, today's women are thrown into the highly contradictory situation of being on the one hand *just housewives* and on the other almost compulsively *adored mothers.*

One can have no hesitation in asserting that American women of all classes take the obligations of the mother role very seriously. That most women, especially those of the middle class, want desperately to learn the ways of being a "good mother" is attested to by the wide sale of books on child rearing, by the many anxious trips to doctors' offices or to baby clinics, by the organization of mothers' clubs and a wide variety of other activities. Recent psychological theories about child rearing are making many of these women more conscientious — and in some cases even more anxious — than ever.

The questions being raised here are of a different order and are, we would maintain, the essential background into which the more narrowly defined psychological theories must be fitted. Very little of that which is being written today on the mother-child relationships gives adequate consideration to the contradictions in the housewife and mother roles. Very little deals at much length with the unsatisfactory nature of many husband-wife relationships or even with the fact of there being too little of the father's influence in the average home of today. Yet these are the very factors which are preventing many women from being the kind of mothers they themselves want, and the whole society expects them, to be. The conscious will is often of the best, but the situation for a realizing of what is willed is not good.

There are many current criticisms of mothers who cling to their young ones in ways that prevent their maturity and not infrequently produce in them neurotic tendencies of one kind and another. Books have been written about *Momism.* It has also been reported that a major

reason for the rejection of many young men for service in the last war was an "abnormal" attachment to their mothers. Almost as frequent as criticisms of this kind are those which berate mothers for a neglect of children while they themselves seek money, prestige, or some other satisfaction in activities outside the home.

Whatever the particular criticisms of particular groups of women may be, the facts we have mentioned are the common ground for all of them. It is only the particular responses which differ. Some women confine their interests to the home, endure isolation and a feeling of being left out of things, give up activities and tasks for which they were once well trained — do all this and more because their feelings of a mother's obligations are strong. Consciously, they may not even be aware of the frustrations which inevitably result. Yet how often these women make known to highly perceptive children their unconscious feelings and give them an uneasy awareness that mother deserves so much because she herself has given up so much for them.

There are other women who really have very few feelings of frustration during the whole of their children's developmental period. They accept the totality of the domestic role with good grace because of the many satisfactions of its mother aspect. Then all too quickly — in this age of few children and many means of staying youthful — they find themselves faced with having to let children go free to become a part of a new generation of independent Americans. Dr. Mead describes the situation in these words:

It is all the harder for the mother of adolescent children when the break comes, when the children leave home for school or jobs and her task is over. Every social pressure to which she is subjected tells her that she should not spoil her children's lives, that she should let them lead their own lives, that she should make them independent and self-sufficient. Yet the more faithfully she obeys these injunctions, the more she is working herself out of a job. Some day, while she is still a young woman, she will have to face a breakfast-table with only one face across it, her husband's, and she will be alone, quite alone, in a home of their own. She is out of a job; her main justification, the work for which she "gave up everything," is gone, and yet there are still two, possibly three, meals a day to get, the door to be answered, the house to be cleaned. But there are only dishes for two and floors do not need to be polished so often when there are no children's feet to track them up. She isn't completely out of a job, but she is on the shelf, kicked upstairs, given one of those placebos by which large organizations whose employees have tenure try to disguise from the employee who is still too young to be retired the fact that he ought to be.[39]

It should not be difficult to understand why it is that so many women are loath to see broken the strong emotional ties between themselves and their children.

Beneath all this confusion, and to some extent more serious than any of it, is the inadequacy for either men or women of the husband-wife relationship. Two of the reasons for the inadequacy were cited above in the quotation from David Cohn's article. American men, he claims, are too much tied to their mothers, are too eternally adolescent to enter fully into a mature man-woman relationship. Or, if this is not the case, they frequently become too absorbed with jobs and business affairs to give the time such a relationship demands. Often both factors are combined. In spite of the somewhat flippant tone of Mr. Cohn's remarks, he was not just being cynical for an effect. Others today are equally concerned with the fact that so many of our men seem to be small boys who want to marry mothers. There is an ever increasing amount of clinical evidence for the verdict of masculine immaturity.

It is not maintained, of course, that all American men are immature or that in contrast all American women are mature. There are countless women who are only little girls grown large and from whom

few adult responses can be expected. The lack of the ability to achieve a successful adjustment in sexual relations is actually more pronounced in the women of our middle class than in the men of the same class. However, both the males and females of this large class in American society show in their sexual adjustments to each other, and in their attitudes toward the whole realm of the sexual, many of the inhibitions of a stern puritan ethic. Even though changes in attitudes are occurring, even though some persons are quite consciously trying to prevent the development in children of too strong attitudes of guilt concerning sexual attitudes and practices, the once firm linkage of sex and sin is far from broken.

It is, therefore, only in relative terms that we are speaking of the greater tendency in American men to continue to display in their behavior many adolescent responses. This immaturity — whether of men or women — is not something which can be changed in a day. Furthermore, there is, in our opinion, some real doubt that it will be achieved simply through alterations in family life. The pressures put upon our men in this society are as important a factor in producing their responses as are patterns of family relationships. Or, at least, let us say that both kinds of factors operate together.

With this qualification we do admit to high-order probability that any change in the feminine role which will serve to reduce the emotional intensity of mother-child, and most especially mother-son, relationships will also make for a greater maturity in American men. But this alone is not enough. American sons, especially those in cities, need more sustained and meaningful relationships with their fathers than most of them now have. Almost everyone who is studying the problems of children agrees that young American boys are too much and too often under the control of women.

Fathers, as we have stated before, are too much outside the home, are put too completely into roles which are autonomous and narrowly defined, while mothers are too much in the home and

---

[39] *Male and Female*, p. 337.

have roles that are both too diffuse and too much lacking in autonomy. The effects of the difference are as serious for the husband-wife relationship as for the maturation process of children. One marked effect — previously mentioned but not discussed — is that of creating a wide separation of the spheres of masculine and feminine interests.

In markedly familistic societies, such as the Spanish-American village groups, allocation of very different tasks and interests to the two sexes creates few problems. The primary reason that it creates few is that all individuals, whether men or women, are expected to accept the welfare and the unity of the total family as a major goal. The family is regarded as an end in and by itself. American values with their much greater emphasis upon the independence of each member's interests would certainly seem to require a different kind of integration of sex-differentiated activities. They also make a truly rigid allocation of interests less feasible.

There is at present too wide a separation of interests into those which are masculine and those which are feminine. Men, by and large, confine their interests to the problems of making a living; women rear the children, take the lead in most community affairs, and engage in the many activities which will help secure the family's social position and give it some claim to having cultivated tastes. On each side there is seldom very much knowledge of, or interest in, what the other one is doing. With the passing of the years the gap between the interests widens until finally even conversations on much besides the sheer commonplaces of everyday life become rare or disappear entirely. That much-hoped-for companionship either does not materialize or is found to lack real depth.

VIII. MODERN WOMEN OUTSIDE THE HOME

What is it that some women seek to find for themselves in pursuing a career or in "holding down a job" either full or part time? What is the meaning of a continuous participation in community groups and organizations for so many other women? Of what importance to women and to the whole country is the fairly large-scale pursuit of cultural interests — the study clubs, adult-education programs, the countless lectures, concerts, and theater performances? What is the effect upon women of the many remaining hours of idleness? These are the major questions which will be used to focus our discussion of the American woman's activities *outside* the home.

Women and Jobs

We know from statistics that fully a third of American women are now gainfully employed in a wide variety of occupations. That a large percentage of the total — approximately 60 per cent — is accounted for by women who either are or have been married is a fact that was mentioned above. Thus, in spite of tenaciously held attitudes, all American women are *not* primarily housewives at all.

Yet we must hastily make corrections in the impressions which raw statistics give. As Dr. Mead once commented, there have never been many sanctions imposed upon the women of the lower economic groups who work outside the home. On the contrary, if women of these groups can provide either necessities or advantages for their families by working for pay, there is more of approval than disapproval. It is an approval which is often mixed with pity, to be sure. Or, perhaps, still more often the attitude rests upon the widely used American rationalization that some people are by nature unable to fit into the ideal patterns. It is also to be remembered that many of the women in the tables of statistics are of another approved kind — those who are forced by family emergencies to take jobs.

Only after removing from the lists all those working from some kind of necessity would we be able to state what percentage of American women — married women, that is — are working as a matter of choice. We do not have complete or accurate enough over-all figures at the present time to come to definite conclusions on the percentages in the several groups. The best figures available are those compiled from the questioning of selected samples of working women. These indicate, as the following quotation will show, that a majority of the married women in the labor force say they are there because of necessity rather than personal desire.

Studies show that a large majority of women workers are financially responsible not only for their own support but for support of dependents as well. In 1944–45, the Women's Bureau found in personal interviews with over 13,000 women employed in 10 war congested areas throughout the country, that 84 percent of the women worked to support themselves and others. An additional 8 percent also gave economic reasons for working, such as to own a home, to be free from debt, or to pay for their children's education. Only 8 percent of the women worked primarily as a way of self expression. Fifteen percent of the women who lived in family groups were the sole wage earners contributing to household expenses. Ninety-two percent of the employed women who lived with their families contributed regularly toward family expenses. Over half of them contributed between 50 and 100 percent of their earnings to the family group. Almost all the women who lived alone (one in every five women) supported themselves; some also had dependents.[40]

However, these statements and figures cannot be allowed to stand without challenge. Because of the prevailing attitudes about the employment of married women, there probably is a tendency on the part of some women to emphasize necessity rather than choice. Also, because the American standard of living is an ever expanding one, it is very often difficult for either the working woman herself or the person interrogating her to draw the line between "necessity" and the type of choice that is determined by a desire for better things.

While it is safe to say that an overwhelming majority of American women want to marry, whether they ever do or not, there is still a large number who deliberately choose careers in preference to marriage. For these women, many of whom are found in the professions and in special kinds of business, the satisfactions derived from the work world are paramount. And, although sometimes of a different order, the rewards given by the job are also primary ones in the lives of unmarried women who work because they have no alternative way to support themselves. In all the crying out against women in the occupations there seems to be some forgetting of the rights of all these women whom the American type of society has either forced into independence or permitted a choice of it. These are the women who are heavily penalized in what they are allowed to be and accomplish both by the prevailing attitudes and by the behavior on the job of their more contingency-minded sisters.

The contingency-minded women are all those who work only when they absolutely must or at those times when some need is felt for additional funds for self or family. It is these women who have few seriously responsible attitudes toward either the work they perform or the organizations in which they work. They quit without proper notice and do not turn up for jobs previously accepted; their absentee rate is high, and their incentives are too slight to make for good performance. These judgments are not mere guesswork, and they do not apply to just one type or one economic class of girls. The placement offices of eastern women's colleges firmly underline their validity. A recent and extensive study of the work habits of girls in the restaurant business of a large city verifies them for another type and class of girl. The wartime records of offices and factories give further ample proof of them.

It is no wonder, therefore, that many employers hesitate to put some kinds of responsibilities on women; that they have a reluctance to spend precious time and money on the training of girls "who will

---

[40] United States Department of Labor, 1947.

marry at a moment's notice and quit." It is also understandable why men think they have good reason to resent feminine competition and often try to keep women confined to certain kinds of jobs.

But this is only one side of the picture. It is the men themselves who are partly responsible for the contingency conception of woman's work. It sometimes is their idealization of women which makes them loath to have wives and daughters work outside the home. Much more often it is a fear that their own status as providers or their reputation for success will be put into jeopardy. It is still another fault of men that they seldom admit to the fact that there are many women who must work and hence are deserving of the same opportunities as they are. Perhaps a main reason for not admitting it is the fairly justified fear that an invasion of women into the occupations on anything like equal terms will leave them very little that is not dominated or strongly influenced by women.

The situation is exceedingly complicated and fast becoming more so. There is at present an evident strengthening of the desire in women — many of them middle-class women who have not in the past figured large in the ranks of the employed — to work as a matter of choice and for reasons of personal fulfillment. Some of these women continue on the job from the very date of their marriages; the greater number begin to look earnestly for work after some five or six years of marriage during which two or three children have been born. In almost all cases it has been the growing dissatisfactions felt in being an isolated housewife, the glimpsing of the widening gap between their own and their husband's interests, or a lack of opportunity to use the training and knowledge in which they had previously invested so much time which makes them fearful of a dreary and empty future.

The present generation of women seems to have a greater awareness than did many of their mothers of the strength and power of the occupational system. They know that success in it is really the only kind of success for which most Americans still have an unqualified respect. Thus, what they are trying to claim for themselves is the opportunity to participate in the total society as man's equal rather than as his symbol. Their claims, when combined with those of unmarried women employees, are the core of the arguments heard everywhere today in discussions of civil rights for women.

There is a great deal in these arguments which merits close attention. As Americans, women do have the right to something more than a symbolic participation in the all-important industrial and business world. And, certainly, all the many women who are forced to work do not warrant the many antagonisms and discriminations they constantly encounter. But if there is no denying the validity of these arguments, neither is it possible to deny that anything like a full-time participation of women in the occupations will so diminish what is left in the domestic component of the feminine role that it will become truly negligible. And as it shrinks down into nothingness the frustrations in the mother role will mount accordingly. There is, in other words, small chance that very many women can be both successful mothers and successful job or career women on a full-time basis. Yet this is precisely what many women are already trying to do and what even more women show signs of wanting to do.

Women in Community Affairs

A not infrequent comment today is that women run our communities. The accusation is not, of course, to be taken too literally. Men still hold many of the responsible positions in town governments and in many voluntary citizens' organizations as well. Nevertheless, the trend toward a feminine domination of community affairs is easily recognized in many places. The most obvious domination is seen in the residential suburbs of large cities. It was a minister of one of the churches in such a suburb who was heard to remark that whenever he had need of the services of the men of his congregation he always put the matter up to the women first. They, not he, could make husbands and sons volunteer.

There are countless illustrations of the growing influence of women. It was chiefly women, for example, who engineered the political campaign in a fairly large eastern city which brought the downfall of a long-entrenched city administration and reared in its place a City Manager form of government. Those particular women were almost all members of the League of Women Voters, which is now a widely recognized and much respected organization.

It is women again who account for most of the membership of Parent-Teacher-Associations. The majority of local welfare organizations, community-relations committees, and a host of other types of community groups also have a predominantly feminine membership. There is, in fact, little need to spell out very far anything so obvious as this greatly increased participation of women in all phases of community life. The main reasons for it — or at least the rationalizations made to explain it — are: Men are busy and women have the time; women also know much more about the needs of the community since they spend so much time in it and men often spend so much time out of it. Obviously a more basic reason is that busy men deliberately leave to women all these activities which would take too much time away from jobs.

There certainly can be no doubt that many of the tasks women undertake in churches, schools, local governments, welfare organizations, and all the rest provide for them a real sense of usefulness and a range of group participation which many have no other way of finding. Furthermore, the work actually is important, and much of it if not all (the country, of course, is greatly *overorganized*) must be done by some one. These facts should not be overlooked.

There probably is less danger however, of their being overlooked than the many other much less favorable facts. There is a great deal to be found in the conditions as they now are which is neither favorable to women as individuals nor to the husband-wife relationship. To go back to the point we raised a moment ago: Whenever a husband — anyone's husband — is found saying "Leave it to the women," whenever he shows real reluctance to give his own time to community matters, there is almost always an implied, though often not well-verbalized, attitude that the tasks in question are of only a secondary importance and significance. Business affairs are those of first importance. If parents must know and talk with teachers, if "the poor" require looking after, if racial-conflict episodes must be investigated or new forms of government introduced, women can handle most of it. If the going becomes rough or the issues appear too critical, then, and then only, are most men found to be willing to step in and "put things on a businesslike basis." (Women do not, of course, have much to say or do with many of the local affairs of areas run by giant political machines. But neither do many middle-class business men.)

A second definite effect of the trend toward a growing feminine and decreasing masculine management of community life is a further separation — a further dichotomizing — of the spheres of masculine and feminine interests. Were men and women, husbands and wives, participating jointly in the affairs of their communities, were their interests in them of equal intensity, common bonds would quickly develop. These bonds are badly needed if the aim is to integrate better the masculine and feminine roles.

There are other dissatisfactions for women in many of these community activities. One is a result of the persistent efforts of Americans to professionalize everything which comes to be regarded as essential or important. There was a time when almost all social-welfare work was volunteer work. Many of the post-Civil War women's clubs took care of much of it. Today most of the welfare organizations are governed by the community or nation, and the responsible positions in them almost all go to professionally trained and salaried workers.

Even the remaining individually supported organizations are for the most part staffed by salaried professionals. Often all that is left to the well-intentioned but untrained volunteer worker is the odd job for which the rewards of accomplishment are small. Or, volunteer services are not accepted at all. Many graduates of the woman's college where I once taught have reported in recent years a firm refusal of their services. They are told to go back to school, obtain the requisite training, and then come back to apply for a paid and scheduled job.

This is not sheer perversity on the part of those who have taken the time to obtain training. It is often stated in treatises on organization that irrefutable evidence proves that volunteer workers are too generally irresponsible to be trusted with many important tasks. It does, indeed, seem to be a fact that in this society a sense of responsibility is not easily developed unless a pay check or some other quite tangible and concrete reward (specific school grades, for example) is forthcoming as a recognition of it.

Another of the unfortunate aspects of community work is the woman's frequent feeling of finding recognition in it only as a representative of her family — often quite specifically as her husband's status symbol. In all such groups as parent-teacher or the others pertaining to children, the mother is clearly representing the family. Other kinds of work may well interest her more, yet she is expected to participate in these particular groups. Her role is not an *autonomous* one; instead it is a symbolic *representative* one.[41] In all that relates to children this is not usually a matter of much seriousness. For some women at least, it becomes a matter of much more significance when they realize they are asked to be directors on various boards not so much because of any proven abilities of their own as because they happen to be the wives of prominent business men.

Of course, not all women participate as family representatives. There are actually two types of community-minded women. In the first group are those who represent families or have the aim of furthering family social and economic interests. It depends both upon the husband's position and their own skill whether they are commended for being helpful to ambitious men or condemned as "social climbers." Good examples of the second group are the women in organizations like the League of Women Voters. These are women who clearly express an independence of action and to whom recognition on an individualistic basis is often freely given.

Women as Culture Bearers

It was stated earlier that one of the significant developments in American middle-class society was that of handing over to women the major responsibility for the pursuit of cultural and aesthetic interests. It was pointed out that in this case, too, the implied attitude was that all such interests were of second-order importance. The attitude has been so strengthened with the passing of the years, particularly the last eighty years of colossal economic expression, that there has been added to it the further idea that women in their role of culture bearer should primarily be *appreciators* rather than creators. Truly creative development in the fields of art, music, and even literature — whether by men or women — has not yet achieved great magnitude in the United States.

This is not to say there has been no creativity at all. A few Americans today are making contributions in the fields of modern art and modern music, but when what they produce is compared with the contributions of a France or an Italy it can be seen to be of minor significance. (This is not allowing, of course, for contributions in the field of popular music, some aspects of which are coming to be highly regarded.) In literature there have been one or two giants — Herman Melville, for example — but for the most part the "best" books have had the utilitarian phrasing of "social protest." A Lewis' *Main Street*, a Steinbeck's *Grapes of Wrath*, and a

---

[41] A distinction introduced by Professor Talcott Parsons in lectures at Harvard University.

Dos Passos' *U.S.A.* are not nearly so much art for art's sake as they are probes for the social conscience. In the case of other types of books, the tendency is to pay small attention to any except those which become "best sellers."

All these attitudes make for a difficult situation for women. Almost all women are made to feel the obligation of developing in themselves and in their children an appreciation for the things of mind and spirit (for religion, too, is largely woman's province today), and then are told that much of what they do is merely supplementary — an embellishment — rather than essential. Of them all only the religious interests are viewed as essential, and, even here, we find a tendency to regard religious and business ethics as being different in degree if not in kind.

Women have tried hard to carry on in their role of culture bearer, but one wonders what the real benefits either to themselves or to the nation are. There is so much of aimlessness in so many of their efforts. One interest is pursued at one moment and another at the next. Book clubs are organized for the discussing of commercially selected books on many unrelated subjects. We find the woman who listens one year to lectures given by some professor borrowed from a nearby university on the subject of geology; the next year she becomes absorbed in a similar course on Mayan archaeology. And literally thousands of women everywhere attend thousands of lectures on thousands of topics. Indeed, this lecturing to audiences composed of culture-seeking women has also become "Big Business."

What is done with all these facts and theories which are so haphazardly presented and as haphazardly absorbed? Something is certainly gained, but how much is the question. Here, too, there is a lack of concentration of aim coupled with some doubt in the minds of many women of the usefulness of it all.

Whiling Away the Hours

There is still another type of American woman for whom none of the affairs of the work world, the community, or any of the cultural interests has much meaning. These are the women who devote all available free time to leisure activities. And, even though we are here pointing to them as a type, let us not forget that almost all American women belong, in varying degrees, to the group. It is commonly expected that married women will find some free time each week — if not each day — to visit with friends, go to luncheons or bridge parties, chat on telephones, or go on shopping sprees. It is, however, only when all such activities are carried to an extreme and the seeking out of them becomes an end in itself that we can speak of the "idle" woman.

Una Bernard Sait, who has given us one of the best of present-day analyses of family life in *New Horizons for the Family,* presents this view of the situation:

Social waste is obviously involved where the community is losing a large part of its potential labor power. According to Lorine Pruette, these women on part-time jobs "from the social standpoint form a social menace. By the thousands they wander up and down city streets, looking for something to fill the idle lonely hours. They are a mark, not only of their husband's ability to keep them in comfort, not only of 'vicarious consumption,' but of social inefficiency, of society's failure adequately to make use of its human material." For the most ominous aspect of the social waste involved is the soul-destroying effect of idleness on the women themselves and through them on their families, their children in particular. Some among them are efficient housekeepers; though where the only interest is in the routine details of daily life, a fussy over-insistence on order and cleanliness is often the result, which may be as destructive of home atmosphere as the inefficient home management which is so often the corollary of an unsupervised, unstandardized performance of household tasks. These are the women who gossip and "window-shop," who become "movie-fans," and "bridge-fiends." Deprived of the discipline of purposeful, efficiently-performed work, they become contented with their lot, in proportion as they grow soft in body and flabby in mind.[42]

Mrs. Sait's statement was made in 1938. Whether she would say the same today, or whether it would be fair of anyone to make similar statements, is a question. In the years since 1938 many more American women have gone into the occupations, many more have begun to take an active part in civic organizations, and there has been an increase in the amount of intelligent study of such problems as child development. However, everyone knows many women whose behavior in whole or some part fits the description. There are still many "bridge-fiends," and many a person has been made uneasy by fussy housewives who empty ash trays before cigarettes are finished. A visit to any large department store or the shops of some famous "avenue" will give ample proof that looking, shopping, the buying of things one day and taking them back the next are the fairly aimless ways in which many women spend the hours of many days.

The status-symbol conception of woman's role and the glamour component come together at this point. However restless idleness may cause women to be, there is still the notion that being free to while away the hours as one chooses has prestige value. The pursuit of the ways and means of remaining youthfully beautiful — of being glamourously young instead of matronly — also brings its satisfaction to many women. Indeed, if once again we judge by advertisements, by woman's pages of newspapers or current magazines, we must say the whole society puts pressure on all women to remain glamourously youthful. It is not strange, therefore, that some women with little else to do and too few other interests make living up to the demand their main goal in life. The chief difference between America and other societies in this respect is that in

this country there are so many more women who follow the patterns. This is a mass-production country which does not confine any luxuries, not even those of beauty, to the select few.

IX. THE ROLE OF THE AMERICAN WOMAN IN THE FUTURE

Let us turn now to a summary of the tentative suggestions for change in the role of the American woman which in one way or another have been either hinted at or openly remarked in the above analysis of the role. These suggestions are only suggestions and are meant to stimulate or provoke discussion and thought, but as suggestions we feel they have the merit of having been derived from an analysis of something more than the apparent and the obvious.

*Broadening of the American
Value System*

Time and again in parts of the previous discussion it was stated that Americans tend to put most of their first-grade "value eggs" in the one basket of the economic. It was said that the affairs of community life, cultural interests, indeed every other aspect of life, are all viewed as having a second — or lower — level of importance. The matters of primary concern are the specific problem of making a living and the general interest in expanding production.

Since this is the pursuit of our main interest — is still the only road on which one can travel to a highly respected success — it is understandable why women are bidding high on the ways and means of traveling it. They are no longer content, being themselves individuals in an individualistic society, to wander down byways which are less well paved, or not paved at all, with the symbolic bricks of success.

The attitudes of American men — attitudes which stress the value of business and industry and make men loath to develop outside interests and loath again to take on many civic responsibilities — were also mentioned. It was seen how the coupling of their own concentra-

---

[42] *New Horizons for the Family*, pp. 448–449.

tion on the economic with their attitude of "leaving to women" so many of the other necessary tasks has produced a self-expanding wedge which pushes farther and farther apart the interest spheres of the two sexes.

Certainly Americans have every right to be intensely proud of their record of economic expansion and proud, too, of the many benefits it has brought to the great majority of American citizens. Both are truly amazing. "Within the past century we have achieved a five-fold increase in net output per man hour. The net output of our economy in 1944 was 27 times as large as in 1850 — $161 billion compared to $6 billion." [43] Health and medical services for many have been enormously increased; in a majority of American homes, even the most unaesthetic ones, comforts of every kind are found. There are some forty million passenger cars on our roads with people in them traveling everywhere, and thirty million more are predicted for the near future unless world events prevent their manufacture. Yes, we have a right to be proud and are even to be forgiven for some of the "headiness" in our pride.

Is this production to continue to increase, will it taper off at some particular level, or will it begin to decline? Optimists see no diminution and even see in the harnessing of atomic energy for industrial purposes the possibilities of greater increase. Pessimists, or realists as they often call themselves, take the opposite view. Neither answer is certain because there are so many factors, known and unknown, which will influence the trend. But one factor which may well prove to be of great importance in family relations is the decrease in satisfaction which many men today feel in their industrial and business activities. Although there are still thousands upon thousands of men who can be called small entrepreneurs, there is no doubt that Big Business is now in control and leads the way. To many men, being a little fish in the pond of Big Business offers fewer incentives and rewards than being the great fish in a private little puddle. They go on working, to be sure, because a living for self and family must be earned, but other interests begin to loom larger in importance than was once the case.

The sheer facts of shorter working days and weeks and an increase in the amount of vacation time are also opening the way for an expansion of interests beyond the job. Herein lies one of the best hopes for a future integration of masculine and feminine interests and for total family interests as well. But it will not just automatically happen. It will depend upon what interests are developed and whether they are of an order of creativity to produce significant joint satisfactions.

It is a striking fact that up to the present time most Americans have tended to regard time off from work as recreation time and spend it, for the most part, in passive forms of amusement. At the movies, in the ball park, seated by the radio, at football games or wandering through the zoo — it makes little difference which, because in them all the individual is seeking ways of having others provide the amusement. Not even traveling about the country in cars is very much different. And how can anyone believe seriously (some say they do) that the quite passive acceptance of television amusement is going to re-create family unity?

In all these things creative drives and expression are absent. Does the absence mean that the boundless energy and creativity for which the country is famous is truly limited to the economic field? Are Americans actually incapable of redirecting some of it into the channels of the intellectual and the aesthetic? Cannot some of it be concentrated on developing new kinds of participation in our communities? So far the signs that it either can or will be are few. Yet this is what will bring real enrichment to the whole American way of life. It is also one of the surest ways of providing the means for men and women to develop the mutual interests which

---

[43] J. Frederick Dewhurst and associates, *America's Needs and Resources* (New York: Twentieth Century Fund, 1947), p. 680.

will bring greater strength and meaning in their relationships with each other.

Domestic Work Needs to Be Reëvaluated

While striving to develop new interests of many kinds, learning to value many different kinds of activities more highly than in the past, it would also seem essential to work for a redefinition of the domestic component of the feminine role and bring back to it some of the prestige it once had. Or, a better way of phrasing the suggestion is that there be created in it a new and richer meaning than it has *ever* had. No one wants American women to be the kind of hard-driven housewives their colonial grandmothers were. It would be ridiculous to imagine that the women of today are going to spend all of their time at home. There is no need for it.

In fact, one of the things most urgently needed is training for the kind of planning and organizing which will cut even deeper than is the case at the moment into the amount of time needed for many household tasks. A part of the time gained may well be spent on activities outside the home, but it is to be hoped that as much, or more of it, will go into a new kind of domestic creativeness.

The country has both the raw products and the equipment necessary for the development of a fine cuisine at a minimum cost of time and energy. Surely the American palate has greater sensitivities than can be pleased or satisfied by the relatively indifferent cooking of most present-day American housewives. The French, the Italian, the Chinese, the Mexican, and many another people have far more interesting food than the United States, and they create it from much less. And what is said of this one particular domestic achievement can be easily said of all the rest — the more aesthetic treatment of home interiors, for example, or more interesting and less stereotyped social gatherings. A complete list of all the potentialities would be a long one.

Admittedly, it is one thing to ask for a new evaluation of domesticity and quite another to achieve it. Neither the attitudes of women nor those of men will be changed quickly, yet change in both will be required. A vital part of the process is certain to be some change in the education of American women (men, too, of course, but our main concern is with women). Women must be better trained both in their own appreciation of what they are doing and also in the actual ways of doing it. If women are different from men, and we would maintain that they inevitably are different in important ways, there must be a systematic allowance for the differences in the education they receive.

A great deal of the education of women as women will necessarily be a matter of home training. This sounds easier than it is because of the many mothers, themselves averse to so much of the domestic, who are producing in daughters the "do it when you have to" attitude. However, once women are more fully aware of the problem than many now are, they will probably work earnestly for change. The women of America have a long, long record of working hard for all sorts of changes and "reform."

At the more formal level of education there are difficulties of greater magnitude. Primary, secondary, and higher education, as well, are on a mass basis and do not allow much for individual differences. The struggle of women, and some men as well, to equalize the educational rights and opportunities of men and women has been too long and is too well rooted in basic values for us even to think of suggesting that we now strive for a new kind of separation of them. Moreover, the rigid separation of boys and girls, of men and women, in our schools and colleges and a marked differentiation in what is taught them would work *against* rather than for the kind of integration of masculine and feminine interests we have been arguing for.

Relative to the sex segregation we now have in education, it is an interesting and telling fact that it is usually the women's colleges which give girls the least training in anything domestic. Originally founded as a means of giving to women educational opportunities equal to men and continuously staffed throughout the years primarily by unmarried women, these colleges have tended always to maximize sameness and minimize difference. A majority of the girls who attend the colleges are themselves uninterested in domesticity and hence accept the emphasis in what they are taught. An effort was made a few years ago in one of the more progressive eastern women's colleges to inaugurate a program in the domestic arts. It failed for the most part because the girls could not be stimulated to a positive response. According to one of the teachers who initiated the program, real interest was stirred only when the college could bring to the lecture platform a brilliant career woman who also happened to have some interest in cooking, household management, or interior decorating. Domestic arts as an exotic adjunct to the prestigeful occupational career are one thing — but for themselves quite another!

Many large universities, some small coeducational colleges, and a larger number of secondary schools do include in their curricula courses which were once called domestic science and now have the more dignified title, "home economics." It is another commentary on the trends of the times, however, that the slanting of what is taught in these courses is toward the scientific rather than the artistic. Of even greater significance is the fact that most of the women who take up home economics as a major field of study have the primary aim of becoming well-trained dieticians, nutritionists, or managers of one sort or another. It is not predominantly the housewives of tomorrow who are found in these college departments.

In contrast to these tendencies and trends we could argue that home life and the domestic tasks which go into the making of it are an important part of a broadly conceived idea of good living. Without in the least urging highly specialized courses in cooking or any other of the domestic arts, it would seem advantageous to include in the education of women more of the teaching of the meaning of what they are learning for home life than is now taught. Men also would benefit from a similar training that has a masculine rather than a feminine focus.

The actual working out of the plan or plans which would allow for these and other developments in general education will not be easy. Fortunately, there are enough persons both in the educational field and outside it who are concerned with the problem for us to expect some significant results in a not too distant future. Several books on the education of women have appeared in the last few years. One specific suggestion which Dr. Margaret Mead is said to have made is that we create a new kind of university in which the men and women would be enrolled in separate "colleges" rather than in one great body. In such a university many of the courses for men and women would be the same; some could be distinctively oriented to the more specific masculine or feminine interests.

Women in the Occupations

The final suggestions we have to offer have to do with the place women can, or should, have in the American occupational system. The greatest of the contradictions in the woman's role would seem to be that which has arisen out of the conflict between the justified feeling of many women that they have a right to participate in that aspect of American life which is still the most important — the economic — and the validly reasoned argument that quite real differences exist between women as mothers and men as fathers. Others derive from the still prominent attitudes which on the one hand make for an idealization of women and on the other require her to be a status symbol.

On whichever side one may choose to stand in this argument, there are some undeniable facts. There actually are many millions of women already in the occupations, and the signs are few that many of them intend to make a full retreat. Some could not retreat even if they so wished. Also, we must recognize that the desire in some families for achieving certain levels of living is such that it demands more than a father's wages. Additionally, there is no overlooking the fact that more and more women are finding more satisfactions in systematically organized jobs than in the more diffuse and less well-organized volunteer activities. Thus, it seems certain that unless some way can be found to give some women full recognition and another way to permit many more women to have their own limited type of occupational interest there will be an increasing number of women seeking to take the man's way — full-time work in an ever increasing variety of occupations. The possible, indeed almost certain, results of this for community life and for the domestic life — even the mother role — have been noted.

In light of all these facts it would seem more to the point to find some substitute or alternative trend than to continue to contest the merits or demerits of the present one. We have three suggestions to offer. The first is that for the women who either must work or who, because of personal desire, choose full-time work, there be no discriminations in the pay they receive, in the positions made available to them, or in their rate of advancement. Even in the highest level of the professions there are still discriminations of all three kinds. One of the country's most brilliant women scientists was denied year after year her promotion to full professorship status primarily because she was a woman. Women physicians, except where they specialize in children's ills, have much more difficulty in establishing themselves than even less able men. Women themselves often refuse to go to women doctors.

A second suggestion is more of a hoped-for result than a proposal for a change in women's occupational interests. Is there not some reason to believe that if ways are found to increase the satisfactions in domestic life, in community services, and in cultural pursuits, fewer women will feel the compelling need to enter the occupations? They will have found other significantly rewarding ways in which they can both fulfill their desire to be essential to the society and achieve a richer and more balanced relationship with husbands and children.

A third suggestion is one that it is believed will be the most applicable to the largest number of women. It is also the most radical, yet not so radical but that one hears talk of it everywhere. One can hardly read anything about women today without encountering the proposal that part-time careers and jobs be created for them. Unfortunately, there is a connotation in the term "part time" of something which is intermittent and inconsequential. What we would propose instead is an occupational interest of "limited scope." There would be no segregation of women in a few particular types of jobs and no giving to them merely the jobs in which there are few requirements of responsibility and initiative. It is possible to develop positions — especially in this age of decreased work hours for everyone — which will have both short and flexibly arranged hours and still be jobs of real importance. Some, but as yet all too few, are being developed. Those few are enough, however, to prove that they are a truly possible answer to the need many women feel to combine domestic life with a job or career.

It may also be that a few highly *particularized* limited positions for married women should be developed. There are many arguments for, and few against, having school children taught in part by *married women who live in the school community*. Yet most school boards still rule against the married woman except as an occasional substitute teacher. Certain types of professional social-welfare work are probably also best handled by women in general and married women in particular. There are undoubtedly many other fields for which the limited work of married women could be as easily and as advantageously used.

There are countless objections which have been and will be raised to proposals of this order. Most of them are without much ground in fact except the argument that the accidents and incidents of home life make married women undependable employees. Here we would hark back to the hope that a new domestic era will give us better-managed homes, hence more time for women to engage in other activities. In addition, there will also be needed the better-organized household services which were previously mentioned as a possibility of the near future. There is really very little in the "limited scope" occupation for women which is not possible of being worked out.

Certainly the advantages would appear to be many. Fewer women will have to face the psychological distress of seeing their job done when children leave. Fewer will have to be content with a makeshift way of resolving the distress because they will have "kept their hand in" throughout the years. They will also, in most cases, have developed a better sense of money value for having had their own experience in earning money. Many of the mothers who now cling emotionally to their few children will

have less reason for the clinging. The husband-wife relationship will gain in closeness for having an added common interest. Even though the occupations of a husband and a wife may be in different fields, some common interest and greater understanding is bound to be achieved. It may also be added that relief for the husband from having to feel himself solely responsible for the support of his family would, in many cases, be considerable. He could soon be made to feel that he was freer to give more of himself to other family activities.

These suggestions may be realizable only in part. Other and better ones may soon be forthcoming. But whatever conceptions any of us now hold or may later develop concerning alterations in the role of American women, let us make no mistake in judgment about the seriousness of the problem. The evidence is conclusive that much of what is to happen in the evolution of American society will be in some large part dependent upon how the role of American women of the future is defined.

CHAPTER X

Value Conflicts

IN ALL human interactions evaluation is constantly taking place; we have to make some value judgments to introduce order and direction into our lives. We have to distinguish between people and events that have positive and negative "value attributes" for us; on these distinctions we base our decisions about future action. We each develop criteria from our interactions with others which permit us to make such distinctions. We learn to recognize quickly people and things "I like" and those "I do not like." In regard to people we often simplify this into terms of categories: "my kind of person" on the one hand, and "different sort of person" on the other. We use various shorthand signs or cues to make distinctions, for example, between adults and adolescents, college graduates and high school graduates, middle-class people and lower-class people, Protestants and Catholics, Christians and Jews, Americans and foreigners. Such cues may be items of clothing, accents of speech, hand gestures, skin color, facial characteristics. We eventually attribute value to the cues themselves in abstraction from the situations in which we originally learned them; they become so important to us that we have strong feelings about them. If our cues become criticized by those who use different ones, we ourselves may feel criticized and respond with anger.

These cues are abstractions drawn from many slightly different experiences which we categorize as similar. Consequently, as is true of all "maps," some details in the "territory" are omitted. We often find ourselves in conflict as a result of this abstraction process. No map which is abstracted from many situations can apply perfectly to any single situation. And, we often come upon a new situation and find that several maps apply partially, but none well. Lowell discusses this problem as "conflicts of principle."[1] He observes that we continue to feel strongly about each of our abstract principles, even though they may not be fully consistent with each other or fully applicable to the situation at hand.

We tend to feel positively toward people who share our principles and values and who employ similar maps in attributing values to experience. Our interactions with such people are apt to be smooth and reassuring. We know, largely without conscious thought, how to act with them and what to expect from them. If we have interacted frequently with people who use different maps or who hold different values, we may learn to understand and share these values and hence feel "comfortable" with a wide variety of people and groups. But if our interactions have been limited, our feelings of "belonging" may be

---

[1] Abbott Lawrence Lowell, "Conflicts of Principle," above, Chapter I. See also S. I. Hayakawa's description of the abstraction ladder, *Language in Thought and Action* (New York: Harcourt, Brace, 1949), chapter 10 (referred to above, Chapter II).

restricted to only a very few groups. For some of us, "my kind of people" hardly means more than the original primary group in which we were raised, the family plus a few neighbors.

As Homans points out, face-to-face groups develop codes of behavior, sets of norms.[2] From the individual's point of view these codes are statements of values about behavior, values which he shares with others, and they facilitate interaction within the group. The individuals in the group also come to share sentiments of solidarity based on the joint norms and the expected interaction they bring. In order to differentiate members from nonmembers, and thus enhance the sentiments of solidarity, groups often overemphasize the differences between their norms and those of outsiders. And they often come to believe that their norms are "better" than those of other groups.

The solidarity thus developed increases our interactions within our group and diminishes interactions with outsiders. Because our interactions with members of groups other than our own are limited, we tend to form oversimplified notions of what their norms actually are, based on superficial or inadequate observations of their behavior. These oversimplifications are often labeled and turn into stereotypes. Once we apply the label, we expect members of the group to behave according to stereotype expectancy, thus failing to observe differences between individuals.[3]

Face-to-face groups in our society overlap, creating a network of interactions that links people into wider aggregates. As a result, group norms become generalized, and large numbers of people who have no *direct* face-to-face contact share these generalized norms. This is what Kluckhohn seems to mean by "value orientations." [4] Thus, two individuals who have never met before might easily become acquainted on a trip. After a short conversation, they might discover that they have quite similar value orientations and use similar maps to attribute value to people and events. They soon feel like old friends — a sentiment which would be strengthened by reference to other types of people with whom they would not desire to associate. To maintain sentiments of solidarity — to avoid threatening isolation — people often bind themselves together by strongly emphasizing their "differences" from other types of people.

We place ourselves on the "social map" by identifying with groups or aggregates of people whose values we share. The particular ones chosen vary in different historical periods. At times the lineal family or local community was most important; other times the aggregate of people whose place in the economic hierarchy was the same ("executives" or "skilled mechanics") considered themselves as the same sort of people. Today nationality seems to be the strongest bond other than the immediate family — so strong that we take it for granted until it is challenged. For instance, if you were to ask a friend to describe himself, you might well get the reply: "My name is John Smith; of course, I am an American . . ." He thus tells you that his family and nationality are more important to him than all other memberships.

In order for national values to serve as common symbols of solidarity for

---

[2] See Chapter IX. Homans defines norm as follows: "A norm, then, is an idea in the minds of the members of a group, an idea that can be put in the form of a statement specifying what the members or other men should do, ought to do, are expected to do, under given circumstances . . . A statement of the kind described is a norm only if any departure of real behavior from the norm is followed by some punishment" (*The Human Group*, New York: Harcourt, Brace, 1950, p. 123).

[3] For examples, see Chapter II and Chapter V, above. See also Osler Memorial Hospital, Vol. II, Case 16, Part C.

[4] See Chapters III and IX, above.

so many different people, they have to be abstract and somewhat vague. They must apply — verbally, at least — to all sorts of situations that differ a great deal from each other. Nevertheless, we "believe" in them; that belief establishes our bond with our compatriots. Being "American" is very important to most of us and anything that seems "un-American" is automatically disavowed. Kluckhohn offered above her description of the core values of American culture, and Gunnar Myrdal supplies a similar one. He calls it the "American Creed":

> These ideals of the essential dignity of the individual, of the basic equality of all men, and of certain inalienable rights to freedom, justice, and fair opportunity, represent to the American people the meaning of the nation's early struggle for independence . . . In all wars, including the last one, the American Creed has been the foundation of national morale. It is remarkable that a vast democracy with so many cultural differences has been able not only to reach agreement on its ideals, but also to make them supreme.[5]

These "supreme" values are so general that in order to be used by individuals they are thought of in terms of particular norms that seem consistent with the general values, yet grow out of each individual's interactions with those immediately around him. Many detailed analyses have been made of the specific group values that coexist under the basic American Creed. Regardless of the particular classification, it seems clear that there are many variations and modifications of the Creed. Some groups consider their version to be the dominant or "official" one. They often feel somewhat superior to other groups who hold variant values. Yet this very feeling of superiority conflicts with certain principles of the basic Creed itself — "equality of opportunity" and "all Americans deserve equal treatment" — in which all Americans tend to believe regardless of whether they hold dominant or variant values.

As has been discussed frequently in these chapters, the application of general principles to specific situations often gives rise to problems that are difficult to handle. Value conflicts thus engendered are common and create important issues that are constantly being dealt with in the interactions between the members of different groups or aggregates. These conflicts could be considered in many different areas. They take place between groups with dominant and variant American values, between men and women, between parents and children, between management and labor, between white and colored people, between Protestants and Catholics and Jews, between upper-, middle-, and lower-class people. All these groups may hold many values in common, but each finds certain values important in interaction within the group that differ from and distinguish it from other groups. For instance, Warner and Lunt show in their Yankee City material[6] that Americans differentiate according to class lines and do not feel that upper-class daughters should marry lower-class sons. It becomes important to "protect" daughters from the difficulties which would be raised by differences in values between those who have widely different class positions.

In order to examine more closely the influence of value conflicts on interaction, it is convenient to focus attention on the example which has been most

---

[5] Gunnar Myrdal, *An American Dilemma*, 2 vols. (New York: Harper, 1944). This quotation is taken from the condensation of Myrdal's work by one of his colleagues, Arnold Rose: *The Negro in America* (New York: Harper, 1948), p. 2.

[6] See Chapter III.

studied by social scientists. They call it interaction between members of the American "majority" (dominant) and different "minorities" (variants). The minorities studied may differ, but the processes are very similar. The reading below considers the Negro and Jewish minorities, although several others would serve as illustrations equally well.

Gunnar Myrdal, a Swede, was called to this country by the Carnegie Corporation to study Negro-white relations with the "objectivity" that it was believed only an outsider could offer. After several years of research with a large staff, his general conclusion was:

> The American dilemma is the ever-raging conflict between, on the one hand, the values which we shall call the "American Creed," where the American thinks, talks, and acts under the influence of high national and Christian morals, and, on the other hand, the values of individual and group living . . . [the facts of] group prejudice against particular persons or types of people.[7]

Myrdal reports on his research in two large volumes entitled *An American Dilemma*. These volumes are summarized by one of his coworkers, Arnold M. Rose, in *The Negro in America*, from which several chapters are listed below. These chapters describe values held by both whites and Negroes, and the many interactions which go counter to the value of "equality." They raise certain questions about why some people act in terms of inequality though believing in the American Creed, and offer hypotheses about the consequences to their thinking of such action when it is in violation of some of their own values. Read

ARNOLD M. ROSE, *The Negro in America* (New York: Harper, 1948), pp. 1–54, 68–81, 124–140, 189–255, 293–321.

Time after time in the pages of *The Negro in America* the "vicious circle" is discussed. This phenomenon has also been called "the self-fulfilling prophecy."[8] It is the circular relationship between beliefs and actions that we explored in earlier chapters.[9] When a person has strong beliefs he tends to perceive the world in such a way that the beliefs are perpetuated. He does not notice facts that do not readily fit into his belief system, and when they are forced upon his attention, he tries to "explain them away." He continually seeks situations that will permit him to act in ways that confirm his beliefs. He has a "vested interest" in them and resists change. The beliefs are useful to him for they order the world in a way he can understand. Contrary ideas create anxiety because they open the way to uncertainty.

Rose and Myrdal say that when the members of a majority that believes in the American Creed deny some privilege to a minority, they tend to develop an elaborate scheme of rationalization for their behavior. The key rationalization is that the "inferior" minority deserves the treatment it gets. The historical accident of the forced inferior position of the Negro when he was brought to America as a slave lends strong support to this rationalization against the colored people. Here we see the self-fulfilling prophecy at its ironic peak: because the minority is believed to be inferior, it is given fewer opportunities in school and at work; because it has fewer opportunities, it is inferior in performance.

---

[7] *The Negro in America*, p. 10.

[8] Robert K. Merton, "A Social Psychological Factor," *Race Prejudice and Discrimination*, ed. Arnold M. Rose (New York: Knopf, 1951).

[9] See particularly Chapters IV and VII.

The belief system of the majority is preserved — they act in ways that make it true.

Belief in the "inferiority" of people who are different from oneself is called "prejudice" in the readings; it leads to "discrimination" or setting the "inferior" people apart to reduce interaction or at least to channel it in certain ways. They may be relegated to lower statuses in the economic and social hierarchy, such as servants or common laborers. Belief systems grow up whose central motif is to prevent change, to keep the lower-status individuals from interacting on a basis of equality with upper-status individuals, to "keep them in their place." When *both* sides accept the beliefs and channel the interactions according to custom, this type of separation can go on for generations without much change or protest. Myrdal and Rose point out, however, that in the United States in recent years we have been educating Negroes (and other minorities) in the values of the American Creed. The Creed teaches them not to be content with a subordinate status; they are now fighting the old customs of discrimination. This has produced considerable change in Negro-white relations; the readings which follow examine several forces both promoting and retarding this change.

There are, of course, important differences between individual members of the "majority" regarding the degree to which they pay attention to their "majority" position. Some are always conscious of it; they are acute observers of the group memberships of other people and immediately upon being introduced to someone try to classify him into some stereotype. Others pay little heed to these matters; they make a new friend without ever bothering to wonder about group classifications.

Recent research appears to indicate two separate factors entering into such differences: one is the cultural tradition or stereotypes about minorities, the other is the personality type which reinforces the tradition. Different areas of the country have different traditions about majority-minority interactions, and it is to be expected that children will generally learn the local rules. Many of those children will as adults move to another part of the country, and they often learn the new rules without difficulty. But there are some individuals who have a personality make-up that leads them to be especially conscious of group memberships and of the "inferiority" of members of minorities. These people will not easily learn new rules; indeed, they become leaders of movements resisting any change which reduces discrimination.

In extreme form, the strong discriminators give evidence of Fromm's "authoritarian personality type." [10] They seem to have an identifiable cluster of related feelings. At the center of the cluster is a feeling of inadequacy, often developed during early childhood experiences. This feeling of inadequacy is then repressed, and there follows, as a means of compensation, a striving toward symbols of superiority. Such people often identify with "powerful" people — those who represent the dominant values of the culture. In response to suspicions they have of their own personal weakness, they strike back and "prove" their strength by devaluing other people. In one of the articles below, Else Frenkel-Brunswick studies these attitudes in children.

Merton's article is an examination of the "self-fulfilling prophecy" which was noted above. He shows how beliefs about "inferiority" can create it even though

---

[10] Erich Fromm, *Escape from Freedom* (New York: Rinehart, 1941). See above, Chapter IV.

"Experience is the best teacher"

Instead of listening to the other fellow, we think of what we're going to say next

it had not previously existed in fact. He demonstrates the subtle relationships between stereotypes and behavior.

The conflicts considered in these articles are not essentially different from those involved in the "Me" thinking contrasted with the "Self" thinking as discussed by Perry.[11] The "Me," in seeking "authoritative" answers to his problems so that he can be "right," becomes involved in two-valued thinking with the predominance of oversimplified classifications. Anxiety about the rightness of his conclusions in respect to the norms of interaction often interferes with his clear observation of the situation around him. Read

ARNOLD M. ROSE, *Race Prejudice and Discrimination* (New York: Knopf, 1951):

Else Frenkel-Brunswick, "A Study of Prejudice in Children," pp. 474–486.
Robert K. Merton, "A Social Psychological Factor," pp. 510–522.

Group loyalty has both a high cultural value and a strong emotional foundation in the threat of isolation that disloyalty might produce. Everyone feels that he wants to follow the values of his own group, yet if their values differ somewhat from the dominant values of the total culture, then he is considered "strange" and "different" by many others with whom he necessarily interacts. Members of minorities hold many beliefs similar to those of the majority. They *feel* just as American as anyone else, so expect to be treated without discrimination. Yet since they *are* treated differently they may come to suspect that there may be "something the matter" with them.

At the present time this process is vividly illustrated by the Negroes and Jews in this country. In their interactions with others they are often treated as if they were inferior, and some of them have come to believe it themselves. They want to be less Negro or less Jewish. They might then respond more readily to the dominant values they have learned, and, in that this might make them seem less different from those around them, they hope it will reduce the discrimination against them.

Such a reaction, involving an observation of the dislike by the majority of many "things" about oneself and thus coming to believe that one is somehow "bad," has been called by Kurt Lewin "self-hatred." He says that it consists of hating part of oneself — a part one cannot change — and putting a chip on one's shoulder in defense of it. One then becomes oversensitive, sees danger where none exists, and generally behaves in ways typical of any individual under stress.[12] The difficulty, Lewin says, is that the individual is fighting a discrimination inside himself just as much as he is fighting one from the outside world. As a psychologist and a Jew, Lewin offers some advice to his fellow Jews about the rearing of their children with a minimum of self-hatred. But he concludes that the situation is created by the majority and cannot be solved by the Jews alone.

Much of Lewin's analysis seems equally applicable to the feelings of Negroes. Signs of self-hatred have long been noticed in the Negroes' stratification of their own community in terms of skin color, giving the higher status to people whose skins are light in shade. They thus accept the dominant American value about skin color and the dominant definition of Negro, namely, any-

[11] See William G. Perry, Jr., "The Student's Response to Teaching," above, Chapter IV.
[12] See Chapter VII, above.

one with a single known Negro ancestor. But as Hayakawa points out, it would be equally logical to define as white anyone with a single known white ancestor. Thus Negroes may criticize their physical traits in terms of a cultural definition. Indeed, much of the material in *The Negro in America* seems congruent with Lewin's theoretical ideas about the Jews. We can see many similarities of response among different minorities that indicate the general processes at work. Read

> Kurt Lewin, *Resolving Social Conflicts* (New York: Harper, 1948), pp. 145–158, 169–200.

So far we have been examining value conflicts as they arise between groups and aggregates of people, especially those within American society. Since group values always seem to differ and to be important, some conflicts of this sort are inevitable. In the attempt to resolve them, individuals in groups will use all the methods discussed in earlier chapters to simplify the problems that thus arise. They will rationalize to support the rightness of their conclusions; they will project their own feelings onto others so that the problem does not seem to be within themselves. And they will displace their feelings of anger from the source of frustration onto someone else who is easier to fight. As a man and wife fighting with each other are able to "forget" their own angers and unite against the neighbor who attempts to stop them, so people can displace hostility arising from a variety of sources onto a minority "scapegoat" group. Many value conflicts are in fact unresolvable without major changes in assumptions that are felt to be basic. Yet life must be lived and these defensive techniques seem to assist. The conflicts are permitted to continue, but the feelings that they arouse are alleviated.

Value conflicts can be handled in other ways. The existence of the conflict is reflected in interactions with others. If interactions between groups are reduced, then value differences can be more easily maintained. Segregation increases group solidarity and avoids some conflict by eliminating contact.

In modern society, however, it is impossible to have complete segregation of any group. All are served by the same mass communications; all read the same newspapers, go to the same schools, read the same books. All people become aware of value differences between groups and respond to them. They learn, for instance, that minorities contribute importantly to the common defense effort; they read the speeches of minority leaders who emphasize the values in the American Creed of equality of opportunity; they learn of scientific research which indicates that all races have equal capacities to learn if given equal educational experiences. As a consequence, value conflict is pointed up; some individuals, instead of falling back on the segregation devices, face the conflict and even join in groups in an attempt to reduce it. They look inside themselves, avoid oversimplifying the problems they find, and recognize the conflicts between principles they have long held. They attempt a new integration: they are willing to modify some values which they had been taught and have long held dear in order to achieve a new synthesis of values which is more consistent.

Such a value synthesis can lead to new interactions with members of other groups. Or, the symbolic process itself can be initiated and reinforced by new interactions that take place without deliberate planning. These interactions tend to occur in situations where people are not entirely free to choose their companions according to their tastes. In business organizations, for example, one of the major values is the adjustment of means for the best attainment of "sound economic goals." Consequently, if labor is scarce, employers will neglect their own prejudices against minorities and hire any competent workers they can obtain. If the employers and the old employees discover from the behavior of the new workers that the values are not so divergent as stereotypes had indicated, they might conclude that these formerly strange people are "my kind of guy" after all.

This process is well illustrated by the story of the firm which started hiring Negro workers during the war because of a labor shortage. The union head and the employer both recognized that there was little choice if the firm was to fulfill its production schedules. They agreed that it would be wise first to hire carefully selected Negroes with a "good appearance" and a high school education. The secretary to the president of the firm, who was the informal leader of the girls in the office, said in advance that she would not work with Negroes; both the boss and the union leader told her that she had no choice. Then she found that the first colored girl who worked near her in the office was a "very pleasant girl," and they soon became friends. One day the boss observed them eating lunch together, and he asked his secretary why she had changed her mind and no longer objected to working with Negroes. The girl replied: "But she's not a Negro, she's Helen."

A similar sort of thing also happened in the army. Rose refers below to research which has shown a correlation between the attitudes about Negro soldiers held by white soldiers and the amount of contact between them. Whites who served in regiments with Negro companies had better opinions of Negroes than whites who had had no such joint experience. And whites who served in nonsegregated companies had the least prejudice of all. These same white soldiers, asked beforehand if they would want to serve with Negroes, said no. After the experience of being with Negroes, they changed their sentiments.

Morton Deutsch and Mary Evans Collins discuss a modification of prejudice which occurred in public-housing developments where whites and Negroes lived in the same projects. In some places, they lived in separate buildings; in others, they were not segregated at all. The attitude researches showed the same results as in the army: the closer the contact, the less the prejudice.

In most of the instances of change in attitudes reported in the articles by Rose and by Deutsch and Collins, people experienced new interactions and reëvaluated their old sentiments. They found themselves in situations where they could not act so as to avoid the new experience; they were not free to choose their companions. The choice was dictated either by the situation itself or by persons in authority in an organization. It seems that one important factor in these situations was the fact that the individuals were engaged in a common activity that provided satisfactions. When the different groups thus acted together, they discovered that their value differences were not so great as they thought and were not so important as the common satisfactions. It is not likely that increased interaction will favorably change sentiments regardless of the circumstances.

Prejudice, for example, seems to increase with general social tension. Under such conditions, people are insecure and seek some group to step on to reassure themselves of their strength (a variant of Fromm's approach). David W. Petegorsky observes:

> In times of social stability and relative prosperity there is little resistance to, and a good deal of acceptance of, the message of brotherhood and good-will. But real dangers emerge during periods of social instability, political chaos and economic stress. Then, a new climate is created. And whatever atmosphere has been generated about good-will through the use of educational techniques and special or mass media approaches is rapidly blown away by far stronger forces generated by our social organism.[13]

Gordon W. Allport agrees with Petegorsky about the complexity of tension reduction. He suggests in the article below a technique for helping the prejudiced person examine his own value conflicts by first "blowing off steam." Once the emotion is expressed, reasoning processes work with less defensiveness. Read

ARNOLD M. ROSE, Race Prejudice and Discrimination (New York: Knopf, 1951):

Arnold M. Rose, "The Influence of Legislation on Prejudice," pp. 545–555.

Morton Deutsch and Mary Evans Collins, "Interracial Housing and Changes in Attitudes," pp. 555–564.

Gordon W. Allport, "Catharsis and the Reduction of Prejudice," pp. 572–580.

This chapter has attempted to indicate the strength of those "vicious circles" created by conflicts in our evaluation of the world about us. In order to avoid seemingly insolvable problems, people often cling to sentiments even though they cause other serious difficulties in interaction. Allport suggests that special techniques might be necessary to help people break out of such vicious circles — deliberate structuring of situations in which sentiments can be reëvaluated without a sense of threat. We cannot expect a prejudiced individual to give up sentiments which aid him in ordering his world to avoid anxiety unless we offer him support. The next chapter examines certain ways of establishing such a bond of support.

ADDITIONAL READINGS

Adorno, T. W., et. al., The Authoritarian Personality (New York: Harper, 1950).

This book reports the most complete research yet made into the personality structure associated with strong prejudice.

Allport, Gordon W., "Prejudice: A Problem in Psychological and Social Causation," Toward a General Theory of Action, ed. Talcott Parsons and Edward A. Shils (Cambridge: Harvard University Press, 1951).

A summary of the major research data on prejudice, balancing "psychological" and "socio-cultural" factors. Includes good bibliography.

Davis, Allison, and John Dollard, Children of Bondage: The Personality Development of Negro Youth in the Urban South (Washington: American Council on Education, 1940).

Case studies of Negro children.

---

[13] "On Combating Racism," Race Prejudice and Discrimination, p. 538.

Dollard, John, *Caste and Class in a Southern Town* (New York: Harper, 1937).
A study of community divided by "caste" (Negro-white) barriers and the effects on the personalities of its inhabitants. An unusually good synthesis of sociological and psychological perspectives.

Drake, St. Clair, and Horace R. Cayton, *Black Metropolis* (New York: Harcourt, Brace, 1945).
The story of "Bronzeville," Chicago's huge Negro district.

Stouffer, Samuel A., *et. al., The American Soldier: Adjustment During Army Life,* vol. I of Studies in Social Psychology in World War II (Princeton: Princeton University Press, 1949), chapter 10, "Negro Soldiers."
The full report on the study of Negro-white attitudes and interactions in the army which was mentioned by Rose.

Warner, W. Lloyd, and Leo Srole, *The Social Systems of American Ethnic Groups,* vol. III of Yankee City Series (New Haven: Yale University Press, 1945).
To quote the preface of the authors: "a detailed study of the social life of a number of ethnic groups, including the Irish, French Canadians, Jews, Armenians, and Poles [in Yankee City]; it explains how they maintain their old cultural traditions but at the same time undergo social changes which make them more and more like the larger American community."

Wright, Richard, *Black Boy* (New York: Harper, 1937).
Autobiography of a prominent Negro author.

CHAPTER XI

Re-evaluating Sentiments

IN THE last chapter the problem of the social strains caused by conflicting social values was considered. Such strains between groups and between individuals are frequently reflected in strains between values inside the individuals themselves. When the values involved are of considerable significance to the individuals — when they feel strongly about them — the difficulties in dealing with them appear to be multiplied many fold. Attitudes, feelings, sentiments come into play that appear to be only indirectly related to the external conflict. People respond in important situations as they feel they should respond and are sometimes surprised to find their responses quite inadequate in the external situation — others continue to behave in unexpected ways. No matter how hard they try to understand the situation, the difficulties may continue to occur and cause them concern and confusion.

These inner conflicts of feelings and values arise in many different ways. We may be faced at any time with conflicts derived from the different roles we are called upon to play, or from different conclusions learned from experiences acquired at different times or with different groups whose values were not identical. Or we might be faced with conflicts between different abstractions and oversimplifications drawn from "essentially the same" experiences, or between our immediate values and more distant or more general values.

Our interactions with others involve a *series* of responses from each side and a *series* of choices which include feelings or values both immediate and more general. An instructor, for example, may respond with anger to an angry student, thus reinforcing and perhaps "justifying" the student's original anger. Yet the instructor may also hold the long-range intention of trying to understand whether the problem back of the student's anger is something the instructor can deal with or not. Hence his immediate reaction to the student's "rudeness" might not represent for him the most adequate appraisal of it, yet from the immediate point of view the anger might have been entirely warranted. In such matters we can observe the same sort of circularity and feedback that we have seen in other aspects of human interaction.

Our choices of response are based on many interlocking sets of data, yet two broad areas can be distinguished: one is our observation of that part of the situation which seems to be outside ourselves, and the other is our observation of our own feelings or sentiments about the situation. Two questions interact very closely but are omnipresent: What *is* the situation? and How do I *feel* about it? All consideration of the elements of choice open to us — whether momentary with ourselves or long, thoughtful consideration with ourselves or others — involves an interweaving of these two questions.

The first question directs our attention to the gathering of material about the nature of the situation itself and might be called the area of orientation. In this area we are concerned with logical, fact-finding inquiry. Here we can properly seek and often obtain the advice of others. We can find out from them answers to a large number of factual questions: do we have enough money to go to college or to get married, do we have enough credits to graduate from college, do we have enough time to drive to Chicago or had we better fly, do we have enough skills to learn to run a lathe or a calculating machine? We can determine or find out what *others* consider a sufficient requirement for adequate action on any course *we* are considering, and such advice may be valuable.

The other question — How do I feel about the situation? — is a much more difficult one. Here we are concerned with a unique, personal appraisal based on our own experience. And all observations, even the advice of others, must pass through our emotional evaluation. Thus even in apparently factual areas it is difficult to determine the adequacy for us of the advice of others because our evaluations are relevant. Our opinion of a "sufficient requirement" may differ materially from theirs. We may not even want a factual answer; we may not want to go to college or we may wish to marry and are merely seeking an acceptable reason for a decision we have already made.

Often our evaluations of a person or situation do not seem to us to reside within ourselves at all but seem to be characteristics of the situation or person observed. We may look upon a house as handsome or an automobile as gaudy. We may consider an instructor as unfair. It appears to us that the unfairness is a quality "of" the teacher, rather than a reaction within ourselves to the teacher's behavior.

With respect to the query How do I feel about the situation? the advice of others is especially difficult to use. Others can tell us how they think they would feel under a particular set of circumstances; they may tell us how they think we *should* feel. If they are skillful and interested enough they may even be able to help us observe (and evaluate) our own feelings. But they cannot tell us what our feelings or sentiments *really are*. These are conclusions we must arrive at for ourselves, and we can only accept as one of the facts of life the possible anxiety that such an isolating activity may arouse.

Fortunately, an awareness of the personal nature of our evaluations is frequently unnecessary; the opinions and observations of others may seem similar to our own — others also may observe the teacher as "unfair." We do not need to understand fully the many ways in which our feelings or sentiments influence our activities and interactions. As we are always a part of a system of relationships with others, so the utility of our sentiments depends largely on their effectiveness in our interactions with others. When our feelings permit our interactions to proceed in ways that continue to produce satisfactions for us, we need hardly consider explicitly the feelings themselves. Often the very social system in which we live will present new data to us in ways that will help us evaluate it effectively without demanding much conscious effort or arousing too great an anxiety.

For example, doing something that is strange to us may be upsetting — we do not know how to act. Yet here we will more readily take guidance from others about how they feel about it, and the activity, by requiring interactions with others, may produce answers to our problems. Our first dance may have been a painful experience, but further dances modified our early impressions; it was not necessary for us to consider explicitly each area of this process. Our first day of school may have been very difficult, but new interaction patterns, feelings, and norms about school developed a system of relationships sufficiently comfortable to permit us to continue.

Often when we are engaged in finding out new things and sizing them up for ourselves, we find pleasure in this expansion of our universe. As we experience something new, we frequently can assimilate it into a value system we already hold with only the smallest change. The "good" things about it are assimilated to our previous ideas of what was "good," and the things we don't like are assimilated to the framework of dislike which we had previously maintained. We are concerned here largely in fitting new evaluations into an old framework. Feelings may not be too strong, and the related evaluations are not too long outstanding or too important to us. Changes required by these evaluations will not arouse much anxiety.

There are times, however, when we seem to stand alone, when our feelings and sentiments about a situation or person seem to differ greatly from those of others. We may be in a situation where all our old standards seem no longer to apply; or the consequences of a failure to act "successfully" may seem too great. Sometimes we seem to be making unique or deviant choices in our responses to others that are preventing us from satisfying our own social purposes; we are not "getting along." Then we are faced with some sort of *reevaluation,* and this is much more difficult than an original evaluation. In such reëvaluation we may be faced with relinquishing values or ways of doing things we had previously felt to be good, or accepting as good things we had previously disliked.

When these values are important and close to us and our feelings about them already well developed, the threat of change is serious to us. At such times anxiety may be intense, and we may take any means at our command to protect us from this apparent threat. We may use any of the mechanisms of defense we discussed in Chapter VII which limit or modify the interactions that seem to be producing the threat. Ordinary social forces cannot then help us, interaction is blocked, we do not take the advice of others in good grace, we try to "escape" from the situation. If the conflict is intense we are only too happy to rid ourselves of it by projecting one side of the debate onto someone else so that we can concentrate our feelings on the other side and see the conflict itself as outside us.

As our need to reëvaluate a person or situation comes to our attention, a need to relate ourselves in some different way to others is also emphasized. Our usual choice of responses seems to have gone awry. Further isolation, which is supported by the mechanisms of defense and which helps us maintain our own integrity, does not seem to relieve the anxiety or resolve the conflict. We apparently cannot "think these problems through" by ourselves; when we try, we tend to defend our accustomed behavior rather than reëvaluate it. At some level of our consciousness we know that something is wrong, that major changes must be accomplished; and we often seem to know that we need the support of others. For this support to be helpful, however, we need a kind of interaction with others very different from the usual relationships — kindly or aggressive — of arguing, advising, guiding, teaching, or disciplining, out of which most of our original evaluations grew. Such relationships, useful as they normally are, tend only to emphasize our own feelings of inadequacy when we are struggling with important reëvaluations.

The special kind of social situation in which such changes can be made is dramatically illustrated by James Finan in the article below. In it he reports briefly the work of Lloyd W. McCorkle in handling discussion groups of criminals in the New Jersey prisons. McCorkle found that he was able to establish a social situation with small groups of even violent prisoners in such a way that they were able to reorient some of their sentiments. They were able to learn how to change their values and feelings in ways that they felt were helpful to them in understanding more clearly their relation to the larger society of which they were a part. It is easy to imagine the reaction this group of people would have had to a lecture on their moral obligations. Such an external evaluation of their moral failure was thoroughly familiar to them, and their defenses against it in support of their own personal integrity were well established. Even if the most sympathetic reasoning had produced a new understanding of the social necessity for the norms they had been violating, it could hardly have affected the underlying, personal evaluations on which their behavior was based. Read

JAMES FINAN, "Inside the Prison," below.

From this article a start can be made on a description of the kind of social situation needed to help us change our value systems and alter our feelings about aspects of our relations with others which are causing us difficulty. Apparently we come to understand our values and feelings best when we become convinced by our interactions with others that they really accept our feelings as part of us. By talking about our feelings, we ourselves can learn and others will agree that they are a useful part of *us* and not merely qualities of the people or situations we have been talking about. Deviant though they may be from many points of view, they may be useful to us and can form a foundation for satisfactory interactions with others.

When others listen carefully to our own unique feelings, the conversation that ensues brings these feelings forward in their own right as interesting and significant. This social process then modifies the disagreements of the others with our feelings. If others indicate their interest in listening to our feelings, they may disagree about whether these feelings are "good" feelings or whether we "should" hold them, but they cannot disagree about whether these feelings of ours exist — after all, on this subject we are the only source of information. And if evaluations by others can be held back, if others will consider orienting themselves to our feelings as they are instead of as they "should be," then disagreement is kept at a minimum. When important disagreement is not offered from outside, when others are listening carefully and sympathetically to our description of our values and feelings, then we may discover for ourselves that the conflicts we have been struggling against so fiercely reside within ourselves and *we* can undertake a reëvaluation. When we stop arguing with others (or ourselves), we become less defensive and can change more readily.

A first requirement, then, in any important reëvaluation is to find at least one person who is willing to listen carefully and try to understand — and help us understand — our feelings and values. In recent years much thought has been given to this kind of listening; much consideration has been given not only to its application in the acute conflicts of psychotherapy but to its more general use in relieving personal and social tensions. Carl R. Rogers in the short article below describes the way in which an untrained USO worker during World War II could provide such listening. In this manner soldiers who were on leave from active duty could obtain an opportunity to work out a reorganization of their feelings when they found themselves in some temporary conflicts. Read

CARL R. ROGERS, "A Counseling Viewpoint for the USO Worker," below.

Rogers is discussing how someone in the USO situation could work usefully with others in respect to feelings or sentiments. It is significant that he uses the word "viewpoint" in the title rather than the word "technique"; he assumes that a great deal of the step-by-step procedure necessary to carry out any role will develop from the interactions of the specific situation if a consistent attitude is kept in mind. Thus he puts his emphasis primarily on the attitude of the counselor. Although he reports in some detail the responses the counselors felt called upon to make in specific situations, it is rather for the purpose of indicating the consequences of maintaining this consistent attitude than to detail any definite procedures that should always be followed. This attitude of real interest in someone else's feelings is characterized by an evident respect for the individual to whom the counselor is listening and a freedom from any wish to "influence" him; the client's feelings, not his, are under consideration. This does not seem to be a common social attitude, and any lack of sincerity on the part of the counselor is readily apparent. If it is to be convincing it must be maintained both verbally and through behavior.

In the book below, Rogers reports more fully on the results that occur when a relationship with another is developed with an appropriate listening attitude well in mind. Rogers is considering here listening to people in a well-defined "counseling" relationship with people who "know" that they have run into problems which more or less seriously interfere with their interactions. They are voluntarily seeking assistance because in some way they feel they need help. These people are seeking for themselves new perceptions which Rogers calls insight. These new perceptions seem to be largely a new understanding of the relation between their feelings and the rest of their behavior. Such insight, Rogers says, involves (a) seeing old facts in a new way, (b) an increase in self-understanding, and (c) a gradual recognition and acceptance of oneself as one is. Much of this change, even though not verbalized, may bring about changes in behavior desired by the client. All the reasons for the modification may not be understood by either client or counselor — and Rogers believes it does not matter. Read

CARL R. ROGERS, *Counseling and Psychotherapy* (Boston: Houghton Mifflin, 1942), pp. 85–114, 131–167, 174–216.

In these pages Rogers defines his views about the creation of a counseling relationship. He considers that it is a unique relationship if it is to be developed at its best; it is not the relationship of parent-child, teacher-pupil, physician-patient, leader-follower, or priest-parishioner. Implications of superior status on the part of the counselor are consciously kept at a minimum. It is not even the relationship of friend to friend, since there "the outstanding characteristic is complete mutuality — mutual understanding, give and take." [1]

He considers that there are "at least four definite qualities which character-ize the most helpful counseling atmosphere . . . *First,* is a warmth and respon-siveness on the part of the counselor which makes rapport possible . . . *Second,* is its permissiveness in regard to the expression of feelings . . . *Third,* there are definite limits to action" that are imposed by the counselor.[2] The counselor limits severely the responsibility he will take for the client's decisions or actions; he imposes a limit of time during which the client may consider problems with him; he imposes a limit on the aggressive action that the client may take against him; he defines the limits of emotional response that he will express. Within these limits and in the manner in which these limits are handled, the *fourth* quality of this relationship is "freedom from any type of pressure or coercion."

Rogers then discusses the ways in which the expression of feelings becomes important in the interview relationship. Here he considers the manner in which the counselor's attitude may be translated into specific responses which might assist the client to express such feelings as "he can helpfully reveal." [3] Implic-itly, he is emphasizing that the vital element is the nature of the process in the interview — the continuity in the sequence of change — the steps that are taken toward the objective. This objective is an expression of the client's feel-ings on the assumption that a clarification of feelings will clarify the other ele-ments of behavior.

Although we do not ordinarily find ourselves in situations where we can or would wish to develop our relation with another with such singleness of purpose, we often find ourselves in situations where *some* clarification of feel-ings is necessary. Then we might want to understand a "viewpoint" which, if maintained persistently, seems to be very helpful in developing such clarifica-tion. Rogers says the key to this viewpoint is "the art of being alert to and responding to the feeling which is being expressed, rather than giving sole attention to the intellectual content. In our culture, most adults are schooled to pay close attention to ideas and none to feeling." [4]

An illustration of the way in which this counseling viewpoint might be significant in our everyday lives can be found in Rogers' brief description of the question of reassurance. Many times situations will come before us where someone is evidently upset. Often our response, in our desire to help, is an attempt to convince the other that his worry is not really so serious as it seems to him. This situation arises frequently in the counseling relationship, and Rogers states that the "only type of reassurance which has any promise of being helpful is that which relieves the client's feeling of peculiarity or isolation . . . A cheery reassurance that the client's problems are not serious, or that he is more normal than he feels or that the solution to his problem is easy . . . denies the client's own feelings." [5] The client is convinced at this moment that his feelings about the situation are of supreme importance. No statement to the contrary can modify his conviction and any such attempt will not in fact reassure.

---

[1] Carl R. Rogers, *Counseling and Psychotherapy* (Boston: Houghton Mifflin, 1942), p. 85.
[2] *Ibid.,* pp. 87–89.
[3] *Ibid.,* p. 114.
[4] *Ibid.,* p. 133.
[5] *Ibid.,* pp. 164–165.

In any particular situation to which we are responding there is, in addition to the questions of orientation and evaluation, the question of control. Beyond the questions, "What is going on here?" and "How do I feel about it?" is the question, "What shall I do about it?" This control question rests on the answers to the other two. But to follow an effective course of action, we must also concern ourselves with the values about the situation that others are expressing through their feelings. The values of others are always a part of the situation to which we must respond and are sometimes the most important part.

Mayo, in the books read in the earlier chapters,[6] describes the behavior necessary to permit a more complete observation of the sentiments and values of others. He was primarily interested in research — in how to observe the behavior of others. Since much of our communication with others is verbal, he considers a technique for "listening" important so that others' feelings may be more clearly expressed by them and understood by us.

Such listening, as he describes it, is no more passive than the somewhat similar behavior in the counseling situation described by Rogers; it is an active response to the type of relationship being established. In social research it is designed to promote a clear expression of another's sentiments so that the total situation involved may be more clearly understood by the researcher. Listening in this way brings to the attention of the social scientist data that would ordinarily be obscure. For the research interview Mayo gives six "rules" of conduct for listening:

1. Give your whole attention to the person interviewed, and make it evident that you are doing so.
2. Listen — don't talk.
3. Never argue, never give advice.
4. Listen to:
    (a) What he wants to say.
    (b) What he does not want to say.
    (c) What he cannot say without help.
5. As you listen, plot out tentatively and for subsequent correction the pattern that is being set before you. To test this, occasionally summarize what has been said and present it for comment. Always do this with caution — that is, abbreviate and clarify but do not add or "twist."
6. Remember that everything said must be considered a personal confidence and not divulged to anyone.[7]

Note that in the first three and the last of these rules Mayo is describing types of overt behavior in the research situation; he is stating how to develop a relationship through responses in order to help someone else clarify his situation for us. In the other rules he states the sort of things to listen for and how to check our observations of what we have heard without disturbing the relationship.

It is of particular significance to understand that these "listening" viewpoints under discussion modify our responses and consequently modify the responses of others to us. Through our changed responses we do obtain a kind of control over the situation that may be important. Although we cannot

[6] Elton Mayo, *Some Notes on the Psychology of Pierre Janet* (Cambridge: Harvard University Press, 1948). See also Mayo, *Human Problems of an Industrial Civilization* (2d ed.; Boston: Division of Research, Graduate School of Business Administration, Harvard University, 1946), pp. 88–91.
[7] *Some Notes on the Psychology of Pierre Janet*, p. 23.

"change the world," we can change our responses to it and through these responses modify the interactions around us. With the viewpoint described as "listening" we respond in ways not usual in ordinary social situations and may obtain more knowledge about another than he knows about himself. This then raises problems of control that are serious. What shall we *do* with this special knowledge? Have we taken an "unfair" advantage of another? Have we put ourselves in a position to manipulate him in ways which he cannot prevent?

This listening viewpoint seems to produce ways of behaving that have useful results for many purposes, be it therapy or research. It brings new knowledge which, like all knowledge, can be used in many ways, well or badly. It can be used on a personal level to assist another to understand the relationship of his feelings to his behavior. It can be used on the control level to assist a superior in dealing with his subordinates. It is, in some sense, special knowledge, and it is helpful if everyone involved understands clearly that it will be used only for mutually acceptable purposes. Mayo's sixth rule regarding the confidential nature of the interview is an attempt to make clear that the interview will not be used in a way detrimental to the individual being interviewed.

Yet behavior is often modified without the interviewee understanding exactly what has happened.[8] Without such understanding the results are always open to the possible interpretation of manipulation. Change has occurred, the interviewee does not feel he has caused the change, therefore the interviewer in some mysterious way must have done it — and possibly for some ulterior purpose of his own. The situation is inherently one where misinterpretations of this kind cannot be precluded, but they can be handled within the context of the relationship itself by a thorough mutual understanding of the objectives to be attained.

Dorothy Baruch, in the book below, faces this problem of control in the training of children by distinguishing between what one does about their behavior and what one does about their feelings. She considers that we must discipline behavior but should only understand and relieve the feelings that are aroused. As parents we must make clear to our children that there are actions we will and will not permit them to do — we must train them to "behave properly." In this training, however, quite justifiable angers may be aroused in both us and the children. Disciplining these angers directly Baruch believes to be ineffective.

As has been discussed earlier, our feelings at all ages are closely tied to our values. In the process of controlling behavior values may be threatened and negative feelings from either side may be aroused. At any age an angry response may be entirely natural. Yet it may be an ineffective response if control of the situation is to be maintained. Disciplining of the anger itself by the parent may produce only further anger, resentment, and further deviant behavior that requires further discipline. Baruch stresses that the important thing is not to discipline the anger but to understand it as a normal response, indicate clearly that we do understand it, and discipline only the behavior that might result. In simple terms, she suggests that we do not say to the child, "Don't be angry with me. That's not a nice way to treat your mother," but rather, "I

---

[8] Brookmay Machinery Company, Vol. II, Case 24, and the changed behavior of Catherine O'Neill in Spofford Fabricated Products Company, Vol. II, Case 19, illustrate this point.

know you are angry, but I cannot let you kick me because of it." The vicious circle requiring continual discipline can only be broken by an understanding and acceptance of the personal nature of the anger. It is not the anger that is "bad" but the behavior that develops in response to it. Read

DOROTHY WALTER BARUCH, *New Ways in Discipline* (New York: McGraw-Hill, 1949), pp. 1–81.

Baruch begins with a brief discussion of the needs of observation — the needs of knowing the child. She proceeds to the importance of letting the child know we understand how he feels. Then as this relationship grows it is necessary to use it in ways that are productive for the ends we have in mind, but also in ways that help the actual needs of the child. When we are using the viewpoint of understanding feelings and when we develop skills in the use of this understanding, we are on safe ground if it is evident that both the parent and the child benefit from it. Baruch's material emphasizes that such relationships are two-sided and that, unless the satisfactions of both are met, the relationship will not be productive.

ADDITIONAL READINGS

Fromm-Reichmann, Frieda, "Notes on the Personal and Professional Requirements of a Psychotherapist," *Psychiatry, XII* (1949), 361–378.
An excellent coverage of factors which interfere with the listening process.

Horney, Karen, ed., *Are You Considering Psychoanalysis?* (New York: W. W. Norton, 1946.)
A helpful book for those who wonder what happens during psychotherapy.

Merton, Robert, and Patricia Kendall, "The Focused Interview," *American Journal of Sociology,* LI, May 1946, 541–557.
This article discusses the interview relationship when the aim is to elicit information about a certain specific area in the life of the subject.

Perry, William G., Jr., and Stanley G., Estes, "The Collaboration of Client and Counselor," *Theory and Research in Psychotherapy,* ed. O. H. Mowrer (New York: Ronald Press, in press, 1952).
A consideration of the balance of responsibility between client and counselor in an educational setting.

Reik, Theodor, *Listening with the Third Ear* (New York: Farrar, Straus, 1948).
This book is a discussion of the doctor-patient relationship during psychoanalysis. Reik emphasizes the importance of the unconscious communication that takes place.

Rogers, Carl R., *Client-Centered Therapy* (Boston: Houghton Mifflin, 1951).
This is the ultimate statement of the assumption that the therapeutic relationship is based completely on "understanding" by the counselor of the feelings of the client.

REVIEW

Charles H. Cooley, "The Roots of Social Knowledge" — see Chapter III.
Cooley discusses his notion of understanding another person through "sympathetic introspection."

Sigmund Freud, "The Origin and Development of Psychoanalysis," *An Outline of Psychoanalysis,* ed. J. S.

Van Teslaar (New York: Modern Library, 1925) — see Additional Readings, Chapter VI.
This is an introduction to Freud's therapeutic methods.

F. J. Roethlisberger and William J. Dickson, *Management and the Worker* (Cambridge: Harvard University Press, 1943) — see Additional Readings, Chapter VIII. Parts II and III describe the development of a research interviewing program at Western Electric. The authors discovered through trial and error an approach to listening which is strikingly similar to that of Rogers. These approaches were developed independently of one another.

Inside the Prison—A New Spark of Hope for Remaking Men*

BY JAMES FINAN

One hot afternoon last July, an angry little holdup man from Trenton convinced me that it really takes a thief to catch a thief.

In the dayroom of a gloomy cell block in Bordentown Reformatory, New Jersey, 18 violent criminals sat around a table. Prison guards had been strictly excluded. The only official present was Lloyd W. McCorkle, vigorous, 32-year-old number-three man of New Jersey's penal system. McCorkle, a beetle-browed fellow with a broken nose and a husky voice, had invited one convict to tell the rest of the group his troubles.

Now the speaker, an oily-tongued robber from a large New Jersey city, confessed that his home town's dishonest politicians were his most worrisome concern. It would be useless for him ever to vote, he complained; all political candidates in his city were corrupt.

Most of the prisoners listened apathetically. But not the little gunman from Trenton. He rasped, "What are you in for, Bud?"

"Robbery," Bud said smoothly.

"Armed robbery — with a gun?" the little convict persisted.

"Yeh," Bud said. "What about it?"

"What about it!" the little man appealed to the rest. "This guy's beefing about crooked politicians. They worry him to death, understand? But he holds up an *honest* citizen with a gun! If the honest citizen don't hand over the lettuce we know what he'll do, right? He pulls the trigger and blows off the top of the honest citizen's head! The same thing goes for you and me and the rest of us. Why don't you get wise to yourself, Bud? *Stop wasting our time!*"

After this session McCorkle commented to me: "That kid from Trenton would not notice such conduct in himself — until he spotted it in the other fellow. And to denounce it he had to adopt normal values. Sometimes a man has begun to change his basic attitudes when he starts using that generous 'we' and 'our' instead of the criminal's habitual 'me' and 'mine.'"

This new method of treating criminals, technically known as Guided Group Interaction, has been in operation for two years throughout New Jersey's penal system. The idea developed during World War II, when the Army faced a crime wave among draftees. Thousands of young soldiers were accumulating in prison stockades. Nearly two thirds of these GI jailbirds had civil-arrest records previous to their Army careers. The discipline of military life had only emphasized their eternal feud against organized society. Wartime pressure demanded that these men be corrected, that every possible individual be returned to active service.

Soon word came from the Rehabilitation Center at Fort Knox, Ky., of a new kind of program. Here Dr. F. Lovell Bixby, ex-Cornell psychologist and acting director of the Army correctional program, and a young sergeant, Lloyd McCorkle, were experimenting with

* Reprinted from *Reader's Digest*, May 1950, by permission of *Reader's Digest* and the author.

group discussion. Encouraged by Colonel Bixby, Sergeant McCorkle would gather prisoners into a barracks hall, let them sit and smoke until they began swapping complaints about Army life — as all soldiers do. Once they were loosened up, it was McCorkle's turn: "Okay. You've had a good gripe session. Now we'll have a *group* session."

Prisoners were required only to listen when another man talked, and to speak, if they spoke at all, about themselves, each other, or the fact of their being in trouble. Before long Fort Knox's return-to-duty rate became so high, and its return-to-prison rate so low, that the Army demanded that *all* court-martialed prisoners be exposed to group sessions.

The scheme worked. The Army restored 42,000 — three divisions — of its long-term military offenders to duty. And 85 percent of these men not only made good but were rated, after their first six months back in service, average or above in performance of duty and in personal conduct. Most striking fact of all: the return-to-prison rate dropped from the dismal 60-plus percent so common to civilian prisons to *below ten percent*.

After the war McCorkle was helping revise the prison system of Japan under MacArthur when New Jersey's prison commissioner, Sanford Bates, and Dr. Bixby, now Jersey's number-two prison man, called him to New Jersey to set up group practices there.

Under the usual New Jersey pattern, 15 to 25 convicts meet for one hour, three times a week. No guards are ever present. There is always resistance among the prisoners at first. "But it's impossible for a man not to take part," says McCorkle.

McCorkle invited me to attend a new group he was starting among the worst offenders at the state prison in Rahway. The 20 members of this "lockup" gang had defied prison rules, refused to work, assaulted guards and other prisoners. The gang's leader, McCorkle explained, was Tony Scala, a rebellious product of Newark's slums.[1] "They'll have heard

something about the group over the prison grapevine, and they won't like it," McCorkle promised. "Scala will have warned them to shut up."

You could sense the hostility in Rahway's auditorium as McCorkle entered. The 20 convicts there stiffened, at a signal from a tall handsome prisoner. Scala glowered icily as McCorkle picked a vacant chair and lit a cigarette, apparently unflustered by 20 pairs of eyes boring in upon him.

Then McCorkle crossed his knees, hunched forward easily, and stared in frank interest from one prisoner's face to another. "Does anybody here know what this group is for?" he finally asked.

There was no reply. McCorkle studied his cigarette, took another drag, then continued. "What are all you people interested in?"

Nobody answers. The convicts look furtively at Scala, who stares with baleful insolence at McCorkle.

"You don't have *anything* you want to say?" McCorkle asks Scala with a show of bland astonishment. Scala spits a bluntly unprintable insult at him.

"*You*," says McCorkle, turning quickly on a rather dull-looking, open-mouthed convict. "What interests *you?*"

The man squirms, finds it impossible to dodge the direct question, mutters, "Gettin' out."

"Right," says McCorkle with vast approval. "It interests us all."

Scala stares contemptuously at the slow-witted man who broke the ice, then spits elaborately on the clean floor and glowers again at McCorkle.

"But can anyone tell us *how* to get out of jail?" McCorkle continues. "*You* seem to know the answers," he urges the stupid convict. "Can't you tell us a way to get out?"

The dull man says gruffly, "Escape."

"Sure, escape. That's one way." McCorkle laughs. Other members of this new-forming group laugh too at their comrade's simplicity. "But isn't there any other way out of prison?"

A prisoner growls, "Die." Another

---

[1] The names of prisoners mentioned, and certain circumstances surrounding their convictions, have been disguised for obvious reasons.

barks, "Pull your full bit." A third says, "Parole."

Like a practiced ballplayer, McCorkle catches and returns each of these sallies. "'Die,'" he repeats. "But how long will that take? How old are *you?*"

The dull convict admits to 23. All convicts chuckle except Scala, who turns his back in disgust.

"Serve your maximum sentence, another man said," McCorkle echoes. "But a full bit at Rahway can be awfully long. This other fellow said, 'Parole.' How many people here want parole?" Reluctantly every man's hand goes up except Scala's.

"Okay," says McCorkle. "How do we get parole?"

Politics, one says. Another says good behavior. But a third member objects that the prison rules are so tough that a man can't keep out of trouble. The men get pretty well drawn into this topic until, the hour suddenly up, McCorkle says, "Well, do you think it's a good idea to get together and talk this out?"

An inmate says grudgingly, "It can't do no harm."

Thus Rahway's "incorrigible" lockup gang became a group.

McCorkle started the following meeting by recapitulating what had been discussed two days earlier. Scala continued to glare. The session seemed a chaotic, disorganized grousing against prison conditions. Some convicts wanted the medical service improved; several others urged McCorkle to "straighten out the guards"; nearly all told McCorkle to "fix the chow," which they claimed was not fit to eat. "Will *you* come down with us tonight and try that chow?" an angry prisoner challenged.

"*Me?* Why should I eat *your* chow?" McCorkle protested, wide-eyed. "*I'm* not in jail." The answer hit home.

Didn't anyone have another problem, McCorkle asked. Nobody seemed to, perhaps because McCorkle was staring directly at the rebel Scala.

"I'll tell you one," said McCorkle. "It's about Tony Scala — the problem of why Scala doesn't like me."

Scala, alert, shifted in his chair, his eyes fixed on McCorkle. There was no sound in the auditorium.

"You men heard the name Scala called me last time," McCorkle continued. "People don't say that to people they like. Why does Scala hate me?"

An intelligent-looking convict muttered under his breath.

"What's that?" McCorkle asked.

"I said, Scala don't *hate* you," said the convict earnestly. "I mean he don't give a damn if you're alive or dead."

"This fellow's right," McCorkle confided to the group. "He *says* Tony doesn't really hate *me*. Isn't it more that he hates what I stand for?" The group seems to agree. "What *does* he hate?"

A convict snickers. Scala looks at him dubiously. "This goddam prison," the convict says.

"Right," says McCorkle. "This jail, the guards, the police, the whole state of New Jersey. Tony hates all authority." The whole session spins about Scala who, McCorkle points out, "always seems to be burned up."

Finally Scala stirs and says: "What the hell, they can't say all them things about me just because I said one single word."

"Then why the hell *did* you say it?" McCorkle asks in a friendlier tone.

"You wouldn't know. I get sick of being locked up so much. But never mind."

"We'll take that up next time," McCorkle says, closing the session.

The next meeting wandered off onto previous topics — parole, chow, prison guards — before talk swung again toward Tony Scala. McCorkle was saying that some people who hate one thing frequently take it out on other things — even to griping about the food. How do people get such attitudes anyway?

After some discussion, a man sitting next to Scala said: "Some guys have a rough time as kids. Maybe they don't get along with their old man — things like that."

McCorkle asked: "Is that what happened to *you?*"

"I don't mean me," said the prisoner lamely. "But I often hear guys say how their old man made it hard for them when they was kids."

Now Scala stirred impatiently and said, perhaps half in defense of his crony, "You wanta know what happens to kids? My old man kicked me around like a piece of dirt, see? I'd be too scared to sleep when he was out gettin' soused — he'd belt me when he come in, understand? He was rotten to my mother, too, until she died. I was eight."

As he spun his tale of a slum boy's sordid home life, Scala seemed to develop genuine feeling. "I hate to say this, but there were times when I almost wanted to kill him."

"Your old man was a louse, Tony," a convict assured him. "What happened?"

Scala grimaced. "I always run away. So they sent me to Jamesburg (State Home for Boys)."

McCorkle: "How did you get along there?"

"What the hell," said Tony Scala blankly. "*I'm here.* Let's talk about somebody else, hey?" And the group left it at that.

Afterward McCorkle remarked to me: "Really tough men like Scala have backgrounds almost too painful for them to talk about, and the future seems hopeless. They've had little capacity for loyal, warm, human relationships. Their strongest tie has been to the gang."

This gang spirit has always plagued penal institutions, molding inmates' attitudes in a basically anti-social way. But the group idea uses this very gang spirit to socialize the criminal. "When a person comes to trust those around him he'll talk."

Recently, I checked at Rahway on Scala. He is still in, with years to go. But he is no longer in the lockup gang. Tony holds a prison job as electrician's helper. Guards, wary of convicts like Scala, admit he gives them no more trouble.

"It's a man's inability to get along in a group that makes him a criminal in the first place," says McCorkle. "Most criminals won't believe that — until group sessions prove it." But, also, it takes a skilled leader to guide a backward convict to the same understanding. The truth

of this grew clear to me during the 11th session of a group at Bordentown.

We were eight armed robbers, three automobile thieves, two payroll bandits, an embezzler, two strong-arm men, a rapist — and Walter, a giant Negro who is serving ten years for attempted murder. Under McCorkle's skillful guidance, Walter has been telling the group why he fights with a guard in the prison kitchen.

Maxwell, the guard, pushes Walter in the back, Walter says. Maxwell makes Walter hate him, strike back — that lands him in solitary confinement. During this recital Walter's eyes bulge with fury.

"That's interesting," McCorkle says calmly. "Why do you think Maxwell treats you like that?"

"Because he's a white man and I'm colored," roars Walter. With deadly vehemence he adds, "No white man's gonna push me around. It's been that way all my life and I won't take it."

"Any of you other colored men work in the kitchen?" asks McCorkle. Several Negroes signify that they do.

"You," says McCorkle, nodding to one of them. "Does Maxwell ever push *you* around?"

"Only once," says the colored robber.

"What did you do then?" McCorkle asks.

"I just turned around, so's Maxwell can see my face," the robber says, with a grin, "so's Maxwell can see I ain't Walter!"

The entire group guffaws at Walter's expense. Clearly whatever lies between Walter and Maxwell must be a personal issue, not racial.

"What kind of guy is Maxwell anyway?" McCorkle asks the colored robber.

The robber looks to his kitchenmates as though for support. Then, staring gravely at Walter, he says: "Maxwell is okay. If a man *do* his work, Maxwell don't bother him none."

Now McCorkle carries the ball. "Whenever some of us feel that people are against us, don't we try to think it's for reasons that can't be our fault, like the color we are? But maybe if people are against us, it's because of things *we've* done to *them*."

"Damn it!" Walter explodes. "You people just talk and talk. This bunch is worse than Maxwell and all the guards. I want out of it."

"What does the group think?" Mac asks.

"Walter's afraid we'll show up his mistakes," a colored prisoner says.

Walter, baffled with emotion, stares hard at the floor. It's not difficult to believe that somehow, inside himself, this big man faces a worse trouncing than he ever received in the squad room of a precinct station. Now McCorkle veers his barrage onto a quiet young white prisoner who is serving 15 years for a payroll robbery. "You haven't said anything today. What do you think?"

"Well," this young convict says hesitantly, "you can't sit in jail without wondering sometimes if you aren't wrong."

"What happens then?" McCorkle asks softly.

"Maybe you think: 'Suppose I'd done that job a little different, maybe I wouldn't have got caught.' Or you think: 'Lots of guys pull tricks like that; why did the cops pick on me?' You can even think: 'Ten years is a hell of a stretch for a two-minute stick-up.' A guy can get sour on everything if he wants to."

"He can," McCorkle agrees. "But can't a guy think some other way while he's in jail?"

"Yeah. But that's tougher. Most guys just pull their time and keep their mouths shut. They talk about different jobs they pulled, and lie about jobs they didn't pull, just to blow themselves up. But they don't talk about the reasons they got that way."

"Why?" persists Mac.

"In prison a guy is locked up mostly inside himself."

"We're all locked up mostly inside ourselves," McCorkle remarks sympathetically.

"You don't trust nobody, see?" the prisoner goes on. "You've got only your-

self to count on, so you don't want to figure you're wrong. If a guy starts figuring *he's* the guy that landed *himself* in jail, he don't have no peace of mind any more."

"And that's what Walter's afraid of?" Mac asks.

"Sure, he's afraid," the young convict affirms. "Plenty of guys would rather do their flat time, with no chance at parole, than have to think of themselves like that. That's why lots of people hate this group business. They're scared of it."

"Do any of you others feel that way?"

McCorkle is a very shrewd leader, and Walter is no longer alone. McCorkle has put that question in seeming innocence. Now it hung unanswered in the smoke-filled room. Some convicts gazed far out through the steel-barred windows. Others studied intently the walls and ceiling of the room. No prisoner looked at another or at McCorkle. But their silence spoke louder than words.

A group meeting, of course, is unrehearsed; the leader takes only the fragments of life experience which members volunteer during the sessions and somehow brings them into a unified framework — "to give members a sense of going somewhere, toward mutually agreed-upon goals." The leader aims at teaching two things: first, your problems are not peculiar to yourself; second, if you want, to change, you can. (In this respect the group resembles Alcoholics Anonymous, our most widespread application of group technique. And AA's national records show that 75 percent of its members achieve their group goal of reform.)

It is surprising how the halting, crude, painfully spoken ideas of 25 convicts are woven into a purposeful theme, finally to be summed up and announced with fresh significance so that convicts recognize the deep application to themselves. And recognize it they do.

I saw this dramatically illustrated at a meeting when the group faced one of the toughest nuts it has to crack — the highly intelligent, superficially cooperative liar.

Phil Kelly, 24, is a superb model of the fawning opportunist whom most convicts scorn as a "handshaker" and "snow-job artist." His sensitive face makes a pleasant impression. But his official record describes him as "shrewd, evasive, unreliable, solitary, antisocial." He was a passive participant in an armed holdup in which the victim was beaten with a gun. He had been transferred to Bordentown from Rahway after attempting bribery of prison officials for a quick release.

As this group's 15th hour opened, Kelly was talking.

"I went before the parole committee yesterday. They let my partner out 16 months ago — but I'm still here. They told me, 'We give you a year to clear up your personality problem.' They didn't tell me what the problem was. I don't know what they mean."

"What do you suppose the committee was getting at?" McCorkle asks.

A quiet, thoughtful-looking prisoner speaks up. "Maybe they figured he wasn't sincere. They thought Kelly was giving them a snow job." The group laughs cruelly, and Kelly frowns.

"Could *you* tell Kelly what his problem is?" McCorkle asks a huge, round-shouldered Negro.

"Shucks," says the big man, puzzled, "Kelly's nice. He ain't here because of his personality. Kelly come here for the *crime* he done."

"Well what are *you* here for?" McCorkle asks.

"Fightin'. I took after a guy with my knife."

"Some of us don't get that angry at people, do we? Isn't that tied up with *your* personality, the kind of guy *you* are?"

"Doggone," says the big fellow, "that's my temper."

"Hadn't you better do some thinking about that?"

"Mightn't be here if I had," the big man says.

"We must think things through," McCorkle says. "We couldn't even get started with Kelly's problem until this group first agreed that what we do is tied up with the kind of people we are.

Now what did those eight parole people see when they looked at Kelly that made them say, 'Look, fella, you gotta make some changes'?"

"They see Kelly's trying to put something over," says the quiet man again. "The committee ain't dopes. They can spot a snow job and a handshaker. They've seen them things before."

"Everybody's smiling," McCorkle observes. To the quiet prisoner, "Why are *you*?"

"I'm smiling because I've been looking at Kelly — and he's smiling. I knew he would be, right now."

"Why is Kelly smiling?"

"Because we're getting mighty close to Kelly, so he'd like to snarl. But he don't want us to know how close we're getting, so he smiles."

Kelly is white and worried.

McCorkle says, "Let's leave Kelly for a moment. Why do some people have difficulty establishing close relationships with others?"

"They don't have confidence."

McCorkle: "We all know people who live pretty much on the surface. They move from place to place, from woman to woman, from job to job. They don't let other people get to know them very well. Why are some people like that?"

Bloor, a little forger, says: "Such a person has something and loses it. That takes confidence away. Perhaps he was deeply attached and something spoiled it. It happened to me."

McCorkle: "When we lose confidence in ourselves, when we feel people won't like us the way we are, we feel the need of saying, 'This is the kind of guy I am,' and put up a false front. I know several people like that."

"But why do they act that way?" the big Negro asks.

"If I were to take a punch at you — we're Outside now — what would be the first thing you'd do?"

"Hit you back."

"You might hit, later. But what's the *first* thing?"

"Put up my hands. I'd see somethin' was comin' that would hurt."

McCorkle: "He'd put up his hands, or

duck, so he wouldn't get hurt. Because people can be hurt in lots of ways, they develop ways to protect themselves; like a fellow learns to put up his dukes and protect his body, people learn to protect their feelings inside.

"But let's get back to Kelly. Kelly, how would you say that you went about developing ways to protect your feelings?"

"I put a lot of trust in my mother," Kelly says. "She died when I was a kid. Then I put my confidence in Dad. He went to State Prison. All the neighborhood kids knew it. I decided I wouldn't count much on other people. They might disappear, or things could blow up again. The way to get by, I figured, was to put up a front. I played horses, drank, gambled, ran around with lots of women. Drifting along, I didn't have any deep contacts with anyone, I guess. So I'd try to cover up that feeling of being by myself."

"That's Kelly's life as he sees it," says McCorkle. "He developed some ways of getting along with people. But he says he felt that, deep down inside, something was missing. Now I wonder" — McCorkle's voice was warm and kindly — "doesn't Kelly use a lot of words just to cover himself up?"

The others: "Sure."

McCorkle: "Perhaps Kelly can tell us something about us, and about himself. Don't people sometimes use words, a swarm of words which they push out in front of them, to keep other people from getting close to them?"

From the group: "Yeah."

McCorkle: "Isn't that why the group used to think of Kelly as a handshaker and a snow-job artist?"

The group says, "That's right." Kelly stares into his hands as he hears their verdict.

McCorkle: "Isn't it interesting that, now we're closer to Kelly, Kelly isn't nearly so talkative?"

The quiet man: "Sure. All these words a guy pushes out ahead of him like a shell. We're sort of made up of shells. First, words; then a shell of silence inside that; then more words. That's why it's hard to get inside some guys. Some guys put out a shell of words, other guys put out a shell of silence, and . . ."

" — and that's *you!*" says McCorkle, delightedly.

"Well, I mean . . ." says the quiet prisoner.

"Isn't it true of him?" McCorkle asks the group. "He has a shell of silence. He discovered that for himself. And Kelly has a shell of words. Sometimes we feel people will like us better if we show them a shell instead of our real selves."

"Which I realize is the case with me," says Bloor, the little forger. "I consciously endeavored to gather a vo-cabulary and lex-i-con of words so that I could, to a certain extent, express myself in a favorable light of the people I would deign to associate with. I desired to give them an impression that I am on the same plane as are they."

"We won't pick that up today," says McCorkle with heroic patience. "But we'll save it, because now Bloor's telling us, from the inside of his own shell, about himself.

"So when the committee told Kelly to take another year, they noticed his shell.

"Kelly's been honest with us today, hasn't he? He must feel that we could like him without any shell. One purpose of this group is to help Kelly and the rest of us find out more things about ourselves. Someday you people will walk out of prison knowing that you can trust people and that they can trust you for what you really are. You'll have left all your shells back here at Bordentown."

Such is the remarkable work being done in New Jersey prisons. Groups are now in operation at Bordentown, Rahway and Anandale, and some progress has been made in the women's prison at Clinton Farms. Beginnings have also been made in the federal-prison system and at San Quentin and other California prisons. The program so far concentrates on the young, who are most malleable, offer best chance of reform — and commit nearly two thirds of all violent crimes.

Up to now, the most that prisons have

been able to do toward rehabilitation of criminals is to reduce their time for good conduct, upgrade them on skills as they show aptitude in prison industries. Austin H. MacCormick, director of the Osborne Association, points out: "Any convict can follow prison rules, then break the community's when he gets out. So many criminals always do. That's where the group idea marks an enormous change in prison thinking."

But obviously, to establish groups will take patience. "The group method cannot be spread over a penal system like paint with a brush," says Sanford Bates, New Jersey's prison commissioner. "It takes a full year to establish the practice in a single institution. After that time the inmates become convinced that there are no boomerangs to what they say in group sessions."

Groups stand at the forefront of several modern sciences — psychiatry, criminology, sociology, penology. Still, whatever may be stated in technical subtleties is summed up in: *"It is not good for man to live alone."* In fact, for man as a social creature it is impossible. Man is accustomed to live in groups.

But how can convicts, when formed into guided groups, influence each other to be better men instead of worse? For the same wonderfully curious reason that impels any of us to get along in his community, reinforcing each other's accepted behavior, disapproving of the other citizen's departure from it — and occasionally, perhaps, as in these prison groups, disapproving of our *own* departures.

In any group, at any moment, he who deviates is one against the disapproving majority. And he will on the next occasion very probably be one of the solid majority, disapproving the man who deviates. Thus we are linked with human

ties more enduring than chains. Tony Scala defied the values of his group until it, and his own feelings, made him accept his group's common standards of conduct.

"Criminal behavior is learned, not predestined," says a leading criminologist. "It grows out of the same motives (wrongly applied) as does noncriminal behavior." In much the same fashion Kelly was forced by his group's disapproval and his own to capitulate and acknowledge the truth about himself — thereupon earning the group's sympathy and approval, and giving them a really inspiring example. Proper behavior tends to be supported in any group — just as in the big Outside group to which most of us belong, and from which these prisoners have been exiled.

Such thoughts stirred one of the country's most eminent psychiatrists to say to me: "You can't work with groups without realizing that the fundamental and unbearable human tragedy for a human being is, by whatever misfortune, whether in sickness or in delinquency, to have shut himself off from society."

Penologists agree that criminals won't be "cured" in prisons by groups or anything else. Steps must be taken, too, outside prison walls — toward improved parole systems, toward removal of the stigma attached to ex-convicts, toward community understanding. We cannot expect an ex-criminal to "go it alone" in a hostile society more successfully than the rest of us could.

As Mr. Bates said the other day, "Return of the Prodigal Son was only half of that famous Bible story. The other half followed when his community welcomed him home."

A Counseling Viewpoint
for the USO Worker*

BY CARL ROGERS

We are facing today a new problem in regard to counseling, the problem of what sort of counseling can be wisely carried on by the person with little professional training or the person whose professional training is in some field other than that of dealing with adjustment problems. It is commonplace knowledge that servicemen, their wives and relatives, servicewomen, and industrial workers who have been transplanted into war production areas, are bringing many problems of personal adjustment to USO workers, chaplains, clergymen, college teachers, and others who have not regarded the task of counseling as their primary responsibility. These workers feel themselves doubtfully equipped to assist in the solution of personal problems. In a great many instances, however, other resources for dealing with the individual are limited or nonexistent.

Among the situations which come to such workers, some typical examples might be mentioned. There is the homesick and lonely inductee; there is the serviceman who is perplexed as to whether or not to get married; there is the servicewoman who is deeply upset because her engagement has been broken; there is the man who is concerned about his wife's behavior while he is far from home; there are the returned servicemen, often bitterly resentful in regard to civilian life and confused as to their own aims and purposes; there are the wounded and handicapped individuals who, in spite of good medical care, feel deeply insecure as they endeavor to face the world; there are the psychoneurotic individuals whose conflicts and instabilities bring them often to the civilian individual in whom they

feel confidence. These are some of the types of adjustment difficulties which come, unheralded and unsought, to every individual whose work brings him in contact with service personnel and war production workers.

The statement is sometimes made that such problems of personal adjustment should be referred to psychiatrists, psychologists, or social case workers. This advice does not take into account the facts of our present war situation. There is not a sufficient number of these professionally qualified people to handle the multitude of personal adjustment problems which have arisen. Their trained services should be reserved for the more serious cases. The basic question is whether there are types of counseling assistance which may be rendered by the USO worker, the clergyman, the teacher, the industrial counselor, to the individual whose problem is not extreme, and to the severely maladjusted individual as a step in referring him to qualified therapists.

It would seem profitable to review briefly two general approaches to counseling, one widely used but inappropriate for the wartime counselor, the other less widely known but much more safe and justifiable for the individual who has a minimum of background in interviewing skills. If we consider counseling in terms of its focal point or emphasis, the two viewpoints we are about to discuss are found at opposite ends of a scale on which there are many intermediate points.

THE COUNSELOR-CENTERED APPROACH

The first type of counseling which we may consider could well be called coun-

* Originally published as a pamphlet by the Program Services Division, United Service Organizations, Inc., ca. 1943, no copyright claimed. Reprinted by permission of the author.

selor-centered. In this type of counseling the significant activities rest with the counselor. The counselor must first of all make a diagnosis, and hence an important part of his effort is concentrated on getting information. Much of this is gained from the individual who comes to him for help and more may be gained from others — spouse, parents, friends, commanding officer, physician, and the like. The counselor may gain information not only through interview and inquiry but also through the use of test procedures, measuring ability, personality characteristics, and other aspects of the individual and his adjustment. In order to make a suitable diagnosis the counselor must know the facts about the adjustment problem in question. If a man complains bitterly about his lack of promotion, the counselor must know whether or not this complaint is justified. If an individual is upset because he believes his wife is "stepping out," the counselor must know whether this is true or a figment of the man's imagination. If a woman war production worker feels that she is unjustly treated by the company, or a serviceman is uncertain as to whether he should marry now or after the war, the counselor must be able to gather all the facts which are relevant to these complex situations.

The second function of the counselor in this method of dealing with the individual is understanding and interpretation of the data. In order to interpret it correctly the counselor must have not only complete information but a thorough knowledge of the psychology of personality and the psychology of adjustment. He must accept a heavy responsibility for a correct diagnosis and interpretation since a mistake in judgment may cause him to deal with the problem in such a way as to make it worse rather than better. He must have the professional skill to know whether his diagnosis of the situation should be kept to himself or should be revealed and interpreted to the client. If he decides upon the latter, he will need skill in handling emotional resistance and must be prepared to find the client upset when truths are unpleasant.

The third function of this type of counselor is to have at hand the solutions for the problems which the client presents. He must know whether marriage is a wise step in this instance, whether divorce is the only solution for the next couple. He must be able to suggest a course of action for the man whose wife is unfaithful, and to advise steps which will lead toward deserved promotion for the war production worker. He must have the solution for homesickness and social maladjustment, for bitterness and discouragement. He must basically have the answers to the client's problems.

This counselor-centered type of counseling is typical of much of the work which is carried on today in this field. Experience would indicate that many professional and lay workers, in educational, religious, industrial, and social welfare organizations, deal with individuals in general accord with the procedures described. Workers in these fields often see the function of the counselor as creating rapport, gathering information, analyzing, diagnosing, interpreting, advising, suggesting, and solving.

Although this is a common viewpoint in many fields of counseling, it is opposed by a growing group of professional workers. It is a viewpoint which, while it may be justified in dealing with the mental defective, the insane, or with some delinquents, is without justification when we are dealing with the serviceman and his wife and family. It demands something very like omniscience on the part of the counselor if he is to solve the problems. It assumes one person may choose to guide and direct another in personal matters, an assumption which is untenable. It is not compatible with a genuinely democratic concept of the individual's responsibility for himself.

It is a viewpoint which is especially inappropriate for the group of wartime counselors to whom this pamphlet is directed. In the first place, the necessary process of gathering information is not feasible for the wartime counselor because it is too costly in time. In the second place, the professional training of most USO workers, clergymen, and other semi-professional counselors is inadequate to make the necessary diagnostic judgments. In the third place, this approach to counseling carries definite risk for the client when the counselor has inadequate professional preparation. Serious harm may be done to an individual by giving him prematurely an interpretation of his behavior which he is not prepared to accept. In the fourth place, this counseling viewpoint is not at all in accord with the free and non-authoritarian atmosphere in which most of these counselors operate. The USO worker, for example, who takes over the responsibility for diagnosing and solving the problems of one of the participants in his group is adopting a viewpoint quite contrary to the democratic and spontaneous atmosphere which prevails or should prevail in the major portion of his work.

THE CLIENT-CENTERED APPROACH

If this approach is so definitely unsuitable for the counselors of whom we are speaking, does it then mean that they must be content to use only a second-rate or ineffective type of counseling approach? Fortunately this is not in the least necessary. Counseling methods which have been developed in the past few years, and which have been crystallized in such institutions as Ohio State University, Western Electric Company, and some of the Child Guidance Centers, offer a safe and exceedingly helpful type of counseling approach which is definitely usable by the individual who does not have complete professional preparation in psychology or social case work. In the judgment of many it is even more helpful to the maladjusted individual than the traditional approach which has been outlined. In contrast with the previous viewpoint we may call it a client-centered type of counseling or, as it is sometimes called, non-directive counseling. In counseling of this sort the deeply significant activities

are those of the client, and the activities of the counselor are only such as will make it easier for the client to guide himself. There are two basic assumptions in this type of counseling which it is well to mention.

It is assumed that we should respect the integrity and the personal autonomy of the individual. It is felt that each person has a right to make his own decisions. He has the right to seek help and to take help, but he also has the right to refuse help. He is responsible for his own life, and every precaution should be taken to build this sense of responsibility, rather than to tear it down.

A second assumption is that the individual has an enormous capacity for adaption and for readjustment. Put in broader terms, the individual has a tremendous drive toward growth and maturity and positive health. The war has shown with striking clarity the capacities for adaption and for growth which exist within each individual. The primary aim of client-centered counseling is to release these forces, to free the individual to go on growing, when conflict, or circumstance, or doubt has halted him. *It is this strength within the individual,* not the strength within the counselor, upon which we must rely.

A growing number of professional people find themselves in accord with these assumptions, but do not carry them through in their counseling, because they know of no way of proceeding in the practical interviewing situation which would be in accord with these basic principles. In the past few years such techniques have been developing and crystallizing and have been described in several references. As we are coming to see the problem more clearly, primarily through more experience in the training of counselors, we become more and more convinced that the basic counseling procedures which implement this viewpoint can be boiled down to certain attitudes and techniques which, if adopted by the counselor, bring about a significant release of the individual growth potentiality and assist the person to become more independent, more responsible, more capable of managing his life problems satisfactorily. To describe them briefly is perhaps to oversimplify, but such a simplification may be of help to the beginning counselor.

In the first place, the attitude of the counselor needs to be one of genuine acceptance and willingness to understand. This does not mean approval of the client nor an uncontrolled sympathy with him. It means a deep and tolerant acceptance of him as a person different from the counselor, and an acceptance of his right to be different. It means an alert willingness to understand, which is perhaps the keynote of client-centered or non-directive therapy. The counselor is free to give his complete attention to understanding this other person, because he is not burdened by all the thought of what he (the counselor) must do about the situation. Instead of concentrating on the completeness of his information, the meaning of it, the probable diagnosis, he is free to give himself wholly to the problem of seeing the situation as it appears to the client.

The second attitude is best described as one of permissiveness. The counselor endeavors to create a relationship in which every expression of attitude is permitted, but none is demanded. The client is helped to feel that he is free to say anything, to discuss any attitude, to bring to the surface all his repressed antagonisms, his guilty feelings, his doubts, his confusions, and to reveal also the very tentative positive impulses which he discovers within himself, but he is not compelled to express any of these things. He is as free to withhold as he is to express.

A third attitude is the conviction on the part of the counselor that the client is capable of being responsible for his own life and capable of managing that life in a manner which will give him reasonable satisfaction. In some extreme instances this confidence is not warranted. The individual is definitely not capable of governing his life. In such cases counseling cannot be in the primary way of giving help. But in the great majority of

problems which arise with service personnel, war production workers, and their families, the individual is competent to direct himself and it is this reliance upon his potential capacity for self-direction which provides the basis for counseling.

USEFUL TECHNIQUES

How does the counselor handle the material which the client brings forth in this kind of atmosphere? There are two techniques above all others which predominate and in which the counselor should develop skill. The first, the major technique of client-centered counseling, is that of reflecting and clarifying the emotionalized personal attitudes which the client has expressed. A few examples may make clear what is meant by this technique. The following is from an interview with a soldier:

Soldier: Service doesn't mean a thing any more! You work hard to get ahead and what do they do but take it away from you again. There's no such thing as getting anywhere!

Counselor: You feel that they're unfair and that you haven't any chance of getting ahead.

Note that the counselor makes no attempt to evaluate the man's complaint or to probe into it. He merely indicates that he understands the attitude and helps the man clarify it for himself. Another example:

Soldier: I have higher ideals than most of the fellows here. I don't enjoy the kind of things they do so consequently I can't talk about them. It seems that they are of a different caste than I am. I have always had trouble in getting along with a group of people.

Counselor: You feel you don't adjust easily because you are really on a higher level than they are.

In this instance the counselor must surely have been tempted to interpret to the young man his obvious feeling of superiority which had doubtless developed out of his feeling of social inadequacy. This would have only aroused defensiveness. The counselor instead shows acceptance of the individual by reflecting his attitudes in a way which implies neither approval nor disapproval of the views expressed. One other example, this time from an interview with a woman war production worker, may also be helpful:

Worker: You know I have no parents. I was brought up in an orphanage. I'm all alone in the world. In case of a layoff what would I do? You know when you're all alone you have a feeling like you're scared sometimes.

Counselor: The possibility of a layoff frightens you because you feel so alone in the world.

Here, rather than giving reassurance, which is always easy but does not reassure, the counselor offers simply a genuine understanding which helps the girl face her own problems more clearly.

The counselor will find it helpful to use this technique of mirroring or reflecting attitudes with all the types of emotionalized response which crop up in the interviewing situation. Attitudes of guilt and self-reproach, attitudes of hostility and resentment, defensive and bragging attitudes, attitudes of fear and depression are all wisely dealt with in this fashion. It is particularly helpful where attitudes are ambivalent and contradictory, since it helps to put more clearly for the client the conflict he is facing.

This technique, which is simplicity itself in principle, is extremely and painfully difficult for counselors to acquire. It runs completely counter to all their previous experience. It requires them to withhold from the situation their own judgment, their own evaluation, their own diagnosis and solution of the difficulty. Instead of focusing upon the usual questions, "what do I think of this?" "What can I do about this?" "What is my judgment of this problem?" it demands a wholehearted immersion in the attitudes of the client and a complete concentration upon the one question, "What attitude is he expressing?" "How does he see this situation?" "How does he feel about this?" No matter how deeply negative, or how absurd, or how unfair these attitudes may seem to be, the counselor

endeavors to reflect them as accurately and fairly as possible.

The second counseling technique which will prove helpful is so simple as to need no comment. It is the technique of simple acceptance: "Yes," "Yes, I see," "M-hm," "I think I understand," and other responses of that sort. It may surprise some that such a simple aspect of counseling even deserves mention, but our study of phonographically recorded counseling reveals that this simplest of techniques is most used when the client is delving most deeply into himself and painfully bringing out significant insights.

And what else does the counselor do? He does nothing else, essentially, though there are some minor techniques at the beginning and end of the counseling situation that may be called into play. But he does not question, he does not probe, he does not analyze, he does not interpret, he does not advise, he does not suggest or coerce. His whole effort has been put into giving the client the deepest understanding of which he is capable and of providing an accepting atmosphere in which the client can work through his problems in his own way.

THREE PHASES OF THE COUNSELING PROCESS

One may well ask, what is the justification for carrying on such a peculiar form of counseling, one which has so little in common with ordinary procedures, which assumes, for example, that help may be given without a diagnosis being made. It is right that such a question should be raised, and increasingly we have a clear and satisfactory answer. On the basis both of clinical experience and a rapidly growing body of research, it can be said that the justification for such procedures is that they work — astonishingly well. The counselor who follows the basic principles and procedures described will find that his clients, in the majority of cases, will go through a definite sequence of events which taken together constitute the counseling process. Ordinarily this process will be achieved through several interviews, though sometimes much may occur in one contact. First comes a period of "talking out," an experience of emotional release, when the client uses the acceptance and permissiveness of the situation to pour out, or painfully to bring out, all the attitudes which surround his life problems. As he discovers that this is a situation in which it is safe to express real feelings, deeper and deeper attitudes are revealed, even those which have been previously repressed and which he has never dared admit even to himself.

It is during this experience of emotional release that the individual talks out not only the superficial aspects of his problem but gradually some of the motivating attitudes which underlie and are responsible for his behavior. For example, a combat man who has had many difficulties since his return to this country is anxious, worried, and insecure. He feels that he is not living up to the expectations of his parents and others. Of his combat experience he says, "Overseas I felt fine. I was scared all the time but I wasn't dependent upon anyone and then my parents were proud of me. I had more peace of mind over there than I have had since my return. Over there you only worried about whether you would be killed. Everything seemed so d—— simple." Much of the dynamics of the man's behavior is revealed in this statement.

A young woman working in a war plant "blows up" because her work is criticized. As she talks out her attitudes to the counselor she brings in the home and family factors which help to explain her behavior. She says of the supervisor who criticized her, "I guess you can't blame her. I'm so tired of having others trying to tell me what to do that I just burn up. I don't mean just here in the factory, but any place. At home my mother always corrected me. I guess I must do everything wrong." (Pause.) "I'm beginning to think I just don't do things right. It was bad enough at home, so I don't want to work and have the same thing happen again. Since I've been with my aunt, well, I have the same

trouble only not as bad as at home." Obviously she is describing not only her behavior but the reasons for it.

Following upon this period of emotional release and catharsis, and to some extent intermingled with it, is the second phase of the counseling process, the development of self-understanding and insight. As the individual gives expression to his more basic attitudes in the very accepting atmosphere which the counselor creates, he finds that he begins to understand himself better. Frequently this increased understanding of self is put into words, though sometimes it is evident only in the changed reactions of the individual. In the case of the young woman just cited a realization of her basic pattern of behavior is expressed in an interesting portion of the interview:

Worker: I would like to do something correct — so at least others would tend to think I did the right thing. Accept what I did as **correct.**

Counselor: You feel you would like to do the right thing. Let's say, do the acceptable thing.

Worker: I believe that's it — I believe that's what I have been trying to explain. I guess I always try to do just the opposite because in the past I've been corrected so much I just do the things that would — well, upset my mother and aunt. I would know underneath that it was wrong — at least it wouldn't make me feel happy. Still I didn't want to give in. Sometimes I knew I would feel worse than they would. Still, I would not give in. Sometimes this would make me so unhappy that I would like to admit I was wrong — but then I would feel I just would not give in.

A young man who has been in a great many difficulties because of his disregard for others and his attempts to do exactly as he wishes in every situation puts his analysis of himself in these words:

Young Man: I wonder how I got so self-centered? When people tell me I'm selfish, I can explain it away and prove that I'm not selfish but when I see what I'm doing —

Counselor: You feel that you're really self-centered, and that explains this seemingly odd attitude about what you put in your letters.

Young Man: Yeah. I think one reason for this is that when I was young, I was cute and admired, especially by the girls. I've had a feeling of wanting everything and giving nothing. I *like* a circle of admirers. I feel they should be interested in me just because I'm me. That's thoroughly ridiculous, of course.

It is impossible in a few words to give any clear notion of the spontaneity, vitality, and depth of these insights. The illustrations may indicate that they have an individual and unique quality which is far more closely related to the real situation than the best "diagnosis" which the counselor might make. They are amazingly effective as stepping stones to new goals. As the client sees himself more clearly, he chooses new directions in which to go.

These reoriented goals and the actions which implement them are the third and final portion of the counseling process. Our research studies show that in the final portion of the counseling contacts, new decisions, new plans, reports of changed behavior, rise to a peak. The young woman in the war plant decides, "I would like to have another chance. That is, I believe I would think before I would do what I did yesterday." A soldier who has gone AWOL and has talked out his situation with a counselor says, "I realize I've got to go back and face the music." He adds realistically, "There is no use in pretending that I won't be afraid when I do go back." The young man who has been so self-centered decides to take a hard manual job for himself in order to learn self-discipline. "I thought I could work for three months at some hard work, and setting that goal and reaching it and the education I would get from it would be worth while. It would be a way of bringing up my confidence. I don't think I would quit. I hope not. I hope it isn't too hard!" The choices and decisions that are made in this spontaneous fashion in a client-centered counseling atmosphere are choices that stick. They are not simply intentions but are actually carried out by the client.

This counseling process is not, to be sure, evident in every case. The wartime counselor must frequently work in a setting very poorly adapted to counseling. His lack of adequate preparation and supervised experience may often reduce the success which might have been achieved. Yet the experience we have had with these counseling methods and the experience we have had in training people to use them cause us to say with the greatest conviction that through such counseling, individuals can reorient their lives. Counselors who have the attitudes described, and who follow the principles presented, find that clients can and do choose to live in a more mature fashion and can markedly improve their personal and social relationships, their marital adjustments, and their educational and vocational purposes, even where these have been destructive or unsatisfactory. Although this type of counseling is relatively new, it is already abundantly clear that the individual can, through this approach, be helped to help himself.

A COUNSELING PROCEDURE FOR THE
WARTIME COUNSELOR

It is this client-centered variety of counseling which is strongly advocated as holding the most promise for the semi-professional counselor who is called upon to deal with the wartime adjustment problems of service personnel and war production workers. In the first place, it is effective — even more effective than more time-consuming therapies. In the second place, it can be taught and taught widely to semi-professional counselors who do not have the full professional preparation which would be necessary for a thoroughly competent handling of all personality maladjustments. Third, it is a procedure which can be used safely. The partially-trained counselor who uses the directive or interpretive methods of the counselor-centered approach may, if he bungles, precipitate a suicide or a psychosis. Client-centered counseling, however, is safe and is temporarily helpful even in the extreme cases in which the counselor's primary function is to refer the situation to a psychiatrist. It is only because it is safe that it is possible to think of short-time training of large numbers of counselors.

Finally, it may be stressed that it is based on a philosophy which is fully consistent with the highest development of democratic living. It is in basic accord with a viewpoint to which we may hope the future belongs — a viewpoint built upon the assumption that the individual has worth and dignity and has the capacity to choose and live a spontaneous, independent, self-directed life.

CHAPTER XII

Executive Leadership

INDIVIDUALS are found to obtain satisfactions from different aspects of group relationships, as we saw in Chapter VIII. Some individuals understand the importance of the activity of the group to the activities of the external system and can convey to others a sense of larger purpose; some know how to train and initiate new members into the group; some are skilled in performing the detailed tasks that are necessary activities of the group. Any of these roles — and many more — are important to the group and produce satisfactions for the individuals who play them. These individuals form their roles out of selected behavior which is their response to the current situation in terms of their total past experience. The various roles help maintain the group's continued existence and the individuals' continued interaction with it, and lead to a feeling of individual usefulness in accomplishing both a personal and a group objective.

In terms of utility to the group the leader's role is often the most crucial, as appeared in Chapter IX. Homans observes that it has certain characteristics that appear to be almost universal and that most face-to-face groups produce a "natural" or informal leader from the ordinary processes of interaction without much, if any, conscious planning. Homans describes him as follows:

> The leader [in the small face-to-face group] is the man who comes closest to realizing the norms the group values highest. The norms may be queer ones, but so long as they are genuinely accepted by the group, the leader, in that group, must embody them. His embodiment of the norms gives him his high rank, and his rank attracts people: the leader is the man people come to; the scheme of interaction focuses on him. At the same time, his high rank carries with it the implied right to assume control of the group, and the exercise of control itself helps maintain the leader's prestige. This control he is particularly well equipped to wield by reason of his position at the top of the pyramid of interaction. He is better informed than other men, and he has more channels for the issuing of orders. He controls the group, yet he is in a sense more controlled by it than others are, since it is a condition of his leadership that his actions and decisions shall conform more closely than those of others to an abstract norm. Moreover, all these elements, and not just one or two of them, come into leadership; all are related to one another and reinforce one another for good or ill.[1]

The leader in such a group through his total response in all his interactions shows his understanding of the norms that are important to the group; his entire behavior both verbal and otherwise steadily communicates this understanding to his group. At all times this communication is directed to an understood context of the group. Others hear him as always in their own frame of reference, but find in their future interactions with him that their understanding and his meaning were very close together.

---

[1] George C. Homans, *The Human Group* (New York: Harcourt, Brace and Company, Inc., London: Routledge and Kegan Paul Ltd., 1950), pp. 188–189.

Face-to-face groups develop leaders as a result of the internal system of relationships. An organization, however, is composed of a number of interlocking groups; these groups have been gathered together to accomplish a series of related tasks which none of them could accomplish alone. Although the organization as a whole has basic purposes shared to some degree by each of its groups, it has other, more general, purposes not wholly shared with any of them. The groups also have purposes and norms developed in their own internal systems which differ from the organizational objectives. Leaders within the groups hold the norms of their groups rather than those of the organization. Although these two sets of norms are not necessarily divergent, they do develop from different sets of interactions and often differ widely.

These groups then do not ordinarily coördinate themselves through their leaders in a way that seems most effective to the organization. Executives and others in "authority" who respond more fully to the general organizational purposes develop in the external system. They derive their strength both from an achieved and ascribed status in the system external to the groups and from their skills in dealing with the groups themselves. An executive is usually placed over a group by the external system and is not often the "natural" leader. At times, however, the norms of the group may be very close to those that the executive feels are most useful to the organizational needs. Then the executive may be able to respond in ways that seem nearly identical with the behavior of a group leader. When the norms diverge the differences in behavior become important: the group leader must follow the norms of his group or lose his leadership, while the executive must follow the organizational norms and still strive to retain control of the group.

Business organizations, for example, are brought together to manufacture and sell certain related products to particular markets. Each group within the organization has some economic norms to which it responds that are related to this objective. But each group also has many other norms which are related to the social interactions within the group and which at particular times may be of greater importance to the group than the economic norms. The leader cannot emphasize the economic norms to an appreciably greater extent than the group feels desirable if he is to remain as leader. But certain economic norms may at times be of overwhelming importance to the organization. Executives, selected by the management partly for their skills in responding to this varying emphasis, keep the organizational purposes before the various groups.

In considering the relationship between superior and subordinate Homans says:

> Although . . . [it] is to some degree the same in every group, it varies greatly in intensity from group to group according to various circumstances, including the relation of the group to its environment, the ability of the subordinate to escape from authority, and the extent to which the superior is chosen by the members of the group. The relationship between sea captain and seaman lies at one end of the spectrum . . . [and] the relationship between Doc and the rest of the Nortons lies close to the other end . . . The closer the situation approaches the former end of the spectrum, the more completely the interaction between the superior and the subordinate is kept down to the amount characteristic of the external system and the greater is the divinity that hedges the superior. In favorable circumstances, especially if he lives up to the norms of the group as a whole, respect for him will be great; in unfavorable circumstances, hostility toward him will be great in like

measure . . . The variations from group to group in the relationships between superior and subordinate are quantitative; in some groups the tie [seems] . . . hardly different from the tie between equals, in others very different indeed.[2]

The divergence between the norms of a group resulting from its internal system of social interaction and the norms of the external system as they are emphasized by an executive brings varying amounts of force to the superior-subordinate relationship. The greater the divergence and the greater the force applied to keep the group operating effectively in its environment, the fewer the interactions between the superior and the subordinate. This decreased interaction may become an ideal in itself: "If you are too close to your men, they will not obey you," or "You must not be too affectionate with your children or they will get out of hand." Such lowered interactions may in fact be necessary to prevent the executive or parent from being too influenced by the subordinate's needs — otherwise he might be swayed too often in the "wrong" direction.

Executives may use many techniques in an attempt to bring the norms of the group into line with the norms considered useful to the company; and in so doing they modify the behavior of their subordinates. The basic process is similar to that used by parents when teaching a child to conform to the standards of the parents' social class. The executives and the parents may say, "I know this is the best thing to do now," or "This is what you should do," or "This is what you must do or I will punish you." Such control, although different from that used by the group leaders, is often necessary and effective; it may seem entirely proper under many circumstances and be widely accepted by all concerned.

The individuals in the group subordinate to the executive will also try to modify the executive's values through their interactions with him wherever the divergence becomes important to them. They will apply such force as they consider possible and appropriate to modify his behavior. Many of the group's problems will be brought to the executive's attention in the form of complaints, indicating that he "should" do something differently. Complaints indicate the strains in the system; they show the difficulties developing in the internal system of relationships, the difficulties between the group and the executive, and the difficulties between the internal and the external systems.

Careful listening by the executive to the complaints of his subordinates, showing a real interest in their problems, is often very effective. Such listening (in the general way discussed in Chapter XI) includes not only the content of the complaints themselves but also the underlying value assumptions and sentiments of the subordinates.[3] If the executive encourages the expression of such matters, he may both understand more fully the nature of the social forces at work and realign some of the feelings to more productive ends. His skills in handling the interactions between the internal and the external system will depend on the clarity of his understanding and the accuracy of his response to the total situation as it will in fact affect his subordinates in the future.

Chester I. Barnard is an executive of wide experience in private industry, government, and philanthropy. He describes in the book below the considerations he believes must be kept in mind by an executive who wishes to operate

---

[2] *The Human Group*, pp. 246–247.

[3] See F. J. Roethlisberger and William J. Dickson, *Management and the Worker* (Cambridge: Harvard University Press, 1939), Chapters IX–XVI.

well in the large organizations of modern society. He describes this book as "an attempt to arrange for orderly presentation hypotheses . . . gradually constructed through several years concerning the executive processes, which are specialized functions in what we know as 'organizations.' If these functions are to be adequately described, the description must be in terms of the nature of organization itself." [4] He says that these hypotheses have been understood implicitly by executives in many fields — indeed, they can communicate their observations to each other in a few words because of common understanding. But he also notes that these same executives have seldom succeeded in explaining themselves to persons who have not shared their type of experience because the assumptions behind their thinking have never been made articulate. Barnard makes explicit in terms of a general theory of organization those assumptions which his experience has indicated to be important. Read

CHESTER I. BARNARD, *The Functions of the Executive* (Cambridge: Harvard University Press, 1938), pp. 55–61, 139–234, 258–284.

The reading from Barnard begins with a definition of the special sense in which he uses the words "effective" and "efficient." "Effective" he relates to the degree of accomplishment of an organization's formal purpose (for example, the making of automobiles or pencils). "Efficient" he relates to the satisfaction of the individual motives of the various members of the organization. This verbal distinction is the key to much of his later material.

Barnard then discusses "The Economy of Incentives." Here he is dealing with the ways people must be "induced to coöperate" by the executives of the organization. In other words, how do executives achieve organizational purpose *through* the satisfaction of individual motives? Since means are limited, special skill is necessary to use them to best effect. Barnard classifies the available means into two types:

> An organization can secure the efforts necessary to its existence . . . either by the objective inducements it provides or by changing states of mind. It seems to me improbable that any organization can exist as a practical matter which does not employ both methods in combination. In some organizations the emphasis is on the offering of objective incentives — this is true of most industrial organizations. In others the preponderance is on the state of mind — this is true of most patriotic and religious organizations.[5]

He goes on to show that the "authority" of an executive grows out of his skillful use of incentives so as to achieve willing acceptance of his orders from his subordinates. "Disobedience [by a subordinate] of . . . a communication is a denial of its authority for him. Therefore . . . the decision as to whether an order has authority or not lies with the persons to whom it is addressed, and does not reside in 'persons of authority' or those who issue these orders." [6]

As part of this concept of "authority," Barnard observes that there is a " 'zone of indifference' in each individual within which orders are acceptable without conscious questioning of their authority." [7] In some situations this zone is wide — that is, almost any suggestion from above will be accepted. In others,

---

[4] Chester I. Barnard, *The Functions of the Executive* (Cambridge: Harvard University Press, 1938), p. vii.

[5] *Ibid.*, p. 141.

[6] *Ibid.*, p. 163.

[7] *Ibid.*, p. 167.

the zone is narrowed sharply — only the most specific orders, clearly aimed at the work process itself, and backed by a full display of official status symbols, will be followed.

In the remaining chapters, Barnard discusses various aspects of the decision-making process from the points of view of both the executive and the subordinate. He distinguishes between decisions that are made on explicitly rational grounds and those that include nonrational factors. He notes that often the decisions of top executives are centered on the resolution of moral or value conflicts: the executive has conflicting feelings of responsibility toward various individuals and groups and must find a way to synthesize these feelings harmoniously.

Barnard recognizes that one of an executive's important functions is the securing of an informal organization with compatible personnel; this is perhaps the most important means for developing and maintaining an adequate system of communication and reducing the necessity for formal decision-making on many detailed matters. In this way the executive makes use of knowledge of the important personal needs of many others, the active utilization of which is so vital to an "efficient" organization.

Barnard's work extends the Homans perspective on leadership in face-to-face groups as discussed above to cover the executive in formal organizations. In contrast to many other writers on this subject, Barnard emphasizes the importance of executive action concordant with the actual interactions, sentiments, and norms of the groups in the organization.

ADDITIONAL READINGS

Dubin, Robert, *Human Relations in Administration: The Sociology of Organization* (New York: Prentice-Hall, 1951).
A collection of readings and cases, tied together by the author's theory of organization.

Gardner, Burleigh B., and David Moore, *Human Relations in Industry* (rev. ed.; Chicago: Irwin, 1950).
An analysis of formal organization in terms of variations in status and lines of communication as expressed in interaction.

Golden, C. S., and H. J. Ruttenberg, *The Dynamics of Industrial Democracy* (New York: Harper, 1942).
Two labor leaders offer industrial executives some strong advice. They suggest that the executive functions can be performed in a way that takes full advantage of the desires of workers and thus enlists the full force of their coöperative energy.

Richardson, F. L. W., and C. R. Walker, *Human Relations in an Expanding Company* (New Haven: Yale University Press, 1948).
A study of the growth of one plant of the International Business Machines Corporation. The conclusions are similar to those of Worthy about Sears, Roebuck and Company.

Smith, E. D., *Technology and Labor* (New Haven: Yale University Press, 1942).
An analysis of the problems faced by executives when they introduce new machinery in their factories which increases the specialization of tasks. Based on a study of textile mills. Can be usefully compared to the article by Warner and Low, Chapter VIII.

Whyte, William F., *Human Relations in the Restaurant Industry* (New York: McGraw-Hill, 1948).
The full report on Whyte's researches in restaurants discussed above in Chapter

VIII. The second half of the volume is meant as a handbook for leaders and executives.

Worthy, James C., "Factors Influencing Employee Morale," *Harvard Business Review*, XXVIII (January 1950), 61–73.

―――― "Organizational Structure and Employee Morale," *American Sociological Review*, XV (April 1950), 169–179.

Discussions by an executive of Sears, Roebuck and Company of researches within their organization relating executive behavior and employee attitudes. He recommends decentralization of authority to encourage "efficient" (in Barnard's sense) informal organization.

CHAPTER XIII

Social Control and Equilibrium

THE LEADER of a group both controls and is controlled by it. The executive in an organization controls the groups under him, is controlled by them, affects and is affected by the total organization. In a similar way, each of us in our relationships with others operates within a framework of dynamic social control which gives continuity to our lives and to society. A wide range of choices seems to be open to us in our interactions with others. We can obtain many different statuses within the groups around us; we can respond to others in different ways and play different roles. But our choices of action are not limitless; we demand that these actions produce some sort of satisfactions for us, and apparently, as part of these personal satisfactions, we usually demand that they produce what we observe as satisfactions in others. Our choices of action are further limited by the consequences of our previous choices. We act, interact, and react at all times within some system of relationships; we are affected by it and it is modified by our actions. Social control seems to be inherent in the social processes.

We learn to operate within social systems in ways that are useful to us and to others. Whether we are participating in a group as a leader or follower, whether we are acting as a critic or observer of the group, we are nevertheless playing some role in respect to it — we ourselves demand that our responses have some constancy — and we are in some way influencing the behavior of others.

As we interact with others, taking part in social control, we are responding to two broad areas of the system of relationships: the total system as we have experienced it up to the present — our conclusion about the way people *are* — and the immediate situation. If our relationships to the current situation are important to us, we will not want to act in ways that we feel will disrupt these relationships and bring about consequences that may seem serious. We estimate, as we must, the potential disruption in terms of our conclusions about our past experiences. But these conclusions may be inadequate or poorly related to this particular situation.

Many of the cases might be used to illustrate this observation. Mrs. Michaelson, Sr., in the Michaelson Family case was responding to her idea of the way in which a "good mother" should behave — a well-established role; her demands and expectations were based on her earlier experience within this family when such behavior was appropriate and useful to it. Some of the difficulties that arose developed from the way in which the situation had changed in time, making her behavior inappropriate. She was responding to her idea of what the situation *should* be, not to the situation as it was. Mary White, in the Spofford Fabricated Products case, was also responding to a series of ideas of her own about what the situation *should* be. Neither of them showed any ability in observing or being influenced by the behavior of others; the degree of conflict in both these situations became high, but still did not lead either of them to modify her behavior toward the group requirements. On the other hand, Catharine O'Neill in the Spofford case was able, with some help, to observe the way people in that situation were behaving, find something reasonable in this behavior, and relate herself to it in productive ways. Richard Carter in the Delman Forge case created relationships during his first few years with the factory that were in accord with the ideas of the employees and supervisors about how he ought to behave; he related himself well to the social system of the factory and apparently enjoyed himself. Later his expectations and norms diverged from theirs; he behaved in response to the situation as he thought it should be without taking their norms into account, and he ran into difficulties.[1]

Still, no matter how inadequate or poorly related our observations are to the situation, we must act. We must do something we consider appropriate — even if the only appropriate action we can conceive is no action at all. This step, a first small one if necessary, may be considered as one in the direction of greater understanding and control. Through it we may test our appraisal of the actual situation by watching carefully the responses of others. An unexpected response to us may lead to a reconsideration of our general conclusions about people or of our immediately preceding behavior. The other persons have responded to us in a way that seemed to them appropriate from some point of view, unexpected though it is to us, and thus have indicated something about their idea of the situation.

The response of others is our clue to their view of the situation, and by our further responses we do several things at once. We continue to test the adequacy of our observation of their view; we express our own view either in affirmation, modification, or denial; and we take steps toward bringing the two views closer together or driving them further apart. An unexpected response from them may lead us to a new view of the situation, which may induce a new response from us, which in turn may elicit a new response from them.

If we are "responding well" to a situation, then it can be said that the results of our testing through our responses have led us to a "good" understanding of this system of relationships. Our "usual" responses have produced behavior from others that is satisfactory to us and does not violate our expectations. Adequate observation at some level of our consciousness is of first importance. In a situation that is producing large amounts of satisfaction for us, no important current observations are required on our part: the necessary observations have already been made by us in the past. However, as the situation changes either because "external" forces require some change or because we wish to relate ourselves to a system in new ways, then we must sharpen our observations and become more aware of what is going on. We must then continually observe more carefully the responses of others, evaluate and reëvaluate our observations in relation to our previous values and sentiments, and decide anew what we mean by "appropriate" responses.

Changes requiring new evaluations of this sort are always taking place. And

---

[1] See these three cases in Vol. II: The Michaelson Family, Case 3; Spofford Fabricated Products Company, Case 19; Delman Forge Company, Case 21.

changes, if they appear to be important, always seem to produce some disagreements between individuals. The problem in group interactions is not so much the disagreements themselves as it is the results of the disagreements. When a new system of relationships is developing following some change, tentative norms about the activities, interactions, and sentiments are set up within the group by a trial-and-error process — as described by Piaget for children's games.[2] The results of these norms are carefully watched and modified by the relationship process as it then exists. If the system develops to a point where coöperation is smooth, then certain norms have become well established. Under these circumstances the departure of any member from these norms will bring about some form of punishment — perhaps even isolation — and will tend to make him return to his previous compliance. This collective punishment in turn serves to reinforce the strength of group allegiance to the norm itself; the members believe in it more strongly because they have effectively met a challenge to it. On the other hand, if the conditions so change that an established norm of behavior no longer seems useful, conflict within the group, often around an "issue" or departure from that norm, tends to bring about a modification of the norms themselves to meet the new circumstances better. Disagreement or conflict is inherent in the process by which these changes are made.

Looked at from the perspective of its members, a social system appears to be a set of expectations that each person has of the way the others will behave. If this set of expectations is relatively stable, then everyone knows how to act. Looked at from an outside perspective, the social system appears to be an interweaving of elements, described by Homans as

> a configuration of dynamic forces. Sometimes the configuration is in balance, and a steady system is maintained; sometimes it is out of balance and continuing change occurs . . . but in both cases our emphasis is on the dynamic forces. Statics, in sociology as in mechanics, is a special case of dynamics. It is not structure but the forces that produce structure that interest us . . .
>
> A regularity of behavior persists, similar events recur in similar circumstances, only because departure from regularity is met by resistance. Nor is the resistance mere inertia. We all discern in human behavior some blind resistance to change, but the amount of sheer change that does take place in society suggests that the inertial force is not very powerful. Custom is not just "natural"; it is a miracle, and its persistence demands more than inertia alone.[3]

Homans goes on to examine the process of social control by which "departure from regularity is met by resistance." Although men join groups to achieve personal goals, group membership in turn modifies as well as creates personal goals. It is through such processes that individual motivations are synthesized into a social system that perpetuates itself. Read

GEORGE C. HOMANS, *The Human Group* (New York: Harcourt, Brace, 1950), pp. 281–312.

The processes of social control produce many different patterns of relationship, many types of social systems. There are systems in which the individuals involved interact smoothly with each other in carrying out the group purposes; then coöperation may be said to be high. There are systems where individual

---

[2] See Chapter V.
[3] *The Human Group*, p. 282.

purposes seem to be widely divergent in consistent ways; then conflict may be said to be high. There are situations where differences of purpose are fully expressed and reconciliation of differences is a part of the system. There are situations where such divergent purposes exist, but are kept carefully concealed and only expressed under extraordinary circumstances. There are situations which are tending toward either increased harmony or increased disharmony, but still can be considered in terms of a system of relationships composed of a large number of mutually dependent variables acting and reacting on each other. When that system is functioning well, we may say it is in a state of dynamic (changing) equilibrium.

Dynamic equilibrium in the system, however, will exist *only when pressures not too great* impinge on the system. A small pressure may be too great for a system that has just reached an effective way of working, and a well-established system may be able to take care of extremely disruptive pressures. In fact, the measure of strength of a system of relationships is the way it withstands a potentially disruptive pressure and reëstablishes an effective operating equilibrium. Social control is not always possible. Sometimes the pressures that impinge on a system are too great. Then the very forces that would have produced a new balance had the outside pressure been less severe may appear to be leading toward "open conflict."

Benjamin M. Selekman, in discussing labor relations in modern industry, considers the importance of the interaction of such forces. Much of the experience that he observes is drawn from situations where the labor-management relations were under conditions of stress — where the equilibrium of the existing system was severely strained. It is his observation that coöperation is never universal but at best predominant, and that conflict is always present:

> Everywhere, as men relate one to another in the diverse activities that constitute daily living, we find cooperation *and* conflict, loyalty *and* rebellion, devotion *and* disaffection reflected in behavior as intermeshed entities. Always the conjunction "and" proves the strategic word, as throughout life these seemingly incongruous sentiments appear together in every social relationship.
>
> Examining more closely these forces at work in the family and other institutions, we discover that cooperative sentiments are proportional to the sense of community developed among the constituent individuals in each instance — to the sense of common interest in common goals. The greater this sense of community, the greater the degree of cooperation; the weaker the sense of community, the greater the friction — the pulling and hauling of individuals and factions . . . The manifestations of conflict are also molded by the character of the relationships binding the individuals in each association. In the family, for instance, negative sentiments rarely find overt acceptance; instead, all the social sanctions are given to the cooperation implicit in the very purposes of the institution. The antagonisms, therefore, are generally pushed into the subconscious, below the threshold of conscious feeling; and the individual who feels hostile to his kin also feels guilty because that sentiment violates his code of what is right and proper.[4]

Social control involves both the adjustment of individuals in face-to-face groups and the adjustment between such groups in various organizational contexts. The state of equilibrium *between* groups affects that *within* groups, and vice versa. Labor-management relations provide a good example. There it can

---

[4] By permission from *Labor Relations and Human Relations*, by Benjamin M. Selekman, pp. 215–216. Copyright, 1947. McGraw-Hill Book Company, Inc.

be seen that the interactions between labor leaders and management executives are always influenced by the relations of labor leaders to workers, and management executives to colleagues. The function of conflict becomes clearer when viewed this way.

William F. Whyte, in the reading below, reports fully the developing relationships between the management and the union of a steel fabricating plant. In this situation the labor leaders and business executives create a new system of interactions that over a period of years produces mutually satisfactory results. Here are reported all the conflicts and struggles that went into the development of this system; here are considered many of the problems that develop in this process and many obstructing assumptions that are so often made. In the concluding chapters of the reading Whyte analyzes the developments that have taken place. The conceptual scheme with which he organizes his observations has much in common with that used by Homans: activities, interactions, and sentiments are its basic elements. Perhaps because Whyte emphasizes the communication process, he uses symbols — "the words or physical objects that *stand for* relations between man and man, and man and physical objects" [5] — as the fourth element in the developing system. Read

WILLIAM FOOTE WHYTE, *Pattern for Industrial Peace* (New York: Harper, 1951), pp. 3–229.

The process of developing a system of relationships in the area of management and labor is of particular importance to our society at this time. Although there are important differences, the process involves many matters that have been discussed above. If a working equilibrium is to be established, the process involves the development of mutually acceptable objectives and standards; it involves the clear acceptance of the importance of the sentiments and norms of others; it usually involves a reëvaluation of well-established sentiments with all the difficulties inherent in this task; it involves a modification of status and role expectations in respect to others. For a new working relationship to grow, the interactions must take place in an atmosphere where the necessary differences can be expressed without arousing diffuse angers that would make a modification of differences impossible. As occurred among the children of Piaget's studies, a system of relationships must develop that includes a *freedom to conflict* in the attainment of goals which are found to be mutually acceptable.

The disagreements and conflicts are often important in themselves. They highlight a need for reëvaluation and modification of the current relationships; something must be done differently if satisfactions are to be enhanced. The arbitrary removal of the source of immediate conflict — a quick acquiescence to a demand, the use of force to prevent discussion, the firing of a man — is often undesirable. Such action may cure only a symptom and ignore more basic problems that further interaction might make evident. Force, for example, may simply reaffirm the existing inadequate relationships, preventing better ones from developing.

Whyte reports such a situation in another article. The union officials, in seeking their objectives, had worked long and carefully for negotiations about higher wages. They took their duties seriously; they prepared figures on the costs of living and marshaled all the reasonable arguments in favor of a wage

[5] William F. Whyte, *Pattern for Industrial Peace* (New York: Harper, 1951), p. 160.

increase; they were ready to show how they deserved the raise through their contributions to the success of the company. Finally, they met with a representative of management. After they had presented their material all afternoon, the management spokesman closed the discussion with these words: "Well, you fellows have done a lot of talking, and I must say I haven't found your arguments very convincing. Still, I think you're a good bunch of fellows, and I tell you what I'll do. I'll give you 10 cents."

Although this was considered a good settlement by the union in terms of higher wages and well in line with similar situations elsewhere, nevertheless a serious strike for higher wages about six months later was narrowly averted. Whyte, in commenting on this situation, says:

> A relationship of even temporary equality requires expression and indications of respect on both sides. It requires that concessions be *won*, not *given away*. You don't make gifts to equals except when they are in a position of making gifts in return. When the top management man said, "I'll give you 10 cents," and took pains to show the men that they had had nothing to do with the offer, he was in effect telling the local officers that they were beneath management — that they did not amount to much.[6]

In the above illustration, as in *Pattern for Industrial Peace*, the men involved are not only responding for themselves but as representatives of groups and organizations — management or labor. They are men whose previous interactions have indicated to their followers that they can be trusted to respond in approved ways. These negotiations are important to all concerned; action is taking place through them, and the behavior of the leaders will be subject to careful scrutiny by their followers. Although they are chosen representatives, if they deviate too far from the values or norms of their followers, sanctions and punishment will be brought to bear upon them. These men, therefore, must act always with thought of the consequences to their relationship with their own groups. Yet as they enter into negotiations a new, face-to-face set of relationships with "opponents" must also be handled. Men who are frequently required to play such representative roles seem to develop skills in handling both sets of relations. Results are apparently accomplished only if the problems of both are dealt with satisfactorily. These men seem to find that, unless ways can be found of disagreeing and conflicting effectively in the face-to-face relationship, they cannot even approach the problems of their organizations.

The important functions of conflict may be easily discerned in the interactions between groups as described by Whyte. But the function of conflict and disagreement is equally important as a part of the process which produces both equilibrium and disequilibrium within face-to-face groups — and even within individuals. An "inner conflict" of an individual personality may lead to crippling disequilibrium, may be side-stepped by any of the protective devices of oversimplification, or may lead to a useful reëvaluation and re-synthesis of the experiences involved, thus giving new flexibility to the personality "system."

Although there are important similarities in the function of conflict within the individual, the group, and the multi-group system, it seems that the influence of any particular factor (or individual) on the outcome of the conflict becomes increasingly restricted as the complexity of the system increases. A

---

[6] Sidney Garfield and William F. Whyte, "The Collective Bargaining Process: A Human Relations Analysis," *Human Organization*, IX (Summer 1950), 10.

large organization, for example, is a social system which emerges from the interactions of many individuals over a long period of time. Often the individual feels rather helpless and does not see how he can influence the totality in any way. He senses that the system itself does not allow any individual to become too powerful. Yet if the system is in dynamic equilibrium, no individual completely lacks influence. He is a part of a set of relationships that have ramifications throughout the system. He does, through his behavior, make his influence felt in his immediate group and through the group somehow influences persons beyond it. Since his behavior always produces change in the system, some conflict is bound to result. The effect of the conflict may be constructive as well as disruptive. The conjugate principles of individualism and collectivism are both true.

ADDITIONAL READINGS

Brinton, Crane, *The Anatomy of Revolution* (New York: W. W. Norton, 1938).
A study of social disequilibrium leading to revolution, based on four historical instances.

Dymond, W. R., "Union-Management Cooperation at the Toronto Factory of Lever Brothers, Limited," *Canadian Journal of Economics and Political Science*, XIII, February 1947.
A case study showing how coöperation between union and management leaders was able to produce constructive change by accepting and utilizing initial hostile reactions of workers to change. The repercussions on shop activities, on the management structure, and on the union hierarchy are all described.

Leighton, Alexander H., *The Governing of Men* (Princeton: Princeton University Press, 1945).
A case study of disorganization of life as a result of mass imprisonment, followed by slow reorganization. This is based on the analysis of a Japanese-American civilian internment camp during World War II.

Parsons, Talcott, *The Social System* (Glencoe, Illinois: The Free Press, 1952).

A major theoretical treatment of social equilibrium.

Redfield, Robert, *The Folk Culture of Yucatan* (Chicago: University of Chicago Press, 1941).
Analysis of the change in a culture as it became urbanized — an example of adjustment to strong outside pressure. Four stages in this process are compared: a primitive and isolated tribe, a tiny country village, a town, and a large city, all existing contemporaneously on the peninsula of Yucatan in Mexico.

Selekman, Benjamin M., *Labor Relations and Human Relations* (New York: McGraw-Hill, 1947).
A discussion of conflict and coöperation as interdependent phenomena observed in labor-management relations.

Thomas, W. I., and Florian Znaniecki, *The Polish Peasant in Europe and America* (5 vols.; Boston: Richard Badger, 1918; 2 vols.; New York, Knopf, 1927).
This classic work contains an account of disorganization followed by reorganization in Polish peasant life in the early years of the twentieth century. See especially vols. I and II (Badger edition).

REVIEW

James L. Halliday, *Psychosocial Medicine* (New York: W. W. Norton, 1948) — see Additional Readings, Chapter VIII.

Index